AI-Driven Assessment Design in Higher Education

Jared Keengwe
https://orcid.org/0009-0002-6935-2189
University of North Dakota, USA

Elizaphan Maina
Kenyatta University, Kenya

Eric Araka
https://orcid.org/0000-0001-9242-7471
Kenyatta University, Kenya

IGI Global
Scientific Publishing
Publishing Tomorrow's Research Today

VP of Publishing Ethics & Research Integrity Melissa Wagner
Director of Acquisitions Mikaela Felty
Director of Book Development Jocelynn Hessler
Production Manager Mike Brehm
Cover Design Jose Rosado

Published in the United States of America by
IGI Global Scientific Publishing
701 East Chocolate Avenue
Hershey, PA, 17033, USA
Tel: 717-533-8845 | Fax: 717-533-7115
Website: https://www.igi-global.com E-mail: cust@igi-global.com

Library of Congress Cataloging-in-Publication Data

Names: Keengwe, Jared, 1973- editor | Maina, Elizaphan, 1976- editor | Araka, Eric, 1988- editor
Title: AI-driven assessment design in higher education / [edited by] Jared Keengwe, Elizaphan Maina, Eric Araka.
Description: Hershey, PA : IGI Global Scientific Publishing, [2027] | Includes bibliographical references and index. | Summary: "Emerging technologies such as Generative Artificial Intelligence (GenAI) are causing a rapid transformation in Higher Education by changing the way knowledge is produced, disseminated, and evaluated. This book explores how the integration of GenAI in assessment can transform assessment practices in higher education"-- Provided by publisher.
Identifiers: LCCN 2026011393 (print) | LCCN 2026011394 (ebook) | ISBN 9798337390901 paperback | ISBN 9798337390895 hardcover | ISBN 9798337390918 ebook
Subjects: LCSH: Generative artificial intelligence in higher education | Artificial intelligence--Educational applications | Educational evaluation
Classification: LCC LB2395.72 .A436 2027 (print) | LCC LB2395.72 (ebook)
LC record available at https://lccn.loc.gov/2026011393
LC ebook record available at https://lccn.loc.gov/2026011394
British Cataloguing in Publication Data
A Cataloguing in Publication record for this book is available from the British Library.

Table of Contents

Detailed Table of Contents

The chapter discusses artificial intelligence (AI) and generative AI, in particular, as it transforms the way assessments are conducted in higher education. The AI systems that have the ability to formulate questions and assess answers as well as give feedback are challenging the traditional assessment methods which largely depend on human judgment. As much as these technologies are favorable in that they provide personalization, efficiency, timely feedback, they also bring up issues to do with validity and fairness, transparency, and ethics and academic integrity. The chapter claims that human-centered approach to AI-based assessment should not be applied so that technology serves to substitute the professional judgment of the teachers. The chapter is balanced by combining the pedagogical harmonization, ethical governance, and institutional preparedness and creates a balanced framework to make AI-enhanced assessments meaningful, fair, and educationally sound.

This chapter investigates the development of assessments powered by Artificial Intelligence (AI) to facilitate Competency-Based Education (CBE) in the realm of higher education. The primary objective of this chapter is to analyze the potential of AI technologies to improve assessment methodologies through the provision of personalized, adaptive, and data-informed evaluations of student competencies. It reviews the foundational principles of CBE, scrutinizes the integration of AI in the design of assessments, and proposes essential guidelines for creating both AI-driven and AI-resilient assessment frameworks. Additionally, the chapter addresses strategies for implementation within digital learning contexts, presents illustrative use cases, and assesses the effectiveness of these approaches. Furthermore, it emphasizes the

The rapid integration of generative artificial intelligence (GenAI) into higher education has transformed assessment practices, yet existing systems remain limited in adaptivity, integrity, trust, and fairness. This chapter proposes a novel framework, Trust-Adaptive Generative Assessment for Competency-Aligned Design (TAGA-CAD), which reconceptualizes assessment as a continuous, adaptive, and ethically governed process. The framework integrates competency-driven task generation, integrity-preserving assessment design, trust-calibrated evaluation mechanisms, and fairness-aware regulation within a unified architecture. By embedding human oversight and closed-loop feedback, TAGA-CAD ensures alignment with learning outcomes while maintaining transparency and reliability in automated grading. A conceptual evaluation model supported by analytical metrics and comparative visualizations demonstrates the superiority of the proposed approach over traditional and existing AI-based systems.

Assessment in higher education is no longer confined to fixed tests, uniform rubrics, or end-point measurement. With the rise of Generative AI, assessment can become more adaptive, dialogic, and responsive to the diverse ways students learn, struggle, and demonstrate understanding. This chapter explores how GenAI can support personalized assessment pathways that adjust tasks, feedback, pacing, and learning evidence according to individual learner needs. Rather than treating assessment as a mechanical process of grading, the chapter frames it as a living pedagogical encounter—one that can guide reflection, reveal hidden misconceptions, and encourage deeper intellectual growth. At the same time, it critically examines concerns around bias, transparency, over-reliance, data ethics, and academic integrity. The chapter argues for a human-centered approach in which GenAI strengthens, rather than replaces, the professional judgment of educators.

Adaptive and personalized assessment systems supported by Generative Artificial Intelligence are transforming evaluation practices in higher education. This chapter examines how AI enables dynamic question generation, real time difficulty adjustment, and personalized feedback to enhance learning outcomes. It explains the pedagogical foundations of adaptive assessment, including constructivism, formative assessment, and competency based learning. The chapter also highlights the role of learning analytics in supporting data driven decision making and continuous improvement. Issues related to academic integrity, bias, and ethical use of AI are discussed along with the importance of human oversight. Practical case examples illustrate real world implementation of adaptive assessment systems. The chapter further explores institutional readiness, policy frameworks, and future directions in AI driven assessment. It provides a clear and structured understanding of how adaptive assessment can support flexible, inclusive, and learner centered education.

Generative Artificial Intelligence (AI) is transforming higher education assessment yet challenging the validity and authenticity of assessment evidence. This chapter argues that the central concern extends beyond academic dishonesty to whether assessment evidence genuinely reflects students' learning, reasoning, and demonstrated competence. Drawing on Messick's unified theory of validity and principles of authentic assessment, the chapter examines how AI may introduce construct-irrelevant variance and weaken the authenticity of assessment evidence. It proposes a framework for preserving valid and authentic assessment evidence through process-based assessment, supervised assessment, multimodal and authentic assessment, and ethical AI-literate engagement. The chapter concludes that sustainable assessment in the AI era requires higher education to move beyond AI detection and prohibition towards assessment practices that generate trustworthy evidence of student learning and competence.

AI-generated feedback is rapidly entering higher education as institutions search for more responsive, scalable, and learner-centered approaches to assessment. Yet its value cannot be reduced to speed, automation, or convenience. This chapter examines AI-generated feedback as a pedagogical tool that can reshape how students interpret their work, revise their thinking, and participate more actively in learning. It explores the opportunities offered by generative AI, including timely formative guidance, personalized explanations, iterative revision support, and expanded access to feedback in large or resource-limited courses. At the same time, it addresses the risks of overdependence, generic responses, hidden bias, weakened teacher judgment, and the possible erosion of meaningful human dialogue. The chapter argues for careful design principles rooted in transparency, contextual sensitivity, student agency, feedback literacy, and human oversight, positioning AI not as a replacement for educators but as a thoughtfully governed partner in assessment design.

Examining the evolving challenge of doctoral supervision in the age of generative artificial intelligence (GenAI) is framed by the question: who is doing the thinking? As AI tools increasingly mediate research processes, supervisors face growing difficulty in distinguishing genuine student cognition and GenAI-assisted outputs. Building on an existing guiding rubric for doctoral supervision in Statistics, an extension is proposed that integrates the responsible, transparent use of GenAI across the doctoral lifecycle, from topic and literature discovery, through methodology and data analysis, to write-up and defence. The revisions proposed for the rubric shift the role of GenAI from a productivity shortcut to a mechanism for enhancing critical thinking. It introduces expanded criteria emphasising transparency, verification, attribution, and development of AI literacy in students and supervisors. A five-level developmental framework is proposed, progressing from uncritical GenAI use to reflexive GenAI stewardship, cultivating independent, ethically grounded researchers.

This chapter explores how artificial intelligence reshapes assessment design in higher education, using Cantonese as a second language as a distinctive lens. Cantonese's tonal and sociolinguistic complexity provides a rigorous case for evaluating AI's role in oral proficiency testing. The discussion highlights the shift toward adaptive, learner-centred formats that move beyond standardised methods. Drawing on Hong Kong's higher education practices, it demonstrates how integrating Automatic Speech Recognition, Large Language Models, and Text-to-Speech enables contextualized tasks, real-time feedback, and alignment with ACTFL and CEFR frameworks. It also addresses challenges of transparency, cultural sensitivity, and human-in-the-loop mediation. Ultimately, AI-driven assessment design fosters flexible, inclusive, and pedagogically robust approaches across multilingual higher education.

This chapter presents a teaching and assessment approach that incorporates generative artificial intelligence (GenAI) into learning while maintaining a focus on students' developing understanding. Drawing on a portfolio-and-interview model implemented in Mathematical Statistics, the approach combines longitudinal portfolios of learning evidence with individual oral interviews. The portfolio records both material collected from external sources, including GenAI where appropriate, and evidence of students' engagement with that material, while the interview provides a complementary opportunity for students to explain and defend their learning. The model is informed by Fink's taxonomy of significant learning, research on desirable difficulties and generative learning, and the AI Assessment Scale. The approach emphasises transparent GenAI use and the cognitive work that remains the responsibility of the student. The chapter describes the creation and assessment of portfolio content, the role of interviews, and practical considerations relating to implementation.

The use of artificial intelligence in assessment design in higher education provides new prospects for economies of scale, personalization and scalable feedback. It is, however, also accompanied by concerning ethical implications around fairness, bias, transparency and accountability of AI-based assessment systems. This paper investigates the problems associated with algorithmic bias in automatic evaluation tools, discussing fairness issues for a varied student population. It focuses on how ethical values such as justice, autonomy and beneficence shape good assessment practice. Safeguards might include the use of bias audits, validation methods and oversight from a human in the loop and culturally responsive design. Strong government oversight and regulatory convergence are needed for AI-powered assessment to facilitate trust, accessibility and academic integrity. Ethical AI evaluation should eventually become a fusion of technological breakthrough, pedagogical responsibility and social equity.

This chapter reviews how the development of generative artificial intelligence (Gen-AI) has quickly become embedded in the assessment of higher education and the consequences of this development on validity, reliability, and academic integrity. Although Gen-AI allows evaluating with a high level of scalability, adapting feedbacks, and guided by data, it also poses severe threats, such as algorithmic bias, lack of transparency, hallucinated results, and undermined authentic learning. In this chapter, according to the authors, the conceptual and normative approach is used in order to synthesize literature, policy frameworks and pedagogical theory in order to overcome these difficulties. It suggests an Ethical Guardrails Framework which inserts the transparency, bias reduction, human-in-the-loop validation and accountability controls into the AI-driven assessment systems. The framework makes Gen-AI an aiding force and not a substitute to human judgment making it fit within the institutional governance and international ethics.

Preface

The rapid development of artificial intelligence (AI), and particularly generative artificial intelligence (GenAI), is reshaping higher education in ways that extend far beyond the adoption of new technologies. Among the areas experiencing some of the most significant transformation is assessment. Traditional approaches to assessment have long relied on established forms of testing, standardized tasks, written assignments, examinations, and instructor judgment to determine what students know and can do. The emergence of AI systems capable of generating questions, evaluating responses, providing feedback, adapting tasks, and supporting learning has introduced new possibilities while simultaneously challenging many of the assumptions upon which assessment practices have been built. This edited volume, *AI-Driven Assessment Design in Higher Education*, brings together diverse perspectives on these developments and considers how assessment can evolve while continuing to provide meaningful, fair, authentic, and educationally sound evidence of student learning.

Our purpose in developing this book is not to present artificial intelligence as either a solution to every challenge in assessment or an unavoidable threat to established educational practices. Rather, the chapters collectively encourage a more thoughtful examination of how AI can be incorporated into assessment while preserving the central role of educators, students, and institutions. Across the contributions, AI is considered in relation to personalization, competency development, adaptive assessment, feedback, academic integrity, validity, authenticity, fairness, transparency, and institutional governance. A recurring principle throughout the volume is that technological capability must remain connected to pedagogical purpose. AI-driven assessment is most meaningful when it strengthens learning and supports educators rather than simply replacing professional judgment with automated processes. This human-centered perspective provides an important foundation for considering the opportunities and limitations of AI in contemporary higher education.

The book also recognizes that the question of assessment in the age of AI cannot be reduced to the detection or prevention of inappropriate technology use. Generative AI has brought renewed attention to a more fundamental question: whether the evidence produced through an assessment genuinely represents a student's learning, reasoning, competence, and intellectual development. Questions of validity and authenticity therefore appear alongside concerns about academic integrity, algorithmic bias, transparency, and accountability. Several contributions move beyond conventional approaches based on prohibition or detection and instead consider how assessment itself can be redesigned to make students' cognitive processes, decision-making, reflection, and engagement more visible. Process-based assessment, authentic and multimodal tasks, portfolios, interviews, and other approaches demonstrate how institutions can respond constructively to the changing assessment environment.

Finally, this volume emphasizes that responsible AI-driven assessment requires collaboration across pedagogical, technological, ethical, and institutional domains. The chapters draw attention to the importance of human oversight, AI literacy, culturally responsive design, bias auditing, transparent use of AI, appropriate governance, and institutional readiness. At the same time, they illustrate the potential for AI to support more adaptive, personalized, timely, and inclusive assessment experiences. We hope this collection will serve as a valuable reference for researchers, faculty members, educational leaders, instructional designers, policymakers, and other professionals seeking to understand and navigate the changing relationship between artificial intelligence and higher education assessment. By bringing together conceptual frameworks, practical approaches, and critical perspectives, this book contributes to an ongoing conversation about how assessment can remain purposeful and trustworthy while responding thoughtfully to technological change.

OVERVIEW OF THE CHAPTERS

The chapters in this volume approach AI-driven assessment from complementary perspectives, beginning with broad questions of assessment design and governance before examining specific applications, challenges, and emerging frameworks.

Chapter 1, "Reconceptualizing Assessment in Higher Education Human-Centered Design and Governance of AI-Driven Assessment Systems," establishes an important foundation for the volume by examining how AI and generative AI are transforming assessment. The chapter considers the benefits of personalization, efficiency, and timely feedback alongside concerns involving validity, fairness, transparency, ethics, and academic integrity. It advocates for a human-centered approach in which AI supports rather than substitutes for the professional judgment of educators, emphasizing pedagogical alignment, ethical governance, and institutional preparedness.

Chapter 2, "Designing AI-Driven Assessments for Competency-Based Education in Higher Education," focuses on the intersection of AI and competency-based education (CBE). The chapter examines how AI can facilitate personalized, adaptive, and data-informed evaluations of student competencies while considering the principles underlying CBE. It also explores AI-driven and AI-resilient assessment frameworks, digital learning implementation, use cases, effectiveness, and the ethical, policy, and governance considerations institutions must address when adopting these approaches.

Chapter 3, "Artificial Intelligence and Academic Integrity: Authentic Assessment and Generative AI Detection Tools," turns attention to one of the most prominent concerns surrounding AI in education: academic integrity. The chapter considers the difficulties of defining effective policies for traditional and AI-related plagiarism, examines concerns associated with AI detection tools, including potential bias affecting neurodivergent thinkers, and considers the perspectives of students, faculty, and administrators. The discussion ultimately introduces AI-resistant assessment as another avenue for maintaining integrity.

Chapter 4, "Swimming in Circles: The Fish Bowl Logic of Assessment, Anthrogogy, and Its Consequences in the Age of Generative AI," offers a conceptual examination of assessment through the metaphor of "fish bowl" logic. The chapter considers how assessments may privilege visible outputs while concealing the reasoning and decision-making behind them. Drawing on reflective essays from postgraduate students in an Indian university, it examines open-source and open-book assessment conditions and positions generative AI as an epistemic stress test that exposes weaknesses in output-based evaluation. The chapter ultimately argues for designing assessment conditions that make meaningful epistemic engagement visible.

Chapter 5, "A Trust-Adaptive Generative AI Framework for Competency-Centered and Integrity-Preserving Assessment in Higher Education," introduces the Trust-Adaptive Generative Assessment for Competency-Aligned Design (TAGA-CAD) framework. The proposed framework brings together competency-driven task generation, integrity-preserving assessment, trust-calibrated evaluation, fairness-aware regulation, human oversight, and closed-loop feedback. Through its conceptual evaluation model, the chapter explores how adaptive and ethically governed AI assessment can maintain alignment with learning outcomes while supporting transparency and reliability.

Chapter 6, "Adaptive and Personalized Assessment Pathways Enabled by GenAI," explores the potential for generative AI to move assessment beyond fixed tests, standardized rubrics, and endpoint measurement. The chapter presents assessment as a more adaptive and dialogic process capable of responding to different learner needs through adjustments to tasks, feedback, pacing, and evidence of learning. At the same time, it considers bias, transparency, over-reliance, data ethics, and academic integrity, reinforcing the importance of maintaining educator judgment within AI-supported assessment practices.

Chapter 7, "Adaptive and Personalized Assessment Systems Using Generative Artificial Intelligence," further examines adaptive assessment by focusing on dynamic question generation, real-time difficulty adjustment, personalized feedback, and learning analytics. The chapter connects these capabilities to pedagogical foundations including constructivism, formative assessment, and competency-based learning. It also considers academic integrity, bias, ethical use, human oversight, institutional readiness, policy frameworks, and practical implementation through case examples.

Chapter 8, "AI-Driven Assessment: Balancing Innovation with Validity and Authenticity of Assessment Evidence," addresses the fundamental question of whether AI-supported assessment produces trustworthy evidence of student learning. Drawing on validity theory and authentic assessment principles, the chapter examines how AI may introduce construct-irrelevant variance and weaken the authenticity of assessment evidence. It proposes approaches including process-based, supervised, multimodal, and authentic assessment, together with ethical AI-literate engagement, to move assessment beyond a narrow emphasis on AI detection and prohibition.

Chapter 9, "AI-Generated Feedback as a Pedagogical Tool: Opportunities & Design Principles," considers feedback as an important area in which AI may contribute to higher education. The chapter examines opportunities for timely formative guidance, personalized explanations, iterative revision support, and expanded access to feedback. At the same time, it emphasizes risks involving overdependence, generic responses, hidden bias, weakened teacher judgment, and diminished human dialogue. Its proposed design principles emphasize transparency, contextual sensitivity, student agency, feedback literacy, and human oversight.

Chapter 10, "Who is doing the thinking? Adapting a Guiding Rubric for Doctoral Supervision to keep pace with rapid advances in generative AI," extends the discussion into doctoral education and supervision. The chapter examines how GenAI can affect the ability of supervisors to distinguish student cognition from AI-assisted outputs. Building on an existing guiding rubric for doctoral supervision in Statistics, it proposes an expanded framework addressing responsible GenAI use throughout the doctoral research lifecycle, including topic development, literature discovery, methodology, data analysis, writing, and defense. Particular attention is given to transparency, verification, attribution, AI literacy, and the development of increasingly reflective and responsible AI use.

Chapter 11, "Artificial Intelligence in Assessment Design for Cantonese Education," provides a distinctive multilingual perspective by examining AI-driven assessment through the context of Cantonese as a second language. The chapter highlights the tonal and sociolinguistic complexity of Cantonese as an important setting for evaluating AI-supported oral proficiency assessment. It explores the use of Automatic Speech Recognition, Large Language Models, and Text-to-Speech technologies to create contextualized tasks and real-time feedback while considering alignment with ACTFL and CEFR frameworks, cultural sensitivity, transparency, and human-in-the-loop mediation.

Chapter 12, "Collaborating with Artificial Intelligence in Higher Education: Portfolios of Learning Evidence and Interview Assessments," presents a portfolio-and-interview model for incorporating GenAI into learning while maintaining focus on students' developing understanding. Through longitudinal portfolios and individual oral interviews, the approach captures both the materials students engage with and their ability to explain and defend their learning. The chapter emphasizes transparent GenAI use and places responsibility for the underlying cognitive work with the student, while also addressing practical considerations for implementing the approach.

Chapter 13, "Ensuring Fairness and Ethical Integrity in AI-Based Assessment Design," examines the ethical dimensions of AI-supported assessment, particularly fairness, bias, transparency, and accountability. The chapter considers algorithmic bias in automated evaluation and connects assessment practice to ethical values including justice, autonomy, and beneficence. It discusses safeguards such as bias audits, validation methods, human oversight, and culturally responsive design, while emphasizing the importance of governance and regulatory oversight in establishing trustworthy AI assessment systems.

Chapter 14, "Ethical Guardrail Framework for Generative AI In Academic Assessment: Ensuring Fairness, Transparency and Authenticity," concludes the collection by returning to the broader ethical and governance questions surrounding GenAI in assessment. The chapter considers challenges related to validity, reliability, academic integrity, algorithmic bias, transparency, hallucinated results, and authentic learning. It proposes an Ethical Guardrails Framework incorporating transparency, bias reduction, human-in-the-loop validation, and accountability, positioning GenAI as an aid to assessment rather than a substitute for human judgment.

CONCLUSION

The chapters in this volume collectively demonstrate that the emergence of artificial intelligence in higher education assessment represents more than a technological transition. It is also an opportunity to reconsider what assessment is intended to accomplish, what constitutes meaningful evidence of learning, and how educators and institutions can ensure that assessment remains aligned with educational goals. Across the contributions, AI is shown to have considerable potential to support personalization, adaptability, timely feedback, competency development, and more responsive learning experiences. Yet these possibilities are accompanied by equally significant questions surrounding fairness, validity, authenticity, transparency, academic integrity, and human judgment. The central challenge, therefore, is not simply determining whether AI should be used in assessment, but determining how it can be used responsibly and purposefully.

A particularly important theme emerging across the volume is the need to move beyond assessment models that focus exclusively on observable outputs. Generative AI makes it increasingly difficult to assume that a submitted product necessarily represents the student's independent thinking or competence. As several chapters illustrate, this challenge creates an opportunity to place greater emphasis on processes of learning, reasoning, reflection, decision-making, and demonstration. Portfolios, interviews, authentic and multimodal assessment, process-based approaches, adaptive pathways, and other forms of evidence can help educators develop a more complete understanding of student learning. In this sense, AI does not simply disrupt existing assessment practices; it can also encourage institutions to examine long-standing assumptions about how learning is demonstrated and evaluated.

At the same time, the responsible adoption of AI-driven assessment requires strong ethical and institutional foundations. The chapters repeatedly emphasize human oversight, transparency, accountability, fairness, bias reduction, culturally responsive design, AI literacy, and appropriate governance. These considerations are especially important as assessment systems become more adaptive and automated. Efficiency and scalability cannot, on their own, define successful assessment. An AI-supported system must also be trustworthy, understandable, equitable, and aligned with the learning outcomes and educational purposes it is intended to serve. The frameworks and approaches presented throughout this book demonstrate that technological innovation and pedagogical responsibility do not need to be competing priorities; rather, they can be integrated through intentional design and thoughtful governance.

Ultimately, we believe that the future of assessment in higher education should not be defined by a choice between human teaching and artificial intelligence. Instead, it should be shaped by purposeful collaboration between educators, students, institutions, and AI technologies. The most promising approaches presented in this volume position AI as a tool that can extend human capabilities while retaining human responsibility for educational judgment. As AI technologies continue to evolve, assessment practices will likewise need to remain adaptable, reflective, and grounded in principles of learning and academic integrity. We hope that *AI-Driven Assessment Design in Higher Education* provides readers with both a critical understanding of the challenges ahead and practical conceptual foundations for designing assessment systems that are innovative while remaining valid, authentic, fair, and centered on meaningful student learning.

Jared Keengwe
University of North Dakota, USA

Elizaphan Maina
Kenyatta University, Kenya

Eric Araka
Kenyatta University, Kenya

Chapter 1
Reconceptualizing Assessment in Higher Education:
Human-Centered Design and Governance of AI-Driven Assessment Systems

Sohom Saha
http://orcid.org/0009-0006-9438-1554
Lakshmibai National Institute of Physical Education, India

Mahendra Kumar Singh
http://orcid.org/0000-0001-9989-9420
Lakshmibai National Institute of Physical Education, India

ABSTRACT

The chapter discusses artificial intelligence (AI) and generative AI, in particular, as it transforms the way assessments are conducted in higher education. The AI systems that have the ability to formulate questions and assess answers as well as give feedback are challenging the traditional assessment methods which largely depend on human judgment. As much as these technologies are favorable in that they provide personalization, efficiency, timely feedback, they also bring up issues to do with validity and fairness, transparency, and ethics and academic integrity. The chapter claims that human-centered approach to AI-based assessment should not be applied so that technology serves to substitute the professional judgment of

DOI: 10.4018/979-8-3373-9089-5.ch001

the teachers. The chapter is balanced by combining the pedagogical harmonization, ethical governance, and institutional preparedness and creates a balanced framework to make AI-enhanced assessments meaningful, fair, and educationally sound.

1. INTRODUCTION AND BACKGROUND

Assessment has been a fundamental part of higher education, as it has long been one of the key tools of assessing learning outcomes, guaranteeing academic standards, and quality assurance (Bearman et al., 2022). Historically, the design of assessments has been dependent on human judgement, standardised rubrics and instructor-based assessment design (Boud and Soler, 2016). But with the emergence of Generative Artificial Intelligence (GenAI), large language models, and adaptive analytics systems, assessment is fundamentally being rethought, designed, and deployed in institutions of higher learning in new ways (Kasneci et al., 2023; Sullivan et al., 2023).

GenAI technologies become progressively able to produce assessment items, analyze complex reactions of a student, give personal feedback, and identify possible instances of academic dishonesty (Rudolph et al., 2023). These skills open up new possibilities of scaling, adaptive and competency-based assessment practices (Zawacki-Richter et al., 2019). Meanwhile, they undermine the traditional beliefs about validity, reliability, transparency, and the contribution of educators as indecisers of the academic judgment (Villasenor, 2023). With the integration of AI systems into the assessment process, institutions need to rethink the definition of authentic learning evidence and the process of making educational decisions (Lodge and Thompson, 2024). Although the recent literature focuses on GenAI-based assessment as having technical affordances, there is a critical lack of integrative frameworks that consider the alignment with pedagogy, ethical management, and human control concurrently (Holmes and Porayska-Pomsta, 2022). Much of the discourse out there is either about the potential of automation or individual ethical risks of the system, without adequately discussing how AI-driven assessment could be built in a human-centered, educationally significant, and institutionally responsible way (Selwyn, 2022).

This chapter addresses this need by conceptualizing the AI-based assessment design in higher education in a human-centered and governance-oriented perspective. It believes that GenAI must be added to human judgment, but not taken away and that responsible assessment innovation demands strong pedagogical models, ethical protection, and institutional preparedness (Williamson and Eynon, 2020). The chapter can help to make an assessment of AI integration more balanced and sustainable by integrating theoretical views, emerging practices, and policy considerations.

2. THEORETICAL AND CONCEPTUAL FOUNDATIONS OF AI-DRIVEN ASSESSMENT

The concept of AI-driven assessment can be explained in several theories, such as assessment of learning, construct validity theory, and socio-technical systems theory (Gikandi et al., 2011; Kane, 2013). Pedagogically, GenAI provides possibilities to replace a static form of assessment with a dynamic one, with plenty of feedback, dynamics (Black and Wiliam, 2009). Adaptive assessment systems have the ability to adapt to the needs of learners, facilitate self-regulation and give timely formative feedback (Luckin et al., 2016).

Assessment for Learning Framework

The assessment paradigm focuses more on the formative role of assessment in facilitating student growth as opposed to measuring achievement (Carless, 2015). GenAI technology is consistent with such a framework as it facilitates sustained, personalized feedback that may inform learning paths (Holmes et al., 2019). Student responses can be analyzed with machine learning algorithms and reveal certain misconceptions and propose a specific intervention on a large scale (Baker and Inventado, 2014). This is a big development in comparison to old evaluation frameworks that tend to give unsatisfactory feedback in a slow way (Shute, 2008).

The introduction of AI into formative assessment, however, makes the nature of feedback questionable. Studies have shown that good feedback has to be timely, specific, and actionable (Hattie and Timperley, 2007). Although the response time of GenAI can be high, there is still a sense of concern regarding the depth, contextual relevance, and pedagogical complexity of feedback generated in an algorithmic manner (Lipnevich and Smith, 2022). The problem here is to make sure that AI-generated feedback facilitates real learning and not the completion of shallow tasks.

Construct Validity and AI Assessment

A validity perspective on AI-generated assessment is that it puts construct congruence, interpretability, and excessive dependence on algorithmic inference into question (Newton and Shaw, 2014). Construct validity is the extent to which an assessment measures what it is supposed to measure (Messick, 1989). When assessment items are created by AI systems, evaluating the work of students, the question appears whether the constructs under evaluation stay aligned with the desired learning outcomes (Williamson et al., 2020).

The AI systems might be biased in favor of some of the forms of knowledge or capability that are more easily measurable or able to be pattern-recognized, excluding more complicated cognitive tasks including critical thinking, creativity and ethical reasoning (Luckin and Cukurova, 2019). This reductionism in algorithms is dangerous to the comprehensiveness and educational legitimacy of assessment practices (Selwyn, 2019). The institutions should thus have a framework of ensuring that AI-assisted assessments are validated to the set learning objectives and discipline standards (AERA et al., 2014).

Socio-Technical Systems Perspective

Socio-technical views underline that AI systems do not work without human values, institutional and policy frameworks (Barocas et al., 2019). The design decisions, data sources, and governance structures incorporated in larger educational ecosystems make assessment outcomes, hence (Eynon, 2021). This is a view that questions technological determinism and that human agency plays a crucial role in defining the application of AI in assessment situations (Selwyn, 2022).

The socio-technical lens shows that the application of AI-based assessment is not only a technical process but a multifaceted interaction between the goals of pedagogy, the interests of institutions, the peculiarities of students, and the possibilities of algorithms (Holmes and Porayska-Pomsta, 2022). This complexity is clear because it is imperative to design assessment systems that can address multiple learning needs and contexts (Williamson and Eynon, 2020).

Table 1. Major Theoretical Perspectives Underpinning Human-Centered AI-Driven Assessment

Theoretical Perspective	Core Principle	Relevance to AI-Driven Assessment	Human-Centered Implication
Assessment for Learning	Assessment promotes continuous learning through feedback	GenAI provides personalized and timely formative feedback	AI should support learner development rather than simply measure achievement
Construct Validity Theory	Assessment should accurately measure intended learning outcomes	AI-generated assessment requires validation of constructs and scoring accuracy	Human experts must verify alignment between AI outputs and educational objectives
Socio-Technical Systems Theory	Technology functions within social and institutional contexts	AI assessment depends on educators, policies, institutional culture, and governance	Human values should guide AI implementation and decision-making

continued on following page

Table 1. Continued

Theoretical Perspective	Core Principle	Relevance to AI-Driven Assessment	Human-Centered Implication
Human-in-the-Loop Framework	Humans retain oversight over automated decisions	AI assists grading, feedback, and analytics while educators make final decisions	Preserves professional judgment and accountability
Learning Analytics Framework	Student data inform instructional improvement	AI identifies learning patterns and predicts academic performance	Data should support learning while respecting ethics and privacy

3. GENAI-ASSISTED DESIGN OF FORMATIVE AND SUMMATIVE ASSESSMENTS

GenAI has the potential to aid in the creation of formative assessments by creating practice, providing adaptive feedback, and scaffolding student reflection (Ouyang et al., 2022). At the summative level, AI could be used to support rubric-based assessment, consistency checking, and management of a large-scale assessment (Zawacki-Richter et al., 2019). These applications can be used to improve efficiency and personalization but also create threats of bias, obscurity, and inconsistency with the learning outcomes.

Formative Assessment Applications

GenAI has a number of uses in the formative assessment setting. Grammar, structure and the quality of arguments in student essays can be digitally assessed on automated writing feedback systems and an immediate response given on how to improve the essay (Wilson and Roscoe, 2020). With the help of intelligent tutoring systems, it is possible to create individualized practice problems based on the learning gaps and allow progressive learning to mastery (Kulik and Fletcher, 2016). Conversational AI agents are able to discuss with students' assessment exercises based on dialogue which explore conceptual knowledge (Kuhail et al., 2023).

It is proven that tools of formative assessment powered by AI can enhance the interest of students and facilitate self-regulated learning when intelligently incorporated into the course design (Pardo et al., 2019). Yet, its efficacy is highly reliant on its compliance with the learning goals, clarity regarding AI opportunities, and constraints, and its connection with human instructional support (Lodge et al., 2018). There is the greatest benefit when AI generated feedback is supplemented with the possibility of human interaction and individual advice to be given to students (Dawson et al., 2019).

Summative Assessment Considerations

GenAI use in summative assessment has unique issues of stakes, validity and accountability. Although AI may be used to mark rubric-based structured responses, the question still remains on its ability to mark more complex and open-ended work that entails finer judgment (Shermis and Burstein, 2013). The research on automated essay scoring indicates that the level of accuracy varies in diverse writing tasks and groups of students, which prompts the issue of equity (Wang et al., 2020).

Moreover, AI implementation in summative assessment that involves high stakes increases the significance of the transparency, explainability, appeal policies (Baker and Hawn, 2021). Students are entitled to know how their assessment is being done and to complain against what they consider as the evaluation being inaccurate or unjustified (Prinsloo and Slade, 2016). Schools should be able to come up with specific policies regulating the application of AI in summative situations, such as the mechanisms of human review and the quality assurance (Selwyn et al., 2020).

Authentic and Competency-Based Assessment

Authentic assessment focuses on the tasks that are reflective of real-life situations and involve the combination of knowledge and skills (Wiggins, 1993). GenAI can be useful to assist in the creation of authentic assessment by creating problems in a scenario, simulating professional conditions, and assessing performance in complicated tasks (Bearman et al., 2022). Nevertheless, it has the threat of encouraging less in-depth involvement in genuine problems and more superficial completion of tasks on the basis of the AI-driven evaluation (Macfadyen et al., 2020).

Competency-based assessment is oriented on the demonstration of the skills and knowledge mastery instead of time-based development (Johnstone and Soares, 2014). Adaptive competency mapping can be facilitated by GenAI technologies where students will be able to advance at a personalized pace and get specific assistance (Ifenthaler and Yau, 2020). However, organizations should make sure that competency frameworks are based on the authentic needs of the profession and discipline rather than the product of a convenient algorithm (Winne and Baker, 2013).

4. ACADEMIC INTEGRITY, ETHICS, AND FAIRNESS

GenAI is associated with important ethical implications in the assessment process, especially academic integrity, bias, and equity (Lancaster, 2023). AI-generated content destabilizes conventional conceptualizations of authorship and originality, and detection software can falsely detect some groups of students (Perkins et al., 2023).

Reframing Academic Integrity

Conventional methods of addressing academic integrity have placed emphasis on the detection of plagiarism and penalties to the offences (Bertram Gallant, 2008). The extensive use of GenAI tools, however, requires a paradigm shift in the expectations of integrity (Sullivan et al., 2023). Instead of trying to ban AI usage in general, the institutions are researching methods of differentiating between proper and improper AI support in a wide range of assessment scenarios (Eaton, 2023).

Such a transition entails effective communication of what can be done with AI, a clear focus on the inclusion of AI literacy in curricula, and assessment models focused on genuine demonstration of learning (Fyfe, 2023). The opportunities of problematic use of AI can be minimized and more effective learning can be encouraged through process-oriented assessment strategies that entail students capturing and documenting their thinking, metacognition, and iterative development (Bearman et al., 2022).

Algorithmic Bias and Fairness

The AI systems have the potential to reproduce and enhance the existing biases of training data, algorithm design, and implementation situations (O'Neil, 2016). In evaluation, it is reflected in the fact that demographic groups of students have varying levels of accuracy in assessment, there is a systematic bias in scoring student work, and unfair access to AI-enhanced learning opportunities (Baker and Hawn, 2021). The studies show that the automated writing evaluation systems are likely to reward linguistic diversity and non-standard varieties of the English language, which negatively impacts multilingual learners and students of minoritized groups (Perelman, 2020).

To ensure fairness, AI-based assessment systems should be audited proactively with respect to bias, diverse stakeholders involved in the development of the system, and continuous monitoring of the results of the assessment disaggregated along the necessary demographic variables (Holstein and Doroudi, 2021). Companies should put in place procedures to detect and counteract bias, such as human inspection of algorithm-tagged individuals and complaint systems of students who think they have been graded unfairly (Prinsloo and Slade, 2016).

Privacy and Data Ethics

The assessment systems developed by AI provide a large amount of information on the learning behaviors, performance tendencies, and personal traits of students (Tsai et al., 2020). On the one hand, this information can be used to inform adaptive instruction and institutional change, but it also has serious implications on privacy (Slade and Prinsloo, 2013). The students might not know well what data is being gathered, how it is being applied, and who can access it (Rubel and Jones, 2016).

Ethical data governance models should be transparent regarding information gathering and use, grant students insightful data management over their educational information, and introduce solid security guidelines to safeguard personal information (Willis et al., 2016). The privacy-by-design principles should be implemented in institutions where the amount of data collected is reduced to the minimum required to achieve the right educational goals and formulated clear policies regarding the storage and erasure of data (Drachsler and Greller, 2016).

Table 2. Opportunities, Challenges, and Human-Centered Responses in AI-Driven Assessment

Dimension	Opportunities	Potential Challenges	Human-Centered Strategy
Personalized Feedback	Immediate individualized feedback	Superficial or inaccurate responses	Teacher verification and contextualization
Assessment Efficiency	Reduced grading workload	Overdependence on automation	Human moderation of assessment outcomes
Academic Integrity	AI-assisted originality checking	False positives and misuse detection	Transparent institutional AI policies
Fairness	Consistent evaluation	Algorithmic bias and discrimination	Regular bias audits and inclusive datasets
Transparency	Explainable assessment decisions	Black-box AI algorithms	Explainable AI and student disclosure
Privacy	Rich learning analytics	Student data misuse	Privacy-by-design and informed consent
Adaptive Assessment	Personalized learning pathways	Unequal assessment experiences	Continuous validation and fairness monitoring

4.1 Learning Analytics and Predictive Assessment

The convergence of GenAI and learning analytics is a major development in assessment practices (Siemens, and Long, 2011). Learning analytics systems are systems that have the capability to work on enormous volumes of data relating to student interaction to make predictions, forecast results and customize learning trajectories (Ferguson, 2012). These systems, combined with the capabilities of GenAI, allow building complex models of predictive assessments that have the potential to predict student challenges prior to them influencing performance on summative tests (Gasevic et al., 2015).

The system of predictive analytics in the context of assessment also carries some significant concerns regarding determinism and self-fulfilling prophecies (Prinsloo and Slade, 2017). In case AI systems guess that some of the students will perform poorly, any intervention founded on these projections will unintentionally restrict opportunities or expectations (Kizilcec and Lee, 2022). The evidence indicates that predictive models can be rather representative of past trends of inequality, which, in turn, might recreates educational inequalities instead of resolving them (Gardner and Brooks, 2018).

Moreover, the majority of predictive algorithms are not transparent, which makes educational accountability difficult (Pasquale, 2015). Professional judgment is limited to algorithmic suggestions, which might or might not reflect pedagogical wisdom, when the educator makes assessment decisions based on machine learning models that are not completely understood by the educator (Ananny and Crawford, 2018). Institutions should consequently develop effective guidelines on how to assess predictive validity, track algorithmic decision-making and make sure that predictions complement and not substitute human assessment practices (Herodotou et al., 2020).

5. ROLE OF EDUCATORS AND HUMAN OVERSIGHT

Responsible AI-based assessment is still primarily human-centered (Holstein et al., 2019). Teachers are very important in the interpretation of AI results, contextualising feedbacks, and final evaluative decisions (Bayne, 2015). GenAI can help educators instead of undermining professional authority, working to de-administer and engage students in deeper learning (Lodge and Thompson, 2024).

Preserving Pedagogical Expertise

AI implementation in evaluation ought to complement, as opposed to substituting teacher knowledge (Selwyn, 2019). The teachers are better placed to have contextual information about the individual students, the nuances of discipline as well as the learning settings in a specific location, which cannot be duplicated by algorithmic systems (Popenici and Kerr, 2017). Good AI-enhanced assessment systems keep the teachers as the main decision-makers who do not accept AI-generated outputs blindly (Knox, 2020).

Professional development programs should empower the educators with knowledge and skills to be effective in AI assessment tools, such as knowledge of algorithmic constraints, interpretation of probabilistic results, and synthesis of AI feedback with personal professional judgment (Crompton & Burke, 2023). This necessitates institutional investment in capacity building of the faculty and learning communities of practice (Eaton, 2023).

Human-in-the-Loop Models

The human-in-the-loop constructs make AI a companion and complementary technology to human decision-making and not an autonomous system of functioning (Holzinger, 2016). At the assessment level, this may include AI-based systems that identify possible problems, propose the use of rubrics, or create rough feedback that teachers can review and revise before providing it to students (Lipnevich and Smith, 2022).

It has been argued that, in cases where they are designed appropriately, both hybrid human-AI estimation systems and either method can be more reliable and valid (Wilson and Roscoe, 2020). Nonetheless, this implementation must have established guidelines on how and when to disregard recommendations of AI and ways of escalating uncertainties to the human interface (Holstein and Doroudi, 2021).

Maintaining Assessment Authenticity

The use of authentic assessment involves tasks that have a genuine signification of the knowledge and skills that the students should have achieved (Wiggins, 1993). With the growth of AI functions, institutions are currently forced to reconsider the definition of what comprises genuine demonstration of learning (Bearman et al., 2022). This can include moving towards formats of assessment more focused on creativity, critical analysis, oral defense, collaborative work, and other formats less prone to AI completion (Villasenor, 2023).

Educators have to juggle the benefits of AI-assisted assessment on efficiency with the possibility of diminishing learning to the levels of what is measurable by the algorithm (Macfadyen et al., 2020). It involves long-term focus on the alignment between the methods of assessment and the desired learning outcomes, so that convenience does not override the purpose of education (Boud and Soler, 2016).

5.1 Multimodal Assessment and GenAI

Multimodal assessment, which entails the use of visual, auditory, and interactive representations, is gradually replacing traditional text-based assessment (Jewitt, 2008). GenAI technologies can provide advanced analysis of a wide range of assessment artifact such as video presentations, digital portfolios, design projects, and collaborative work products (Knight et al., 2020). The principles of visual design can be evaluated with the help of computer vision algorithms, oral communication skills can be assessed by speech recognition systems, and collaborative discourse patterns can be analyzed with the help of natural language processing (Southavilay et al., 2013).

Multimodal assessment provides a chance to appreciate a wide range of competence and cater to the different preferences of learning (Kress, 2010). Students with difficulties when it comes to the traditional written tests can have a deep level of understanding in other forms (Cope and Kalantzis, 2015). Multimodal assessment, however, also presents some new challenges to validity, with the various modalities being capable of measuring different constructs or favoring specific cultural communication standards (Archer and Breuer, 2015).

GenAI systems that are mainly trained on the mainstream cultural patterns can be confused or underestimated when it comes to multi-modal utterances by diverse student groups (Noble, 2018). As an illustration, the accuracy of automated speech assessment systems has been lower with speakers of non-standard forms of language (Koenecke et al., 2020). The visual assessment algorithms can not detect culturally specific design conventions or symbolic meanings (Crawford and Paglen, 2019). It is thus necessary that institutions that are applying multimodal GenAI assessment should focus on cultural validity and make sure that algorithmic decisions should be adjusted in such a manner that they can identify various types of excellence (Montenegro and Jankowski, 2020).

5.2 Adaptive and Personalized Assessment Pathways

Adaptive assessment systems apply AI algorithms that dynamically change the difficulty of questions, the focus of the content, and the format of the assessment using responses given by the individual students (Aleven et al., 2016). Such systems are said to be more effective and accurate in measuring knowledge of students since the focus of assessment is on the edge of student competence instead of giving the same tests to all students (van der Linden and Glas, 2010). GenAI utilizes adaptive assessment that creates individually relevant items on-the-fly and offers complex diagnostic feedback (Baraniuk et al., 2016).

The studies on computerized adaptive tests show that the measurement accuracy and test anxiety are better than in fixed-form testing (Wainer et al., 2000). According to the students, they find assessments based on their ability level more engaging, and there is no loss of reliability when the format is adjusted, because adaptive formats can decrease testing time (Magis et al., 2017). Nevertheless, adaptive assessment presents some peculiar fairness issues as well since students are not offered comparable assessment experiences, which are not necessarily comparable (Zenisky and Hambleton, 2012).

Many adaptive algorithms are black box and, therefore, transparency and contestability are questioned (Mittelstadt et al., 2016). Students do not necessarily get an explanation of why they are being given specific things and how their performance is being assessed in an individualized assessment pathway (Regan and Jesse, 2019). Also, adaptive systems have high item bank requirements and advanced psychometric models which pose a challenge to resource-limited institutions to implement (Yan et al., 2014). To perform effective adaptive assessment, it is necessary to strike a balance between the benefits of personalization and transparency, fairness, and practical feasibility (Holstein et al., 2018).

6. INSTITUTIONAL READINESS AND POLICY FRAMEWORKS

To achieve successful implementation of AI-based assessment, institutions must be institutionally ready on the technological, pedagogical, and policy levels (Martin et al., 2020). Data privacy, accountability, professional growth, and quality assurance have to be covered by governance frameworks (Selwyn et al., 2020). To make sure that GenAI is used responsibly and with agreement, institutions should invest in faculty capacity building and digital literacy (Eaton, 2023).

Developing Institutional Policies

Detailed institutional policies must create explicit requirements of AI use in assessment, such as what it can be used to do, the degree of transparency, and accountability structures (Lancaster, 2023). The policies should strike a balance between innovation and risk reduction to allow experimentation and protect education standards and the rights of students (Zawacki-Richter et al., 2019).

To develop an effective policy, there must be an inclusive approach to stakeholder participation which involves faculty, students, educational technological, and institutional research practitioners (Williamson and Eynon 2020). The policies are to be improved sequentially in accordance with the experience of their implementation and new findings regarding the effectiveness and influence of AI (Holmes and Porayska-Pomsta, 2022).

Infrastructure and Technical Capacity

The AI-based assessment would demand a well-developed technological system, such as efficient platforms, data integration, and support infrastructure (Bond et al., 2020). The institutions need to evaluate their preparedness in various aspects, such as network capacity, data security measures, interoperability, and user support services (Ifenthaler & Yau, 2020).

The decisions to allocate resources must focus on fair accessibility, and AI improved assessment opportunities must be accessible to all students irrespective of their socioeconomic status or institutional affiliation (Baker and Haw, 2021). It might be necessary to make specific investments in technology access initiatives and support in digital literacy of underserved groups (Tsai et al., 2020).

Faculty Development and Support

The professional development of educators should be fully equipped to apply AI assessment tools in an effective and ethical way (Crompton & Burke, 2023). The professional development must be focused on technical skills, the concept of pedagogical integration, the critical assessment of AI products, and the moral side of the matter (Eaton, 2023). Learning opportunities among the faculty must not be in the form of a single training event, but continuous because AI technologies are rapidly developing (Popenici & Kerr, 2017).

The institutional support frameworks are to comprise of available documentation, programs of mentoring peers, and specific assistance with instructional design of the faculty using AI-assisted assessment (Martin et al., 2020). The system of recognition and rewards should appreciate well-considered pedagogical improvisation and sound principles of technology acceptance (Selwyn et al., 2020).

Quality Assurance Mechanisms

Good quality assurance mechanisms are a necessity to authenticating assessment practices that are supported by AI (AERA et al., 2014). Before widely implementing AI-generated assessments, institutions must formulate guidelines on how they can assess their reliability, validity, and fairness (Kane, 2013). This involves pilot testing on different student groups, a comparative study with other well-known assessment strategies, and continued evaluation of the results (Newton and Shaw, 2014).

Quality assurance is no longer a focus on technical performance but should also include educational effectiveness, student experience, and the identification with institutional mission and values (Bearman et al., 2022). The issue of whether AI assessment tools are meeting the expected learning goals and whether unintended implications are being found should be regularly audited (Holstein and Doroudi, 2021).

6.1 Student Agency and Assessment Literacy

With the further embedding of AI into the assessment process, student agency and assessment literacy emerge as the key concerns (Tai et al., 2018). The students should be aware of the principles of AI systems operation, their capabilities and limitations, and how they can engage effectively with AI-mediated assessment (Carless and Boud, 2018). Assessment literacy does not only involve knowledge of evaluation standards but also the ability to see the influence of AI tools on assessment procedures and results (Smith et al., 2013).

To empower students to practice agency in situations involving AI-mediated assessment, it is necessary to have a clear disclosure of the use of AI, the possibilities to provide feedback on AI-generated assessment, and the way of contesting the potential of algorithmic decisions (Slade and Prinsloo, 2013). They should not be seen as recipients of algorithmical judgment as students are supposed to be partners in the design of the assessment (Bovill, 2020). Participatory approach may raise issues of fairness and unintended impacts and make assessment innovations to be student focused and student oriented (Cook-Sather et al., 2014).

The literature shows that students have varied attitudes towards AI in assessment with some positively enjoying its personalization and efficiency and others having negative views due to concerns about privacy, equality, and the disappearance of a human touch (Crawford et al., 2023). Institutions should establish platforms where they engage in a continuous discussion on AI evaluation practices, making sure that the voices of students are incorporated into the decisions made in the process of policy creation and implementation (Dollinger et al., 2019). Development of assessment literacy and agency entails a deliberate pedagogical focus as opposed to a technical one (Boud et al., 2018).

6.2 Cross-Cultural and Linguistic Considerations

The evaluation systems based on AI are often created in specific cultural and language settings, which may be full of assumptions that discriminate against students with other backgrounds (Hutson et al., 2018). NLP systems that have been trained mostly on standard academic English might not be able to handle multilingualism in writing, code-switching, or culturally-based rhetorical choices (Blodgett et al., 2020). The automated essay scoring systems have shown to be systematically biased against the essays written by learners who use English language and minorities racial groups (Elliot, 2016).

The AI systems might fail to interpret the cultural differences in communication style, patterns of arguing, and knowledge representation as differences, but as weaknesses (Young, 2014). One instance of this is where collectivist forms of knowledge building may be reprimanded by systems that need to drive personal novelty (Biggs and Watkins, 2001). Multimodal and visual assessment instruments are not able to identify culturally distinct aesthetic principles or symbolic systems (Banks, 2019).

To handle these issues, AI assessment should be designed in a culturally responsive way, including a variety of views in the creation of algorithms, validation research carried out in diverse cultural backgrounds, and continuous observations of dissimilar performance in various groups of students (Gay, 2018). Educational institutions that have international and multicultural student populations have to be especially attentive to the aspect of cultural validity so that AI assessment tools can identify and appreciate other types of competence (De Wit & Altbach, 2021). This can include creating more localized or tailored AI models and not using generalized systems (Holmes et al., 2022).

7. TOWARD A HUMAN-CENTERED FRAMEWORK FOR AI-DRIVEN ASSESSMENT

Based on the above considerations, the chapter develops a human-centered system of AI-driven assessment design based on the five fundamental principles, namely the provision of pedagogical alignment, transparency and explainability, the maintenance of human judgment, the promise to fairness and inclusion, and the guarantee of ongoing quality assurance (adapted from Holmes and Porayska-Pomsta, 2022; Williamson and Eynon, 2020).

Table 3. Comparison of Existing AI Assessment Frameworks and the Proposed Human-Centered Framework

Framework	Primary Focus	Strengths	Limitations	Proposed Chapter Contribution
AI Ethics Framework	Responsible AI	Ethical principles	Limited pedagogical integration	Integrates ethics with pedagogy and governance
Learning Analytics Framework	Student performance prediction	Data-informed learning	Limited human oversight	Emphasizes educator decision-making
AI Assessment Frameworks	Assessment automation	Efficiency and scalability	Insufficient governance perspective	Combines AI efficiency with institutional accountability
Educational Technology Models	Technology adoption	Technology integration	Limited attention to assessment validity	Prioritizes validity, fairness, and educational quality
Proposed Human-Centered Framework	Integrated AI assessment governance	Combines pedagogy, ethics, governance, educator oversight, institutional readiness, and quality assurance	Provides comprehensive implementation guidance	Novel contribution of this chapter

Figure 1. Conceptual Framework for Human-Centered Governance of AI-Driven Assessment in Higher Education

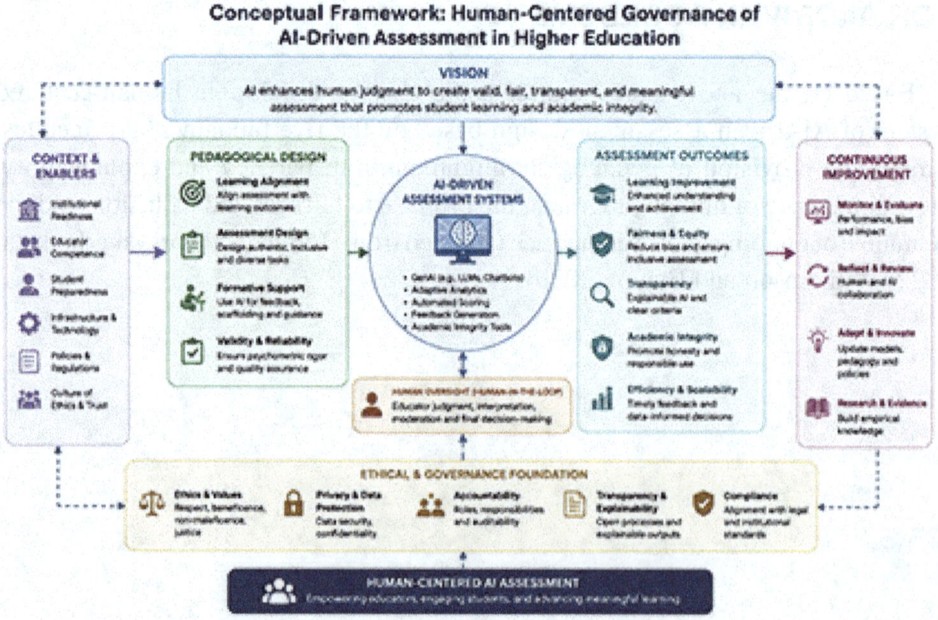

Figure 1. Proposed conceptual framework illustrating the integration of pedagogical alignment, ethical governance, institutional readiness, human oversight, and continuous quality assurance for the responsible implementation of AI-driven assessment in higher education. The framework positions AI as a tool that augments rather than replaces educator judgment while promoting fairness, transparency, accountability, and meaningful student learning.

Principle 1: Pedagogical Alignment

The AI assessment tools to be used should be chosen and configured according to the clear educational intentions in accordance with learning outcomes as opposed to technological possibilities (Macfadyen et al., 2020). The design of the assessments should start with the questions concerning what students should learn and how they will demonstrate learning, and the decisions related to AI integration should be based on these pedagogical backgrounds (Boud and Soler, 2016).

Principle 2: Transparency and Explainability

Learners and teachers are supposed to know the functionality of AI systems, the type of data they process, and how they make decisions (Barocas et al., 2019). Transparency is not limited to technical documentation, but rather available communication regarding the application of AI in assessment, such as the constraints and ambiguity in the outputs of the algorithms (Prinsloo and Slade, 2016).

Principle 3: Preservation of Human Judgment

The teachers should maintain the ultimate responsibility in decision-making on assessment, and AI systems should be seen as powerful supplements and not as independent decision-makers (Bayne, 2015). The human control should be substantial and not formal, and the systems of professional judgment must have a way to override the algorithms when necessary (Holstein et al., 2019).

Principle 4: Commitment to Fairness and Inclusion

The assessment systems based on AI should be created and supervised in such a way that they deliver fair results to the student population of different categories (Baker and Hawn, 2021). This involves taking active steps against bias, culturally sensitive design and disaggregated analysis of assessment outcomes (O'Neil, 2016). The concerns of fairness must be applied to every phase of AI evaluation development and application (Holstein and Doroudi, 2021).

Principle 5: Continuous Quality Assurance

Assessment that is based on AI must be evaluated and improved on a regular basis depending on the provision of evidence of the educational efficacy, technical accomplishment, and the experience of stakeholders (Kane, 2013). The quality assurance procedures ought to be systematic, transparent, and sensitive to new arising concerns (AERA et al., 2014). Organizations are encouraged to set transparent performance standards and guidelines on the termination of AI use that is not beneficial or even damaging (Selwyn et al., 2020).

7.1 Professional Development and AI Competencies

There should be long-term professional development in the field of AI implementation, encompassing technical, pedagogical, and ethical aspects of assessment (Caena & Redecker, 2019). Teachers should have a chance to gain practical experience with AI evaluation instruments and critically assess their affords and constraints as well as determine pedagogically valid ways of implementation (Ranieri et al., 2023). The professional development should go beyond training with tools to explore more in-depth questions regarding the purpose of assessment, its validity, and the role of human judgment that is currently changing (Trust et al., 2023). Communities of practice are beneficial frameworks of collaborative learning on AI assessment innovation (Wenger, 1998).

Sharing experiences, challenges, and solutions with members of different disciplines and institutional contexts, the members of the faculty create more advanced understandings of risks and opportunities (Voogt et al., 2015). The most suitable methods to AI-integrated assessment can be developed through interdisciplinary cooperation between educators, instructional designers, data scientists, and ethicists than any one of the perspectives separately (Bozkurt et al., 2021).

Professional development should not be supported by institutions in isolated instances, but an ongoing process, as AI technologies and best practices have yet to be discovered (Tondeur et al., 2012). Faculty should have secure experiment time, expert consultation, and reward mechanisms, which appreciate reflective pedagogical change (Henderson et al., 2017). The lack of institutionally-backed professional capacity building can lead to the poor implementation of AI assessment tools, which only lead to the worsening of educational difficulties instead of their solution (Ertmer & Ottenbreit-Leftwich, 2010).

7.2 Regulatory Compliance and Legal Considerations

The AI-driven assessment functions in a complex regulatory space such as laws in data protection, accessibility, and educational quality standards (Tsai et al., 2020). The General Data Protection Regulation (GDPR) in Europe sets high standards of processing student data, which includes the right to explanation, access, and erasure (Voigt and Von dem Bussche, 2017). The United States has a similar law, the Family Educational Rights and Privacy Act (FERPA), which limits the use of educational data, but with less extensive protections (Reidenberg and Schaub, 2018). The regulations of accessibility like the Americans with Disabilities Act (ADA) and Web Content Accessibility Guidelines (WCAG) stipulate that AI assessment tools should support a variety of learning requirements (Seale, 2020).

The systems of assessment based on algorithms have to offer the same experience to students with assistive technologies and not to cause prejudice to students with disabilities (Treviranus, 2018). Nevertheless, not all AI tools are accessible enough to allow students using the screen reader or alternative input devices, among other access methods (Whittaker et al., 2019). New AI-specific laws, such as the European Union AI Act, offer risk-based constructs of AI systems in education (Samoili et al., 2021). Assessment applications that demand high stakes have enhanced requirements of transparency, human supervision, and impact assessment (Floridi et al., 2018). Compliance frameworks should be created by institutions to cope with the current and upcoming regulation and be capable of adapting to the changing legal environment (Cath et al., 2018).

7.3 Sustainability and Long-Term Viability

Assessment founded on AI is not only sustainable in the short term but also in the long term, meaning that it requires maintenance, updating, and adaptation (Mor et al., 2015). The AI systems should be constantly improved because the curricula are always developing, students are changing, and new teaching methods appear (Roll and Wylie, 2016). The institutions need to strategize on long-term resource commitment such as technical infrastructure, personnel skills as well as financial sustainability (Adams Becker et al., 2017).

The use of vendors poses threats to institutional independence and survival in the long term (Williamson, 2018). In cases where the assessment systems are based on proprietary AI platforms, the institution can experience lock-in effects, cost increase, and restricted control over the evolution of the system (Audrin and Audrin, 2022). Open-source alternatives are more transparent and customizable, but demand a significant internal technical capability (Papamitsiou and Economides, 2014). Commercial convenience and long-term strategic control have to be assessed with care considering a trade-off in institutions (Selwyn et al., 2020). Environmental sustainability is also a more critical factor that is gaining momentum because AI systems use a large amount of computation and power (Strubell et al., 2019).

The process of training large language models consumes a lot of carbon, and the evaluation of AI-based assessment might be costly in terms of the environment (Schwartz et al., 2020). Achieving sustainability requires balancing AI affordances and environmental effects as the institution might prefer small, resource-efficient models to resource-intensive ones (Bender et al., 2021).

7.4 Implementation Roadmap

An effective application of human-centered AI evaluation cannot be achieved instantly by replacing the entire system of evidence-based phases (McNely and Teston, 2015). Pilots need to concentrate on the low-stakes formative contexts in which the risks are as low as possible and learning opportunities as high as possible (Conole, 2013). Strong assessment systems should also be introduced in pilot implementation to analyze technical work, pedagogical efficiency, student experience and equity implications (Mor & Winters, 2007). Reproduction of pilots to comprehensive implementation should be keen to aspects of contexts such as disciplinary variation, the nature of student's population and institutional cultural (Dede, 2006). Things that have been successful in one setting would entail a lot of adjustment in another setting (Cohen, 1987).

Evidence-based decision points should also be included in the implementation roadmaps to assess the pilot outcomes, refine approaches, and decide whether to continue with the expansion or not (Fixsen et al., 2005). By involving the stakeholders in the implementation cycles, it is possible to make sure that various opinions should guide the decision-making processes and that the concerns are addressed in advance (Freeman et al., 2020). Constant communication on the progress of implementation, challenges, and results helps build trust and contribute to shared learning (Grunwald, 2018). The end result of successful AI assessment implementation lies in human factors, institutional leadership, commitment of faculty, student trust and collective willingness to engage constructively with innovation as much as technical capabilities (Cuban, 2001).

Table 4. Practical Implementation Roadmap for Human-Centered AI Assessment in Higher Education

Implementation Phase	Institutional Actions	Responsible Stakeholders	Expected Outcomes
Phase 1: Readiness Assessment	Evaluate infrastructure, faculty competencies, institutional policies	Institutional leaders, IT teams	Organizational readiness
Phase 2: Pilot Implementation	Introduce AI in low-stakes formative assessments	Faculty, instructional designers	Initial evidence of effectiveness
Phase 3: Faculty Capacity Building	Conduct professional development and AI literacy programs	Academic development units	Improved educator competence
Phase 4: Ethical Governance	Develop AI governance policies, privacy safeguards, transparency protocols	Ethics committees, administrators	Responsible AI implementation
Phase 5: Continuous Quality Assurance	Monitor validity, fairness, bias, student satisfaction, and learning outcomes	Quality assurance offices	Sustainable AI-enhanced assessment
Phase 6: Continuous Improvement	Revise policies, update AI tools, incorporate stakeholder feedback	Institutional leadership	Long-term sustainable assessment ecosystem

8. CONCLUSION

The increasing necessity to rethink the practices of assessment in tertiary education is emphasized in this chapter as the integration of artificial intelligence rapidly extends. Since AI tools are more likely to shape the evaluation of learning, the use of traditional assessment models will become inadequate to tackle new pedagogical, ethical, and institutional issues. The chapter explains the need of such reconceptualization by showing that AI is efficient, scalable and able to provide personalized feedback, but also poses threats of bias, loss of transparency, low validity and weaker human judgment. The discussion underlines that assessment is not an insulated process but very human and a value-oriented process. Unless AI-based assessment is governed and pedagogically aligned, it is likely to focus more on that which is easily quantifiable rather than that which is an important part of the education. Thus, this chapter highlights the need to have human control, fairness and inclusiveness, student agency and data privacy. It also highlights how teachers play a critical role of being interpreters, decision-makers, and ethical custodians within the AI-assisted assessment settings. Besides, the chapter defines the institutional preparedness by setting explicit policies, faculty preparation, quality assurance systems, and long-term implementation plans. The chapter offers an ethical and practical guide to the institutions that are undergoing the integration of AI by proposing a human-centered model based on transparency, accountability, and constant testing. On the whole, this chapter is needed to help the stakeholders of higher education to move towards responsible, balanced, and future-oriented assessment that does not undermine the essence of education but rather welcomes the technological innovation.

REFERENCES

Adams Becker, S., Cummins, M., Davis, A., Freeman, A., Hall Giesinger, C., & Ananthanarayanan, V. (2017). *NMC horizon report: 2017 higher education edition*. The New Media Consortium., DOI: 10.1111/cura.12022

Aleven, V., McLaughlin, E. A., Glenn, R. A., & Koedinger, K. R. (2016). Instruction based on adaptive learning technologies. In Mayer, R. E., & Alexander, P. A. (Eds.), *Handbook of research on learning and instruction* (pp. 522–560). Routledge., DOI: 10.4324/9781315736419

American Educational Research Association (AERA), American Psychological Association (APA), & National Council on Measurement in Education (NCME). (2014). *Standards for educational and psychological testing*. American Educational Research Association. DOI: 10.2307/j.ctvr43hg2

Ananny, M., & Crawford, K. (2018). Seeing without knowing: Limitations of the transparency ideal and its application to algorithmic accountability. *New Media & Society*, *20*(3), 973–989. DOI: 10.1177/1461444816676645

Archer, A., & Breuer, E. (Eds.). (2015). *Multimodality in writing: The state of the art in theory, methodology and pedagogy*. Brill., DOI: 10.1163/9789004297197

Audrin, C., & Audrin, B. (2022). Key factors in digital literacy in learning and education: A systematic literature review using text mining. *Education and Information Technologies*, *27*(6), 7395–7419. DOI: 10.1007/s10639-021-10832-5

Baker, R. S., & Hawn, A. (2021). Algorithmic bias in education. *International Journal of Artificial Intelligence in Education*, *32*(4), 1052–1092. DOI: 10.1007/s40593-021-00285-9

Baker, R. S., & Inventado, P. S. (2014). Educational data mining and learning analytics. In Larusson, J. A., & White, B. (Eds.), *Learning analytics: From research to practice* (pp. 61–75). Springer., DOI: 10.1007/978-1-4614-3305-7_4

Banks, M. (2019). Fighting the tyranny of the pixel: The visual culture reader as a resource for the methodological development of visual research. *Visual Studies*, *34*(2), 181–190. DOI: 10.1080/1472586X.2019.1653223

Baraniuk, R. G., Burrus, C. S., Johnson, D. H., & Jones, D. L. (2016). Adaptive assessment and training using the Web. *Proceedings of the IEEE International Conference on Acoustics, Speech, and Signal Processing*, *6*, 3868–3871. DOI: 10.1109/ICASSP.1997.604701

Barocas, S., Hardt, M., & Narayanan, A. (2019). *Fairness and machine learning: Limitations and opportunities*. MIT Press., DOI: 10.7551/mitpress/12200.001.0001

Bayne, S. (2015). Teacherbot: Interventions in automated teaching. *Teaching in Higher Education, 20*(4), 455–467. DOI: 10.1080/13562517.2015.1020783

Bearman, M., Dawson, P., Bennett, S., Hall, M., Molloy, E., Boud, D., & Joughin, G. (2022). How university teachers design assessments: A cross-disciplinary study. *Higher Education, 74*(1), 49–64. DOI: 10.1007/s10734-016-0027-7

Bender, E. M., Gebru, T., McMillan-Major, A., & Shmitchell, S. (2021). On the dangers of stochastic parrots: Can language models be too big? *Proceedings of the 2021 ACM Conference on Fairness, Accountability, and Transparency*, 610-623. DOI: 10.1145/3442188.3445922

Bertram Gallant, T. (2008). *Academic integrity in the twenty-first century: A teaching and learning imperative*. Jossey-Bass., DOI: 10.1002/9781118638521

Biggs, J., & Watkins, D. (2001). Insights into teaching the Chinese learner. In Watkins, D., & Biggs, J. (Eds.), *Teaching the Chinese learner: Psychological and pedagogical perspectives* (pp. 277–300). Comparative Education Research Centre., DOI: 10.1007/978-94-011-3620-1_16

Black, P., & Wiliam, D. (2009). Developing the theory of formative assessment. *Educational Assessment, Evaluation and Accountability, 21*(1), 5–31. DOI: 10.1007/s11092-008-9068-5

Blodgett, S. L., Barocas, S., Daumé, H.III, & Wallach, H. (2020). Language (technology) is power: A critical survey of "bias" in NLP. *Proceedings of the 58th Annual Meeting of the Association for Computational Linguistics*, 5454-5476. DOI: 10.18653/v1/2020.acl-main.485

Bond, M., Zawacki-Richter, O., & Nichols, M. (2020). Revisiting five decades of educational technology research: A content and authorship analysis. *British Journal of Educational Technology, 51*(3), 1854–1877. DOI: 10.1111/bjet.12899

Boud, D., Ajjawi, R., Dawson, P., & Tai, J. (Eds.). (2018). *Developing evaluative judgement in higher education: Assessment for knowing and producing quality work*. Routledge., DOI: 10.4324/9781315109251

Boud, D., & Soler, R. (2016). Sustainable assessment revisited. *Assessment & Evaluation in Higher Education, 41*(3), 400–413. DOI: 10.1080/02602938.2015.1018133

Bovill, C. (2020). Co-creation in learning and teaching: The case for a whole-class approach in higher education. *Higher Education*, *79*(6), 1023–1037. DOI: 10.1007/s10734-019-00453-w

Bozkurt, A., Karadeniz, A., Baneres, D., Guerrero-Roldán, A. E., & Rodríguez, M. E. (2021). Artificial intelligence and reflections from educational landscape: A review of AI studies in half a decade. *Sustainability (Basel)*, *13*(2), 800. DOI: 10.3390/su13020800

Caena, F., & Redecker, C. (2019). Aligning teacher competence frameworks to 21st century challenges: The case for the European Digital Competence Framework for Educators. *European Journal of Education*, *54*(3), 356–369. DOI: 10.1111/ejed.12345

Carless, D. (2015). *Excellence in university assessment: Learning from award-winning practice*. Routledge., DOI: 10.4324/9781315740621

Carless, D., & Boud, D. (2018). The development of student feedback literacy: Enabling uptake of feedback. *Assessment & Evaluation in Higher Education*, *43*(8), 1315–1325. DOI: 10.1080/02602938.2018.1463354

Cath, C., Wachter, S., Mittelstadt, B., Taddeo, M., & Floridi, L. (2018). Artificial intelligence and the 'good society': The US, EU, and UK approach. *Science and Engineering Ethics*, *24*(2), 505–528. DOI: 10.1007/s11948-017-9901-7

Cohen, D. K. (1987). Educational technology, policy, and practice. *Educational Evaluation and Policy Analysis*, *9*(2), 153–170. DOI: 10.3102/01623737009002153

Conole, G. (2013). *Designing for learning in an open world*. Springer., DOI: 10.1007/978-1-4419-8517-0

Cook-Sather, A., Bovill, C., & Felten, P. (2014). *Engaging students as partners in learning and teaching: A guide for faculty*. Jossey-Bass., DOI: 10.1002/tl.20106

Cope, B., & Kalantzis, M. (2015). *A pedagogy of multiliteracies: Learning by design*. Palgrave Macmillan., DOI: 10.1057/9781137539724

Crawford, J., Cowling, M., & Allen, K. A. (2023). Leadership is needed for ethical ChatGPT: Character, assessment, and learning using artificial intelligence (AI). *Journal of University Teaching & Learning Practice*, 20(3), 02. DOI: 10.53761/1.20.3.02

Crawford, K., & Paglen, T. (2019). Excavating AI: The politics of images in machine learning training sets. *AI & Society*, *36*(4), 1105–1116. DOI: 10.1007/s00146-019-00934-z

Crompton, H., & Burke, D. (2023). Artificial intelligence in higher education: The state of the field. *International Journal of Educational Technology in Higher Education, 20*(1), 1–22. DOI: 10.1186/s41239-023-00392-8

Cuban, L. (2001). *Oversold and underused: Computers in the classroom.* Harvard University Press., DOI: 10.4159/9780674030107

Dawson, P., Henderson, M., Mahoney, P., Phillips, M., Ryan, T., Boud, D., & Molloy, E. (2019). What makes for effective feedback: Staff and student perspectives. *Assessment & Evaluation in Higher Education, 44*(1), 25–36. DOI: 10.1080/02602938.2018.1467877

De Wit, H., & Altbach, P. G. (2021). Internationalization in higher education: Global trends and recommendations for its future. *Policy Reviews in Higher Education, 5*(1), 28–46. DOI: 10.1080/23322969.2020.1820898

Dede, C. (2006). Scaling up: Evolving innovations beyond ideal settings to challenging contexts of practice. In Sawyer, R. K. (Ed.), *The Cambridge handbook of the learning sciences* (pp. 551–566). Cambridge University Press., DOI: 10.1017/CBO9780511816833.034

Dollinger, M., Lodge, J. M., & Coates, H. (2019). Co-creation in higher education: Towards a conceptual model. *Journal of Industry-University Collaboration, 1*(1), 45–59. DOI: 10.1108/JIUC-01-2018-0003

Drachsler, H., & Greller, W. (2016). Privacy and analytics: It's a DELICATE issue. *Proceedings of the 6th International Conference on Learning Analytics & Knowledge*, 89-98. DOI: 10.1145/2883851.2883893

Eaton, S. E. (2023). ChatGPT and other AI text generators: Strategies for promoting academic integrity. *Innovations in Education and Teaching International.* Advance online publication. DOI: 10.1080/14703297.2023.2190148

Elliot, N. (2016). A theory of ethics for writing assessment. *Journal of Writing Assessment, 9*(1). Advance online publication. DOI: 10.5281/zenodo.55756

Ertmer, P. A., & Ottenbreit-Leftwich, A. T. (2010). Teacher technology change: How knowledge, confidence, beliefs, and culture intersect. *Journal of Research on Technology in Education, 42*(3), 255–284. DOI: 10.1080/15391523.2010.10782551

Eynon, R. (2021). What should be the role of AI in education? *AI & Society, 36*(4), 1199–1203. DOI: 10.1007/s00146-020-01040-4

Ferguson, R. (2012). Learning analytics: Drivers, developments and challenges. *International Journal of Technology Enhanced Learning*, *4*(5-6), 304–317. DOI: 10.1504/IJTEL.2012.051816

Fixsen, D. L., Naoom, S. F., Blase, K. A., Friedman, R. M., & Wallace, F. (2005). *Implementation research: A synthesis of the literature*. University of South Florida., DOI: 10.1037/e525602012-001

Floridi, L., Cowls, J., Beltrametti, M., Chatila, R., Chazerand, P., Dignum, V., Luetge, C., Madelin, R., Pagallo, U., Rossi, F., Schafer, B., Valcke, P., & Vayena, E. (2018). AI4People, An ethical framework for a good AI society: Opportunities, risks, principles, and recommendations. *Minds and Machines*, *28*(4), 689–707. DOI: 10.1007/s11023-018-9482-5

Freeman, R. E., Phillips, R., & Sisodia, R. (2020). Tensions in stakeholder theory. *Business & Society*, *59*(2), 213–231. DOI: 10.1177/0007650318773750

Fyfe, P. (2023). How to cheat on your final paper: Assigning AI for student writing. *AI & Society*, *38*(4), 1395–1405. DOI: 10.1007/s00146-022-01397-z

Gardner, J., & Brooks, C. (2018). Student success prediction in MOOCs. *User Modeling and User-Adapted Interaction*, *28*(2), 127–203. DOI: 10.1007/s11257-018-9203-z

Gay, G. (2018). *Culturally responsive teaching: Theory, research, and practice* (3rd ed.). Teachers College Press.

Gikandi, J. W., Morrow, D., & Davis, N. E. (2011). Online formative assessment in higher education: A review of the literature. *Computers & Education*, *57*(4), 2333 2351. DOI: 10.1016/j.compedu.2011.06.004

Grunwald, A. (2018). Societal engagement in the age of artificial intelligence. *AI & Society*, *33*(3), 477–478. DOI: 10.1007/s00146-018-0846-4

Hattie, J., & Timperley, H. (2007). The power of feedback. *Review of Educational Research*, *77*(1), 81–112. DOI: 10.3102/003465430298487

Henderson, M., Selwyn, N., & Aston, R. (2017). What works and why? Student perceptions of 'useful' digital technology in university teaching and learning. *Studies in Higher Education*, *42*(8), 1567–1579. DOI: 10.1080/03075079.2015.1007946

Herodotou, C., Rienties, B., Hlosta, M., Boroowa, A., Mangafa, C., & Zdrahal, Z. (2020). The scalable implementation of predictive learning analytics at a distance learning university: Insights from a longitudinal case study. *The Internet and Higher Education*, *45*, 100725. DOI: 10.1016/j.iheduc.2020.100725

Holmes, W., Anastopoulou, S., Schaumburg, H., & Mavrikis, M. (2022). *Technology-enhanced personalised learning: Untangling the evidence.* Robert Bosch Stiftung. DOI: 10.25656/01:25412

Holmes, W., Bialik, M., & Fadel, C. (2019). *Artificial intelligence in education: Promises and implications for teaching and learning.* Center for Curriculum Redesign., DOI: 10.1007/s40593-021-00237-x

Holmes, W., & Porayska-Pomsta, K. (2022). *The ethics of artificial intelligence in education: Practices, challenges, and debates.* Routledge., DOI: 10.4324/9780429329067

Holstein, K., & Doroudi, S. (2021). Equity and artificial intelligence in education: Will "AIEd" amplify or alleviate inequities in education? *arXiv preprint.* /arXiv.2104.12920DOI: 10.48550

Holstein, K., Hong, G., Tegene, M., McLaren, B. M., & Aleven, V. (2018). The classroom as a dashboard: Co-designing wearable cognitive augmentation for K-12 teachers. *Proceedings of the 8th International Conference on Learning Analytics and Knowledge*, 79-88. DOI: 10.1145/3170358.3170377

Holstein, K., McLaren, B. M., & Aleven, V. (2019). Co-designing a real-time classroom orchestration tool to support teacher-AI complementarity. *Journal of Learning Analytics*, *6*(2), 27–52. DOI: 10.18608/jla.2019.62.3

Holzinger, A. (2016). Interactive machine learning for health informatics: When do we need the human-in-the-loop? *Brain Informatics*, *3*(2), 119–131. DOI: 10.1007/s40708-016-0042-6

Hutson, J., Taft, J. G., Barocas, S., & Levy, K. (2018). Debiasing desire: Addressing bias & discrimination on intimate platforms. *Proceedings of the ACM on Human-Computer Interaction*, 2(CSCW), 1-18. DOI: 10.1145/3274342

Ifenthaler, D., & Yau, J. Y. K. (2020). Utilising learning analytics to support study success in higher education: A systematic review. *Educational Technology Research and Development*, *68*(4), 1961–1990. DOI: 10.1007/s11423-020-09788-z

Jewitt, C. (2008). Multimodality and literacy in school classrooms. *Review of Research in Education*, *32*(1), 241–267. DOI: 10.3102/0091732X07310586

Johnstone, S. M., & Soares, L. (2014). Principles for developing competency-based education programs. *Change*, *46*(2), 12–19. DOI: 10.1080/00091383.2014.896705

Kane, M. T. (2013). Validating the interpretations and uses of test scores. *Journal of Educational Measurement*, *50*(1), 1–73. DOI: 10.1111/jedm.12000

Kasneci, E., Sessler, K., Küchemann, S., Bannert, M., Dementieva, D., Fischer, F., Gasser, U., Groh, G., Günnemann, S., Hüllermeier, E., Krusche, S., Kutyniok, G., Michaeli, T., Nerdel, C., Pfeffer, J., Poquet, O., Sailer, M., Schmidt, A., Seidel, T., & Kasneci, G. (2023). ChatGPT for good? On opportunities and challenges of large language models for education. *Learning and Individual Differences*, *103*, 102274. DOI: 10.1016/j.lindif.2023.102274

Kizilcec, R. F., & Lee, H. (2022). Algorithmic fairness in education. In Khosrow-Pour, M. (Ed.), *Encyclopedia of information science and technology* (5th ed., pp. 1–15). IGI Global., DOI: 10.4018/978-1-7998-9220-5.ch132

Knight, S., Shum, S. B., Ryan, P., Sándor, Á., & Wang, X. (2020). Designing academic writing analytics for civil law student self-assessment. *International Journal of Artificial Intelligence in Education*, *28*(1), 1–28. DOI: 10.1007/s40593-016-0121-0

Knox, J. (2020). Artificial intelligence and education in China. *Learning, Media and Technology*, *45*(3), 298–311. DOI: 10.1080/17439884.2020.1754236

Koenecke, A., Nam, A., Lake, E., Nudell, J., Quartey, M., Mengesha, Z., Toups, C., Rickford, J. R., Jurafsky, D., & Goel, S. (2020). Racial disparities in automated speech recognition. *Proceedings of the National Academy of Sciences of the United States of America*, *117*(14), 7684–7689. DOI: 10.1073/pnas.1915768117

Kress, G. (2010). *Multimodality: A social semiotic approach to contemporary communication*. Routledge., DOI: 10.4324/9780203970034

Kuhail, M. A., Alturki, N., Alramlawi, S., & Alhejori, K. (2023). Interacting with educational chatbots: A systematic review. *Education and Information Technologies*, *28*(1), 973–1018. DOI: 10.1007/s10639-022-11177-3

Kulik, J. A., & Fletcher, J. D. (2016). Effectiveness of intelligent tutoring systems: A meta-analytic review. *Review of Educational Research*, *86*(1), 42–78. DOI: 10.3102/0034654315581420

Lancaster, T. (2023). Academic integrity challenges in the era of ChatGPT. *Journal of Academic Ethics*. Advance online publication. DOI: 10.1007/s10805-023-09478-1

Lipnevich, A. A., & Smith, J. K. (2022). *The Cambridge handbook of instructional feedback*. Cambridge University Press., DOI: 10.1017/9781009180344

Lodge, J. M., Kennedy, G., & Lockyer, L. (2018). Digital learning environments, the science of learning, and the relationship between the teacher and the learner. In Lodge, J. M., Horvath, J. C., & Corrin, L. (Eds.), *Understanding and shaping student learning* (pp. 1–14). Springer., DOI: 10.1007/978-3-319-72669-5_1

Lodge, J. M., & Thompson, K. (2024). Generative artificial intelligence and learning analytics. *Journal of Learning Analytics*, *11*(1), 1–8. DOI: 10.18608/jla.2024.8255

Luckin, R., & Cukurova, M. (2019). Designing educational technologies in the age of AI: A learning sciences-driven approach. *British Journal of Educational Technology*, *50*(6), 2824–2838. DOI: 10.1111/bjet.12861

Luckin, R., Holmes, W., Griffiths, M., & Forcier, L. B. (2016). *Intelligence unleashed: An argument for AI in education*. Pearson. DOI: 10.13140/RG.2.2.30194.84164

Macfadyen, L. P., Dawson, S., Pardo, A., & Gašević, D. (2020). Embracing big data in complex educational systems: The learning analytics imperative and the policy challenge. *Research & Practice in Assessment*, *9*, 17–28.

Magis, D., Yan, D., & Von Davier, A. A. (2017). *Computerized adaptive and multistage testing with R: Using packages catR and mstR*. Springer., DOI: 10.1007/978-3-319-69218-0

Martin, F., Sun, T., & Westine, C. D. (2020). A systematic review of research on online teaching and learning from 2009 to 2018. *Computers & Education*, *159*, 104009. DOI: 10.1016/j.compedu.2020.104009

McNely, B. J., & Teston, C. B. (2015). Tactical and strategic: Qualitative approaches to the digital humanities. In Ridolfo, J., & Hart-Davidson, W. (Eds.), *Rhetoric and the digital humanities* (pp. 111–126). University of Chicago Press., DOI: 10.7208/chicago/9780226177274.003.0008

Messick, S. (1989). Validity. In Linn, R. L. (Ed.), *Educational measurement* (3rd ed., pp. 13–103). American Council on Education/Macmillan.

Mittelstadt, B. D., Allo, P., Taddeo, M., Wachter, S., & Floridi, L. (2016). The ethics of algorithms: Mapping the debate. *Big Data & Society*, *3*(2), 2053951716679679. DOI: 10.1177/2053951716679679

Montenegro, E., & Jankowski, N. A. (2020). A new decade for assessment: Embedding equity into assessment praxis. *Occasional Paper No. 42*. National Institute for Learning Outcomes Assessment. DOI: 10.7282/t3-kbtn-ex80

Mor, Y., Craft, B., & Hernández-Leo, D. (2015). The art and science of learning design [Editorial]. *Research in Learning Technology*, *21*. Advance online publication. DOI: 10.3402/rlt.v21i0.22513

Mor, Y., & Winters, N. (2007). Design approaches in technology-enhanced learning. *Interactive Learning Environments*, *15*(1), 61–75. DOI: 10.1080/10494820601044236

Newton, P. E., & Shaw, S. D. (2014). *Validity in educational and psychological assessment*. SAGE Publications., DOI: 10.4135/9781446288856

Noble, S. U. (2018). *Algorithms of oppression: How search engines reinforce racism*. NYU Press., DOI: 10.18574/nyu/9781479833641.001.0001

O'Neil, C. (2016). *Weapons of math destruction: How big data increases inequality and threatens democracy*. Crown., DOI: 10.1080/2330443X.2018.1436530

Ouyang, F., Zheng, L., & Jiao, P. (2022). Artificial intelligence in online higher education: A systematic review of empirical research from 2011 to 2020. *Education and Information Technologies*, *27*(6), 7893–7925. DOI: 10.1007/s10639-022-10925-9

Papamitsiou, Z., & Economides, A. A. (2014). Learning analytics and educational data mining in practice: A systematic literature review of empirical evidence. *Journal of Educational Technology & Society*, *17*(4), 49–64.

Pardo, A., Jovanovic, J., Dawson, S., Gašević, D., & Mirriahi, N. (2019). Using learning analytics to scale the provision of personalised feedback. *British Journal of Educational Technology*, *50*(1), 128–138. DOI: 10.1111/bjet.12592

Pasquale, F. (2015). *The black box society: The secret algorithms that control money and information*. Harvard University Press., DOI: 10.4159/harvard.9780674736061

Perelman, L. (2020). E-rater® doesn't rate: The validity of automated essay-scoring programs. *Journal of Writing Assessment*, *13*(1). Advance online publication. DOI: 10.5281/zenodo.3747603

Perkins, M., Roe, J., Postma, D., McGaughran, J., & Hickerson, D. (2023). Detection of GPT-4 generated text in higher education: Combining academic judgement and software to identify generative AI tool misuse. *Journal of Academic Ethics*. Advance online publication. DOI: 10.1007/s10805-023-09490-5

Popenici, S. A., & Kerr, S. (2017). Exploring the impact of artificial intelligence on teaching and learning in higher education. *Research and Practice in Technology Enhanced Learning*, *12*(1), 1–13. DOI: 10.1186/s41039-017-0062-8

Prinsloo, P., & Slade, S. (2016). Student vulnerability, agency, and learning analytics: An exploration. *Journal of Learning Analytics*, *3*(1), 159–182. DOI: 10.18608/jla.2016.31.10

Prinsloo, P., & Slade, S. (2017). An elephant in the learning analytics room: The obligation to act. *Proceedings of the 7th International Conference on Learning Analytics & Knowledge*, 46-55. DOI: 10.1145/3027385.3027406

Ranieri, M., Raffaghelli, J. E., & Bruni, I. (2023). Data literacy in teacher education: A scoping review and conceptual framework. *Teaching and Teacher Education*, *125*, 104049. DOI: 10.1016/j.tate.2023.104049

Regan, P. M., & Jesse, J. (2019). Ethical challenges of edtech, big data and personalized learning: Twenty-first century student sorting and tracking. *Ethics and Information Technology*, *21*(3), 167–179. DOI: 10.1007/s10676-018-9492-2

Reidenberg, J. R., & Schaub, F. (2018). Achieving big data privacy in education. *Theory and Research in Education*, *16*(3), 263–279. DOI: 10.1177/1477878518805308

Roll, I., & Wylie, R. (2016). Evolution and revolution in artificial intelligence in education. *International Journal of Artificial Intelligence in Education*, *26*(2), 582–599. DOI: 10.1007/s40593-016-0110-3

Rubel, A., & Jones, K. M. (2016). Student privacy in learning analytics: An information ethics perspective. *The Information Society*, *32*(2), 143–159. DOI: 10.1080/01972243.2016.1130502

Rudolph, J., Tan, S., & Tan, S. (2023). ChatGPT: Bullshit spewer or the end of traditional assessments in higher education? *Journal of Applied Learning and Teaching*, *6*(1), 342–363. DOI: 10.37074/jalt.2023.6.1.9

Samoili, S., Cobo, M. L., Gomez, E., De Prato, G., Martinez-Plumed, F., & Delipetrev, B. (2021). *AI watch. Defining artificial intelligence 2.0*. Publications Office of the European Union., DOI: 10.2760/019901

Schwartz, R., Dodge, J., Smith, N. A., & Etzioni, O. (2020). Green AI. *Communications of the ACM*, *63*(12), 54–63. DOI: 10.1145/3381831

Seale, J. (2020). *Simplifying accessibility in educational technologies and practices*. Routledge., DOI: 10.4324/9780429398650

Selwyn, N. (2019). *Should robots replace teachers? AI and the future of education*. Polity Press.

Selwyn, N. (2022). The future of AI and education: Some cautionary notes. *European Journal of Education*, *57*(4), 620–631. DOI: 10.1111/ejed.12532

Selwyn, N., Hillman, T., Bergviken Rensfeldt, A., & Perrotta, C. (2020). Digital technologies and the automation of education: Key questions and concerns. *Postdigital Science and Education*, *2*(3), 541–547. DOI: 10.1007/s42438-020-00150-7

Shermis, M. D., & Burstein, J. (Eds.). (2013). *Handbook of automated essay evaluation: Current applications and new directions*. Routledge., DOI: 10.4324/9780203122761

Shute, V. J. (2008). Focus on formative feedback. *Review of Educational Research*, *78*(1), 153–189. DOI: 10.3102/0034654307313795

Siemens, G., & Long, P. (2011). Penetrating the fog: Analytics in learning and education. *EDUCAUSE Review*, *46*(5), 30–32.

Slade, S., & Prinsloo, P. (2013). Learning analytics: Ethical issues and dilemmas. *The American Behavioral Scientist*, *57*(10), 1510–1529. DOI: 10.1177/0002764213479366

Smith, C. D., Worsfold, K., Davies, L., Fisher, R., & McPhail, R. (2013). Assessment literacy and student learning: The case for explicitly developing students 'assessment literacy'. *Assessment & Evaluation in Higher Education*, *38*(1), 44–60. DOI: 10.1080/02602938.2011.598636

Southavilay, V., Yacef, K., Reimann, P., & Calvo, R. A. (2013). Analysis of collaborative writing processes using revision maps and probabilistic topic models. *Proceedings of the 3rd International Conference on Learning Analytics and Knowledge*, 38-47. DOI: 10.1145/2460296.2460307

Strubell, E., Ganesh, A., & McCallum, A. (2019). Energy and policy considerations for deep learning in NLP. *Proceedings of the 57th Annual Meeting of the Association for Computational Linguistics*, 3645-3650. DOI: 10.18653/v1/P19-1355

Sullivan, M., Kelly, A., & McLaughlan, P. (2023). ChatGPT in higher education: Considerations for academic integrity and student learning. *Journal of Applied Learning and Teaching*, *6*(1), 31–40. DOI: 10.37074/jalt.2023.6.1.17

Tai, J., Ajjawi, R., Boud, D., Dawson, P., & Panadero, E. (2018). Developing evaluative judgement: Enabling students to make decisions about the quality of work. *Higher Education*, *76*(3), 467–481. DOI: 10.1007/s10734-017-0220-3

Tondeur, J., Van Braak, J., Sang, G., Voogt, J., Fisser, P., & Ottenbreit-Leftwich, A. (2012). Preparing pre-service teachers to integrate technology in education: A synthesis of qualitative evidence. *Computers & Education*, *59*(1), 134–144. DOI: 10.1016/j.compedu.2011.10.009

Treviranus, J. (2018). Learning differences and digital equity. In *The Cambridge handbook of computing education research* (pp. 420–443). Cambridge University Press., DOI: 10.1017/9781108654555.016

Trust, T., Maloy, R. W., & Edwards, S. (2023). Learning about AI through five big ideas: A guide for secondary teachers. *TechTrends*, *67*(2), 325–334. DOI: 10.1007/s11528-022-00809-4

Tsai, Y. S., Rates, D., Moreno-Marcos, P. M., Muñoz-Merino, P. J., Jivet, I., Scheffel, M., Drachsler, H., Kloos, C. D., & Gašević, D. (2020). Learning analytics in European higher education, Trends and barriers. *Computers & Education, 155*, 103933. DOI: 10.1016/j.compedu.2020.103933

van der Linden, W. J., & Glas, C. A. (Eds.). (2010). *Elements of adaptive testing*. Springer., DOI: 10.1007/978-0-387-85461-8

Villasenor, J. (2023). How ChatGPT can improve education, not threaten it. *Scientific American*. Advance online publication. DOI: 10.1038/scientificamerican0323-12

Voigt, P., & Von dem Bussche, A. (2017). *The EU General Data Protection Regulation (GDPR): A practical guide*. Springer., DOI: 10.1007/978-3-319-57959-7

Voogt, J., Fisser, P., Pareja Roblin, N., Tondeur, J., & van Braak, J. (2015). Technological pedagogical content knowledge – A review of the literature. *Journal of Computer Assisted Learning*, *29*(2), 109–121. DOI: 10.1111/j.1365-2729.2012.00487.x

Wainer, H., Dorans, N. J., Flaugher, R., Green, B. F., & Mislevy, R. J. (2000). *Computerized adaptive testing: A primer* (2nd ed.). Lawrence Erlbaum Associates., DOI: 10.4324/9781410605931

Wang, Y., Liu, O. L., & Zhao, C. M. (2020). Evaluating automated essay scoring in mass assessment of English writing in China: Accuracy, validity, and fairness. *Educational Measurement: Issues and Practice*, *39*(3), 26–35. DOI: 10.1111/emip.12346

Wenger, E. (1998). *Communities of practice: Learning, meaning, and identity*. Cambridge University Press., DOI: 10.1017/CBO9780511803932

Whittaker, M., Crawford, K., Dobbe, R., Fried, G., Kaziunas, E., Mathur, V., West, S. M., Richardson, R., Schultz, J., & Schwartz, O. (2019). *AI now report 2018*. AI Now Institute at New York University.

Wiggins, G. (1993). *Assessing student performance: Exploring the purpose and limits of testing*. Jossey-Bass.

Williams, J. E., & III, J. D. (2016). Student privacy in learning analytics. In C. Haythornthwaite, R. Andrews, J. Fransman, & E. M. Meyers (Eds.), *The SAGE handbook of e-learning research* (pp. 438-457). SAGE Publications. DOI: 10.4135/9781473955011.n21

Williamson, B. (2018). The hidden architecture of higher education: Building a big data infrastructure for the 'smarter university'. *International Journal of Educational Technology in Higher Education*, *15*(1), 1–26. DOI: 10.1186/s41239-018-0094-1

Williamson, B., Bayne, S., & Shay, S. (2020). The datafication of teaching in higher education: Critical issues and perspectives. *Teaching in Higher Education*, *25*(4), 351–365. DOI: 10.1080/13562517.2020.1748811

Williamson, B., & Eynon, R. (2020). Historical threads, missing links, and future directions in AI in education. *Learning, Media and Technology*, *45*(3), 223–235. DOI: 10.1080/17439884.2020.1798995

Wilson, J., & Roscoe, R. D. (2020). Automated writing evaluation and feedback: Multiple metrics of efficacy. *Journal of Educational Computing Research*, *58*(1), 87–125. DOI: 10.1177/0735633119830764

Winne, P. H., & Baker, R. S. (2013). The potentials of educational data mining for researching metacognition, motivation and self-regulated learning. *JEDM-Journal of Educational Data Mining*, *5*(1), 1–8. DOI: 10.5281/zenodo.3554619

Yan, D., Von Davier, A. A., & Lewis, C. (Eds.). (2014). *Computerized multistage testing: Theory and applications*. CRC Press., DOI: 10.1201/b16858

Young, V. A. (2014). Other people's English and a other rhetorical dispositions. In Schroeder, C., Fox, H., & Bizzell, P. (Eds.), *ALT DIS: Alternative discourses and the academy* (pp. 49–60). Boynton/Cook., DOI: 10.2307/j.ctt5hjqkx.7

Zawacki-Richter, O., Marín, V. I., Bond, M., & Gouverneur, F. (2019). Systematic review of research on artificial intelligence applications in higher education – where are the educators? *International Journal of Educational Technology in Higher Education*, *16*(1), 1–27. DOI: 10.1186/s41239-019-0171-0

Zenisky, A. L., & Hambleton, R. K. (2012). Developing test score reports that work: The process and best practices for effective communication. *Educational Measurement: Issues and Practice*, *31*(2), 21–26. DOI: 10.1111/j.1745-3992.2012.00231.x

Chapter 2
Designing AI-Driven Assessments for Competency-Based Education in Higher Education

Meta Amalya Dewi
http://orcid.org/0000-0001-5353-9921
Binus University, Indonesia

ABSTRACT

This chapter investigates the development of assessments powered by Artificial Intelligence (AI) to facilitate Competency-Based Education (CBE) in the realm of higher education. The primary objective of this chapter is to analyze the potential of AI technologies to improve assessment methodologies through the provision of personalized, adaptive, and data-informed evaluations of student competencies. It reviews the foundational principles of CBE, scrutinizes the integration of AI in the design of assessments, and proposes essential guidelines for creating both AI-driven and AI-resilient assessment frameworks. Additionally, the chapter addresses strategies for implementation within digital learning contexts, presents illustrative use cases, and assesses the effectiveness of these approaches. Furthermore, it emphasizes the ethical, policy, and governance implications, offering strategic recommendations for educational institutions seeking to incorporate AI-enhanced assessment systems.

DOI: 10.4018/979-8-3373-9089-5.ch002

1. INTRODUCTION

1.1 Concept of Competency-Based Education (CBE)

Competency-Based Education (CBE) represents a significant evolution in the realm of higher education, placing paramount importance on the achievement of explicitly articulated competencies as opposed to the mere completion of time-bound instructional segments. In contrast to conventional paradigms that emphasize seat time and uniform progression, CBE prioritizes the observable mastery of knowledge, skills, and competencies that correspond to established learning outcomes. This shift in educational philosophy fosters more adaptable, individualized, and learner-focused experiences, which are increasingly essential in rapidly changing, technology-oriented contexts (Ponomarioviené et al.2025).

Competency-Based Education (CBE) is fundamentally rooted in the principles of Outcome-Based Education (OBE), which emphasize the clear articulation of learning objectives that are quantifiable and aligned with practical applications. The competencies are generally organized to encompass cognitive, technical, and interpersonal skills, allowing students to advance based on their mastery of content rather than predetermined timeframes. This structure facilitates self-paced learning, addressing various learning preferences and existing knowledge bases. Consequently, CBE fosters greater student autonomy and encourages deeper engagement with the material by prioritizing application and performance over mere memorization (Hamidi et al.2024).

A fundamental aspect of competency-based education (CBE) is the incorporation of genuine assessment methodologies. These assessments are structured to assess learners' capacities to utilize knowledge in real-world scenarios, typically employing project-based assignments, simulations, or portfolio assessments. This approach harmonizes educational objectives with industry standards, guaranteeing that graduates acquire skills pertinent to employment needs. Recent research indicates that competency-based models enhance employability by closing the divide between academic education and professional competencies (Rhoney et al.2024).

Furthermore, the implementation of CBE is increasingly supported by digital technologies and learning analytics. Data-driven insights enable educators to monitor student progress, identify competency gaps, and provide targeted interventions. The integration of Artificial Intelligence (AI) further enhances CBE by enabling adaptive learning pathways and personalized assessment strategies. These technologies facilitate continuous feedback and support individualized learning trajectories, reinforcing the core principles of CBE (Adabor et al., 2025).

Despite its advantages, the adoption of CBE presents several challenges. These include the complexity of defining measurable competencies, ensuring assessment validity and reliability, and redesigning institutional structures to support flexible learning pathways. Additionally, faculty readiness and the need for robust data governance frameworks remain critical considerations in scaling CBE effectively.

1.2 Assessment in CBE Context

Assessment plays a central role in Competency-Based Education (CBE), functioning as the primary mechanism for verifying whether learners have achieved predefined competencies. Unlike traditional assessment models that often emphasize summative testing and standardized measurement, assessment in CBE is designed to evaluate mastery through continuous, authentic, and performance-oriented approaches. This shift reflects the broader transition from content coverage to demonstrable learning outcomes, where assessment is not merely evaluative but also developmental (Chen et al.2024).

Within a Competency-Based Education (CBE) framework, assessments are meticulously aligned with well-defined competencies and learning outcomes. Each assessment task is purposefully crafted to evaluate particular skills or domains of knowledge, thereby promoting transparency and consistency in the educational process. This alignment allows educators to ascertain whether students can effectively apply their learnings in relevant and practical situations, rather than merely reciting information. Consequently, formative assessment is deemed especially significant, as it offers continuous feedback that aids learners in attaining mastery at their individual rates (Zaky, 2026).

Authentic assessment is a defining feature of CBE. It involves tasks such as case studies, simulations, portfolios, and project-based assignments that mirror real-world challenges. These approaches allow students to demonstrate higher-order thinking skills, including analysis, synthesis, and problem-solving. Research indicates that authentic assessments not only enhance learning engagement but also improve the transferability of skills to professional environments (Wan and Zaini, 2025). Furthermore, such assessments support the development of transversal competencies, including collaboration, communication, and critical thinking, which are essential in the modern workforce.

Another critical aspect of assessment in CBE is flexibility. Learners are allowed multiple opportunities to demonstrate competence, and assessments can be adapted to individual learning pathways. This flexibility supports personalized learning and accommodates diverse learner needs, including prior knowledge and varying learning speeds. Digital technologies and learning analytics further enhance this process by enabling real-time tracking of student progress and providing data-driven insights into competency development (Waladi and Lamarti, 2024).

The integration of Artificial Intelligence (AI) is increasingly shaping assessment practices in CBE. AI-driven tools can automate feedback, support adaptive testing, and analyze complex performance data to provide more precise evaluations of student competencies. These capabilities not only improve efficiency but also enable more granular and personalized assessment strategies. However, challenges remain, including ensuring fairness, transparency, and ethical use of student data (Deepshikha, 2026).

1.3 Challenges in Traditional Assessment Approaches

Conventional assessment methods in higher education have faced significant scrutiny due to their inadequacy in evaluating the multifaceted competencies necessary for modern educational landscapes. Primarily dependent on standardized tests, examinations with time restrictions, and summative assessments, these techniques frequently prioritize the memorization of information over the practical application of skills in authentic scenarios. As higher education progressively embraces Competency-Based Education (CBE), the shortcomings of traditional assessment frameworks become increasingly evident, particularly regarding their failure to effectively assess higher-order cognitive processes and transferable skills (Fagbohun et al. 2024).

A significant issue associated with conventional assessment methods is their insufficient alignment with specified learning outcomes. Frequently, assessments are developed in isolation from well-articulated competencies, which leads to a disconnect between instructional content and evaluative measures. This lack of alignment compromises the validity of assessment results and constrains their effectiveness in gauging whether students have met the designated learning objectives. Moreover, traditional assessment approaches typically employ a uniform strategy that does not consider the varying learning requirements, prior knowledge, and individual learning rates of students (Zhao et al. 2023).

Another noteworthy constraint is the inadequate provision of formative feedback. Conventional assessments typically emphasize summative evaluations, thereby offering few opportunities for students to obtain prompt and constructive feedback that could facilitate their learning process. This deficiency curtails the advancement of self-regulated learning and diminishes students' capacity to recognize and rectify their own skill deficits. Conversely, competency-based education (CBE) underscores the importance of ongoing assessment and iterative feedback, elements that are predominantly missing in traditional assessment frameworks (Mani, 2025).

Furthermore, conventional assessment strategies frequently fail to adequately gauge intricate and genuine performance. Abilities including critical thinking, problem-solving, collaboration, and creativity prove challenging to quantify through multiple-choice examinations or written assessments. Consequently, students may achieve high scores on these evaluations without necessarily demonstrating the competencies that are essential in professional environments. This disjunction further exacerbates the established disparity between academic success and preparedness for the workforce (Tai et al. 2023).

Scalability and efficiency pose significant challenges in the educational assessment landscape. Although conventional assessments are generally more straightforward to implement on a large scale, they fail to capitalize on the advantages offered by digital technologies for delivering tailored evaluations. The absence of integration with learning analytics constrains educators' capacity to track student progress in real-time and to make decisions informed by data. Additionally, concerns regarding academic integrity, including instances of cheating and plagiarism, become increasingly difficult to address within traditional assessment structures, particularly in the context of online and hybrid learning settings (McIntosh et al., 2025).

CHAPTER 2: THE ROLE OF ARTIFICIAL INTELLIGENCE IN ASSESSMENT DESIGN

2.1 Overview of AI Technologies in Education

Artificial Intelligence (AI) has swiftly reshaped the framework of higher education by facilitating adaptive, data-centric, and individualized learning experiences. Specifically, within the realm of assessment design, AI technologies present notable opportunities to improve the precision, effectiveness, and scalability of student competency evaluations. In a broader sense, AI in the educational sector includes a variety of technologies such as machine learning (ML), natural language processing (NLP), and generative AI, each of which plays a distinctive role in the advancement of sophisticated assessment systems (Chookaew et al., 2024).

Machine learning serves as a fundamental element in the realm of artificial intelligence applications within the educational sector. It empowers systems to discern patterns within extensive datasets, including metrics related to student performance, engagement, and learning behaviors. By employing predictive analytics, machine learning models are capable of forecasting student outcomes, identifying learners who may be at risk, and facilitating adaptive assessment methodologies. Such functionalities enable educators to customize assessments in accordance with individual learning pathways, thereby aligning with the foundational tenets of Competency-Based Education (CBE) (Huang et al., 2025).

Natural language processing (NLP) is fundamental in facilitating the capacity of artificial intelligence systems to comprehend and assess textual information.

Various NLP methodologies are employed in processes such as automated essay evaluation, grading of short answers, and the generation of feedback. Through the examination of linguistic characteristics, semantic cohesion, and the structure of arguments, NLP-based systems are capable of delivering prompt and uniform assessments of student submissions. This advancement not only alleviates the burden on instructors but also guarantees the provision of timely feedback, which is crucial for formative assessment within competency-based education (CBE) frameworks. (Olaniyan et al., 2025).

In recent developments, generative artificial intelligence, especially large language models (LLMs), has opened up innovative avenues for the design of assessments. These systems possess the capability to create assessment items, replicate interactive learning environments, and furnish tailored feedback contingent on students' responses. Generative AI enables the establishment of dynamic and adaptive assessment settings, wherein tasks can be modified in real time in accordance with learners' competency levels. Moreover, it aids in the formulation of authentic assessment tasks that accurately represent real-world challenges, thus improving the validity of competency evaluations (Khlaif et al., 2025).

Artificial intelligence is intricately linked to learning analytics, a process that encompasses the gathering and examination of educational data to guide decision-making. Systems employing learning analytics utilize AI to generate insights regarding student progression, pinpoint deficiencies in competencies, and suggest specific interventions. Such insights are especially beneficial in the formulation of ongoing and individualized assessment strategies that facilitate mastery learning (Chiu et al., 2024).

Despite these advancements, the adoption of AI technologies in education raises important challenges. Issues related to algorithmic bias, data privacy, and transparency must be carefully addressed to ensure ethical and equitable assessment practices. Additionally, the effectiveness of AI-driven assessment systems depends on the quality and diversity of the data used to train them.

2.2 AI-Driven Assessment Mechanisms

AI-driven assessment systems are revolutionizing the evaluation of student competencies within higher education by facilitating more adaptive, efficient, and data-informed methodologies. In contrast to conventional assessment frameworks, which tend to be fixed and uniform, AI-enhanced systems utilize sophisticated technologies, including machine learning, natural language processing (NLP), and generative AI, to dynamically customize assessment processes for individual learners. These advanced mechanisms are especially compatible with Competency-Based

Education (CBE), in which the ongoing assessment of mastery and individualized feedback are critical components (Alfaleh, 2026).

A notable application of artificial intelligence in education is the implementation of automated grading and feedback mechanisms. Employing natural language processing (NLP) alongside supervised machine learning models, AI systems demonstrate a remarkable capability to assess written responses, essays, and short-answer queries with a high level of consistency. These systems perform analyses of linguistic patterns, semantic coherence, and structural composition of arguments to deliver prompt feedback to learners. Such an expedited feedback process enhances formative assessment methodologies by allowing students to recognize deficiencies in their understanding and engage in iterative improvement. Research has indicated that AI-facilitated feedback can substantially enhance educational outcomes while concurrently alleviating the burden on instructors, particularly within large-scale course settings (Mahamad et al., 2025).

Another important mechanism is adaptive testing, which customizes evaluations according to a learner's performance in real time. Artificial intelligence algorithms modify the difficulty and nature of the questions based on the student's responses, ensuring that assessments remain suitably challenging and correspond to the learner's level of competency (Contrino et al., 2024). This methodology not only improves the accuracy of assessments but also boosts student engagement by preventing frustration caused by either excessively difficult or overly simplistic tasks. Adaptive assessment systems are extensively implemented in digital learning platforms and are especially beneficial in facilitating mastery-based progression within Competency-Based Education (CBE) settings.

Artificial Intelligence (AI) facilitates the processes of competency mapping and predictive assessment. Through the examination of extensive datasets reflecting student interactions, AI systems are capable of detecting patterns that suggest proficiency in particular competencies. Learning analytics dashboards, driven by AI technology, offer educators valuable insights into the progress of students, emphasizing their strengths as well as areas that necessitate additional support. Furthermore, predictive models have the ability to anticipate future performance, enabling proactive assistance and the implementation of targeted instructional methodologies. This approach, grounded in data analysis, improves decision-making and fosters ongoing assessment in accordance with established competency frameworks (Hochstetter-Diez et al., 2025).

Generative artificial intelligence significantly enhances assessment methodologies by facilitating the automated generation of assessment items and situational contexts. Advanced language models are capable of producing questions, case studies, and simulations that incorporate complex, realistic challenges. This capability promotes authentic assessment methodologies and fosters a variety of assessment tasks, thereby minimizing the potential for performance based on rote memorization. Furthermore, generative AI can create interactive assessment environments, exemplified by conversational agents, which provide real-time evaluations of students' reasoning processes (Salinas-Navarro et al., 2024).

Notwithstanding these benefits, AI-based evaluation systems pose certain challenges, particularly with respect to issues of bias, transparency, and the ethical utilization of data. The pursuit of fairness and accountability within automated frameworks continues to be an essential domain for both investigation and practical application.

2.3 Opportunities and Risks of AI in Assessment

The incorporation of Artificial Intelligence (AI) into assessment design offers considerable potential to improve the efficacy, efficiency, and customization of evaluative practices within higher education. Concurrently, it brings forth various risks that necessitate judicious management to uphold ethical, equitable, and credible assessment frameworks. In the realm of Competency-Based Education (CBE), where ongoing and personalized evaluation is paramount, it is essential to comprehend both the advantages and the constraints associated with AI (Memarian & Doleck, 2024).

A significant advantage provided by artificial intelligence in the realm of assessment is the enhancement of efficiency and scalability. AI-powered systems are capable of automating grading procedures, creating assessment materials, and delivering immediate feedback, which alleviates the burden on educators and facilitates prompt responses to students. This capability is especially beneficial in extensive or online educational settings, where traditional assessment methods can be labor-intensive. Furthermore, AI facilitates adaptive assessment, whereby tasks are fluidly modified according to learners' performance, thus promoting personalized learning trajectories and enhancing student engagement (Deepshikha, 2025).

Artificial intelligence significantly improves the accuracy and comprehensiveness of assessments by utilizing data-driven insights. Through the application of learning analytics, AI systems have the capacity to examine patterns related to student behavior and performance, thereby pinpointing areas of competency deficiency and forecasting potential future achievements. This capability facilitates more focused interventions and promotes mastery-based advancement, a fundamental aspect of competency-based education (CBE). Furthermore, generative AI technologies are capable of producing genuine and contextually rich assessment scenarios, which allows for the evaluation of advanced cognitive skills, such as problem-solving and critical thinking (Xu et al., 2024).

Notwithstanding the aforementioned benefits, the implementation of artificial intelligence in evaluative processes presents numerous significant risks. A primary concern pertains to algorithmic bias, wherein AI systems may yield unjust or discriminatory results stemming from prejudiced training datasets or deficient model architectures. Such biases can compromise the validity and equity of assessment outcomes, especially for heterogeneous student cohorts. Achieving fairness and inclusivity in AI-based assessment necessitates meticulous curation of datasets, transparency in the development of models, and continuous oversight (Hanna et al., 2025).

A noteworthy concern pertains to the transparency and explainability of artificial intelligence systems. Numerous AI frameworks, especially those grounded in intricate machine learning algorithms, function as "black boxes," thereby hindering both educators and students from comprehending the rationale behind assessment decisions. This deficiency in transparency may undermine confidence in AI-enhanced systems and complicate attempts to validate assessment results. The concept of Explainable AI (XAI) has been suggested as a potential remedy; however, its application within educational settings continues to pose significant challenges (Marey et al., 2024).

The considerations of data privacy and security are of paramount importance. Artificial intelligence systems depend extensively on substantial quantities of student data, which prompts significant concerns regarding the methodologies employed for the collection, storage, and utilization of this data. Educational institutions are obliged to adhere to data protection regulations and to implement comprehensive governance frameworks designed to protect student information effectively.

Ultimately, there exists a potential hazard of excessive dependence on artificial intelligence, which could undermine the significance of human discernment in evaluative processes. Although AI has the capacity to bolster and improve assessment methodologies, it must not supplant the pedagogical proficiency possessed by educators. An equitable approach that harmonizes human supervision with the functionalities of AI is crucial.

CHAPTER 3: DESIGNING AI-DRIVEN ASSESSMENTS FOR CBE

3.1 Principles of AI-Driven Assessment Design

The creation of AI-driven assessments within Competency-Based Education (CBE) necessitates a systematic methodology that harmonizes pedagogical principles, technological potential, and ethical considerations. Fundamentally, the design of AI-driven assessments must be anchored in well-articulated learning outcomes and competencies (Elshall & Badir, 2025). This structural alignment guarantees that assessment activities accurately evaluate the knowledge, skills, and competencies that learners are anticipated to exhibit. In CBE contexts, where advancement is determined by the attainment of mastery rather than the passage of time, assessments should be explicitly aligned with competency frameworks and organized to reflect diverse proficiency levels (Mani, 2025).

A foundational tenet of education is the personalization that centers on the learner. Artificial intelligence technologies facilitate the tailoring of assessment routes according to the distinct profiles of individual learners, which encompass their prior knowledge, rate of learning, and performance trends. Adaptive assessment frameworks responsively modify the difficulty of tasks and the content presented based on student responses, thereby ensuring that learners are consistently confronted with suitably challenging material. This level of personalization not only amplifies student engagement but also aids in achieving a more precise evaluation of competencies, as students are assessed in contexts that mirror their unique educational journeys (Adabor et al., 2025).

An additional fundamental principle is the incorporation of continuous and formative assessment. Systems powered by artificial intelligence enhance the provision of immediate feedback via automated evaluation and analytics, which permits students to incrementally enhance their performance. In competency-based education (CBE), timely, data-informed feedback is critical, as it promotes self-regulated learning and assists learners in recognizing deficiencies in their competencies. Furthermore, ongoing assessment allows educators to track student progress over time and intervene as needed, thereby cultivating a more adaptable and supportive educational environment (Goldhamer et al., 2022)

The collaboration between humans and artificial intelligence is fundamental to the successful design of assessments. Although AI possesses the capability to automate various processes and generate insights, the presence of human oversight is indispensable to guarantee pedagogical validity and contextual appropriateness. Educators are essential in interpreting the results produced by AI, crafting meaningful assessment tasks, and upholding academic integrity. This "human-in-the-loop" methodology harmonizes the efficiency of AI with the specialized knowledge and ethical discernment of educators (Park & Derakhshan, 2026).

Transparency and explainability represent a fundamental principle in the context of AI-driven assessment systems. It is imperative that these systems offer comprehensive and intelligible explanations regarding the basis upon which evaluation decisions are derived, especially in the context of high-stakes assessments. The implementation of Explainable AI (XAI) significantly contributes to fostering trust and accountability, as it enables both students and educators to comprehend the reasoning underlying the assigned scores and provided feedback. This aspect is crucial in mitigating issues pertinent to bias and fairness in automated systems.

Finally, it is imperative that ethical considerations and data governance principles are integrated into the design framework of AI systems. Given that these systems depend on extensive collections of student data, there is a critical need for comprehensive policies addressing data privacy, security, and informed consent. Educational institutions are responsible for ensuring that assessments driven by AI technologies are equitable, inclusive, and adhere to established regulatory standards.

3.2 Conceptual Framework for AI-Driven CBE Assessment

Figure 1. Conceptual Framework for AI-Driven Competency-Based Assessment in Higher Education

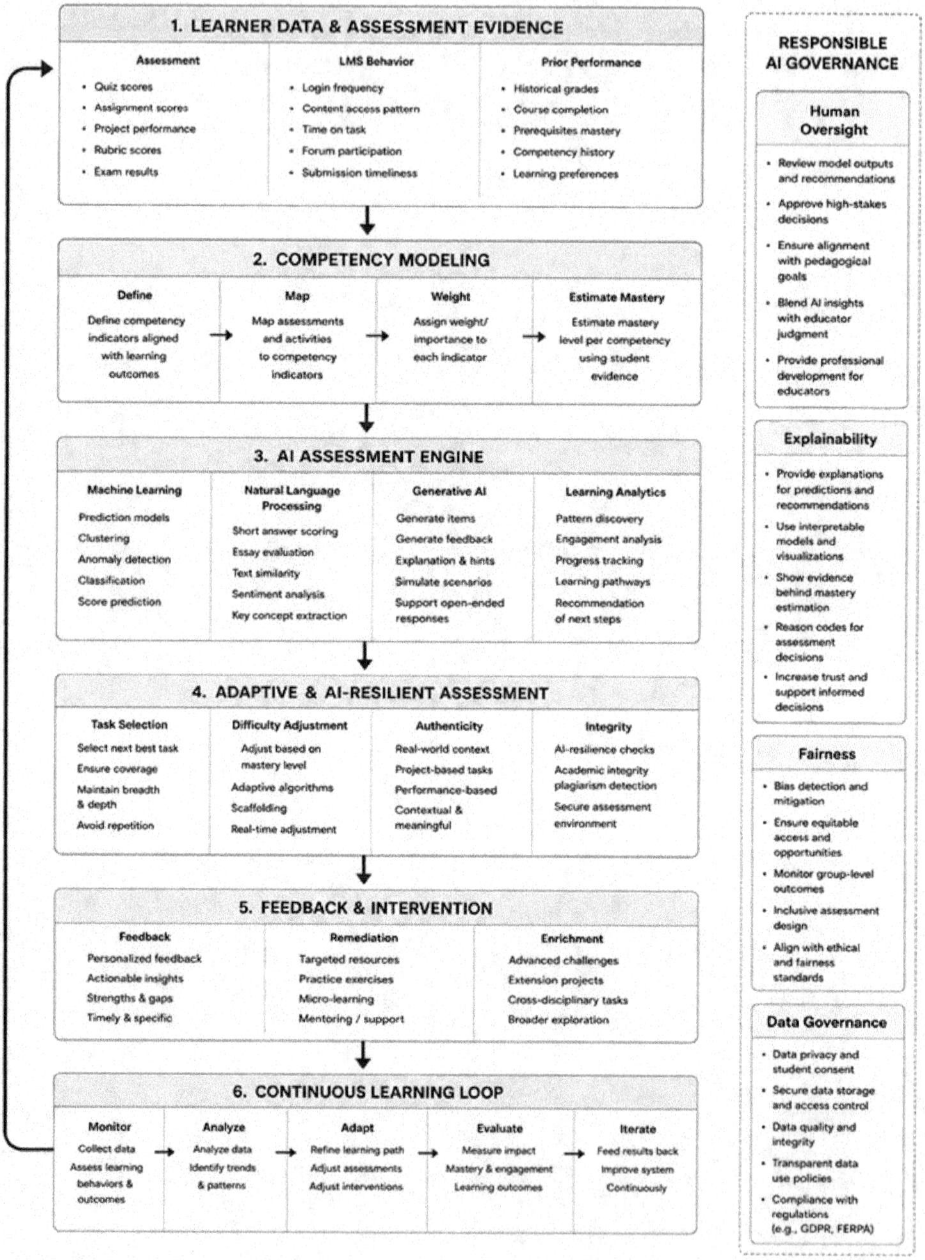

A comprehensive conceptual framework is essential for guiding the design and implementation of AI-driven assessments in Competency-Based Education (CBE). As illustrated in Figure 1, the proposed framework integrates learner evidence, competency modeling, intelligent assessment technologies, adaptive and AI-resilient assessment, feedback and intervention, and a continuous learning loop. These components are supported by responsible AI governance mechanisms encompassing human oversight, explainability, fairness, and data governance. Such integration ensures that assessment processes remain aligned with competency development, learner needs, and pedagogical objectives (Avilés Mariño & Sarasa Cabezuelo, 2025).

The first stage, Learner Data and Assessment Evidence, provides the foundation for competency evaluation. This stage incorporates assessment results, LMS behavioral data, and prior performance, including quiz scores, assignments, project performance, examination results, learning interactions, historical grades, and competency history. Such multidimensional evidence provides a more comprehensive representation of learner development than isolated assessment scores. Learning analytics can transform these data into meaningful insights concerning learning behaviors, engagement, and competency progression (Mahamad et al., 2025).

The second stage, Competency Modeling, translates learning outcomes and competency standards into measurable indicators. Assessments and learning activities are mapped to relevant competency indicators, and weights are assigned according to their relative importance. Competency achievement can be represented through a Weighted Competency Score (WCS):

where C_i represents the competency score of learner *i*, x_{ij} represents normalized performance on indicator *j*, w_j represents the indicator weight, and m denotes the number of competency indicators. The resulting score can be interpreted against a context-specific mastery threshold:

where $M_i = 1$ indicates demonstrated mastery, $M_i = 0$ indicates that mastery has not yet been demonstrated, and τ represents the minimum mastery threshold established according to institutional, program-level, or course-specific requirements. This formulation allows competency standards to be adapted to different educational contexts rather than imposing a universal threshold.

Following competency estimation, the framework introduces an adaptive assessment function to determine the difficulty of subsequent assessment tasks. Let D_t denote the current assessment difficulty, P_t represent learner performance at time *t*, *T* denote the target performance level, and α represent the adaptation rate. The subsequent difficulty level can be expressed using a bounded adjustment function:

where D_{t+1} represents the difficulty of the subsequent assessment task, while D_{min} and D_{max} define the permissible difficulty range. When learner performance exceeds the target level ($P_t > T$), the system increases task difficulty to provide an appropriate challenge. Conversely, when performance is below the target ($P_t < T$), the system reduces task difficulty or may provide scaffolding and remedial activities. When performance is close to the target level, the difficulty can be maintained. This formulation provides a simplified mathematical representation of adaptive assessment and can be extended through more sophisticated approaches, including machine learning and other adaptive algorithms.

The third stage, AI Assessment Engine, provides the analytical capabilities required to process learner evidence and support assessment decisions. Machine learning can support prediction, classification, clustering, anomaly detection, and score estimation; natural language processing (NLP) can evaluate open-ended responses; generative AI can support assessment-item generation and contextualized feedback; and learning analytics can identify patterns in learner progression (Ofori-Boateng et al., 2024). These technologies can operate independently or in combination depending on the assessment objectives, data characteristics, and institutional requirements.

The fourth stage, Adaptive and AI-Resilient Assessment, uses competency estimates and AI-generated insights to determine subsequent assessment activities. Task selection and difficulty can be dynamically adjusted, while authentic and contextualized tasks can be employed to evaluate the application of knowledge and skills. AI-resilient mechanisms, including process evidence, AI-use disclosure, oral demonstrations, and academic integrity safeguards, help ensure that assessment outcomes continue to represent authentic learner competencies (Yeganeh et al., 2025).

The fifth stage, Feedback and Intervention, transforms assessment results into actionable learning support. Learners who demonstrate competency gaps may receive targeted remediation, whereas those demonstrating mastery may receive enrichment activities and more advanced challenges. AI-supported feedback can therefore facilitate timely formative assessment while educators retain responsibility for interpreting results and determining appropriate interventions. Educator dashboards can further support monitoring and intervention decisions by presenting competency profiles and learner progress (Sajja et al., 2025).

Finally, the Continuous Learning Loop connects new learner evidence with subsequent monitoring, analysis, adaptation, evaluation, and iteration. This closed-loop mechanism enables learner profiles, assessment strategies, and intervention recommendations to be continuously refined. Across all stages, Responsible AI Governance provides cross-cutting safeguards through human oversight, explainability, fairness, and data governance. Human oversight ensures that educators remain involved in high-stakes decisions, while explainability supports transparency of AI-generated recommendations. Fairness mechanisms address potential algorithmic bias, and data governance ensures appropriate privacy, security, consent, and data management. Consequently, the framework positions AI as an augmentation of pedagogical decision-making rather than a replacement for educator judgment.

3.3 Designing AI-Resilient Assessments

The swift expansion of generative Artificial Intelligence (AI) tools within higher education has presented novel challenges to the integrity of assessments, prompting the need for the creation of assessment designs that are resilient to AI influences. Such AI-resilient assessments are formulated to guarantee that learning outcomes accurately represent students' genuine comprehension and skill sets, even in contexts where AI tools are readily available. This issue is especially pertinent within the framework of Competency-Based Education (CBE), where assessments are fundamentally linked to the exhibition of mastery rather than mere participation or course completion (Singh & Mohamad, 2025).

A fundamental tenet of assessments designed to withstand the challenges posed by artificial intelligence is the prioritization of process-driven evaluation. Instead of concentrating exclusively on the end products, assessments ought to encompass the learning journey, particularly the methodologies employed by students to reach their conclusions. This concept can be implemented through reflective elements, metacognitive inquiries, and repeated submissions that necessitate students to articulate their rationale and decision-making processes. Such methodologies not only complicate the dependence on responses generated by AI but also promote enhanced learning and self-regulatory skills (Khlaif et al., 2024).

A noteworthy strategy involves the integration of genuine and contextualized evaluation tasks. Assessments that are resilient to artificial intelligence often necessitate that students tackle real-world issues, analyze case studies, or interact with personalized scenarios which are challenging to replicate through generic AI outputs. By embedding assessment within particular contexts—such as local case studies, project-oriented tasks, or experiential learning opportunities—educators can more effectively assess students' capacity to utilize knowledge in significant ways. Empirical studies suggest that authentic assessments not only increase engagement but also improve the validity of competency evaluations (Quinlan et al., 2025).

The transparency of human-AI interaction constitutes an essential element of AI-resilient design. Instead of disallowing the utilization of AI altogether, certain assessment frameworks advocate for students to maintain records of their engagements with AI tools. This practice encompasses the systematic documentation of prompts, outputs, and any subsequent adjustments made. Such methodologies not only foster academic integrity but also enhance the understanding of students' critical thinking skills and their capacity to assess AI-generated information. This approach is consistent with evolving viewpoints that consider AI as a collaborative instrument rather than merely a facilitator of academic dishonesty (Ncube et al., 2026).

Furthermore, the design of assessments ought to integrate validation mechanisms, which may include oral defenses, live demonstrations, or in-class problem-solving exercises. Such approaches enable educators to ascertain students' comprehension and confirm that the work submitted accurately represents their individual capabilities. The integration of asynchronous tasks supported by artificial intelligence with synchronous validation activities results in a more comprehensive and reliable assessment framework (Hung et al., 2024).

Ethical considerations are critically important in the context of AI-resilient assessment. Educational institutions are tasked with developing precise guidelines regarding the permissible use of AI, ensuring that assessment criteria are transparent, and fostering equity among a diverse array of student populations. Furthermore, it is essential that educators receive adequate training to successfully formulate and execute strategies that are resilient to AI influences.

CHAPTER 4: IMPLEMENTATION AND USE CASES IN HIGHER EDUCATION

4.1 Implementation in Learning Management Systems (LMS)

The incorporation of artificial intelligence (AI)-driven assessments in Learning Management Systems (LMS) constitutes a significant advancement in the realization of Competency-Based Education (CBE) in the realm of higher education. LMS platforms function as the primary framework for content delivery, assessment management, and monitoring of student progression (Simelane-Mnisi, 2023). The integration of AI technologies within LMS settings enables educational institutions to improve assessment methodologies through mechanisms such as automation, tailored learning experiences, and decisions informed by data analytics (Afolabi et al., 2025).

A fundamental component of this implementation is the incorporation of AI-driven assessment instruments directly within the functionalities of Learning Management Systems (LMS). These instruments encompass automated grading frameworks, intelligent feedback systems, and adaptive testing configurations. For instance, Natural Language Processing (NLP) can be integrated into LMS platforms to assess written submissions and deliver timely, formative feedback. This integration diminishes the time necessary for manual grading while guaranteeing consistency and scalability, particularly in the context of large classes or online educational environments (Alotaibi, 2024).

An additional significant characteristic is the implementation of adaptive assessment within Learning Management System (LMS) frameworks. Artificial intelligence algorithms examine student interactions, performance metrics, and learning behaviors to modify the difficulty and content of assessments in real time. This process facilitates personalized learning trajectories that correspond with individual competency levels, which is a fundamental tenet of Competency-Based Education (CBE). By means of adaptive quizzes and assignments, students are afforded the opportunity to advance at their own pace, encountering specific challenges that enhance mastery learning (Contrino et al., 2024).

Learning analytics plays a central role in supporting AI-driven assessment within LMS. Data collected from student activities—such as quiz performance, time on task, and interaction patterns—are analyzed to generate insights into competency development. Dashboards within LMS platforms provide educators with real-time visibility into student progress, enabling early identification of learning gaps and timely intervention. These analytics also support predictive modeling, allowing institutions to anticipate student performance and enhance retention strategies (Mahamad et al., 2025).

Interoperability and system integration constitute essential factors in contemporary educational technology. Current Learning Management System (LMS) platforms are required to facilitate integration with external artificial intelligence services, including generative AI applications and analytics frameworks, via application programming interfaces (APIs). This capability guarantees both adaptability and expansiveness in the deployment of sophisticated assessment functionalities. Moreover, cloud-based architectures empower educational institutions to manage substantial data volumes and to enable real-time processing, which is vital for applications driven by artificial intelligence (Maciel et al., 2024).

Notwithstanding the aforementioned advantages, a number of challenges warrant attention. Data privacy and security emerge as significant concerns, given that Learning Management System (LMS) platforms manage sensitive information pertaining to students. It is imperative for institutions to establish comprehensive data governance policies and adhere to applicable regulations to safeguard the ethical application of artificial intelligence. Additionally, training for faculty members is crucial to equip educators with the necessary skills to design and analyze AI-driven assessments within LMS settings effectively (Babu, 2025).

4.2 Case Studies of AI-Driven Assessment

The utilization of Artificial Intelligence (AI) in assessment has attracted substantial attention through various applications in higher education, demonstrating its potential to support Competency-Based Education (CBE). Existing cases illustrate how intelligent systems can facilitate personalized assessment, enhance feedback processes, and align evaluation with competency development. These applications provide practical perspectives for understanding how the conceptual framework proposed in this chapter can be operationalized in higher education settings.

A significant application involves adaptive assessment systems implemented through digital learning platforms. These systems employ machine learning algorithms to modify the difficulty and sequencing of assessment items according to learner performance. Adaptive quizzes, for example, can respond dynamically to students' answers, enabling subsequent tasks to remain appropriate to their estimated competency levels. Empirical studies indicate that adaptive learning approaches can enhance engagement and learning outcomes by providing individualized challenges and reducing unnecessary cognitive load (Mahmud & Kurt, 2026). This approach is particularly relevant to CBE, in which learner progression is determined by demonstrated mastery rather than predetermined instructional timelines.

A second application concerns automated feedback and grading using Natural Language Processing (NLP). Higher education institutions increasingly employ AI-based tools to evaluate essays and short-answer responses and provide timely feedback concerning content, coherence, and argument quality (Smerdon, 2024). Such systems can support formative assessment by enabling students to revise their work iteratively. AI-augmented feedback may therefore contribute to improvements in writing proficiency and academic performance while reducing the routine assessment burden experienced by educators (Mekheimer, 2025).

A third application involves project-based and authentic assessment supported by generative AI. AI technologies can generate realistic scenarios, case-based tasks, and interactive assessment environments that simulate professional contexts. Students may engage with AI systems to explore alternative solutions while demonstrating competencies such as critical thinking, creativity, problem-solving, and decision-making. Such applications are consistent with CBE because they emphasize the application of knowledge and skills in meaningful contexts rather than the reproduction of factual information (Kotsis, 2025).

Learning analytics dashboards represent another important application. These systems integrate student performance and behavioral data to generate insights into competency development. Educators can monitor progress, identify competency gaps, and formulate targeted interventions using predictive analytics. Early-warning mechanisms, for example, can identify learners who may require additional support, enabling intervention before performance deteriorates substantially (Paulsen & Lindsay, 2024). These applications demonstrate how assessment can evolve from periodic evaluation toward continuous, evidence-informed competency monitoring.

To demonstrate how the proposed framework can operate in practice, Table 1 presents a hypothetical scenario in which three assessment indicators—Quiz, Project, and Case Analysis—are mapped to a target competency. The competency score is calculated using the Weighted Competency Score presented in Section 3.2.

For illustrative purposes, the three indicators are assumed to have equal weights, and a mastery threshold of 75 is applied. The values are hypothetical and are provided solely to illustrate the operationalization of the proposed framework; they do not represent empirical findings.

Table 1. Illustrative AI-Driven Competency Assessment Output

Student	Quiz	Project	Case Analysis	Competency Score	Status	AI-Supported Decision
S1	88	91	86	88.3	Mastered	Advanced task
S2	72	78	70	73.3	Developing	Targeted practice
S3	61	68	64	64.3	Not Yet Mastered	Remedial assessment
S4	82	80	85	82.3	Mastered	Advanced task

The illustrative output demonstrates how assessment evidence can be transformed into competency profiles and subsequent AI-supported decisions. Learners who demonstrate mastery may receive more complex or authentic tasks, whereas learners below the mastery threshold may be directed toward targeted practice or remedial assessment. The process therefore connects assessment evidence, competency estimation, adaptive decision-making, and intervention, reflecting the continuous learning loop presented in Figure 1.

Despite these opportunities, existing applications also highlight challenges related to data privacy, algorithmic bias, transparency, academic integrity, and faculty readiness. Consequently, AI-driven assessment requires careful instructional design and responsible governance to ensure that technological capabilities remain aligned with pedagogical objectives and equitable competency evaluation.

4.3 Evaluation of Effectiveness

Evaluating the effectiveness of AI-driven assessment requires a multidimensional approach that considers not only whether learners achieve the intended competencies but also whether the underlying AI models, assessment processes, and educational systems perform reliably. Within Competency-Based Education (CBE), effectiveness should therefore be evaluated through learning and competency outcomes, AI model performance, and system and user effectiveness. This broader evaluation perspective is consistent with the principles of CBE, which emphasize demonstrated mastery, continuous improvement, and evidence-based decision-making rather than solely relying on final grades or time-based progression (Ilieva et al., 2025).

The first dimension concerns the extent to which AI-driven assessments accurately support competency development and learning improvement. Competency attainment rate can be used to determine the proportion of learners who achieve the predefined mastery threshold. This measure is particularly relevant to CBE because it directly indicates whether learners have demonstrated the required competency. In addition, learning gain can be used to examine changes in learner performance between an initial and subsequent assessment. AI-enabled learning analytics can provide more detailed evidence of competency development by integrating behavioral patterns, engagement indicators, and performance trends rather than relying exclusively on individual assessment scores (Xu, 2024).

The effectiveness of AI-generated or AI-supported feedback should also be considered. Feedback effectiveness can be evaluated through indicators such as feedback usefulness, relevance, timeliness, and subsequent learner improvement. AI-supported assessment can provide more immediate and personalized feedback, potentially strengthening formative assessment and supporting learners in identifying and addressing competency gaps. Student perceptions are also important because the effectiveness of adaptive assessment depends partly on whether learners perceive AI-generated feedback and assessment pathways as relevant and supportive (Owan et al., 2023).

The second dimension evaluates the technical performance of the AI models underlying the assessment process. The appropriate metric depends on the type of prediction or decision produced by the model. When the system classifies learners into categories such as *Mastered* and *Not Yet Mastered*, classification metrics including accuracy, precision, recall, and F1-score are appropriate. When the system predicts a continuous competency score, regression metrics such as Mean Absolute Error (MAE), Root Mean Square Error (RMSE), and are more appropriate. For adaptive recommendations, Precision@K, Recall@K, and recommendation acceptance rates can be used to assess whether recommended assessment tasks or interventions are relevant to learner needs.

The third dimension addresses the operational and educational effectiveness of AI-driven assessment systems. Response time can measure how efficiently the system generates assessment results, feedback, or recommendations. Usability can be evaluated through standardized usability instruments or task-completion measures, while student satisfaction can capture perceptions of personalization, fairness, transparency, and usefulness. From the educator perspective, instructor workload reduction can indicate whether AI automation effectively decreases repetitive grading and feedback activities without compromising assessment quality (Lee, 2023). AI-driven assessment can also provide institutional benefits by supporting data-informed decisions concerning curriculum design, instructional strategies, and student support. Predictive analytics can identify learners who may require intervention, while alignment between assessment evidence and competency frameworks can strengthen the relevance of educational outcomes to professional and industry requirements.

The transition from traditional assessment to AI-driven CBE assessment involves more than replacing manual grading with automated technologies. It represents a shift in the timing, evidence, personalization, progression, and decision-making mechanisms of assessment. Table 2 compares the two approaches across several dimensions.

Table 2. Comparison of Traditional and AI-Driven CBE Assessment

Dimension	Traditional Assessment	AI-Driven CBE Assessment
Assessment timing	Periodic	Continuous and iterative
Assessment pathway	Standardized	Adaptive and personalized
Feedback	Delayed and generally uniform	Timely and personalized
Competency evidence	Primarily assessment scores	Multidimensional assessment and learning evidence
Task difficulty	Generally fixed	Dynamically adjusted
Learner progression	Course- or time-based	Mastery-based
Data utilization	Limited use of learning data	Learning analytics-driven
Instructor role	Primary evaluator	Evaluator, interpreter, and AI supervisor
Scalability	High for standardized assessment	High with personalized assessment
Transparency	Primarily based on assessment criteria and rubrics	Requires transparency of assessment criteria and AI decisions
Primary risks	Limited personalization and delayed feedback	Algorithmic bias, privacy, explainability, and over-reliance on automation

The comparison demonstrates that AI-driven assessment offers opportunities for greater personalization, continuous evidence collection, and adaptive decision-making. However, these advantages should not be interpreted as evidence that AI-driven assessment is inherently superior in every context. Traditional assessments may remain appropriate for specific learning outcomes, particularly when standardized and highly controlled measurement is required. Conversely, AI-driven approaches introduce additional requirements for data quality, algorithmic transparency, infrastructure, and human oversight. The principal distinction therefore concerns the capacity to dynamically use multiple sources of evidence to support competency-oriented decisions, rather than a simple replacement of traditional assessment by AI.

The recommended evaluation dimensions and metrics are summarized in Table 3.

Table 3. Recommended Metrics for Evaluating AI-Driven CBE Assessment

Assessment Function	Expected Output	Recommended Metrics
Competency classification	Mastered / Not Yet Mastered	Accuracy, Precision, Recall, F1-score
Competency score prediction	Continuous competency score	MAE, RMSE,
Adaptive recommendation	Assessment task/intervention	Precision@K, Recall@K, Acceptance Rate
AI-generated feedback	Personalized feedback	Usefulness, Relevance, Timeliness, Response Time
Learning effectiveness	Competency development	Learning Gain, Mastery Rate
System effectiveness	Operational performance	Response Time, Usability, Reliability
User effectiveness	Learner and educator experience	Student Satisfaction, Instructor Workload Reduction

The final consideration concerns validity, fairness, and reliability. Quantitative performance metrics alone cannot establish that an AI-driven assessment is educationally appropriate. Data quality, algorithmic bias, transparency, and explainability may influence the reliability and equity of assessment outcomes. Therefore, technical evaluation should be complemented by human review, expert judgment, and fairness analysis. Such validation is necessary to ensure that high-performing AI models do not inadvertently produce inappropriate or inequitable educational decisions. Consequently, the effectiveness of AI-driven CBE assessment should be understood as a combination of competency achievement, model reliability, system performance, user experience, and responsible AI implementation.

CHAPTER 5: FUTURE DIRECTIONS AND STRATEGIC IMPLICATIONS

5.1 Emerging Trends in AI-Driven Assessment

The swift advancement of Artificial Intelligence (AI) is influencing the trajectory of assessment design in higher education, especially regarding Competency-Based Education (CBE). Current trends suggest a movement toward more sophisticated, transparent, and cohesive assessment frameworks that emphasize personalization, immediate feedback, and continuous learning. Such innovations are transforming the methods by which competencies are assessed and verified in ever-complex educational settings (Rahiman & Kodikal, 2024).

A notable trend is the progression of Explainable Artificial Intelligence (XAI) within assessment frameworks. As the use of AI-based evaluations gains traction, the demand for transparency and comprehensibility has increased. XAI seeks to render algorithmic determinations comprehensible for both educators and learners, thereby fostering trust and accountability. In the realm of assessment, this translates to the necessity of offering explicit rationales for scores, feedback, and suggestions. Empirical studies underscore that explainability is essential for promoting fairness and mitigating issues related to bias in automated evaluation systems (Deck et al., 2024).

A notable trend in contemporary education is the emergence of real-time adaptive assessment ecosystems. In contrast to conventional assessment methods and earlier adaptive systems, next-generation artificial intelligence platforms engage in continuous analysis of learner data to dynamically modify assessment tasks (Mallik & Gangopadhyay, 2023). These innovative systems amalgamate learning analytics, behavioral data, and contextual factors to deliver immediate feedback and tailored learning pathways. The capacity for real-time responsiveness fosters mastery learning and correlates significantly with the principles of Competency-Based Education (CBE), allowing students to advance according to their exhibited competencies, rather than adhering to predetermined timelines.

The incorporation of generative artificial intelligence and conversational agents signifies a pivotal trend in educational assessment. Large language models (LLMs) are progressively being employed to develop interactive assessment frameworks in which students participate in dialogue-driven problem-solving activities. Such systems are capable of simulating intricate scenarios, evaluating reasoning methodologies, and delivering contextualized feedback. This methodology facilitates the assessment of advanced cognitive skills, including critical thinking, creativity, and decision making, which are challenging to quantify through conventional evaluative measures (Agostini & Picasso, 2024).

An additional significant avenue pertains to the integration of AI-driven assessment within lifelong learning and micro-credentialing frameworks. As educational paradigms shift towards modular and continuous formats, artificial intelligence systems are increasingly employed to monitor and authenticate competencies across various learning environments, encompassing formal, informal, and professional contexts. The utilization of digital badges and competency portfolios, augmented by AI analytics, enables learners to showcase their skills progressively and across diverse platforms. This development signifies the rising necessity for adaptable and skills-focused educational approaches that are attuned to the dynamic requirements of the labor market (Alfaleh, 2026).

Notwithstanding these developments, emerging trends underscore the significance of ethical and governance-related aspects. Concerns regarding data privacy, algorithmic bias, and equitable access continue to be pivotal in the responsible integration of artificial intelligence in assessment practices. Educational institutions are required to implement comprehensive governance structures to guarantee that AI-driven systems operate transparently, inclusively, and in accordance with educational principles.

5.2 Policy, Ethics, and Governance

The incorporation of Artificial Intelligence (AI) into the framework of assessment design necessitates a thorough examination of pertinent policy, ethical, and governance issues that must be effectively navigated to facilitate responsible and sustainable deployment within higher education contexts (Schicktanz et al., 2023). This concern is amplified in Competency-Based Education (CBE), where the results of assessments significantly influence both mastery and learners' progression. Consequently, educational institutions are required to develop comprehensive frameworks that reconcile innovation with accountability, thereby guaranteeing that AI-enhanced assessments uphold principles of fairness, transparency, and consistency with established educational values (Khlaif et al., 2025).

A principal policy issue pertains to data governance, given that artificial intelligence systems depend extensively on substantial amounts of student data, which encompasses performance metrics, behavioral engagements, and personal details. Robust data governance frameworks are required to manage aspects of data collection, storage, access, and utilization, while ensuring adherence to privacy regulations and institutional guidelines. Moreover, transparency in data handling practices is crucial to uphold student trust and mitigate the risk of misuse. Recent research underscores that well-defined data governance policies are essential for the ethical implementation of learning analytics and artificial intelligence within educational settings (Carroll et al., 2023).

Ethical considerations hold significant importance, particularly in relation to fairness, bias, and equity. Artificial intelligence (AI) systems are prone to algorithmic bias, which can emerge from unrepresentative training datasets or inadequate model architecture. These biases can lead to disproportionate effects on specific student demographics, resulting in unequal assessment results. To mitigate these issues, it is essential to implement ongoing monitoring, validation, and the integration of diverse datasets during the model development process. Furthermore, ethical AI frameworks promote inclusivity and accessibility, thereby ensuring that AI-based assessments are capable of accommodating a variety of learning needs and contexts (Ferrara, 2024).

Transparency and explainability constitute fundamental governance principles in the realm of artificial intelligence. Assessment systems that are powered by AI are required to offer coherent and interpretable rationales for their determinations, especially in contexts where the implications are significant. Explainable AI (XAI) promotes accountability by facilitating comprehension among educators and students regarding the processes that lead to assessment results. This understanding is essential for fostering trust and supporting informed decision-making. In the absence of transparency, AI systems may be regarded as enigmatic and unreliable, which could hinder their integration into educational environments (Teixeira et al., 2025).

Institutional governance frameworks are crucial for supervising the implementation of artificial intelligence (AI). It is imperative for universities to formulate policies that delineate permissible applications of AI in evaluation processes, encompassing standards for academic integrity, student consent, and the necessity of human oversight. The principle of "human-in-the-loop" governance guarantees that educators are continually engaged in the interpretation of AI-generated outputs and in rendering conclusive assessment judgments. This model seeks to harmonize technological efficiency with pedagogical expertise and ethical accountability.

Moreover, regulatory and accreditation entities are progressively impacting the integration of artificial intelligence within educational settings. Emerging standards and guidelines governing the application of AI in assessment are being established, with a focus on quality assurance, equity, and accountability. It is imperative for institutions to align their practices with these developing standards to maintain credibility and ensure compliance.

5.3 Strategic Recommendations for Higher Education

The successful integration of AI-based assessments within higher education necessitates a thorough strategic framework that harmonizes technological advancements with educational objectives and institutional preparedness. In the realm of Competency-Based Education (CBE), it is imperative for universities to transition from sporadic implementation to structured strategies that promote sustainability, scalability, and educational effectiveness. Consequently, strategic planning becomes crucial to optimize the advantages of Artificial Intelligence (AI) while addressing potential risks (Luo et al., 2025).

A fundamental recommendation involves the formulation of institutional readiness frameworks to facilitate the adoption of artificial intelligence (AI). It is imperative for universities to evaluate their technological infrastructure, data management proficiency, and organizational culture as preliminary steps prior to the deployment of AI-enhanced assessment systems. This evaluation necessitates significant investment in robust digital platforms, including Learning Management Systems (LMS), while ensuring compatibility with AI tools. Furthermore, institutions are required to develop comprehensive roadmaps that effectively synchronize AI initiatives with educational objectives and competency-based curricula (Warren et al., 2026).

An additional essential strategy pertains to the enhancement of faculty capabilities and ongoing professional development. Educators are pivotal in the creation, execution, and analysis of assessments powered by artificial intelligence. Consequently, educational institutions are required to offer ongoing training that encompasses AI literacy, assessment design, and ethical frameworks. Faculty members must be armed with both technical competencies and pedagogical methodologies to effectively incorporate AI into their teaching and assessment methodologies. Scholarly research underscores that faculty preparedness is a critical factor influencing the successful integration of AI in educational contexts (Al-Maskari et al., 2024).

The incorporation of human-AI collaborative frameworks is of significant importance. AI ought not to supplant educators; instead, it should enhance their competencies by automating repetitive tasks and offering data-informed insights. A strategic approach should prioritize a "human-in-the-loop" methodology, wherein educators maintain authority over assessment determinations while utilizing AI to improve efficiency and personalization. This equilibrium guarantees that assessment procedures remain pedagogically valid and contextually pertinent (Luckin, 2025).

It is essential for institutions to give precedence to the development of assessment frameworks that are resilient to artificial intelligence and aligned with competencies. This necessitates the integration of assessment methods that are genuine, process-oriented, and adaptable, thereby mirroring the practical application of knowledge and skills in real-world contexts. Ensuring strategic coherence between the design of assessments and competency frameworks is critical, as it allows AI-driven systems to effectively evaluate student mastery and facilitate substantial learning outcomes.

Moreover, data governance and ethical adherence ought to be integrated into institutional strategies. Higher education institutions should formulate policies that focus on data privacy, algorithmic transparency, and equitability. This encompasses the establishment of mechanisms for bias monitoring, ensuring interpretability, and safeguarding student information. Robust governance frameworks are critical for cultivating trust among stakeholders and promoting the responsible utilization of artificial intelligence.

Finally, it is essential for educational institutions to implement a structured methodology for ongoing assessment and enhancement. Evaluation systems powered by artificial intelligence require regular evaluations to determine their efficacy, usability, and influence on student learning outcomes. Input from students, faculty, and administrators should guide iterative enhancements, ensuring that these systems continue to be pertinent and effective within the dynamic context of education.

6. CONCLUSION

This chapter has explored the intricacies involved in the design and implementation of AI-enhanced assessments within the context of Competency-Based Education

(CBE) in higher education. It posits that conventional assessment methodologies are increasingly inadequate for capturing the multifaceted nature of real-world competencies, which necessitates the adoption of more adaptive, data-informed, and learner-centered evaluation frameworks. Through the integration of Artificial Intelligence (AI) technologies such as machine learning, natural language processing, and generative AI, assessment systems can achieve greater levels of personalization, scalability, and alignment with explicitly defined learning outcomes. A notable contribution of this chapter is the suggestion of principled methodologies for the design of AI-driven assessments, emphasizing the alignment with specified competencies, the provision of continuous and formative feedback, the fostering of human-AI collaboration, and the establishment of assessments resilient to AI influences. Additionally, the chapter underscores the critical necessity of incorporating ethical considerations, transparency, and data governance into the design and implementation of AI-enabled assessment systems.

The ramifications of these advancements permeate various domains, including policy formulation, practical applications, and educational cultures. From a policy standpoint, higher education institutions are obligated to create comprehensive governance structures that address critical issues such as data privacy, algorithmic equity, and accountability concerning the deployment of artificial intelligence. These governance frameworks should be in alignment with evolving regulatory criteria and facilitate responsible innovation. Regarding practical applications, educators must embrace new responsibilities that merge pedagogical expertise with proficiency in AI, thereby equipping them to design impactful assessments and effectively analyze insights generated by AI systems. Consequently, institutions are necessitated to allocate resources towards faculty development and infrastructure improvements to facilitate this transition. In terms of educational culture, AI-enhanced assessments promote a shift towards more student-centered, adaptable, and lifelong learning approaches. By placing an emphasis on mastery, ongoing feedback, and genuine performance, these assessment systems enhance student engagement and support the cultivation of transferable skills that are pertinent to the rapidly evolving professional landscape.

REFERENCES

Adabor, E. S., Addy, E., Assyne, N., & Antwi-Boasiako, E. (2025). Enhancing sustainable academic course delivery using AI in technical universities: An empirical analysis using adaptive learning theory. *Sustainable Futures : An Applied Journal of Technology, Environment and Society*, *10*, 100828. Advance online publication. DOI: 10.1016/j.sftr.2025.100828

Afolabi, I. Y., Ugah, J. O., Igwe, J. S., & Nwali, M. E.Afolabi I.YUgah J.OIgwe J.SNwali M.E. (2025). Development of an ai-driven adaptive learning management system using data analytics. *International Journal of Scientific Research in Modern Science and Technology*, *4*(7), 52–63. DOI: 10.59828/ijsrmst.v4i7.349

Agostini, D., & Picasso, F. (2024). Large language models for sustainable assessment and feedback in higher education: Towards a pedagogical and technological framework. *Intelligenza Artificiale*, *18*(1), 121–138. DOI: 10.3233/IA-240033

Al-Maskari, A., Al Riyami, T., & Ghnimi, S. (2024). Factors affecting students' preparedness for the fourth industrial revolution in higher education institutions. *Journal of Applied Research in Higher Education*, *16*(1), 246–264. DOI: 10.1108/JARHE-05-2022-0169

Alfaleh, M. (2026). Sustainable AI-Driven Assessment in Higher Education: A Systematic Review of Fairness, Transparency, Pedagogical Innovation, and Governance. *Sustainability (Basel)*, *18*(2), 785. DOI: 10.3390/su18020785

Alotaibi, N. S. (2024). The impact of AI and LMS integration on the future of higher education: Opportunities, challenges, and strategies for transformation. *Sustainability (Basel)*, *16*(23), 10357. DOI: 10.3390/su162310357

Avilés Mariño, E., & Sarasa Cabezuelo, A. (2025). AI-Enhanced PBL and Experiential Learning for Communication and Career Readiness: An Engineering Pilot Course. *Algorithms*, *18*(10), 634. DOI: 10.3390/a18100634

Carroll, S. R., Garba, I., Figueroa-Rodríguez, O. L., Holbrook, J., Lovett, R., Materechera, S., Parsons, M., Raseroka, K., Rodriguez-Lonebear, D., Rowe, R., Sara, R., Walker, J. D., Anderson, J., & Hudson, M. (2023). The CARE principles for indigenous data governance. Open Scholarship Press Curated Volumes: Policy. *Data Science Journal*, *19*(1), 43. DOI: 10.5334/dsj-2020-043 PMID: 37810187

Chen, A. M., Kleppinger, E. L., Churchwell, M. D., & Rhoney, D. H. (2024). Examining competency-based education through the lens of implementation science: A scoping review. *American Journal of Pharmaceutical Education*, *88*(2), 100633. DOI: 10.1016/j.ajpe.2023.100633 PMID: 38092089

Chiu, T. K., Ahmad, Z., Ismailov, M., & Sanusi, I. T. (2024). What are artificial intelligence literacy and competency? A comprehensive framework to support them. *Computers and Education Open*, *6*, 100171. DOI: 10.1016/j.caeo.2024.100171

Chookaew, S., Kitcharoen, P., Howimanporn, S., & Panjaburee, P. (2024). Fostering student competencies and perceptions through artificial intelligence of things educational platform. *Computers and Education: Artificial Intelligence*, *7*, 100308. DOI: 10.1016/j.caeai.2024.100308

Contrino, M. F., Reyes-Millán, M., Vázquez-Villegas, P., & Membrillo-Hernández, J. (2024). Using an adaptive learning tool to improve student performance and satisfaction in online and face-to-face education for a more personalized approach. *Smart Learning Environments*, *11*(6), 6. Advance online publication. DOI: 10.1186/s40561-024-00292-y

Contrino, M. F., Reyes-Millán, M., Vázquez-Villegas, P., & Membrillo-Hernández, J. (2024). Using an adaptive learning tool to improve student performance and satisfaction in online and face-to-face education for a more personalized approach. *Smart Learning Environments*, *11*(1), 6. DOI: 10.1186/s40561-024-00292-y

Deck, L., Schoeffer, J., De-Arteaga, M., & Kühl, N. (2024). A critical survey on fairness benefits of explainable AI. In *Proceedings of the 2024 ACM conference on fairness, accountability, and transparency 1579*-1595. DOI: 10.1145/3630106.3658990

Deepshikha, D. (2025). A comprehensive review of AI-powered grading and tailored feedback in universities. *Discover Artificial Intelligence*, *2025*(5), 251. DOI: 10.1007/s44163-025-00517-0

Deepshikha, D. (2026). *A systematic review on the future of educational assessment: AI-driven grading and personalised feedback in higher education.* Artificial Intelligence in Education., DOI: 10.1108/AIIE-03-2025-0036

Elshall, A. S., & Badir, A. (2025). Balancing AI-assisted learning and traditional assessment: The FACT assessment in environmental data science education. *Frontiers in Education*, *10*, 1596462. Advance online publication. DOI: 10.3389/feduc.2025.1596462

Fagbohun, O., Iduwe, N. P., Abdullahi, M., Ifaturoti, A., & Nwanna, O. M. (2024). Beyond traditional assessment: Exploring the impact of large language models on grading practices. Journal of Artificial Intelligence. *Machine Learning and Data Science*, *2*(1), 1–8. DOI: 10.51219/JAIMLD/oluwole-fagbohun/19

Ferrara, E. (2024). The butterfly effect in artificial intelligence systems: Implications for AI bias and fairness. *Machine Learning with Applications*, *15*, 100525. Advance online publication. DOI: 10.1016/j.mlwa.2024.100525

Goldhamer, M. E. J., Martinez-Lage, M., Black-Schaffer, W. S., Huang, J. T., Co, J. P. T., Weinstein, D. F., & Pusic, M. V. (2022). Reimagining the clinical competency committee to enhance education and prepare for competency-based time-variable advancement. *Journal of General Internal Medicine*, *37*(9), 2280–2290. DOI: 10.1007/s11606-022-07515-3 PMID: 35445932

Hamidi, H., Hejran, A. B., Sarwari, A., & Edigeevna, S. G. (2024). The effect of outcome based education on behavior of students. *European Journal of Theoretical and Applied Sciences*, *2*(2), 764–773. DOI: 10.59324/ejtas.2024.2(2).68

Hanna, M. G., Pantanowitz, L., Jackson, B., Palmer, O., Visweswaran, S., Pantanowitz, J., Deebajah, M., & Rashidi, H. H. (2025). Ethical and bias considerations in artificial intelligence/machine learning. *Modern Pathology*, *38*(3), 100686. Advance online publication. DOI: 10.1016/j.modpat.2024.100686 PMID: 39694331

Hochstetter-Diez, J., Negrier-Seguel, M., Diéguez-Rebolledo, M., Candia-Garrido, E., & Vidal, E. (2025). From Mapping to Action: SmartRubrics, an AI Tool for Competency-Based Assessment in Engineering Education. *Sustainability (Basel)*, *17*(13), 6098. DOI: 10.3390/su17136098

Huang, J., Xin, Y. P., & Chang, H. H. (2025). The application of machine learning to educational process data analysis: A systematic review. *Education Sciences*, *15*(7), 888. Advance online publication. DOI: 10.3390/educsci15070888

Hung, C. T., Wu, S. E., Chen, Y. H., Soong, C. Y., Chiang, C. P., & Wang, W. M. (2024). The evaluation of synchronous and asynchronous online learning: Student experience, learning outcomes, and cognitive load. *BMC Medical Education*, *24*(1), 326. DOI: 10.1186/s12909-024-05311-7 PMID: 38519950

Ilieva, G., Yankova, T., Ruseva, M., & Kabaivanov, S. (2025). A framework for generative AI-driven assessment in higher education. *Information (Basel)*, *16*(6), 472. DOI: 10.3390/info16060472

Khlaif, Z. N., Alkouk, W. A., Salama, N., & Abu Eideh, B. (2025). Redesigning assessments for AI-enhanced learning: A framework for educators in the generative AI era. *Education Sciences*, *15*(2), 174. Advance online publication. DOI: 10.3390/educsci15020174

Khlaif, Z. N., Ayyoub, A., Hamamra, B., Bensalem, E., Mitwally, M. A., Ayyoub, A., Hattab, M. K., & Shadid, F. (2024). University teachers' views on the adoption and integration of generative AI tools for student assessment in higher education. *Education Sciences*, *14*(10), 1090. DOI: 10.3390/educsci14101090

Kotsis, K. T. (2025). Integrating artificial intelligence into higher education curricula: Challenges and opportunities for science-based programs. International Journal of Artificial Intelligence Engineering and Transformation, 6(1), 04-12. DOI: 10.54660/IJAIET.2025.6.1.04-12

Lee, A. V. Y. (2023). Supporting students' generation of feedback in large-scale online course with artificial intelligence-enabled evaluation. *Studies in Educational Evaluation*, *77*, 101250. Advance online publication. DOI: 10.1016/j.stueduc.2023.101250

Luckin, R. (2025). Nurturing human intelligence in the age of AI: Rethinking education for the future. *Development and Learning in Organizations*, *39*(1), 1–4. DOI: 10.1108/DLO-04-2024-0108

Luo, J., Zheng, C., Yin, J., & Teo, H. H. (2025). Design and assessment of AI-based learning tools in higher education: A systematic review. *International Journal of Educational Technology in Higher Education*, *22*(1), 42. DOI: 10.1186/s41239-025-00540-2

Maciel, R. S. P., Valle, P. H. D., Santos, K. S., & Nakagawa, E. Y. (2024). Systems interoperability types: A tertiary study. *ACM Computing Surveys*, *56*(10), 1–37. DOI: 10.1145/3659098

Mahamad, S., Chin, Y. H., Zulmuksah, N. I. N., Haque, M. M., Shaheen, M., & Nisar, K. (2025). Technical review: Architecting an AI-driven decision support system for enhanced online learning and assessment. *Future Internet*, *17*(9), 383. DOI: 10.3390/fi17090383

Mahamad, S., Chin, Y. H., Zulmuksah, N. I. N., Haque, M. M., Shaheen, M., & Nisar, K. (2025). Technical review: Architecting an AI-driven decision support system for enhanced online learning and assessment. *Future Internet*, *17*(9), 383. DOI: 10.3390/fi17090383

Mahmud, S. K., & Kurt, M. (2026). Enhancing Inclusive Sustainability-Oriented Learning in Higher Education Using Adaptive Learning Platforms and Performance-Based Assessment. *Sustainability (Basel)*, *18*(3), 1489. DOI: 10.3390/su18031489

Mallik, S., & Gangopadhyay, A. (2023). Proactive and reactive engagement of artificial intelligence methods for education: A review. *Frontiers in Artificial Intelligence*, *6*, 1151391. Advance online publication. DOI: 10.3389/frai.2023.1151391 PMID: 37215064

Mani, Z. A. (2025). Transitioning to competency-based education in nursing: A scoping review of curriculum review and revision strategies. *BMC Nursing*, *24*(1), 1111. Advance online publication. DOI: 10.1186/s12912-025-03319-y PMID: 40855546

Marey, A., Arjmand, P., Alerab, A. D. S., Eslami, M. J., Saad, A. M., Sanchez, N., & Umair, M. (2024). Explainability, transparency and black box challenges of AI in radiology: Impact on patient care in cardiovascular radiology. *The Egyptian Journal of Radiology and Nuclear Medicine*, *55*(1), 183. DOI: 10.1186/s43055-024-01356-2

McIntosh, T. R., Susnjak, T., Liu, T., Watters, P., Xu, D., Liu, D., & Halgamuge, M. N. (2025). From Google Gemini to OpenAI Q*(Q-Star): A survey on reshaping the generative artificial intelligence (AI) research landscape. *Technologies*, *13*(2), 51. DOI: 10.3390/technologies13020051

Mekheimer, M. (2025). Generative AI-assisted feedback and EFL writing: A study on proficiency, revision frequency and writing quality. *Discover Education*, *4*(1), 170. Advance online publication. DOI: 10.1007/s44217-025-00602-7

Memarian, B. & Doleck, T. (2024). A review of assessment for learning with artificial intelligence. Computers in Human Behavior: Artificial Humans. DOI: 10.1016/j.chbah.2023.100040

Ncube, P. D. N., Dzvapatsva, G. P., Matobobo, C., & Ranga, M. M. (2026). Redefining student assessment in AI-infused learning environments: A systematic review of challenges and strategies for academic integrity. *AI and Ethics*, *6*(68), 68. Advance online publication. DOI: 10.1007/s43681-025-00871-w

Ofori-Boateng, R., Aceves-Martins, M., Wiratunga, N., & Moreno-Garcia, C. F. (2024). Towards the automation of systematic reviews using natural language processing, machine learning, and deep learning: A comprehensive review. *Artificial Intelligence Review*, *57*(200), 200. Advance online publication. DOI: 10.1007/s10462-024-10844-w

Olaniyan, J., Verkijika, S. F., & Obagbuwa, I. C. (2025). NLP-Based restoration of damaged student essay archives for educational preservation and fair reassessment. *Electronics (Basel)*, *14*(16), 3189. Advance online publication. DOI: 10.3390/electronics14163189

Owan, V. J., Abang, K. B., Idika, D. O., Etta, E. O., & Bassey, B. A. (2023). Exploring the potential of artificial intelligence tools in educational measurement and assessment. *Eurasia Journal of Mathematics, Science and Technology Education, 19*(8), em2307. Advance online publication. DOI: 10.29333/ejmste/13428

Park, Y., & Derakhshan, A. (2026). From Gutenberg to the classroom: Large-scale generation and validation of vocabulary-controlled EFL reading materials. *Language Testing in Asia, 16*(1), 13. Advance online publication. DOI: 10.1186/s40468-026-00429-5

Paulsen, L., & Lindsay, E. (2024). Learning analytics dashboards are increasingly becoming about learning and not just analytics-A systematic review. *Education and Information Technologies, 29*(11), 14279–14308. DOI: 10.1007/s10639-023-12401-4

Ponomarioviene, J., Jakavonytė-Staškuvienė, D., & Torterat, F. (2025). Implementing competency-based education through the personalized monitoring of primary students' progress and assessment. *Education Sciences, 15*(2), 252. DOI: 10.3390/educsci15020252

Quinlan, K. M., Sellei, G., & Fiorucci, W. (2025). Educationally authentic assessment: Reframing authentic assessment in relation to students' meaningful engagement. *Teaching in Higher Education, 30*(3), 717–734. DOI: 10.1080/13562517.2024.2394042

Rahiman, H. U. & Kodikal, R. (2024). Revolutionizing education: Artificial intelligence empowered learning in higher education. Cogent Education. 11:1, 2293431, DOI: DOI: 10.1080/2331186X.2023.2293431

Rhoney, D. H., Chen, A. M., Churchwell, M. D., Daugherty, K. K., Jarrett, J. B., Kleppinger, E. L., Nawarskas, J. J., Sibicky, S. L., Stowe, C. D., & Meyer, S. M. (2024). The need for competency-based education. *American Journal of Pharmaceutical Education, 88*(6), 100706. DOI: 10.1016/j.ajpe.2024.100706 PMID: 38705241

Sajja, R., Sermet, Y., Cwiertny, D., & Demir, I. (2025). Integrating AI and learning analytics for data-driven pedagogical decisions and personalized interventions in education. Technology, knowledge and learning, 1-31. DOI: 10.1007/s10758-025-09897-9

Salinas-Navarro, D. E., Vilalta-Perdomo, E., Michel-Villarreal, R., & Montesinos, L. (2024). Designing experiential learning activities with generative artificial intelligence tools for authentic assessment. *Interactive Technology and Smart Education, 21*(4), 708–734. DOI: 10.1108/ITSE-12-2023-0236

Schicktanz, S., Welsch, J., Schweda, M., Hein, A., Rieger, J. W., & Kirste, T. (2023). AI-assisted ethics? Considerations of AI simulation for the ethical assessment and design of assistive technologies. *Frontiers in Genetics*, *14*, 1039839. Advance online publication. DOI: 10.3389/fgene.2023.1039839 PMID: 37434952

Simelane-Mnisi, S. (2023). Effectiveness of LMS digital tools used by the academics to foster students' engagement. *Education Sciences*, *13*(10), 980. DOI: 10.3390/educsci13100980

Singh, H. K. D., & Mohamad, S. K. (2025). *Designing an AI-Resilient Assessment Framework in Open and Distance Learning*. Innovative Teaching and Learning Journal., DOI: 10.11113/itlj.v9.202

Smerdon, D. (2024). AI in essay-based assessment: Student adoption, usage, and performance. *Computers and Education: Artificial Intelligence*, *7*, 100288. Advance online publication. DOI: 10.1016/j.caeai.2024.100288

Tai, J., Ajjawi, R., Bearman, M., Boud, D., Dawson, P., & Jorre de St Jorre, T. (2023). Assessment for inclusion: Rethinking contemporary strategies in assessment design. *Higher Education Research & Development*, *42*(2), 483–497. DOI: 10.1080/07294360.2022.2057451

Teixeira, B., Carvalhais, L., Pinto, T., & Vale, Z. (2025). Explainable AI framework for reliable and transparent automated energy management in buildings. *Energy and Building*, *374*, 116246. Advance online publication. DOI: 10.1016/j.enbuild.2025.116246

Waladi, C., & Lamarti, M. S. (2024). Adaptive AI-driven assessment for competency-based learning scenarios. In *Innovative instructional design methods and tools for improved teaching* (pp. 215–226). IGI Global Scientific Publishing., DOI: 10.4018/979-8-3693-3128-6.ch010

Warren, S. J., Boston Vogt, E., Tincher, B., & Yang, J. (2026). Enhancing quality assurance through strategic artificial intelligence integration: A framework for higher education digital transformation. *Quality Assurance in Education*, *34*(2), 205–222. DOI: 10.1108/QAE-09-2024-0183

Xu, Y., Zhu, J., Wang, M., Qian, F., Yang, Y., & Zhang, J. (2024). The impact of a digital game-based AI chatbot on students' academic performance, higher-order thinking, and behavioral patterns in an information Technology Curriculum. 14(15), 6418; .DOI: 10.3390/app14156418

Xu, Z. (2024). *AI in education: Enhancing learning experiences and student outcomes*. Applied and Computational Engineering., DOI: 10.54254/2755-2721/51/20241187

Yeganeh, L. N., Fenty, N. S., Chen, Y., Simpson, A., & Hatami, M. (2025). The future of education: A multi-layered metaverse classroom model for immersive and inclusive learning. *Future Internet*, *17*(2), 63. DOI: 10.3390/fi17020063

Zaky, H. (2026). Reimagining Higher Education: The Promise and Challenges of Competency-Based Learning in the Digital Age. Available at *SSRN* 6131446. http://dx.doi.org/DOI: 10.3390/knowledge6030015

Zhao, L., Zhao, B., & Li, C. (2023). Alignment analysis of teaching–learning-assessment within the classroom: How teachers implement project-based learning under the curriculum standards. *Disciplinary and Interdisciplinary Science Education Research*, *5*(1), 13. DOI: 10.1186/s43031-023-00078-1

Chapter 3
Artificial Intelligence and Academic Integrity: Authentic Assessment and Generative AI Detection Tools

Colleen Halupa
http://orcid.org/0000-0002-7469-184X
Saint Joseph's College, USA

ABSTRACT

The purpose of this chapter is to discuss academic integrity in the age of artificial intelligence (AI). The chapter begins with a discussion of the challenges of defining and creating effective policies for both traditional and AI plagiarism. Problems with use of AI detection software, such as bias to neurodivergent thinkers, are addressed, as well as the major concerns of students, faculty and administration about AI, assessment and academic integrity. Last, a discussion of AI resistant assessment is presented.

INTRODUCTION

Academic integrity has always been a challenging issue since there is no standard, widely accepted definition. In addition, different values and behaviors are associated with academic integrity. This already complex issue has been further impacted by the free availability of generative artificial intelligence (AI) programs, such as ChatGPT and Gemini starting in December of 2022. These generative AI programs have disrupted higher education, particularly regarding assessment. Students need to be able to effectively use AI tools, while faculty need to ensure students are learning

DOI: 10.4018/979-8-3373-9089-5.ch003

to think critically and can successfully complete assessments on their own. This has made the issue of academic integrity difficult to manage.

Traditional assessments used to measure higher levels of learning include research papers, case studies, analyses, and other written works. These types of assessments can be easily completed on generative AI programs. Although in the beginning, AI was somewhat ineffective in creating quality academic work, it has continued to improve. In addition, generative AI tools are now embedded in programs such as Microsoft Office and Google. Although there are AI-detection tools that can be used to determine if students are using AI to complete their assignments rather than doing their own work, these tools are problematic. Higher education is at a stalemate currently; faculty cannot prove students are using AI, and students cannot prove that they are not.

Both a thematic and chronological approach was used to synthesize the literature. The purpose of this chapter is to discuss the impact of generative AI on academic integrity and assessment. It includes a discussion of academic integrity and AI academic integrity issues including the potential impact of generative AI on student critical thinking, volition and creative thought. In addition, the concerns of faculty, students and administration about AI and the use of AI detectors to ensure academic integrity are discussed. Last, AI resistant assessment is addressed.

ACADEMIC INTEGRITY

There is no universally accepted "gold standard" definition of academic integrity (Jamieson & Moore Howard, 2019). In its inception, academic integrity first became important related to copyright and financial issues related to copyright infringement. The term "academic integrity" was first used in 1964 in a dissertation by William Bowers, and since that point the term has become widely adopted. Even though it is a common term in academia, there are no definitions of academic honesty in dictionaries as there are for most terms in wide use (Jamieson & Moore Howard, 2019). Jamieson and Moore Howard lamented there was no standard definition even in library databases after they conducted an extensive search.

In 1999, the International Center for Academic Honesty (ICAH) published a definition of academic integrity in their guide *The Fundamentals of Academic Integrity* listing five key values. In 2014, the sixth value of courage was added. Per the 2014 definition they defined it as,"…a commitment, even in the face of adversity, to six fundamental values: honesty, trust, fairness, respect, responsibility and courage" (p. 1). They noted these values lead to principles of behavior and principled action. In 2024 on the EBSCO Database Research Starter page, Rholetter (2024) used ICAH's definition of academic integrity which signals wider adoption of this definition.

ICAH (2014) further breaks down each value that comprises academic integrity. Honesty includes being truthful, giving credit to the owner of a written work, providing factual evidence, and being objective and without bias. They defined trust, the second value as "assured reliance...on the truth of someone or something" (p. 6). This includes *not* falsifying work. The third value is fairness which was defined as students doing their own original work, citing appropriately, and upholding institutional academic integrity policies. The next value of respect was in reference to properly citing scholars and giving credit to their work and not representing it as one's own. The value responsibility was defined as standing up against wrongdoing including cheating and resisting peer pressure. Courage was defined as "acting in accordance with one's convictions" (p. 10) where students hold themselves and others to the highest standards of academic integrity. Although ICAH's definition incorporates the values included in many university academic integrity policies, the problem with defining values in any instance is that values are a personal, introspective process that takes place in the human mind. Values are important in maintaining societal order, but they are also important in understanding human motivation. Publishing a policy requiring that students have these values does not mean students will internalize them, particularly if they are in conflict with their personal values, or that they will motivate positive action. Schwartz (2012) notes the relative importance of a value will guide action. If a student values doing well on an assignment at any cost more than honesty, he will cheat on the assignment.

In 2018, the European Network for Academic Integrity published a glossary of terms. In this glossary, they defined academic integrity as "compliance with ethical and professional principles, standards, practices and a consistent system of values that serve as guidance for making decisions and taking actions in education, research and scholarship" (p. 8). This definition is more straightforward and less nebulous than ICAH's definition. Compliance is a call to action rather than just commitment to academic integrity. A student can easily be committed to doing something and not follow through because it is difficult. Compliance can be measured more objectively to a defined set of standards.

Colleges and universities also have very different definitions of academic integrity. Several different examples follow. Penn State University's 2026 policy is:

> *Consistent with the Pennsylvania State University's core ethical aspirations of Integrity, Respect, Responsibility, Discovery, Excellence and Community, we are committed to high standards of honesty in our academic efforts. Academic integrity is a basic guiding principle for the Penn State University community as it allows the pursuit of scholarly activity in an open, honest, and responsible manner. All students should act with personal integrity, respect everyone's dignity, rights, and property, and help create and maintain an environment in which all can succeed through the fruits of their efforts (p. 1).*

Harvard University's 2025-2026 policy is as follows, "Members of the Harvard College community commit themselves to producing academic work of integrity — that is, work that adheres to the scholarly and intellectual standards of accurate attribution of sources, appropriate collection and use of data, and transparent acknowledgment of the contribution of others to our ideas, discoveries, interpretations, and conclusions" (p. 1).

In addition, some specific examples are outlined in these policies. At Penn State they are:

Violations of academic integrity include, but are not limited to, copying, plagiarism, fabrication of information or citations, facilitation of acts of academic dishonesty by others, unauthorized possession of examinations, submitting work of another person or work previously used without informing the instructor, and tampering with the academic work of other students. Academic integrity includes a commitment by all members of the University community to not engage, regardless of intent, in acts of dishonesty, falsification, misrepresentation, or deception, as these acts violate the fundamental ethical principles of the University community and compromise the worth of work completed by others (p. 1).

Harvard has a much more detailed and comprehensive list of criteria with extensive explanations of each. These include plagiarism and collaboration, submitting the same assignment to more than one course (self-plagiarism), and using tutoring, school and term paper companies.

The Australian Government Tertiary Education Quality and Standards Organization (2026) list several behaviors that are considered violations of academic integrity in Australia: plagiarism, recycling or resubmitting work, fabricating information, collusion, exam cheating, contract cheating and impersonation. In the United States, each school sets what it considers academic integrity violations. Some other behaviors which may be included in individual university or college policies in the United States include things such as impersonation and sabotage (Stony Brook University, 2026), the use of any unauthorized electronic or mechanical communication devices (University of Massachusetts Boston, 2026), technological misconduct including attempting to obtain access codes, classroom misconduct, and out-of-classroom misconduct during internships or practicums (Indiana University of Pennsylvania, 2026). In Europe, behaviors include deceit of any type (University of Edinburgh, 2026), while Sheffield Hallam University (2026) lists poor academic practice which they define as slightly breaking any academic integrity rules. Johansen et al. (2026) in a survey of academic integrity across educational levels in four European countries queried students about practices such as comparing answers with other students before handing in an assignment, handing in an assignment where the student had significant help without acknowledging it, or adding a student as a co-author of assignments when they did not contribute. They found students have difficulty interpreting scenarios that deal with academic integrity; there were several gray-zone academic integrity violations that were not effectively identified by any category of higher education students from freshman to PhD students. This demonstrates there is still considerable confusion in interpreting academic integrity standards and language in actual practice.

Yet even with policies in place, Stillman (2025) notes that the estimated percentage of college students that cheat was 60%; DiPaulo (2022) noted students with degrees in education (who are those who will in the future police academic honesty in students) was up to 80%. It is interesting to note that as of the time of this writing, many university policies do not include detailed information about academic integrity and artificial intelligence (AI). This is likely because even three years after the release of the free version of ChatGPT to the public, the academic community is still struggling with the issue of academic integrity and AI. AI has further muddled the issue of academic integrity which was already confusing in application for many students and faculty.

Academic Integrity and AI

Advances in technology have significantly improved resources available to students, but it has also increased the ability of students to engage in academic integrity violations. In response to this, the creation of plagiarism detection software has become a multi-million-dollar industry. Artificial intelligence, which can generate papers and projects and answer questions with the minimal human intervention of textual prompts, has significantly accelerated the ability of students to engage in actions that are considered academically dishonest. Ballalle and Pannilage (2025) note the AI language model " does not have the understanding, critical thinking, or personal insights needed to produce authentic scholarly work" (p. 1). Wahle (2022) reported that AI writing is difficult to detect by both humans and software used to detect AI plagiarism. Perkins and Roe (2023) remarked as AI gets better at paraphrasing material, it will be much more difficult to detect in the future. They, along with other researchers (Crawford et al., 2023; Sullivan et al., 2023) observed it is crucial for higher education institutions to develop extensive guidelines regarding appropriate and inappropriate AI use.

Bannister et al. (2024) in a study of AI-based academic integrity policies in tertiary students in 10 countries throughout the world commented there were "significant gaps and inconsistencies" (p. 151) in these policies, and that these policies have been created in relative isolation (p. 151). Perkins and Roe (2023) in a review of 142 academic integrity policies referred to the "silence" (p. 5) that has been surrounding AI usage and specific AI policies in their evaluation of higher education institutions worldwide; they found significant variability in AI policy. Out of the

142 university policies evaluated, only one had specifically addressed AI in their academic integrity policy. Although this has increased in the three years since then, there continues to be significant gaps not only in policy, but in procedure as well. Rodrigues et al. (2025) said institutions tend to be reactive rather than proactive in responding to changes such as generative AI. Alsharefeen and Al Sayari (2025) who surveyed 71 faculty from 37 nations reported policies about generative AI were only moderately effective and insufficient, and that policies for traditional academic integrity were clearer and more adequate.

In 2021, UNESCO published a document that outlined some potential concerns with AI use in education. They noted a lack of agreed upon guidelines for the ethical use of AI in education. In 2023, all 24 Russell Group universities (including Oxford and Cambridge) in the United Kingdom (UK) collaborated on a set of guiding principles. These universities banned the use of AI and indicated students who used it would be expelled. In addition, some opted out of plagiarism detection programs because they wanted to ensure students were not falsely accused of cheating. However, these universities also pledged to incorporate it in education since students needed to know how to use AI in the workplace (Ngila, 2023). The Russell group universities developed the following principles regarding AI:

- Universities will support students and staff to become AI-literate.
- Staff should be equipped to support students to use generative AI tools effectively and appropriately in their learning experience.
- Universities will adapt teaching and assessment to incorporate the ethical use of generative AI and support equal access.
- Universities will ensure academic rigor and integrity is upheld.
- Universities will work collaboratively to share best practice as the technology and its application in education evolve (Russell Group, 2023).

Chan (2023) attempted to create a framework for AI policy based on feedback from students and faculty in Hong Kong. She noted faculty are not the only ones that are concerned about the issues of AI and academic integrity. Students were also concerned that their peers would use AI to "get ahead" (p. 9) in their assignments, devaluing the work of those who did their own work ($\bar{x}$=3.67, SD=1.22) and reported its use undermined the value of a university education(($\bar{x}$=3.29, SD=1.25). Students also reported generative AI would hinder their educational development in skills such as teamwork and problem solving (($\bar{x}$=3.30, SD=1.33). In addition, both students and teachers were unsure if teachers could accurately detect AI (with or without detectors). As part of the AI Ecological Policy Framework she created from her study, Chan reported that rethinking assessments and exams were a significant part of the framework. She stated universities need to develop a master plan for AI use in teaching, learning and assessment as did Bin-Nashwan et al. (2023).

Like Johansen at al. (2026) in their study of traditional academic integrity violations, Lund et al. (2025a) reported although most students realize that using a complete paper generated on AI is a violation, they have difficulty determining if more subtle uses are violations or not. This was also echoed by Chang in two separate studies in 2023 and 2024. In addition, Lund et al. (2025b) found students who perceive AI use as ethical also view academic integrity violations as less serious, while students who perceived AI use to be unethical took academic integrity much more seriously.

Gonsalves (2025) reported in 2025 at King's College in London that students were required beginning in 2023 to complete a course coversheet which required them to acknowledge AI use. If students disclosed AI use and followed assignment guidelines, then this would not negatively impact grades according to university policy. The students had to indicate if AI was used and if it was, specify how they used it in their work. Even with this initiative, 74% of students did not comply with completing the coversheet, particularly the acknowledgement of AI use portion even though the coversheet was freely available through the university learning management system.

To determine the cause of this issue, Gonsalves (2025) researched the reasons why students did not want to acknowledge AI use. She surveyed 57 undergraduate and graduate students; 63% of the population was undergraduate. She also conducted interviews to triangulate her data. She found 79% of students used AI, but only 65% disclosed it. Even though students were told their grades would not be affected, students still feared reduction in grades or being accused of academic integrity violations. In addition, they also had difficulty separating ethical and non-ethical AI use.

This study demonstrates that even when policies are created that allow free use of AI without penalty, there is still student confusion and unwillingness to admit to use of AI. Students indicated in Gonsalves (2025)'s study that if such a process is used, then there must be very clear detailed information about AI use. However, students also acknowledged that creating a long worksheet that allowed for detailed information would be an additional deterrent to its use. Gonsalves also reported students perceived AI as "personal aids" (p. 599) and felt use should remain private. They perceived acknowledging AI use as "invasive" (p. 599) and desired autonomy in their work. Some students felt AI was no different than a calculator even though generative AI is much, much more. Some students also reported if they did not use it and others did, they were "missing out" and were "stupid" (p. 600). Gonzalves concluded AI policies needed to be detailed and consistent and rolled out gradually to the student body. In addition, she noted that rather than making policies appear punitive, it might be more beneficial to focus on innovation and what AI can do in the learning process. More information about ethical and proper use of AI to reduce student fear of disclosure was needed in the institution's policy. She said clarity of institutional policies is key in promoting appropriate AI-related student behaviors.

Kramm and McKenna (2023) contend that trying to assure students have done their own work and not used AI is a "waste of time…and ethically troublesome" (p. 2173). They reported significant problems with even traditional plagiarism detection programs which in fact are not that at all, but text-match programs. They indicated they are particularly concerned in the software company "arm's race" (p. 2173) that puts these software companies in the "unquestioned position of power" (p. 2173). They note rather than police use, higher education institutions need to transform to work toward knowledge and learning. Instead, academic policies related to AI should not be targeted towards students, but to the institution itself with creating assessments that effectively use or deter the use of AI as needed.

The American Psychological Association (APA) was an early adopter of ethical principles and a code of conduct for research, teaching and publications for faculty and then students (Keith-Spiegel, 1994). APA has provided guidance in citing AI in academic work (McAdoo et al., 2025). The APA website (2026) notes use of AI must be disclosed and that AI cannot be "named as an author in a scholarly publication" (p. 1)

The Modern Language Association (MLA) in their 9th edition of their MLA handbook also has rules for citing AI in student work, although they specifically state AI should *not* be treated as an author. However, they do provide guidelines for citing and referencing specific pieces of content generated with AI (MLA Style Center, 2026). The Chicago Manual of Style (Turabian) in the 17th edition (2026) also has guidelines for AI citation and documentation of sources, and notes that AI "stands in as author of the content" (p. 1). This demonstrates even the three major organizations that publish standards for citation styles cannot agree about AI. Since faculty and institutions often consult professional organization guidance in policy creation, this clouds the issue of AI even more.

Universities have been struggling with implementing policies for appropriate student use of AI. However, Elom et al. (2025) reported even if policies exist, they may not be as effective as hoped in deterring improper use. Rather, many researchers believe compliance is more related to individual personality traits (Athar, 2025; Lund et al., 2025a; Lund et al., 2025b; Song & Liu, 2025).

Although there has never been a gold standard definition of academic integrity, prior to the introduction of generative AI, faculty, administration and students were, in general, in agreement about issues of academic integrity and what constituted "cheating." This is no longer the case with generative AI. There is significant confusion about how generative AI should be used in the academic environment, ethical versus unethical use and most importantly the impact on student learning and cognition. This has resulted in a significant delay in university policy and procedures in response to this issue and/or nebulous policies that do not effectively manage student and faculty behaviors or provide clear guidance.

The learning curve for university faculty, administration and students regarding generative AI has been extremely steep. The issue of generative AI is not a "one size fits all" approach for every institution, faculty member or even individual assessment as many other challenges (such as traditional plagiarism) have been in the past from a policy perspective. This is exacerbated by the fact that AI continues to improve and change almost instantaneously. The concerns of students, faculty and administration about generative AI are essential to the issue of academic integrity, educational assessment and the preparedness of graduates to enter the workplace with appropriate skills and competencies.

WHAT IS ALL THE CONCERN ABOUT?

After addressing the conundrum of academic integrity policies in the age of AI, it is important to address why faculty, administrators and students are so concerned about it. All three are concerned for very different reasons.

Students

Student concerns are fairly obvious. They do not want to be accused of an academic integrity violation when they have not committed one. Because of the issues with AI detection tools which are discussed later in this chapter, they cannot in fact prove they did not use AI. In many cases, they may have inadvertently used AI without even knowing it as AI becomes more embedded in the software they use for their research and assessments.

At this point in time, there is a paucity of research about how students truly feel about this issue. Mumtaz et al. (2025) evaluated graduate business college students in various countries and noted student culture significantly impacts student perception of generative AI use. Although this was a small study, Asian students were more likely than North American, European, and Arab students to perceive using generative AI to answer a question in an academic setting as unethical. They note this is because Western cultures are more individualized and see academic success as a personal achievement which makes them more likely to cheat, while Asian cultures are more collective in nature.

Han et al. (2025) reported AI applications have been developed for higher education in several major areas: assessment, prediction, personalized systems that are adaptive, and intelligent tutoring systems. Faculty and administration who are attempting to keep up with the rapid changes in AI in higher education are familiar with AI in assessment and beginning to implement it. Some may even be familiar with predictive tools which are usually algorithms that analyze student data such as retention or academic success. Personalized adaptive systems are being created to attempt to respond to the unique educational needs of individual students; some are based on Maria Montessori's concept of individualized education, as well as Bloom's mastery learning (Fortuna et al., 2025). These AI-based systems automatically create learning materials tailored to a student's academic level, as well as provide personalized feedback. These systems can adapt as the student changes and adapts. Intelligent tutoring systems also provide student-specific tutoring information based on student performance.

Han et al. (2025) looked at students' perceptions of personalized adaptive systems that could detect student behavior in the classroom to predict student weaknesses and learning. These systems can also provide custom learning suggestions for the professor for students exhibiting behaviors that indicate weaknesses or a lack of learning. The researchers used the Story Completion Method (SCM) to create scenarios to evaluate student's perceptions of AI use in the higher education classroom to detect behaviors. Two scenarios addressed their feelings towards AI being used for facial and emotional recognition to detect student potential confusion and engagement so the teacher could intervene. Facial and emotional recognition AI-based tools in education include gaze tracking, voice recognition, body language and facial expression detectors to evaluate potential emotions (Wei, 2024).

The patterns that are tracked and used are proprietary information for the companies that are developing these software programs since they are in competition with one another, so detailed information on how they work is not freely available. In Han et al.'s research, Scenario 1 used student AI monitoring during a lecture. In Scenario 2, monitoring occurred during group activities. Scenario 3 asked students to address the intended benefits of these AI tools. Students were asked to complete what they felt would be the end result of each narrative for them as students. The research population included higher education students from freshman through PhD's in Australia and China. The researchers performed qualitative analysis on 71 different participants of which 54% were male and 46% were female.

Students acknowledged that there were some benefits to classroom AI predictive technology in that they could provide personalized guidance. However, most of the identified themes were more negative in nature. Overall, students felt the predictive AI analysis "oversimplifies human behavior" (Han et al., 2025, p. 9), and that there was no connection between their facial expressions and their own human thoughts. They rated this predictive analysis as "shallow" (p. 9) and inaccurate. For example, one student was predicted to be bored, but he was just in fact tired from working late the night before. Students also felt that AI technology such as this "decontextualizes" (p. 9) the learning process, and that if a person is learning or not cannot be that easily detected based on just a few observations or factors. One student commented learning is not linear for all learners, but AI would never be able to detect this. Students also felt use of these technologies neglects cultural differences and diversity and could result in unfair consequences for students. They perceived these systems as not being fair to all students because AI could not consider all possible human considerations. Students reported human judgement rather than AI was crucial to enhance their learning and to judge their performance and only other humans could understand human nuance. They felt these systems were inherently biased both intentionally and unintentionally. In addition, they felt AI prediction systems could also result in the Hawthorne effect where students modify their behavior because they are being observed which is a well-known behavioral reaction.

Students also addressed power dynamics and felt that it was difficult to address and determine how much power and credence should be put into AI prediction and analysis (Han et al., 2025). It is important to note this is the exact same issue and concern that is occurring with AI plagiarism detectors as well. In this study, students did not trust the predictive AI just like they do not trust AI plagiarism detectors.

Fošner and Aver (2025) evaluated student perceptions of chatbots in higher education by deploying a survey to 422 participants in business programs in Slovenia. They reported 70% of the students felt that chatbots generated human-like results, but 76% rated them as unreliable. Most students (86%) felt they should not be prohibited in education; 75% felt using them was not cheating, and only 20% felt their use was morally wrong. There were no significant differences in responses across levels of study, but there were statistically significant differences based on the field of study. Students felt it was more acceptable to use chatbots for academic tasks in some fields more than others. In addition, students were concerned that students in some fields could become dependent on chatbots which was viewed as a negative effect.

Chan (2023) in her study of 487 students in Hong Kong reported students felt they could become over-reliant on generative AI, but also strongly felt universities should have a plan for the potential risks of students using AI inappropriately. They also moderately agreed that generative AI undermines the value of a university education, as well as hinders their problem-solving skills. In a 2025 study of 393 students in Hong Kong of student perceptions of AI plagiarism, Chan also reported students seemed to understand that they could not use AI to generate specific content for an assignment or discussion or to paraphrase content. However, they did not understand more subtle uses of AI as violating academic integrity. This included using it to generate ideas, refine work, searching for resources and checking for grammar. Overall, she concluded although students understand ethical implications of AI use, they cannot effectively interpret more "nuanced scenarios" (p. 8098).

Chan reported students are even more confused about AI-plagiarism than they are about traditional plagiarism.

Lund et al. (2025a) surveyed primarily graduate students at several major universities in the United States and received 277 complete and valid surveys. In this study, 84% of students were aware that platforms such as Grammarly use generative AI which could be detected by AI plagiarism detection tools. These students reported using AI to generate an entire paper was ethically wrong as well and that using AI is a form of cheating; in addition, they considered cheating as not okay even if students got away with it. It is important to note that since this study sample was composed of 91% graduate students, these students are likely more aware of academic integrity issues of all types than undergraduates are.

Students also are concerned that their faculty know how to use and interpret AI detectors. Agomuoph (2023) reported in 2023 a professor at Texas A& M Commerce failed an entire class when he ran all of his papers through ChatGPT to test them for AI plagiarism, not realizing that ChatGPT could not detect AI plagiarism. The students' diplomas were held because of this.

There are significant valid student concerns about AI use and academic policy. Faculty are not consistent in dealing with traditional academic honesty violations consistently, let alone AI violations, which is a significant concern for students and institutions. Part of this is because of lack of clarity in policy and the continually changing environment.

Faculty

Faculty have many general concerns about AI and AI academic integrity. Buele and Llerena-Aguirre (2025) commented that faculty perceptions of generative AI are ambivalent because although they see significant potential, they also see very significant problems including institutional and technological barriers.

The first significant concern is faculty feel they cannot definitively detect if a student is using AI in an unethical manner or not. Chan et al. (2023) in a study of 180 faculty in Hong Kong universities reported faculty believed they could not effectively determine inappropriate AI use for class assignments ($\bar{x}$=2.72, SD=1.62). In Alsharefeen and Al Sayari's (2025) study, faculty reported the most significant factor to policy ineffectiveness was technological insufficiencies or the problems with AI plagiarism detectors. The faculty did not trust the results of these detectors. In addition, they stated no matter what they did, technology changed so rapidly that students could circumvent the system and continue to use AI in unethical manners. The faculty noted they really could not prove student AI use. Perhaps the most significant finding described by these researchers is the large disparity between student and faculty attitudes towards AI use.

Islam et al. (2024) surveyed 115 faculty in 22 private universities and found almost 70% of faculty were significantly concerned about generative AI and academic integrity, and almost 96% felt AI posed significant academic integrity challenges for faculty. Only 5% reported existing policies were sufficient, only approximately 14% felt they prevented misuse of AI tools, and only 7% felt AI tools were effective.

The second major concern of faculty is that students are using AI for course work when they should not be or are not using it in an ethical manner. In a small pilot study of 31 faculty in diverse disciplines in Oman, Mishra and Varshney (2024) reported slightly more than half of students were likely adhering to academic integrity policies including the use of AI; however, most faculty felt they could positively impact bad student behavior. However, going back to the first concern, without AI detectors that can with certainty detect AI use and keep up with the rapid changes, faculty cannot fix behaviors if they do not definitively know if they are occurring.

Colleges and universities have been slow to respond to the issue of AI which is the third major faculty concern. Jiang et al. (2025) in a qualitative study and interview of seven faculty at various universities noted faculty are still waiting on universities to establish clear AI use policies. Alsharefeen and Al Sayari (2025) related faculty rated AI plagiarism policies as lacking in availability, visibility, clarity, adequacy and effectiveness. In addition, faculty felt policies should be more educational than punitive, although only about 80% of faculty allowed students to resubmit the work where AI integrity violations occurred. In this study, 76% of faculty also said that AI has increased academic integrity violations; however, only about 62% of faculty said they reported them. When the researchers reviewed institutional records, the actual percentage of faculty reporting violations was much lower even though each institution had a policy that any violations need to be reported.

Some universities have attempted simple across the board policies which may not be the most effective. Some have added a statement about AI to their traditional academic integrity policies and have just indicated AI cannot be used, or it cannot be used unless specified in the assignment itself. Other universities such as Vanderbilt, Michigan State, Northwestern and the University of Texas (Quach, 2023) turned off the AI detector function in Turnitin and are not checking for AI use as policy. Universities that use Blackboard with the SafeAssign traditional plagiarism detection tool are not checking for AI at all because this common detector does not detect AI (Blackboard, 2026). From a policy perspective, some universities who used Turnitin to detect traditional plagiarism opted to turn off the AI detection feature because the false positive rate was too high and even with a 20% false positive rate (Chechitelli, 2023) thousands of students would be accused of unwarranted AI-based academic integrity violations (Quach, 2023).

Some researchers have tried to further explore what faculty really want to see in AI academic integrity policies. Islam et al. (2024) in Bangladesh used the Technological Acceptance Model (TAM) to frame their study of university faculty. In this model, technologies are more likely to be accepted if they are useful as well as easy to use and will lead to positive outcomes. Although plagiarism detectors are easy to use, they do not necessarily lead to positive outcomes if a faculty member accuses a student of unethical use of AI when it in fact did not occur.

Gustilo et al. (2024) used TAM as a basis to understand faculty perceptions of generative AI in a triangulated research study. In Gustilo et al.'s study, faculty very strongly agreed that generative AI was dangerous if clear policies were not set for its use. They agreed students should be required to report generative AI use, but digital writing assistants such as Grammarly were acceptable to use. In this study, 100% of faculty felt AI use for coursework, short essays, reports, theses and dissertations should be regulated or banned. They also recommended it be banned for mathematical calculations. When queried about the allowable percentage of AI matches, most faculty indicated no higher than 15%. This was likely impacted by Turnitin's reported 20% false positive rate (Chechitelli, 2023). Ethical concerns listed by the faculty in Gustilo et al.'s study included academic dishonesty which was the major concern, concerns over reliability of sources and data generated by AI, dependency on AI tools for students and faculty, and hindrance of the development of skills.

Gustilo et al. (2024) also queried faculty on the types of resources they would like their institutions to provide. This included policy guidelines on how to use and regulate generative AI, training on ethical use of AI, and processes that ensured equitable access for faculty and students. Overall, faculty felt that while generative AI should be banned in the tasks listed above, it could be used with supervision in some assessments and tasks. The researchers also noted some faculty's inexperience with AI tools may impact their attitudes toward it. Educators reported it is almost impossible to keep pace with new AI tools, and institutional response to AI policies was lagging and most institutions were at a discussion phase. The researchers concluded "institution heads may not be adequately informed or prepared to address the challenges of AI integration in education" (p. 30).

A fourth concern of faculty was procedural limitations in policy escalation when multiple instances occur in addition to differing faculty responses. These are all concerns that have also existed with traditional plagiarism policies. However, the burden of proof with AI academic integrity violations is considered much more significant (Alsharefeen & Al Sayari, 2025).

Overall, faculty seem to desire detailed policies for student AI use, as well as for faculty reporting and escalation. However, since there are so many nuances with AI use, this type of policy can be very difficult to write. In addition to cheating and policy concerns, faculty also have significant concerns about cognitive and behavioral impacts on students.

Cognitive and Behavioral Concerns

One of the major purposes of higher education has been to promote critical thinking. John Dewey first introduced the concept of critical thinking in 1910 but thought it could only be done through experiential learning. Piaget and Montessori, two important educational theorists concurred (Ültanir, 2012). According to other classic literature on critical thinking, it has three components: logic and reasoning, the ability to be thoughtful and reflect, and the ability to apply the first two components (Glaser, 1941). Faculty have struggled for decades trying to find ways to teach critical thinking since higher education is primarily cognitive rather than psychomotor or affective in nature.

In 1990, Facione for the American Psychological Association expanded the cognitive skills needed for critical thinking to include interpretation, analysis, evaluation, inference, explanation and self-regulation. In theory, these things sound wonderful; in practice it is a lot more difficult for university faculty to create assessments and experiences that promote critical thinking. Critical thinking is a construct which in and of itself has an abstract nature composed of various parts (Merriam Webster, 2026). Like academic integrity, there is no gold standard definition of what critical thinking is (Lau, 2024).

Akbar (2025), Basit (2025), and Xiu et al. (2025) all found faculty are concerned about the impact of AI on critical thinking. Other than self-regulation, generative AI can do all the things in both Glaser's and Facione's definitions. Although previously AI was not the best at being thoughtful and reflective, as it has "learned," it has significantly improved on this ability since it was first released, particularly if it is told to be reflective. Self-regulation, the one thing AI cannot do because it is not human, is the one thing students need to do. But, with the ready availability of AI, many students do not have any self-regulation and use AI even if they should not. Bauer et al. (2025) found over-reliance in AI led to reduced cognitive engagement in students.

Some researchers feel AI can teach critical thinking including Akbar (2025) and Wu (2024) who evaluated AI use in an art appreciation course. But it takes significant faculty time and education to be able to do this. Wu (2025) felt faculty needed to teach "why" and "how" and discussed scaffolding and educational theorists such as Piaget. However, in scaffolding, faculty must ensure students understand basic concepts of most any field before they can get to the why and how. However, since Wu did look at art appreciation, AI can provide rich experiences that were not available before improvements in technology. Melisa et al. (2025) in a meta- analysis of 19 research articles concluded ChatGPT does have a positive impact on critical thinking; he inferred this based on previous studies done in 2023 and 2024; however, seven of the authors he cited did not explicitly conclude it improves critical thinking.

In 2024, the editors of the Academy of Management Learning and Education (AMLE) wrote a statement on critical thinking and generative AI appealing to those in the business management field to pay increased attention to critical thinking because of AI. They wrote that although AI helps students gain wider points of view quite easily, if students use it, then they are not fostering critical thinking cognitively themselves. There is also significant concern about information quality since generative AI extracts from the internet where there is a plethora of incorrect information (Buchanan et al., 2024; Hannigan et al., 2024, Watson, 2024). The editors of AMLE also concluded generative AI would inhibit critical thinking since humans trust it too much and defer to it as an "expert." They note this trust is cognitive as well as emotional, and the very nature of the way AI presents information makes it more likely for a student to use it. Part of critical thinking is recognizing bias which AI does not necessarily do. The other concern they had was the sheer ease; the use of AI for classwork is too tempting for many students. All these factors cause students to "uncritically" (p. 375) rely on it.

In the past through Socratic dialogue and dialectic thinking, or even with just discussion, critical thinking was more of a social event where humans bounced ideas and concepts off one another and argued for their point of view. Generative AI totally changes this interaction from a social interaction to an interaction between man and machine which is a solitary pursuit. Feng (2025) found that generative AI use in learning and assessment limits interaction with peers and has a negative impact on human dialogue which is a key soft skill highly desired by employers.

Grinshgl et al. (2021) looked at the consequences of cognitive offloading before AI even existed. They defined cognitive offloading as the use of a tool that decreases cognitive demand. Before cell phones came into regular use, children were required by their parents to memorize their home phone number and address. Children also memorized the phone numbers of the friends and family they called regularly. Cell phones with contact lists provided cognitive offloading for these tasks.

There are cases where humans have to offload certain cognitive tasks or they will be overwhelmed. Grinschgl et al. (2021) report offloading can improve problem-solving and memory, but offloading too much can lead to "impoverishment of internal abilities"(p. 478). To correlate this with students, if they offload too much, they lose critical thinking and what is considered actual intelligence or the ability to think. Gringshl et al. (2021) also said when cognitive information is offloaded that may be needed in the long term, students may not be able to do the tasks they are required to do and memory is negatively impacted. These findings were also supported by other researchers (Richmond & Taylor, 2025; Risko & Gilbert, 2016)

There is absolutely no doubt that generative AI provides for cognitive offloading. The problem is the potential and likelihood humans will offload too much and know too little themselves. If a student goes through his entire career in higher education using generative AI to complete almost all of his assignments, then his critical thinking, memory and ability to apply what he has learned on the job he has prepared for with his college degree will be significantly negatively impacted.

Gerlich (2025) looked specifically at the impact of cognitive offloading and AI in relation to critical thinking. He surveyed 666 participants across various ages and educational backgrounds and conducted in-depth interviews. He found AI use decreased critical thinking because of cognitive offloading, and those ages 17-25 were highly dependent on generative AI and had much lower critical thinking scores than older participants. The one ray of hope in this study is that he found the higher the education level the student attained, the better his/her critical thinking skills were regardless of AI usage. Although this might have been true in 2025 when his study was done, this may not necessarily be true in the future. Since generative AI only became available in early 2023, the majority of people in this study who attained higher education levels would have only done so prior to the availability of AI. In the future, for generative AI "natives" there may in fact be no difference.

Yan et al. (2025) noted significant research is needed concerning the impact of generative AI use on human knowledge construction and cognitive load management. In other words, will the creation of AI cause humans to store less and less information in the human brain and rely more on technology? Yan et al. question whether AI will in fact " reshape the very nature of the human mind" (p. 7). They note there is not enough information at this point in time to understand how prolonged use of generative AI impacts deeper cognitive processes. There is also little information on the overuse of AI and its impact on human cognition.

There is so much researchers and educators do not know at this time regarding how AI use impacts student learning and cognition in the long-term. The true impact on the human brain and learning will not be able to be ascertained until AI natives complete their primary and secondary education and enter the workplace.

Overall, the impact of generative AI on student cognition and learning is perhaps the most significant concern of faculty and humanity as well. Although most faculty clearly acknowledge AI can be beneficial, it also presents significant challenges regarding assessment design to facilitate the transversal skills defined by Bauer et al. (2025) which include: critical thinking, problem-solving, information and technology literacy, collaboration, communication, AI literacy and creativity.

Creativity

Critical thinking and impact on human cognition is not the only concern of faculty. Hoa (2023) found half of faculty and administrators felt generative AI would negatively impact student creativity as well. Researchers have generally defined creativity as the ability to formulate ideas that are "novel and appropriate" (Jia,

2025, p. 1). Bosen (2004) who is credited as beginning the cognitive evaluation of creative thinking noted creativity is the ability to also come up with something that is surprising and has value. Mouzzi (2025) in a theoretical discussion of AI and creativity posited at this time, many researchers believe AI does not meet the definition of creativity because it just draws from other existing sources and it lacks its own authenticity since it does not produce anything new.

Like critical thinking, human creativity is a cognitive function. In a study of 128 students at Southwest University, Jia et al. (2025) looked at creativity and the impact of metacognitive disfluency, which is the difficulty or effort of solving complex problems or doing complex tasks. They found the difficulty or metacognitive disfluency in a task enhanced creative and divergent thinking. In other words, for students to be able to be creative in analyzing and solving problems, they must struggle to a certain extent. Wang and Huang (2025) in a study of 2,531 undergraduates supported this finding and reported AI does not directly shape creativity; rather, creativity is dependent on self-regulated learning (2025). In essence, generative AI has almost taken this issue of cognitive struggle and self-reliant learning totally off the table since it can provide answers in just a few seconds.

In 2024 Habib et al. examined the effect of generative AI on creative thinking on 100 undergraduate students at a major university in the United States. Although AI was helpful for brainstorming, there were still negative effects on creativity. Since creative thinking is related to self-efficacy, AI negatively impacted students' self-efficacy in relation to creative thinking, and stifled divergent thinking and student confidence in themselves to think creatively. They noted "reliance on AI might fixate thoughts rather than expand them" (p. 4). This negative impact was echoed by Brem and Hörauf (2025).

Looking synergistically at both cognitive offloading and the hindrance of creative thinking that AI facilitates, this may have a negative impact on what is currently perceived as human intelligence. This was supported by Lin and Chen (2024) who supported Habib et al. 's (2024) premise that in undergraduate students, AI was helpful in brainstorming initial ideas, but overall constrains creative thinking and innovation. Of course, there are opposing studies (Han et al., 2026; Mahmoud, 2025) that have found that AI can also increase student creativity, but only in certain types of assessment. It is important to note that Mahmoud's conclusions were not based on original research, but in looking at research of others' work about AI-generated quizzes and games.

Analytical Thinking

Alter et al. in 2007 asserted the metacognitive difficulty of a task also increases analytic reasoning in addition to creativity. This was supported by studies done by Alon-Barkat & Busuioc (2021) who evaluated three separate studies of 2,854 people who were making decisions on which teachers to hire in a theoretical scenario. When AI was used, the respondents would default to taking the advice of an AI algorithm, ignoring contradictory cues from other human sources. In other words, like with creative thinking, humans tend to rely on AI rather than on their own thoughts and intuition when AI is used. This demonstrates a negative impact on analytical reasoning.

Hassen (2025) examined the effects of generative AI on problem-solving and analytics skills in college students. He indicated use of student AI in an unethical manner can result in a cascade of negative effects since skills are not isolated. For example, first students no longer read their text, but instead use an AI summarizer on an e-text. Then, the student is asked to write an evaluation of the text. Since he did not read it and relied on AI, he cannot critically think since his engagement was superficial and knowledge was shallow which impacts his analytical abilities. Therefore, he again uses AI. Then, if the student is given an additional complex problem based on the concepts in the text, this again impacts analysis and problem-solving abilities which leaves the student to continue to use AI once again. He calls this cognitive dependency. Consequently, there are some studies that found AI has a positive impact on analytic skills (Ilgun Dibek et al. (2025), but this was dependent on assessment type and even discipline so there was significant variability.

Volition

Some faculty fear that generative AI may negatively impact students' motivation to continue to put forth effort in doing their own work and enhancing their own learning. But perhaps more so than motivation, student volition is what really comes into play. Motivation is a cognitive process where students intend to do something (such as use generative AI for their classwork when they are pressed for time even though they shouldn't). Volition takes this a step farther from intent into action (Haggard, 2019) or execution of a behavior. At this point in time, research studies on AI and volition are non-existent.

Although there are not currently studies on volition and student use of generative AI, there are some studies that looked at AI and student motivation. Motivation and volition are of concern in two respects: a) motivation/volition to do one's own work no matter what the external circumstances and b) motivation/ volition to use AI in an unethical manner so one does not have to do one's own work yet reaps the benefit of college credit and degrees. The more confident students become in using AI, the more likely it is they will use it. If a college student sees his peers use AI to do work everyone is supposed to do on their own and get away with that, will that continue to impact student volition to use AI for classroom work in an unethical manner? This is a possibility considering AI detectors are viewed as unreliable, and faculty cannot really prove when students are using AI. Giray et al. (2026) found peer influence is an important factor in normalizing AI use whether it is allowed or not and this significantly impacts student motivation and behavior. They also noted a lack of clear institutional policies was interpreted by students as "silent approval of their actions" (p. 1) and when challenged by time constraints students view cheating as wrong but make excuses as to why they are engaging in it.

Abbas et al. (2025) in a study of 394 college students that looked at motivation for use of AI, found use of AI can lead to AI addiction and a tolerance for cheating. Tutor et al. (2026) said student motivation to use AI to cheat was driven by the desire for a passing grade. Some research in these areas can be informed by research on traditional teaching and motivation for student cheating, but more research is needed on generative AI and student motivation and volition. In addition, strategies are needed to try to motivate students to *not* act upon the temptation to use AI. These are particularly needed for students whose personality traits make them inclined to cheat.

This overview of faculty concerns about generative AI and academic integrity was not all encompassing. However, it provided an overview of some of the major faculty concerns. Both students and faculty have concerns about generative AI and academic integrity and are looking toward higher education administration for guidance.

Administration

Bassett et al. (2026) notes the burden of proof of AI-based academic integrity violations is on administration. Currently there is very little information in the research literature about higher education administration perceptions of generative AI and academic integrity even though they are the ones responsible for crafting the policies. Karakose and Tulabas (2025) indicated educational leaders must have significant problem-solving skills to manage in the age of AI. Gustillo et al. (2024) called for administration in higher education to drive educational reforms in the rigor of assessments in response to AI and for the complete overhaul of institutional academic integrity policies, particularly about generative AI use. Yet, Hoa (2023) found administrators' experience level with generative AI was about the same as faculty; experience was very slightly higher with ChatGPT and Grammarly, but the same with other AI applications. Faculty were slightly more cautious about using AI in academic writing than administrators, but both groups were considered cautious rather than accepting.

Tarisayi (2024, p. 9) theorized the following key leadership roles in higher education to respond to the proliferation of generative AI:

- Articulate a strategic vision
- Foster and institutional culture of experimentation
- Gather and allocate resources
- Seek external partnerships

However, it is important to note, this guidance did not really provide significant information about academic integrity. Overall, administrators are called upon to provide guidance and policy on generative AI to assist both students and faculty, but they are having difficulty coming up with effective policies. This, in turn, causes them as administrators more challenges and problems in interpreting the very individual nature of academic integrity offenses. Administrators have struggled in the past doing this for traditional academic honesty offenses since many of these offenses are gray rather than black or white. Generative AI has exacerbated an already problematic issue.

Evaluation of Concerns

In the issue of generative AI, students, faculty and administration have valid concerns. Students fear that they may be unjustly accused of academic integrity violations which could negatively impact their academic career. Faculty are experiencing an unprecedented change in the way they need to create and manage student assessment. Previous technological advances facilitated students in doing their own work; human effort was still required. Faculty are now faced with generative AI that can do the work for the students with little effort on the students' part. Faculty have no effective way to determine if students are doing their own work or having AI do the work for them. Particularly after the advent of online learning, assessment moved outside of the classroom with online testing as well as papers and projects that were checked with traditional plagiarism detection programs and submitted online through a learning management system. With generative AI, faculty feel powerless to create processes and AI-resistant assessments to replace traditional assessment practices and fear their students may not be learning. With a constantly changing AI landscape, university administration is having difficulty responding quickly and effectively to create policies and procedures that address student and faculty needs regarding AI use and academic integrity.

Soon employers will be faced with their first group of graduates who could have used generative AI in lieu of completing their own work for a large portion of an entire bachelor's degree. Will this generation of graduates lack analytical and critical thinking, creativity and volition in the workplace? Will they be too dependent on technology and powerless to respond in situations where technology cannot provide the quick and easy answer? If students do not have these skills, then this may reflect negatively on the faculty and universities that taught them and allowed them to graduate.

Generative AI detectors use and associated challenges were identified as a concern for all three groups. These tools were meant to help faculty detect violations and educate students on improper AI use to encourage students to do their own work. But they have caused even more confusion in the issue of academic integrity and institutional policy.

AI DETECTORS

AI detectors/classifiers use proprietary mathematics to detect similarities between human-written and typical AI-generated text and are inherently unreliable (Crockett & Howe, 2024. p. 187). They report AI-generated text is more predictable with similar sentence and paragraph breaks that are determined using an algorithm. However, when users keep re-entering prompts for a specific topic and ask for different wording and phrasing, this can break these patterns and make AI less detectable. There are also humanizing programs.

Waked et al. (2024) reported since academic writing is somewhat rote in structure, and the probability is higher it will be detected as AI writing rather than human. They noted that often the students who worked the hardest on a quality assessment such as a research paper are "most at risk for falling victim to false detection" (p. 577). Pratama (2024) reported in detection of AI in faculty journal article submissions, that the writing styles of some disciplines were more likely to cause an AI match than others. One reason is because AI detectors are trained to detect perplexity (how unpredictable the text is) and burstiness (which is variation in sentence length and structure. If a student is writing up a laboratory report for an experiment that uses the scientific method and commonly associated terminology, this student's work is more likely to come up as an AI match even if the student did not use it.

Other problems noted by Waked et al. (2024) include the fact AI detectors are based on probability which is only likelihood, and one of the reasons software creators do not necessarily stand behind the accuracy of their products. In their study of AI detection in 90 freshman students in four different sections of an introductory writing course, Waked et al. evaluated students creating descriptive, comparison and contrast, informative, and argumentative papers. They deployed a handwritten midterm and final essay exam that was done in class over a period of two hours for each exam. Research was conducted on the final essay exam. Grades on the essay exams were categorized into three groups: high performing, median and low performing. The researchers then used six different AI detection programs on these original handwritten samples. They found the AI detection programs detected a match for all of the original handwritten work at varying probabilities. Students who were performing well on the exam had much higher rates of AI match.

Lund et al. (2025a) reported that because of the level of sophistication in algorithmic detection programs, this makes it difficult to detect and respond to academic integrity violations. This is supported by Waked et al. (2024) who said that while AI detection programs serve an important role in deterrence of unethical use of AI, there is no guarantee that it is accurate in differentiating human and AI-generated text. AI and AI detectors cannot necessarily separate "good" from "bad" information; if a high volume of incorrect information is present on the Internet, AI will include it; Crockett and Rowe called this a "hallucination" (2024, p. 179).

Part of the issue lies in the deployment of the AI detection feature on Turnitin, a widely used plagiarism detection tool in higher education. It was first released in April of 2023 and a few months after release in June 2023, Annie Chechitelli, the Chief Product Officer of Turnitin reported higher false positive rates were found in documents with less than a 20% AI match (2023) that had not been previously disclosed. This occurred after faculty had already reported students for academic integrity violations. Kaner (2025) concluded current AI detection tools encounter "significant technological, ethical and pedagogical challenges" (p. 242); he felt this made them inappropriate for decision-making, particularly in high stakes situations such as when a student may fail a course, be placed on probation or removed from programs of study.

However, savvy users of AI through multiple prompting and humanizing programs can create text that is less likely to be detected (Crocket & Howe, 2024). One reason is that no two detection programs were "taught" using the same datasets. In addition, the percentage of human and AI-generated writing used to train the AI is also different.

Non-Native Speakers

Several studies have concluded AI detectors are significantly biased against non-native speakers. In 2023 Liang et al. used seven different AI detectors to evaluate 91 Test of English as a Foreign Language (TOEFL) essays written by humans and not generated by AI and compared them to 88 essays written by United States eighth grade students. All of the detectors accurately classified the junior high student essays, while on average, 61.3% of the TOEFL essays were flagged as AI when it was not. They concluded this was because the TOEFL essay did not have the element of unpredictability that Waked et al. (2024) indicated AI detector algorithms look for.

Ibrahim in 2023 compared two AI detectors on 240 essays (human and AI-generated) and concluded detection accuracy was inconsistent in English as a second language students. Bannister et al. (2024) declared there are significant challenges for international students whose writing may cause an AI-match with current AI detectors when one does not exist. Liange et al. (2023) reported humans sometimes write in AI-like ways (Liang et al., 2023) and that in particular, international students tend to use simpler sentence structure which AI detectors classify as machine-driven text. Caner (2025) in a meta-analysis of 25 peer-reviewed research articles published from 2022-2025 concluded, "Empirical evidence indicates a constant, ethically significant bias against multi-lingual writers" (p. 243). He agreed with Bannister (2024) that this was caused by reduced word diversity in writing and more predictable, simple phrasing. Jiang et al. (2024) noted when AI systems are trained, non-native speakers are underrepresented and this contributed to AI detector bias. Hadra et al. (2026) in a study of AI detectors looked at the effectiveness of the Turnitin AI detector and Originality detector in English as a foreign language (EFL) students in 192 texts. He used human, AI-generated and hybrid texts which were 50% human and 50% AI generated; it was ensured the texts demonstrated continuity and coherence. He found Turnitin did not detect many AI generated texts and instead categorized them as human writing although it was effective in detecting human writing. The Originality tool performed similarly, but both detection systems performed very poorly in classifying hybrid texts. It can be surmised that one reason this occurred is because AI detectors are biased against non-native speakers and they cannot differentiate them from AI generated text. The bias of AI detectors against certain groups is a critical ethical and policy issue. Research in this area is ongoing. However, problems have also been found in native speakers as well.

Divergent Writers

Many students are classified as neurodivergent including those with dyslexia, attention-deficit hyperactivity disorder (ADHD), and autism, but it can also be considered a natural variation in human brain function and cognitive differences that are not classified as disabilities (Eaton, 2025). It is important to consider that not everyone who is neurodiverse or is a neurotypical thinker has a medical condition or diagnosis, although the limited research that exists on AI detectors and divergency looks at those with medical diagnoses. A neurodivergent person may be very creative, can easily solve complex problems others cannot, or just think differently (Johns Hopkins University, 2026). In the case of AI detectors, these people may also in fact just write differently as well.

Eaton (2025) found overall there is a significant lack of literature regarding divergent students and academic integrity, and bias in AI detectors disproportionately identified neurodivergent individuals as using AI when they were not. This can lead to significant psychological distress for an already marginalized population. Chakaborty et al. (2024) asserted not all texts by humans contain the variability that AI detectors look for in phrasing, word use and syntax. An example was given earlier on how research writing has a certain style and format, and specific words are more likely to be used. Gegg-Harrison and Quarteman (2024) reported neurodivergent writers (which may not just include those with cognitive disabilities) are more likely to be flagged as using AI when they have not. Sayeed (2026) concurred AI detectors have bias against neurodivergent writers because they are more consistent in sentence structure and length; on the other side, it also may detect writing from neurodivergent writers that is too unusual as well.

Whitney Gegg-Harrison (2023) from the University of Rochester who has a background in computational linguistics ran her own papers that were written prior to AI through an AI detector. The detector indicated her original work had been produced by AI when it was not. In the past she had always been told her writing was very precise. Elise Gomes (2026) who is a professional writer and game creator, says she writes "like a robot" (p. 1) and considers herself a divergent writer; in addition, English is her second language. She indicated texts she wrote 20 years ago are being flagged as being written by AI and wrote neurodivergent people are being excluded. This author also has had personal experiences with two different students who were completing their master's capstone projects. The first student did an applied research project and his entire paper was about more or less a mini ethnography where he documented what he saw in his organization and what he heard from others about deploying a new electronic medical record system and analyzed it. The organization which was a military facility and implementation of medical records in these organizations is not usually addressed in the literature. Most of the information included in his paper were his interpretations, thoughts, and recommendations specific to that organization. Although the paper had a literature review, it was rather short as it was an applied project. When this paper was run through Turnitin, he had a 100% AI match. He had not used Grammarly even to spellcheck his essay. Another student who was doing a theoretical capstone project which was a large literature review also had a 100% match. Her paper was 40 pages long. The author ensured the student turned off AI on her Microsoft Office program, ensured she did not use Grammarly or other AI spell-checkers, and the student then rewrote her entire paper. When it went through Turnitin, it still showed a 100% AI match. This occurred two days after Turnitin updated their AI detector to better detect humanizing programs in late 2025.

In 2024, Davalos and Yin in *Businessweek* and *Bloomberg News* reported on a student named Moira Olmstead, an adult learner who was enrolled in online courses at Central Methodist University. Her writing was continually flagged as written by AI when she insisted it was not; she had autism spectrum disorder. It is evident more research is needed in this area and that people who are divergent thinkers and writers could be accused of using AI when they have not. Students are not the only ones who say they have been falsely targeted. David Mingay, (2026) a faculty member, reported he wrote a journal article without the use of AI and the paper was flagged by the AI detector used by the editors as being too uniform as well as too "fluent" (p. 1). He noted in essence he was penalized for writing well since his paper was not accepted. Mingus makes this wonderful point, how can he accuse his students of using AI for their assessments when he himself was falsely accused?

Problems with AI detectors have only exacerbated an already problematic issue for students, faculty and university administration. Faculty may have access to these detectors, but they cannot depend on them to ascertain whether a student has committed an academic honesty offense by using generative AI. Students fear they may be unfairly targeted by these software programs when they do not use AI in an unethical manner solely because of their personal cognitive characteristics. University administration, at this point in time, risks possible student litigation if it uses AI detectors as a basis for academic action such as class failure or probation. Yet, inaction by administration regarding AI academic integrity violations frustrate both faculty who report these events and students who are being ethical and doing their own work. This miasma has created a significant problem higher education still has not been successful in trying to solve.

IMPACT OF AI ACADEMIC INTEGRITY ISSUES ON ASSESSMENT

Traditional assessment focuses on assessing student knowledge, competency and performance. At this point in time, the literature demonstrates different points of view regarding AI and assessment. Some researchers call for free use of AI by students and the turning off of AI detectors. Others call for a more cautious approach to attempt to get students to do their own work since working through new concepts enhances learning. Yet others are calling for sweeping changes in traditional assessment methods in higher education because of AI. At this point in time, traditional assessment methods are truly not AI-proof unless students are directly supervised and are not allowed to have any devices (including smart watches) while completing an assessment. Some universities are moving back to oral exams and handwritten exams. Northern Michigan University calls this" going medieval" (2026, p. 1). This was echoed by Muladzi & Hamilton (2025. In a qualitative study; they recommended in-class components be added to assessment to ensure ethical use of AI.

While this may be possible for tests, it is not possible to physically supervise a student doing a research paper or large project that must be done outside of class. While this might work for some assessments in face-to-face education, it is much more challenging to ensure students have not used AI in homework or in online classes and have written the paper or solved the problem themselves. Even online proctoring programs can be "fooled" by astute students in virtually proctored tests.

In essence, there is at least some merit in all of these various points of view; however, there are also detractors in each as well. If students no longer have to do their own work and can use AI freely, are they learning anything and will they be able to apply it in the workplace in the future? If higher education faculty continue to use AI detectors to flag potential AI plagiarism will students (particularly divergent and non-native populations) be falsely targeted? AI is changing so rapidly that AI detectors just cannot keep up. Even as they do, in response students will find some other way around the issue if they really want to cheat. Sweeping educational assessment is the choice that is likely to make the most impact to ensure student learning, but the sheer scope of doing a change like this in higher education is completely overwhelming. Traditional educational assessment methods have been used for well over 100 years in their current forms.

AI-Resistant Assessment

When examining the point of view that AI should be used freely, most faculty would not disagree students need to be taught how to use AI as it becomes ubiquitous in the workplace. There are numerous researchers and authors who have evaluated this very issue (Charles et al., 2025; Topping et al., 2025). Outside of the realm of student learning, there are numerous benefits to using AI from an administrative or faculty perspective for improving assessment. Faculty can create higher quality assessments much more quickly using AI. Al-Zahrani and Alasmari (2024) noted AI can help faculty evaluate automated grading and learning analytics for quick intervention and student support, as well as personalize student learning experiences. Doğan et al. (2025) discusses the benefits of using AI to detect and assist at-risk learners.

However, the challenge is to create assessments that are AI-resistant, particularly in work that is not done under direct faculty supervision in a physical classroom. With the popularity and proliferation of online learning, this makes this issue extremely challenging. This author wrote a conference paper just two years ago (Halupa, 2024) that discussed how to create assessments that were more AI resistant and many of these suggestions are no longer of any practical value. AI now can more effectively write self-reflection essays and can effectively answer case studies. Even the use of multiple drafts and use of portfolios as recommended by Matrogiacomi (2023) is no longer AI-proof for savvy students. The key to a good AI-generated paper is to give the AI multiple prompts until the desired product is obtained. This also makes it less detectable. This may be additional work, but many students will put more work into figuring out how to cheat when they could have done the work themselves in just about the same amount of time. This is one reason AI detectors were adopted by many educational institutions.

While screening assessments, Ardito (2025) argues AI detectors have numerous shortcomings and vulnerabilities and liken them to "academic malpractice" (p. 16). Akbar (2025) notes they are "fundamentally inadequate" (p. 1). Even with traditional plagiarism detection, software companies have never "guaranteed" the accuracy of the detector; however, the student match could be independently validated from the original source that was identified as a match. In other words, faculty are just taking the "word" of the AI plagiarism detector and have no way of validating its accuracy. He says detectors are not verifiable, yet they are still widely in use because they have been heavily marketed to academics. AI is not going to go away, and he states telling students not to use it is not a viable option and could cause students to shy away from using the very technologies they will be required to do in the workplace. He recommends educational outcomes that instead harness the potential of AI tools but does not specify how this could be done. He does acknowledge students need to have crucial skills themselves outside of AI use but feels this should be done without using AI detectors.

Bassett et al. (2026) agree with Ardito and note AI detection is "conceptually unsound" (p. 13) and an "unworkable solution" (p. 13) and call for assessment design that recognizes AI's role in learning, as well as realizing that assessments that are not done under supervision cannot be policed. Blommerde et al. (2024) at Northumbria University posit AI detectors should be turned off, particularly since the methodology behind the detection is "opaque" (p. 8). They provide examples of well-respected universities in the United States, Ireland and the UK choosing to turn off the detection and indicate universities who do so are "leading the way in exploring alternate assessment" (p. 8). They say this results in more holistic educational practices that should be followed by other institutions. This is a call for sweeping change, but there is not enough research on how this should be done in practice. There are numerous other researchers who have indicated they feel AI should be more freely used, but specific research studies and concrete information on how to create assessments that truly measure student knowledge and skills without AI use that can be done without direct supervision are theoretical at this point as AI continues to learn.

Authors such as Wu (2026) in the education of physicians, and Corbin et al. (2025), Antara et al. (2025) and Chiu (2026) in higher education have examined educational frameworks around AI use since faculty struggle with how to implement alternate types of assessment. Zaphir et al. (2024) suggested using the MAGE Framework to make assessments more AI-resistant. MAGE stands for mapping, vulnerability testing, grading and evaluation. However, doing this takes a very significant amount of time for one assessment.

Akbar (2025) posited faculty should create AI-resistant assessments rather than using AI detectors after the fact. He used a web-based Python tool that integrated Bloom's Taxonomy with advanced processing language techniques and term frequency-inverse document frequency (TF-IDF) to evaluate if AI could solve assessments. He evaluated 50 assessments in various disciplines. He did not indicate if they were assessments done in-class with supervision, outside of class or online. He reported 66% of the assessments had a 65% chance or more of being done by AI. However, AI has improved since this study was done and this rate could in fact be higher.

From Theory to Practice

At this point in time, there is very little practical or feasible information on how to make assessments more AI resistant in a way that can be done by all faculty. Most faculty do not have the knowledge or capacity to create tools such as the one discussed by Akbar (2025) previously. The Northern Michigan University Center for Teaching and Learning (2026) provides some suggestions for more AI-resistant assignments; however, many of these are not feasible for all types of assessment. In addition to going back to pen and paper assessments which traditionally have been difficult to read, they emphasize assessments should be created that allow students to solve complex problems or integrate different sources of information. The problem is AI has gotten better at doing just these things. They also recommend tailoring assignments to individual students or events and including reflective components; however, AI has also gotten much better at doing this as well. Another suggestion is to use drafts, but again if the student is doing the draft outside of class, it is still difficult to ascertain if it was done with AI or not unless it is required to be handwritten. Even in that case, a student could run it in AI and just handwrite out what AI gave him/her and the faculty member would have no idea.

One suggestion is for faculty to test their assessments with AI to see if it can be effectively answered (Akbar, 2025; Northern Michigan University, 2026). The author tried this very thing and created a masters level case study in business marketing stream analysis in ChatGPT with five questions that required synthesis of these concepts. The author then asked AI to make the assessment "AI proof." ChatGPT responded," *You can't fully "AI-proof" an assignment—but you can redesign it so AI alone is not enough to succeed. The key is to require original data, personal/observational inputs, iterative reasoning, and defensible decisions tied to evidence students must generate themselves. Here's a redesigned version of your case that is much harder to complete using AI alone"* (OpenAI, 2026a). Even AI itself indicated it is not possible to effectively make an assignment AI-proof. The author then asked ChatGPT for suggestions on making an assessment more AI-resistant. It indicated reflective and complex assessments. Then, the author indicated AI can effectively do self-reflective and complex assessments, so now what? ChatGPT indicated, " there is no longer a type of *question* that AI can't answer " (Open AI, 2026a).

The author then asked ChatGPT for some practical suggestions on AI resistant assessments. According to ChatGPT, "Faculty needed to use better assessment environments and evidence of learning" (OpenAI, 2026b). ChatGPT then provided a list that included making students perform, oral defenses, live problem-solving sessions and group debates. It indicated reduced time can reduce AI use (just as reduced time can reduce using a text for an online exam taken at home). It also noted AI can fake reflection. One worthwhile suggestion was to check to see if an assessment is done in drafts if the student actually incorporated specific feedback given to him/her by a faculty member (Open AI, 2026b). But again, even AI cannot provide many practical suggestions on how to create assessments that are AI resistant without a face-to-face component.

The University of Chicago recommends having students create concept maps since these cannot be effectively done with free AI programs (2026). Dr. Luke Hobson (2025) on his blog suggests having students record their reflection and journal assessments and having students record interviews, listen to each other's recordings and note the key issues addressed by the interviewee. This may be AI resistant, but is it the most effective way to assess the student? Mulder et al. (2026) write a guide for faculty in how to redesign assessments in response to AI also suggests audio and video-recorded assessments as more AI-resistant options. However, a student could do the assessment on AI and then just consult it for the video. Washington University in Saint Louis (2026) recommends requiring students to use annotation tools that require them to directly interact with their assigned readings using text (Hypothesis) or video (Annoto).

The answers faculty really want about how to implement AI resistant assessments quickly become outdated as AI improves. Second, practical application methods of creating AI-resistant assessments are very sparse with going back to face-to-face assessment which was noted as one of the primary methods in research and internet informational articles to avoid AI use by students. However, this is not a viable option for every assessment and is very difficult and time-consuming to do in an online format. There is significant potential for additional research in the practical aspects of assessment redesign, as well as a potential market for software products that can detect resistance to AI in assessments.

In the research as well as in the educational press, there is very little to no practical guidance for faculty on how to create authentic assessments that allow students to appropriately use generative AI, yet ensure that students are able to function on their own, are actually learning something, and are not just obtaining a grade for something done by AI. Advances in AI have made even the suggestions for AI-resistant assessment in the literature that were valid just two short years ago obsolete.

The field of authentic assessment saw significant strides in the last 20 years as varied, problem-based and authentic assessments could be done outside of the physical classroom and submitted online. This left more time in the physical classroom for coverage of needed content. Generative AI has negated these strides for faculty who want to definitively ensure that students truly have learned required content on their own and can use the information effectively. The only valid suggestions for AI-resistant assessment require faculty to physically observe students during assessment. This regresses assessment back to 20th century practices where student performance is directly observed in the physical classroom on objective assessments rather than authentic assessments. This has been evidenced by many universities moving back to oral and supervised written exams.

CONCLUSION AND A CALL TO ACTION

There are three major schools of thought on how faculty should deal with and assess in the age of generative AI. The first is to allow students to freely use AI and not use detectors to police students. This "free rein" view needs significant research to ensure that students still possess required knowledge, critical thinking, analytical thinking, creativity and the ability to think and strategize on their own is not negatively impacted when AI use goes unchecked in the academic environment. It is critical to ensure that such a step does not result in a negative impact on human cognition, higher order thinking, and executive functioning.

The second school of thought regarding assessment and generative AI is to use detectors to determine unethical or unapproved AI use in assessment. This view assumes that traditional assessment methods are still effective and AI should not be used in all assessments. More research is also needed on the effectiveness of AI detectors, particularly in divergent students. Strides need to be taken to improve AI detectors so that they are reliable and effective indicators of AI use by a student. These tools need to undergo significant validation testing of their validity and reliability as well as cross-product comparison testing and standardization. Detection methods need to be more transparent so students and faculty truly know what a detection match means, and software companies need to stand by their products rather than using disclaimers. This would drive product improvement. This option would allow faculty choice in determining when AI use was appropriate in assessment and when it was used when it should not have been. However, since AI learns and changes so rapidly, this may in fact be an impossible task.

The last school of thought is that sweeping changes in traditional assessment methods are needed. At the time of this writing, there is no detailed information on what these sweeping changes in assessment might be in the literature or in the popular educational press. It is a theoretical concept. There is a body of research incorporating the use of generative AI into assessment. However, there is no body of literature on what sweeping changes in assessment should be, or how to create new and different types of assessment that are truly AI resistant when faculty desire to ensure students are actually learning and not relying on AI.

Faculty need practical guidance on how to move from traditional assessment methods to alternate assessment methods where faculty can effectively measure transversal skills and even required knowledge when AI assistance is not optimal or desired. Particularly in large classrooms, there is not enough time in a 16-week class that meets for an hour three times a week to physically assess 60 or more students in assessments that measure higher levels of learning; it is only possible with objective assessment (such as multiple choice testing) which most often tests comprehension instead of analysis and synthesis. Objective tests that measure analysis and synthesis are notoriously difficult to write and most faculty do not know how to effectively write these types of questions. This practical guidance must include how to assess when AI use is not desired outside of the physical constraints of a classroom, particularly in online learning.

These postulated theoretical sweeping changes may be the best alternative in the long term to ensure students can utilize learned concepts and critically think without AI assistance and retain the strengths, adaptability and creativity of human cognition and not become unduly dependent on AI. However, this is not a time where these alternate methods exist in a practical sense. It will take significant time to postulate alternate assessment methods and validate them. Until that time, students, faculty and administration will continue to struggle with assessment and generative AI. This is exacerbated by the ever-learning and ever-improving nature of generative AI.

Practical information and guidance is what students, faculty and administration truly need to assist them through this transition period until these sweeping changes in assessment finally occur. It is possible that these sweeping changes may in fact be free rein use of generative AI by students. It could become as common as a calculator or an internet search. But if this is the case, educational institutions still owe their students, faculty and the future employers of their students assurance that future graduates can function in the real world of the workplace on their own when the power goes out.

Academic integrity and assessment in the age of AI is a contentious and controversial issue. Whether AI detectors should be used is an issue with varying opinions. Universities are having a great deal of difficulty responding to these issues with effective policies and practices. Faculty, students and administration have very significant concerns on how to navigate the minefield of AI and its impact on student learning. In addition, liability is a concern for institutions who use AI detectors and accuse students of academic dishonesty when the student has not used AI such as with divergent writers and thinkers and non-native speakers. There is a significant paucity of practical information on how to assess outside of a face-to-face classroom to ensure a student does not use AI and does not suffer possible cognitive effects of AI overuse and misuse on critical thinking, creativity and volition. Although technology has disrupted the educational landscape in the past, before technologies were assistive rather than generative in nature. This is perhaps the most challenging time in the history of assessment in higher education.

ADDITIONAL RESOURCES

Since the issues discussed in this chapter are evolving so rapidly, additional resources were not provided. Instead, it is recommended the reader consult the most current literature on the topics outlined in this chapter.

REFERENCES

Abbas, M., Khan, T. I., & Jam, F. A. (2025). Avoid excessive usage: Examining the motivations and outcomes of generative artificial intelligence usage among students. *Journal of Academic Ethics*, *23*(4), 2423–2442. DOI: 10.1007/s10805-025-09659-3

Agomuoph, F. (2023, May 18). *Professor flunks entire class based on ChatGPT's false claims. Digital Trends.* https://www.digitaltrends.com/computing/chatgpt-dupes-professor-trying-to-catch-ai-plagiarism/

Akbar, M. S. (2025). Beyond detection: designing AI-resilient assessments with automated feedback tool to foster critical thinking. *arXiv preprint arXiv:2503.23622.*

Al-Zahrani, A. M., & Alasmari, T. M. (2024). Exploring the impact of artificial intelligence on higher education: The dynamics of ethical, social, and educational implications. *Humanities & Social Sciences Communications*, *11*(1), 1–12. DOI: 10.1057/s41599-024-03432-4

Alon-Barkat, S., & Busuioc, M. (2021). Human-AI interactions in public sector decision making: Automation bias and selective adherence to algorithmic advice. *Journal of Public Administration: Research and Theory*, *33*(1), 153–159. DOI: 10.1093/jopart/muac007

Alsharefeen, R., & Al Sayari, N. (2025, June). Examining academic integrity policy and practice in the era of AI: A case study of faculty perspectives. *Frontiers in Education*, *10*, 1621743. Advance online publication. DOI: 10.3389/feduc.2025.1621743

Alter, A. L., Oppenheimer, D. M., Epley, N., & Eyre, R. N. (2007). Overcoming intuition: Metacognitive difficulty activates analytic reasoning. *Journal of Experimental Psychology. General*, *136*(4), 569–576. DOI: 10.1037/0096-3445.136.4.569 PMID: 17999571

American Psychological Association. (2025). *APA journals policy on generative AI.* https://www.apa.org/pubs/journals/resources/publishing-tips/policy-generative-ai

Antara, P., Mohd Beta, R. M. D., Ibrahim, N. A. & Talip, I. (2025, October 23). Beyond the algorithm: Towards a human-centered AI pedagogy. *International Journal of Research and Innovation in the Social Sciences.* DOI: 10.47772/IJRISS.2025.903SEDU0570

Ardito, C. G. (2025). Generative AI detection in higher education assessments. *New Directions for Teaching and Learning*, *2025*(182), 11–28. DOI: 10.1002/tl.20624

Athar, M. E. (2025, May). The constructive, over reliant and irresponsible use of artificial intelligence tools in academia: Personality correlates and implications for academic integrity. *Computers in Human Behavior Reports, 18*, 100679. Advance online publication. DOI: 10.1016/j.chbr.2025.100679

Australian Government Tertiary Education Quality and Standards Association. (2026, February 28). *What is academic integrity?* https://www.teqsa.gov.au/students/understanding-academic-integrity/what-academic-integrity

Bannister, P., Alcalde, Peñalver, E. & Santamaria Urbieta, A. (2024). International students and generative artificial intelligence: A cross-cultural exploration of HE academic integrity policy. *Journal of International Students, 14*(3), 149-170. ISSN: ISSN-2162-3104

Basit, I., Safdar, U., & Malik, F. (2025).Artificial intelligence and academic integrity: A study of faculty perceptions in higher education. *Policy Journal of Social Science Review* 3(4), 212-221. ISSN 3006-4627.

Bassett, M. A., Bradshaw, W., Bornsztejn, H., Hogg, A., Murdoch, K., Pearce, B., & Webber, C. (2026). Heads we win, tails you lose: AI detectors in education. *Journal of Higher Education Policy and Management*, 1–16. DOI: 10.1080/1360080X.2026.2622146

Bauer, E., Greiff, S., Graesser, A. C., Scheiter, K., & Sailer, M. (2025). Looking beyond the hype: Understanding the effects of AI on learning. *Educational Psychology Review, 37*(2), 45. DOI: 10.1007/s10648-025-10020-8

Bin-Nashwan, S. A., Sadallah, M., & Bouteraa, M. (2023). Use of Chat-GPT in academia: Academic integrity hangs in the balance. *Technology in Society, 75*, 102370. Advance online publication. https://www.sciencedirect.com/science/article/pii/S0160791X23001756. DOI: 10.1016/j.techsoc.2023.102370

Blackboard. (2026). *SafeAssign.* https://safeassign.blackboard.com/

Blommerde, T., Bright, W., Musgrave, E., Mitchell, R., & Heselton, R. (2024). AI detectors in universities: Time to turn them off and embrace AI for enhanced learning. *Educational Developments, 25*(4), 8–11.

Brem, A., & Hörauf, D. (2025). Artificial creativity? AI's short-and long-term impact on creativity. *Research Technology Management, 68*(2), 54–58. DOI: 10.1080/08956308.2025.2450756

Buchanan, J., Hill, S., & Shapoval, O. (2024). ChatGPT hallucinates non-existent citations: Evidence from economics. *The American Economist, 69*(1), 80–87. Advance online publication. DOI: 10.1177/05694345231218454

Buele, J., & Llerena-Aguirre, L. (2025, July). Transformations in academic work and faculty perceptions of artificial intelligence in higher education. *Frontiers in Education, 10*, 1603763. Advance online publication. DOI: 10.3389/feduc.2025.1603763

Caner, H. N. (2025). AI detection tools: A systematic review of empirical evidence and their implications for education. *Khazar Journal of Humanities and Social Sciences, 28*(4), 4. DOI: 10.5782/2223-2621.1580

Chan, C. K. Y. (2023). A comprehensive AI policy education framework for university teaching and learning. *International Journal of Educational Technology in Higher Education, 20*(1), 38. Advance online publication. DOI: 10.1186/s41239-023-00408-3

Charles, K. A., Yousuf, A., Chua, H. C., Matthews, S., Harnett, J., & Hinton, T. (2025). AI in action: Changes to student perceptions when using generative artificial intelligence for the creation of a multimedia project-based assessment. *European Journal of Pharmacology, 998*, 177508. DOI: 10.1016/j.ejphar.2025.177508 PMID: 40086582

Chechitelli, A. (2023, June 6). *Understanding the false positive rate for sentence es of our AI writing detection capability.* Turnitin Blog. https://www.turnitin.com/blog/understanding-

Chicago Manual of Style. (2026). *Citation, documentation of sources.* https://www.chicagomanualofstyle.org/qanda/data/faq/topics/Documentation/faq0422.html

Chiu, T. K. F. (2026). Human-Centric Artificial Intelligence Pedagogy (HCAP) framework developed from TPACK through integration of artificial intelligence literacy and competency. *Interactive Learning Environments*, 1–16. DOI: 10.1080/10494820.2026.2615818

Corbin, T., Dawson, P., Nicola-Richmond, K., & Partridge, H. (2025). Where's the line? It's an absurd line: Towards a framework for acceptable uses of AI in assessment. *Assessment & Evaluation in Higher Education, 50*(5), 705–717. DOI: 10.1080/02602938.2025.2456207

Crawford, J., Cowling, M. and Allen, K.-A. (2023) Leadership is needed for ethical ChatGPT: character, assessment, and learning using artificial intelligence AI. *Journal of University Teaching & Learning Practice 20*(3), 02.

Crockett, R., & Howe, R. (2024). The inherent uncertainties of AI-text detection and the implications for education institutions: An overview. In Mahmud, S. (Ed.), *Academic integrity in the age of artificial intelligence* (pp. 175–198). IGI Global. DOI: 10.4018/979-8-3693-0240-8.ch010

Davalos, J., & Yin, L. (2024, October 18). *AI detectors falsely accuse students of cheating with big consequences.* Businessweek. https://news.bloomberglaw.com/private-equity/ai-detection-tools-are-falsely-accusing-students-of-cheating

Dewey, J. (1910). *How we think.* Prometheus Books. DOI: 10.1037/10903-000

DiPaulo, D. (2022). Do preservice teachers cheat in college, too? A quantitative study of academic integrity among preservice teachers. *International Journal for Educational Integrity, 18*(1), 3. DOI: 10.1007/s40979-021-00097-3

Doğan, M., Celik, A., & Arslan, H. (2025). AI in higher education: Risks and opportunities from the academician perspective. *European Journal of Education, 60*(1), e12863. DOI: 10.1111/ejed.12863

Eaton, S. E. (2025). Neurodiversity and academic integrity: Toward epistemic plurality in a post plagiarism era. *Teaching in Higher Education*, 1–20. DOI: 10.1080/13562517.2025.2583456

Editors Academy of Management Learning and Education. (2024). From the editors: Critical thinning in the age of generative AI. *Academy of Management Learning and Education Journal*, 23(3). 373-378. DOI: 10.5465/amle.2024.0338

European Network for Academic Integrity. (2018, October 26). *Glossary for academic integrity.* https://www.academicintegrity.eu/wp/glossary/

Facione, P. (1990). *Delphi report.* Committee on Pre-College Philosophy, American Psychological Association. https://assessment.trinity.duke.edu/documents/Delphi_Report.pdf

Feng, S. (2025). Group interaction patterns in generative AI-supported collaborative problem solving: Network analysis of the interactions among students and a GAI chatbot. *British Journal of Educational Technology, 56*(5), 2125–2145. DOI: 10.1111/bjet.13611

Fortuna, A., Prasetya, F., Dwingo Samala, A., Rawas, S., Criollo, S., Kaya, D., & Nabawi, N. (2025). Artificial intelligence in personalized learning: A global systematic review of current advancements and shaping future opportunities. *Social Sciences & Humanities Open, 12*, 102114. Advance online publication. DOI: 10.1016/j.ssaho.2025.102114

Fošner, A., & Aver, B. (2025). AI chatbots in higher education: Students' beliefs and concerns. *Sustainable Futures: An Applied Journal of Technology, Environment and Society, 9*, 100734. Advance online publication. DOI: 10.1016/j.sftr.2025.100734

Gegg-Harrison, W. (2023). Against the use of GPTZero and other LLM-detection tools on student writing. *Write Rethink*. https://writerethink.medium.com/against-the-use-of-gptzero-and-other-llm-detection-tools-on-student-writing-b876b9d1b587

Gegg-Harrison, W., & Quarterman, C. (2024). AI detection's high false positive rates and the psychological and material impacts on students. In Mahmud, S. (Ed.), *Academic integrity in the age of artificial intelligence* (pp. 199–219). IGI Global. DOI: 10.4018/979-8-3693-0240-8.ch011

Gerlich, M. (2025). AI tools in society: Impacts on cognitive offloading and the future of critical thinking. *Societies (Basel, Switzerland)*, *15*(1), 6. Advance online publication. DOI: 10.3390/soc15010006

Giray, L., Jacob, J., Encanto, V., & Mansilungan, C. J. (2026). Cheating writing with generative AI: Exploring student motivations using the Theory of Planned Behavior. *Journal of Academic Ethics*, *24*(1), 1–23. DOI: 10.1007/s10805-025-09695-z

Glaser, E. M. (1941). *An experiment in the development of critical thinking*. Teacher's College, Columbia University.

Gomes, E. (2026). *The AI that isn't: AI bias against neurodivergent and non-native writers*. Elise. https://www.elisegomes.com/en/post/the-ai-that-isn-t-false-ai-positives-and-the-harm-to-neurodivergent-writers

Gonsalves, C. (2025). Addressing student non-compliance in AI use declarations: Implications for academic integrity and assessment in higher education. *Assessment & Evaluation in Higher Education*, *50*(4), 592–606. DOI: 10.1080/02602938.2024.2415654

Grinschgl, S., Papenmeir, F., & Meyeroff, H. (2021). Consequences of cognitive offloading: Boosting performance, but diminishing memory. *Quarterly Journal of Experimental Psychology*, *74*(9), 1477–1496. DOI: 10.1177/17470218211008060 PMID: 33752519

Gustilo, L., Ong, E., & Lapind, M. R. (2024). Algorithmically-driven writing and academic integrity: Exploring educators' practices, perceptions and policies in the AI era. *International Journal for Educational Integrity*, *20*(3), 3. Advance online publication. DOI: 10.1007/s40979-024-00153-8

Habib, S., Vogel, T., Anli, X., & Thorne, E. (2024). How does generative artificial intelligence impact student creativity? *Journal of Creativity*, *34*(1), 100072. Advance online publication. DOI: 10.1016/j.yjoc.2023.100072

Hadra, M., Cambridge, K., & Mesbah, M. (2026). Evaluating the accuracy and reliability of AI content detectors in academic contexts. *International Journal for Educational Integrity*, *22*(1), 4. DOI: 10.1007/s40979-026-00213-1

Haggard, P. (2019). The neurocognitive bases of human volition. *Annual Review of Psychology*, *70*(1), 9–28. DOI: 10.1146/annurev-psych-010418-103348 PMID: 30125134

Han, B., Coghlan, S., Buchanan, G., & McKay, D. (2025). Who is helping whom? Student concerns about AI-teacher collaboration in higher education classrooms. *Proceedings of the ACM on Human-Computer Interaction*, USA, *9*(2), 1-32. DOI: 10.1145/371110

Han, Y., Ren, W., & Li, X. (2026). Can artificial intelligence assistance enhance creativity in university students? An experimental study. *New Ideas in Psychology*, *82*, 101246. DOI: 10.1016/j.newideapsych.2026.101246

Hannigan, T., McCarthy, I. P., & Spicer, A. (2024). Beware of botshit: How to manage the epistemic risks of generative chatbots. *Business Horizons*, *4678265*(5), 471–486. Advance online publication. DOI: 10.1016/j.bushor.2024.03.001

Harvard University. (2025). *Student handbook academic integrity.* https://oaisc.fas.harvard.edu/find-resources/

Hassen, M. (2025). The impact of AI on students' reading, critical thinking, and problem-solving skills. *American Journal of Education and Information Technology*, *9*(2), 82–90. DOI: 10.11648/j.ajeit.20250902.12

Ibrahim, K. (2023). Using AI-based detectors for control AI-assisted plagiarism in ESL writing: "The Terminator vs. the machines. *Language Testing in Asia*, *13*(46), 46. Advance online publication. DOI: 10.1186/s40468-023-00260-2

Ilgun Dibek, M., Sahin Kursad, M., & Erdogan, T. (2025). Influence of artificial intelligence tools on higher order thinking skills: A meta-analysis. *Interactive Learning Environments*, *33*(3), 2216–2223. DOI: 10.1080/10494820.2024.2402028

Indiana University of Pennsylvania. (2026). *Types of violations.* https://www.iup.edu/academicaffairs/for-faculty/academic-integrity/types-of-violations.html

International Center for Academic Integrity. (2014). Fundamental values of academic integrity. {Pamphlet}. https://www.academicintegrity.org/aws/ICAI/pt/sp/values

Islam, M., Hasan, M. M., & Mahmud, R. (2024). EFL teachers' perceptions of AI's impact on academic integrity and pedagogy in Bangladeshi universities. *Language Literacy: Journal of Linguistics, Literature, and Language Teaching*, *8*(2), 564–579. DOI: 10.30743/ll.v8i2.10082

Jamieson, S., & Moore Howard, R. (2019). Rethinking the relationship between plagiarism and academic integrity. *International Journal of Technologies in Higher Education*, *16*(2), 69. Advance online publication. DOI: 10.18162/ritpu-2019-v16n2-07

Jia, X., Li, P., & Li, W. (2025, February 24). The role of creative mindsets in the relationship between metacognitive experience and divergent thinking: A metacognitive perspective. *Journal of Intelligence*, *13*(3), 27. Advance online publication. DOI: 10.3390/jintelligence13030027 PMID: 40137059

Jiang, Y., Hao, J., Fauss, M., & Li, C. (2024). Detecting Chat-GPT-generated essays in a large-scale writing assessment: Is there a bias against non-native speakers? *Computers & Education*, *217*, 105070. Advance online publication. DOI: 10.1016/j.compedu.2024.105070

Jiang, Y., Xie, L., & Cao, X. (2025). Exploring the effectiveness of institutional policies and regulations for generative AI usage in higher education. *Higher Education Quarterly*, *79*(4), e70054. DOI: 10.1111/hequ.70054

Johansen, M. W., Goddiksen, M. P., Clavien, C., Hogan, L., Olsson, I. A. S., Santos, J. B., dos Santos, R. A., Wall, P. J., Sandøe, P., & Lund, T. B. (2026, March). Academic integrity across educational levels: Exploring students' engagement with grey-zone and non-compliant practices in four European countries. *PLoS One*, *21*(3), e0342227. Advance online publication. DOI: 10.1371/journal.pone.0342227 PMID: 41779692

Johns Hopkins University. (2026). *Neurodivergence at a glance.* https://imagine.jhu.edu/blog/2022/10/05/neurodivergence-at-a-glance/

Karakose, T., & Tulubas, T. (2025). The role of educational leaders in the age of artificial intelligence (AI). *Educational Process: International Journal*, *16*(1), e2025267. DOI: 10.22521/edupij.2025.16.267

Keith-Spiegel, P. (1994). Teaching psychologist and the new APA ethics code: Do we fit in? *Professional Psychology, Research and Practice*, *25*(4), 362–268. DOI: 10.1037/0735-7028.25.4.362 PMID: 12186089

Kramm, N., & McKenna, S. (2023). AI amplifies the tough question: What is higher education really for? *Teaching in Higher Education, 28*(8), 2173–2178. DOI: 10.1080/13562517.2023.2263839

Lau, J. Y. F. (2024). Revisiting the origin of critical thinking. *Educational Philosophy and Theory, 57*(7), 724–733. DOI: 10.1080/00131857.2024.2320199

Liang, W., Yuksekgonul, M., Mao, Y., Wu, E., & Zou, J. (2023). GPT detectors are biased against non-native English writers. *Patterns (New York, N.Y.), 4*(7), 1–4. DOI: 10.1016/j.patter.2023.100779 PMID: 37521038

Lin, H., & Chen, Q. (2024). Artificial intelligence (AI)-integrated educational applications and college students' creativity and academic emotions: Students and teachers' perceptions and attitudes. *BMC Psychology, 12*(1), 487. DOI: 10.1186/s40359-024-01979-0 PMID: 39285268

Lund, B., Mannuru, N. R., Teel, Z. A., Lee, T. H., Ortega, N. J., Simmons, S., & Ward, E. (2025b, September). Student perceptions of AI-assisted writing and academic integrity: Ethical concerns, academic misconduct, and use of generative AI in higher education. *AI in Education, 1*(1), 2. DOI: 10.3390/aieduc1010002

Lund, B., & Wang, T. (2023, January). *Chatting about ChatPGT*: How *may AI and GPT impact academia and libraries*. Library Hi Tech News. https://www.research gate.net /profile/Brady-Lund/publication/367161545_Chatting_about_ChatGPT_How_ may_AI_and _GPT_impact_academia_and_libraries/links/6412235c315df-b4cce80f0e4/ Chatting-about-ChatGPT-How-may-AI-and-GPT-impact-academia-and-libraries.pd

Lund, B. D., Lee, T. H., Mannuru, N. R., & Arutla, N. (2025a). AI and academic integrity: Exploring student perceptions and implications for higher education. *Journal of Academic Ethics, 23*(3), 1545–1565. DOI: 10.1007/s10805-025-09613-3

Mahmoud, E. (2025). Artificial intelligence solutions and college students' assessment: Exploring potential influences on their creative thinking skills. *Journal of Information Systems Engineering and Management*, 2468-4376. ISSN: 2468-4376

McAdoo, T., Denneny, S., & Lee, C. (2025, September 9). *Citing generative AI in APA style: Part I reference formats*. APA Style Blog. https://apastyle.apa.org/blog/cite-generative-ai-references

Melisa, R., Ashadi, A., Triastuti, A., Hidayati, S., Salido, A., Ero, P. E. L., & Fuad, Z. A. (2025). Critical thinking in the age of AI: A systematic review of AI's effects on higher education. *Educational Process: International Journal, 14*(1), e2025031. DOI: 10.22521/edupij.2025.14.31

Merriam Webster Dictionary. (2026). *Construct.* https://www.merriam-webster.com/dictionary/construct

Mingay, D. (2026, January 9). *After being falsely branded an AI plagiarist how can I accuse students?* The Times Higher Education. https://www.timeshighereducation.com/opinion/after-being-falsely-branded-ai-plagiarist-how-can-i-accuse-students

Mishra, D. R., & Varshney, D. (2024, April). Academic integrity in higher education: Faculty perceptions, strategies, and digital challenges in the digital age. *International Journal of All Research Education and Scientific Methods, 12(*4). ISSN 2455-6211.

MLA Style Center. (2026). *How do I cite generative AI in MLA style?* https://style.mla.org/citing-generative-ai-updated-revised/

Moruzzi, C. (2025). Artificial intelligence and creativity. *Philosophy Compass, 20*(3), e70030.1 of 8 DOI: 10.1111/phc3.70030

Mulaudzi, L. V., & Hamilton, J. (2025). Lecturer's perspective on the role of AI in personalized learning: Benefits, challenges, and ethical considerations in higher education. *Journal of Academic Ethics, 23*(4), 1571–1591. DOI: 10.1007/s10805-025-09615-1

Mulder, R., Baik, C., & Ryan, T. (n.d.) *Rethinking assessment in response to AI.* https://melbourne-cshe.unimelb.edu.au/ai-aai/home/ai-assessment/designing-assessment-tasks-that-are-less-vulnerable-to-ai

Mumtaz, S., Carmichael, J., Weiss, M., & Nimon-Peters, A. (2025). Ethical use of artificial intelligence-based tools in higher education: Are future business leaders ready? *Education and Information Technologies, 30*(6), 7293–7319. DOI: 10.1007/s10639-024-13099-8

Ngila, F. (2023, July 5). *The UK's top universities reached an agreement on how to deal with generative AI.* Tech and Innovation. https://qz.com/russel-uk-universities-generative-ai-students-1850603771

Nguyen, Q. H. (2023). AI and plagiarism: Opinion from teachers, administrators and policymakers. *Proceedings of the AsiaCALL International Conference*, Vietnam, *4*, 75–85. DOI: 10.54855/paic.2346

Northern Michigan University Center for Teaching and Learning. (2026). *Creating AI-resistant assignments, activities and assessments (designing out).* https://nmu.edu/ctl/creating-ai-resistant-assignments-activities-and-assessments-designing-out

Open, A. I. (2026a, March 22). *Create a masters' level case analysis with five questions that is AI-resistant. ChatGPT.* https://chatgpt.com/?utm_source=google&utm_medium=paid_search&utm_campaign =GOOG_C_SEM_GBR_Core_CHT_TST_ACQ_PER_MIX_ALL_NAMER_US_EN_031126&c_id=23637266097&c_agid=196969197591&c_crid=799723648506&c_kwid=kwd-1927051708782&c_ims= &c_pms=1026339&c_nw=g&c_dvc=c&gad_source =1&gad_campaignid=23637266097&gbraid=0AAAAA-I0E5epYRlgKduzSFX-sQOYZrHef1&gclid =Cj0KCQjwpv7NBhCzARIsADkIfWxDJjoqHUIN0piKd-KEuMidNeKrijJxK7yIxxo2OYST42UoXiXurfI8aAtfyEALw_wcB

Open, A. I. (2026b, March 22). *How do I make university student assessments AI-resistant?* ChatGPT. https://chatgpt.com/?utm_source=google&utm_medium =paid_search&utm_campaign=GOOG_C_SEM_GBR_Core_CHT_TST_ACQ _PER_MIX_ALL_NAMER_US_EN_031126&c_id=23637266097&c_agid=196969198031&c_crid=799723648692&c_kwid=kwd-693063707937&c_ims =&cpms=1026339&c_nw=g&c_dvc=c&gad_source=1&gad_campaign id=23637 266097&gbraid=0AAAAA-I0E5epYRlgKduzSFXsQOYZrHef1&gc lid=Cj0KC-Qjwpv7NBhC zARIsADkIfWypQK5HNuacRkifSNdZESQ7RdWBUiW_X8B6X-saJMCOCrkIeYxBKvN waAqvc EALwwcB

Penn State University. (2026). *University College academic integrity procedures.* https://www.campuses.psu.edu/university-college-academic-integrity-procedures

Perkins, M., & Roe, J. (2023). Decoding academic integrity policies: A corpus linguistics investigation of AI and other technological threats. *Higher Education Policy*, *37*(3), 633–650. DOI: 10.1057/s41307-023-00323-2

Pratama, A. R. (2025). The accuracy-bias trade-offs in AI text detection tools and their impact on fairness in scholarly publication. *PeerJ. Computer Science*, *11*, e2953. DOI: 10.7717/peerj-cs.2953 PMID: 40989485

Quach, K. (2023, September 23). *Colleges snub Turnitin's AI-writing detector over fears it will wrongly accuse students.* The Register. https://www.theregister.com/2023/09/23/turnitin_ai_detection/#:~:text=Various%20American%20universities%2C%20however%2C%20including,cheating%2C%20as%20noted%20by%20Bloomberg

Rholetter, W. (2024). *Academic integrity*. EBSCO Knowledge Advantage Research Starters. https://www.ebsco.com/research-starters/education/academic-integrity

Richmond, L. L., & Taylor, R. G. (2025). The benefits and potential costs of cognitive offloading for retrospective information. *Nature Reviews Psychology*, *4*(5), 312–321. DOI: 10.1038/s44159-025-00432-2

Risko, E. F., & Gilbert, S. J. (2016). Cognitive offloading. *Trends in Cognitive Sciences*, *20*(9), 676–688. DOI: 10.1016/j.tics.2016.07.002 PMID: 27542527

Rodrigues, M., Silva, R., Borges, A. P., Franco, M., & Oliveira, C. (2025, March). Artificial intelligence: Threat or asset to academic integrity? A bibliometric analysis. *Kybernetes, International Journal of Cybernetics. Kybernetes*, *54*(5), 2939–2970. DOI: 10.1108/K-09-2023-1666

Russell Group. (2023). *Russell Group principles on the use of generative AI tools in education*. https://www.russellgroup.ac.uk/policy/policy-briefings/principles-use-generative-ai-tools-education

Sayeed, S. (2026, January 19). *Can AI detectors mistake neurodivergent writing for AI-generated text?* AI Writing. https://deceptioner.site/blog/can-ai-detectors-flag-neurodivergent-writing-styles

Schwartz, S. H. (2012). An overview of the Schwartz Theory of Basic Values. *Online Readings in Psychology and Culture,* 2(1). htp://DOI: 10.9707/2307-0919.1116

Sheffield Hallam University. (2026). *Definitions of academic misconduct*. https://www.shu.ac.uk/myhallam/university-life/university-rules-and-regulations/student-conduct/academic-conduct-regulation/definitions-of-academic-misconduct

Song, J., & Liu, S. (2025, July 1). Dark personality traits are associated with academic misconduct, frustration, negative thinking, and generative AI use habits: The case of Sichuan art universities. [P]. *BMC Psychology*, *13*(1), 633. DOI: 10.1186/s40359-025-02949-w PMID: 40598633

Stillman, T. (2025). Maintaining academic integrity through AI-trap questions. *Journal of Educators Online,* 22(4). EISSN-1547-500. https://www.thejeo.com/archive/archive/2025_223~2/25rea0023_jeo_sept_30_stillmanpdf

Stoney Brook University. (2026). *Categories of academic dishonesty*. https://www.stonybrook.edu/commcms/academic_integrity/faculty-and-staff/categories-of-academic-dishonesty.php

Sullivan, M., Kelly, A., & McLaughlan, P. (2023). ChatGPT in higher education: Considerations for academic integrity and student learning. *Journal of Applied Learning and Teaching*, *6*(1). Advance online publication. DOI: 10.37074/jalt.2023.6.1.17

Tarisayi, K. S. (2024, March). Strategic leadership for responsible artificial intelligence adoption in higher education. *CTE Workshop Proceedings, 11,* 4-14. DOI: 10.55056/cte.616

The-false-positive-rate-for-sentences-of-our-ai-writing-detection-capability

Topping, K. J., Gehringer, E., Khosravi, H., Gudipati, S., Jadhav, K., & Susarla, S. (2025). Enhancing peer assessment with artificial intelligence. *International Journal of Educational Technology in Higher Education*, *22*(1), 3. DOI: 10.1186/s41239-024-00501-1

Tutor, B. O. D., Lopez-Tutor, M. J., & Bernardo, L. M. A. (2025, June). Motivations of tertiary-level students to use generative artificial intelligence (GenAI) to cheat. *International Conference on Frontiers of Educational Technologies Proceedings*, Singapore, 509-519. Springer. DOI: 10.1007/978-981-95-2521-8_36

Ültanır, E. (2012). An epistemological glance at the constructivist approach: Constructivist learning in Dewey, Piaget, and Montessori. *International Journal of Instruction, 5*(2). ISSN: 1694-609X

UNESCO. (2021). *AI and education: Guidance for policymakers.* UNESCO. https://unesdoc.unesco.org/ark:/48223/pf0000376709

University of Chicago. (2026). *Generative AI at UChicago.* https://genai.uchicago.edu/resources/faculty-and-instructors/strategies-for-designing-ai-resistant-assignments

University of Edinburgh. (2026). *Academic misconduct.* https://registryservices.ed.ac.uk/academic-services/staff/discipline/academic-misconduct

University of Massachusetts Boston. (2026). T*ypes of academic integrity errors.* https://www.umb.edu/academics/provost/academic-integrity/integrity-errors/

University of Northern Michigan. (2026). *Creating AI-resistant assignments, activities and assessments (designing out).* Center for Teaching and Learning. https://nmu.edu/ctl/creating-ai-resistant-assignments-activities-and-assessments-designing-out

University of Washington at Saint Lewis. (2026). *AI resilient assignments.* https://ctl.wustl.edu/resources/ai-resistant-assignments/

Wahle, J. P., Ruas, T., Kirstein, F., & Gipp, B. (2022, December). How large language models are transforming machine-paraphrased plagiarism. *Proceedings of the 2022 Conference on Empirical Methods in Language Processing, Society for Computational Linguistics*, Abu Dhabi, UAE. https://aclanthology.org/2022.emnlp-main.62/

Waked, S. N., Abdelsalem, A., Wagar Ashraf, M., & El Alaoui, K. (2024). T*he impact of falsely detecting AI-generated text on academic assessment. Proceedings of the* International Society *for Technology, Education and Science*, Antalya Turkey. https://eric.ed.gov/default.aspx?q=descriptor%3A%22Plagiarism%22&ff1=pubSpeeches%2FMeeting+Papers&id=ED673127

Wang, S., & Huang, Y. (2025). Facilitation or Inhibition: The impact of generative artificial intelligence on college students' creativity. *Frontiers of Education in China, 20*(1), 38–53. DOI: 10.3868/s110-020-025-0003-0

Watson, A. P. (2024). Hallucinated citation analysis: Delving into student-submitted AI-generated sources at the University of Mississippi. *The Serials Librarian, 85*(5-6), 172–280. DOI: 10.1080/0361526X.2024.2433640

Wei, X. (2024, July 3). *How AI detects student engagement to transform classrooms.* Digital Promise. https://digitalpromise.org/2024/07/03/how-ai-detects-student-engagement-to-transform-classrooms/

Wu, Y. (2024). Critical thinking pedagogics design in an era of ChatGPT and other AI Tools-Shifting from teaching" what" to teaching" why" and" how." *Journal of Education and Development*, 8(1). ISSN 2529-7996

Wu, Y. (2026, February). Future-proofing medical assessment: Evaluating collaborative intelligence in the age of artificial intelligence. *Academic Medicine, 101*(2), 152–159. DOI: 10.1093/acamed/wvaf039 PMID: 41620848

Xu, B., Li, J., & Zhang, S. (2022). Artificial intelligence in academic writing: Opportunities, limitations, and ethical concerns. *Journal of Educational Technology & Society, 25*(4), 76–89.

Yan, L., Pammer-Schindler, V., Mills, C., Nguyen, A., & Gašević, D. (2025). Beyond efficiency: Empirical insights on generative AI's impact on cognition, metacognition and epistemic agency in learning. *British Journal of Educational Technology, 56*(5), 1675–1685. DOI: 10.1111/bjet.70000

Zaphir, L., Lodge, J. M., Lisec, J., McGrath, D., & Khosravi, H. (2024). How critically can an AI think? A framework for evaluating the quality of thinking of generative artificial intelligence. *arXiv preprint arXiv:2406.14769.*

KEY TERMS AND DEFINITIONS

Academic Integrity: when a student does his/her work, only uses designated assistance and properly cites others' work

Artificial Intelligence: (AI): the conceptual definition used in this chapter is for generative artificial intelligence (AI) that can create new, original content on its own in response to user prompts

AI Academic Integrity: when students only use AI when allowed; ethical use of AI

AI Detectors: software that uses algorithmic structural variations and predictability analysis to detect writing created by AI

AI-Resistant Assessment: assessments that cannot effectively be done by AI

Assessment: assignments and methods educators use to evaluate student learning

Critical Thinking: ability to analyze, evaluate and synthesize multiple sources of information to solve a problem or issue

Creativity: original thought

Student Motivation: The desire to do something

Volition: goes beyond motivation or intent to do something to the focused effort and action of completing a task even when difficult or outside distractions exist

Chapter 4
Swimming in Circles:
The Fish Bowl Logic of Assessment, Anthrogogy, and Its Consequences in the Age of Generative AI

Shree Deepa
http://orcid.org/0000-0002-0083-5783
University of Hyderabad, India

Geetha Durairajan
http://orcid.org/0009-0000-5844-5174
English and Foreign Languages University, India

ABSTRACT

This chapter conceptualises higher education assessment as operating within a "fish bowl" logic that privileges visible outputs while obscuring underlying reasoning and decision-making. Grounded in validity theory and an anthrogogic orientation, it analyses reflective essays from postgraduate students in an Indian university who experienced open-source and open-book summative examinations. The findings show that open-source conditions expand access but shift constraints into internal decision-making, while open-book formats stabilise engagement without reducing the demand for judgement. Generative AI is treated not as a disruption but as an epistemic stress test exposing the fragility of output-based evaluation. The chapter argues for reframing assessment as the design of conditions that make epistemic engagement visible.

DOI: 10.4018/979-8-3373-9089-5.ch004

INTRODUCTION

Higher education assessment has long relied on environments that make performance visible, comparable, and manageable within constrained conditions. Written examinations, structured assignments, and time-bound tasks are routinely treated as credible indicators of student capability, even though it is acknowledged that they can never capture the full range of intellectual capability that needs to be measured. Observable consistent evaluation is valued much more than a complete representation of the construct: it is accepted as the representative token of its type only because observable performance in forms that can be evaluated with reliable consistency is perceived as providing a better basis for a valid inference of the construct being measured. Assessment scholarship has repeatedly cautioned that when visibility becomes the governing principle of design, there is a risk of conflating what can be displayed with what is actually learned. The under representation of the construct and irrelevant variances come to the fore (Messick, 1989). In such situations, the assessment does not merely measure learning; it begins to redefine it in terms of what can be seen and judged within the observable boundaries of measurable performance.

This chapter conceptualises this condition as the "fish bowl" logic of assessment. The term is used here not as a rhetorical flourish but as a structural description of how assessment environments operate. Learners are placed within bounded spaces where their intellectual work must take a visible, stable form, and judgments are made on the basis of that visible output. Thus maximum performance is expected, even though the predictions are often about performances under typical performance conditions (Cronbach, 1970). The processes that constitute intellectual engagement: hesitation, doubt, iterative reasoning, and the ethical negotiation of choices are the typical conditions that remain inaccessible in what we would like to term as 'fish bowl' assessment. The image of the fish bowl is instructive here not because of its familiarity, but because of what it reveals about constrained environments. A goldfish placed in a bowl appears manageable, contained, and fully visible, yet this very containment alters its development; in more natural conditions, the same organism grows differently, shaped by space, movement, and ecological complexity. What is seen in the bowl is therefore not a neutral representation, but a product of the conditions imposed upon it. In assessment terms, this suggests that what is made visible within bounded evaluative settings is not simply evidence of learning, but an outcome shaped by the constraints of the environment itself. Such an assessment is not very far from the evaluation that takes place under a panopticonical gaze (Foucault, 1991).

From a validity perspective, this raises a central concern. If the constructs that higher education claim to assess include reasoning, methodological judgment, and ethical positioning, then the extent to which these are captured—or obscured—within visible performance becomes a matter of not just social but individual consequence as far as the interpretation and use of the score or grade is concerned (Messick, 1989). The problem is not just that the assessment is partial, but that its partiality is often mistaken for completeness.

The emergence of generative artificial intelligence has intensified this concern in ways that are difficult to ignore. Systems capable of producing fluent, coherent, and academically structured responses at speed do not simply introduce a new form of academic misconduct; they expose an existing fragility in how assessment evidence is interpreted. When acceptable academic performance can be generated with minimal epistemic engagement, the long-standing reliance on mere linguistic fluency and structural coherence as indicators of understanding, as valued at that point in time, (Bachman & Palmer, 1996; Canale & Swain, 1980) becomes unstable today in the 21st century. Contemporary work in AI ethics highlights the risks of automation bias, the over-reliance on system outputs, and the diffusion of responsibility in human–AI interaction (Floridi et al., 2018; Mittelstadt et al., 2016). Within assessment contexts, these concerns take on a specific form: they challenge the assumption that visible output can be straightforwardly linked to individual intellectual labour.

From the standpoint of argument-based validation, the meaning of an assessment lies not in the conceptualisation and realisation of the task prompts and response formats alone but in the chain of inferences that connect observed performance with warrants and evidence that link it to claims about underlying ability (Kane, 2006). With reference to language assessment a clear and relevant at that point in time articulation and justification of this perspective was presented by Bachman and Palmer (2010) but today, Generative AI disrupts this chain by weakening the link between output and inference. If a well-structured response can be produced without sustained engagement with the problem, then the inference that such a response reflects reasoning, understanding, or judgment becomes questionable. This does not render assessment invalid in itself, but it exposes the extent to which interpretive assumptions have been taken for granted. The issue, therefore, is not the presence of AI as an external threat, but the way in which it reveals a misalignment between what assessment claims to measure and what it is structurally equipped to capture.

Assessment scholarship in the context of generative artificial intelligence has understandably focused on redesigning tasks, strengthening authenticity, safeguarding academic integrity, and developing assessment practices that are resilient to AI-assisted production (Balducci, 2024; Kaldaras et al., 2024; Lye & Lim, 2024). These developments, however, continue to operate largely within inherited assessment paradigms. Anthrogogy shifts the discussion to a more fundamental level by arguing that adult education cannot simply be treated as an extension of child-centred pedagogy oriented educational theory: it requires an independent theoretical construal grounded in adulthood as a distinct educational condition with corresponding implications for teaching, learning, and assessment (Deepa, 2026). Assessment in higher education, therefore, cannot be viewed merely as a mechanism for verifying content acquisition or the reproduction of disciplinary knowledge. Instead, it must be the intrinsic and most important part of a broader educational enterprise that recognises adult students as autonomous individuals whose prior experiences, disciplinary identities, multilingual repertoires, and capacity for independent judgement constitute legitimate educational resources rather than variables to be controlled or ignored. Such a reconceptualisation provides an important theoretical foundation for reconsidering the role of assessment in AI-mediated higher education, where access to information is increasingly ubiquitous and educational value lies less in information recall than in responsible judgement, interpretation, and decision-making.

In the context of such an anthrogogic perspective, assessment itself requires a theoretical re-examination. Durairajan (2026) argues that existing testing theory does not make any distinction between children and adults despite age being routinely acknowledged as a test-taker characteristic, resulting in pedagogic assumptions being transferred unquestioningly into higher education. Anthrogogic assessment privileges assessments over tests because they provide stronger predictive validity for adult life, beyond the space of an educational institution, leading to a wash-forward and not a mere washback (Deepa & Durairajan, 2023) while simultaneously repositioning adult students as primary users of assessment rather than passive recipients of externally generated judgements. This perspective extends prevailing validity theory by arguing that authentic assessment should prepare adults for the realities of professional and social life instead of confining them to artificial examination conditions that reward memorisation and regurgitation. Assessment tasks should therefore mirror the authentic environments in which graduates will subsequently function, incorporate dialogue, collaboration, negotiated responsibility, and meaningful feedback, and generate evidence that supports informed educational and professional decisions rather than merely allocating grades. Such arguments assume renewed significance in the era of generative artificial intelligence, where the educational challenge is no longer the protection of closed-book recall but the design of assessments whose validity derives from authentic performance, responsible use of available resources, and the quality of the inferences that can legitimately be drawn with reference to adult capability (Durairajan, 2026).

This chapter therefore examines how the interpretation and use of any assessment needs to be renegotiated when generative AI becomes part of the academic environment. The focus is not on prohibition, detection, or technological regulation. Instead, the concern is with the conditions under which intellectual work becomes visible, and the consequences that these conditions have for how learners engage with knowledge. It is no longer sufficient for us to be aware of the conditions of language learning (Spolsky, 1989). The conditions of all assessment, not just in terms of how it can be assessed in a reliable manner, which are to a large extent subsumed under irrelevant variance, but the plausible real time conditions under which students can and will write and how it will reflect a wash-forward beyond the classroom (Deepa & Durairajan, 2023) needs to be taken into account. Assessment is treated here as an epistemic environment that shapes not only what learners produce but how they come to understand their own role as knowers (Boud & Falchikov, 2007).

Central to this chapter is an anthrogogic orientation to assessment. The term "anthrogogy," originally construed by Trott (1991), refers to an approach that recognises adult learners as epistemically responsible agents capable of reflexive engagement, ethical judgment, and self-positioning within knowledge practices. Unlike pedagogic models that are organised around transmission, guidance, and controlled progression, an anthrogogic stance assumes that learning at the postgraduate level involves negotiating complexity, making informed decisions, and taking responsibility for the consequences of those decisions. In this sense, assessment is not merely an evaluative checkpoint but a site where intellectual maturity is enacted. More recent work has extended this orientation by foregrounding constructs such as thought seeds, (Deepa, 2022a) verbal disposition, (Deepa, 2022b) and reflective positioning as central to adult academic development, emphasising that learning emerges through engagement with disturbance, not through compliance with predetermined structures (Deepa & Durairajan, 2023).

The study is situated within a postgraduate academic context in which assessment was deliberately designed to value such an anthrogogic orientation. Assessment tasks were structured around complex, scenario-based problems that required interpretation, positioning, and justification rather than reproduction. In this environment, generative AI was not excluded but recognised as part of the contemporary research and argumentation landscape. Students were encouraged to engage with it critically, to distinguish between assistance and substitution, and to remain accountable with reference to how it informed their work. This approach aligns with emerging perspectives that position responsible AI use as a matter of cultivated judgment rather than enforced restriction (Floridi et al., 2018).

The initial summative assessment adopted in this context was open-source, permitting unrestricted access to digital resources, including AI tools. The intention was to approximate the conditions under which research is actually conducted: open, resource-rich, and situated. However, the evaluation of student responses revealed a tension that could not be reduced to individual behaviour. A number of submissions demonstrated high levels of fluency and coherence while raising questions about the depth of underlying engagement. This was not treated as a problem of integrity alone, but as a signal that the assessment environment continued to privilege what could be displayed within its visible frame. Generative AI, in this sense, did not create the problem; it made it undeniable.

At this point, the fish bowl logic becomes analytically central. Expanding access to resources did not alter what the assessment recognised as evidence of competence. As long as evaluation remained anchored in visible outputs, namely structured prose, confident tone and orderly argumentation, the system continued to reward what could be produced within the bowl. With respect to validity, this raises concerns not only about the nature of construct representation but also about the consequences of assessment decisions based on such representations (Messick, 1989). If performance that is decoupled from reasoning is treated as evidence of learning, then the meanings and values attached to grades and scores become unstable.

In response to such a validity predicament, the assessment was redesigned as a time-bound open-book examination. This shift was not a retreat into control, nor a punitive response to AI use. It functioned as an intervention aimed at altering what the assessment environment makes visible. By restricting access to real-time digital generation while allowing pre-selected materials, the open-book format introduced conditions that required learners to rely more directly on internalised understanding. The emphasis shifted from producing polished outputs to engaging in reasoning under constraint. From an interpretive perspective, this redesign sought to strengthen the link between observed performance and the inferences drawn about underlying capability (Kane, 2006).

The empirical basis of this chapter lies in reflective essays written by postgraduate students across two courses operating within this shared anthrogogic assessment framework. These reflections are treated not as opinion statements but as situated accounts of epistemic experience under specific assessment conditions. They provide access to how learners interpret the availability of resources, how they respond to constraints, and how they negotiate questions of responsibility, authorship, and understanding. Selected moments within these accounts are approached as analytically significant incidents, consistent with qualitative traditions that treat experience as constructed and interpretable rather than self-evident (Flanagan, 1954; Tripp, 1993). In this sense, the data are not used to report what students felt in a general sense, but to examine how assessment conditions shape the ways in which learners think, decide, and position themselves.

What emerges from these accounts is not a simple preference for one assessment format over another, but a patterned difference in how intellectual conduct is enacted. Under open-source conditions, students describe both a sense of freedom and a susceptibility to over-reliance on external outputs. Under open-book conditions, they report increased pressure alongside a heightened awareness of their own reasoning processes. These differences are not incidental; they reflect the ways in which assessment environments regulate the relationship between the learner and knowledge. Generative AI, in this context, functions less as a cause of change and more as a catalyst that makes existing dynamics visible.

The argument developed in this chapter is that the central challenge facing higher education is not how to exclude AI from assessment, but how to design assessment environments in such a way that epistemic labour becomes visible again. The fish bowl cannot be removed entirely, as assessment necessarily involves framing and selection. However, it can be redesigned so that it does not reduce complex intellectual activity to surface performance. By bringing together validity theory, anthrogogic principles, and empirical student accounts, the chapter examines how the interpretation and use of assessment scores can be renegotiated in the age of generative AI and its implications for the future of assessment and testing in academic contexts.

ASSESSMENT, VISIBILITY, AND VALIDITY

Assessment in higher education is often treated as a technical exercise in measurement, but its operations are more accurately understood as interpretive and consequential. What is selected for evaluation, how it is elicited, and how it is interpreted together determine not only what is measured, but what comes to count as knowledge within a given academic context. The concern is not simply whether assessment is reliable or efficient, but whether it meaningfully and responsibly represents the constructs it claims to assess. This concern is at the centre of validity theory.

Messick's unified view of validity positions construct representation and consequential implications as inseparable (Messick, 1989). An assessment is not valid merely because it produces consistent scores: what is validated is the inference made on the basis of the score obtained. As such, there should be a clear indication that the inferences drawn from those scores are grounded in an adequate representation of the intended construct. When assessment environments privilege what is easily observable—structured writing, fluency, formal correctness—they risk underrepresenting more complex dimensions of intellectual work such as reasoning, judgment, and ethical positioning. This is not a marginal issue. It reflects what Messick describes as construct under representation, where important aspects of ability remain outside the scope of measurement, and also construct-irrelevant variance, where performance is influenced by factors not central to the construct itself.

The problem becomes sharper when visibility is mistaken for adequacy. In many assessment settings, the assumption persists that if a response appears coherent and well-formed, it is sufficient evidence of understanding. This assumption relies on a stable link between performance and cognition, where what is produced is taken to reflect what has been internally processed (Bachman & Palmer, 2010). However, this link has always been fragile. Even prior to the emergence of generative AI, students could reproduce forms of academic discourse without fully engaging with underlying ideas. What generative AI has done is to make this fragility unmistakably discernible. When systems can generate linguistically polished responses with minimal human intervention, the reliance on visible textual performance as evidence of learning becomes increasingly difficult to justify.

Kane's argument-based approach to validation provides a useful framework for examining this issue (Kane, 2006). Rather than treating validity as a property of a test, Kane conceptualises it as a chain of inferences that move from observed performance to claims about underlying ability. Each step in this chain—scoring, generalisation, extrapolation, and implication—requires justification. The introduction of generative AI disrupts this chain most directly at the level of extrapolation, which is related to predictive validity. If the observed performance can no longer be assumed to originate in the learner's own reasoning processes, then the inference from performance to competence becomes unstable. The issue is not that inference is impossible, but that it requires stronger warrants than those traditionally relied upon.

Within the fish bowl logic of assessment, this instability is compounded by the conditions under which performance is produced. When assessment environments are tightly bound and oriented toward visible output, they create incentives for learners to optimize for what is recognisable within those bounds. Fluency, structure, and conformity to expected academic forms become central, not necessarily because they reflect deeper understanding, but because they are what can be evaluated. This leads to a narrowing of what is treated as legitimate evidence. As a result, the assessment may successfully distinguish between performances, but fail to capture the constructs it is intended to represent.

The consequences of such misalignment are not confined to measurement error; they extend to how learners understand knowledge itself. Assessment can play a formative role in shaping students' conceptions of learning (Boud and Falchikov, 2007) for assessment could be learning oriented (Turner & Purpura, 2016). When assessment rewards reproduction and surface features, learners may orient themselves toward those features at the expense of deeper engagement. This is akin to negative washback (Alderson & Wall, 1993). Conversely, when assessment demands interpretation, justification, and ethical positioning, learners are more likely to develop capacities associated with sustained intellectual work. In this sense, assessment is not merely evaluative but constitutive: it shapes the very practices it seeks to measure.

This constitutive role becomes particularly visible when assessment formats shift. Open-book examinations, with a long history in higher education, were originally introduced to reduce the emphasis on memorisation and to encourage understanding and application (Stalnaker & Stalnaker, 1934). Subsequent research has shown that open-book formats can support deeper engagement with material, while also placing greater demands on learners' ability to synthesise and apply knowledge under time constraints (Heijne-Penninga et al., 2008; Williams & Wong, 2009). Later studies further indicate that open-book conditions do not necessarily make assessment easier; rather, they shift the locus of difficulty from recall to reasoning and decision-making (Durning et al., 2016).

Parallely, digitally mediated forms of assessment—often described as open-web or open-source—have emerged as responses to changing knowledge environments. These formats allow unrestricted access to online resources, including search engines and, more recently, generative AI tools. Early work on open-web examinations suggests that such environments more closely approximate authentic problem-solving contexts, where information is accessed, evaluated, and integrated dynamically rather than retrieved from memory (Williams, 2006). More recent analyses of online assessment environments underscore the complexity of designing tasks that promote genuine engagement in resource-rich contexts, particularly when digital tools can mediate large portions of the response process (Ellis et al., 2020; Jervis & Brown, 2020).

What becomes evident across this body of work is that changes in assessment formats are not merely neutral adjustments; they reconfigure the relationship between the learner, knowledge, and evidence. Open-book conditions reduce reliance on memorisation but increase dependence on internalised understanding and rapid synthesis. Open-source conditions expand access and align more closely with real-world practices, but they also create situations in which the distinction between engagement and substitution becomes less visible. In both cases, the issue is not simply one of difficulty, but about what the assessment environment makes possible and what it renders visible.

Generative AI intensifies these dynamics by altering the balance between effort and output. The availability of tools that can produce immediate, well-structured responses shifts the conditions under which performance is generated. What previously required extended engagement can now be produced rapidly, creating a situation in which the appearance of competence is more easily achieved than the competence itself. This does not eliminate the need for learning, but it complicates the relationship between process and product. Within such a context, continued reliance on visible output as the primary basis for evaluation risks reinforcing a system in which performance is decoupled from epistemic labour.

The ethical dimensions of this shift have been widely discussed in AI scholarship, particularly when linked to responsibility, accountability, and human oversight (Floridi et al., 2018; Mittelstadt et al., 2016). In assessment contexts, these concerns intersect with validity in specific ways. If learners rely on AI-generated outputs without critical engagement, the issue that needs to be sorted is not only one of integrity but of representation. The assessment outcome will no longer provide a clear indication of the learner's capability, raising questions about the legitimacy of decisions based on that outcome. At the same time, attempts to prohibit AI use without reconsidering assessment design leave intact the underlying assumption that visible performance is an adequate proxy for understanding.

This brings the discussion back to the conditions of visibility that define the fish bowl. The problem is not simply that assessment is visible, but that it is selectively visible in ways that privilege certain forms of output over others. Reasoning processes, moments of uncertainty, and the negotiation of competing possibilities are typically compressed into final responses, leaving little trace of the intellectual work that produced them. Generative AI, by producing such stabilised outputs efficiently, exposes the extent to which assessment has relied on these compressed representations.

A validity-oriented response to this situation requires more than tightening controls or refining scoring procedures. It requires reconsidering what is to be accepted as evidence and how such evidence is elicited. If the construct being evaluated includes reasoning, judgment, and ethical engagement, then assessment designs must create conditions in which these can be observed, at least in part. The distinction between open-source and open-book assessment conditions, as examined in this chapter, is therefore not a matter of format preference but of epistemic visibility. Each configuration brings into view certain aspects of learning while obscuring others. The task, then, is not to choose between them in the abstract, but to understand how they shape the relationship between performance and inference, and how that relationship can be aligned more closely with the constructs that higher education seeks to value.

ANTHROGOGY AS EPISTEMIC POSITIONING IN ASSESSMENT

The present chapter proceeds from the need to stabilise a construct that has remained insufficiently recognised within dominant educational discourse. The term *anthrogogy*, first articulated by Trott (1991), does not extend pedagogy nor refine andragogy; it repositions the adult human being within teaching–learning–assessment environments (Deepa, 2026). Where pedagogic orientations have historically operated through deficit assumptions and externally regulated progression, anthrogogy begins with the recognition that adult participants are already embedded in linguistic, cultural, and experiential worlds and are capable of acting as epistemically responsible agents within them. This is not a matter of instructional preference but a shift in ontological positioning.

Within this framework, the adult is not treated as a learner approximating to competence but as a language user negotiating meaning, consequence, and responsibility in real contexts. Empirical work in Indian higher education has consistently demonstrated that when such positioning is enacted, learners do not simply respond to instruction; they participate in shaping the terms of engagement, including the design and interpretation of the assessment itself (Deepa, 2022c, 2026; Deepa & Durairajan, 2023, 2025a, 2026). This repositioning is central to the present chapter, as it reframes assessment from an external mechanism of evaluation to an internal site of epistemic engagement.

The distinction and shift from pedagogic orientations is therefore structural. In pedagogic assessment regimes, even at advanced levels of education, learners are frequently positioned as deficient, requiring demonstration of correctness within tightly controlled formats. Assessment, in such contexts, privileges stability, uniformity, and compliance. Anthrogogic environments, by contrast, dismantle this hierarchy by recognising teacher and student as co-participants in a shared epistemic space. Assessment is not designed unilaterally but emerges through negotiated processes, as exemplified in the development of the Anthrogogic Question Paper (AQP), which stands in contrast to the imposed and pre-structured Pedagogic Question Paper (PQP) (Deepa & Durairajan, 2025a). The difference between these formats is not procedural but epistemological: one regulates performance within predefined limits, while the other invites engagement with complexity and responsibility.

This shift necessitates a reconsideration of what is being assessed. Conventional constructs such as linguistic accuracy and communicative competence, while not irrelevant, are insufficient for capturing the full scope of adult language use. Anthrogogic work has therefore proposed the construct of *language potentiality*, which foregrounds the consequences of language use rather than its formal properties alone (Deepa, 2022b; Deepa & Durairajan, 2023, 2025b). Language, in this sense, is not simply a system to be mastered or a tool for communication; it is a medium through which individuals enact constructive, neutral, or destructive possibilities in relation to others. The same utterance, structurally correct and contextually appropriate, may function differently depending on how it positions the speaker and affects the listener. Assessment that remains confined to correctness or appropriacy cannot account for this dimension.

Anthrogogic assessment responds to this limitation by designing tasks that require learners to engage with situations, make choices, and account for those choices. This includes adaptations of established formats, such as discourse completion tasks, to elicit not only pragmatic responses but evidence of ethical and epistemic positioning (Deepa & Durairajan, 2025b, 2026). What is made visible in such tasks is not merely what learners know or can produce, but how they recognise situations, weigh alternatives, and take responsibility for the consequences of their responses. Assessment, therefore, becomes a site where judgement is enacted rather than inferred indirectly through surface performance.

The empirical grounding of this chapter rests on reflective essays, student responses, and assessment artefacts generated within such anthrogogic environments.

These materials are treated as qualitative data and therefore should not be dismissed as mere illustrative commentary. Consistent with incident-based and interpretive traditions, the focus is on analytically significant moments that reveal how participants experience and negotiate assessment conditions (Flanagan, 1954; Tripp, 1993). Reflective accounts are approached as sites of articulation in which learners make visible their reasoning, uncertainties, and decisions. Such data are not reduced to coded categories but interpreted as constructed representations of experience, allowing for a nuanced examination of epistemic engagement (Charmaz, 2014). This approach aligns with the anthrogogic premise that knowledge is not externally transmitted but emerges through situated interaction and reflection.

The relevance of this framework becomes particularly evident in the context of AI-mediated academic environments. Recent analyses of generative artificial intelligence in education have highlighted its capacity to produce linguistically fluent and structurally coherent outputs with minimal human intervention, thereby complicating the relationship between performance and underlying understanding (Dwivedi et al., 2023; Kasneci et al., 2023). From a pedagogic assessment perspective, this introduces concerns about authorship, originality, and the integrity of evaluation. However, from an anthrogogic standpoint, these developments do not constitute a disruption as much as an exposure. When assessment is anchored in outputs that can be replicated or generated independently of sustained engagement, its construct validity is already compromised. AI renders this condition visible.

Anthrogogic assessment, by contrast, is less susceptible to such substitution because it is not centred on the production of decontextualised outputs. Its emphasis on judgement, positioning, and responsibility situates assessment within domains that cannot be easily externalised. The question is no longer whether a response meets formal criteria, but whether it reflects a considered engagement with the situation and an accountable stance toward its consequences. In this sense, AI operates as a stress test that distinguishes between assessment systems that rely on surface indicators of competence and those that engage with deeper dimensions of epistemic activity.

The argument advanced here is that anthrogogy does not offer an alternative technique within existing assessment paradigms; it redefines the grounds on which assessment operates. By repositioning adult participants as epistemic agents, expanding the construct of language use to include potentiality, and grounding analysis in lived experiences, it provides a framework that is capable of responding to the challenges posed by contemporary educational environments. The sections that follow build on this foundation by examining the manner in which such an orientation interacts with specific assessment conditions and how the resulting data can be interpreted within a validity framework that takes both the complexity of human language use and the changing ecology of academic work seriously in the age of generative AI.

METHODOLOGICAL FRAMING

This chapter adopts an interpretive qualitative orientation centred on examination experiences as articulated by test takers themselves. It does not engage with either scores, performance outcomes, or judgments of correctness. The focus is on how participants experience the examination as an event: how they interpret the task, negotiate available resources, make decisions under constraint, and account for those decisions in their own words. The examination is therefore approached not as a mechanism for measuring ability but as a situated condition, not of only learning as conceptualised by Lave & Wenger (1991) but of assessment, within which forms of reasoning, uncertainty, and responsibility become visible. Within this orientation, validity is not treated as a statistical property of scores but as an interpretive concern regarding the nature and type of assessment conditions that enable or constrain in relation to participants' engagement with knowledge (Messick, 1989; Kane, 2006).

This shift from measurement to interpretation is not merely procedural; it reflects a different understanding of what assessment is and what it does. In conventional assessment frameworks, validity is often tethered to the stability of scores and the reliability of instruments. However, when the object of inquiry is examination experience, such a framing becomes insufficient. What requires a major scrutiny instead is the relationship between the conditions under which participants engage with the assessment and the kinds of intellectual activity that such conditions make possible or suppress. In this sense, validity is relocated from the test as an object to the examination as an environment—an environment that shapes how participants think, decide, and act.

The epistemic stance of this study is anthrogogic. Participants are approached as adult language users capable of reflexive engagement, ethical positioning, and accountable decision-making within assessment environments (Deepa & Durairajan, 2023, 2025a; Durairajan, 2026). This stance is not limited to theoretical positioning; it has direct methodological consequences. It demands that participants' articulations of their experience be treated as meaningful data in their own right, rather than as a secondary commentary on performance. It also expects that analysis should focus on how participants position themselves in relation to the examination—whether as compliant responders, strategic navigators, or responsible decision-makers—rather than evaluating them against externally imposed criteria of correctness and more importantly, situating them as the subject of scrutiny.

Within such an anthrogogic orientation, any examination needs to be understood and valued as a site where intellectual life is enacted rather than tested. Participants do not simply produce answers; they engage in acts of meaning where the narrative is a mode of thought (Bruner, 1990) and also in acts of plausible judgement under assessment conditions that may either enable or constrain their capacity to act responsibly. The method of analysis or interpretation, as such, cannot proceed by abstracting responses from their context or reducing them to measurable units. Instead, it must remain attentive to the situated nature of participants' engagement and to the ways in which that engagement is articulated through reflective accounts.

Reflective writing is central to this methodological orientation. The study treats reflective essays not as supplementary or anecdotal material but as analytically constructed accounts of experience. This treatment is grounded in constructivist qualitative inquiry, which recognises that accounts are shaped through processes of selection, articulation, and positioning (Charmaz, 2014). Participants do not simply report what happened; they construct narratives that reveal their thought processes, how they interpret their actions, how they justify their decisions, and how they understand their role within the examination. The analytic value of such accounts lies precisely in this constructedness, as it provides access to the interpretive work through which participants make sense of their engagement.

This approach also necessitates a departure from analytic procedures that privilege coding, categorisation, and frequency as primary means of establishing rigour. The study does not seek to produce thematic summaries or generalisable patterns across participants. Such approaches, while valuable in other contexts, risk flattening the complexity of the examination experience by reducing it to recurring categories. Instead, the analysis focuses sharply on moments within the participants' accounts that are analytically significant because they reveal tensions, uncertainties, or shifts in how the examination has been experienced by them.

These moments are approached through the construction of analytic episodes. Episodes are not treated as pre-existing units within the data but as outcomes of analytic attention, consistent with the view that incidents are constituted rather than discovered (Tripp, 1993). Their significance is not determined by frequency but by their capacity to illuminate underlying dynamics within the examination experience, in line with the critical incident tradition (Flanagan, 1954). For example, a single instance in which a participant articulates uncertainty about the use of generative AI may be analytically more revealing than multiple instances of routine description, because it exposes a point at which responsibility, authorship, and decision-making intersect.

Interpretation of the data proceeds through iterative engagement with these constructed episodes, moving between individual accounts and the broader conceptual framework of the study. Concepts such as responsibility, positioning, and language potentiality function as sensitising concepts that guide analytic attention without reducing the data to fixed categories (Charmaz, 2014). This allows the analysis to remain responsive to the specificity of participants' accounts while maintaining coherence with the anthrogogic orientation of the study.

Importantly, this methodological design makes explicit what the study does not attempt to do. It does not aim to either evaluate student performance, compare achievement across conditions, or to establish causal relationships between assessment formats and outcomes. It also does not seek to generalise findings beyond the specific contexts in which the data were generated. Its purpose is to examine how examination conditions were experienced and how those experiences revealed the ways in which participants understand and enact their role within assessment.

In this sense, the methodological approach is inseparable from the argument of the chapter. By focusing on the examination as a lived experience, by treating reflective accounts as analytically constructed data, and by privileging interpretive depth over measurement, the study creates the conditions for examining how assessment operates not merely as a system of evaluation but as an environment in which epistemic life is enacted, constrained, and made consequential.

CONTEXT, DATASET, AND ANALYTICAL APPROACH

The study is situated within a central university in India, drawing on postgraduate English studies classrooms across two course environments: a Research Methods course and a course in Indian Knowledge Systems (IKS). In both courses, the assessment that is the focus of this study was conducted as part of formal end-semester summative examinations within the institutional framework of the programme. Summative assessment is understood here as assessment of learning, usually with the use of examinations conducted at the end of a defined instructional period for the purpose of certifying learning within institutional structures (Black & Wiliam, 1998). These examinations constitute high-stakes academic events in which students are required to respond under defined temporal and procedural constraints. The concern of the present study, however, is not with evaluating outcomes to function as an assessment of learning, but with examining how such conditions are experienced and interpreted by those who participate in them.

Across both courses, assessment was designed within an anthrogogic framework that foregrounds interpretation, positioning, and responsibility rather than reproduction or correctness (Deepa & Durairajan, 2023, 2025a, 2026). The tasks required participants to engage with situations, justify their choices, and articulate their reasoning within conditions that did not prescribe singular correct responses. In this sense, the examination functioned not as a mechanism for testing pre-specified knowledge but as an environment in which participants enacted and revealed their judgement under constraint, consistent with an anthrogogic orientation to assessment as a site of epistemic engagement.

Two distinct examination conditions were implemented across cohorts, each constituting a different configuration of openness and constraint. The first was a time-bound open-source examination in which students had unrestricted access to digital resources, including generative artificial intelligence tools. Under this condition, participants could consult online materials, draw upon multiple sources, and engage with AI systems in the process of constructing their responses. The second was a time-bound open-book examination in which students were permitted access to pre-selected materials but were restricted from engaging in real-time external generation. Open-book formats are understood as assessment conditions that allow access to authorised materials during the examination while maintaining constraints on time and task completion (Heijne-Penninga et al., 2008; Durning et al., 2016). These conditions are not treated as variables for comparison but as distinct epistemic environments that shape how participants experience decision-making, authorship, and responsibility.

The dataset consists primarily of reflective essays written by the postgraduate students following the completion of these summative examinations. These essays were produced as part of the examination process itself and required students to articulate their experience of engaging with the examination, including how they approached the tasks, the resources they used, the decisions they made, and the uncertainties they encountered. Reflective writing in this context is treated as an integral component of the assessment experience, capturing participants' own accounts of how they navigated the examination environment. Such accounts are understood as analytically constructed representations of experience, shaped through processes of articulation and positioning rather than as transparent reports of internal states (Charmaz, 2014).

In addition to reflective essays, selected student responses and examination artefacts are drawn upon where they illuminate how participants describe and make sense of their engagement. These materials are not treated as indicators of performance or correctness but as extensions of participants' accounts, providing further insight into how they negotiate the conditions of the examination. The analytic focus remains on experience as expressed by the participants rather than on externally defined measures of success.

The analytical approach adopted in this chapter is the construction and interpretation of analytic episodes derived from these materials. Episodes are identified at points where participants explicitly engage with tensions central to the study, such as negotiating the use of generative AI, expressing uncertainty about authorship, responding to constraints in open-book conditions, or recognising shifts in their approach to reasoning and decision-making. These moments are treated as analytically significant not because of their frequency but because of their capacity to illuminate how participants experience and interpret the examination.

Consistent with an incident-based approach to qualitative analysis, such episodes are not treated as pre-existing units within the data but as constructs emerging through analytic attention (Tripp, 1993). Their selection is guided by analytic relevance rather than representativeness, in line with the critical incident tradition in which significance is attributed to events that reveal underlying structures rather than those that occur most frequently (Flanagan, 1954). Interpretation proceeds through iterative engagement with these episodes, moving between individual accounts and the broader conceptual concerns of the chapter. Concepts such as responsibility, positioning, and language potentiality function as sensitising concepts that orient analytic attention without imposing fixed categories (Charmaz, 2014; Deepa & Durairajan, 2023).

By grounding the analysis in reflective essays produced within summative examination contexts and by treating these essays as analytically constructed data, the study establishes a clear relationship between context, data, and interpretation. It enables an examination of how different configurations of assessment—open-source and open-book—operate as distinct epistemic environments that shape how participants understand, negotiate, and enact their role within examination conditions.

ANALYSING THE EXAMINATION EXPERIENCE UNDER OPEN-SOURCE CONDITIONS

The analysis that follows examines analytically constructed episodes drawn primarily from reflective essays written by postgraduate students after summative open-source examinations in the Indian Knowledge Systems (IKS) course, alongside selected retrospective references from Research Methods (RM) students who had previously experienced the same open-source format in an earlier course and for this course, had taken an open book examination. Participants are referred to using anonymised identifiers (IKS1, IKS2...; RM1, RM2...), where identifiers indicate course context but not examination type in isolation. Episodes are selected not for frequency but for their analytic intensity in revealing how participants construct their examination experience with reference to both open-source conditions and their prior encounters with more conventional closed-book formats (Flanagan, 1954; Tripp, 1993).

A participant (IKS2) writes:

"This was the first time I felt like I was not limited by the exam. Usually, I keep thinking about what I remember, but here I was thinking about what I can do with what I find."

This account establishes the open-source examination as a departure from closed-book expectations. The participant contrasts two orientations: one centred on recall ("what I remember") and another on engagement ("what I can do with what I find"). The shift is not merely procedural but epistemic. The examination is no longer experienced as a test of retained knowledge but as a space of active interaction with available resources. What is significant here is not the presence of resources per se, but the redefinition of what counts as engagement within the examination. It is not just the student's sense of plausibility in teaching-learning contexts (Deepa & Ambati, 2026) that is possible. In this context, it is essential to invoke a participant test taker's sense of plausibility under examination conditions that comes into play.

A related articulation appears in another account (IKS4):

"In other exams, I try to bring out what I studied before. Here I was constantly checking, reading, and thinking at the same time. It did not feel like writing an exam in the usual way."

This participant foregrounds simultaneity—*"checking, reading, and thinking at the same time"*—as a defining feature of the experience, which again is evidence of test taker plausibility. In contrast to the sequential structure of closed-book examinations (study → recall → write), the open-source condition produces a layered engagement in which multiple processes occur concurrently. The phrase "not ... in the usual way" signals a disruption of established examination scripts. The participant is not simply performing differently; they are operating within a differently structured activity.

This disruption, however, does not always translate into ease. A participant (IKS1) reflects:

"I had access to everything, but that made it harder to decide what to focus on. I kept going from one source to another without feeling settled."

Here, abundance generates instability. The availability of multiple sources does not resolve uncertainty; it amplifies it by expanding the range of possible directions. The participant's difficulty lies not in accessing information but in stabilising attention. Thus, The examination becomes a space in which direction must be actively constructed by the test/examination taker, and not be externally guided through administrative constraints.

This instability is further elaborated in the following account (IKS5):

"I found many different explanations for the same concept, and all of them made sense in different ways. I had to choose which one I wanted to go with, but I was not sure on what basis to choose."

The multiplicity of valid explanations displaces the notion of a single correct answer. The participant is required to select among alternatives that cannot be hierarchically ordered through correctness alone. The question shifts from "which is right?" to "which do I adopt?" This introduces a form of epistemic responsibility, originating in a sense of what is plausible, in which the participant must justify their choice in the absence of definitive criteria. The act of answering becomes inseparable from the act of positioning.

A temporal dimension to this experience is articulated by another participant (IKS3):

"I spent a lot of time searching because I felt there might be something better. By the time I started writing properly, I had less time left."

This participant's engagement is shaped by the possibility and plausibility of improvement. The search process becomes difficult to terminate because each new source introduces the potential for a better response. Time, in this context, does not merely limit performance; it exposes the absence of a clear endpoint. The participant must decide when to stop searching, but this decision is not externally regulated. It becomes a matter of judgement under uncertainty.

The relationship between availability and ownership is explicitly addressed in the following account (IKS6):

"Even when I found good points, I was not sure if I should use them because I did not fully understand them. I did not want to write something that was not really mine."

This episode foregrounds a distinction between access and ownership. The participant recognises that the presence of material does not guarantee its legitimacy within their response. The hesitation to include points that are not fully understood indicates an awareness of the limits of appropriation. The examination thus becomes a space in which participants must negotiate what can be legitimately claimed as their own, even when access is unrestricted.

A similar tension is visible in another account (IKS7):

"It was easy to collect information, but difficult to decide what I actually wanted to say. I had to stop and think about my own understanding."

The participant identifies a gap between accumulation and articulation. Information can be gathered readily, but transforming that information into a coherent response requires a different form of engagement. The moment of having to "stop and think" marks a shift from external sourcing to internal processing. The examination thus demands not only access to information but the capacity to integrate and organise that information into a position that can be sustained. Such stopping to think moments usually happen only during assignments or projects which are written over a period of time, not during timed one shot writing (Wiegle, 2002) in an examination hall.

Retrospective reflections from the RM students further illuminate this shift by contrast. A participant (RM2), reflecting on their earlier open-source experience, writes:

"Compared to regular exams, I remember feeling that I had more freedom but also more responsibility. There was no clear limit, so I had to decide everything myself."

This account reinforces the redistribution of constraints observed in the IKS data. The participant explicitly links freedom with responsibility, indicating that the removal of external limits does not eliminate constraint but relocates it within the participant's own decision-making processes. The phrase *"I had to decide everything myself"* captures the extent to which the participant becomes responsible for structuring their engagement.

Across these episodes, a pattern of hesitation and decision-making becomes visible. Participants repeatedly encounter moments where they must determine without clear criteria: what to focus on, when to stop searching, what to include, and how to justify their choices. These moments are not peripheral; they constitute the core of the examination experience under open-source conditions. Their analytic significance lies in revealing how participants experience the redistribution of constraint from external structures to internal deliberation (Flanagan, 1954; Tripp, 1993).

The open-source examination thus operates as an expanded epistemic condition in which the range of possible actions increases while the criteria for action become less explicit. In contrast to closed-book examinations, where boundaries are externally imposed, the open-source format requires participants to construct their own boundaries of engagement. This redistribution aligns with an anthrogogic orientation in which participants are positioned as responsible agents required to navigate conditions rather than comply with instructions (Deepa & Durairajan, 2023, 2025a, 2026).

However, this repositioning is not uniformly experienced as enabling. For some participants, the expanded condition provides flexibility and opportunities for exploration. For others, it introduces instability, making it difficult to sustain direction and arrive at closure. What remains consistent across these variations is the requirement to assume responsibility for decisions that are no longer externally regulated.

From an analytic perspective, these episodes make visible a shift from externally regulated performance to internally negotiated engagement. The examination ceases to function as a bounded task defined by recall and reproduction and becomes an open field in which participants must actively constitute the terms of their participation. In doing so, it reveals dimensions of examination experience—selection, hesitation, positioning, and ownership—that remain largely obscured in conventional closed-book formats.

ANALYSING THE OPEN-BOOK EXAMINATION EXPERIENCE POST OPEN-SOURCE EXPOSURE

The analytic episodes in this section examine how postgraduate students in the Research Methods (RM) course articulate their experience of a time-bound open-book examination after having previously encountered open-source assessment conditions in an earlier course. Participants are referred to using anonymised identifiers (RM1, RM2, etc.). The analysis does not treat the open-book examination as an isolated format; rather, it examines how it is experienced relationally—through comparison with prior open-source engagement. Episodes are selected for their analytic intensity in revealing how boundaries, responsibility, and decision-making are recalibrated when openness is partially restructured through constraint (Flanagan, 1954; Tripp, 1993).

A participant (RM4) writes:

"Compared to the open-source exam we had earlier, this felt more controlled. I knew what I had with me and what I could use, so I could start writing faster."

This account immediately frames the open-book condition through contrast. The sense of "control" emerges not as an inherent property of the format, but as a relational experience following exposure to open-source conditions. The participant's ability to "start writing faster" is linked to the finiteness of available resources. Unlike the open-source environment, where the possibility of further searching delays commitment, the open-book condition stabilises the point of entry into response construction. The boundary between preparation and writing, previously dissolved, is partially restored.

However, this restoration does not imply a return to conventional closed-book logic. Another participant (RM1) reflects:

"It was not like a closed-book exam where I just write what I remember. I still had to think and connect things, but I was not distracted by looking for more sources."

Here, the participant distinguishes the open-book condition from both open-source and closed-book formats. The absence of distraction from continuous searching allows for sustained engagement with available material, yet the task still requires active thinking and connection-making. The examination is experienced as a bounded but not reductive space—one that limits expansion without eliminating the need for interpretation and integration.

This recalibration becomes more visible in the following account (RM6):

"In the open-source exam, I felt like I was exploring while answering. In this one, I felt like I had to rely on my own clarity and understanding."

The contrast between "exploring" and "relying on my own clarity" marks a shift in the locus of engagement. Under open-source conditions, the participant's activity extends outward into a field of resources; under open-book conditions, it turns inward toward consolidation. The participant is no longer navigating an expansive field but working within a defined set of materials, requiring them to draw more directly on their own understanding. The examination thus becomes a space where internal coherence is foregrounded over external exploration.

Temporal experience is also reconfigured in this transition. A participant (RM2) notes:

"There was still time pressure, but it felt more focused. I was not switching between sources all the time. I could stay with my answer and develop it."

Time, which in the open-source condition is dispersed across searching and decision-making, becomes concentrated in the open-book format. The participant experiences time not as fragmented but as directed. The ability to "stay with" an answer indicates a stabilisation of attention. The examination demands sustained engagement with a line of thought rather than continuous negotiation of multiple possibilities.

The relationship between resource use and ownership is articulated in another account (RM5):

"Even with the books, I realised I could not just take from them directly. I had to understand quickly and then write in my own way."

Here, the participant recognises that access to material does not eliminate the need for transformation. The constraint on real-time expansion means that available resources must be interpreted and rearticulated within the time frame of the examination. Authorship is not dissolved by access; it is reconfigured as the ability to work with material in a way that reflects one's own understanding. The examination thus continues to demand ownership, but within a more bounded field.

A further dimension of this boundedness is evident in the following account (RM3):

"I had fewer options compared to open-source, so it was easier to decide what to include and what to leave out. The decisions were still there, but they felt more manageable."

The participant explicitly identifies a reduction in the scale of decision-making. The need to choose remains, but the range of possibilities is narrowed. This does not eliminate the cognitive demand of selection; it recalibrates it. Decision-making becomes more contained, allowing the participant to arrive at closure with greater confidence. The examination thus retains its requirement for judgement while providing clearer parameters within which that judgement operates.

Another participant (RM7) reflects on the role of prior experience:

"After the open-source exam, I became more aware of how I use material. In the open-book exam, I was more careful about what I included because I knew I had to stand by it."

This account demonstrates how prior exposure to open-source conditions continues to shape engagement even when those conditions are no longer present. The participant carries forward an awareness of responsibility and authorship, applying it within a more constrained environment. The open-book examination is thus not experienced in isolation; it is informed by earlier encounters with expanded conditions that have made certain aspects of engagement more visible.

This continuity is further articulated in another account (RM8):

"In earlier exams, I never thought much about whether the answer was really mine. After the open-source experience, I kept thinking about it even in the open-book exam."

Here, the participant indicates that the open-source condition has introduced a lasting shift in how examination engagement is understood. Questions of ownership and responsibility, once implicit, become explicit and persist across formats. The open-book condition does not erase this awareness; it provides a different context in which it is enacted.

Across these episodes, the open-book examination emerges not as a return to restriction but as a recalibrated condition shaped by prior epistemic expansion. The boundaries reintroduced in this format—limited materials, time constraints—do not simply constrain action; they reorganise it. Participants are no longer navigating an indefinite field of possibilities but operating within a defined set of resources that require interpretation, selection, and integration.

At the same time, the presence of boundaries does not reduce the demand for responsibility. Instead, it concentrates it. Participants must work more directly with what they have, drawing on their understanding to transform available material into a coherent response. The examination thus becomes a space of focused engagement, where decision-making remains central but is exercised within clearer limits.

From an analytic perspective, these episodes demonstrate that the experience of open-book assessment cannot be understood independently of prior exposure to open-source conditions. The latter introduces a form of epistemic awareness—of decision-making, authorship, and responsibility—that persists even when the conditions change. The open-book format, in this sense, functions as a site where this awareness is recalibrated rather than diminished.

The contrast between open-source and open-book conditions therefore does not lie in a simple opposition between openness and constraint. Rather, it lies in how constraint is structured and experienced. In the open-source condition, constraint is diffused and internally negotiated; in the open-book condition, it is reintroduced in a more defined form, allowing for stabilisation without eliminating the need for judgement. The examination, across both conditions, emerges as an environment in which participants continuously negotiate the relationship between resource, understanding, and responsibility—albeit under differently configured parameters.

ANTHROGOGIC ASSESSMENT CONDITIONS AND GOLD FISH BOWL SWIMMING: CONSEQUENCES IN THE GENERATIVE AI AGE

The preceding analyses have shown that changes in assessment conditions do not simply alter what students produce; they reconfigure how engagement itself is structured, experienced, and interpreted. The metaphor of the fish bowl offers a way of theorising this relationship between the environment and intellectual activity. Within the fish bowl, movement is visible, contained, and manageable. The observer can see the organism at all times, and its activity appears continuous and coherent. Yet this visibility is achieved only through constraint. The space is limited, the range of movement is predetermined, and the conditions under which the organism develops are shaped by the boundaries imposed upon it. What is observed is not a neutral expression of capacity but a form of activity conditioned by the environment itself.

In such assessment, the logic that operates is through the privileging of visible, stable outputs as evidence of learning. Written responses and structured arguments, assuming that closed book examinations of the timed one shot type do belong to the genre of planned and not unplanned discourse (Ochs, 1979) particularly because all such writing samples carry organisation as an analytic scoring category, along with linguistically fluent performances are taken as indicators of competence because they can be observed, compared, and evaluated. However, as validity theory has long argued, the visibility of performance does not guarantee the adequacy of construct representation (Messick, 1989). What becomes visible within assessment is always selective. Processes such as hesitation, uncertainty, iterative reasoning, and the negotiation of competing possibilities are compressed into final responses, leaving little trace of the intellectual work that produced them. The fish bowl, in this sense, does not merely reveal performance; it produces a particular form of constrained writing.

The notion of "swimming in circles" captures the patterned nature of this production. Within bounded assessment environments, learners encounter recurring task structures and evaluative expectations. Over time, they learn to orient their responses towards what is recognisable within these constraints. The repetition of such patterns creates a form of circular movement: responses become predictable, aligned with expected formats, and optimised for evaluation. One such example is the over use of cohesive devices, as a result of tutoring, which gets actually marked down in assessments of writing samples in timed examinations like IELTS (Banerjee, et al. 2007; Cotton, et al. 2011). This type of circularity, which is an outcome of test wiseness, identified as part of construct irrelevant variance (Messick, 1989) is, in closed book examinations, also mistaken for stability and, by extension, for competence. Yet what it reflects is the internalisation of environmental constraints rather than the full range of intellectual engagement.

The analytic episodes presented earlier illuminate how this circularity is disrupted when the boundaries of the fish bowl are altered. Under open-source conditions, the containment that produces predictable movement is loosened. Participants are no longer restricted to a fixed set of resources or a predetermined pathway from question to response. Instead, they encounter an expanded field in which multiple directions are possible. However, the disruption of circularity does not immediately produce clarity. Rather, it introduces uncertainty. Participants describe difficulty in determining when to stop searching, how to prioritise among competing sources, and how to justify the inclusion of material that is available but not fully understood. The absence of externally imposed limits requires the construction of internal criteria for action.

This shift from externally regulated constraint to internally negotiated engagement is central to understanding the limits of the fish bowl logic. In tightly bounded environments, constraint is visible and manageable. In expanded environments, constraint does not disappear; it gets redistributed. Participants must now decide what counts as sufficient, relevant, and legitimate. These decisions are not ancillary to the task; they constitute its core. The examination becomes less about producing an answer and more about navigating conditions under which answering is not only possible but plausible. Under such circumstances, test takers are also likely to begin developing their own sense of plausibility (Deepa & Ambati, 2026) not only in learning but also in testing and assessment contexts.

Yet the persistence of circularity is evident even within these expanded conditions. Participants often continue to search for optimal responses, delay closure, and rely on externally available formulations. The logic of the fish bowl remains operative, not as a physical constraint but as an internalised orientation toward producing evaluatively acceptable outputs. The expectation that there exists a "better answer" somewhere within the available resources reflects a continued alignment with assessment as optimisation rather than engagement. The movement may no longer be physically constrained, but it remains patterned by prior conditioning.

The open-book condition, as experienced by participants with prior exposure to open-source environments, reveals a further reconfiguration of this logic. Here, boundaries are reintroduced, but in a moderated form. Participants operate within a finite set of materials and a defined time frame, which stabilises the process of engagement. The need to continuously search is reduced, allowing for sustained attention to a line of reasoning. However, the awareness developed under open-source conditions does not disappear. Participants continue to reflect on questions of ownership, responsibility, and justification. The circularity of movement is not reinstated in its original form; it is recalibrated. Constraint and openness are brought into a different relation, enabling movement that is directed without being entirely predetermined.

From an anthrogogic perspective, this reconfiguration is significant because it foregrounds the learner as an epistemically responsible agent. Within the fish bowl logic, learners are positioned as performers who must demonstrate competence within predefined limits. Their task is to produce responses that align with expected forms. In contrast, anthrogogic environments position participants as individuals who must navigate complexity, make decisions, and take responsibility for those decisions (Deepa & Durairajan, 2023; 2025a, Durairajan, 2026). The shift from circular movement to navigational engagement reflects this repositioning. Learners are no longer confined to repeating established patterns; they are required to construct their own pathways through available resources and to justify the positions they adopt, thereby evolving their own sense of what we would like to term as 'assessment response plausibility, taking off from the student sense of plausibility as articulated by Deepa, & Ambati (2026). Such assessment oriented plausibility may even lead to an examination being perceived as a joyful experience (Durairajan, 2026).

The social and individual consequences of these differing configurations of assessment are not trivial. When learners are repeatedly engaged in environments that reward predictable, structured responses, they may internalise a preference for certainty and conformity. Intellectual risk-taking becomes less attractive, as it may not align with evaluative expectations. The emphasis on producing correct or acceptable answers can discourage exploration of alternative perspectives, particularly when such exploration cannot be easily accommodated within the format of the assessment. Over time, this may contribute to the development of what can be described as a "correct answer culture," in which knowledge is approached as something to be reproduced rather than interrogated.

In contrast, environments that require navigation, decision-making, and justification can foster different dispositions. Participants are compelled to confront uncertainty, to weigh alternatives, and to take responsibility for their choices. These are not merely cognitive skills but forms of intellectual conduct that have implications beyond the examination context. They shape how individuals engage with knowledge, how they respond to complexity, and how they position themselves in relation to others' ideas. Assessment, in this sense, participates in the formation of epistemic habits that extend into broader academic and professional practices.

The presence of generative AI intensifies these dynamics by altering the relationship between effort and output. Within the fish bowl logic, where visible performance is the primary basis for evaluation, AI-generated responses can replicate the expected features of competence with remarkable efficiency. Fluency, coherence, and structural organisation—long treated as indicators of understanding—can be produced without sustained engagement. This does not introduce a new problem as much as it exposes an existing one. The reliance on visible output as evidence of learning is revealed to be fragile, as the connection between performance and underlying reasoning can no longer be assumed.

At the same time, AI complicates the notion of authorship in ways that extend beyond questions of integrity. When participants engage with AI as part of their process, the boundaries between assistance and substitution become blurred. The issue is not simply whether a response is "original," but how the participant positions themselves in relation to the tools they use. This positioning involves decisions about what to accept, what to modify, and what to reject. It requires a form of judgement that cannot be captured solely through the final output. The fish bowl, oriented toward visible performance, is ill-equipped to account for such processes.

This exposure creates an imperative to reconsider the logic of assessment itself. If the aim is to move beyond circular patterns of reproduction, then assessment environments must be designed to make alternative forms of engagement visible. This does not entail abandoning structure but rethinking its function. Constraint can be used not to limit movement to predetermined paths but to create conditions under which decision-making, reasoning, and responsibility become observable. The goal is not to eliminate the fish bowl but to transform it into an environment that supports directional movement rather than circular repetition.

The metaphor of "swimming in circles" thus serves as both a diagnosis and a point of departure. It reveals how assessment environments can produce patterns of engagement that are mistaken for competence, and it highlights the need to reconfigure these environments in the light of contemporary conditions. In the age of generative AI, where the production of acceptable outputs can be automated, the limitations of a visibility-driven assessment logic become increasingly apparent. What is required is an approach that attends not only to what is produced but to how it is produced, and to the conditions that shape this production.

In this sense, the fish bowl is not merely a constraint to be removed but a structure to be redesigned. By attending to the relationship between constraint, visibility, and engagement, assessment can move toward configurations that do not confine learners to circular patterns but enable forms of movement that reflect the complexity of intellectual life.

IMPLICATIONS FOR ASSESSMENT DESIGN IN THE AI-MEDIATED CONTEXT

The analyses presented in this chapter necessitate a reconsideration of what assessment is understood to be based on evidence presented and discussed with reference to assessment experience. The issue is not that generative AI introduces a new threat to academic integrity, but that it renders untenable a long-standing assumption: that visible textual performance can reliably stand in for underlying intellectual engagement. When linguistically coherent, structurally organised responses can be produced without sustained epistemic labour, the inferential link between performance and competence is weakened. From the standpoint of construct validity, this is not a peripheral concern but a structural problem. What is being observed is no longer a stable representation of the construct, and the inferences drawn from that observation require re-examination (Messick, 1989; Kane, 2006).

Within the fish bowl logic of assessment, this instability has been masked by the apparent reliability of observable outputs. Coherence, fluency, and alignment with academic conventions have functioned as proxies for understanding because they are visible and evaluable. Generative AI does not disrupt this logic; it exposes its fragility. When the same surface features can be reproduced independently of the learner's reasoning processes, the assumption that these features index understanding collapses. The problem, therefore, cannot and should not be identified and located as the presence of AI, but in the continued reliance on forms of evidence that are no longer defensible as indicators of epistemic engagement.

This has direct implications for how assessment must be conceptualised. Assessment can no longer be treated primarily as a mechanism for capturing outputs. It must be understood as the design of conditions under which particular forms of intellectual activity become visible. The question is not whether a response is correct or well-formed, but whether the conditions of its production allow for the observation of reasoning, decision-making, and responsibility. In this sense, assessment design becomes an exercise in configuring visibility: determining what aspects of engagement are made accessible to interpretation and what remains obscured.

The distinction between open-source and open-book conditions, as examined in this chapter, illustrates that changes even in format reconfigure this visibility rather than simply increasing or decreasing difficulty. Open-source environments expand access and align more closely with contemporary knowledge practices, but they also distribute the constraints and move them into the participant's own decision-making processes. What becomes visible are moments of hesitation, selection, and uncertainty—dimensions of engagement that are typically suppressed in more controlled settings. At the same time, the absence of clear boundaries can lead to instability, making it difficult to arrive at closure. Open-book conditions, particularly when experienced after open-source exposure, reintroduce boundaries that stabilise engagement while retaining an awareness of responsibility and authorship. These configurations demonstrate that assessment is not a choice between openness and restriction, but a matter of how constraint is structured to shape engagement.

From an anthrogogic perspective, the implications of this shift are significant. If adult learners are positioned as epistemically responsible agents, then assessment must engage with their capacity to make decisions, justify positions, and account for the consequences of their choices. This requires a movement away from assessment designs that privilege compliance with predefined forms and toward those that foreground positioning and responsibility. The central question becomes not whether a learner can reproduce acceptable responses, but whether they can navigate complex conditions and articulate the basis of their engagement.

This repositioning has consequences for how evidence obtained from student responses is perceived and valued within assessment. Evidence can no longer be restricted to final products that compress the processes through which they are generated. It must include traces of engagement that make visible how participants arrive at their responses. Reflective articulations, justification of choices, and the explicit negotiation of resources become integral, not supplementary, to the assessment process. These are not add-ons designed to deter misuse of AI; they are necessary components of an assessment system that seeks to align its evidence with the constructs it claims to represent.

At the same time, the incorporation of such elements cannot be reduced to procedural adjustments. Simply requiring reflection or explanation does not in itself guarantee meaningful engagement. The issue is not the inclusion of additional components but the orientation of the assessment as a whole. If the primary evaluative emphasis is primarily on the quality of the final output, as is the case in most summative assessment and definitely in the context of sit down examinations, then reflective elements risk becoming performative extensions of the same logic. What is required is a shift in what counts as central: from the product of performance to the process of engagement.

This shift also reconfigures the role of constraint. Rather than functioning solely as a mechanism for control, constraint becomes a design resource for making particular forms of engagement possible. Time limits, curated materials, and task structures can be used as conditions of language assessment (in this context sit down open source examinations) to direct attention and stabilize decision-making without reducing the complexity of the task. The aim is not to eliminate uncertainty but to situate it within conditions where it can be productively navigated. In this sense, constraint is not opposed to openness; it is part of how openness is made manageable through performance conditions.

The presence of generative AI further underscores the need for such reconfiguration. Attempts to exclude AI through stricter control risk reinforcing the very conditions that the fish bowl logic embodies: environments in which performance is tightly bounded and evaluated on the basis of visible output. Such approaches do not resolve the underlying problem; they preserve it. If assessment continues to rely on outputs that can be generated without engagement, then the validity of its inferences remains compromised, regardless of the mechanisms used to enforce compliance.

An alternative approach is to recognise AI as part of the contemporary epistemic environment and to design assessment in ways that engage with its presence. This does not imply uncritical acceptance but requires that the use of AI be situated within a framework of responsibility. Participants must not only decide whether and how to use such tools, but also account for the role they play in shaping their responses. The focus shifts from detection of misuse to evaluation of engagement: how learners interact with available resources, how they exercise judgement, and how they position themselves in relation to the knowledge they produce.

From a validity perspective, this reorientation strengthens the interpretive basis of assessment and its use. By making visible the processes through which responses are constructed, it provides more robust grounds for linking observed performance to claims about underlying capability. It does not eliminate uncertainty—no assessment can—but it aligns the conditions of observation more closely with the constructs being evaluated. In doing so, it addresses both construct underrepresentation and the various risks of construct-irrelevant variance (Messick, 1989) that arise when surface features are taken as proxies for deeper engagement.

The implications of this shift extend beyond individual assessment tasks to the broader architecture of academic evaluation. If assessment continues to operate within a fish bowl logic that privileges visible output, it risks reinforcing patterns of engagement that are increasingly disconnected from the realities of knowledge work in the age of generative AI. Learners may become adept at producing acceptable performances while remaining distanced from the processes of reasoning and judgement that such performances are assumed to represent. Conversely, assessment environments that foreground navigation, positioning, and responsibility have the potential to cultivate forms of engagement that are more closely aligned with contemporary epistemic demands.

The central implication, therefore, is not the adoption of a particular format, but a shift in how assessment itself needs to be construed. It must move from an orientation toward capturing performance to one that attends to the conditions under which such performance is produced. In the AI-mediated context, this involves recognising that what is at stake is not merely the integrity of assessment, but the visibility of epistemic labour itself.

REFRAMING ASSESSMENT: CONCLUDING REFLECTIONS

This chapter has argued that what is at stake in contemporary assessment is not merely the adoption of new formats or the regulation of emerging technologies, but a deeper reconsideration of how assessment constructs visibility and, through it, meaning. The long-standing reliance on observable performance as evidence of learning has rested on an assumption that what is produced in response to assessment tasks can stand in for the intellectual processes that generate it. This assumption, while always partial, has been sustained by the relative stability of assessment environments in which constraints rendered performance manageable and interpretable. In such environments, the fish bowl logic of assessment operated largely unnoticed: bounded conditions produced visible, patterned responses that could be evaluated with consistency, and these patterns were taken as indicators of competence.

The analyses in this chapter have sought to demonstrate that this logic is neither neutral nor sufficient. The metaphor of the fish bowl makes explicit that visibility is achieved through constraint, and that what becomes visible is shaped by the environment itself. Within such environments, learners will always move in predictable ways, aligning their responses with what is recognisable and evaluatable. The notion of "swimming in circles" captures this patterned movement: repetition becomes normalised, and stability is mistaken for depth. The assessment does not simply reveal competence; it conditions the forms in which competence can appear.

When the boundaries of this environment are reconfigured, as in the open-source examination condition, the circularity becomes visible by its disruption. Participants no longer operate within a closed system of recall and reproduction but within an expanded field in which access, selection, and integration must be actively negotiated. The absence of externally imposed limits requires the construction of internal criteria: when to stop searching, what to prioritise, what to include, and what to claim. These decisions are not peripheral; they constitute the core of engagement. Constraint, in this context, does not disappear but is redistributed, shifting from external regulation to internal deliberation.

The open-book condition, particularly when experienced after such expansion, reveals that the reintroduction of boundaries need not restore the earlier circularity. Instead, it can stabilise engagement while retaining the awareness of responsibility that the open-source condition foregrounds. Participants operate within finite limits but continue to attend to questions of ownership, justification, and positioning. The examination becomes a site of directed reasoning rather than unbounded exploration, demonstrating that constraint can be reconfigured to support engagement rather than confine it.

From an anthrogogic perspective, these shifts are not incidental but foundational. When learners are positioned as epistemically responsible agents, assessment should not be limited to the verification of performance within predefined formats. It must engage with the capacity to navigate complexity, to make decisions under conditions of uncertainty, and to account for those decisions. The movement away from circular performance toward navigational engagement reflects this repositioning. Learners are no longer confined to demonstrating what they can reproduce; they are required to take a stance in relation to knowledge and to recognise the consequences of that stance.

The emergence of generative AI intensifies the significance of these findings. By enabling the rapid production of coherent and structurally acceptable responses, AI disrupts the assumed link between visible performance and underlying understanding. What appears as competence can no longer be taken as evidence of epistemic engagement. In this sense, AI does not introduce a new problem so much as it renders an existing one unavoidable. The fish bowl, long relied upon to make learning visible, is revealed to be insufficient for capturing the processes it claims to represent.

This exposure has consequences that extend beyond questions of academic integrity. It brings into focus the individual and social consequences of assessment design. When learners are repeatedly engaged in environments that reward predictable, surface-level performance, they may come to internalise these patterns as the expected mode of intellectual activity. The capacity to engage with uncertainty, to weigh competing possibilities, and to take responsibility for one's choices may be underdeveloped, not because learners are incapable, but because the assessment environments do not require or recognise such engagement. In this sense, assessment participates in the shaping of epistemic dispositions, influencing how knowledge is approached and enacted beyond the examination context. Social and individual consequences then extend far beyond gate keeping and move into enabling a wash-forward beyond the classroom.

Reframing assessment, therefore, requires more than the modification of formats or the inclusion of additional components. It requires recognising assessment as an epistemic environment and attending to how its conditions shape what becomes visible as evidence. The central question is not how to eliminate the fish bowl, but how to redesign it so that it does not confine learners to circular patterns of reproduction. Constraint must be rethought as a resource for structuring engagement rather than limiting it, enabling movement that is directed but not predetermined.

REFERENCES

Alderson, J. C., & Wall, D. (1993). Does washback exist? *Applied Linguistics*, *14*(2), 115–129. DOI: 10.1093/applin/14.2.115

Bachman, L. F., & Palmer, A. S. (1996). *Language testing in practice: Designing and developing useful language tests*. Oxford University Press.

Bachman, L. F., & Palmer, A. S. (2010). *Language assessment in practice: Developing language assessments and justifying their use in the real world*. Oxford University Press.

Balducci, B. (2024). AI and student assessment in human-centered education. *Frontiers in Education*, *9*, 1383148. Advance online publication. DOI: 10.3389/feduc.2024.1383148

Banerjee, J., Franceshina, F., & Smith, A. M. (2007). Documenting features of written language production typical at different IELTS band score levels In IELTS Academic Writing Task 2. In Taylor, L., & Flavey, P. (Eds.), *IELTS Research Reports* (Vol. 7, pp. 191–237). Cambridge ESOL.

Black, P., & Wiliam, D. (1998). Assessment and classroom learning. *Assessment in Education: Principles, Policy & Practice*, *5*(1), 7–74. DOI: 10.1080/0969595980050102

Boud, D., & Falchikov, N. (2007). *Rethinking assessment in higher education: Learning for the longer term*. Routledge. DOI: 10.4324/9780203964309

Bruner, J. (1990). *Acts of meaning*. Harvard University Press.

Canale, M., & Swain, M. (1980). Theoretical bases of communicative approaches to second language teaching and testing. *Applied Linguistics*, *1*(1), 1–47. DOI: 10.1093/applin/1.1.1

Charmaz, K. (2014). *Constructing grounded theory* (2nd ed.). Sage.

Cotton, F., Falvey, P., & Kent, S. (2011). An investigation of examiner rating of coherence i IELTS Academic Writing TAsk 2. In Taylor, L., & Flavey, P. (Eds.), *IELTS Research Reports* (Vol. 11, pp. 235–286). Cambridge ESOL.

Cronbach, L. (1970). *Essentials of psychological testing* (3rd ed.). Harper.

Deepa, S. (2022a). Thought seeds in anthrogogic learning contexts. *Journal of Indian Education*, *48*(2), 58–70.

Deepa, S. (2022b). Verbal disposition: The need for language potentiality in anthrogogic spaces. *Journal of English Language Teaching, 64*(6), 17–24. DOI: 10.66121/x2e8ay04

Deepa, S. (2022c). Options in multiple choice questions: Oh Really! Yours sincerely Adult learners! *Language and Language Teaching: A peer reviewed journal.* Vol 11.2.22. (pp 81-86.)

Deepa, S. (2026). Principles of anthrogogic language education. In Deepa, S., & Durairajan, G. (Eds.), *Anthrogogy in Use: A Handbook for Language Educators* (pp. 3–26). Orient BlackSwan.

Deepa, S., & Ambati, A. (2026). Anthrogogic Contexts and Student Sense of Plausibility in Language Materials. In Sarkeshikian, A. (Ed.), *Exploring the Psychology of Language Materials Development* (pp. 245–278). IGI Global Scientific Publishing., DOI: 10.4018/979-8-3373-2995-6.ch008

Deepa, S., & Durairajan, G. (2023). Learning through assessment in anthrogogic contexts: Wash-forward. In Gokturk-Saglam, A. L., & Sevgi-Sole, E. (Eds.), *Emerging practices for online language assessment, exams, evaluation, and feedback* (pp. 99–118). IGI Global., DOI: 10.4018/978-1-6684-6227-0.ch006

Deepa, S., & Durairajan, G. (2025a). Students and Teachers as Equal Learning Collaborators: Reflections on an Anthrogogic Course in India. In Aftab, A. (Ed.), *Materials for Language Assessment* (pp. 91–111). Cambridge Scholars Publishing., https://www.cambridgescholars.com/product/978-1-0364-5693-1

Deepa, S., & Durairajan, G. (2025b). Assessing Language Potentiality in an Anthrogogic Classroom in India. In Aftab, A. (Ed.), *Materials for Language Assessment* (pp. 131–147). Cambridge Scholars Publishing., https://www.cambridgescholars.com/product/978-1-0364-5693-1

Deepa, S., & Durairajan, G. (2026). Language learner versus user in anthrogogic contexts: The case of idioms in multiple choice items. In Tomlinson, B., & Masuhara, H. (Eds.), *Materials Development for L2 Communicative Ability: Theory and Practice* (pp. 393–406). Bloomsbury Academic.

Durairajan, G. (2026). Principles of anthrogogic testing and assessment: The need for joyful humane practices. In Deepa, S., & Durairajan, G. (Eds.), *Anthrogogy in use: A handbook for language educators* (pp. 27–55). Orient BlackSwan.

Durning, S. J., Dong, T., Ratcliffe, T., Schuwirth, L., Artino, A. R.Jr, Boulet, J. R., & Eva, K. (2016). Comparing open-book and closed-book examinations: A systematic review. *Academic Medicine, 91*(4), 583–599. DOI: 10.1097/ACM.0000000000000977 PMID: 26535862

Dwivedi, Y. K., Hughes, L., Ismagilova, E., Aarts, G., Coombs, C., Crick, T., Duan, Y., Dwivedi, R., Edwards, J., Eirug, A., Galanos, V., Ilavarasan, P. V., Janssen, M., Jones, P., Kar, A. K., Kizgin, H., Kronemann, B., Lal, B., Lucini, B., & Williams, M. D. (2023). So what if ChatGPT wrote it? Multidisciplinary perspectives on opportunities, challenges and implications of generative conversational AI for research, practice and policy. *International Journal of Information Management, 71*, 102642. DOI: 10.1016/j.ijinfomgt.2023.102642

Ellis, R. A., Goodyear, P., O'Hara, A., & Prosser, M. (2020). Students' experiences of e-assessment in higher education: The ecology of assessment for learning. *Assessment & Evaluation in Higher Education, 45*(2), 316–330. DOI: 10.1080/02602938.2019.1638117

Flanagan, J. C. (1954). The critical incident technique. *Psychological Bulletin, 51*(4), 327–358. DOI: 10.1037/h0061470 PMID: 13177800

Floridi, L., Cowls, J., Beltrametti, M., Chatila, R., Chazerand, P., Dignum, V., Luetge, C., Madelin, R., Pagallo, U., Rossi, F., Schafer, B., Valcke, P., & Vayena, E. (2018). AI4People—An ethical framework for a good AI society: Opportunities, risks, principles, and recommendations. *Minds and Machines, 28*(4), 689–707. DOI: 10.1007/s11023-018-9482-5 PMID: 30930541

Foucault, M. (1991). *Discipline and Punish: The Birth of the Prison*. Vintage Books. (Original work published 1978)

Heijne-Penninga, M., Kuks, J. B. M., Hofman, W. H. A., & Cohen-Schotanus, J. (2008). Influence of open-book tests on study behaviour: A discrete choice experiment. *Advances in Health Sciences Education : Theory and Practice, 13*(2), 263–273. DOI: 10.1007/s10459-006-9038-y PMID: 17063381

Jervis, C. G., & Brown, L. R. (2020). The prospects of sitting 'end of year' open book exams in the light of COVID-19: A medical student's perspective. *British Journal of Educational Technology, 51*(5), 1865–1870. DOI: 10.1111/bjet.12980 PMID: 32432953

Kaldaras, L., Akaeze, H. O., & Reckase, M. D. (2024). Developing valid assessments in the era of generative artificial intelligence. *Frontiers in Education, 9*, 1399377. Advance online publication. DOI: 10.3389/feduc.2024.1399377

Kane, M. T. (2006). Validation. In Brennan, R. L. (Ed.), *Educational measurement* (4th ed., pp. 17–64). Praeger.

Kasneci, E., Sessler, K., Küchemann, S., Bannert, M., Dementieva, D., Fischer, F., Gasser, U., Groh, G., Günnemann, S., Hüllermeier, E., Krusche, S., Kutyniok, G., Michaeli, T., Nerdinger, F. W., Pfeffer, J., Poquet, O., Sailer, M., Schmidt, A., Seidel, T., & Kasneci, G. (2023). ChatGPT for good? On opportunities and challenges of large language models for education. *Learning and Individual Differences*, *103*, 102274. DOI: 10.1016/j.lindif.2023.102274

Lave, J., & Wenger, E. (1991). *Situated learning: Legitimate peripheral participation*. Cambridge University Press. DOI: 10.1017/CBO9780511815355

Lye, C. Y., & Lim, L. (2024). Generative artificial intelligence in tertiary education: Assessment redesign principles and considerations. *Education Sciences*, *14*(6), 569. DOI: 10.3390/educsci14060569

Messick, S. (1989). Validity. In Linn, R. L. (Ed.), *Educational measurement* (3rd ed., pp. 13–103). Macmillan.

Mittelstadt, B. D., Allo, P., Taddeo, M., Wachter, S., & Floridi, L. (2016). The ethics of algorithms: Mapping the debate. *Big Data & Society*, *3*(2), 2053951716679679. Advance online publication. DOI: 10.1177/2053951716679679

Ochs, E. (1979). Planned and unplanned discourse. IN T. Givon (Ed.). Syntax and semantics. Vol. 12. Discourse and syntax. (pp. 51-80. Academic Press. Spolsky, B. (1989). Conditions for second language learning: Introduction to a general theory. Oxford University Press

Stalnaker, J. M., & Stalnaker, R. C. (1934). The effect of open-book examinations. *School and Society*, *39*, 533–535.

Tripp, D. (1993). *Critical incidents in teaching: Developing professional judgement*. Routledge.

Trott, D. C. (1991, October). *Anthrogogy*. (Paper presentation). Meeting of the American Association for Adult and Continuing Education, Montreal, Quebec.

Turner, C. E., & Purpura, J. E. (2016). Learning-oriented assessment in second and foreign language classrooms. In Tsagari, D., & Banerjee, J. (Eds.), *Handbook of second language assessment* (pp. 255–274). De Gruyter Mouton., DOI: 10.1515/9781614513827-018

Wiegle, S. (2002). *Assessing writing*. Cambridge University Press. DOI: 10.1017/CBO9780511732997

Williams, J. B. (2006). The place of open-book, online exams in supporting deep learning. *Australasian Journal of Educational Technology*, *22*(1), 1–14. DOI: 10.14742/ajet.1299

Williams, J. B., & Wong, A. (2009). The efficacy of final examinations: A comparative study of closed-book, open-book and cheat sheet examinations. *Assessment & Evaluation in Higher Education*, *34*(3), 335–345. DOI: 10.1080/02602930801956029

Chapter 5
A Trust-Adaptive Generative AI Framework for Competency-Centered and Integrity-Preserving Assessment in Higher Education

Dhinakaran Damodaran
http://orcid.org/0000-0002-3183-576X
Vel Tech Rangarajan Dr. Sagunthala R&D Institute of Science and Technology, India

S. Edwin Raja
http://orcid.org/0000-0002-2948-9669
Vel Tech Rangarajan Dr. Sagunthala R&D Institute of Science and Technology, India

ABSTRACT

The rapid integration of generative artificial intelligence (GenAI) into higher education has transformed assessment practices, yet existing systems remain limited in adaptivity, integrity, trust, and fairness. This chapter proposes a novel framework, Trust-Adaptive Generative Assessment for Competency-Aligned Design (TAGA-CAD), which reconceptualizes assessment as a continuous, adaptive, and ethically governed process. The framework integrates competency-driven task generation, integrity-preserving assessment design, trust-calibrated evaluation mechanisms, and fairness-aware regulation within a unified architecture. By embedding human

DOI: 10.4018/979-8-3373-9089-5.ch005

oversight and closed-loop feedback, TAGA-CAD ensures alignment with learning outcomes while maintaining transparency and reliability in automated grading. A conceptual evaluation model supported by analytical metrics and comparative visualizations demonstrates the superiority of the proposed approach over traditional and existing AI-based systems.

1. INTRODUCTION: RETHINKING ASSESSMENT IN THE GENERATIVE AI ERA

Assessment has been the main tool that evaluates higher education in its manner and form of learning outcomes, competency acquisition and academic progression. Nonetheless, traditional evaluation systems have been mostly inert, standardized as well as disconnected with the cognitive developmental pattern of the learners. Standardized tests, standard scoring rubrics and time restrictions were initially developed to make testing scalable and grading fair but tend to miss individual learning dynamics, abstract thinking processes, and problem-solving in context. With the growing inclusiveness in student populations, both in terms of background and learning rate and the level of competency development, hard-and-fast assessment systems can no longer give much valuable information as to the actual mastery of knowledge (Ilieva et al., 2025). This alienation has led to increasing anxieties surrounding the superficial learning, memorization through assessment and insufficient formative feedback that is insufficient to sustain the development of skills. The advent of Generative Artificial Intelligence (GenAI) brings about both the unparalleled opportunities and drastic changes in the academic assessment ecosystem (Gruenhagen et al., 2024). It is now possible to have large language models and generative systems produce examination questions, adaptive quizzes, feedback stories, grading rubrics, and even grading performances at scale. Although these capabilities provide an efficiency benefit, as well as potential personalization, their uncontrolled implementation has proven to give rise to serious concerns regarding academic integrity, content validity, automated grading reliability, and ethical responsibility. Access to the tools of GenAI to create responses in an extremely effortless way makes the concept of authorship and originality less distinct in a manner that diminishes the credibility of conventional assessment methods. At the same time, non-transparent AI-generated scoring systems pose the risk of increasing the hidden bias, discrepancy, and the mismatch with the curricular competencies, which endangers the equity and credibility of the education results (Xia et al., 2024).

Such tensions show that there is some basic difference between technological capacity and assessment design which is sound as a pedagogical instrument. GenAI is not the solution to the more profound genetic assessment requirements of traditional assessment forms since it only automates them and does not solve the further requirements of adaptive, competency-based, and ethically-regulated assessment systems. Meaningful changing the paradigm to intelligent assessment structures that dynamically react to learner achievement, that maintain academic honesty by designing authentic tasks, and that incorporate trust, transparency, and fairness as a normative component of operations and not post hoc remedies is needed (Agostini & Picasso, 2024). These systems should combine the role of human control with AI-powered intelligence to allow educators to mentor, certify, and constantly benchmark AI-oriented operations and enjoy the benefits of customization and scale. To address these issues, the chapter proposes a new research-based framework that is known as the Trust-Adaptive Generative Assessment of Competency-Aligned Design (TAGA-CAD). The suggested model redefines assessment as an adaptive, ongoing and ethically controlled learning process as opposed to a measurement occurrence. TAGA-CAD is a comprehensive architecture of next-generation AI-based assessment in higher education through integrating generative task synthesis, competency modeling, integrity-preserving assessments and evaluation structures, trust-calibrated mechanisms and fairness-conscious controls (Chiu, 2024). Conceptual The chapter formalizes workflows in adaptive assessment, methodology through the introduction of trust and integrity modeling in generative systems, and practice through describing an implementation pathway toward ethically sound AI application in academic assessment. In this research-oriented manner, the chapter will focus on the way of moving the conversation past automation to intelligent, responsible, and pedagogically transformative assessment ecosystems.

2. RESEARCH GAPS IN EXISTING AI-BASED ASSESSMENT SYSTEMS

Although the field of higher education has developed at a fast pace, moving to the implementation of AI-based technologies, the contemporary evaluation framework remains unintegrated and does not provide the required level of coordination with the educational philosophy. Most of the existing AI-based frameworks are primarily concerned with efficiency in terms of automated question generation and grading, and do not necessarily apply the competency-based learning frameworks to the very working of the systems. This means that tests will tend to test the superficial knowledge memory rather than mastery or critical thinking or progressive acquisition of skills. This discontinuity limits the ability of such systems to bear any significant indication of learner development or to take part in long-term learning outcomes. The dissonance between the idea of academic integrity in AI-based assessment context also is a significant one. The current approaches largely view integrity as an external enforcement mechanism, which is implemented on the principle of plagiarism detectors and after assessment monitoring. However, such reactive practice does not address the underlying problem since learners can use generative AI tools to compose seemingly original but not original answers that cannot be identified by conventional means. Absence of integrity-sensitive test design i.e. examinations resistant to cheating has continued to destroy the feasibility of assessment processes.

In addition, the automated grading systems lack the systems of the trust calibration always. Through opaque scoring outputs, it is commonly understood that opaque scoring outputs are not transparent in presenting decisions, no perception of confidence or uncertainty and reliability is given. This leads to the issue of uniformity and reliability of AI-generation assessment particularly in large-scale. At the same time, such issues as algorithmic bias and fairness are not effectively resolved. The currently existing systems barely incorporate the constant bias tracking and remedial measures, which is why the potential gap in evaluation outcomes of various groups of learners, cultures, and educational histories appears. Above all things, perhaps, the oversatisfaction with the automation is being laid upon the sacrifices of the pedagogical governance. The teachers are usually placed at its periphery and never featured in the justification, validation or navigation of the AI-based processes. This enables not only to circumvent the supervision of instructions, but also to reduce the level to a point of destroying academic responsibility and trust in institutional evaluation process. All these limitations illuminate the insufficiency of holistic and competency-based and ethically-founded AI assessment frameworks, and more integrated and accountable forms need to be created as swiftly as they can.

3. PROBLEM FORMULATION AND DESIGN OBJECTIVES

To circumvent the limitations of the existing AI-based assessment systems, they should be reimagined in terms of how the generative technologies will be incorporated into the educational evaluation systems. The current paradigm looks at generative artificial intelligence as primarily a tool to provide a supporting mechanism that automates single areas of evaluation such as generation of questions or grading. However, this fragmented union fails to indicate the more challenging pedagogical, ethical and systematic requirements of the contemporary higher education. The problem needs to be reorganized in such a way as a system, in which AI is not an appendage utility, but an asset and a liability of a clever, receptive and accountable analysis system (Dhinakaran et al., 2026). It is necessary that this change demands architectural designs that are more technologically advanced and at the same time pedagogically competent, ethically grounded and capable of responding dynamically to the evolving needs of various learners.

The cause of such an issue is to establish adaptable evaluation systems which are capable of discerning and responding to the capable condition of learners at a particular time. The traditional evaluation systems rest on the fixed models, in which the assessment is performed after a period of time with the use of the standardized instruments. By its very nature, these methods are limited by their inability to define the fluid and non-linear nature of learning. In its turn, the next-generation assessment systems are to be in the form of continuous procedures where the performance of the learner will be observed immediately, and the tasks of the assessment will be changed dynamically with the reflection of the level of mastery at the moment (Khlaif et al., 2025). It requires that comprehensive competency representation frameworks must be developed which have the potential to encode multidimensional learning states, including the conceptual knowledge, procedural knowledge and cognitive participation. Such representations should then be used by the system to generate contextually relevant tasks that are not too difficult to the learner, but are rather difficult enough to be challenging. The inability to achieve this balance can result in either cognitive over-load or disengagement and this is detrimental to the effectiveness of learning.

At the same time, the adaptive system design should also be able to tackle the major problem of academic integrity in a time when generative AI tools are easily available to students. The conventional method of identifying wrongdoing when the assessment is finished is becoming not enough, with generative systems able to generate advanced and context-sensitive answers or reactions that do not fall under the popular undergo detection procedures. The issue, therefore, becomes the method of creating tests that are less prone to abuse (Agostini & Picasso, 2024). This entails the incorporation of authenticity in task structures, where unless one genuinely comprehends, situates well, and constructs a response individually, then the task cannot be solved successfully. The tasks need to be created in a way that they have variability, dependency and reflection in them so that they are not easily duplicated or can be externally created without having to engage in meaningful thinking. In such a way, integrity preservation becomes more of a design idea than corrective action, which changes the very way assessments are conceptualized and put into practice.

It is also imperative that the generative products should be regulated by trust sensitive evaluation systems. The automated system of grading and feedback, although efficient, has major issues to do with transparency, reliability and accountability. Most current systems have the evaluation processes as black boxes, and it is not so evident how the scores are calculated or how the feedbacks are formed. Such inability to interpret weakens confidence in the minds of teachers and students, and prompts the question of equity and precision. Thus, the issue is projected to the creation of trust-calibrated evaluation models that will be able to measure and report the credibility of AI-generated products (Xia et al., 2024). These models should include ways of estimating confidence, verifying consistency, and detecting anomalies, which the stakeholders can use to determine the trustworthiness of automated decisions. Moreover, the issues of explainability should be incorporated into the evaluation procedure where the user can comprehend why something is graded and why the feedback stories are provided. In the absence of these abilities, the implementation of AI-based assessment systems will be limited by the problem of trust and acceptance.

4. PROPOSED TAGA-CAD FRAMEWORK ARCHITECTURE

The Trust-Adaptive Generative Assessment for Competency-Aligned Design (TAGA-CAD) framework is proposed as a closed-loop, modular, and intelligent assessment architecture that redefines evaluation as a continuous, adaptive, and ethically regulated process. Unlike conventional assessment systems that operate as discrete and static events, TAGA-CAD models assessment as a dynamic interaction between learner competency states, generative intelligence, and pedagogical governance (Dhinakaran et al., 2025). The architecture integrates multiple interdependent modules that collectively enable personalized task generation, integrity-preserving evaluation, trust-aware grading, and continuous system calibration as shown in Figure 1.

Figure 1. TAGA-CAD System Architecture (Core Framework)

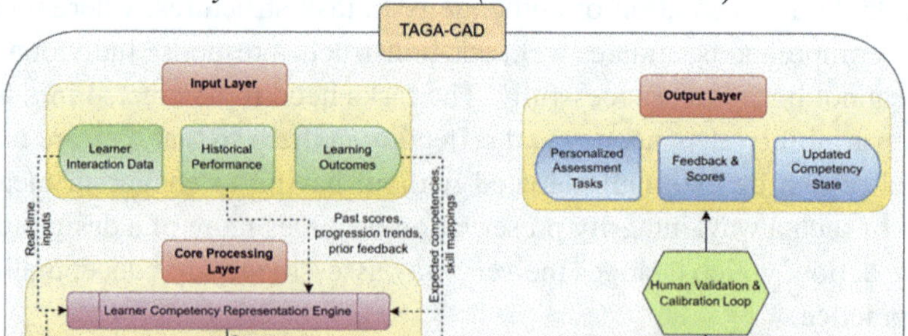

The Learner Competency Representation Engine (LCRE) is at the heart of the structure where a multidimensional competency vector is built about every learner. It is not an absolute score but a moving representation that is based on historical performance data, indicators of cognitive engagement, consistency of responses and changes in progression throughout assessment cycles. Formally, the competency state of a learner at time step t could be given as: $C(t) = \{c\ (t), c\ (t), \ldots, c\ (t)\}$ whereby every component $c_i\ (t)$ is related to a particular skill or dimension of learning outcome. This type of evolution is controlled by incremental updates that are determined by the performance of the assessment to allow the system to track the mastery progression and gaps in knowledge in real time. These competency vectors are fed into the Generative Assessment Construction Unit (GACU) that synthesizes personalized assessment tasks. The process of generation is primed around three major parameters namely, competency state C(t), desired level of difficulty D(t) and mapping learning outcomes L. Task generation role can be defined as: $T = G(C(t), D(t), L)$ where T is the assessment task generated. This designation is such that every activity is clearly related in terms of capability and the goals of the curricula that does not produce generic or irrelevant work by the learner. One important innovation in the context of TAGA-CAD is the Integrity-Resilient Task Generator (IRTG) that inserts authenticity in task design. This module implements context-driven variability and reflection-based structures as opposed to using external plagiarism detection.

The generated tasks are presented as multi-layered situations that involve sequential reasoning, justification, and adaptation to context. This drastically diminishes the capability of generating answers directly with the assistance of AI where answers have to be constructed according to individualised inputs and the changing conditions of the problem. The Trust-Adaptive Evaluation Layer (TAEL) proposes a new trust calibration algorithm of automated grading. Instead of the deterministic scores, the evaluation process gives out a tuple: $E = (S, \tau, \rho)$. S is the score, τ is confidence level, and rho is reliability consistency in terms of assessment criteria. Model agreement, response coherence, and stability of the grading generated by historical means provides confidence, whereas reliability is evaluated by evaluating cross-validation of the scoring patterns (Zhang et al., 2020). Also, the mechanisms of anomaly detection are incorporated to detect abnormal response patterns or inconsistencies that can reflect misuse or uncertainty of the model. To overcome the ethical issues, Ethical Constraint and Bias Regulator (ECBR) is constantly checking the fairness among the groups of learners. The deviation of bias may be defined as: $\beta = |\mu\ - \mu_b|$ and μ and μ_b are mean performance scores in various demographic or contextual populations. When β is greater than a predetermined threshold, the system dynamically modifies task generation parameters and evaluation weights to reestablish some fairness level. This will make the results of assessment fair and impartial in the long run.

The Human Validation and Continuous Calibration Loop (HVCCL) are a very important governance layer of the architecture. The teachers are actively involved in the active review of AI-generated works, grading system appraisal, and system revision. The loop is a way of supporting corrective intervention and the contextuality of judgment and pedagogical alignment, which is why AI is not a single system but a co-intelligent system that can be steered by human beings. The overall flow of information in TAGA-CAD can be defined in a cyclic manner: the competency vectors update is provided through the interaction of the learner, which in turn triggers the generation of the tasks; the tasks generated are evaluated by trust-calibrated processes, and their results are audited to ensure fairness and integrity; human operator manages the work of the systems as well (Dhinakaran et al., 2025). This is a closed-loop design, which enables constant adaptation, resilience and moral uprightness. With the integration of generative intelligence system and modeling of trust, integrity, and human governance, TAGA-CAD offers a new and integrated system of AI-based assessment in the higher education.

5. ADAPTIVE GENAI ASSESSMENT GENERATION MECHANISM

The competency-based generative workflow the TAGA-CAD model is based on is the adaptive assessment process that transforms the assessment into the dynamic and constantly evolving process. TAGA-CAD takes advantage of real-time competency profiles of all learners to create personalized assessment activities to contrast with more traditional systems that only utilize fixed question banks and difficulty levels to create assessments. Such an approach would also imply that each instance of the assessment is pegged uniquely to the prevailing state of mastery of the learner and clearly aligned to the desired learning outcomes. It trains the generative procedure on the competency vector, learning objective space, and a dynamically adjusted difficulty parameter enabling the system to produce contextually dependent and pedagogically meaningful evaluation exercises (Sai Aswin et al., 2023). On the ground-based competency, one can utilize the synthesis of tasks to generate questions, applied, and performance-based challenges that represent specific competency areas of the competency profile of the learner. Another type of personalization is dynamic difficulty modulation, this adds more complexity to the cognition based on the prior performance measures, confidence score, and mastery level. This ensures that the learners are neither overstretched nor understretched but are in an optimal level to be competent to use their brain fully. Simultaneously with this, individualized learning path modeling forecasts potential competency disruptions through longitudinal performance analysis and allows the system to anticipate future development of specific assessment procedures that will focus on the identification of particular areas of weakness.

The adaptive feedback orchestration is the major innovation of this mechanism. After the completion of the task, the system provides real time, context sensitive feedback not only to assess the correctness but also to provide the reasoning pathways, misconceptions, and improvement strategies. Such a feedback loop enhances learning and at the same time corrects the competency vector of the learner (Smolansky et al., 2023). The update can be formulated as: $C(t+1) = C(t) + \Delta(P, F)$, where Δ is the adjustment of performance P and feedback interpretation F. The adaptive assessment algorithm is continuously used to track the response of the learners and when mastery gaps occur it triggers the regeneration cycles. Regeneration logic provides variability of the task, unique context, and incremental progression of complexity, which is used to reduce memorization and exploitation of patterns. Also, mastery progression tracking combines the longitudinal performance indicators to confirm the learning over time improvement and re-calibrate the difficulty parameters. The result of this closed-loop adaptive process is that assessment becomes more of an intelligent learning accelerator, allowing more profound engagement and long-term advancement, as well as competency-based educational achievements.

6. INTEGRITY-PRESERVING ASSESSMENT DESIGN STRATEGY

The TAGA-CAD model redefines academic integrity as an inherent design of assessment as opposed to a post-hoc enforcement mechanism. The framework also checks integrity constraints within the generative assessment pipeline as opposed to using external detection tools to detect misconduct once the submission is received. This is done, by context-specific scenario generation, in which individual learners are introduced to dynamically-generated, real-world problem situations, under parameterization with either individual variable, data, or situational parameters (Dhinakaran et al., 2022). Formally, a task instance can be represented as $T = G(C(t), \theta)$, where θ denotes learner-specific contextual parameters. This inconsistency makes sure that no two learners face the same problem formulations and thus makes the answer replication or the generalized AI-assisted response generation much more difficult.

To make the point of authenticity even more substantial, TAGA-CAD also integrates reflection at problem structures that results in the evaluation does not center around end products, but instead the thinking of the people. The students have to come up with a method of reasoning, justifying middle-ground decisions and also be capable of criticizing other approaches. This reflective layer produces a dependency between expression and knowledge and it is difficult to get external generative tools to produce coherent and context-consistent instances without real knowledge. Multistage reasoning tasks are also used where solving a problem is in stages and the answers given form the basis of the subsequent stage. The dependency chains could be defined as the following: $S_k = f(S_k - 1, R_k)$ so the stage k depends on the previous state and the answers of the learner and therefore the generation of solutions cannot take place in one step and gradual reasoning is required.

It also involves application of realistic performance-based evaluation which are simulations of actual work-life tasks as system design, analysis of a case and applied modeling. These are synthesis, adaptation and contextualizing, which are equivalent to evaluation and practice activities in competency application compared to abstract remembrance. Such tests cannot be automated either and require original communication as well as they are personal interpretation and refinement which is an iterative process. These mechanisms make assessment design hard against abuse, resulting in a positive paradigm of integrity-sustaining mechanisms. TAGA-CAD makes the generative AI use less dangerous as it provides contextual uniqueness, reflective reasoning, problem-solving using stages and simulated settings, and promotes a more comprehensive conceptual perception, critical thought, and the creation of transferrable skills that can be used to solve problems in real life.

Figure 2. Trust–Integrity–Fairness Control Loop

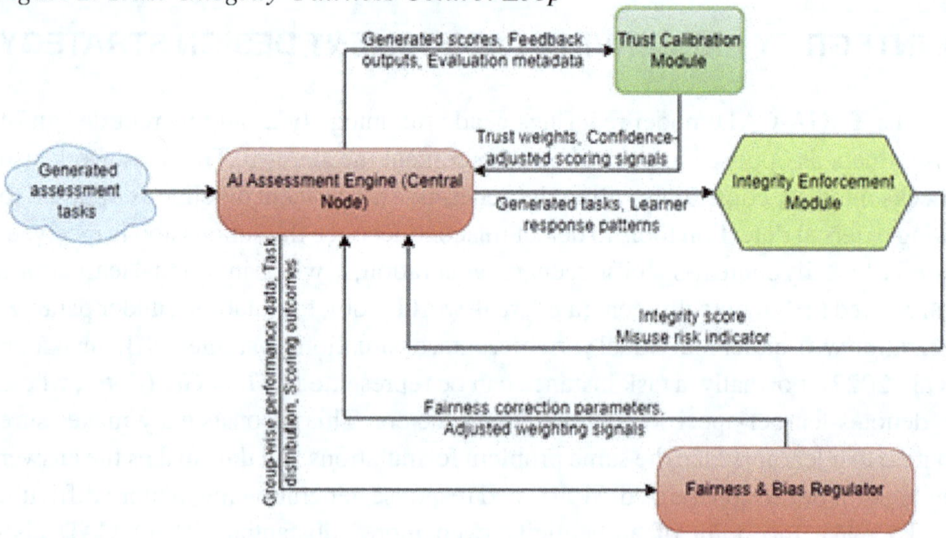

7. TRUST, BIAS, AND FAIRNESS MODELING LAYER

To guarantee reliability, transparency, and ethical soundness, the TAGA-CAD paradigm applies a Trust-Adaptive Assessment Calibration Model (TACM) to regulate the generative deliverables and automated assessment procedures. This layer converts the trust and fairness as an abstract policy principle to measurable and functional system property. In its essence, TACM presents the idea of AI output confidence scoring whereby a reliability weight is given to every single generated artifact, such as an assessment task, a feedback narrative, a grading decision, etc. The computation of this confidence score is by combining historical accuracy patterns, inter model consensus, coherence between responses and estimates of uncertainty. It can be formulated formally as confidence: $\tau = f(\alpha, \mu, \kappa)$ in which τ is the confidence, α is alignment with historical accuracy, μ is the uncertainty of the model and κ is consistency in the appraisal criteria. It means that every automated output will have an interpretable degree of reliability, allowing the system-level filtering alongside the consideration of the human-trained validation. Similar to the estimation of confidence, the framework incorporates monitoring of bias deviation to identify and measure the difference between the results of the assessment used on various groups of learners (Aruna Jasmine et al., 2021). This process reviews statistical differences in scoring patterns, distribution of tasks difficulty and feedback nature. The metric of a bias deviation may be represented as follows:

$$\beta = |E(S) - E(S_b)|$$

$E(S)$ and $E(S_b)$ are expected scores of various groups of learners. The continual violations of acceptable levels cause corrective actions in the system. In order to balance out such imbalances, the fairness constraint tuning dynamically changes both generative and evaluative parameters as illustrated in Figure 2. This involves re-calibration of difficulty distributions, adjustment of patterns of feedback generation, and re-calibration of scoring standards in order to bring equity in the treatment of different demographic, cultural and academic settings. Notably, these adjustments are not fixed but change constantly in response to the arriving assessment data, making possible the enforcement of fairness in an adaptive manner.

In addition to these mechanisms, continuous reliability auditing examines longitudinal consistency in scored decisions, consistency in feedback, and consistency with predetermined competency frameworks. This is associated with monitoring changes in the scoring behavior, identifying deviations, and confirming that the assessment results are not changing and do not have a pedagogical value over time. The auditing process serves as a systemic check, which enforces the fact that the AI is not drifting or inconsistent by guaranteeing adherence to the educational goals

(Nguyen Thanh et al., 2023). These elements, collectively, constitute a closed-loop system of calibration where trust, bias and fairness are constantly examined, judged and polished. With these controls integrated into the operational pipeline, TAGA-CAD will create a transparent, accountable and ethically based assessment environment with automated decisions being not only efficient, but also reliable, interpretable and justifiable.

8. CONCEPTUAL EVALUATION FRAMEWORK

In order to objectively evaluate the efficacy of the suggested TAGA-CAD framework, a conceptual evaluation model is created based on analytically defined metrics, which reflect pedagogical alignment, system intelligence, ethical robustness and operational reliability. In contrast with the traditional types of empirical judgments, which are based on the benchmark datasets only, this framework embraces a hybrid approach to validation that involves both the formulation of theoretical metrics and the comparative and simulation-based analysis, as shown in Figures 3 to 5. The metrics are thoroughly crafted to demonstrate a measure of the performance efficiency but also more meaningful levels of educational validity and reliability. Competency attainment accuracy provides the degree to which the results of the assessment give a true reflection of the mastery of a learner along specific dimensions of competency. It is a measure assessing how well the generated tasks, responses of the learners, and the anticipated learning outcomes match. One can take it as the relationship between the expected competency levels and the actual performance development in the long run. When the value is high, it means that the system is capturing depth of knowledge as opposed to its superficial essence. Figure 3 indicates that TAGA-CAD models a better competency alignment because it is based on the constant updating of its competency vectors and the generation of tasks based on outcomes.

Figure 3. Conceptual Comparative Performance Across Assessment Models

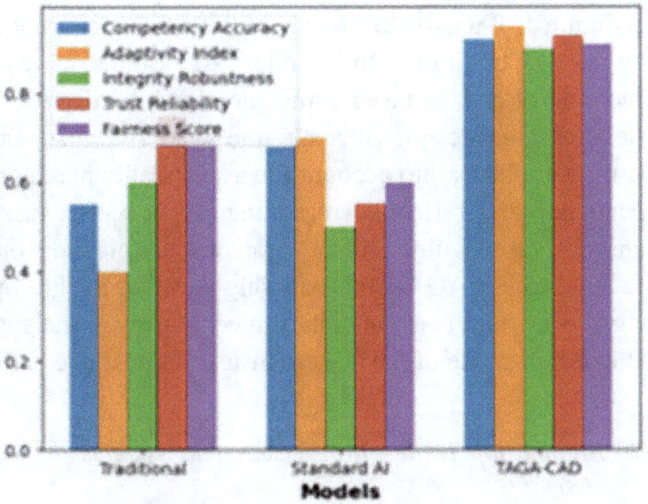

Figure 4. Adaptive Learning Progression Across Assessment Models

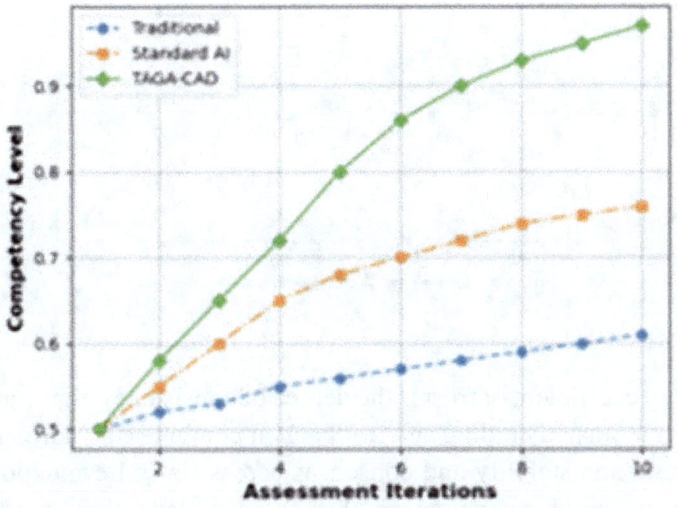

Assessment adaptivity index measures the dynamically changing difficulty and structure of tasks in a system according to the changing states of the learners. These are being responsive to changes in performance, combinability of personalisation, and rapid adaptation between assessment cycles. F formally, adaptivity may be linked to the rate of change in task complexity in regard to competency updates. As mentioned in Figure 4, TAGA-CAD demonstrates much more rapid progression curve of learning than the traditional and standard AI systems, which points to the effective adaptive control and its faster time learning. Integrity robustness score measures how the assessment design withstands the generative misuse and academic dishonesty. This measure takes into account the aspects of contextual uniqueness, multi-stage dependency and reflective reasoning needs within tasks. Increased robustness means decreased vulnerability to answer duplication or AI-assisted shortcuts. Figure 3 indicates TAGA-CAD has a high level of integrity performance because the integrity-resistant task generation mechanisms in the system ensures authenticity in the design phase of the system instead of post hoc detection.

Figure 5. Trust vs Automation Trade-off in Assessment Systems

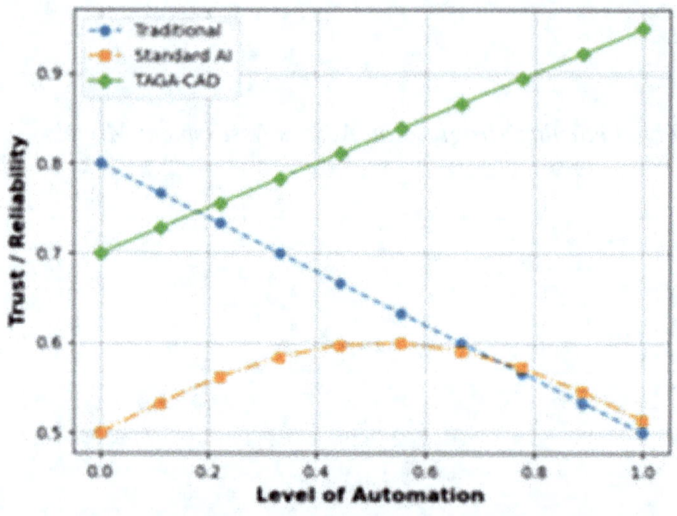

The reliability coefficient of trust is the degree of consistency, transparency, and trust relating to automated grading and feedback. It combines the normalization of confidence, evaluation stability and consensus across several evaluation criteria. This indicator is essential in showing whether AI-generated ratings can be deemed reliable when making academic decisions. Figure 5 shows that TAGA-CAD preserves and even improves reliability by its trust-adaptive calibration model unlike the traditional trade-offs where more automation results in less trust. The rate of bias deviation is used to assess fairness by estimating the differences in the results of assessments among groups of learners. It examines whether the system yields fair outcomes irrespective of the differences by demographics, culture and academic differences. Less deviation means more inclusiveness and fairness. TAGA-CAD includes fairness constraint tuning with a continuous bias monitoring making sure the deviations do not exceed reasonable limits. TAGA-CAD can be applied to empirically validate itself in a controlled educational context with longitudinal data on learners. Experimental design would include the comparisons between the TAGA-CAD and baseline systems through several assessment cycles and determining the improvements in competency development, decreases in the number of integrity violations, consistency of the grading results, and level of fairness among the learner groups. Adaptive behavior can also be tested through simulation studies that model the behavior of various learners and monitor system responsiveness. Together, these assessment constructs and pictorial studies form a stringent basis of validating TAGA-CAD as a credible, adaptable and morally upright AI-based assessment model.

9. COMPARATIVE RESEARCH ANALYSIS

In order to place the proposed TAGA-CAD framework in its context, a comparative analysis of the system level is done with three prevailing paradigm assessment, traditional Learning Management System (LMS)-based assessment, typical AI-enabled auto-grading tools, and fixed online quiz systems. This analogy does not stop at the level of functional abilities but goes deeper to the higher levels of pedagogical fit, moral strength, and adaptive intelligence. Conventional LMS-based assessment (systems) is mainly focused on being scalable and convenient to the administration, based on a fixed bank of questions, preset grading rubrics and have a periodic cycle of evaluation. Although these systems have a fairly high degree of institutional trust because of human control, they are not adaptive and do not reflect the dynamic progress of the learners. Competency alignment is frequently informal instead of being explicitly modelled, which means that it has only a little support to individual learning paths.

Partially automated Standard AI-based auto-grading tools allow quick grading of assignments and feedback generation. But these systems are normally limited to the use of the fixed input formats and do not have the competency-based task generation. In addition, they have their lack of transparency as well as a lack of trust calibration mechanisms, which brings about the issue of reliability and fairness concerns. The preservation of integrity is poor as well, and these tools do not inherently resist the generative misuse, but rely on external detection. The most limited type of AI-assisted assessment is the form of assessment that utilizes static online quiz platforms, which are commonly utilized in digital education settings. Such systems are based on non-authorable questions and have low levels of personalization, which mean low adaptivity and low correspondence to higher-order learning outcomes. Even though they are simple to implement, they are prone to memorization effects and cannot provide integrity-aware and context-sensitive evaluation.

In comparison, TAGA-CAD framework proposes a common architecture whereby adaptivity, trust, integrity, fairness, and competency alignment is closed looped into a system. In contrast to the current methods, TAGA-CAD generates assessment tasks in real-time and depending on competency states, which guarantees the strict adherence to the learning goals. Its trust-adaptive evaluation layer improves reliability by scoring on confidence and consistency validation and the integrity-resistant task design reduces abuse by introducing authenticity into the assessment design. Moreover, the concept of fairness is proactively controlled by bias monitoring and adaptive correction systems, which guarantee equal results in different groups of learners. The comparative analysis in all important dimensions is summarized in Table 1.

Table 1. System-Level Comparison of Assessment Paradigms

Dimension	Traditional LMS	Standard AI Tools	Static Quizzes	TAGA-CAD
Adaptivity	Low	Moderate	Very Low	High
Trust Calibration	High (manual)	Low	Low	High (adaptive)
Integrity Preservation	Moderate	Low	Very Low	High (design-embedded)
Fairness Regulation	Limited	Minimal	None	Continuous & dynamic
Competency Alignment	Implicit	Partial	Weak	Explicit & dynamic
Feedback Quality	Static	Semi-dynamic	Limited	Real-time & contextual
Personalization	Minimal	Moderate	None	Fully adaptive

This comparative analysis clearly demonstrates that existing systems operate in isolation across individual dimensions, whereas TAGA-CAD provides a holistic and integrated solution. By simultaneously addressing adaptivity, trust, integrity, fairness, and competency alignment, the proposed framework establishes a new paradigm for AI-driven assessment. The results align with the conceptual evaluation presented in Section 8, reinforcing the theoretical superiority and practical relevance of TAGA-CAD as a next-generation assessment architecture.

10. IMPLEMENTATION PATHWAY FOR HIGHER EDUCATION SYSTEMS

Implementing the TAGA-CAD framework in higher education centers successfully necessitates an organized and multi-layered implementation channel that incorporates the technological infrastructure, educational processes, administrative policies, and moral protection. In contrast to traditional evaluation instruments, which can be implemented as freestanding systems, TAGA-CAD is an ecosystem level architecture, which requires the co-ordination of institutional, instructional and technical realms. On system level, the system model should be able to support the smooth interoperability of TAGA-CAD modules with the current digital learning platforms like Learning Management Systems (LMS), student information systems, and analytics platforms. This is possible via a modular service-oriented architecture where all the core components, competency representation engine, generative assessment unit, trust evaluation layer and bias regulator are independent and yet interrelated services. The exchange of real-time data is provided by APIs and middleware layers, which allow constantly updating learner competency profiles, building dynamically generated tasks. Notably, both directions of data flow should be supported by integration, as the learner interactions should threaten the system adaptation and the system output should be reflected in the institutional performance tracking. The deployment model on the clouds can also be used to increase the factor of scalability, whereby the institution can effectively handle high and diverse number of learners and still be computationally cffcctivc.

The design of faculty oversight work flows is equally of key importance to implementation since it ensures that the educators are at the center of the assessment process. In the TAGA-CAD model, the role of the instructor is changed by the role of the supervisor, who is evaluated as a calibrator of the system and a grader that is not manual. The interfaces of the faculties should be transparent and allow access to AI-driven tasks, feedback, and confidence rates as well as indicators of fairness to allow informed review and intervention. Teachers need to be capable of authenticating generated materials, reverse automated judgments as needed, and alter system settings to conform to disciplinary imperatives. The workflow pipelines must have human checking points at critical points which include task approval, grading validation, and anomaly remedy. Also, the faculty training initiatives are necessary in order to develop digital literacy and confidence in dealing with AI-based systems so that human expertise will not replace but support the work of algorithmic intelligence.

The TAGA-CAD implementation is based on the institutional foundations of governance alignment. Universities have to develop effective policies and operational guidelines that present the acceptable use of generative AI in assessment. This involves establishment of transparency, accountability, and auditability standards of AI-generated outputs. The governing systems ought to include supervisory committees that would manage the performance of the systems, review the bias reports, and make sure that the academic regulations are adhered to. The governance of data is especially important because TAGA-CAD is based on the constant gathering and processing of data on learners. Strict data protection systems, anonymization, and access controls should be implemented to protect the privacy of students in institutions. Additionally, the governance models are expected to facilitate an ongoing audit of the system, in which such performance indicators as trust reliability, bias deviation, and integrity robustness are regularly assessed and reported.

A deployment plan is necessary, which must be ethical to make sure that the combination of TAGA-CAD is in line with the greater values and expectations of society. The issues of ethics need to be incorporated throughout the lifecycle of deployment, including system design and its actual use. There should be transparency mechanisms that would inform the learners about the way the assessments are created, graded and modified to gain trust and acceptance. The explainability capabilities in the trust-adaptive evaluation layer can give justifiable explanations of grading decisions and feedbacks and allow learners to comprehend and participate in the assessment process. Inequality should be actively corrected by observing bias and adapting to its introduction where it is necessary, especially in multicultural and diverse schools. Besides, the institutions are advised to use a gradual implementation strategy that will start with pilot implementation in chosen courses or departments. This enables experimentation, refinement, and feedback of the stakeholders prior to the full-scale adoption. Pilot studies may test the performance of the system on varied disciplines, learner types, and types of assessment that may give informative findings on the scalability and flexibility. Feedback must be incorporated systematically in both educator and learner to improve usability, acceptance and pedagogical effectiveness. Lastly, the mechanisms of continuous improvement should be entrenched in the implementation pathway. TAGA-CAD must not be considered a fixed system, but rather, it is a dynamic system that adjusts to new educational demands, changes in technology, and the progress of policies. Generative models, calibration parameters, and ethical guidelines need to be updated on a regular basis, to keep the system relevant and reliable. The TAGA-CAD implementation can help institutions of higher education to evolve into intelligent, trustworthy, and future-proof assessment ecosystems by implementing system-level interoperability, human-centred workflows, governance structures, and ethical protections.

11. RESEARCH CHALLENGES AND FUTURE DIRECTIONS

The development of AI-assessment systems like TAGA-CAD creates a revolutionary opportunity and, at the same time, increases the complex research issues that need to be explored over time. The shift in generative technology usage should focus more on understanding the model that is more functional and how it can influence learning in the future, rather than on the interpretability, inclusivity, scalability, and long-term educational effects. However, despite the fact that the suggested framework provides a powerful basis of adaptive, trustful, and integrity-based assessment, there are a number of essential dimensions that can be developed further. They are the necessity to have explainable generative assessment systems, the multimodal competency assessment integration, creation of cross-cultural fairness models, and the addition of longitudinal learning analytics. These issues are necessary not only to improve the functioning of the system but to guarantee that AI-based assessment is relevant to various educational settings and is responsive to the changing requirements of the pedagogue. In the below subsections, there are presented major research directions that could be used to expand and improve the TAGA-CAD framework to more comprehensive, transparent, and internationally applicable assessment ecosystems.

11.1 Explainable GenAI Assessment Systems

The most urgent issue concerning AI-based assessment is the inability to explain generative models that are employed in the creation of tasks, grading, and providing feedback. Although TAGA-CAD presents the idea of trust calibration, the insider-processes of generative AI-based systems tend to be obscure, preventing educators and learners to understand them. Explainable GenAI assessment systems could help address this gap by offering clear and human-readable explanations of generated tasks and evaluation results. This is done by creating models that are capable of tracing explicitly how the parameters of input, e.g. the competency vectors and difficulty levels, affect the task generation and scoring decisions.

One direction of research is to incorporate explainability layers that can break down AI outputs into explainable entities, e.g., reasoning patterns, feature significance, and decision logic. As an example, the grading of outputs may be supplemented by detailed explanations of what details in the response of a learner earned the most points in the overall grade. Likewise, generation of feedback may be accompanied by rationale-based accounts that may be congruent with the pedagogical expectations. The second significant element is the creation of interactive explanation interfaces where educators can ask, confirm, and update the AI decisions in real-time. But, the explainability of generative systems is technically difficult, especially with large language models, which are complex and non-deterministic. They have to balance model performance and interpretability as a trade-off. Future studies should be addressed on the hybrid techniques in which symbolic reasoning is integrated with generative abilities to produce both good quality as well as transparent decision-making. The development of explainable GenAI assessment systems will become essential to inspire trust, responsibility, and general acceptance in the educational setting.

11.2 Multimodal Competency Evaluation

In this section, the study will assess multimodal competency by conducting an evaluation of the objective domains: verbal, non-verbal, knowledge, and skills domains. In this section, the research will evaluate multimodal competency through the objective domains that will be evaluated; the verbal, non-verbal, knowledge and skills domains. In the majority of forms of traditional assessment systems, including most AI-based methods, the primary inputs and outputs are in the form of text, thus restricting the range of competencies that these methods can assess. Educational settings in the modern world are becoming more and more demanding regarding the assessment of various skills that include visual reasoning, problem-solving, teamwork, and practice and cannot be properly evaluated based on textual responses alone. Multimodal competency evaluation is the answer to this limitation, as it suggests engaging various data modalities, such as text, audio, video, and interaction patterns in the assessment process. In the context of TAGA-CAD, a multimodal input competency representation would allow the more sophisticated and detailed learner profiling. To take an example, the knowledge of a student about a concept might be tested using the combination of written explanations, verbal answers, and demonstrations. Equally, performance type activities, which might include simulations, coding activities or design projects, can be used to get more insight into applied skills. Multimodal assessment tasks, including interactive or problem-solving problems, can be adapted to generative AI models and make them more engaging and authentic. Nevertheless, multimodal assessment creates tremendous problems pertaining to data integration, model complexity and standardization. It is necessary to have complex fusion mechanisms and effective validation schemes to ensure that the interpretation is consistent across various modalities. Also, the gathering and processing of multimodal data have issues of privacy, storage and computing overhead. Future studies should aim at coming up with unified multimodal frameworks that can easily combine different data sources without compromising scalability and reliability. Multimodal evaluation can help AI-based systems of assessment become much more relevant and effective by allowing one to evaluate the competencies of a learner holistically.

11.3 Cross-Cultural Fairness Modeling

With AI-based assessment systems being applied in a variety of educational settings, the problem of fairness in terms of culture, language, and socio-economic background becomes one of the most pressing issues. Current models of fairness are usually concerned with the idea of demographic parity or reduction in statistical biases but do not take into consideration a broader cultural dimension that can affect the nature of learning, its communication patterns, and how to interpret assessment activities. The cross-cultural fairness modeling is aimed to overcome these limitations and introduce contextual awareness into designing and evaluating the AI-based assessment systems. Fairness in the TAGA-CAD should not just be limited to handle the numerical bias in a specific manner, but rather apply cultural sensitivity to the task generation, feedback provision and evaluation criteria. An example is that the generative models must be able to adjust the complexity of languages, contextual references, and problem situations to the culture of the learners. Equally, grading systems should take into consideration the differences in the form of expression, and way of reasoning so that the learners are not disadvantaged because of cultural backgrounds.

The creation of such models will demand the combination of various training data, culturally sensitive representation of features, and adaptive assessment approaches. Nevertheless, in some cases, it is difficult to define fairness in heterogeneous situations and prevent over-generalization or stereotyping. Also, the transparency and accountability must be ensured in making fair adjustments to ensure trust. Future studies ought to examine setting-specific justices systems that are capable of dynamically adjusting to cultural changes without compromising consistency and justice. This will be critical especially to the international educational systems and transnational learning systems.

11.4 Longitudinal Learning Analytics

The key shortcoming of most available systems of assessment is that they concentrate more on short-term evaluation as opposed to long-term learning trajectory. Longitudinal learning analytics is a solution to this issue that examines the performance of learners over longer durations, which allows a deeper understanding of knowledge building, skills acquisition, and learning behaviours. In the context of the TAGA-CAD, longitudinal analytics can go a long way to improve the competency modeling and adaptive assessment mechanisms. The system also helps to detect trends by monitoring performance in a series of evaluation periods, including consistent growth, stagnation, or decline in particular dimensions of competencies. This allows making assessment tasks and interventions more specific. Indicatively, students who exhibit enduring deficiencies in definite skills can be given special tests and feedback that targets the gaps. Also, predictive analytics can be supported by longitudinal data, as the system can be able to predict the future performance trends and change the learning pathways ahead.

Nonetheless, the application of longitudinal analytics is associated with data management, scaling, interpretation, and challenges. Historical data in large quantities need to be stored, processed and analyzed effectively and data privacy and security maintained. Furthermore, to extract meaningful information using longitudinal data, the highest level of modeling is needed that can address the effects of time and changes in context. Future studies ought to involve coming up with scalable analytics systems, incorporation of time modeling procedures and establishment of standard measurements of evaluating long-term learning. Through the insights of the long run, AI-based assessment systems are able to leave episodic evaluation in favor of continuous and sustained learning optimization.

CONCLUSION

The fast adoption of generative AI in higher education assessment has the potential to transform assessment and introduce significant pedagogical threats. Although currently used AI-based technology has been mostly focused on automation and efficiency, it is not always able to meet fundamental educational needs of competency alignment, academic integrity, trustworthiness and ethical accountability. This chapter developed the discussion by suggesting the Trust-Adaptive Generative Assessment framework (TAGA-CAD) as a new systems-oriented architecture that redefines assessment as an ongoing, accommodative and ethically mediated learning experience. Through the combination of competency-based task synthesis, integrity-conscious evaluation systems, trust-calibrated evaluation systems, regulation of fairness, and human monitoring integrated within a combined closed-loop framework, TAGA-CAD will go beyond AI adoption on the surface toward intelligent assessment ecosystems, which are pedagogically based.

The model also brings into focus the strategic utility of the generative technologies to customize learning pathways, facilitate profound cognitive process and improve formative feedback whilst maintaining the academic integrity at the same time. Furthermore, introduction of the trust-adaptive calibration and ethical control layers provides a viable avenue towards bias reduction, reliability, and transparency in the automated assessment systems. All of this makes TAGA-CAD one of the potential foundational research models of an AI-assisted assessment design in the next generation. This study may be further expanded in future research by means of empirical validation, multimodal competency assessment, and explainable assessment intelligence, which will further underpin the position of generative AI as a responsible and transformative agent in higher education.

REFERENCES

Agostini, D., & Picasso, F. (2024). Large language models for sustainable assessment and feedback in higher education. Intelligenza Artificiale., 10.3233_IA-240033. DOI: 10.3233/IA-240033

Aruna Jasmine, J., Nisha Jenipher, V., Richard Jimreeves, J. S., Ravindran, K., & Dhinakaran, D. "A traceability set up using digitalization of data and accessibility," International Conference on Intelligent Sustainable Systems (ICISS), IEEE Xplore, Tirunelveli, India, pp. 907-910, 2021. DOI: DOI: 10.1109/ICISS49785.2020.9315938

Chiu, T. K. (2024). Future research recommendations for transforming higher education with generative AI. *Computers and Education: Artificial Intelligence, 6*, 100197. DOI: 10.1016/j.caeai.2023.100197

Dhinakaran, D., Edwin, S., Gopalakrishnan, S., Selvaraj, D., & Lalitha, S. D. (2025). UNCA: A Neutrosophic-Based Framework for Robust Clustering and Enhanced Data Interpretation. *International Journal of Neutrosophic Science, 25*(4), 176–192. DOI: 10.54216/IJNS.250415

Dhinakaran, D., Gopalakrishnan, S., Selvaraj, D., Girija, M. S., & Prabaharan, G. (2025). Mining privacy-preserving association rules using transaction hewer allocator and facile hash algorithm in multi-cloud environments. *MethodsX, 14*, 103317. DOI: 10.1016/j.mex.2025.103317 PMID: 40331027

Dhinakaran, D., Kumar, D. A., Dinesh, S., Selvaraj, D., & Srikanth, K. Recommendation System for Research Studies Based on GCR, *2022 International Mobile and Embedded Technology Conference (MECON)*, Noida, India, (2022) 61-65, DOI: 10.1109/MECON53876.2022.9751920

Dhinakaran, D., Ramani, R., Edwin Raja, S., & Selvaraj, D. (2026). Enhancing clinical data security with the contextual polynomial-based data protection model (CPDPM). *Biomedical Signal Processing and Control, 111*, 108329. DOI: 10.1016/j.bspc.2025.108329

Gruenhagen, J. H., Sinclair, P. M., Carroll, J., Baker, P. R., Wilson, A., & Demant, D. (2024). The rapid rise of generative AI and its implications for academic integrity: Students' perceptions and use of chatbots for assistance with assessments. *Computers and Education: Artificial Intelligence, 7*, 100273. DOI: 10.1016/j.caeai.2024.100273

Ilieva, G., Yankova, T., Ruseva, M., & Kabaivanov, S. (2025). A Framework for Generative AI-Driven Assessment in Higher Education. *Information (Basel), 16*(6), 472. Advance online publication. DOI: 10.3390/info16060472

Khlaif, Z. N., Alkouk, W. A., Salama, N., & Eideh, B. A. (2025). Redesigning Assessments for AI-Enhanced Learning: A Framework for Educators in the Generative AI Era. *Education Sciences*, *15*(2), 174. Advance online publication. DOI: 10.3390/educsci15020174

Nguyen Thanh, B., Vo, D. T. H., Nguyen Nhat, M., Pham, T. T. T., Thai Trung, H., & Ha Xuan, S. (2023). Race with the machines: Assessing the capability of generative AI in solving authentic assessments. *Australasian Journal of Educational Technology*, *39*(5), 59–81. DOI: 10.14742/ajet.8902

Sai Aswin, B. G., Vishnubala, S., Dhinakaran, D., Kumar, N. J., Udhaya Sankar, S. M., & Mohamed Al Faisal, A. M. (2023). "A Research on Metaverse and its Application," 2023 World Conference on Communication & Computing (WCONF), RAIPUR, India, pp. 1-6, DOI: 10.1109/WCONF58270.2023.10235216

Smolansky, A., Cram, A., Raduescu, C., Zeivots, S., Huber, E., & Kizilcec, R. F. (2023). Educator and Student Perspectives on the Impact of Generative AI on Assessments in Higher Education. In Proceedings of the Tenth ACM Conference on Learning @ Scale (L@S '23). Association for Computing Machinery, New York, NY, USA, 378–382. DOI: 10.1145/3573051.3596191

Xia, Q., Weng, X., Ouyang, F., Lin, T. J., & Chiu, T. K. F. (2024). A scoping review on how generative artificial intelligence transforms assessment in higher education. *International Journal of Educational Technology in Higher Education*, *21*(1), 40. DOI: 10.1186/s41239-024-00468-z

Xia, Q., Weng, X., Ouyang, F., Lin, T. J., & Chiu, T. K. F. (2024). A scoping review on how generative artificial intelligence transforms assessment in higher education. *International Journal of Educational Technology in Higher Education*, *21*(1), 40. DOI: 10.1186/s41239-024-00468-z

Zhang, L., Yang, S., & Carter, R. A. (2020). Personalized learning and ESSA: What we know and where we go. *Journal of Research on Technology in Education*, *52*(3), 253–274. DOI: 10.1080/15391523.2020.1728448

Chapter 6
Adaptive and Personalized Assessment Pathways Enabled by GenAI

Mustafa Kayyali
http://orcid.org/0000-0003-3300-262X
Maaref University of Applied Sciences, Syria

ABSTRACT

Assessment in higher education is no longer confined to fixed tests, uniform rubrics, or end-point measurement. With the rise of Generative AI, assessment can become more adaptive, dialogic, and responsive to the diverse ways students learn, struggle, and demonstrate understanding. This chapter explores how GenAI can support personalized assessment pathways that adjust tasks, feedback, pacing, and learning evidence according to individual learner needs. Rather than treating assessment as a mechanical process of grading, the chapter frames it as a living pedagogical encounter—one that can guide reflection, reveal hidden misconceptions, and encourage deeper intellectual growth. At the same time, it critically examines concerns around bias, transparency, over-reliance, data ethics, and academic integrity. The chapter argues for a human-centered approach in which GenAI strengthens, rather than replaces, the professional judgment of educators.

INTRODUCTION

Assessment has always carried a quiet tension within higher education (Sharma & Gupta, 2023). On the surface, it appears to be a practical mechanism: students submit

DOI: 10.4018/979-8-3373-9089-5.ch006

work, instructors evaluate it, marks are recorded, and institutions certify achievement. Yet beneath this administrative routine lies something far more consequential. Assessment shapes how students understand knowledge, how they judge their own abilities, how they decide whether they belong in a discipline, and how teachers interpret the hidden movements of learning. It is never merely a final checkpoint. It is a signal system, a mirror, a gate, a conversation, and sometimes, unfortunately, a source of anxiety that narrows the very learning it is supposed to support.

For decades, many assessment systems in higher education have depended on standardization. This is understandable. Universities need fairness, comparability, accountability, and evidence (Aloisi, 2023). A class of two hundred students cannot always be assessed through deeply individualized dialogue. A department must defend its grading practices. A degree must mean something beyond the subjective judgment of one instructor. Standardized rubrics, fixed exams, common assignments, and uniform marking criteria have therefore played an important role in protecting academic credibility. Still, the cost of this standardization has become increasingly visible. Students do not enter higher education with identical histories, learning rhythms, linguistic resources, cultural expectations, disciplinary confidence, or cognitive habits. A single assessment pathway may appear fair because it treats everyone the same, but sameness is not always justice. Sometimes it merely hides difference under a neat institutional surface.

This is where the idea of adaptive and personalized assessment pathways becomes especially significant. Rather than asking every learner to move through the same assessment route at the same pace and in the same form, adaptive assessment seeks to respond to the learner's development as it unfolds. It asks a different set of questions. What does this student already understand? Where is the misunderstanding located? What kind of feedback might help at this moment? Should the next task be more challenging, more scaffolded, more reflective, more applied, or more diagnostic? What evidence of learning matters most here? Such questions move assessment away from a rigid model of measurement and toward a more responsive model of educational guidance.

Generative AI adds a powerful and complicated new layer to this discussion. Unlike earlier digital assessment tools that mainly automated scoring or delivered pre-set quizzes, GenAI systems can generate questions, simulate dialogue, offer formative feedback, adapt prompts, summarize patterns of performance, and support students in revising their understanding over time (Webb, M., & Galamba, 2026). Used thoughtfully, these systems can make assessment feel less like a closed judgment and more like an evolving pathway. A student struggling with a concept in economics, engineering, language learning, medicine, or teacher education may receive immediate explanations, alternative examples, practice tasks, and feedback loops that would be difficult for one instructor to provide continuously at scale.

Similarly, teachers may gain richer diagnostic insight into where students are confused, how their reasoning develops, and what kinds of support are needed before failure becomes permanent.

Yet the promise of GenAI should not be romanticized. Higher education has seen many technologies arrive with inflated claims of transformation. Too often, the language of innovation conceals older problems in newer packaging. A tool that personalizes badly may reinforce bias. A system that gives instant feedback may also give shallow or misleading feedback. An adaptive pathway may become a quiet form of tracking if students are placed into narrower learning routes based on incomplete data. A chatbot may encourage reflection, but it may also tempt students into dependence, shortcutting, or intellectual passivity. The central issue, therefore, is not whether GenAI can be used in assessment. It already can. The more urgent question is how it can be designed, governed, and pedagogically situated so that it supports human learning rather than simply accelerating institutional efficiency.

This chapter approaches GenAI-enabled assessment as both a technical possibility and a pedagogical responsibility. It argues that adaptive and personalized assessment should not be reduced to algorithmic adjustment or automated convenience. At its best, it is a deeply educational practice rooted in attentiveness: attentiveness to learners' needs, to disciplinary standards, to context, to equity, and to the fragile relationship between judgment and growth. GenAI may help instructors create more varied forms of assessment, provide timely formative feedback, support self-regulated learning, and recognize diverse demonstrations of competence (Yilmaz et al, 2026). However, these benefits depend on careful design. The educator's role does not disappear; in fact, it becomes more important. Teachers must interpret, question, frame, validate, and humanize what AI systems produce.

The chapter therefore examines how GenAI can enable adaptive assessment pathways in higher education while also confronting the ethical and pedagogical risks that accompany such systems. It considers the shift from one-size-fits-all assessment toward flexible evidence-based progression, the role of AI-generated feedback in supporting learner agency, and the challenges of transparency, bias, data privacy, academic integrity, and over-automation. Above all, it insists that assessment should remain a human-centered practice. GenAI may widen the possibilities of assessment, but it should not be allowed to flatten its moral and educational meaning. The real task is not to build assessment systems that are merely faster or more personalized in a superficial sense. The task is to design pathways that help students become more aware of their thinking, more capable of improvement, and more confident in their own intellectual development.

RETHINKING ASSESSMENT IN THE AGE OF GENERATIVE AI: FROM STANDARDIZATION TO RESPONSIVENESS

Assessment in higher education has long lived under the shadow of standardization (Awashreh et al, 2024). The logic is familiar, almost comforting in its neatness: define learning outcomes, design tasks, apply criteria, assign grades, record achievement. It sounds orderly. It sounds fair. It sounds, at least on paper, like the kind of system a university can defend before students, accreditation bodies, employers, and society at large. Yet anyone who has spent real time in classrooms, laboratories, studios, seminars, or online learning spaces knows that learning rarely unfolds with such administrative tidiness. Students do not understand at the same speed. They do not misunderstand in the same way. They do not bring equal confidence, language resources, disciplinary habits, prior schooling, emotional resilience, or familiarity with academic conventions. The standardized assessment model may promise fairness by treating learners uniformly, but uniform treatment can become strangely indifferent when human difference is not a marginal detail but the very substance of education.

This does not mean that standardization has no value. It would be too easy, and frankly too naïve, to dismiss it as a bureaucratic relic. Higher education needs shared expectations. It needs recognizable standards. A medical student cannot be assessed through pure personal preference. An engineering graduate must demonstrate competence that reaches beyond private interpretation. A teacher, architect, nurse, lawyer, scientist, or researcher must be judged against criteria that protect public trust. Standardization, at its best, gives assessment a common language. It reduces arbitrariness. It helps institutions avoid the chaos of purely subjective evaluation. The problem begins when standardization hardens into sameness, when it mistakes procedural consistency for educational justice, and when it assumes that the same task, given under the same conditions, tells the whole truth about what students know, can do, or are becoming capable of doing.

The age of Generative AI unsettles this arrangement in a profound way (Manu, 2024). Not because it simply introduces new tools into existing assessment routines, but because it exposes the fragility of those routines. A fixed essay, a take-home assignment, a generic quiz, or a conventional reflective response no longer carries the same evidentiary certainty it once did. Students can now generate drafts, explanations, summaries, code, arguments, translations, and problem-solving steps within seconds. Some educators have responded to this with suspicion, even alarm, and the reaction is understandable. Assessment has always depended on a delicate assumption: that the submitted work meaningfully represents the student's own effort and understanding. GenAI complicates that assumption. But it also forces a more honest question. Were many conventional assessment tasks ever as authentic, personal, or intellectually revealing as universities imagined them to be?

A standardized assessment often captures performance at a particular moment, under particular conditions, in response to a predetermined task (Mancuso et al, 2024). That can be useful, but it is limited. It may show what a student can reproduce, organize, or perform when prompted. It may not show how the student thinks when confused, how they revise after feedback, how they transfer knowledge across contexts, how they negotiate ambiguity, or how they grow over time. Generative AI, if treated merely as a threat to academic integrity, narrows the conversation. If treated more thoughtfully, it invites a shift from assessment as static verification toward assessment as responsive inquiry. The central issue becomes less "How do we prevent students from using AI?" and more "What kinds of assessment remain meaningful when intelligent tools are part of the learning environment?"

Responsiveness begins with the recognition that assessment should not only measure learning after it has happened. It should participate in learning while it is still taking shape. This distinction matters. A standardized test may identify that a student failed to grasp a concept, but a responsive assessment system asks why, where, and what might help next. Is the difficulty conceptual? Linguistic? Procedural? Motivational? Does the student lack background knowledge, or are they applying knowledge in an unfamiliar form? Have they memorized terminology without internalizing relationships? Are they afraid to take intellectual risks because previous schooling rewarded obedience more than inquiry? These questions cannot be answered by a score alone. They require interpretation, feedback, adjustment, and, above all, attention.

Generative AI can support this movement toward responsiveness by making formative interaction more available. It can generate alternative explanations when students stumble. It can produce practice tasks at varying degrees of difficulty. It can help learners compare their reasoning against models, identify gaps in drafts, rehearse arguments, or receive immediate feedback before submitting final work. For instructors, GenAI may assist in identifying patterns across student responses, suggesting differentiated prompts, creating scenario-based tasks, or designing iterative assessment sequences. In large classes especially, where the teacher's desire to give meaningful feedback often collides with the cruel arithmetic of time, such support can be significant. The promise is not that AI will replace teacher judgment. The promise, more modest and more powerful, is that it may help create spaces where feedback is less delayed, less generic, and less detached from the learner's immediate struggle.

Figure 1. Shift from Standardized Assessment toward Responsive GenAI-Enabled Assessment

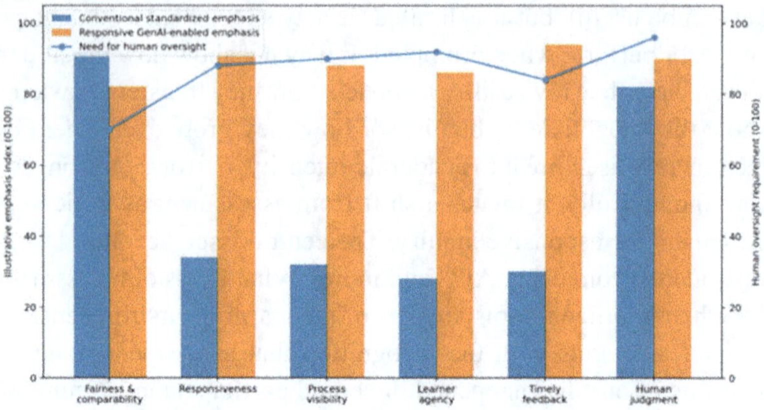

Still, responsiveness must not be confused with endless customization. There is a subtle danger here. In the language of educational technology, personalization is often presented as an unquestioned good, as if adapting everything to the individual automatically produces deeper learning. But higher education is not a private consumer service, and students are not merely users moving through optimized content streams. They are participants in intellectual traditions, communities of practice, disciplinary debates, and public forms of knowledge. A responsive assessment pathway should not isolate each learner inside a personalized bubble where challenge is softened too quickly or standards become invisible. Sometimes students need support. Sometimes they need friction. Sometimes they need to sit with difficulty longer than they would prefer. Good assessment does not simply adapt to the learner's comfort; it adapts to the learner's growth.

This is why GenAI-enabled assessment must be guided by pedagogy rather than novelty. A system that automatically adjusts tasks based only on previous performance may appear intelligent, yet still operate with a narrow understanding of learning. If a student performs poorly, should the next task become easier? Perhaps. Or perhaps the student needs a different representation of the concept, a peer discussion, a worked example, a reflective pause, or a more authentic problem that gives meaning to abstract material. Human teachers often understand these nuances because they read more than answers. They read hesitation, tone, context, effort, silence, and the small signs of emerging confidence. GenAI can help surface data, but it cannot fully inhabit the relational texture of teaching. Responsiveness without human interpretation risks becoming adaptive machinery: efficient, impressive, and educationally thin.

The shift from standardization to responsiveness also asks universities to reconsider what counts as evidence. In traditional assessment, evidence is often treated as a product: an exam paper, a report, a presentation, a portfolio, a project. In a GenAI-rich environment, the process behind the product becomes more important. How was the work developed? What decisions did the student make? Where did they use AI, and why? How did they evaluate its output? What did they reject, revise, question, or extend? A polished final answer may reveal less than a messy trail of thinking. The draft, the annotation, the oral explanation, the revision history, the critique of AI-generated material, the reflective commentary—these may become central pieces of assessment evidence. In this sense, GenAI does not necessarily weaken assessment. It may push assessment toward richer forms of intellectual visibility (Montebello, 2025).

There is also an equity dimension that cannot be brushed aside. Standardized assessment often assumes that all students have equal access to the codes of academic performance. They do not. Some students know how to write in ways that please the university before they even arrive. Others must learn not only the subject matter but the hidden grammar of academic success: how to frame an argument, how to interpret a rubric, how to signal confidence, how to ask for clarification, how to recover from critique without feeling personally diminished. GenAI tools may help demystify some of these codes by providing explanations, examples, and rehearsal opportunities. Yet the same tools may deepen inequality if access is uneven, if wealthier students use more advanced systems, or if AI feedback privileges dominant linguistic and cultural styles. Responsiveness, then, must be ethical as well as technical. It must ask who benefits, who is misread, who is nudged into lower expectations, and who is silently excluded by the assumptions built into the system.

The more one thinks about it, the more assessment begins to look less like a technical procedure and more like a moral practice. To assess a student is to make a claim about their learning, but also to influence their future learning. A careless grade can close a door in the student's mind. A timely piece of feedback can reopen one. A rigid assessment structure can tell students, without saying it openly, that there is only one acceptable way to be intelligent. A responsive structure can say something different: that learning has patterns, detours, hesitations, recoveries, and multiple forms of evidence. This does not dilute academic rigor. On the contrary, it may deepen it. Rigor is not the same as inflexibility. Serious learning requires standards, but standards become more educationally meaningful when students are given thoughtful pathways toward meeting them.

Generative AI has entered higher education at a moment when assessment was already under pressure (Sol et al, 2025). Massification, online learning, diverse student populations, employability demands, academic integrity concerns, and mental health challenges had already stretched conventional models. GenAI did not create all these tensions; it made them harder to ignore. The old assessment bargain—same task, same deadline, same criteria, final grade—will not disappear, nor should it in every context. But it can no longer stand as the unquestioned center of assessment design. Universities now have an opportunity, perhaps even an obligation, to imagine assessment as something more dialogic, developmental, and responsive.

The real question is not whether higher education should abandon standardization. It should not. The question is where standardization is necessary, where it is insufficient, and where it has quietly become a substitute for genuine educational attention. GenAI can either reinforce the old model by making standardized assessment faster, cheaper, and more automated, or it can help open a different path—one in which assessment listens more carefully, responds more intelligently, and treats students not as identical units moving through a system, but as developing thinkers whose learning deserves to be seen in motion (Lee, 2025). That, perhaps, is the deeper promise: not assessment made easier, but assessment made more alive.

ADAPTIVE ASSESSMENT PATHWAYS: PERSONALIZATION, LEARNER AGENCY, AND EVIDENCE-BASED PROGRESSION

Adaptive assessment pathways begin from a simple but often neglected premise: students do not move through learning in straight, identical lines. Some advance quickly at first and then stumble when abstraction deepens. Others appear hesitant for weeks, almost invisible in the classroom rhythm, before suddenly producing work that shows a quiet and rather beautiful consolidation of thought. Some students need more examples; others need fewer examples and more space to wrestle with uncertainty. A few are harmed by over-scaffolding, because too much guidance can make intellectual risk feel unnecessary. Others are harmed by premature independence, where the institution celebrates autonomy while leaving them stranded in a fog of unclear expectations. Assessment that ignores these variations may still produce grades, but it does not necessarily produce insight.

The idea of an adaptive assessment pathway is not merely to "personalize" tasks in a decorative or superficial way (Rani & Rani, 2025). It is not about giving each student a different worksheet, a different quiz, or a different automated prompt and then calling the system innovative. At its most serious, adaptive assessment is a structured yet flexible arrangement through which evidence of learning is gathered, interpreted, and used to guide the next meaningful step. It treats assessment as a journey of progressive clarification. What does the learner understand now? What kind of evidence supports that claim? What remains unstable, partial, borrowed, memorized, or poorly transferred? What should happen next so that the student is not simply judged, but moved closer to genuine competence?

In higher education, this matters deeply because learning is rarely confined to the acquisition of information. Students are expected to enter disciplinary ways of thinking. They must learn how historians weigh evidence, how engineers define constraints, how nurses make responsible judgments under pressure, how educators interpret learner behavior, how business students read uncertainty, how researchers distinguish between a plausible claim and a defensible one. These are not small cognitive adjustments. They require repeated encounters with feedback, practice, failure, self-correction, and increasingly complex forms of demonstration. A single assessment event can hardly capture such development. It may freeze learning at one moment, but it cannot easily show the route by which understanding has been built.

Generative AI introduces new possibilities here, particularly because it can support assessment as a sequence rather than an isolated event (Bandi et al, 2023). A GenAI-enabled system may help generate diagnostic tasks at the beginning of a module, identify patterns in student responses, offer individualized feedback, suggest practice activities, and help instructors design branching routes through later assignments. A student who demonstrates conceptual fluency may be invited into a more complex applied challenge. Another student, whose work shows confident terminology but weak reasoning beneath it, may be guided toward explanation, comparison, or concept mapping. A third student may need to revisit foundational assumptions through a conversational tutorial or a reflective micro-task before moving forward. The pathway is not random. It is responsive to evidence.

Yet personalization must be handled with care, almost with suspicion as well as hope. The word itself has become fashionable, and fashionable educational words often lose their sharpness. Personalization can mean attentiveness to learner need, but it can also slide into soft academic consumerism, where the student is treated as a client whose preferences must be continuously accommodated (Johnson, 2024). That is not the purpose of adaptive assessment. Higher education cannot simply ask students how they would like to be assessed and then dissolve standards into comfort. Learning sometimes requires discomfort—the productive kind, the kind that unsettles easy answers and forces the mind to stretch. A personalized pathway should not remove challenge. It should place challenge more intelligently.

This is where learner agency becomes central. Adaptive assessment should not be something done to students by invisible systems. It should be something students learn to participate in, question, and eventually manage with increasing independence. Agency is not the same as choice, although choice may support it. A student may choose between topics and still remain intellectually passive. Genuine agency emerges when learners understand the criteria of quality, monitor their own progress, interpret feedback, make strategic decisions, and recognize what kind of evidence is needed to demonstrate growth. In other words, agency is not a menu. It is a cultivated capacity.

GenAI can either strengthen or weaken this capacity. If students use AI-generated feedback as a substitute for self-evaluation, agency shrinks (Poh & Lee, 2026). If the system simply tells them what to fix, what to write, what to revise, and when they are "ready," then personalization becomes another form of dependency. The student moves, but not necessarily with awareness. On the other hand, if GenAI is used to prompt reflection, compare alternative explanations, ask students to justify their revisions, or help them trace the difference between an early draft and a more mature response, then it can support metacognitive growth. The important question is not whether AI gives feedback, but what kind of learner the feedback helps to create.

Figure 2. Educational Value Surface: Personalization × Learner Agency

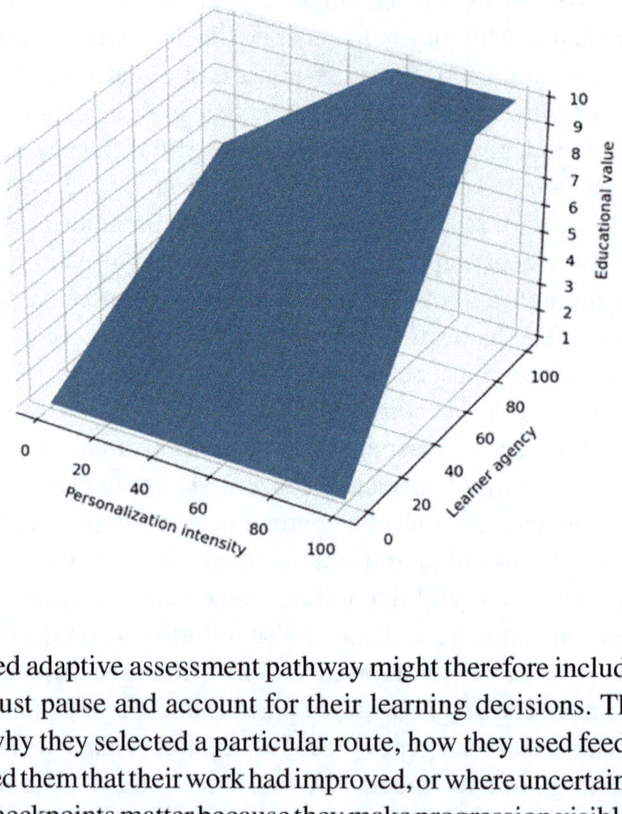

A well-designed adaptive assessment pathway might therefore include moments where students must pause and account for their learning decisions. They may be asked to explain why they selected a particular route, how they used feedback, what evidence convinced them that their work had improved, or where uncertainty remains. These reflective checkpoints matter because they make progression visible. They also resist the false smoothness of automation. Learning is not always sleek. Sometimes it is clumsy, uneven, resistant, and full of half-formed insight. Assessment should have room for that texture. A student's ability to say, "I misunderstood this before, and here is how my understanding changed," may be more educationally valuable than a polished answer with no trace of intellectual struggle.

Evidence-based progression is the backbone of this model. Without evidence, personalization becomes guesswork. Without progression, feedback becomes scattered advice. The pathway must be anchored in carefully interpreted signs of learning: performance data, drafts, peer interaction, self-assessment, oral explanation, practical application, simulations, portfolios, and instructor observation. GenAI may assist in collecting and organizing some of this evidence, but the interpretation cannot be surrendered entirely to the system. Evidence is never self-explanatory. A weak answer may indicate poor understanding, but it may also reflect language difficulty, anxiety, unfamiliarity with the task format, or lack of confidence in academic expression. A strong answer may show competence, or it may show that the student has learned to imitate disciplinary language without grasping its deeper logic. Human judgment remains essential because educational evidence is layered, contextual, and sometimes frankly ambiguous.

Table 1. Adaptive Assessment Pathway Design Matrix

Assessment Stage	GenAI-Supported Function	Learner Agency / Evidence	Human Oversight Requirement
Diagnostic entry	Generate or adapt low-stakes diagnostic prompts and identify possible knowledge gaps	Student explains prior understanding and uncertainties; multiple evidence sources are collected	Teacher validates whether the apparent gap is conceptual, linguistic, procedural, or contextual
Targeted scaffolding	Offer alternative explanations, examples, practice tasks, and just-in-time hints	Student selects or rejects supports and explains what was useful	Teacher ensures scaffolding does not lower the intended learning standard
Formative progression	Provide iterative feedback and suggest increasingly complex tasks when evidence supports readiness	Drafts, self-assessment, revision decisions, peer input, and performance evidence inform progression	Teacher checks that the pathway remains open and does not become deterministic tracking
Demonstration of competence	Support rehearsal, comparison, scenario generation, or rubric interpretation	Student produces defensible evidence of competence and discloses relevant AI assistance	High-stakes judgment remains accountable to qualified educators
Reflection and next step	Summarize patterns in performance and generate reflective prompts	Student identifies growth, remaining uncertainty, and preferred next challenge	Teacher interprets progress across context, discipline, and longer-term development

This ambiguity should not be seen as a flaw. It is part of the human reality of assessment. In fact, one of the dangers of AI-driven systems is that they may make assessment appear more certain than it is (Babu, 2025). Dashboards, scores, predictive indicators, color-coded progress maps—these can be useful, but they can also seduce institutions into premature conclusions. A student marked as "at risk" may become trapped beneath that label. Another student classified as "advanced" may stop receiving the kinds of challenge needed for further growth. Adaptive pathways must be designed against such quiet determinism. They should keep routes open, allow students to surprise the system, and treat every data point as a signal requiring interpretation rather than a verdict demanding compliance.

There is also a democratic dimension to learner agency. Students should have some understanding of how adaptive assessment decisions are made. If AI-supported systems recommend certain tasks, feedback, or progression routes, learners deserve transparency. Why am I receiving this activity? What evidence led to this recommendation? Can I challenge it? Can my instructor override it? Can I take a more demanding route if I am ready, or a more scaffolded one if I need support? These questions are not technical luxuries. They are part of academic fairness. When assessment pathways become opaque, students may feel managed rather than educated. The pathway then loses its moral legitimacy, even if it appears efficient.

Adaptive assessment also invites educators to rethink the relationship between equality and equity (Ferreira & Richetto, 2025). Equality often gives everyone the same assessment structure. Equity asks what different learners need in order to demonstrate meaningful achievement without diluting the standard itself. This distinction is delicate. Universities must avoid creating lower expectations for students who need support. At the same time, they must avoid pretending that identical assessment conditions automatically produce fairness. GenAI may help by offering differentiated preparation, feedback, examples, and revision opportunities, but only if the system is designed with vigilance (Ahmer, 2025). Otherwise, it may reproduce old inequalities through new mechanisms—privileging students who know how to prompt effectively, who have access to better tools, or who already possess the confidence to use AI strategically.

The most promising adaptive pathways are not those that make assessment easier (Adeoye et al, 2025). They are those that make learning more visible, more navigable, and more intellectually honest. They allow students to encounter assessment not as a single threatening event, but as a sequence of opportunities to show growth. They allow instructors to see more than final products. They create space for correction before failure becomes fixed. They value movement. And perhaps most importantly, they remind higher education that progression should be earned through evidence, but supported through humane design.

In this sense, adaptive assessment is not a retreat from rigor. It is a richer form of rigor. It asks for standards, but also for responsiveness. It asks for evidence, but also for interpretation. It asks for personalization, but not indulgence. It asks for learner agency, but not abandonment. GenAI can contribute to this vision, though it cannot guarantee it. The real work lies in the educational architecture built around the technology: the prompts, tasks, rubrics, reflection points, teacher interventions, ethical safeguards, and institutional cultures that determine whether adaptive assessment becomes a pathway of growth or merely another automated corridor. At its best, it helps students understand not only where they stand, but how they might move—and why that movement matters.

GENERATIVE AI AS AN ASSESSMENT PARTNER: FEEDBACK, SCAFFOLDING, AND DIAGNOSTIC INSIGHT

To describe Generative AI as an assessment partner is not to grant it the authority of a teacher, nor to imagine it as some tireless digital examiner hovering above the classroom with perfect judgment. That would be a dangerous fantasy, and not even a very interesting one. The more compelling possibility is quieter: GenAI may become a mediating presence in assessment, helping teachers and students notice what might otherwise remain unseen (Luo, 2025). It can offer feedback before confusion hardens into failure. It can provide scaffolding at the exact moment when a learner is close to understanding but not yet able to stand alone. It can help instructors detect patterns across student work that would be difficult to trace manually, especially in large, diverse, and fast-moving higher education environments. In this sense, GenAI is not best understood as a replacement for assessment expertise, but as a conversational instrument that can widen the field of educational attention.

Feedback is perhaps the most immediate area where this partnership becomes visible. Students often receive feedback too late, too briefly, or in language too compressed to be genuinely useful. A comment such as "develop your argument," "be more critical," or "clarify your methodology" may be accurate, but accuracy alone does not guarantee learning. Many students do not know what such phrases actually require them to do. They may read the comment, nod vaguely, feel disappointed, and then repeat the same mistake in the next assignment. The feedback has technically been given, yet pedagogically it has not landed. This is one of the small tragedies of higher education: teachers spend hours marking, students glance at the grade, and the richest part of the assessment encounter evaporates almost unnoticed.

GenAI can interrupt this pattern by making feedback more dialogic (Magne et al, 2025). A student who receives a brief instructor comment can ask an AI system to unpack it, generate examples, compare weak and stronger versions of a paragraph, or suggest questions for revision. A draft can be examined not only for surface-level grammar but for coherence, evidence, conceptual depth, and alignment with assessment criteria. Used carefully, such feedback does not have to spoon-feed the student. It can ask, "What is the claim here?" "Which evidence directly supports it?" "Where might a reader challenge your assumption?" These questions matter because they keep the learner intellectually active. They turn feedback from a verdict into an invitation.

Yet the temptation to over-automate feedback is real. AI-generated comments can sound fluent while remaining generic, polite, and oddly weightless. They may praise too easily, criticize without contextual understanding, or mistake stylistic polish for analytical strength. In disciplines where meaning depends on nuance, evidence, ethical judgment, or methodological precision, feedback cannot be reduced to textual smoothness. A beautifully written answer may be conceptually hollow. A clumsy sentence may contain the beginning of a strong idea. Human teachers know this, not always perfectly, but often through accumulated sensitivity to disciplinary thinking. For this reason, AI feedback should be positioned as provisional, interrogable, and secondary to educational judgment. Its value lies not in being final, but in being available, generative, and open to critique.

Scaffolding is another crucial dimension of GenAI-enabled assessment (Jha & Atif, 2025). In traditional assessment design, support is often front-loaded: instructions are given, rubrics are explained, perhaps a sample is shown, and then students are expected to produce the required work. But learning difficulties rarely appear neatly at the beginning. They emerge halfway through a task, in the awkward middle, when the student realizes that they can define a concept but cannot apply it, or that they understand a theory in isolation but not in relation to a messy case. This is where many learners quietly lose momentum. They may not ask for help because they feel embarrassed, or because the deadline is close, or because they cannot yet name what they do not understand.

GenAI can provide a form of just-in-time scaffolding, offering hints, guiding questions, partial models, alternative explanations, or step-by-step prompts without necessarily giving away the final answer (Skripchuk, 2025). A student preparing a research proposal, for example, may be guided to distinguish between a broad topic and a researchable problem. A student in statistics may receive a sequence of questions that clarifies why a particular test fits one dataset but not another. A student in teacher education may be invited to analyze a classroom scenario from multiple pedagogical perspectives before writing a final reflection. In each case, the AI-supported scaffold is not the assessment itself; it is the temporary structure that helps the learner approach the assessment with greater clarity.

Good scaffolding, however, must eventually recede. This is easy to forget. If GenAI remains constantly present, always suggesting, correcting, phrasing, and reorganizing, students may produce stronger work while developing weaker independence. The appearance of progress can become deceptive. A learner may seem more capable because the output is cleaner, yet the underlying capacity to reason, select, evaluate, and revise may not have matured. Assessment designers must therefore ask uncomfortable but necessary questions: At what point does support become substitution? How much AI assistance is compatible with the learning outcome being assessed? Should students disclose the nature of the support they received? Can they defend their work orally or through reflective commentary? Can they reproduce the reasoning without the tool? These questions should not be treated as obstacles to innovation. They are part of responsible design.

The diagnostic potential of GenAI may be even more significant than its role in feedback or scaffolding. Diagnosis in assessment is not merely about identifying wrong answers. It is about locating the structure of misunderstanding. Two students may arrive at the same incorrect response through entirely different routes. One may have misread the question. Another may hold a flawed prior assumption. A third may understand the concept but fail to express the reasoning in accepted disciplinary language. A fourth may be guessing, borrowing phrases, or imitating examples without internal comprehension. Traditional grading often compresses these differences into a single mark. Diagnostic assessment tries to recover the hidden paths beneath the mark.

GenAI can assist by analyzing patterns in student responses, clustering common misconceptions, identifying recurring weaknesses in argumentation, or highlighting gaps between rubric expectations and actual performance (Chen et al, 2025). For instructors, this can be valuable. Instead of discovering after the final exam that half the class misunderstood a foundational concept, teachers may notice the issue earlier and adjust instruction. Instead of treating every weak assignment as an isolated failure, departments may recognize broader curriculum problems: perhaps students are not being taught how to synthesize sources, interpret data, or connect theory to practice. In this way, GenAI-supported diagnosis can move assessment beyond individual correction toward program-level learning improvement.

Still, diagnostic insight must be handled with caution. AI systems do not "understand" students in the human sense. They infer patterns from data and language. They may detect correlations while missing lived realities. A student's sparse answer may indicate confusion, but it may also reflect fatigue, linguistic insecurity, disability-related barriers, unfamiliar assessment culture, or personal circumstances that no algorithm can ethically or accurately infer from a submission alone. The danger is not only technical error; it is interpretive arrogance. When institutions begin to trust dashboards more than dialogue, diagnosis can become surveillance wearing the clothes of support.

This is why GenAI should be placed within a broader ecology of assessment partnership (Webb & Galamba, 2026). The student, the teacher, the peer group, the curriculum, the discipline, and the technological system all contribute different forms of evidence. No single source should dominate. AI-generated diagnostic suggestions may help a teacher ask better questions, but they should not close the case. Feedback generated by AI may help a student revise, but the student must still learn to judge whether the feedback is appropriate. Scaffolds may help learners move through difficulty, but they must be designed to cultivate independence rather than dependency. Partnership, in this context, means distributed responsibility, not delegated authority.

There is also a subtle emotional dimension here. Assessment is not only cognitive. Students often experience it as exposure. Their work is placed before someone else and judged. For some, especially those who have repeatedly received discouraging feedback, assessment becomes associated with shame, defensiveness, or withdrawal. GenAI may provide a lower-stakes space for rehearsal. Students can ask "basic" questions without fear of appearing weak. They can test ideas, receive preliminary responses, and return to the human classroom with more confidence. This is not trivial. Confidence is not a decorative addition to learning; it often determines whether students remain engaged long enough to improve.

At the same time, emotional safety should not become intellectual softness. A useful assessment partner does not merely reassure. It challenges, unsettles, and presses for better evidence. The best use of GenAI may be to create a feedback environment where students feel supported enough to face difficulty honestly (Noroozi et al, 2025). A system that only flatters them is useless. A system that overwhelms them with corrections is equally poor. The art lies somewhere in between: feedback that is candid without being cruel, scaffolded without being controlling, diagnostic without being reductive.

Generative AI, then, can serve as an assessment partner when it helps make learning more visible and improvement more attainable (Yan et al, 2024). Its promise lies in the spaces between teacher and student: the draft before submission, the misconception before it spreads, the feedback comment before it is misunderstood, the moment of hesitation before the learner gives up. But this promise depends on disciplined imagination. AI must be embedded in assessment cultures that value transparency, student agency, ethical use, and human interpretation. Otherwise, the partner becomes a proxy, and the proxy quietly becomes the judge.

The better path is more demanding. It asks educators to design assessment practices in which GenAI expands feedback without cheapening it, strengthens scaffolding without removing intellectual labor, and supports diagnosis without pretending to know the whole learner. That is not a small task. Yet it may be precisely the kind of task higher education now faces: to use intelligent machines not to escape the complexity of assessment, but to engage that complexity with greater patience, humility, and pedagogical care.

ETHICAL AND PEDAGOGICAL RISKS: BIAS, TRANSPARENCY, ACADEMIC INTEGRITY, AND OVER-AUTOMATION

The ethical risks of GenAI-enabled assessment do not sit outside the technology like optional concerns to be handled after the "real" design work is finished (Su et al, 2026). They are inside the design from the beginning. Every decision about data, feedback, task generation, scoring, personalization, access, disclosure, and teacher oversight carries assumptions about what learning is, who students are, and how academic judgment should be exercised. This is why the conversation cannot remain trapped in the language of efficiency. Efficiency is attractive, of course. Universities are under pressure. Teachers are overloaded. Students want faster feedback. Administrators want scalable systems. Yet assessment is not a warehouse process, and learners are not parcels moving along a conveyor belt. The moment assessment becomes too smooth, too automated, too quietly managed by systems students cannot see or question, something educationally delicate begins to disappear.

Bias is one of the most persistent dangers, partly because it rarely announces itself openly. It does not always appear as obvious discrimination or blunt unfairness. More often, it enters through patterns: the language a system treats as "clear," the examples it considers typical, the forms of argument it rewards, the cultural references it assumes, the kinds of errors it interprets as weakness rather than difference. In higher education, where students may come from varied linguistic, social, economic, and educational backgrounds, these hidden preferences matter enormously. An AI-generated assessment system may evaluate a student's writing as vague when, in fact, the student is using rhetorical conventions shaped by another academic culture (Amirjalili et al, 2024). It may reward polished surface fluency while underestimating original but awkwardly expressed thinking. It may generate scenarios that feel familiar to some students and alien to others. The result is not always dramatic injustice. Sometimes it is quieter: a series of small misreadings that accumulate into unequal opportunity.

This is especially troubling when GenAI is used to support adaptive pathways. A system that recommends easier tasks for a student based on early weak performance may appear supportive, but it could also narrow the student's future without anyone noticing. A learner who needs temporary scaffolding may be quietly positioned as "low ability." Another who writes in fluent academic English may be pushed forward despite conceptual fragility. Bias, in this context, is not only about who receives a higher or lower mark. It is also about who is invited into complexity, who is protected from challenge, who is treated as promising, and who is managed through reduced expectations. That is a deeply pedagogical issue, not merely a technical defect.

Transparency, then, becomes more than a policy requirement. It becomes part of the moral architecture of assessment. Students should know when GenAI is involved in generating tasks, giving feedback, analyzing performance, or shaping progression routes (Jönsson, 2024). They should understand, at least in accessible terms, what the system is doing and what it is not doing. A black-box assessment process weakens trust because it asks learners to accept judgments whose origins remain obscure. This is not a small matter. Assessment already carries power. It affects progression, confidence, scholarships, employability, and identity. When AI enters that space invisibly, students may feel that they are being evaluated by a mechanism rather than engaged by an educator.

Yet transparency should not be reduced to a checkbox statement buried in a course handbook. "AI may be used in assessment support" tells students almost nothing. Meaningful transparency requires explanation: what kind of AI support is used, what data are considered, who reviews the output, whether students can question AI-generated feedback, and how final academic decisions are made. It also requires humility from institutions. No system should be presented as neutral simply because it is computational. Algorithms do not float above human judgment; they are built from it, trained on it, constrained by it, and sometimes distorted by it. A transparent university does not pretend that AI systems are infallible. It makes their limits visible.

Academic integrity is perhaps the most publicly discussed risk, but the discussion is often too narrow. Much of it centers on detection: how to identify whether students used GenAI to complete assignments. This is understandable, but it can easily become a dead end. AI-detection tools are imperfect, and over-reliance on them can create new injustices, especially when false accusations damage student trust. More importantly, a purely policing-oriented approach keeps assessment trapped in an old model: the institution sets a task, students submit a product, and teachers investigate whether the product is "authentic." GenAI makes that model increasingly fragile. Instead of asking only how to detect misuse, universities must ask how to design assessments in which meaningful authorship, reasoning, and learning process are visible.

This does not mean academic integrity should be softened or ignored. Quite the opposite. GenAI makes integrity more complex and, in some ways, more intellectually serious. Students need to learn the difference between using AI as a brainstorming partner and outsourcing thinking; between receiving language support and disguising someone—or something—else's intellectual labor as their own; between critique of AI-generated material and passive acceptance of it. These distinctions are not always obvious, especially for students entering higher education at a time when digital assistance is woven into everyday life. Institutions cannot simply say "do not use AI" and expect clarity. Nor can they say "use it responsibly" without defining responsibility in relation to specific tasks, disciplines, and learning outcomes.

A more mature approach would treat AI literacy as part of academic integrity. Students should be taught how to disclose AI use, evaluate AI-generated content, identify hallucinated references, question automated feedback, and explain their own intellectual contribution (Elsayed, 2024). Assessment tasks may include process logs, annotated drafts, oral defenses, reflective commentaries, in-class components, collaborative critique, or applied scenarios that require situated judgment. These practices do not eliminate misconduct, but they make it harder for learning to be reduced to polished output. They also shift the tone from suspicion to formation. Integrity is not only about catching wrongdoing; it is about helping students understand what honest intellectual work looks like in a changed environment.

The risk of over-automation cuts across all these concerns. It may be the most seductive danger because it often arrives disguised as progress. Automated feedback, automated task generation, automated scoring, automated analytics, automated recommendations—each may have a useful role. Together, however, they can create an assessment culture in which human judgment is gradually displaced, not by one dramatic decision, but by hundreds of small conveniences. The teacher checks less carefully because the system has already flagged the issue. The student reflects less deeply because the system has already suggested revisions. The institution asks fewer questions because the dashboard looks clean. Slowly, the educational encounter becomes thinner.

Over-automation is not simply the excessive use of technology. It is the surrender of interpretation. Assessment requires interpretation because student learning is not self-evident (Apostolopoulos et al, 2023). A piece of work must be read in relation to criteria, context, prior development, disciplinary expectations, and sometimes the student's own account of their process. AI can support parts of this work, but it cannot carry the full human responsibility of academic judgment. There is a danger in allowing machine-generated certainty to replace teacherly hesitation. And hesitation matters. A teacher who pauses over a student's strange answer, wondering whether it is wrong or unexpectedly insightful, is practicing a form of intellectual care that no automated rubric can fully replicate.

There is also the question of dependence. Students who constantly turn to GenAI for feedback, phrasing, structure, explanation, and correction may become more productive while becoming less self-reliant (Karnabi, 2025). This is a strange paradox. Their assignments may improve, but their internal capacity to judge quality may remain underdeveloped. They may learn to ask the tool better questions without learning to ask themselves harder ones. Higher education must be attentive to this possibility. Scaffolding is meant to be temporary; if it never recedes, it becomes a crutch. The goal is not to produce students who can assemble acceptable work through AI mediation, but graduates who can think, decide, critique, and create with discernment, including when AI is present.

A related pedagogical risk is the flattening of feedback. GenAI can produce abundant commentary, but abundance is not the same as significance. Too much feedback can overwhelm students. Too much generic encouragement can dull their sense of quality. Too many automated suggestions can pull their work toward safe, conventional patterns. In creative, interpretive, and research-intensive fields, this matters greatly. Some of the best student work begins unevenly. It may contain an odd phrase, a bold but underdeveloped claim, a peculiar connection that does not yet know what it wants to become. Automated systems may tidy such work too early. They may sand down the rough edges where originality sometimes begins.

The ethical use of GenAI in assessment therefore requires deliberate restraint (Le, 2024). Not everything that can be automated should be automated. Not every data point should be collected. Not every student action should be tracked. Not every assignment needs AI-generated feedback. The question should always return to educational purpose: What does this use of GenAI help students understand, practice, demonstrate, or reflect upon? What might it obscure? Who might it disadvantage? What human conversation must remain in place? These questions keep the technology in its proper position—as a support for educational judgment, not its substitute.

Figure 3. Accumulation and Mitigation of Risks in GenAI-Enabled Adaptive Assessment

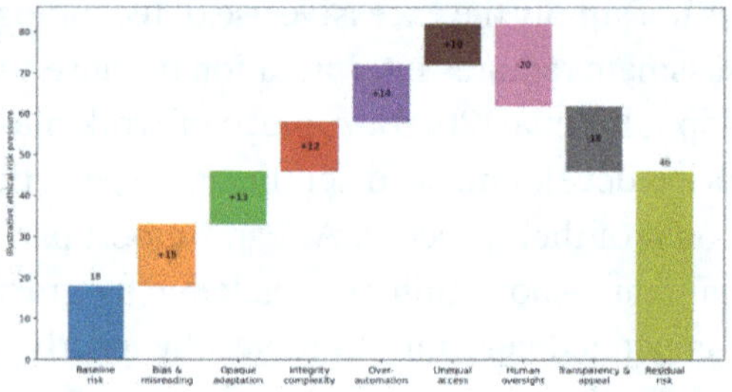

For institutions, the path forward requires governance, but governance alone is insufficient. Policies are necessary, yes, especially around data privacy, consent, disclosure, appeal mechanisms, accessibility, and teacher oversight. But ethical assessment also depends on culture. Teachers need time to redesign tasks, not just instructions to "integrate AI." Students need guidance, not vague warnings. Departments need shared language, because inconsistency across courses can create confusion and resentment. Leaders need to resist the fantasy that GenAI will solve workload problems without changing the conditions that created them. A rushed adoption of AI assessment systems may give the appearance of modernization while deepening the very pressures it claims to relieve.

The challenge, then, is not to reject GenAI out of fear, nor to embrace it with breathless optimism. The challenge is to build assessment practices that remain answerable to students as human learners (Andrew & Mueller, 2025). Bias must be examined, not denied. Transparency must be lived, not merely declared. Academic integrity must be reimagined as intellectual formation, not reduced to surveillance. Automation must be disciplined by human judgment, pedagogical purpose, and institutional responsibility. GenAI can make assessment more responsive, but it can also make it more opaque, more unequal, and more mechanical if universities allow convenience to outrun conscience.

At its best, assessment helps students become more honest about their own thinking. That honesty is fragile. It cannot be manufactured by an algorithm, though it may be supported by well-designed tools. It grows in environments where feedback is trusted, standards are clear, support is available, and judgment is fair enough to be taken seriously. GenAI may become part of such environments, but only if higher education remembers that the ethical question is never merely "Can this system assess?" The more searching question is: "What kind of learner, teacher, and institution does this system help us become?"

TOWARD HUMAN-CENTERED GENAI ASSESSMENT MODELS IN HIGHER EDUCATION

A human-centered model of GenAI assessment begins with a modest but demanding conviction: technology should serve the educational relationship, not quietly reorganize it around its own logic (Palalas et al, 2025). This sounds obvious, perhaps even too obvious, yet higher education has repeatedly learned that tools do not remain neutral once they enter institutional routines. They reshape expectations. They alter time. They change what teachers notice, what students value, what administrators measure, and what counts as evidence of learning. GenAI is no exception. If introduced carelessly into assessment, it may strengthen the very habits universities should now be questioning: excessive standardization, feedback without dialogue, grading as administrative closure, and learning reduced to visible output. If designed with pedagogical imagination, however, it can help create assessment systems that are more responsive, more reflective, and, strangely enough, more human.

Human-centered assessment does not mean sentimental assessment. It does not mean lowering standards, avoiding difficulty, or treating student comfort as the highest educational good. Higher education has obligations that extend beyond individual preference. It must protect academic credibility, disciplinary integrity, professional competence, and public trust. A nurse, engineer, teacher, pharmacist, researcher, accountant, or architect cannot be certified on the basis of vague encouragement.

There must be evidence. There must be standards. There must be judgment. The human-centered question is not whether standards should remain, but how students are supported in approaching them, how fairly their progress is interpreted, and how assessment can become a means of intellectual formation rather than a narrow mechanism of sorting.

In this sense, the first principle of a human-centered GenAI assessment model is pedagogical primacy (Hsu, & Lao, 2025). The design must begin with learning purposes, not with technological features. A university should not ask, "How can we use this AI tool in assessment?" as if the tool itself were the starting point. The better question is more patient: "What kind of learning are we trying to cultivate, and where might GenAI support that learning without displacing the learner's responsibility?" In some cases, GenAI may help students rehearse explanations, receive formative feedback, generate alternative problem scenarios, or compare the strength of different arguments. In other cases, its use may be inappropriate because the task is designed precisely to assess unaided recall, spontaneous reasoning, manual technique, clinical judgment, or embodied practice. Human-centered design knows the difference. It does not force AI into every assessment space simply because it is available.

A second principle is teacher authority with transparent mediation. GenAI may assist in feedback generation, rubric alignment, diagnostic analysis, and adaptive task design, but final academic judgment should remain accountable to qualified educators. This is not professional defensiveness; it is educational responsibility. Teachers bring disciplinary knowledge, contextual awareness, ethical sensitivity, and relational understanding that cannot be replicated by predictive systems. They can recognize when a student's unconventional answer contains a promising line of thought. They can distinguish between genuine confusion and a temporary failure of expression. They can interpret silence, hesitation, revision, and effort in ways that exceed the data trail. A human-centered model may use GenAI to widen the teacher's field of attention, but it should not allow the system to become the unseen examiner behind the curtain.

Transparency is essential here. Students should not have to guess whether AI has shaped the feedback they receive, the tasks they are assigned, or the progression route they are advised to follow (Hooda et al, 2022). They deserve to know when GenAI is being used, for what purpose, and with what limits. They also need pathways to question or appeal decisions influenced by AI-supported analysis. Without such openness, personalization can begin to feel like quiet management. Learners may sense that decisions are being made about them, but not with them. That is a dangerous feeling in education because trust is not decorative; it is the atmosphere in which meaningful feedback becomes usable.

A third principle is learner agency through reflective participation. Human-centered assessment should help students become more capable judges of their own work. GenAI can contribute to this only if students are not positioned as passive recipients of machine-generated advice (Dolský, 2025). They should be asked to engage with AI feedback critically: Which suggestions are useful? Which are superficial? What did the system misunderstand? What changes did the student accept, reject, or modify? Why? Such questions turn AI use into an object of learning rather than a hidden shortcut. They also develop a form of academic maturity increasingly needed in contemporary life: the ability to work with intelligent systems without surrendering judgment to them.

This has practical implications for assessment design. Instead of assessing only final products, universities may need to assess processes more deliberately. Draft histories, reflective statements, oral defenses, annotated AI interactions, learning journals, peer critique, and revision rationales can help reveal how students think and how they use support. A final essay or project may still matter, but it should not carry the entire burden of evidence. In a GenAI-rich environment, the route toward the product becomes educationally significant. A polished submission tells one story; the student's account of how it was developed tells another. Sometimes the second story is more revealing.

A fourth principle is equity without simplification. GenAI tools may help reduce some barriers by offering language support, practice opportunities, explanatory feedback, and individualized scaffolding (Lee et al, 2026). For students who feel intimidated by office hours, who study in a second or third language, or who need repeated low-stakes rehearsal, this can be genuinely valuable. Yet equity cannot be assumed simply because tools are available. Access differs. AI literacy differs. Confidence differs. Some students will know how to prompt, evaluate, and strategically use GenAI; others may use it clumsily, excessively, or not at all. A human-centered model must therefore include explicit guidance, institutional access, and discipline-specific examples of responsible use. Otherwise, GenAI may reward the already advantaged while appearing, on the surface, to democratize support.

Equity also means resisting deficit-based personalization. Adaptive systems should not quietly reduce the intellectual horizon of students who struggle early. Support must not become containment (Mokhtar & Manganelli, 2026). A student who performs weakly on an initial task may need a different explanation, more time, a peer discussion, or a concrete example—not a permanently simplified pathway. Human-centered assessment keeps challenge alive. It assumes that learners can grow beyond their first data point. This is crucial because educational systems sometimes mistake early evidence for destiny, and AI can make that mistake look scientific.

A fifth principle is productive restraint. Universities must learn not only how to use GenAI, but when not to use it. This may be one of the hardest lessons, because technological adoption is often driven by institutional excitement, vendor promises, and the seductive appeal of scale. But assessment is too consequential to be governed by convenience alone. Some feedback should remain personal. Some judgments should require conversation. Some tasks should be conducted without AI assistance. Some student data should not be collected at all. The human-centered university understands that restraint is not backwardness. It is a form of wisdom.

From these principles, a possible model begins to emerge. At the design stage, instructors define the learning outcomes and decide where GenAI can support formative development without compromising the integrity of the final evidence. At the student level, learners are taught how to use GenAI ethically, how to disclose assistance, and how to critique AI output. During assessment, GenAI may provide low-stakes feedback, generate practice variations, support self-assessment, or help identify misconceptions (Hazra et al, 2026). Teachers then interpret student progress using multiple forms of evidence, not merely AI-generated analytics. At the institutional level, policies protect privacy, require transparency, ensure accessibility, and maintain human oversight. This model is not glamorous. It does not promise effortless transformation. But it is educationally defensible.

Table 2. Human-Centered Governance Framework for GenAI-Enabled Assessment

Governance Principle	Practical Requirement	Risk Controlled	Evidence / Indicator
Pedagogical primacy	Use GenAI only where it clearly supports the intended learning outcome and assessment purpose	Technology-driven assessment and superficial personalization	Documented rationale linking AI use to learning outcomes
Transparency and contestability	Explain AI involvement, recommendation logic, limits, and routes for questioning or appeal	Opaque pathway decisions and loss of student trust	Student understanding of why a route or feedback response was recommended
Human accountability	Keep educators responsible for interpretation and all consequential decisions	Automated judgment replacing professional responsibility	Human review records for high-stakes or ambiguous cases
Equity without simplification	Monitor access, language effects, early-risk labels, and differential progression	Bias, deficit tracking, and lower expectations for some learners	Equity audit by learner group and evidence of pathway mobility
Privacy and data restraint	Collect only necessary learning evidence and use approved systems with clear data practices	Surveillance, inappropriate data use, and privacy loss	Data minimization review and accessible student privacy information
Continuous evaluation	Review learning value, dependence, fairness, accuracy, and teacher workload over time	Normalization of ineffective or harmful AI practices	Periodic evaluation using student voice, outcomes, teacher judgment, and error monitoring

The cultural dimension matters just as much as the technical structure. Human-centered GenAI assessment requires a shift in how universities speak about students. If learners are described mainly as risks to be monitored, assessment becomes surveillance. If they are treated mainly as consumers to be satisfied, assessment becomes service delivery. If they are understood as developing thinkers, capable of error, revision, responsibility, and growth, assessment becomes something richer. GenAI can fit into any of these cultures. The tool will not decide the moral direction. Institutions will.

There is a quiet irony here. The arrival of powerful artificial intelligence may force higher education to clarify what is most human in assessment. Not because humans are always fair, wise, or attentive; they are not. Teachers can be biased, exhausted, inconsistent, and rushed. But human-centered assessment does not romanticize human judgment. It disciplines it. It asks educators to use technology to become more attentive, not less accountable; more responsive, not more mechanical; more transparent, not more obscure. GenAI should help teachers see patterns they might miss, help students rehearse thinking they might otherwise avoid, and help institutions design pathways that recognize difference without abandoning rigor.

The future of assessment in higher education will not be shaped simply by the sophistication of AI systems. It will be shaped by the values embedded in their use (Katsamakas et al, 2024). A human-centered GenAI assessment model insists that learning is not merely the production of correct answers, polished texts, or measurable outputs. It is a gradual formation of judgment, confidence, discipline, curiosity, and ethical responsibility. Assessment should make that formation visible and support it with care. GenAI can be part of this work, but only as a partner held within human purposes. The machine may generate, suggest, summarize, and adapt. The university must still ask what kind of learning is worth cultivating, what kind of evidence is worth trusting, and what kind of person the assessment process is helping the student become.

CONCLUSION

Adaptive and personalized assessment pathways enabled by GenAI invite higher education to reconsider one of its most familiar practices with fresh seriousness. Assessment has often been treated as the final act of teaching, the moment when learning is measured after the real educational work has already taken place. This chapter has argued for a different understanding. Assessment can be part of learning itself. It can guide, provoke, diagnose, reassure, challenge, and redirect. It can help students see not only what they have achieved, but how they are thinking, where they are hesitating, and what kind of effort might move them forward. In this sense, assessment is not simply a tool of judgment. It is a form of educational care, though one that must be disciplined by fairness, rigor, and intellectual honesty.

Generative AI makes this rethinking both more possible and more urgent. Its ability to generate differentiated tasks, offer immediate feedback, simulate tutorial dialogue, and adapt learning activities to individual needs opens pathways that were previously difficult to sustain, especially in large and diverse higher education settings. Instructors who face heavy workloads and varied student preparedness may use GenAI to support formative assessment more consistently. Students may receive guidance at moments when they would otherwise remain silent, confused, or embarrassed to ask for help. Assessment may become less episodic and more continuous, less punitive and more developmental, less attached to a single performance and more attentive to growth over time.

However, the value of GenAI in assessment does not lie in automation alone. Indeed, automation is perhaps the least interesting part of the story. The deeper value lies in the possibility of creating richer feedback ecologies, more flexible routes through learning, and more humane ways of recognizing student progress. A personalized assessment pathway should not mean that each student is enclosed inside a private algorithmic tunnel. It should mean that each student receives meaningful opportunities to engage, revise, demonstrate, and extend understanding in ways that remain connected to shared academic standards. Personalization without standards becomes fragmentation. Standards without personalization can become exclusion. The challenge is to hold both together.

This balance is not easy. GenAI systems can reproduce bias, misread student work, generate inaccurate feedback, or create a false sense of objectivity. They may privilege certain forms of expression, penalize linguistic difference, or encourage institutions to treat students as data profiles rather than complex human beings. There is also the continuing problem of academic integrity. When students can use GenAI to produce essays, solve problems, or simulate competence, traditional assessment formats become less reliable. But this should not lead universities into panic or surveillance-heavy responses. A more constructive response is to redesign assessment so that process, reflection, oral defense, iterative development, authentic problem-solving, and contextual judgment become more central. In other words, GenAI does not merely threaten assessment; it exposes weaknesses that were already there.

The role of educators remains essential. No AI system can fully understand the emotional climate of a classroom, the history of a struggling learner, the disciplinary nuance behind a partially correct answer, or the ethical weight of a high-stakes academic judgment. GenAI can assist with feedback, variation, diagnosis, and support, but it should not be treated as the final authority over student learning. Human teachers must remain interpreters of evidence, designers of meaningful tasks, guardians of fairness, and mentors in intellectual growth. Their professional judgment is not made obsolete by AI; it is made more visible. The more powerful the technology becomes, the more carefully human responsibility must be articulated.

For institutions, the adoption of GenAI-enabled adaptive assessment requires more than technical access. It demands policy, training, transparency, and a culture of thoughtful experimentation. Universities need clear guidelines on data use, student consent, feedback reliability, AI disclosure, and the boundaries between assistance and authorship. Teachers need professional development that goes beyond tool demonstrations and engages with assessment theory, ethics, and discipline-specific practice. Students also need support in learning how to use GenAI responsibly—not as a substitute for thinking, but as a resource for questioning, drafting, testing, and refining their ideas. Without such preparation, personalization may remain a slogan rather than a serious educational practice.

Ultimately, the future of AI-driven assessment in higher education should not be imagined as a coldly efficient system in which algorithms quietly sort learners into predetermined categories. A better future is possible. It is one in which assessment becomes more responsive without losing rigor, more flexible without becoming vague, more technologically supported without becoming dehumanized. GenAI can help build this future, but only if universities resist the temptation to equate innovation with speed, scale, or novelty. The real measure of success will be whether students become more reflective, more capable, more ethically aware, and more engaged in their own learning.

Adaptive and personalized assessment pathways, then, are not merely a technical upgrade. They represent a philosophical shift in how higher education understands learning evidence. They ask institutions to move from asking, "How do we grade everyone efficiently?" toward a richer and more difficult question: "How do we help each learner produce, understand, and act upon meaningful evidence of growth?" That question cannot be answered by GenAI alone. But with careful design, critical oversight, and a deeply human educational imagination, GenAI can become part of the answer.

Recommendations

Higher education institutions should introduce GenAI-enabled adaptive assessment through deliberate pedagogical design rather than technology-first adoption. Assessment pathways should begin with clear learning outcomes and shared academic standards, while allowing differentiated scaffolding, practice, feedback, and progression where evidence justifies it. Students should be taught how adaptive decisions are made, why particular tasks or supports are recommended, and how they can question or challenge an AI-supported pathway. Universities should assess process as well as final products by incorporating drafts, revision histories, oral explanations, reflective commentaries, portfolios, and documented AI use. GenAI feedback should strengthen learner agency by prompting self-evaluation and justification rather than supplying complete solutions. Human educators must retain final responsibility for high-stakes judgment, interpretation of ambiguous evidence, and decisions affecting progression. Institutions should establish governance for bias, privacy, transparency, academic integrity, accessibility, and unequal access to advanced AI tools. Adaptive systems should also be audited for deficit-based tracking so that early weakness does not become a permanent lower-expectation route. Finally, institutions should evaluate these models through student learning, fairness, independence, feedback quality, teacher judgment, and the capacity of learners to progress with greater awareness rather than dependence.

Limitations of the Research

This chapter is conceptual and analytical rather than empirical, so it does not present original experimental, survey, or longitudinal data. The figures and numerical values are analytical illustrations derived from the chapter's arguments, not measured results from a particular GenAI assessment system. Adaptive assessment practices may vary considerably across disciplines, institutions, learner populations, technologies, and regulatory contexts. The framework therefore requires contextual adaptation rather than mechanical application. Future research should test GenAI-enabled assessment pathways through comparative classroom studies, longitudinal progression data, equity analyses, student voice research, and evaluations of teacher judgment and workload.

REFERENCES

Adeoye, M. A., Prastikawati, E. F., & Riwayatiningsih, R. (2025). Beyond traditional testing: Exploring the efficacy of adaptive assessments in shaping future learners. *Journal of Nonformal Education, 11*(1), 153–169. DOI: 10.15294/jone.v11i1.19934

Ahmer, S. (2025). Designing adaptive lessons with GenAI to meet diverse learning preferences.

Aloisi, C. (2023). The future of standardised assessment: Validity and trust in algorithms for assessment and scoring. *European Journal of Education, 58*(1), 98–110. DOI: 10.1111/ejed.12542

Amirjalili, F., Neysani, M., & Nikbakht, A. (2024, March). Exploring the boundaries of authorship: A comparative analysis of AI-generated text and human academic writing in English literature. [). Frontiers Media SA.]. *Frontiers in Education, 9*, 1347421. DOI: 10.3389/feduc.2024.1347421

Andrew, M., & Mueller, B. (2025). Is that all there is?" Work-integrated learning educators meet GenAI: upskilling journeys to "the deep end. In *Handbook of Artificial Intelligence in Higher Education* (pp. 300–314). Edward Elgar Publishing. DOI: 10.4337/9781035338764.00028

Apostolopoulos, I. D., Tzani, M., & Aznaouridis, S. I. (2023). ChatGPT: ascertaining the self-evident. The use of AI in generating human knowledge. arXiv preprint arXiv:2308.06373.

Awashreh, R., Al-Naqbi, S., & Gharib, M. (2024). Ethical decision making by Arab universities' advisory and shadow committees: Forms of corruption, implications, and solutions. *Kurdish Studies, 12*(1), 4197–4209.

Babu, M. S. (2025). AI-Driven Educational Assessments: Navigating the Intersection of Innovation, Equity, and Ethical Concerns for Future Learning. Journal of Cultural Analysis and Social Change, 1368-1382.

Bandi, A., Adapa, P. V. S. R., & Kuchi, Y. E. V. P. K. (2023). The power of generative ai: A review of requirements, models, input–output formats, evaluation metrics, and challenges. *Future Internet, 15*(8), 260. DOI: 10.3390/fi15080260

Chen, J., Huang, K., Lai, C., & Jin, T. (2025). The Impact of GenAI-Based Collaborative Inquiry on Critical Thinking in Argumentation: A Case Study of Blended Argumentative Writing Pedagogy. *TESOL Quarterly, 59*(S1), S150–S182. DOI: 10.1002/tesq.3407

Dolský, M. (2025). Reassembling Learning Collectives: An Ethnography of Student Entanglements with Generative AI in Czech Higher Education.

Elsayed, H. (2024). The impact of hallucinated information in large language models on student learning outcomes: A critical examination of misinformation risks in AI-assisted education. *Northern Reviews on Algorithmic Research, Theoretical Computation, and Complexity*, *9*(8), 11–23.

Ferreira, W. J., & Richetto, K. C. D. S. (2025). Education towards equity: Adapting assessment practices in the multicultural context of mathematics education. *Educar em Revista*, *41*, e93725. DOI: 10.1590/1984-0411.93725

Hazra, R., Chatterjee, P., & Ghosh, S. (2026). Assessment and Feedback Through Generative AI Intelligent Tutoring Systems. In Collaborative Paradigms of Generative AI and Human Intelligence for Equitable Learning Futures (pp. 121-148). IGI Global Scientific Publishing. DOI: 10.4018/979-8-3373-6063-8.ch005

Hooda, M., Rana, C., Dahiya, O., Rizwan, A., & Hossain, M. S. (2022). Artificial intelligence for assessment and feedback to enhance student success in higher education. *Mathematical Problems in Engineering*, *2022*(1), 5215722. DOI: 10.1155/2022/5215722

Hsu, T. C., & Lao, N. (2025). From Policy to Pedagogy–Building Human-Centered AI Literacy Across Educational Contexts. *Informatics in Education*, *24*(4), 645–651. DOI: 10.15388/infedu.2025.00

Jha, M., & Atif, A. (2025). Reimagining pedagogy for the GenAI era: Frameworks, challenges and institutional strategies. *Australasian Journal of Educational Technology*, *41*(5), 56–73. DOI: 10.14742/ajet.10645

Johnson, T. K. A. (2024). Humanization in Higher Education: A Grounded Theory Study on the Impact That Customer Service Practices Have on the Student Academic Journey (Doctoral dissertation, Morgan State University).

Jönsson, A. (2024). Prompting for progression: How well can GenAI create a sense of progression in a set of multiple-choice questions?.

Karnabi, S. (2025). Exploring International Master's Students' Perceptions on the Use of Generative AI tools for.

Katsamakas, E., Pavlov, O. V., & Saklad, R. (2024). Artificial intelligence and the transformation of higher education institutions: A systems approach. *Sustainability (Basel)*, *16*(14), 6118. DOI: 10.3390/su16146118

Le, X. (2024). Assessment reform in higher education: An ethical approach to harness the power of generative artificial intelligence. *Education Research and Perspectives*, *51*, 156–185. DOI: 10.70953/ERPv51.2412007

Lee, A. V. Y. (2025). The double-edged sword of generative AI for assessment: efficiency versus homogenization. In *Navigating Generative AI in Higher Education* (pp. 128–143). Edward Elgar Publishing. DOI: 10.4337/9781035337873.00012

Lee, S., Choe, H., Zou, D., & Jeon, J. (2026). Generative AI (GenAI) in the language classroom: A systematic review. *Interactive Learning Environments*, *34*(1), 335–359. DOI: 10.1080/10494820.2025.2498537

Luo, J. (2025). How does GenAI affect trust in teacher-student relationships? Insights from students' assessment experiences. *Teaching in Higher Education*, *30*(4), 991–1006. DOI: 10.1080/13562517.2024.2341005

Magne, V., Vince, S., Mace, R., & Hooper, S. (2025). AI as a dialogic partner: Rethinking feedback in higher education. *Assessment & Evaluation in Higher Education*, •••, 1–15.

Mancuso, V., Sarcinella, E. D., Bruni, F., Arlati, S., Di Santo, S. G., Cavallo, M., Cipresso, P., & Pedroli, E. (2024). Systematic review of memory assessment in virtual reality: Evaluating convergent and divergent validity with traditional neuropsychological measures. *Frontiers in Human Neuroscience*, *18*, 1380575. DOI: 10.3389/fnhum.2024.1380575

Manu, A. (2024). Generative AI as a disruptor. In *Transcending imagination* (pp. 147–162). Chapman and Hall/CRC. DOI: 10.1201/9781003450139-15

Mokhtar, T., & Manganelli, J. (2026). *Coexistence and Coevolution of Humans and Intelligent, Adaptive Environments*. CRC Press. DOI: 10.1201/9781003441953

Montebello, M. (2025). Rethinking Pedagogy and Assessment in the Age of Generative AI.

Noroozi, O., Haddadian, G., Gao, X., Schunn, C., Alqassab, M., & Banihashem, S. K. (2025). The value of GenAI for peer feedback provision: Student perceptions and impacts. *International Journal of Educational Technology in Higher Education*, *22*(1), 61. DOI: 10.1186/s41239-025-00558-6

Palalas, A., Pegrum, M., Gunawardena, C. N., Robertson, R. S., & Ventura, J. (2025). The 'Tragic Dilemma' of GenAI in Education: An Exploratory Human-AI Conversation. *Postdigital Science and Education*, *7*(4), 1451–1477. DOI: 10.1007/s42438-025-00600-w

. Poh, S. K., & Lee, I. (2026). Generative Artificial Intelligence (GenAI) for Feedback in School Writing: Friend or Foe?. Teaching English as a Second or Foreign Language—TESL-EJ.

Rani, D., & Rani, M. D. (2025). Adaptive Assessment: Personalizing Evaluation in the Digital Age. *International Journal of Engineering Science & Humanities, 15*(4), 506–513.

Sharma, S., & Gupta, B. (2023). Investigating the role of technostress, cognitive appraisal and coping strategies on students' learning performance in higher education: A multidimensional transactional theory of stress approach. *Information Technology & People, 36*(2), 626–660. DOI: 10.1108/ITP-06-2021-0505

Skripchuk, J. (2025). *Effective Help-Seeking in Programming Outside the Classroom: Challenges, Motivations, and Pedagogy*. North Carolina State University.

Sol, K., Sok, S., & Heng, K. (2025). *Rethinking assessment in higher education in the age of generative AI. Encyclopedia of educational innovation.* Springer., DOI: 10.1007/978-981-13-2262-4_327-1

Su, F., O'Dea, M., Wood, M., & Seidl, E. (2026). Embracing a new world: authentic assessment designs in an age of generative artificial intelligence (GenAI). Perspectives: Policy and Practice in Higher Education, 1-12.

Webb, M., & Galamba, A. (2026). Transforming pedagogy with GenAI-supported formative assessment: Challenges for teacher education. *British Journal of Educational Technology, 57*(3), 690–706. DOI: 10.1111/bjet.70051

Yan, L., Greiff, S., Teuber, Z., & Gašević, D. (2024). Promises and challenges of generative artificial intelligence for human learning. *Nature Human Behaviour, 8*(10), 1839–1850. DOI: 10.1038/s41562-024-02004-5

Yilmaz, M., Temur, H. B., Emmungil, L., Çelik, E., Gauthier, A., & Cukurova, M. (2026). Supporting self-regulated learning through generative AI feedback in online higher education: The importance of student perceptions of the source of feedback. *International Journal of Educational Technology in Higher Education, 23*(1), 16. DOI: 10.1186/s41239-026-00592-y

KEY TERMS AND DEFINITIONS

Adaptive Assessment Pathways: structured but flexible assessment routes that respond to evidence of student learning and guide appropriate next steps.

Evidence-Based Progression: movement through assessment stages based on multiple interpreted signs of learning rather than fixed sequencing or a single score.

Generative AI Assessment: the use of GenAI to support task generation, formative feedback, scaffolding, diagnostic analysis, reflection, and adaptive assessment design.

Human-Centered Assessment: assessment that keeps educational purpose, professional judgment, fairness, transparency, learner dignity, and development at the center of technological use.

Learner Agency: the student's capacity to interpret criteria, make learning decisions, use feedback critically, and participate actively in assessment progression.

Personalized Assessment: assessment designed to respond to differences in learner readiness, support needs, progression, and demonstration of competence without lowering shared standards.

Responsible Automation: the selective use of automated assessment support within clear boundaries of transparency, accountability, privacy, equity, and human oversight.

Chapter 7

Adaptive and Personalized Assessment Systems Using Generative Artificial Intelligence

Sushil Bhardwaj
http://orcid.org/0000-0001-5184-3866
RIMT University, Mandi Gobindgarh, India

Indu Sharma
http://orcid.org/0009-0001-9402-4702
Chandigarh University, Punjab, India

Neeraj Kumar Sharma
http://orcid.org/0009-0005-9794-2129
Punjab University, Chandigarh, India

Harpominder Jit Kaur
http://orcid.org/0009-0000-3821-9057
Chandigarh University, Punjab, India

Santosh Bali
http://orcid.org/0009-0003-0658-7092
CGC University, Punjab, India

ABSTRACT

Adaptive and personalized assessment systems supported by Generative Artificial Intelligence are transforming evaluation practices in higher education. This chapter examines how AI enables dynamic question generation, real time difficulty adjust-

DOI: 10.4018/979-8-3373-9089-5.ch007

ment, and personalized feedback to enhance learning outcomes. It explains the pedagogical foundations of adaptive assessment, including constructivism, formative assessment, and competency based learning. The chapter also highlights the role of learning analytics in supporting data driven decision making and continuous improvement. Issues related to academic integrity, bias, and ethical use of AI are discussed along with the importance of human oversight. Practical case examples illustrate real world implementation of adaptive assessment systems. The chapter further explores institutional readiness, policy frameworks, and future directions in AI driven assessment. It provides a clear and structured understanding of how adaptive assessment can support flexible, inclusive, and learner centered education.

INTRODUCTION

Adaptive and personalized assessments are modern approaches that improve how student learning is evaluated in higher education. These approaches recognize that learners differ in their pace, ability, background knowledge, and learning preferences. Traditional assessment methods often fail to capture these differences. As a result, many students are either under challenged or overburdened during evaluation. Adaptive and personalized assessment shifts the focus from uniform testing to flexible and learner centered evaluation. Through these approaches, learners are identified as individuals who vary in their learning pace, capability, background knowledge and learning preferences. These differences tend not to be reflected in traditional assessment methods. Consequently, a large number of learners are either under worked or overworked in the assessment process. Individualized and adaptive testing turns the emphasis on standard testing to adaptive and learner centered testing. These strategies are supposed to ensure that every learner is presented with a suitable amount of challenge as well as meaningful feedback (Maity & Deroy, 2024). Such systems have become more feasible and scalable with the integration of digital technologies and artificial intelligence. These practices are being embraced by institutions in order to enhance the effectiveness and quality of assessment practices. Adaptive assessment is a technique whereby the level of difficulty and order of question are adjusted based on the answers of the learner.

The system is used to constantly track the performance and to modify the assessment in real time as illustrated in Fig.1. Upon a learner giving the correct answer to a question, a more difficult question is presented by the system. When the learner gives the wrong answer, the system will give a simpler question or will give more support. This is done to determine the real level of understanding of the learner than the fixed assessments.

The concept of adaptive assessment is closely linked with computerized adaptive testing. In such systems, algorithms are used to determine the next question based on previous responses (Arslan et al., 2024). The goal is to estimate the learner's ability with fewer questions while maintaining accuracy. This makes the assessment process efficient and focused.

Figure 1. Flow of Adaptive Assessment Based on Learner Responses

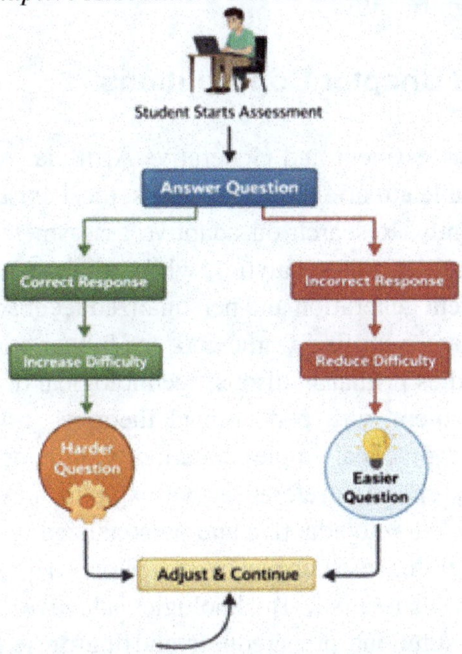

Personalized assessment extends this idea by considering broader learner characteristics. It focuses on tailoring the assessment experience according to individual learning needs. Factors such as prior knowledge, learning speed, strengths, weaknesses, and learning goals are taken into account. Personalized assessment may include customized tasks, varied question formats, and specific feedback that supports individual improvement.

These approaches emphasize continuous assessment rather than one time evaluation. They support ongoing interaction between the learner and the system. Learners receive feedback during the assessment process, which helps them improve their understanding. This creates a more engaging and supportive learning environment. Adaptive and personalized assessment are also aligned with learner centered education (Bouguettaya et al., 2025). They encourage active participation and self reflection. Students are not only evaluated but are also guided to improve their performance. This makes assessment an integral part of the learning process rather than a separate activity.

With the advancement of artificial intelligence, these systems have become more powerful. AI can analyze large amounts of learner data and generate appropriate questions and feedback. This enhances the accuracy and effectiveness of assessment. It also allows institutions to implement these methods on a larger scale without increasing workload significantly.

Research Gap and Chapter Contributions

Although adaptive assessment and Generative Artificial Intelligence (GenAI) have received considerable attention in recent years, most existing studies examine these topics independently. Research on adaptive assessment mainly focuses on computerized testing and learning analytics, while studies on Generative AI emphasize automated content generation and personalized feedback. Limited research integrates these areas into a unified framework for higher education assessment. Furthermore, many studies primarily discuss technological developments without adequately connecting them with pedagogical theories, institutional readiness, ethical governance, and practical implementation. Consequently, educators and institutions lack a comprehensive reference that explains how Generative AI can be systematically integrated into adaptive and personalized assessment systems.

This chapter addresses this research gap by presenting an integrated discussion of pedagogical foundations, Generative AI technologies, adaptive assessment strategies, ethical considerations, institutional preparedness, and future research directions within a single framework. The chapter also highlights how AI-supported assessment can enhance learning while maintaining fairness, transparency, and human oversight.

The major contributions of this chapter are summarized below.

- Presents an integrated view of adaptive and personalized assessment using Generative Artificial Intelligence.
- Connects pedagogical theories with AI-driven assessment practices.
- Explains the role of AI in question generation, adaptive testing, personalized feedback, and learning analytics.
- Discusses ethical issues, academic integrity, and institutional readiness for AI adoption.
- Identifies future research directions for developing trustworthy and learner-centered assessment systems.

Traditional Vs. Adaptive Assessment

Conventional evaluation techniques have predetermined design. A common set of questions is administered to all learners irrespective of their personal capacities or learning levels. This strategy is easy to adopt and does not address the idea of diversity among learners. Consequently, it can be used to give little information about the true knowledge of students. In conventional systems, the assessments tend to be done at a certain point like mid term or final examination. The feedback is usually given upon the completion of the assessment. Such a delay minimizes the chances of the learners to enhance the process. The emphasis is primarily on grading, as opposed to learning. Adaptive assessment is more responsive and flexible. The system will raise or lower the difficulty level depending on the performance of the learner. This makes certain that every learner is at the appropriate level of assessment. It helps decrease the possibility of boredom among the advanced learners and frustration among struggling learners. The other significant difference is the type of feedback. The adaptive assessment systems have the ability to give instantaneous and sustained feedback. The assessment process helps learners to know their errors and rectify them. This helps in more in-depth learning and improved memory (Ismail et al., 2024). Conventional tests can have many questions that are needed to measure the learners. Contrastingly, the adaptive systems are capable of doing the same or even better accuracy using less questions. These systems are effective by being relevant in the subject matter of the assessment process.

Diagnostic evaluation is also facilitated by adaptive assessment. It assists in detecting certain areas that a learner requires to improve on. Teachers can use this information to develop specific interventions. It also assists learners to concentrate on their areas of weakness. Adaptive assessment is also improved through the use of technology. Responses, patterns and content modification can be monitored, analyzed, and modified on digital platforms automatically (Yadav et al., 2025). This saves on manual work and enhances uniformity. It can as well be applied on a large scale in institutions of higher learning.

Relevance in Higher Education

Higher education institutions deal with a diverse group of learners. The students belong to various academic and learning environments and levels of preparedness. Standardized evaluation method will not be effective in dealing with these differences. Adaptive and personalized assessment is a solution, which offers options in the evaluation process to be flexible. These strategies underpin competency based education which is gaining more relevance in higher education. The learning process is moving away towards memorization and towards skill and competency development. Adaptive assessment aids in the measurement of these competencies by providing tasks that are at the level of competence of a learner. Individualized evaluation is also effective in enhancing the quality of feedback. In a case where feedback is done in relation to individual performance, learners would be in a position to know clearly their strengths and areas that they need to improve on. This assists in building up self awareness and promoting perpetual learning (Ahmed & Mejri, 2025). Adaptive assessment aids in ongoing assessment as opposed to using final tests. This will enable teachers to keep track of the student development during the process of learning. Learning gaps are identified early on to support students in a timely manner. These systems are enhanced further by the incorporation of artificial intelligence and learning analytics. Schools are able to gather and examine data that pertains to student achievement. This information can be utilized to enhance teaching practices and curricula. It also facilitates evidence based decision making. These strategies increase student engagement as well.

Learners get encouraged to take part when they believe that the assessment is in line with their level. Adaptive systems are interactive and therefore enhance the learning process to be more interesting and meaningful. Assessment that is adaptive and individualized also helps in inclusivity in education. More effective accommodation of learners with various abilities and learning needs can be provided. This aids in the provision of a fair learning environment where every student stands a chance to excel. These systems can be applied on a scale, provided they use digital platforms. Adaptive assessment can be incorporated into learning management systems at Universities. This aids in effective administration and in uniformity of evaluation practices within courses. In general, the adaptive and personalized assessment are in line with the objectives of higher education in the modern context (Tariq, 2024). They promote skill building, lifelong learning and student centred learning. They also equip them with the real world challenges as they understand and apply as opposed to rote learning.

ROLE OF GENERATIVE ARTIFICIAL INTELLIGENCE IN ASSESSMENT DESIGN

Generative AI (Kaddouri et al., 2025) is revolutionizing higher education assessment design by facilitating dynamic, flexible, and learner centered assessment systems. It aids in the development of assessment material, modifies levels of difficulty dynamically, and offers valuable feedback to students. These functionalities enhance effectiveness and quality of assessment practices. Artificial intelligence based systems will decrease constraints of fixed assessments and enable institutions to adopt scalable and responsive assessment frameworks.

AI Based Question Generation

AI based question generation can be defined as the application of Generative Artificial Intelligence in the automatic generation of assessment items. These questions may consist of multiple choice questions, short answer questions, descriptive questions and case based problems. Questions are created by the system based on the objectives of learning, course material and difficulty levels as specified by the educators. In large amounts of academic text (textbooks, lecture notes, question banks, etc.), generative AI models can be used to analyze academic material. According to this analysis, they are able to come up with relevant and structured questions, which are consistent with the curriculum. This saves on the teacher workload and consistency in assessment design. The possibility to generate several variations of the same question can be considered one of the main benefits of AI based question generation. This aids in decreasing the instances of academic dishonesty by offering various questions to various learners yet they have the same learning outcomes. It also aids in large scale testings where it becomes complicated to create questions manually. AI is also able to categorize questions according to difficulty levels including basic, intermediate and advanced. This classification assists adaptive assessment systems to choose the right questions to the particular learner. The system also has a capability to make sure that the questions are at various levels of cognition like understanding, application and analysis. The other advantage is that it has the ability to produce context based and real world problems. AI is able to generate scenario based questions that challenge more practical knowledge and critical thinking. This enhances the relevance of the evaluation of higher education. Teachers continue to be significant in question review and validation of AI generated questions. Human control makes sure that the content is correct, significant and that is consistent with academic standards. Such combination of AI efficiency and human judgement results in improved assessment design.

Dynamic Difficulty Adjustment

One of the main characteristics of AI driven assessment systems is dynamic difficulty adjustment. It enables the system to adjust the level of difficulty depending on the performance of the learner in real-time. This will make sure that every learner is tested on the right level. Generative AI involves algorithms and data analysis, which are used to identify the level of difficulty of questions. The system challenges the learner by presenting more difficult questions when he/she answers correctly. The system makes the task easier or offers assistive questions in case of a learner giving a wrong answer. This is done during the assessment. The strategy assists in ensuring a balance between challenge and support. easy questions do not bore or difficult questions discourage learners. It makes them interested and motivated in the process of assessment. Inaccurate assessment is also enhanced by dynamic difficulty adjustment. It is concerned with determining the true level of ability of the learner as opposed to the number of correct answers given. The system changes depending on the responses of the learner and gives a more accurate assessment. Performance data, like response time, accuracy and error patterns, are utilized in AI systems to adjust difficulty levels (Alali & Wardat, 2024). This statistical method is more efficient in decision making and can be fair in evaluation. The technique is especially effective in a big classroom setting and within an online classroom (Bhardwaj et al., 2025). It enables institutions to offer personalized assessment experience without augmenting administrative work. It also facilitates ongoing evaluation through tasks modification over the period of time. Competency based education is consistent with dynamic difficulty adjustment. It assists the learners to advance at their own pace and master certain fields. This renders assessment more meaningful and effective.

Technical Foundations of Adaptive Assessment

Adaptive assessment systems rely on established measurement techniques together with artificial intelligence. Two important methods are Item Response Theory (IRT) and Computerized Adaptive Testing (CAT).

Figure 2. Relationship Between Generative AI, IRT, and CAT in Adaptive Assessment

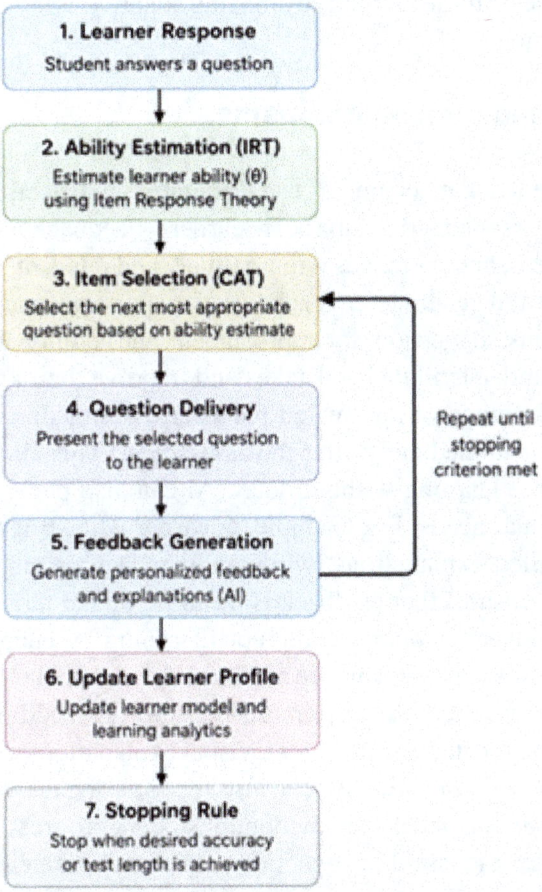

Item Response Theory (IRT) estimates a learner's ability by considering the relationship between learner performance and question difficulty. Each assessment item is assigned characteristics such as difficulty and discrimination. Based on learner responses, the system estimates the learner's current ability level and selects appropriate questions.

Computerized Adaptive Testing (CAT) uses the learner's estimated ability to dynamically select the next assessment item. Students answering correctly receive more challenging questions, whereas incorrect responses lead to comparatively easier questions. This process continues until sufficient evidence is collected to estimate learner competency accurately.

Generative Artificial Intelligence enhances these techniques by automatically generating multiple assessment items, creating question variations, and producing personalized explanations and feedback. Instead of replacing IRT and CAT, Generative AI complements these methods by making adaptive assessment more scalable, flexible, and efficient.

Automated Feedback Mechanisms

Automated feedback mechanisms use Generative Artificial Intelligence to provide instant and personalized feedback to learners. Feedback is an essential part of the learning process, and AI makes it more timely and relevant. AI systems analyze learner responses and generate feedback based on performance. This feedback can include explanations, suggestions for improvement, and additional learning resources. It helps learners understand their mistakes and improve their knowledge.

One major advantage of automated feedback is immediacy. Learners receive feedback during or immediately after the assessment. This allows them to correct errors and reinforce learning without delay. AI can also personalize feedback according to individual needs. For example, a learner who struggles with a concept may receive detailed explanations, while another learner may receive advanced suggestions. This ensures that feedback is meaningful and targeted.

Automated feedback supports continuous learning by encouraging reflection. Learners can review their performance and identify areas that require improvement. This promotes self directed learning and responsibility. In addition, AI can provide feedback in different formats such as text, visual explanations, or hints. This makes learning more engaging and accessible. It also supports diverse learning preferences.

Educators can use feedback data to monitor student progress and adjust teaching strategies. This creates a strong connection between assessment and instruction. It helps in improving overall learning outcomes. Human oversight remains important in automated feedback systems. Educators need to ensure that the feedback is accurate, unbiased, and aligned with learning objectives. The combination of AI and human guidance leads to effective and reliable assessment practices.

Table 1. Comparison of Adaptive Assessment Approaches

Approach	Advantages	Limitations
Rule-based Adaptive System	Simple implementation	Limited flexibility
Computerized Adaptive Testing	Accurate ability estimation	Requires calibrated item bank
Learning Analytics	Tracks learner progress	Depends on data quality
Generative AI	Dynamic question generation and personalized feedback	May generate inaccurate or biased content

Each approach has distinct strengths and limitations. Traditional adaptive systems provide reliable measurement but require extensive manual preparation of assessment items. Learning analytics offers valuable insights into learner performance but depends on the availability of quality data. Generative Artificial Intelligence enhances assessment flexibility by automatically generating questions and personalized feedback; however, it requires human supervision to verify accuracy, fairness, and alignment with learning objectives. Therefore, combining AI with established adaptive assessment techniques provides a balanced and effective assessment framework.

PEDAGOGICAL FOUNDATIONS OF ADAPTIVE ASSESSMENT

Adaptive assessment is not only a technological advancement but also a pedagogically grounded approach. It is based on well established learning theories that emphasize active learning, continuous improvement, and skill development. These foundations ensure that assessment supports learning rather than only measuring performance. By integrating adaptive systems with pedagogical principles, higher education can create meaningful and effective learning environments. The alignment of assessment with learning theories helps in improving student engagement, understanding, and long term retention of knowledge. The pedagogical foundations of adaptive assessment are illustrated in Fig. 2.

Figure 3. Pedagogical Foundations of Adaptive Assessment

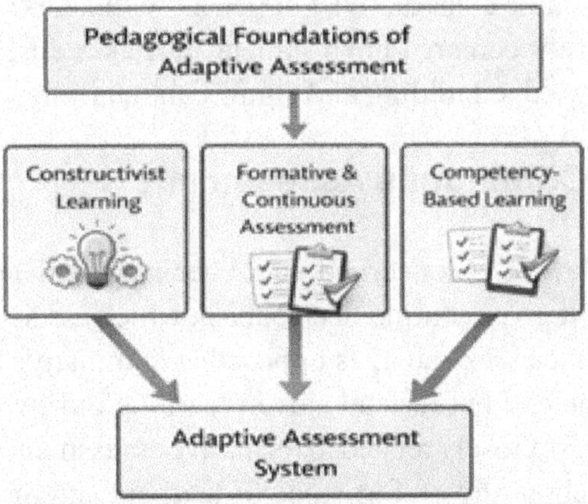

Constructivist Learning Theory

According to constructivist learning theory, learners have a role to play in the construction of knowledge based on their experiences and interactions. Learning does not refer to as an inactive process of information receivership but rather the active process of constructing meaning. All learners have a different interpretation of information depending on knowledge and experiences. Adaptive assessment is in line with constructivist ideals. It offers learners activities that are within their present understanding. Learners can construct knowledge successfully when exposed to questions that are not too challenging or too simple. This system encourages learning at a slow pace through suitable challenges. Feedback is significant in constructivist learning. Adaptive assessment has timely feedback that enables the learners to reflect on their feedback. This reflection helps in further insight and helps learners to learn by correcting their errors. It also promotes self learning and independent thinking. Another key aspect of constructivism is learner engagement. Adaptive systems have the benefit of keeping the learners on the edge of their seats by making changes on the content depending on their performance. This forms a dynamic learning environment in which learners are constantly engaging with the learning content. The adaptive assessment also promotes individual learning. Every learner has a different way of progressing and the system is flexible enough to accommodate this. This appreciates the differences in learners and offers a more customized learning experience. Problem solving and critical thinking are also highlighted in constructivist theory. Scenario based and application oriented questions can be considered as adaptive assessment. Such questions make the learners use their knowledge in practice. Combination of constructivist concepts with adaptive assessment assists in developing a learner centered environment. It makes sure that assessment is a contribution to knowledge building and significant learning.

Formative and Continuous Assessment

Formative assessment is concerned with checking the learning progress in the process of learning. It gives continuous feedback which assists the learners to better themselves. Formative assessment, as opposed to summative assessment, does not assess learning at the end but instead aids in learning during the course. Adaptive assessment systems are closely related to formative assessment. They also constantly gather information about the performance of learners and modify the assessment. This will enable learners to have feedback at each point of the process. Constant monitoring makes learning an ongoing process and not at a given time. Adaptive systems help to sustain this strategy through regular and diverse evaluation activities. These activities aid in the detection of learning gaps at an early stage and give a chance of improvement. Immediate feedback is one of the advantages of formative assessment. Adaptive systems give immediate feedback in response to the learners. This aids learners to be aware of what they are doing wrong and rectify them immediately. It strengthens proper knowledge too and develops confidence. Self regulation is also aided by formative assessment. Students are made conscious of their learning and become responsible learners. Adaptive assessment systems give in-depth information about performance, which is useful in goal setting, and in improving performance. Flexibility is another plus. Adaptive assessment enables the learners to learn at their own speed. The individuals who learn fast can proceed whereas other individuals may need more time and encouragement. This provides an equal learning environment. Formative and continuous assessment are also beneficial to educators. They are provided with real time information on student performance. This assists them in adjusting teaching techniques and give special attention where necessary.

Constant evaluation minimizes the stress involved with high stakes tests. Students are tested in the long run, and this is better placed to give a clear view of their talents. It also promotes regular work and activity. Adaptive assessment enhances formative practices by ensuring that they are efficient and scalable. It enables institutions to carry out continuous evaluation in both small and large classes.

Competency Based Learning

Competency based learning emphasizes on the acquisition of particular skills and abilities as opposed to the mere course content coverage. It focuses on learning outcomes mastery and gives learners the opportunity to advance when they exhibit competence. Adaptive assessment helps in competency based learning by offering tasks that are of a suitable level of ability to the learner. Difficulty varies with performance and this will be used in determining whether a learner has mastered a specific area or not. Achievement is a basis of progress in competency based learning as opposed to time. Adaptive assessment enables the learners to proceed at a pace that suits them. Students who show proficiency can graduate at a fast rate and those who lag are given more assistance until they get to the level it requires. Evaluation in this method is in line with well-specified learning outcomes. Questions that can be created through adaptive systems can be specific to competencies. This ensures that assessment is focused and meaningful. Feedback is an important part of competency based learning (Ahmed et al., 2024). Adaptive assessment gives feedback in detail, which enables the learners to know the strengths and weaknesses. This helps in unending skills growth. Another important aspect is personalization. Competency based learning recognizes that learners have different abilities and learning speeds.

Adaptive assessment offers individualized trajectories that help in individual development. This practice enhances assessment transparency as well. The learners are well aware of the expectations and the method of assessment of their performance. This enhances motivation and responsibility. Real world tasks are another task that is supported by adaptive assessment (Khlaif et al., 2024). It may involve application based questions where practical skills are tested. This equips students with the real world and work situations. Educators are able to monitor competency development by using performance data. This assists in the development of specific interventions as well as curriculum design. Adaptive assessment with competency based learning provides a robust background to skill oriented education. It makes sure that the learners attain meaningful learning outcomes and are ready to meet the challenges in the future.

PERSONALIZED FEEDBACK AND LEARNING ANALYTICS

Personalized feedback and learning analytics are significant aspects of contemporary assessment systems. They assist in enhancing the quality of learning by giving an insight on the student performance and learning behavior. Feedback can be given to individual learners in real time and made customized with the help of Generative Artificial Intelligence. Learning analytics enables institutions and teachers to use performance information to explore trends that can be used to enhance teaching and evaluation (Xu et al., 2025). These strategies move the evaluation beyond mere evaluation to an ongoing improvement. Students are guided according to their feedback and teachers acquire meaningful data to aid in teaching. The combination of feedback and analytics will provide a data informed learning environment that benefits the process of teaching and learning.

AI Driven Personalized Feedback

AI driven personalized feedback is the application of Generative Artificial Intelligence to give feedback that is specific to the performance of each learner. Learners get specific suggestions to their responses and level of understanding instead of generic ones. The AI systems process the answers of learners and provide feedback immediately. This feedback can comprise the explanations of correct answers, the detection of mistakes and recommendations on how to improve. Timely feedback enables the learners to rectify the errors and reinforce their learning in the process. One of the major aspects of AI based feedback is personalization. Students who excel can be given more intensive instructions or more challenges. Students experiencing the problem might also be given simplified instructions or hints. This guarantees that feedback is pertinent and useful to each person. The tone and depth of the feedback can also be adapted by AI. An example is that the novice can be given elaborate explanation, whereas the more advanced learner might be given terse feedback centered on the more advanced concepts. Such flexibility enhances the learning process and makes the learners involved. Another important aspect is consistency. The feedback of AI systems is formed on the basis of predetermined rules and data analysis, which minimizes variation and bias. This guarantees equality in assessment and feedback provision. Recommendations to further learning can also be part of AI driven feedback. Students can be instructed to go to other sources like readings, video or practice. This helps in lifelong learning after the assessment. Teachers are able to examine AI generated feedback to ascertain whether they are accurate and meet the learning goals. It is necessary to have human control to ensure quality and relevance. With the efficiency of AI and the human judgment, effective feedback practices can be achieved. Individual feedback that is generated by AI makes student interactions more active and motivating. Learners find it easier to reflect and improve when the feedback given on their performance is shown to be directly related to their performance. This renders evaluation a participatory element of the learning process.

Role of Learning Analytics

Learning analytics involves the collection, measurement, and analysis of data related to student learning. It helps in understanding how learners interact with content, perform in assessments, and progress over time. In adaptive assessment systems, learning analytics plays a central role. AI systems collect data such as response accuracy, time taken to answer questions, frequency of attempts, and patterns of errors. This data is analyzed to identify trends and learning behaviors. These insights help in understanding the strengths and weaknesses of learners.

Learning analytics supports personalized learning by providing detailed information about individual performance (Janardhana et al., 2025). Educators can use this information to design targeted interventions. For example, students who struggle with specific topics can be provided additional support (Mimoudi, 2025). Another important function of learning analytics is monitoring progress. It allows educators to track student development over time. This helps in identifying whether learners are improving and achieving learning objectives.

Learning analytics also supports adaptive assessment by informing decision making within the system. The system uses data to adjust question difficulty and provide appropriate feedback. This creates a responsive learning environment (Manokore et al., 2024). Visualization tools such as dashboards make learning analytics more accessible. Educators and learners can view performance data in graphical form. This helps in easy interpretation and better understanding of progress.

Learning analytics also contributes to institutional improvement. Data collected from multiple learners can be used to evaluate course effectiveness and teaching methods. Institutions can identify areas that require improvement and take necessary actions. Ethical use of data is important in learning analytics. Institutions must ensure privacy, transparency, and responsible use of student data. Proper policies and safeguards are required to maintain trust and integrity (AlMohsen, 2025). Learning analytics enhances the effectiveness of adaptive assessment by providing data driven insights. It supports informed decision making and improves overall learning outcomes.

Data Driven Decision Making

Data driven decision making is a decision making process that utilizes data and analytics to make decisions in education. Adaptive assessment systems make decisions based on data and not assumptions regarding teaching, assessment design, and learner support. AI and learning analytics generate large amounts of data about student performance. This information can offer useful information about the learning patterns, the level of engagement, and the areas of weaknesses. This information can be used to make informed decisions by educators. Instructional planning is one of the applications. Teachers are able to know areas that the students are struggling and revise their teaching techniques. This assists in enhancing delivery of instruction. Individualized learning is also supported by the use of data driven decision making. Teachers are able to develop interventions that are in line with individual needs. As an illustration, those students who require more practice can be given extra practice whereas the advanced learners can be given challenging tasks. Data can also be used to improve assessment design. Teachers will be able to discuss which questions are effective and which should be changed. This assists in making quality assessments that are effective in measuring learning outcomes. Policy making and academic planning can be done at the institutional level using data. Institutions are able to assess program performance, student performance patterns and resource use. This helps in strategic decision making. Early identification of at risk students is another factor. It can be used to determine struggling learners, which can be done through data analysis. It is possible to intervene in time and help these students to be retained. Accountability and transparency are also encouraged in data driven approaches. Evidence is used when deciding which enhances trust in the system. It also helps in the continuous enhancements in teaching and assessment practices. Although data driven decision making has numerous advantages, it involves adequate management of data. Institutions should guarantee the accuracy of data, its security and ethical application. Human judgment will still play a role in data interpretation and balanced decisions. Modern education has a solid foundation through the integration of AI, learning analytics, and data driven decision making (Leon, 2024). It facilitates successful evaluation, individualized learning and endless enhancement in higher education systems.

ACADEMIC INTEGRITY AND ETHICAL CONSIDERATIONS

The use of Generative Artificial Intelligence in assessment brings significant benefits, but it also raises important concerns related to academic integrity and ethics. As assessment systems become more automated and data driven, it is necessary to ensure that fairness, honesty, and transparency are maintained. Institutions must carefully design and monitor AI based systems to prevent misuse and maintain trust in the evaluation process. Ethical considerations play a key role in ensuring that technology supports learning without compromising academic standards.

Academic Integrity Challenges

Academic integrity refers to honesty and ethical behavior in learning and assessment. In AI supported assessment systems, maintaining integrity becomes more complex due to increased automation and digital access. One major challenge is the misuse of AI tools by learners. Students may use external AI systems to generate answers, which can reduce genuine learning and create unfair advantages.

Another challenge is related to question predictability and content sharing. In digital environments, assessment items can be shared easily among learners. Even when adaptive systems generate different questions, there is still a risk of collaboration or unauthorized assistance. This makes it difficult to ensure that the assessment reflects individual performance.

Plagiarism is also a concern in AI driven assessments. Learners may submit AI generated responses without proper understanding. Detecting such content can be challenging because AI generated text may appear original and well structured. This requires the use of advanced detection tools and careful evaluation by educators.

Over reliance on automated systems can also affect academic integrity. If assessments are fully automated without human review, errors in evaluation may go unnoticed. This can lead to unfair grading and reduced accountability. To address these challenges, institutions need to develop clear policies and guidelines. Assessment design should include measures such as randomized questions, time limits, and application based tasks. Educators should also play an active role in monitoring and validating assessment outcomes. Promoting academic integrity also involves educating students about ethical use of AI. Learners should understand the importance of honesty and the value of independent learning. A balanced approach that combines technology with human oversight can help maintain integrity in AI supported assessment systems.

Bias and Fairness in AI Systems

Bias in AI systems is an unfair outcome that is caused by the information or algorithms employed in the system. Bias may also influence the process of assessment, i.e., the way the questions are formulated, the way the responses are rated, and the way of providing feedback. This may result in inequalities among learners. AI systems are trained on big data, and such data might be biased. Unless the training data is representative of a wide range of learners, then the system will give biased results. As an illustration, some language patterns or cultural settings might be preferred over others. This might be a disadvantage to learners of other backgrounds. Fairness is an important requirement in assessment. There should be equal opportunities to show the knowledge and abilities of all learners. The AI systems should also be developed with caution to avoid discrimination on basis of language, gender or socio economic status. The other issue is algorithmic decision making. Based on the data trends, AI systems can change the level of difficulty or give feedback. When such patterns are skewed, the system will not gauge the ability of learners accurately. This may impact on student performance and confidence. Various and high quality datasets should be used to minimize bias. To detect and address bias, AI systems should be tested and evaluated regularly. Algorithms can be designed in transparent fashion and assist in comprehending the manner in which decisions are arrived at. Human supervision is important in enhancing equity. Teachers are to analyze AI generated materials and testing scores to make sure that they are correct and impartial. The integration of AI and human judgment would enhance the reliability and trust in the system. Just and impartial evaluation systems promote inclusivity in education. They make sure that every learner is rated according to his/her abilities and is not influenced by outside factors.

Ethical Principles and Transparency

The ethical considerations inform the responsible application of AI in assessment. Such values are fairness, accountability, transparency, and privacy. They make sure that the assessment systems are created and applied in such a manner that they are beneficial to the learners and that they are also trustworthy. Transparency is an important aspect of ethical assessment. Students must be aware of the process of the assessment system, generation of questions, and the evaluation of performance. Effective communication can assist in establishing trust and minimizing misunderstandings. The extent of accountability holds significance and is attributed to institutions and educators in the management of AI systems. Human stakeholders are still in charge of making sure that assessment processes are just and precise even in circumstances where AI is utilized. The AI-based decisions must be tested and checked. Another important issue is privacy. Systems based on AI gather and process extensive data about learners. Such information has to be secured to avoid abuse. Learner information should be kept safe and institutions should adhere to appropriate data protection policies. Over automation is another ethical application of AI. Machines should not be entirely relied on in assessment. The interpretation of results, guidance, and meaningful evaluation require human input. There should be clear guidelines and policies on the use of AI in assessment. These policies must establish the acceptable practice, responsibilities and constraints of AI systems. Training should be provided to educators and learners to promote ethical use. Another element of transparency is articulating feedback that is presented by AI systems. Learners ought to know the purpose of providing some feedback or scores. This aids in learning and helps in self improvement. Transparent ethics contribute to establishment of an environment of trust in assessments. They make sure AI is not implemented as a substitute to human judgment, but as an assistant.

ROLE OF EDUCATORS AND HUMAN OVERSIGHT

Generative Artificial Intelligence as a tool of assessment does not eliminate the role of the educators. Rather, it transforms their roles and enhances their significance in the process of learning. Questions can be generated and feedback provided and performance analysis can be automated by AI. Nevertheless, human judgment is still needed to guarantee quality, equity, and correspondence to the learning objectives. Teachers are at the front line in designing, monitoring and validating AI supported assessment systems. They make sure that the practices of assessment are meaningful, ethical and student centered. Human supervision assists in the discovery of limitations of AI systems, including bias, wrong responses, or absence of contextual comprehension. Through the integration of AI and educator skills, institutions have the potential to develop balanced and effective assessment systems.

Human in the Loop Assessment

Human in the loop assessment refers to a system in which educators actively participate in the design, monitoring, and evaluation of AI driven assessment processes (Tarun et al., 2025). In this approach, AI supports assessment activities, but final control and validation remain with human experts. Educators are involved in setting learning objectives, defining assessment criteria, and reviewing AI generated content. This ensures that the assessment aligns with academic standards and course requirements. AI may generate questions and feedback, but educators verify their accuracy and relevance before use.

Human involvement is also important in monitoring the performance of AI systems. Educators can identify errors or inconsistencies in generated content. They can make necessary adjustments to improve the quality of assessment. This continuous supervision helps in maintaining reliability.

Human in the loop systems also support ethical practices. Educators ensure that AI does not introduce bias or unfair evaluation. They can review assessment results and make corrections where needed. This helps in maintaining fairness and transparency. Another important role is providing contextual understanding. AI systems may not fully understand the specific learning context or student needs. Educators can interpret results and provide additional support to learners.

This approach creates a collaborative environment where AI and educators work together. AI improves efficiency, while human oversight ensures quality and trust. Human in the loop assessment is essential for responsible use of AI in education.

Teacher as Facilitator and Evaluator

In AI supported assessment systems, the role of teachers shifts from traditional instruction to facilitation and guidance. Teachers act as facilitators who support learners in understanding concepts and improving their performance. They use insights from AI systems to provide targeted support. As facilitators, teachers help learners interpret feedback and apply it to improve learning. They guide students in setting goals and developing strategies for improvement. This supports active and self directed learning. Teachers also act as evaluators who ensure that assessment results are accurate and meaningful. They review AI generated questions, responses, and feedback. This helps in maintaining the quality of assessment.

Another important role is addressing individual learning needs. Teachers can use performance data to identify students who require additional support. They can provide personalized guidance and interventions to improve learning outcomes. Teachers also help in developing critical thinking and problem solving skills. While AI can provide automated feedback, human interaction is necessary to encourage deeper understanding. Teachers can ask questions, provide explanations, and engage students in discussions. In addition, teachers play a role in maintaining academic integrity. They ensure that students use AI tools responsibly and follow ethical practices. They can design assessments that reduce misuse of AI.

The role of the teacher becomes more interactive and supportive in AI driven environments. Teachers focus on guiding learning rather than only delivering content. This improves student engagement and overall learning experience.

Balancing AI and Human Judgment

The effective assessment systems require balancing AI and human judgment. Although AI is efficient and scalable, it can never substitute human knowledge and decision making. A middle way will make sure that technology and human expertise are both utilized effectively. AI technologies are capable of handling huge volumes of data and deliver prompt output. They are able to create questions, appraise answers and give feedback. Nevertheless, AI can be out of context and may give erroneous or biased results. Results should be interpreted by human judgment and be accurate. Teachers are major players in ensuring this equilibrium. They determine the way AI tools are applied and in which areas human intervention is required. As an example, AI can be applied to routine tasks, whereas more intricate assessments should be checked by humans. There are also ethical considerations in balancing. Teachers make sure that AI technologies are applied fairly and transparent. They are able to recognize and rectify assessment biases. This assists in sustaining confidence amongst the learners. Another aspect is flexibility. There are various learning scenarios that might demand varying degrees of AI participation. Teachers have the opportunity to adapt the application of AI depending on the situation and learning aims. There is also the human judgment which is crucial in offering emotional and motivational support. AI is not able to comprehensively understand the emotions of a learner and encouragement as a teacher would do. Learning cannot be effective without human interaction. A balanced solution would develop a system of efficiency fostered by AI and quality taught by the educators. This mix will result in positive evaluation and learning outcomes in higher education.

INSTITUTIONAL READINESS AND POLICY FRAMEWORKS

Institutional readiness is essential in the successful implementation of adaptive and personalized assessment systems. To implement Generative Artificial Intelligence in assessment, higher education institutions must be ready in terms of technological infrastructure, human resources, and policy frameworks. The application of AI can result in inefficiency, inconsistency, or even ethical issues without adequate preparation. Institutional readiness refers to the alignment of technology, people, and processes with objectives of modern assessment (Zhang, 2024). It necessitates a clear knowledge on how AI can facilitate learning and assessment. The institutions should make sure that systems are reliable, secure, and scalable. They should also establish a culture that trains and helps educators to adopt new technologies. Policies frameworks are significant to inform the application of AI in assessment. Political transparency, accountability and fairness are maintained with the aid of clear policies. They determine the collection of data, the use of AI systems and decision making. Universities should also take into account the ethical aspect and make sure that technology is used responsibly. An institution that is well prepared can easily incorporate adaptive assessment in the academic practices. This results in enhanced learning, student interaction and effective assessment procedures. Figure 3 shows the key elements of institutional readiness.

Figure 4. Institutional Readiness Framework for AI-based Assessment

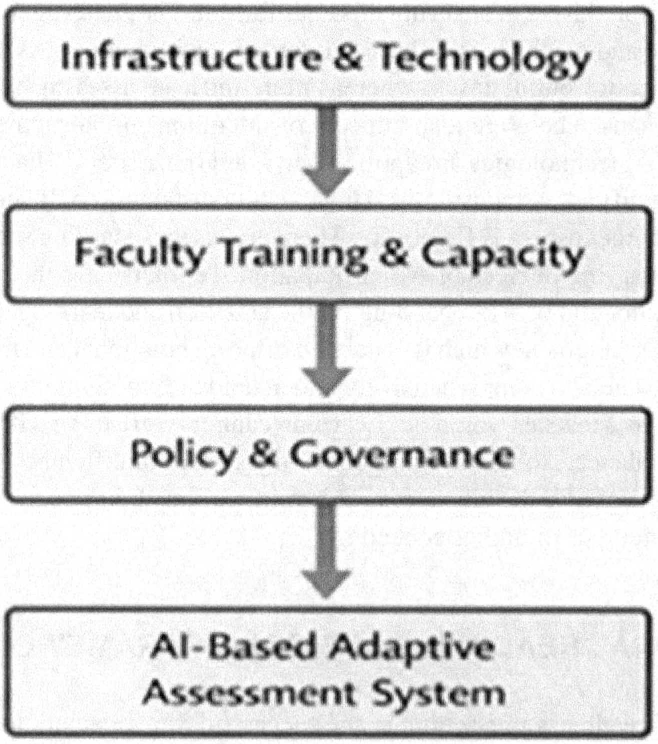

Infrastructure and Technological Readiness

Infrastructure and technological readiness are essential for implementing AI based assessment systems. Institutions must ensure that they have the necessary digital platforms, hardware, and software to support adaptive assessment.

Learning management systems play a key role in this process. These systems should be capable of integrating AI tools that support question generation, adaptive testing, and feedback delivery. The platform must be stable and able to handle large numbers of users without performance issues. Reliable internet connectivity is another important requirement. Students and educators should have access to high speed and stable internet to participate in online assessments. This ensures smooth operation of adaptive systems and reduces disruptions.

Data management is also a critical component. AI systems rely on large amounts of data to function effectively. Institutions must have systems in place to store, manage, and analyze this data securely. Proper data management ensures accuracy and supports learning analytics.

Security is an important concern in technological readiness. Institutions must protect student data from unauthorized access. Secure systems help in maintaining trust and compliance with data protection regulations. Scalability is another key factor. The system should be able to support increasing numbers of users and courses. This is important for institutions that plan to expand the use of adaptive assessment. Technical support is also necessary. Institutions should provide support services to help users resolve technical issues. This ensures smooth implementation and user satisfaction.

Faculty Training and Capacity Building

Faculty training is essential for the successful adoption of AI based assessment systems. Educators need to understand how to use AI tools effectively and how to integrate them into their teaching practices. Training programs should focus on both technical and pedagogical aspects. Educators should learn how to use AI platforms, interpret data, and manage adaptive assessment systems. They should also understand how these systems support learning and assessment.

Capacity building involves developing skills and confidence among educators. Teachers should be comfortable using technology and should be able to guide students in using AI tools responsibly. This requires continuous professional development (May et al., 2025). Workshops, seminars, and hands on training sessions can help in building these skills. Institutions should provide regular opportunities for educators to learn and update their knowledge. This ensures that faculty members remain competent in using new technologies.

Collaboration among educators can also support capacity building. Sharing experiences and best practices helps in improving teaching and assessment methods. It also creates a supportive learning environment for faculty. Faculty training should also include ethical considerations. Educators need to understand issues related to bias, data privacy, and academic integrity. This helps in ensuring responsible use of AI.

Support from the institution is important for effective training. Institutions should provide resources, time, and incentives for faculty development. This encourages participation and improves adoption. Well trained educators play a key role in the success of adaptive assessment systems. They ensure that technology is used effectively and that learning objectives are achieved.

Policy and Governance Frameworks

Policy and governance frameworks provide guidelines for the use of AI in assessment. They make sure that the practices of assessment are equal, impartial and transparent. Clear policies can assist institutions to deal with AI risks. The use of AI systems in assessment should be outlined in policies. They are supposed to define the roles and duties of teachers, administrators and pupils. This assists in keeping accountability. Data governance is an important part of policy frameworks. Institutions need to specify collection, storage and use of student data. Policies ought to provide protection of data as well as its responsible use. This also involves adhering to data protection laws. Ethical guidelines should also be included in policy frameworks. These should deal with aspects of fairness, transparency and bias. Learning institutions should make sure that AI systems do not discriminate against a group of learners. Academic integrity should also be dealt with by the policies. Easy to follow regulations must be put in place to ensure AI tools are not abused. This assists in keeping trust on the assessment process. There are governance mechanisms that are required to oversee and assess AI usage. Educational establishments need to formulate committees or teams to monitor the implementation of AI. Such bodies are able to check the performance of the systems and correct the problems. Designing of policy is about flexibility. Technology should be reviewed with new policies being introduced to align with the changes. The constant review is one way in which the policies are kept up to date. Communication of policies is also essential. There must be guidelines and expectations of educators and students. Effective communication aids in compliance and minimizing misunderstandings. Effective policy and governance frameworks assist in the responsible use of AI in assessment (Iswari, 2025). They make sure that technology does not compromise ethical and academic standards but improves learning.

CASE EXAMPLES OF ADAPTIVE ASSESSMENT IMPLEMENTATION

Adaptive assessment is now used in many higher education systems through digital platforms and AI tools (Suna & Özer, 2025). Real life implementations show how adaptive testing, personalized feedback, and competency based evaluation improve learning outcomes. These case examples demonstrate practical use of technology and highlight how institutions apply adaptive assessment in real environments. They also show how flexibility, feedback, and data driven approaches support effective learning.

AI Based Adaptive Online Assessments

AI based adaptive online assessments are widely implemented in universities and online learning platforms. A well known example is the use of adaptive testing in the *Graduate Record Examination (GRE)*. The test adjusts the difficulty of questions based on the candidate's responses. If a student answers correctly, the next question becomes more difficult. If the answer is incorrect, the system presents a simpler question. This helps in accurately measuring the ability level of each candidate.

Another example is *Coursera*, which uses adaptive quizzes in many of its courses. The platform provides different question sets based on learner performance. Students receive questions that match their level, which improves engagement and understanding. The system also tracks performance and adjusts future assessments accordingly.

In universities, learning management systems such as *Moodle* and *Canvas* are used to implement adaptive assessments. These systems include plugins and tools that allow educators to create question banks with different difficulty levels. The system selects questions dynamically based on student responses. This approach is used in subjects such as mathematics, programming, and science courses.

AI based adaptive assessments are also used in placement tests. For example, many institutions use adaptive testing to assess student readiness in subjects like English and mathematics. The test identifies the correct level of the student and places them in appropriate courses. These implementations show that adaptive online assessments improve accuracy, reduce test length, and provide a fair evaluation for all learners.

Personalized Feedback Systems

Personalized feedback systems are implemented in various online learning environments to support student learning. A common example is *Duolingo*, which uses AI to provide feedback based on learner responses. The system identifies mistakes and provides immediate corrections. It also adjusts future exercises based on performance, which supports continuous improvement.

Another example is *Khan Academy*, which provides personalized feedback in subjects such as mathematics. The platform analyzes student responses and offers hints, step by step solutions, and recommendations for further practice. Learners receive feedback that matches their level of understanding.

In higher education, many universities use AI based feedback tools integrated into learning management systems. These tools provide automated feedback on assignments and quizzes (Liu, 2025). For example, programming courses often use systems that evaluate code and provide suggestions for improvement. Students receive feedback instantly, which helps them correct errors and learn effectively.

Some institutions also use AI based writing assistants to provide feedback on essays and reports. These tools analyze grammar, structure, and clarity, and provide suggestions for improvement. This helps students improve their writing skills. Personalized feedback systems also support formative assessment. Students receive feedback during the learning process, which helps them improve before final evaluation. Educators can monitor this feedback data to identify areas where students need additional support. (EL Fougour & Erradi, 2025). These examples show that personalized feedback systems enhance learning by providing timely, relevant, and targeted guidance.

Competency Based Assessment Models

Competency based assessment models are used in many institutions to evaluate skills and knowledge rather than only theoretical understanding. One example is *Western Governors University (WGU),* which follows a competency based education model. Students progress through courses by demonstrating mastery of specific skills. Assessment is based on performance rather than time spent in class.

Another example is the use of competency based platforms in professional certification programs. For instance, *Microsoft Learn* provides assessments that test practical skills in technology areas. Learners complete tasks and projects to demonstrate their competency. The system adapts to the learner's progress and provides appropriate challenges.

In higher education, many institutions use competency based assessment in technical and vocational courses. For example, engineering and computer science programs use project based assessments. Students are evaluated based on their ability to apply knowledge in real world scenarios. Adaptive systems support this by providing tasks that match the learner's skill level.

Competency based models are also used in medical education. Students are assessed on clinical skills and decision making abilities. Adaptive assessment systems provide case based scenarios that test practical knowledge. These models allow learners to progress at their own pace. Students who achieve mastery can move forward, while others receive additional support. Feedback is provided to help learners improve their skills. Competency based assessment models show how adaptive systems can support skill oriented education. They focus on practical learning and prepare students for professional environments.

FUTURE DIRECTIONS IN AI DRIVEN ASSESSMENT

The use of Artificial Intelligence in assessment is still evolving and offers many opportunities for future development. As technology advances, assessment systems are expected to become more intelligent, responsive, and inclusive. AI driven assessment will move beyond simple automation and focus more on supporting learning, skill development, and real time evaluation.

Future systems will integrate advanced technologies such as machine learning, natural language processing, and data analytics to create more accurate and personalized assessment experiences. Institutions will also focus on making assessment systems more inclusive and accessible for diverse learners. At the same time, new research areas will emerge to address challenges related to ethics, fairness, and effectiveness of AI based assessment.

Emerging Technologies in Assessment

Emerging technologies are expected to play a major role in shaping the future of assessment. Machine learning algorithms will improve the ability of systems to analyze learner behavior and predict performance. This will help in creating more accurate and adaptive assessment models.

Natural language processing will enhance the evaluation of descriptive and open ended responses. AI systems will be able to understand and assess written answers more effectively. This will allow for more comprehensive assessment beyond objective questions.

Another important development is the use of real time analytics. Assessment systems will be able to track learner performance continuously and provide instant feedback. This will support ongoing learning and improvement. Virtual and augmented reality technologies are also expected to be used in assessment. These technologies can create realistic environments where learners can demonstrate practical skills. For example, students in medical or engineering fields can be assessed through simulated scenarios.

Blockchain technology may be used to store assessment records securely. This will ensure transparency and authenticity of academic achievements. It can also support the verification of skills and competencies. These emerging technologies will make assessment more interactive, accurate, and aligned with real world applications.

Inclusive and Accessible Assessment Design

The assessment systems in the future will work on inclusivity and accessibility. The possibility of AI driven systems to offer equal chances to learn to all the students irrespective of their abilities and backgrounds is a possibility. Adaptive assessment is able to assist learners with varying learning speeds and styles. Appropriate tasks and feedback can be offered to those students who require more time or assistance. This facilitates breaking of learning barriers. Features like accessibility like text to speech, speech to text, and multilingual will be more prevalent. Such characteristics will assist disabled or language learners to actively engage in testing. It is also possible to customize the format of the questions by AI systems to suit the needs of the learners. As an illustration, the visual learners can get graphical questions, whereas the rest can get text based questions. This enhances comprehension and interaction. Also inclusive assessment design entails minimizing bias. A variety of data should be trained to AI systems to make them fair. Assessment systems should be checked on a regular basis in institutions to enable them to detect and address bias. Another important aspect is flexibility. Students must be in a position to get the tests at various devices and places. This promotes online learning and enhances access. Assessment systems will be inclusive and accessible to establish a more equitable learning environment. They make sure that every learner is given a chance to showcase his/her skills.

Research Opportunities and Trends

AI driven assessment opens many opportunities for research and development. Researchers are exploring new methods to improve the accuracy, fairness, and effectiveness of assessment systems. One important area of research is improving adaptive algorithms. Researchers are working on developing models that can better understand learner behavior and provide more precise assessment. This will improve the reliability of AI systems.

Another area is the study of learning analytics. Researchers are analyzing large datasets to understand learning patterns and predict student performance. This information can be used to improve teaching strategies and assessment design.

Ethical issues are also a key focus of research. Studies are being conducted to address concerns related to bias, privacy, and transparency. Researchers aim to develop guidelines for responsible use of AI in assessment.

Research is also exploring the integration of AI with competency based education. This includes developing systems that can accurately measure skills and support continuous learning.

Interdisciplinary research is becoming more important. Experts from education, computer science, and psychology are working together to improve assessment systems. This collaboration helps in developing more effective and user friendly solutions. Future trends include the use of explainable AI, which helps users understand how decisions are made by AI systems. This increases trust and transparency. Research and innovation will continue to shape the future of AI driven assessment. These developments will support better learning outcomes and more effective education systems.

CONCLUSION

Generative Artificial Intelligence Generative AI is changing the way higher education is evaluated in adaptive and personalized assessment systems. These systems no longer follow the one size fits all methods and they emphasize on learner centered assessment. They help to better assess student learning by using data driven insights, personalized feedback, and adjusting the difficulty of questions. The chapter has indicated how adaptive assessment is consistent with key pedagogical concepts like constructivism, formative assessment and competency based learning. These pillars will make sure that assessment is used to support learning and acquisition of skills and not just to gauge performance. The contributions of AI in question generation, difficulty levels, and feedback demonstrates how technology can be effective and efficient in quality improvement. Concurrently, the chapter also emphasizes the role of human control. Teachers are still at the heart of the assessment. They play a critical role in validating AI outputs, being fair, and setting guidance to learners. An integrated system of AI and human judgment creates reliable and effective evaluation systems. Another important factor is institutional readiness. Implementation would need adequate infrastructure, faculty education, and effective policy guidelines to be successful. Institutions should make sure that AI systems are implemented in a responsible manner and in line with educational objectives. Academic integrity, bias, and data privacy are some of the ethical aspects that need to be considered to ensure the system is trusted. The examples given in the case illustrate that adaptive assessment is already being implemented in actual educational contexts. These implementations demonstrate an increase in engagement, flexibility, and outcomes of learning. The further evolution of AI and new technologies will lead to the further improvement of these systems and make them more inclusive and available. On-to-one and adaptive testing is a significant move towards education modernization. They advocate lifelong learning, knowledge building and equitable assessment. These systems can also be used to establish effective and learner centered learning environments with responsible use and guidance.

REFERENCES

Ahmed, A. M., & Mejri, M. (2025). Generative AI for cybersecurity awareness training. Proceedings, 1–10. DOI: 10.1109/IECON58223.2025.11221870

Ahmed, Z., Shanto, S. S., Khanom Rime, M. H., Morol, M. K., Fahad, N., Hossen, J., & Abdullah-Al-Jubair, M. (2024). The generative AI landscape in education: Mapping the terrain of opportunities, challenges and student perception. *IEEE Access : Practical Innovations, Open Solutions*, *1*, 147023–147050. Advance online publication. DOI: 10.1109/ACCESS.2024.3461874

Alali, R. M., & Wardat, Y. (2024). *Opportunities and challenges of integrating generative artificial intelligence in education.* International Journal of Religion., DOI: 10.61707/8y29gv34

AlMohsen, F. (2025). Ethical integration of generative AI in higher education assessments. Advances in Computational Intelligence and Robotics Book Series, 275–288. DOI: 10.4018/979-8-3693-7332-3.ch017

Arslan, B., Lehman, B., Tenison, C., Sparks, J. R., López, A. A., Gu, L., & Zapata-Rivera, D. (2024). Opportunities and challenges of using generative AI to personalize educational assessment. *Frontiers in Artificial Intelligence*, *7*, 1460651. Advance online publication. DOI: 10.3389/frai.2024.1460651 PMID: 39434872

Bhardwaj, S., & Sharma, I. (2025). Exploring the effects of AI-powered personalized classroom management strategies. In *Transforming education with AI-powered personalized learning* (pp. 25–48). IGI Global., DOI: 10.4018/979-8-3693-5443-8.ch002

Bouguettaya, S., Pupo, F., Chen, M., & Fortino, G. (2025). A meta-survey of generative AI in education: Trends, challenges, and research directions. *Big Data and Cognitive Computing*, *9*(9), 237. DOI: 10.3390/bdcc9090237

EL Fougour, W., & Erradi, M. (2025). Enhancing formative assessment with AI. Advances in Computational Intelligence and Robotics Book Series, 307–332. DOI: 10.4018/979-8-3373-7579-3.ch010

Ismail, A., Tanweer, M., & Farooq, S. (2024). Transforming assessments with generative AI. Advances in Educational Technologies and Instructional Design Book Series, 379–404. DOI: 10.4018/979-8-3693-2418-9.ch014

Iswari, N. M. S. (2025). Personalized learning system based on artificial intelligence to enhance learning effectiveness: A bibliometric analysis. *G-Tech*, *9*(3), 1436–1446. DOI: 10.70609/g-tech.v9i3.7355

Janardhana, D. R., Arif, H., Bhat, U. H., Rukmini, T., Hanumanthappa, H., & Gaikwad, V. (2025). Personalized learning systems using AI enhancing adaptive education. *International Journal of Environmental Sciences*, •••, 668–676. DOI: 10.64252/ps80c806

Kaddouri, M., Mhamdi, K., Jabri, A., Boukare, M., & Jmad, S. (2025). Generative artificial intelligence and assessment of learning. Advances in Educational Technologies and Instructional Design Book Series, 277–326. DOI: 10.4018/979-8-3693-6527-4.ch010

Khlaif, Z. N., Odeh, A., & Bsharat, T. R. K. (2024). Generative AI-powered adaptive assessment. Advances in Educational Technologies and Instructional Design Book Series, 157–176. DOI: 10.4018/979-8-3693-6397-3.ch007

Leon, M. (2024). Generative AI as a new paradigm for personalized tutoring in modern education. *International Journal of Integrating Technology in Education, 15*(3), 49–63. DOI: 10.5121/ijite.2024.13304

Liu, L. (2025). Beyond one-size-fits-all: An AI-driven approach for personalized quizzes using clustering and ChatGPT. *International Journal of Information and Education Technology (IJIET), 15*(9), 1768–1776. DOI: 10.18178/ijiet.2025.15.9.2378

Maity, S., & Deroy, A. (2024). Generative AI and its impact on personalized intelligent tutoring systems. https://doi.org/DOI: 10.35542/osf.io/kawr5

Manokore, K., Manokore, A. S., & Chigora, T. B. (2024). Educational assessments in the age of generative AI. Advances in Educational Marketing, Administration, and Leadership Book Series, 59–92. DOI: 10.4018/979-8-3693-6351-5.ch003

May, T. A., Provinzano, K., Koskey, K. L. K., Sondergeld, C. J., Stone, G. E., Archer, J., & Rimkunas, N. (2025). Expanding the team: Integrating generative artificial intelligence into the assessment development process. *Applied Sciences (Basel, Switzerland), 15*(18), 9976. DOI: 10.3390/app15189976

Mimoudi, A. (2025). Generative AI to bridge the educational divide: Personalized learning and challenges. *Social Sciences & Humanities Open, 12*, 102140. DOI: 10.1016/j.ssaho.2025.102140

Suna, H. E., & Özer, M. (2025). Assessment in higher education in the era of generative AI. Advances in Computational Intelligence and Robotics Book Series, 241–274. DOI: 10.4018/979-8-3373-7579-3.ch008

Tariq, M. U. (2024). Advancing inquiry-based learning through generative AI-enabled assessments. Advances in Educational Marketing, Administration, and Leadership Book Series, 179–206. DOI: 10.4018/979-8-3693-6351-5.ch007

Tarun, B., Du, H., Kannan, D., & Gehringer, E. F. (2025). Human-in-the-loop systems for adaptive learning using generative AI. arXiv. /arxiv.2508.11062DOI: 10.1109/FIE63693.2025.11328658

Xu, Y., Ding, Z., Zhang, Z., Zhou, L., Zhou, Y., & Ge, Z.-G. (2025). Personalized learning resources created by generative artificial intelligence: A systematic review. Proceedings, 84–89. DOI: 10.1109/ICETT66247.2025.11137092

Yadav, R., Huzooree, G., Yadav, M., & Gangodawilage, D. (2025). Generative AI for personalized learning content creation. Advances in Computational Intelligence and Robotics Book Series, 107–130. DOI: 10.4018/979-8-3693-8744-3.ch005

Zhang, Q. (2024). Harnessing artificial intelligence for personalized learning pathways: A framework for adaptive education management systems. *Applied and Computational Engineering*, *82*(1), 167–172. DOI: 10.54254/2755-2721/82/20241102

KEY TERMS AND DEFINITIONS

Academic Integrity in AI Assessment: It refers to maintaining honesty, fairness, and ethical behavior in AI supported evaluation systems. It involves preventing misuse of AI tools, ensuring originality of student work, and maintaining transparency in assessment processes. Challenges include plagiarism, unauthorized use of AI, and bias in automated systems. Institutions address these issues through policies, monitoring, and human oversight. Maintaining academic integrity ensures trust in assessment outcomes and supports meaningful learning.

Adaptive Assessment: It is an evaluation approach in which the sequence and difficulty of questions change based on the learner's responses. The system continuously analyzes performance and adjusts the level of challenge in real time. Correct responses lead to more complex questions, while incorrect responses lead to simpler or supportive tasks. This method helps in identifying the learner's actual ability level more accurately than fixed assessments. It also improves engagement by maintaining an appropriate level of difficulty throughout the assessment process.

Competency Based Assessment: It evaluates learners based on their ability to demonstrate specific skills and knowledge. It focuses on mastery of learning outcomes rather than completion of course content. Learners progress when they achieve required competencies. Adaptive assessment supports this approach by presenting tasks that match the learner's ability level. This ensures accurate measurement of skills and allows learners to improve at their own pace. It is widely used in skill oriented and professional education.

Formative Assessment: It is an ongoing evaluation process that takes place during learning. It focuses on providing continuous feedback to help learners improve their performance. Unlike final examinations, formative assessment supports learning throughout the course. Adaptive systems enhance formative assessment by offering real time feedback and adjusting tasks based on performance. This approach helps learners identify their strengths and weaknesses and encourages continuous improvement and active engagement in the learning process.

Generative Artificial Intelligence: It is a type of AI that can create new content such as text, questions, feedback, and learning materials. In assessment, it is used to generate questions, evaluate responses, and provide personalized feedback. It works by analyzing large datasets and learning patterns to produce meaningful outputs. This technology helps in automating assessment design and improving efficiency. It also supports adaptive systems by generating dynamic and varied assessment items aligned with learning objectives.

Human in the Loop: It refers to the involvement of educators in AI driven assessment systems. While AI performs automated tasks such as question generation and evaluation, educators supervise and validate the process. This ensures accuracy, fairness, and alignment with learning objectives. Human oversight helps in identifying errors, reducing bias, and maintaining academic integrity. It creates a balanced system where technology supports efficiency and human judgment ensures quality and ethical practices.

Learning Analytics: It involves the collection, analysis, and interpretation of data related to student learning. It includes data such as performance scores, response patterns, and engagement levels. This information is used to understand learning behavior and improve teaching and assessment practices. Learning analytics supports adaptive assessment by providing insights that help adjust question difficulty and feedback. It also helps educators identify learning gaps and provide targeted support to students, leading to better academic outcomes.

Personalized Assessment: It refers to the design of evaluation methods that consider individual learner characteristics such as prior knowledge, learning pace, strengths, and weaknesses. Each learner receives tasks and feedback that match their specific needs. This approach supports inclusivity and fairness by recognizing differences among students. Personalized assessment also enhances learning by providing relevant challenges and targeted guidance. It allows learners to progress at their own pace and improves overall learning outcomes in higher education.

Chapter 8
AI-Driven Assessment:
Balancing Innovation With Validity and Authenticity of Assessment Evidence

Kristofina Junias
http://orcid.org/0009-0008-5206-1880
Namibia University of Science and Technology, Namibia

ABSTRACT

Generative Artificial Intelligence (AI) is transforming higher education assessment yet challenging the validity and authenticity of assessment evidence. This chapter argues that the central concern extends beyond academic dishonesty to whether assessment evidence genuinely reflects students' learning, reasoning, and demonstrated competence. Drawing on Messick's unified theory of validity and principles of authentic assessment, the chapter examines how AI may introduce construct-irrelevant variance and weaken the authenticity of assessment evidence. It proposes a framework for preserving valid and authentic assessment evidence through process-based assessment, supervised assessment, multimodal and authentic assessment, and ethical AI-literate engagement. The chapter concludes that sustainable assessment in the AI era requires higher education to move beyond AI detection and prohibition towards assessment practices that generate trustworthy evidence of student learning and competence.

INTRODUCTION

The emergence and adoption of Artificial Intelligence (AI) technologies are transforming higher education in unprecedented ways. Universities globally inte-

DOI: 10.4018/979-8-3373-9089-5.ch008

grate AI tools into teaching, learning, research, administration, and student support systems (Mariam, 2024; Mudenda, 2025; Rao & Suhasini, 2025; Shwedeh, 2024). Generative AI tools such as ChatGPT, Gemini, Copilot and others have attracted significant attention due to their ability to generate human-like responses, provide instant feedback, summarise information, and support content creation (Boral & Mondal, 2025). The usage of these generative AI tools has introduced both opportunities and challenges for higher education institutions, particularly in relation to assessment practices.

Assessment is one of the most disrupted domains in higher education due to the capabilities of generative AI. Traditionally, assessment has served as a mechanism for measuring student learning, demonstrating competence, and generating evidence upon which judgments about student performance are made. However, the increasing use of AI tools by students during assessment activities is reshaping the nature of assessment evidence and challenging long-standing assumptions about authorship, originality, and the demonstration of competence (Montebello, 2025; Trajkovski & Hayes, 2025). Assessment tasks that were previously assumed to represent students' independent thinking and understanding can now be completed, enhanced, or generated through AI platforms.

The growing use of AI in assessment contexts has resulted into intense debates within the higher education landscape. Earlier debates focused on concerns related to academic dishonesty and plagiarism. However, the implications of AI extend beyond conventional concerns about cheating. The emergence of generative AI raises important assessment questions regarding validity, authenticity, fairness, and the interpretation of assessment results (Kaldaras et al., 2024; Matheis & Jubin, 2025). When students rely heavily on AI-generated responses, assessments may no longer accurately measure the intended competencies (Karadağ, 2023; Zhao et al., 2024), but rather their ability to effectively prompt, manipulate, and refine outputs produced by AI tools. This introduces construct-irrelevant variance and threatens the validity of interpretations made from assessment results (Messick, 1989).

Furthermore, the integration of AI into assessment practices challenges the authenticity of assessment evidence. Traditionally, authentic assessment emphasises the demonstration of meaningful learning, application of knowledge in real world contexts, and the production of evidence that reflects student competence (Wiggins, 1990). In this era of AI, distinguishing between student-generated and AI-generated work becomes increasingly difficult, raising concerns about the credibility and integrity of qualifications awarded by higher education institutions (Alshanetsky, 2025; Revell, 2024). The debate surrounding AI in assessment is not only about preventing misconduct, but about safeguarding the quality, trustworthiness, and meaningfulness of assessment systems in contemporary higher education.

Despite these concerns, AI should not be viewed exclusively as a threat to assessment. AI-powered tools also present significant pedagogical opportunities for both academics and students. For academics, AI can support the efficient design of assessment tasks, alignment of assessments with learning outcomes, generation of authentic assessment tasks, designing of marking rubrics, and provision of timely feedback (Ahmad, 2022; Owan et al., 2023; Tang, 2024; Zawacki-Richter, 2019). For students, AI tools can improve learning through personalised support, immediate feedback, clarification of difficult concepts, and assistance with assessment preparation (Gligorea, 2023; Lin, 2023; Sajja, 2024; Strielkowski, 2025) The challenge facing higher education institutions is not whether AI should be prohibited or not embraced, but how assessment practices can be rebalanced to preserve validity, authenticity, and fairness while leveraging the educational benefits of AI.

Drawing on Messick's unified theory of validity, this chapter argues that the increasing presence of AI in higher education necessitates a fundamental reconsideration of assessment design and evidence generation. Take-home assessments and unsupervised written tasks are becoming vulnerable in the era of AI. Thus, there is a need for higher education institutions to adopt assessment approaches that place greater emphasis on process-based assessment, supervised tasks, multimodal evidence, and authentic demonstrations of learning. The chapter contends that sustainable assessment practices in the era of AI must move beyond product-oriented approaches and towards assessment systems that verify students' competencies.

The chapter is organised into several sections. The first section conceptualises Artificial Intelligence within the context of higher education assessment and discusses the growing integration of AI-powered tools in assessment practices. The second section examines the theoretical foundations underpinning the chapter, with particular focus on validity, authenticity, and assessment integrity. The third section analyses how generative AI threatens the validity and authenticity of assessment evidence through construct-irrelevant variance and challenges to authorship and fairness. The fourth section explores strategies for rebalancing assessment practices in higher education. The chapter then proposes a conceptual framework for balancing innovation with validity and authenticity in AI-mediated assessment environments. Finally, the chapter discusses implications for higher education institutions and concludes by reflecting on the future of assessment in the age of Artificial Intelligence.

CONCEPTUAL APPROACH

This chapter adopts a conceptual approach to examine how generative Artificial Intelligence is reshaping the nature and credibility of assessment evidence in higher education. The chapter synthesises contemporary scholarship on generative AI and higher education assessment and interprets emerging assessment challenges through established theoretical perspectives. Attention is given to literature addressing AI-mediated assessment, assessment validity, authentic assessment, AI literacy, and changing approaches to assessment in higher education. The conceptual analysis is anchored in Messick's unified theory of validity and principles of authentic assessment. These perspectives provide the theoretical basis for examining whether assessment evidence generated in AI-mediated environments continues to support valid interpretations of student learning and authentically represents students' knowledge, reasoning, engagement, and demonstrated competence. Through this theoretical synthesis, key challenges posed by generative AI to assessment evidence are identified and connected to corresponding assessment response mechanisms. These relationships inform the development of the Framework for Preserving Valid and Authentic Assessment Evidence in AI-Mediated Higher Education, which represents the chapter's principal conceptual contribution

CONCEPTUALISING AI IN EDUCATION

Wang (2019) argued that artificial intelligence is fraught with definitional problems pointing a definition influencing the path of the research. For the sake of this work, AI refers to the capability of computer systems to perform tasks that typically require human intelligence, such as reasoning, problem-solving, decision-making, language processing, pattern recognition, and learning from data (Russell & Norvig, 2021). In educational contexts, AI involves the use of intelligent technologies to support teaching, learning, assessment, administration, and student engagement (Ahmad et al., 2022). AI technologies have expanded the ways in which higher education institutions interact with digital learning environments, particularly through tools capable of generating content, analysing student data, and adapting instructional experiences to individual student needs.

Advancements in machine learning, natural language processing, and Large Language Models (LLM) has accelerated the integration of AI in higher education. These technologies enable AI systems to process large amounts of information, generate human-like responses, and provide real-time support to users (Nallamothu, 2024; Shakoor,2024). As a result, AI-powered tools are now being used by both academics and students for pedagogical purposes making AI one of the most transformative developments in contemporary higher education. AI can be broadly categorised into generative AI, predictive AI, and adaptive AI, each serving different functions within the education context:

Generative Artificial Intelligence

These are AI systems capable of creating new content such as text, images, audio, code, and responses based on prompts provided by users (Harrington, 2024. These systems generate outputs by analysing patterns from large datasets and generate new data (Eysenbach, 2023; Harrington, 2024; Rashidi et al, 2025). In higher education, generative AI tools are used to draft essays, summarise content, generate assessment questions and answers, provide explanations, support academic writing etc. (Pang & Wei, 2025; Poellhuber & Lepage, 2024). Examples of generative AI tools include ChatGPT developed by OpenAI, Gemini developed by Google, and Microsoft Co-pilot and others. The emergence of these tools has transformed assessment practices because students can now generate responses within seconds, raising important questions about authorship, originality, and the authenticity of assessment evidence.

Predictive Artificial Intelligence

Predictive AI analyse existing data to forecast future outcomes or behaviours (Harrington, 2024; Khare, 2023). In higher education, predictive AI is commonly used in learning analytics systems to identify patterns related to student performance, engagement, progression, and retention (Darbyshire & Beitsayadeh, 2025; Rodríguez-Ortiz et al, 2025). For example, predictive AI can be used to identify students at risk of academic failure, predict learning outcomes based on engagement patterns, and support institutional decision-making regarding student support interventions. These systems rely on data analysis and pattern recognition to assist educators and institutions in making informed academic decisions.

Adaptive Artificial Intelligence

These are intelligent systems that personalise learning experiences based on individual student needs, behaviours, and performance. Adaptive learning technologies analyse student interactions and adjust instructional content, difficulty levels, feedback, and learning pathways accordingly (Lin et al, 2023; Sajja et al,2024; Zawacki-Richter et al., 2019). In educational settings, adaptive AI can provide personalised quizzes, customised learning resources, and differentiated feedback tailored to students' levels of understanding. Such systems are valuable for their potential to support student-centred learning and enhance student engagement through personalised educational experiences.

Although these categories of AI perform different functions, they may intersect within contemporary higher education systems. Generative AI tools may incorporate adaptive features, while predictive AI systems can inform personalised learning pathways. As a result, AI technologies are becoming deeply embedded within the broader teaching, learning, and assessment ecosystem of higher education institutions. However, among these categories, generative AI has generated the greatest concern within assessment discourse because of its ability to produce responses that may appear indistinguishable from student-generated work posing a threat to assessment integrity (Kofinas, 2025; Leaton & Parapadakis, 2025; Lye & Lim, 2024; Yeo, 2023). This development has profound implications for how higher education institutions conceptualise assessment evidence, academic integrity, and the demonstration of competence in AI-mediated learning environments.

INTEGRATION OF AI IN ASSESSMENT PRACTICES

The integration of AI within assessment systems in higher education is shifting the ways assessments are designed, administered, evaluated, and interpreted. Higher education institutions are now adopting AI technologies to enhance efficiency, improve student support, and modernise assessment-related processes. The integration of AI into assessment practices reflects a broader shift towards digitally mediated learning environments in which data-driven technologies play a significant role in educational decision-making.

One of the major areas in which AI is being used is assessment design. Academics use generative AI tools to assist in the creation of assessment tasks and marking rubrics (Ilieva et al., 2025; Khlaif et al,2024; Owoseni et al,2024). Generative AI tools can generate diverse assessment items aligned with specific learning outcomes reducing the time and workload associated with assessment preparation. AI-generated question banks can also support assessment diversification by producing multiple versions of assessment items, thereby reducing predictability and opportunities for academic dishonesty. In addition, AI tools can assist academics to design authentic and contextualised assessment tasks (Nguyen Thanh et al., 2023) by generating real-world scenarios. Such capabilities are particularly valuable in large classes where academics are often required to produce multiple assessment variations while maintaining consistency and alignment with curriculum outcomes.

The second area is the use AI in automated marking and grading processes. Automated marking systems have been associated with improved efficiency, consistency, and faster feedback turnaround times, particularly in higher education contexts characterised by large student enrolments (Balfour, 2013; Luckin et al., 2016). Automated marking systems have long been used to mark objective items. However, in the current era of AI technologies, automated systems are now able to evaluate more complex student responses viz; the subjective responses. AI-powered marking systems can analyse grammar, coherence, structure, argumentation, and language patterns to generate provisional grades and scoring recommendations (Mammadova et al. 2025; Murff, 2025). Furthermore, AI-assisted grading can support academics by reducing repetitive marking tasks and enabling greater focus on higher-level instructional responsibilities (Tan et al., 2025).

In addition to automated marking is the use of AI in feedback generation. Timely and constructive feedback is recognised as a critical component of effective learning and assessment. AI-powered tools can provide immediate feedback to students. AI technologies can identify errors, suggest corrections, explain concepts, and provide personalised recommendations for improvement (Kochmar et al., 2022). In writing-intensive subjects such as languages, AI-based writing assistants can offer feedback on grammar, sentence structure, referencing, clarity, and organisation (Bahari, 2025). The capacity of AI systems to provide immediate and personalised feedback has the potential to enhance student engagement, support self-regulated learning, and improve assessment preparation.

Another important application of AI in assessment involves AI detection and academic integrity management. Higher education institutions have adopted AI-powered AI detection software to identify similarities between student submissions and existing sources. Tools such as Turnitin and others are commonly used to detect copied content, inappropriate paraphrasing, and potential breaches of academic integrity policies. Of recent, AI detection tools have emerged with the aim of identifying whether student submissions were generated by AI systems. These tools analyse linguistic patterns, sentence structures, and probability models to estimate the likelihood of AI-generated content (Rodrigues et al., 2025). However, the reliability and accuracy of AI-detection technologies remain highly contested, with growing concerns regarding false positives, bias, and the inability to conclusively determine authorship (Dalalah & Dalalah, 2023; Elkhatat et al., 2023; Krishna et al., 2023; Weber-Wulff et al., 2023). Thus, the use of AI in AI detection has generated complex ethical and pedagogical debates concerning trust, surveillance, and fairness in higher education assessment.

Furthermore, AI is transforming assessment through adaptive testing systems. Adaptive assessment technologies use AI algorithms to adjust the difficulty and sequencing of assessment items in real time based on student responses and performance patterns (Ince & Özbay, 2025; Khine, 2024). In adaptive testing environments, students who demonstrate higher levels of competence may receive more advanced questions, while those experiencing difficulties may receive additional support or simpler items. Such systems aim to provide more personalised and accurate measurement of student learning by tailoring assessment experiences to individual student ability levels. Adaptive testing enhances efficiency, improve student engagement, and generate detailed performance data (Khine, 2024).

The last area on how AI is integrated in assessment is the role of AI powered learning analytics systems in supporting assessment-related decision-making. Learning analytics involves the collection, analysis, and interpretation of student data to understand and optimise learning processes (Ray & Saeed, 2018). AI-powered learning analytics systems can track student participation, engagement, submission patterns, assessment performance, and learning behaviours across digital platforms (Kumar et al, 2025). Through predictive modelling, institutions can identify students at risk of academic failure, monitor progression trends, and implement targeted support interventions. Learning analytics can assist academics in identifying difficult content areas, evaluating assessment effectiveness, and informing curriculum improvements.

The integration of AI across these various dimensions of assessment practices proves that AI is no longer an add on technological innovation within higher education assessment, but an embedded component of contemporary educational practice. AI-powered technologies are reshaping how assessments are designed, administered, evaluated, and experienced by both academics and students. While these developments present significant opportunities, they also raise important questions regarding validity, authenticity, authorship, and the integrity of assessment evidence. Thus, necessitating critical examination of how higher education institutions can preserve meaningful and trustworthy assessment practices within AI-mediated learning environments.

Pedagogical Opportunities of AI-Driven Assessment

The increasing integration of Artificial Intelligence into higher education assessment is driven not only by technological advancement, but also by the growing demand for more efficient assessment practices. Higher education institutions across the globe are facing issues such as massification, student diversity, expansion of online and blended learning environments (Castro, 2019; Nyagope, 2024; Obizue et al., 2025), yet academics are expected to provide timely and meaningful assessment support. It is within such a context that AI-driven technologies are viewed as tools capable of enhancing assessment practices and supporting student learning in ways that may not be feasible through traditional approaches alone. Thus AI-driven assessment offers the following pedagogical opportunities:

Enhancing Efficiency and Responsiveness in Assessment

Assessment activities such as question development, marking, moderation, and feedback provision often require substantial time and administrative effort from academics (Nkealah, 2023). In large classes, these demands can delay feedback, reduce opportunities for personalised engagement, and increase academic workload pressures (Nilson & Stanny, 2023; Nkealah, 2023. AI technologies have the potential to automate repetitive assessment tasks and support faster processing of assessment activities, thereby improving institutional responsiveness (Holmes et al., 2019). AI-assisted assessment systems support quicker turnaround times for grading and feedback, enabling students to receive responses within shorter timeframes. This is important because timely feedback offers opportunities for reflection, correction of misconceptions, and continuous learning. In this way, AI technologies may contribute towards more sustainable assessment practices by reducing administrative burdens while supporting continuity in teaching and learning processes.

Supporting Personalised and Student-Centred Learning

AI-driven technologies create opportunities for more personalised and student-centred approaches to assessment and learning support. Traditional assessment practices often apply uniform approaches to diverse student populations despite significant differences in learning pace, prior knowledge, academic readiness, and learning preferences (Tomlinson, 2017). However, AI technologies have the capacity to analyse student interactions, performance trends, and engagement patterns and provide customised learning experiences and targeted academic support (Holmes et al., 2019; Khaliq et al., 2025). Such personalisation may enhance student engagement and improve students' ability to take ownership of their learning processes. This implies that AI has the potential to strengthen student autonomy and support inclusive educational environments within higher education institutions.

Strengthening Formative Assessment Practices

Formative assessment focuses on supporting learning during the instructional process through continuous feedback, monitoring, and improvement. Effective formative assessment requires timely feedback, active student participation, and opportunities for students to identify and address learning gaps (Irons & Elkington, 2021; Morris et al., 2021). However, providing frequent and individualised formative feedback can be difficult in contexts characterised by heavy teaching workloads and large class sizes (Nkealah, 2023). AI technologies can support formative assessment by providing immediate and ongoing feedback during learning activities (Kasneci et al., 2023; Tlili et al., 2023). Students can receive instant responses regarding errors, misconceptions, and areas requiring improvement while engaging with learning tasks. AI systems can facilitate iterative learning processes where students continuously revise and improve their work based on automated guidance and feedback. This way AI technologies may contribute towards assessment approaches that emphasise learning progression rather than a measurement of final performance outcomes.

Expanding Opportunities for Authentic and Innovative Assessment

Traditional assessment approaches have often been criticised for overemphasising memorisation, reproduction of information, and decontextualised testing practices (Heidari & House, 2025; Ghosh et al., 2020). In contrast, authentic assessment emphasises the application of knowledge, problem-solving, critical thinking, and performance in real contexts (Koh, 2017; Oroh et al., 2025). Generative AI systems can assist academics in developing contextualised assessment tasks that mirror real-world situations. It can facilitate multimodal assessment approaches incorporating text, visuals, simulations, and interactive activities (Gonsalves, 2025), thereby expanding opportunities for students to demonstrate learning in diverse ways. These developments imply a shift from content-focused assessment towards more competency-oriented and experiential forms of learning evaluation.

Supporting Data-Informed Assessment Decision-Making

Traditional assessment systems often generate isolated performance outcomes such as grades but provide limited insight into the broader learning behaviours and engagement patterns underlying student performance (Lim, 2024; Sharma et al., 2025). AI-powered learning analytics systems can overcome this limitation by analysing large volumes of student data to identify patterns related to engagement, participation, progression, and academic performance (Kumar et al, 2025).. Assessment data generated through AI systems can assist educators in evaluating the effectiveness of assessment tasks, identifying difficult content areas, and refining curriculum design.

THEORETICAL FOUNDATIONS: VALIDITY AND AUTHENTICITY OF ASSESSMENT EVIDENCE

The integration of Artificial Intelligence into higher education assessment raises fundamental questions regarding the meaning, credibility, and interpretation of assessment evidence (Bearman et al., 2022; Kasneci et al., 2023). Most of the contemporary discourse surrounding AI in education focuses on technological capabilities and concerns about academic dishonesty however, the implications of AI extend far beyond AI detection or policy compliance (Tlili et al., 2023; Perkins, 2023). At the centre of the debate lies a deeper educational question concerning whether assessment practices in AI-mediated environments still generate valid, authentic, and trustworthy evidence of student learning and competence. Thus, understanding the impact of AI on assessment requires engagement with foundational assessment theories relating to validity, authenticity, and assessment integrity.

Understanding Educational Assessment

Educational assessment plays a central role in teaching and learning processes. Assessment is not only about allocating marks or certifying student achievement, but a systematic process through which evidence of learning is generated, interpreted, and used to make judgments about student competence (Suskie, 2018). Through assessment, higher education institutions seek to determine whether students have achieved intended learning outcomes and developed the competencies associated with a particular qualification or programme of study.

Traditionally, assessment serves multiple purposes within higher education viz; formative purposes aimed at supporting learning and improvement during the instructional process, as well as summative purposes concerned with grading, certification, progression, and accountability (Archer, 2017; Flahive, 2026; Suskie, 2023). Assessment also performs diagnostic functions by identifying learning gaps and informing instructional decisions (Suskie, 2023). Regardless of these different purposes, the credibility of assessment depends on whether the evidence generated genuinely reflects what students know, understand, and can do.

Central to educational assessment is the notion of assessment as evidence of learning. Assessment tasks are designed to elicit observable performances, responses, or products from which inferences about student competence can be made. Therefore, assessment does not directly measure learning itself but rather relies on evidence generated through student performance in relation to specific tasks. The validity of assessment therefore depends on the extent to which the evidence produced accurately represents the intended learning outcomes and competencies being assessed (Messick, 1989; Nitko & Brookhart, 2014). This relationship highlights the importance of alignment between learning outcomes, assessment tasks, and assessment judgments (Biggs & Tang, 2011). Learning outcomes define the knowledge, skills, attitudes students are expected to achieve. Assessment tasks are then designed to provide opportunities for students to demonstrate achievement of these outcomes. Then assessment judgments are made which involve interpreting the evidence produced through student performance to determine the extent to which the intended outcomes have been achieved. The principle in assessment practices assumes that the work submitted by students constitutes credible evidence upon which valid interpretations and judgments can be based. However, the emergence of generative AI challenges this foundational assumption (Bearman et al., 2022; Cotton et al., 2023). In AI-mediated assessment environments, the relationship between student competence, assessment tasks, and assessment evidence becomes complex because the submitted work may no longer solely represent the intellectual effort, reasoning, or understanding of the student. Instead, assessment evidence may partly reflect the capabilities of AI systems used during task completion. This development raises critical concerns regarding whether assessment results can still be interpreted as valid indicators of student learning and competence.

Messick's Unified Theory of Validity

The concept of validity occupies a central position in educational assessment because it is concerned with the legitimacy and appropriateness of interpretations made from assessment results. Among the most influential contributions to validity theory is Messick's unified theory of validity, which reconceptualised validity as an integrated and comprehensive construct rather than a collection of separate validity types (Messick, 1989). Messick conceptualised validity as the extent to which assessment results can be appropriately interpreted and used to make meaningful judgments about students' competencies. Thus, validity is not just a property of a test or assessment instrument itself, but a judgment concerning the appropriateness, meaningfulness, and consequences of score interpretation (Kane, 2013).

Messick conceptualised validity as a unified form of construct validity supported through multiple interrelated sources of evidence viz, content, substantive, structural, generalisability, external, and consequential aspects. Together, these dimensions provide a comprehensive framework for evaluating the quality and validity of assessment interpretations.

The content dimension of construct validity concerns the extent to which assessment tasks adequately represent the domain of knowledge, skills, and attitudes intended to be assessed. Assessment tasks should therefore align with learning outcomes and curriculum expectations (Messick, 1989; Kane, 2013). In AI-mediated environments, concerns emerge when assessment tasks become vulnerable to AI-generated responses that may not genuinely reflect students' understanding of the intended content domain.

The substantive dimension of construct validity focuses on the cognitive processes and reasoning engaged during assessment performance. This aspect emphasises whether students engage in the intended intellectual processes required by the assessment task (Messick, 1989). Generative AI introduces concerns in this regard because students may rely on AI-generated responses rather than independently engaging in analysis, reasoning, problem-solving, or knowledge construction processes expected by the assessment.

The structural dimension of construct validity relates to the internal structure of assessment tasks and scoring processes. It examines whether assessment scoring reflects the intended constructs being measured (Messick, 1989). In AI-mediated assessment, the structural integrity of assessment may be compromised when scoring systems reward polished AI-generated outputs without distinguishing between genuine student competence and technologically assisted production.

The generalisability dimension of construct validity concerns the consistency and stability of assessment interpretations across tasks, contexts, and conditions. Valid assessment should produce dependable interpretations regardless of variations in assessment settings or administration conditions (Messick, 1989; Kane, 2013). However, unequal access to AI technologies, differences in students' AI literacy, and different institutional policies may introduce inconsistencies that affect the comparability and fairness of assessment outcomes.

The external dimension of construct validity examines relationships between assessment outcomes and other relevant measures or indicators of competence. Assessment results should meaningfully correspond with broader demonstrations of knowledge, performance, or professional capability (Messick, 1989; Kane, 2013).. In AI-mediated assessment environments, concerns arise regarding whether assessment results continue to predict actual competence if students rely on AI-generated responses during assessment tasks.

The consequential dimension of construct validity focuses on the social consequences and implications of assessment practices and interpretations. According to Messick, validity cannot be separated from the consequences arising from assessment use. Assessment systems that generate misleading interpretations about student competence may produce harmful educational and societal consequences. For example, within higher education this concern becomes important when graduates receive qualifications that may not accurately reflect their independent knowledge, skills, or professional readiness due to extensive reliance on AI-generated assessment responses.

Messick's unified theory is relevant in the context of Artificial Intelligence because it shifts the assessment debate beyond concerns about cheating towards deeper questions regarding the meaning and legitimacy of assessment interpretations. The issue is not only whether students use AI, but whether assessment practices in AI-rich environments still generate valid evidence upon which trustworthy judgments about competence can be made. Therefore, validity concerns in the age of AI extend to the integrity of the entire assessment interpretation process.

Authenticity in Assessment

The concept of authenticity is closely related to validity in assessment. Authentic assessment emphasises the demonstration and application of knowledge, skills, and competencies in real world contexts (Gulikers et al., 2004; Ghosh et al., 2020). Unlike traditional assessment approaches that often prioritise memorisation and reproduction of information (Heidari & House, 2025; Ghosh et al., 2020), authentic assessment seeks to evaluate students' ability to apply learning in ways that resemble real-world situations, professional practice, and complex problem-solving environments. Authentic assessment is grounded in the principle that meaningful learning is best demonstrated through performances, tasks, and activities that reflect application of knowledge and competence. Such assessments often involve case studies, simulations, portfolios, projects, presentations, practical demonstrations, workplace-based tasks, and problem-solving activities that require students to integrate and apply learning rather than merely recall information (McTighe et al., 2020).

An important dimension of authentic assessment is ownership of learning. Authentic assessment assumes that the evidence produced represents students' own understanding, reasoning, reflection, and performance (Black & Warhurst, 2025; Khatter, 2024). The credibility of assessment judgments therefore depends on the extent to which students engage in the learning and production processes demanded by assessment tasks. However, generative AI complicates traditional notions of authenticity in assessment (Cotton et al., 2023; Perkins et al., 2023). AI systems are now capable of generating sophisticated essays, reflections, analyses, problem solutions, and academic responses that may appear highly credible and academically polished. As a result, distinguishing between authentic student performance and AI-generated production becomes difficult (Perkins, 2023). This raises important questions regarding whether assessment evidence still represents students' actual competence, reasoning processes, and intellectual engagement, a fundamental question of validity.

The point of departure is that the use of AI challenges conventional assumptions regarding originality and independent work. In some cases, students may combine their own ideas with AI-generated responses thereby blurring the boundaries between assistance and substitution. Hence, authenticity in assessment can no longer be understood only in terms of whether plagiarism has occurred but must consider the extent to which assessment evidence genuinely reflects students' independent learning and competence.

AI AND THE THREAT TO VALIDITY AND AUTHENTICITY OF ASSESSMENT EVIDENCE

The growing integration of generative AI into higher education assessment presents profound challenges to the validity and authenticity of assessment evidence. While AI technologies offer significant pedagogical opportunities, they at the same time disrupt fundamental assumptions underpinning educational assessment. Traditional assessment practices are premised on the assumption that student submissions represent authentic evidence of students' own understanding, reasoning, and competence. However, the growing capabilities of generative AI complicate this assumption because assessment outputs may reflect the capabilities of AI systems rather than the independent intellectual engagement of students. Therefore, the rise of AI necessitates critical reconsideration of what assessment evidence represents and whether assessment results can continue to support valid and trustworthy judgments about student learning.

Construct-Irrelevant Variance in AI-Mediated Assessment

One of the most significant threats posed by generative AI to educational assessment relates to construct-irrelevant variance. According to Messick (1989) validity theory, construct-irrelevant variance occurs when assessment performance is influenced by factors unrelated to the intended construct being measured. When that happens, assessment outcomes may no longer accurately reflect the competencies that the assessment was designed to evaluate. Instead, extraneous variables influence performance and distort the interpretation of assessment results.

The emergence of generative AI introduces new forms of construct-irrelevant variance within higher education assessment. Traditional written assignments, take-home examinations, reflective tasks, and online assessments are now vulnerable to AI-assisted production of responses (Cotton et al., 2023; Perkins, 2023). In many cases, students may use AI technologies to generate responses that appear sophisticated, coherent, and academically sound (Kasneci et al., 2023; Tlili et al. 2023). Thus, assessment tasks intended to measure students' critical thinking, problem-solving, reasoning, writing ability, or conceptual understanding may instead become measures of students' ability to effectively prompt AI tools, manipulate, edit, or refine AI-generated outputs. This development fundamentally changes the nature of assessment evidence. For example, when an essay assessment is completed with substantial AI assistance, the resulting product may no longer provide valid evidence of the student's independent writing competence, analytical ability, or conceptual understanding. Rather, the final output may partly reflect the capabilities of large language models, students' prompting skills, or their ability to curate AI-generated content. As a result, the relationship between assessment tasks and intended learning outcomes becomes weakened.

Generative AI also challenges the substantive dimension of construct validity because students may not engage in the cognitive processes intended by assessment tasks. Traditionally, assessment activities are designed not merely to produce final products, but to engage students in reasoning, analysis, synthesis, reflection, and knowledge construction processes. However, AI technologies are now able to perform many of these intellectual functions on behalf of students (Bearman et al.,

2022; Perkins, 2023). This results in students bypassing critical learning processes yet producing high-quality assessment outputs. The result is a situation where assessment products appear academically acceptable with limited evidence of genuine intellectual engagement.

Furthermore, AI-mediated assessment environments may undermine the interpretability of assessment results. Academics typically interpret assessment outcomes as indicators of students' independent competence and readiness for progression or professional practice. However, when assessment evidence is shaped by AI-generated production, it becomes difficult to determine what assessment results genuinely represent. This raises important validity concerns because the interpretations and decisions derived from assessment outcomes may no longer accurately correspond to students' actual knowledge and capabilities.

The challenge presented by construct-irrelevant variance therefore extends beyond concerns about academic misconduct. The issue is not simply whether students use AI during assessment, but whether assessments continue to measure the constructs they claim to assess. Thus, generative AI challenges the credibility of the evidence used to make assessment judgments in higher education.

AI and the Erosion of Authentic Assessment Evidence

Compounding to validity concerns, generative AI poses significant threats to the authenticity of assessment evidence. Authentic assessment is concerned with the extent to which assessment tasks and responses genuinely reflect students' own learning, reasoning, and demonstrated competence. The credibility of authentic assessment therefore depends on confidence that assessment evidence represents students' independent intellectual engagement and application of knowledge. However, generative AI complicates the authenticity of assessment evidence because AI systems can produce sound academic responses that may appear indistinguishable from student-generated work. Essays, reports, reflections, literature syntheses, problem solutions, and discussion responses generated through AI technologies may demonstrate coherence, academic language, and conceptual sophistication despite limited student involvement in the actual production process. Thus, the authenticity of submitted assessment evidence becomes uncertain.

The growing use of AI in assessment contexts blurs the boundaries between educational assistance and intellectual substitution (Dawson, 2020; Perkins, 2023). Traditionally, educational support tools such as spell checkers, grammar correction software, dictionaries, or tutoring services were generally viewed as supplementary aids that supported student learning without replacing students' intellectual contribution. Generative AI, however, differs significantly because it can independently generate responses that may replace significant portions of students' cognitive work.

As a result, distinguishing between acceptable support and inappropriate substitution becomes difficult within AI-mediated assessment environments. This blurring of boundaries creates important challenges regarding ownership of learning and demonstration of competence. Authentic assessment assumes that students actively engage in the learning, reasoning, reflection, and production processes underlying assessment tasks. However, when AI systems perform substantial aspects of these processes, the submitted assessment evidence may no longer genuinely represent students' independent competence. In such cases, assessment products risk becoming demonstrations of technological mediation rather than authentic demonstrations of student learning.

The erosion of authentic assessment evidence is particularly problematic in higher education because assessment outcomes are used to support progression, certification, and professional qualification decisions (Carter et al., 2025). Higher education institutions rely on assessment evidence to determine whether graduates possess the competencies required for employment, professional practice, and societal contribution. However, if assessment evidence no longer authentically reflects students' actual capabilities, confidence in the credibility of qualifications may gradually weaken.

Moreover, the challenge of authenticity extends beyond issues of originality or plagiarism. AI-generated responses may be entirely original in wording and structure while still failing to authentically represent students' own understanding and intellectual engagement. Therefore, authenticity in AI-mediated assessment environments cannot simply be reduced to whether copied material is detected. The central concern should be whether assessment evidence genuinely reflects students' independent learning and demonstrated competence.

Consequential Implications for Higher Education Assessment

The threats posed by generative AI to validity and authenticity have broader implications for higher education assessment systems and the credibility of qualifications. According to Messick's consequential dimension of construct validity, assessment practices cannot be separated from the educational and societal consequences arising from their interpretation and use (Messick, 1989). When assessment evidence becomes compromised, the consequences extend beyond individual assessment tasks to affect institutional trust, professional competence, and public confidence in higher education qualifications.

One major implication concerns the potential misrepresentation of student competence. If assessment systems reward AI-assisted outputs that do not accurately reflect students' own knowledge and abilities, then higher education institutions may certify graduates whose demonstrated assessment performance other than their actual competence (Bearman et al., 2022). This creates concerns regarding graduates' preparedness for work, especially in fields where independent reasoning, ethical judgment, problem-solving, and communication are essential.

Degrees and academic credentials derive their value from the assumption that they represent reliable evidence of learning and competence (Tholen, 2020). However, if employers, professional bodies, and society begin to question whether assessment outcomes reflect students' capabilities, they lose trust in the qualifications awarded by higher education institutions. Therefore, higher education institutions are pressurred to redesign assessment practices in ways that preserve the credibility and legitimacy of assessment evidence.

REBALANCING ASSESSMENT IN THE ERA OF AI

The growing capabilities of generative AI suggest a shift in assessment methods. Traditional assessment approaches that rely on independently produced written submissions and unsupervised take-home assignments are now vulnerable in AI-mediated learning environments. Thus, higher education institutions are now forced to reconsider assessment approaches capable of generating valid, authentic, and trustworthy evidence of student learning and competence. The challenge is therefore not whether Artificial Intelligence should be prohibited within higher education, but how assessment systems can be redesigned to preserve the credibility and legitimacy of assessment evidence while acknowledging the realities of AI-rich educational contexts.

Rebalancing assessment in the era of AI requires a shift from assessment methods that focus mainly on final products towards methods that provide full evidence of learning processes, reasoning, participation, and demonstrated competence. This rebalancing does not imply abandoning innovation or technological advancement, but rather strengthening assessment practices in ways that preserve validity and authenticity within increasingly AI-mediated educational environments.

From Product-Based to Process-Based Assessment

Traditional assessment methods in higher education have often prioritised final products such as essays, reports, assignments, and written examinations. However, in AI-rich environments, final products alone may no longer provide sufficient evidence of students' independent learning and intellectual engagement (Bearman et al., 2022; Cotton et al., 2023) because AI systems can generate academically sound outputs. There is need for a paradigm shift from product to process. Process-based assessment shifts attention from only evaluating completed products towards examining how learning occurs throughout the assessment journey. Process based assessment emphasise students' reasoning processes, developmental progression, reflection, and active engagement in knowledge construction. This shift towards process-based assessment aligns closely with Lawrence Stenhouse's process model of curriculum, which emphasises learning as an active process of inquiry, exploration, reflection, and intellectual development rather than the achievement of predetermined outcomes (Stenhouse, 1975). From a process-oriented perspective, the educational value of assessment lies not only in the final product submitted by students, but also in the learning processes, reasoning, engagement, and intellectual growth demonstrated throughout the learning journey. In the context of generative AI, this perspective becomes significant because process-oriented assessment methods may provide credible and authentic evidence of students' independent learning and demonstrated competence than product-oriented assessment methods.

The first strategy for strengthening process-oriented assessment is draft submissions. Academics may break tasks into smaller components requiring students to submit multiple drafts. This allows academics to observe the evolution of students' thinking, argumentation, and writing development over time. Iterative submissions can provide evidence of conceptual progression, revision processes, and engagement with feedback, thereby making learning more visible within assessment practices (Morrell, 2021; Yan et al., 2021). For example:

In a History course and other social science disciplines, students may be required to submit a sequence of assessment components beginning with a topic proposal, followed by an annotated bibliography, draft analysis sections, peer-review reflections, and a final research essay or project. Through these iterative submissions, academics can observe how students refine arguments, engage with sources, incorporate feedback, and progressively develop analytical reasoning over time.

In Engineering or Design-based disciplines, students may submit initial design concepts, prototype sketches, simulation results, testing reports, and revised models before presenting a final product. These staged assessment processes provide evidence of students' problem-solving approaches, decision-making processes, and technical development throughout the learning journey rather than evaluating only the final output.

In a teacher education programme, student teachers may submit lesson plans, reflective journals, classroom observations, peer feedback reports, and revised teaching portfolios across different stages of practicum experiences. These iterative submissions allow academics to evaluate pedagogical growth, reflective practice, and the progressive development of professional competence. In each of these cases, assessment moves beyond judging isolated products towards examining learning as an evolving and developmental process.

The second strategy is reflective practices which may strengthen assessment authenticity by requiring students to explain their reasoning, learning strategies, decision-making processes, and intellectual development. Reflection encourages students to articulate how they approached assessment tasks, justify choices made during the learning process, and evaluate their own understanding (Miller & Konstantinou, 2022). These reflective practices may provide insight into students' genuine engagement with learning tasks beyond the final assessment product only. For example:

In a History course, reflective practices may require students to explain how they selected historical sources, justified interpretations of historical events, evaluated conflicting perspectives, and revised arguments throughout the research process. This can reveal students' historical reasoning and analytical decision-making beyond the final essay itself.

In Engineering, students may reflect on design choices, testing failures, modifications made during prototype development, and the rationale underlying technical decisions. These reflections provide insight into students' problem-solving processes and application of engineering principles throughout the project lifecycle.

In teacher education programmes, student teachers may produce reflective journals discussing lesson planning decisions, classroom management strategies, learner engagement challenges, and adjustments made during teaching practice. This allows lecturers to evaluate pedagogical reasoning, professional growth, and reflective practice beyond observable teaching performance alone.

Oral defenses and viva-style discussions can support process-based assessment by allowing academics to verify students' understanding, reasoning, and ownership of submitted work. Through questioning and dialogue, students may be required to explain arguments, defend interpretations, clarify methodologies, and demonstrate conceptual understanding (Abuzied & Nabag, 2023; Frank et al., 2025). These assessment methods can strengthen confidence that assessment evidence genuinely reflects students' own competence and intellectual engagement. For example:

In a History course, students may be required to orally defend interpretations presented in research essays, explain source selection decisions, and respond to questions regarding historical arguments and evidence.

In Engineering, students may present and defend design solutions, explain technical calculations, justify material selections, or respond to scenario-based problem-solving questions related to their projects.

In teacher education, oral discussions may require student teachers to justify instructional strategies, explain assessment decisions, defend classroom interventions, and reflect on teaching experiences during practicum placements.

The use of generative AI by students is inevitable. Thus, in AI-mediated learning environments, process-based assessment may also require greater visibility of how students engage with generative AI during assessment tasks. Academics must not only evaluate final AI-assisted products, they may require students to document and reflect on their interactions with AI systems throughout the learning process. Such practices may include submission of prompt histories, screenshots of AI interactions, reflective commentaries explaining how AI-generated outputs were evaluated and refined, and explanations of why particular responses were accepted, modified, or rejected. This approach strengthens the validity and authenticity of assessment evidence by shifting attention beyond the final product towards students' reasoning processes, judgment, disciplinary understanding, and intellectual engagement during AI-assisted learning. Through visibility of AI interaction processes, academics may be better positioned to determine whether submitted work genuinely reflects students' own competence and engagement with the intended learning outcomes rather than uncritical dependence on AI-generated responses alone. This way, the quality of students' interaction with AI may itself become valuable evidence of learning, critical thinking, and AI literacy.

Supervised and Controlled Assessment Methods

The growing usage of Generative AI has renewed interest in supervised and controlled methods of assessment. The renewed emphasis on supervised and directly observable assessment practices reflects what may be described as a "back to basics, back to pen and paper" movement within higher education assessment discourse. In the era of generative AI, traditional assessment methods such as in-class writing, handwritten tasks, oral examinations, and supervised demonstrations are regaining significance because they provide greater assurance that assessment evidence genuinely reflects students' independent reasoning, understanding, and demonstrated competence. This does not imply rejection of technological innovation, but rather recognition that certain foundational assessment practices remain important for preserving validity and authenticity in AI-mediated educational environments.

Invigilated assessment tasks continue to offer important mechanisms for ensuring that assessment evidence reflects students' own reasoning and performance under controlled conditions (Dawson, 2020). Although traditional invigilated examinations have often been criticised for encouraging memorisation and surface learning, supervised assessment approaches may still play an important role in verifying foundational knowledge, problem-solving ability, and independent intellectual engagement within AI-rich environments.

In-class writing activities such as analytical writing exercises, timed reflections, short essays, case analyses, or problem-solving activities provide opportunities for academics to observe students' independent thinking and communication abilities.

These activities may strengthen confidence that submitted work reflects students' own understanding and reasoning processes.

Live demonstrations, practical tasks, and studio or laboratory-based assessments may also become increasingly important in disciplines requiring applied competence and performance-based skills. In such assessment environments, students demonstrate practical abilities, procedures, techniques, and problem-solving processes directly under observation. Therefore, practical assessment approaches may provide more authentic evidence of competence than independently produced written outputs alone.

Oral examinations represent another potentially valuable assessment approach in AI-mediated educational contexts. Oral assessment enables academics to directly engage students in discussion, questioning, explanation, and justification of ideas. This can reveal depth of understanding, conceptual clarity, reasoning ability, and students' capacity to apply knowledge. Oral examinations may reduce opportunities for overreliance on AI-generated responses because students are required to demonstrate understanding in dynamic and interactive contexts.

Multimodal and Authentic Assessment

The capabilities of generative AI are disruptive to traditional assessment methods that rely mainly on text-based written submissions such as essays, reports, and take-home assignments. Because AI systems generate academically sound written responses, overreliance on a single method of assessment may weaken confidence that submitted work reflects students' own understanding and demonstrated competence. Therefore, rebalancing assessment in the era of AI requires greater emphasis on multimodal and authentic forms of assessment capable of generating richer and more diverse evidence of learning.

Multimodal assessment methods allow students to demonstrate competence through multiple forms of evidence and communication rather than relying exclusively on written text. These methods may incorporate combinations of written work, oral presentations, visual artefacts, portfolios, simulations, digital media, practical demonstrations, collaborative inquiry, and project-based activities. By diversifying assessment modes, academics are better positioned to evaluate applied understanding, reasoning processes, creativity, communication skills, contextual problem-solving, and disciplinary competence across different learning contexts (Govender & Rajkoomar, 2021; Ross, 2020).

Authentic multimodal assessments are particularly valuable in AI-mediated educational environments because they emphasise meaningful application of knowledge within realistic or professionally relevant situations. Examples may include workplace-based projects, case analyses, simulations, community engagement activities, portfolios documenting developmental progress, and performance tasks requiring students to apply disciplinary knowledge to real-world challenges. These methods shift assessment emphasis from reproduction of information towards demonstration of understanding, participation, performance, and contextualised application of learning.

Ethical and Intelligent Engagement with Artificial Intelligence

Generative Artificial Intelligence is increasingly becoming embedded within higher education and broader society, making its use by students both inevitable and difficult to regulate. AI technologies are no longer used only by students but are integrated into the everyday professional practices of academics and institutions themselves, including drafting emails, generating ideas, summarising information, supporting research activities, and assisting with administrative tasks. The inconsistency emerges when higher education institutions attempt to position generative AI solely as an unacceptable tool for students while academics and professionals increasingly rely on the same technologies in their own daily practices. As AI technologies become more accessible, sophisticated, and integrated into everyday practices, attempts to completely prohibit student use of generative AI are unlikely to be sustainable or effective in the long term (Tlili et al., (2023). Therefore, the challenge facing higher education institutions is no longer whether students will use AI, but how students can engage with AI technologies responsibly, critically, and ethically in ways that continue to support meaningful learning and intellectual development.

The emergence of AI in education shares similarities with earlier technological developments such as the introduction of calculators in mathematics education. When calculators were first introduced, concerns were raised that students would stop thinking independently and become overly reliant on technology. However, calculators did not eliminate mathematical thinking; rather, meaningful use of calculators still depended on learners' understanding of mathematical concepts, problem interpretation, and procedural reasoning. I would liken this calculator scenario to the advent of generative AI. I argue that generative AI does not automatically replace thinking or understanding. The quality, accuracy, and relevance of AI-generated outputs often depend significantly on the knowledge, judgment, critical thinking, and guidance provided by the user.

Effective engagement with generative AI therefore requires students to possess sufficient disciplinary understanding to thoroughly evaluate AI-generated responses, identify inaccuracies, refine outputs, and meaningfully direct AI interactions on AI literacy (Ng et al., 2021). Students who lack foundational understanding may accept incorrect, superficial, or misleading AI-generated information without critical interrogation. In this way, AI should not be viewed as a replacement for human thinking, but as a tool whose educational value depends largely on the intellectual engagement and critical judgment of the user.

It is against this context that higher education institutions should place greater emphasis on AI literacy as an important component of contemporary learning. AI literacy extends beyond technical ability to use AI tools. It should include understanding the capabilities, limitations, ethical implications, and potential risks associated with generative AI technologies. Students should be guided on how to use AI to support idea generation, reflection, feedback, organisation of information, and conceptual clarification while still maintaining ownership of learning and independent intellectual engagement.

Transparent and ethical engagement with AI may also require the development of disclosure practices within assessment contexts. Rather than treating all AI use as inherently inappropriate, institutions may need to differentiate between responsible AI-assisted learning and forms of AI use that undermine the authenticity of assessment evidence. This may encourage honesty, accountability, and critical engagement rather than purely punitive or surveillance-oriented responses.

Ultimately, the future of higher education assessment may depend not only on redesigning assessment tasks, but also on developing students' capacity to engage intelligently, critically, and ethically with Artificial Intelligence. In increasingly AI-mediated learning environments, the goal should not be to eliminate AI from education, but to ensure that human reasoning, judgment, reflection, and demonstrated competence remain central to the learning process.

FRAMEWORK FOR PRESERVING VALID AND AUTHENTIC ASSESSMENT EVIDENCE IN AI-MEDIATED HIGHER EDUCATION

The preceding discussion demonstrated that Artificial Intelligence presents both opportunities and challenges for assessment in higher education. On one hand, AI technologies offer considerable benefits through enhanced assessment design, automated feedback, personalised learning support, learning analytics, and improved assessment efficiency. On the other hand, the growing use of generative AI introduces important concerns regarding construct-irrelevant variance, the erosion of authentic assessment evidence, and the validity of interpretations made from assessment results. These developments challenge traditional assumptions that assessment evidence represents students' own knowledge, reasoning, and demonstrated competence.

The current discourse surrounding AI in higher education mostly focuses on issues of academic dishonesty, AI detection, and the regulation of AI use, this chapter has introduced a more fundamental concern relates to the quality and trustworthiness of assessment evidence. The fundamental question is no longer whether students use AI technologies, but whether assessment practices in AI-mediated learning environments continue to generate evidence that supports valid, authentic, and meaningful judgments about student learning and competence. Therefore, assessment responses that focus exclusively on prohibition, surveillance, or AI detection technologies may be insufficient to address the broader educational implications of AI.

In response to these challenges, this chapter proposes the framework for preserving valid and authentic assessment evidence in AI-mediated Higher Education. The framework is grounded in Messick's unified theory of validity and principles of authentic assessment. It recognises that AI is becoming a permanent feature of higher education and that sustainable assessment practices must move beyond attempts to eliminate AI from educational contexts. Instead, the framework seeks to guide higher education institutions in balancing innovation with the preservation of validity, authenticity, and evidence of competence. The framework positions assessment evidence as the central consideration in assessment decision-making and proposes a set of interconnected assessment responses aimed at safeguarding the credibility of assessment judgments and the integrity of higher education qualifications in AI-mediated learning environments.

Figure 1. A framework for preserving valid and authentic assessment evidence in AI-Mediated Higher Education

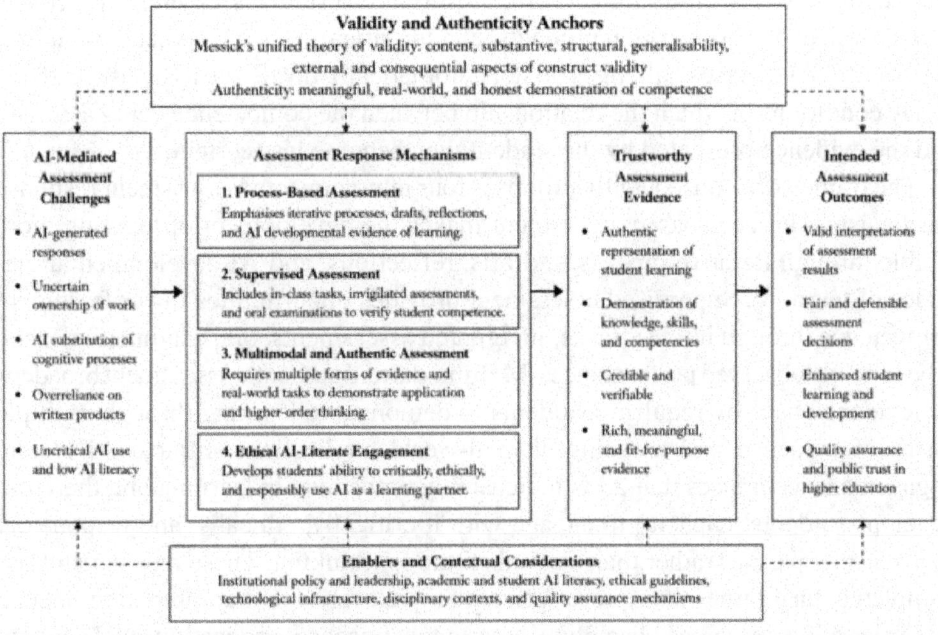

Source: Author's own illustration, (Junias, 2026)

Figure 1 presents the Framework for Preserving Valid and Authentic Assessment Evidence in AI-Mediated Higher Education. The framework responds to the central argument advanced in this chapter: that the fundamental assessment challenge presented by generative AI is not simply whether students use AI, but whether the evidence generated through assessment remains capable of supporting valid judgments about students' learning and authentically representing their demonstrated competence. The framework therefore shifts attention from detecting AI use towards preserving the quality and trustworthiness of assessment evidence.

The framework is anchored in validity and authenticity. Validity is informed by Messick's unified theory, encompassing the content, substantive, structural, generalisability, external, and consequential aspects of construct validity. These aspects provide a basis for examining whether assessment evidence supports appropriate interpretations of student learning and competence. Authenticity complements validity by emphasising meaningful and contextualised demonstrations of competence and, importantly within AI-mediated assessment, the extent to which the evidence genuinely represents students' own learning and intellectual engagement. These anchors extend across the framework because they provide the principles against which AI-mediated assessment challenges, assessment responses, evidence, and resulting judgments should be evaluated.

The framework begins by identifying AI-mediated assessment challenges that may weaken confidence in assessment evidence. These include AI-generated responses, uncertain ownership of submitted work, substitution of students' cognitive processes by AI, overreliance on written products, and uncritical AI use associated with limited AI literacy. These challenges do not automatically invalidate assessment. They create conditions in which the relationship between the competence being assessed and the evidence presented by the student may become less certain.

The framework consequently proposes four interconnected assessment response mechanisms. Process-based assessment makes the development of learning more visible through iterative processes, drafts, reflections, and AI developmental evidence of learning. Supervised assessment provides opportunities to verify student competence through in-class tasks, invigilated assessments, oral examinations, and other directly observed performances. Multimodal and authentic assessment broadens the evidence base by requiring students to demonstrate learning through multiple forms of evidence and meaningful, real-world applications. Ethical AI-literate engagement recognises that AI is increasingly embedded in learning and therefore develops students' capacity to engage with it critically, ethically, and responsibly as a learning partner rather than as a substitute for thinking. These mechanisms are complementary rather than prescriptive; their relevance and combination depend on the learning outcomes, discipline, assessment purpose, and institutional context.

These response mechanisms seek to strengthen trustworthy assessment evidence. Within the framework, such evidence authentically represents student learning, demonstrates relevant knowledge, skills, and competencies, is credible and verifiable, and is sufficiently rich, meaningful, and fit for the intended assessment purpose. Trustworthiness therefore does not necessarily require assessment evidence to be completely free from AI involvement. Instead, it requires sufficient confidence that the evidence provides a defensible basis for judging what the student knows, understands, and can do.

Trustworthy assessment evidence, in turn, supports the intended assessment outcomes of the framework: valid interpretations of assessment results, fair and defensible assessment decisions, enhanced student learning and development, and strengthened quality assurance and public trust in higher education. This progression highlights the broader significance of assessment evidence. Where evidence does not adequately represent student competence, the credibility of subsequent assessment decisions, qualifications, and institutional quality assurance processes may also be weakened.

The framework recognises that its implementation is shaped by enablers and contextual considerations. Institutional policy and leadership, academic and student AI literacy, ethical guidelines, technological infrastructure, disciplinary contexts, and quality assurance mechanisms influence how effectively the proposed assessment responses can be implemented. Their placement across the base of the framework emphasises that preserving valid and authentic assessment evidence is not the responsibility of individual academics alone. It requires an enabling institutional environment and context-sensitive implementation.

In a nutshell, the framework conceptualises the preservation of assessment evidence as a systemic rather than purely technological response to generative AI. Its distinctive contribution lies in repositioning the debate from *whether AI was used* to the more educationally consequential question of *whether the available assessment evidence remains sufficiently valid, authentic, credible, and meaningful to support judgments about student competence*. Thus, the framework provides a basis for rethinking assessment practice without positioning either AI prohibition or AI detection as the primary solution.

Operationalising the Framework in Higher Education

The value of the proposed framework lies not only in its conceptual contribution but also in its practical application within higher education institutions. The framework can serve as a guide for academics, curriculum designers, quality assurance practitioners, and institutional leaders when reviewing and redesigning assessment practices in response to the growing influence of generative AI.

For academics, the framework provides a lens through which assessment tasks can be evaluated to determine whether they generate credible evidence of student learning and competence. Rather than focusing exclusively on detecting AI use, academics are encouraged to consider how assessment methods can strengthen the visibility of learning processes, independent reasoning, and authentic demonstrations of competence.

For curriculum designers, the framework highlights the importance of constructive alignment i.e. aligning learning outcomes, teaching and learning activities, and assessment strategies with the realities of AI-mediated learning environments. Assessment planning should therefore incorporate opportunities for students to demonstrate competence through multiple forms of evidence while promoting responsible engagement with AI technologies.

For quality assurance units and accreditation bodies, the framework provides a basis for evaluating whether assessment systems continue to support valid and authentic interpretations of student achievement. In this way, assessment quality should be judged by the credibility of evidence generated rather than by the mere absence of AI use.

At an institutional level, the framework supports the development of policies that move beyond prohibition-oriented approaches towards strategies that emphasise AI literacy, ethical engagement, transparency, and assessment integrity. Such policies should recognise that AI is becoming a permanent feature of higher education and that sustainable responses require adaptation rather than resistance.

Finally, operationalising the framework requires a shift in institutional thinking. The future of assessment in higher education may depend less on preventing students from accessing AI technologies and more on ensuring that assessment systems continue to generate trustworthy evidence capable of supporting valid judgments about learning and competence in increasingly AI-mediated educational environments.

IMPLEMENTATION CHALLENGES AND LIMITATIONS

The proposed framework provides a conceptual pathway for preserving valid and authentic assessment evidence in AI-mediated higher education however, its implementation is not without drawbacks. The feasibility of the proposed assessment response mechanisms is likely to vary across disciplines, institutions, class sizes, and resource contexts. Process-based assessment, for example, may require academics to review drafts, reflections, AI interaction records, and other evidence generated throughout the learning process. Similarly, oral defences, iterative feedback, and multimodal assessment may increase assessment and feedback workloads, particularly in programmes characterised by large student enrolments. Institutions therefore need to balance the need for richer and more trustworthy assessment evidence with the manageability and sustainability of assessment practices.

Institutional capacity also influences the feasibility of implementing the framework. Supervised, multimodal, digitally supported, and AI-integrated assessment approaches may require appropriate infrastructure, technological resources, professional development, and institutional support. Moreover, disciplinary differences need to be recognised. Assessment mechanisms that are appropriate for teacher education, engineering, medicine, or other practice-oriented disciplines may not necessarily be equally applicable in all fields. The framework should therefore not be interpreted as prescribing a uniform assessment model, but rather as providing principles and response mechanisms that can be adapted to specific disciplinary and institutional contexts.

AI literacy and digital inequality present additional challenges. Ethical AI-literate engagement assumes that both academics and students have sufficient understanding of generative AI to evaluate its outputs and use it responsibly. However, differences in access to AI technologies, digital infrastructure, disciplinary knowledge, and AI literacy may create unequal opportunities for students to benefit from AI-supported learning. Requiring students to submit evidence of their interactions with AI, such as prompts, screenshots, or conversation histories, may also raise privacy and ethical concerns. Institutions adopting such practices therefore need clear policies regarding what evidence should be disclosed, how it will be used, and how student data and privacy will be protected.

There is also a risk of overcorrecting in response to generative AI. Excessive reliance on invigilated, controlled, or surveillance-oriented assessment may strengthen confidence in authorship while simultaneously reducing opportunities for independent inquiry, creativity, collaboration, and authentic learning. The purpose of rebalancing assessment should therefore not be to eliminate unsupervised or AI-supported learning, but to create an appropriate combination of assessment approaches capable of generating sufficient and credible evidence of student competence.

The proposed framework is conceptual and has not yet been empirically validated across different disciplinary and institutional contexts. Its effectiveness, feasibility, and applicability therefore require further investigation. Future research should examine how the framework operates in practice, how academics and students experience its different assessment mechanisms, and the conditions under which it strengthens the validity and authenticity of assessment evidence. Empirical investigation would enable further refinement of the framework and contribute to the development of context-sensitive approaches to assessment in AI-mediated higher education.

IMPLICATIONS FOR HIGHER EDUCATION

The growing integration of AI into higher education has implications that extend beyond individual assessment tasks and classroom practices. The arguments advanced in this chapter suggest that generative AI is reshaping fundamental assumptions about assessment, evidence of learning, and the demonstration of competence. Therefore, higher education institutions may need to reconsider how assessment systems are designed, implemented, and governed in AI-mediated learning environments.

A major implication concerns assessment policy and governance. Traditional institutional responses to emerging technologies have often focused on regulation, prohibition, and academic misconduct detection. However, the inevitable usage of generative AI suggest that prohibition-oriented approaches alone are unlikely to provide sustainable solutions. Higher education institutions may therefore need to develop assessment policies that recognise AI as an enduring feature of contemporary education while establishing clear expectations regarding ethical use, disclosure, transparency, and responsible engagement. Such policies should focus not only on preventing misuse but also on preserving the validity and authenticity of assessment evidence.

The chapter suggests the need for a reconsideration of what constitutes acceptable evidence of learning and competence. In traditional assessment practices, independently produced written assignments have been accepted as credible indicators of student achievement. However, the capabilities of generative AI challenge this assumption by making it increasingly difficult to determine the extent to which written products represent students' own intellectual effort. As a result, higher education institutions may need to place greater emphasis on assessment methods that generate richer and more diverse forms of evidence, including evidence of learning processes, reasoning, reflection, participation, and demonstrated performance. So, assessment practices may shift from evaluating what students produce to examining how learning is developed and demonstrated.

The implications are significant for professional and occupational programmes where assessment outcomes have direct consequences for workplace performance and public trust. Fields such as medicine, engineering, teacher education, law, and technical and vocational education rely on assessment systems to verify competence and readiness for professional practice. If assessment evidence fails to accurately represent students' actual capabilities, the credibility of qualifications and confidence in graduates may be undermined. Therefore, institutions offering professional programmes may face increasing pressure to adopt assessment methods capable of verifying demonstrated competence within authentic and supervised contexts.

A further implication concerns the importance of AI literacy as a graduate capability. As generative AI becomes integrated into professional and everyday life, the ability to engage critically, ethically, and intelligently with AI technologies may become an essential competence for graduates. The challenge for higher education is therefore not simply to teach students how to use AI tools, but to develop their capacity to evaluate AI-generated information, identify inaccuracies, exercise professional judgment, and apply disciplinary knowledge in AI-supported environments. From this perspective, AI literacy may become a component of graduate preparedness for participation in knowledge-based societies and workplaces.

The point of departure here is that the emergence of generative AI presents higher education with an opportunity to rethink assessment in more meaningful ways. Rather than viewing AI solely as a threat to academic integrity, institutions may use this moment to strengthen assessment practices, improve the quality of assessment evidence, and place greater emphasis on authentic demonstrations of learning and competence. These developments have the potential to enhance the credibility, relevance, and sustainability of higher education assessment in the digital era.

CONCLUSION

The emergence of generative Artificial Intelligence has introduced both unprecedented opportunities and significant challenges for assessment in higher education. While AI technologies offer valuable support for assessment design, feedback generation, personalised learning, and academic productivity, they simultaneously challenge traditional assumptions regarding the validity and authenticity of assessment evidence. As AI systems become more capable of generating original and sound academic responses, concerns arise regarding the extent to which assessment outcomes continue to represent students' own knowledge, reasoning, and demonstrated competence.

This chapter has argued that the central assessment challenge in the era of generative AI extends beyond issues of academic dishonesty and plagiarism. Rather, the more fundamental concern relates to the quality and trustworthiness of the evidence upon which assessment judgments are based. Drawing on Messick's unified theory of validity and principles of authentic assessment, the chapter demonstrated how AI-mediated assessment environments may introduce construct-irrelevant variance, weaken the authenticity of assessment evidence, and compromise the credibility of assessment interpretations and decisions.

The chapter has also argued that attempts to prohibit the use of AI will not provide sustainable solutions. Generative AI has become an indispensable part of everyday life, making responsible and intelligent engagement with AI a more realistic and productive response than prohibition. Thus, higher education institutions must reconsider how assessment practices generate, verify, and interpret evidence of learning and competence in AI-mediated environments.

To address these challenges, the chapter proposed the framework for preserving valid and authentic assessment evidence in AI-mediated Higher Education. The framework positions trustworthy assessment evidence as the central concern of contemporary assessment practice and identifies process-based assessment, supervised assessment, multimodal and authentic assessment, and ethical AI-literate engagement as key mechanisms for strengthening the credibility of assessment evidence. The framework further emphasises validity, authenticity, fairness, and demonstrated competence as essential anchors for assessment decision-making.

In a nutshell, the future of higher education assessment may depend less on the ability to detect or eliminate AI use and more on the capacity of institutions to design assessment systems that continue to generate trustworthy evidence of student learning. As higher education adapts to AI-mediated learning environments, preserving valid and authentic assessment evidence will remain essential for ensuring credible qualifications, graduate competence, and public confidence in higher education. In this context, the challenge is not whether AI should exist within higher education, but whether assessment systems can evolve in ways that ensure human learning, judgment, and demonstrated competence remain at the centre of educational practice.

REFERENCES

Abuzied, A. I. H., & Nabag, W. O. M. (2023). Structured viva validity, reliability, and acceptability as an assessment tool in health professions education: A systematic review and meta-analysis. *BMC Medical Education*, *23*(1), 531. DOI: 10.1186/s12909-023-04524-6 PMID: 37491301

Ahmad, S. F., Alam, M. M., Rahmat, M. K., Mubarik, M. S., & Hyder, S. I. (2022). Academic and Administrative Role of Artificial Intelligence in Education. *Sustainability (Basel)*, *14*(3), 1101. DOI: 10.3390/su14031101

Alshanetsky, E. (2025). When AI Dissolves Trust: Education Can Pioneer New Infrastructure. *Society*, *62*(6), 982–987. DOI: 10.1007/s12115-025-01149-x

Archer, E. (2017). The Assessment Purpose Triangle: Balancing the Purposes of Educational Assessment. *Frontiers in Education*, *2*, 41. DOI: 10.3389/feduc.2017.00041

Bahari, A. (2025). Balancing syntactic complexity and clarity: The role of AI in enhancing academic writing proficiency. *Saudi Journal of Language Studies*, *5*(4), 271–290. DOI: 10.1108/SJLS-10-2024-0062

Balfour, S. P. (2013). Assessing Writing in MOOCs: Automated Essay Scoring and Calibrated Peer Review. 8. https://files.eric.ed.gov/fulltext/EJ1062843.pdf

Bearman, M., Ajjawi, R., Boud, D., Tai, J., & Dawson, P. (2022). *Re-imagining university assessment in a digital world*. Springer Nature.

Biggs, J., & Tang, C. (2011). *Teaching for quality learning at university* (4th ed.). Open University Press.

Black, K., & Warhurst, R. (2025). Democratising the curriculum: inclusive learning through students' ownership of assessment. In Handbook of Inclusive Learning and Teaching in Business and Management. Cheltenham, UK: Edward Elgar Publishing. Retrieved May 27, 2026, from DOI: 10.4337/9781035325733.00008

Boral, K., & Mondal, K. K. (2025). Comparing AI-Generated Responses: A Study on ChatGPT, Gemini, and Copilot in Education. *Journal of Educational Technology Systems*, *54*(2), 291–309. DOI: 10.1177/00472395251368385

Carter, S., Bennett, S., Hawkins, J., & Southam, D. (2025). Programmatic assessment: A literature review of challenges, opportunities and useful tools to support student transition to the workplace. *Assessment & Evaluation in Higher Education*, •••, 1–18. DOI: 10.1080/02602938.2025.2567538

Castro, R. (2019). Blended learning in higher education: Trends and capabilities. *Education and Information Technologies, 24*(4), 2523–2546. DOI: 10.1007/s10639-019-09886-3

Cotton, D. R. E., Cotton, P. A., & Shipway, J. R. (2023). Chatting and cheating: Ensuring academic integrity in the era of ChatGPT. *Innovations in Education and Teaching International, 61*(2), 228–239. Advance online publication. DOI: 10.1080/14703297.2023.2190148

Dalalah, D., & Dalalah, O. M. (2023). The false positives and false negatives of generative AI detection tools in education and academic research: The case of ChatGPT. *International Journal of Management Education, 21*(2), 100822. DOI: 10.1016/j.ijme.2023.100822

Darbyshire, P., & Beitsayadeh, C. (2025). Enhancing Student Success through GAI and Predictive Analytics. *International Journal for Educational Media and Technology, 19*(2). https://www.ijemt.org/index.php/journal/article/view/392

Dawson, P. (2020). *Defending assessment security in a digital world.* Routledge. DOI: 10.4324/9780429324178

Elkhatat, A. M., Elsaid, K., & Almeer, S. (2023). Evaluating the efficacy of AI content detection tools in differentiating between human and AI-generated text. *International Journal for Educational Integrity, 19*(1), 17. DOI: 10.1007/s40979-023-00140-5

Eysenbach, G. (2023). The Role of ChatGPT, Generative Language Models, and Artificial Intelligence in Medical Education: A Conversation With ChatGPT and a Call for Papers. *JMIR Medical Education, 9*, e46885. https://mededu.jmir.org/2023/1/e46885. DOI: 10.2196/46885 PMID: 36863937

Flahive, E. (2026). Assessment in Higher Education: Purpose, Practice, and Feedback. In Linguistics and Language Teaching Conference 2024 (p. 196). Zayed University Press.

Frank, R., Black, P. E., & Jeff, C. (2025). Testing by Talking: Rethinking Oral Examinations. *American Journal of Pharmaceutical Education, 89*(12), 101892. Advance online publication. DOI: 10.1016/j.ajpe.2025.101892 PMID: 41177357

Ghosh, S., Brooks, B., Ranmuthugala, D., & Bowles, M. (2020). Authentic Versus Traditional Assessment: An Empirical Study Investigating the Difference in Seafarer Students' Academic Achievement. *Journal of Navigation, 73*(4), 797–812. DOI: 10.1017/S0373463319000894

Gligorea, I., Cioca, M., Oancea, R., Gorski, A.-T., Gorski, H., & Tudorache, P. (2023). Adaptive Learning Using Artificial Intelligence in e-Learning: A Literature Review. *Education Sciences*, *13*(12), 1216. Advance online publication. DOI: 10.3390/educsci13121216

Gonsalves, C. (2025). Contextual Assessment Design in the Age of Generative AI. *Journal of Learning Development in Higher Education*, (34). Advance online publication. DOI: 10.47408/jldhe.vi34.1307

Govender, R., & Rajkoomar, M. (2021). A multimodal model for learning, teaching and assessment in higher education. COVID-19: Interdisciplinary explorations of impacts on higher education,57. DOI: 10.52779/9781991201195/04

Gulikers, J. T. M., Bastiaens, T. J., & Kirschner, P. A. (2004). A five-dimensional framework for authentic assessment. *Educational Technology Research and Development*, *52*(3), 67–86. DOI: 10.1007/BF02504676

Harrington, L. (2024). Comparison of generative artificial intelligence and predictive artificial intelligence. *AACN Advanced Critical Care*, *35*(2), 93–96. Advance online publication. DOI: 10.4037/aacnacc2024225 PMID: 38848562

Heidari Tabrizi, H., & House, J. (2025). Moving Beyond Conventional Tests: Performance Assessment as an Alternative for Evaluating Students' Academic Translations. Contrastive Pragmatics, 1-32. DOI: 10.1163/26660393-bja10139

Holmes, W., Bialik, M., & Fadel, C. (2019). *Artificial Intelligence in Education Promises and Implications for Teaching and Learning* (1st ed.). Center for Curriculum Redesign.

Ilieva, G., Yankova, T., Ruseva, M., & Kabaivanov, S. (2025). A Framework for Generative AI-Driven Assessment in Higher Education. *Information (Basel)*, *16*(6), 472. DOI: 10.3390/info16060472

Ince, A. H., & Özbay, S. (2025). AI-Enhanced Adaptive Testing: Integrating Response Time with IRT Models. *KSII Transactions on Internet and Information Systems*, *19*(8). Advance online publication. DOI: 10.3837/tiis.2025.08.005

Irons, A., & Elkington, S. (2021). *Enhancing learning through formative assessment and feedback*. Routledge. DOI: 10.4324/9781138610514

Kaldaras, L., Akaeze, H. O., & Reckase, M. D. (2024). Developing valid assessments in the era of generative artificial intelligence. *Frontiers in Education*, *9*, 1399377. DOI: 10.3389/feduc.2024.1399377

Kane, M. T. (2013). Validating the interpretations and uses of test scores. *Journal of Educational Measurement*, *50*(1), 1–73. DOI: 10.1111/jedm.12000

Karadağ, N. (2023). The impact of artificial intelligence on online assessment: A preliminary review. *Journal of Educational Technology & Online Learning*, *6*(4), 822–837. DOI: 10.31681/jetol.1351548

Kasneci, E., Seßler, K., Küchemann, S., Bannert, M., Dementieva, D., Fischer, F., Gasser, U., Groh, G., Günnemann, S., Hüllermeier, E., Krusche, S., Kutyniok, G., Michaeli, T., Nerdel, C., Pfeffer, J., Poquet, O., Sailer, M., Schmidt, A., Seidel, T., & Kasneci, G. (2023). ChatGPT for good? On opportunities and challenges of large language models for education. *Learning and Individual Differences*, *103*, 102274. DOI: 10.1016/j.lindif.2023.102274

Khaliq, A., Muhammad, N., & Qamar, N. (2025). Enhancing Student Engagement and Academic Performance through AI-Based Tutoring Systems: A Comparative Study of Traditional vs. AI-Driven Education Models. *The Critical Review of Social Sciences Studies*, *3*(4), 824–834. DOI: 10.59075/m9g5pc96

Khare, Y. (2023). Generative AI vs Predictive AI: What is the Difference. Analytics Vidhya. https://www. analyticsvidhya. com/blog/2023/09/generative-ai-vs-predictive-ai/

Khatter, A., Thalaachawr, K., & Blyth, M. (2024). Student engagement and fostering ownership of learning. *Journal of Applied Learning & Teaching*, *7*(1), 291–302. https://search.informit.org/doi/10.3316/informit.T2025091900007891326081625

Khine, M. S. (2024). Using AI for Adaptive Learning and Adaptive Assessment. In Khine, M. S. (Ed.), *Artificial Intelligence in Education*. Springer., DOI: 10.1007/978-981-97-9350-1_3

Khlaif, Z. N., Ayyoub, A., Hamamra, B., Bensalem, E., Mitwally, M. A. A., Ayyoub, A., Hattab, M. K., & Shadid, F. (2024). University Teachers' Views on the Adoption and Integration of Generative AI Tools for Student Assessment in Higher Education. *Education Sciences*, *14*(10), 1090. DOI: 10.3390/educsci14101090

Kochmar, E., Vu, D. D., Belfer, R., Gupta, V., Serban, I. V., & Pineau, J. (2022). Automated Data-Driven Generation of Personalized Pedagogical Interventions in Intelligent Tutoring Systems. *International Journal of Artificial Intelligence in Education*, *32*(2), 323–349. DOI: 10.1007/s40593-021-00267-x

Kofinas, A. K., Tsay, C.-H., & Pike, D. (2025). The impact of generative AI on academic integrity of authentic assessments within a higher education context. *British Journal of Educational Technology*, *56*(6), 2522–2549. DOI: 10.1111/bjet.13585

Koh, K. H. (2017). Authentic Assessment. In Kathy Hytten (ed.), Oxford Research Encyclopedia of Education (New York, NY, online edn, Oxford Academic, 9 June 2016 -), DOI: 10.1093/acrefore/9780190264093.013.22

Krishna, K., Song, Y., Karpinska, M., Wieting, J., & Iyyer, M. (2023). Paraphrasing evades detectors of ai-generated text, but retrieval is an effective defense. *Advances in Neural Information Processing Systems, 36*, 27469–27500. DOI: 10.52202/075280-1195

Kumar, K. P., Ponnuchamy, K., Bala, N. M., Santhoshini, M. V., Himasri, K., & Jagadeesh, K. (2025). An AI-Powered Smart Learning Platform Integrating Adaptive Assessments, Personalized Learning Paths, and Performance Analytics, 2025 4th International Conference on Applied Artificial Intelligence and Computing (ICAAIC), Salem, India, 2025, pp. 1283-1288, DOI: 10.1109/ICAAIC64647.2025.11330782

Leaton Gray, S., Edsall, D., & Parapadakis, D. (2025). AI-Based Digital Cheating At University, and the Case for New Ethical Pedagogies. *Journal of Academic Ethics, 23*(4), 2069–2086. DOI: 10.1007/s10805-025-09642-y

Lim, K. (2024). Assessing beyond grades: Unravelling the implications on student learning and engagement in higher education. *Assessment & Evaluation in Higher Education, 49*(5), 665–679. Advance online publication. DOI: 10.1080/02602938.2024.2314703

Lin, C. C., Huang, A. Y. Q., & Lu, O. H. T. (2023). Artificial intelligence in intelligent tutoring systems toward sustainable education: A systematic review. *Smart Learning Environment, 10*(41), 41. Advance online publication. DOI: 10.1186/s40561-023-00260-y

Luckin, R., Holmes, W., Griffiths, M., & Forcier, L. B. (2016). *Intelligence unleashed: An argument for AI in education*. Pearson.

Lye, C. Y., & Lim, L. (2024). Generative Artificial Intelligence in Tertiary Education: Assessment Redesign Principles and Considerations. *Education Sciences, 14*(6), 569. DOI: 10.3390/educsci14060569

Mammadova, I., Ismayilli, F., Aliyeva, E., & Mammadova, N. (2025). The Role of Artificial Intelligence in Shaping Assessment Practices in Higher Education. *Educational Process: International Journal, 18*(1), e2025439. DOI: 10.22521/edupij.2025.18.439

Mariam, G., Adil, L., & Zakaria, B. (2024). The integration of artificial intelligence (ai) into education systems and its impact on the governance of higher education institutions. *International Journal of Professional Business Review*, *9*(12), 13. DOI: 10.26668/businessreview/2024.v9i12.5176

Matheis, P., & Jubin, J. (2025). Assessment renaissance: authentic design in the era of generative AI. In *Generative AI in Higher Education*. Edward Elgar Publishing., DOI: 10.4337/9781035326020.00020

McTighe, J., Doubet, K. J., & Carbaugh, E. M. (2020). *Designing authentic performance tasks and projects: Tools for meaningful learning and assessment*. ASCD.

Messick, S. (1989). Validity. In Linn, R. L. (Ed.), *Educational measurement* (3rd ed., pp. 13–103). American Council on Education/Macmillan.

Miller, E., & Konstantinou, I. (2022). Using reflective, authentic assessments to embed employability skills in higher education. *Journal of Work-Applied Management*, *14*(1), 4–17. DOI: 10.1108/JWAM-02-2021-0014

Montebello, M. (2025). Rethinking Pedagogy and Assessment in the Age of Generative AI. In *Artificial Intelligence*. IntechOpen., DOI: 10.5772/intechopen.1012982

Morrell, L. J. (2021). Iterated assessment and feedback improves student outcomes. *Studies in Higher Education*, *46*(3), 485–496. DOI: 10.1080/03075079.2019.1643301

Morris, R., Perry, T., & Wardle, L. (2021). Formative assessment and feedback for learning in higher education: A systematic review. *Review of Education*, *9*(3), e3292. DOI: 10.1002/rev3.3292

Mudenda, S. (2025). Impact of Artificial Intelligence on College and University Students: A Global Transformation of the Education System. *Creative Education*, *16*(11), 1801–1828. DOI: 10.4236/ce.2025.1611112

Murff, M. J. (2025). AI-Enabled Innovations in Automated Essay Scoring and Feedback Systems. Theses and Dissertations. 10933. https://scholarsarchive.byu.edu/etd/10933

Nallamothu, T. K. (2024). The age of smart living how AI is shaping our daily lives in real time. *International Journal of Research and Applied Innovations*, *7*(5), 11456–11468. DOI: 10.34218/IJAIRD_02_02_017

Ng, D. T. K., Leung, J. K. L., Chu, K. W. S., & Qiao, M. S. (2021). AI Literacy: Definition, Teaching, Evaluation and Ethical Issues. *Proceedings of the Association for Information Science and Technology*, *58*(1), 504–509. DOI: 10.1002/pra2.487

Nguyen Thanh, B., Vo, D. T. H., Nguyen Nhat, M., Pham, T. T. T., Thai Trung, H., & Ha Xuan, S. (2023). Race with the machines: Assessing the capability of generative AI in solving authentic assessments. *Australasian Journal of Educational Technology*, *39*(5), 59–81. DOI: 10.14742/ajet.8902

Nilson, L. B., & Stanny, C. J. (2023). *Specifications Grading: Restoring Rigor, Motivating Students, and Saving Faculty Time* (2nd ed.). Routledge., DOI: 10.4324/9781003447061

Nkealah, N. (2023). Unravelling an assessment puzzle: Reflections on reconciling effective assessment and workload management in South African higher education. *Assessment & Evaluation in Higher Education*, *48*(8), 1092–1102. DOI: 10.1080/02602938.2023.2173139

Nyagope, T. S. (2024). Massification at higher education institutions; challenges associated with teaching large classes and how it impacts the quality of teaching and learning in South Africa. *International Journal of Environmental, Sustainability, and Social Science*, *5*(1), 209–220. DOI: 10.38142/ijesss.v5i1.852

Obizue, M. N., Otuonye, C. E., & Daw, A. (2025). Massification and internationalization of higher education: problems and prospects. International journal of economics, finance, accounting and management, 1(2), 14-30. https://journals.iempsglobal.org/index.php/IJEFAM/article/view/34

Oroh, E. Z., Ali, M. I., Pelenkahu, N., Usman, H., & Rorintulus, O. A. (2025). Authentic assessment in higher education to increase critical thinking and develop metacognitive awareness. *Studies in English Language and Education*, *12*(2), 827–844. DOI: 10.24815/siele.v12i2.45077

Owan, V. J., Abang, K. B., Idika, D. O., Etta, E. O., & Bassey, B. A. (2023). Exploring the potential of artificial intelligence tools in educational measurement and assessment. *Eurasia Journal of Mathematics, Science and Technology Education*, *19*(8), em2307. Advance online publication. DOI: 10.29333/ejmste/13428

Owoseni, A., Kolade, O., & Egbetokun, A. (2024). Applications of generative AI in summative assessment. In *Generative AI in higher Education: Innovation strategies for teaching and learning* (pp. 97–122). Springer Nature Switzerland. DOI: 10.1007/978-3-031-60179-8_4

Pang, W., & Wei, Z. (2025). Shaping the Future of Higher Education: A Technology Usage Study on Generative AI Innovations. *Information (Basel)*, *16*(2), 95. DOI: 10.3390/info16020095

Perkins, M. (2023). Academic integrity considerations of AI large language models in the post-pandemic era: ChatGPT and beyond. *Journal of University Teaching & Learning Practice*, *20*(2), 1–10. DOI: 10.53761/1.20.02.07

Poellhuber, B., Roy, N., & Lepage, A. (2024). Artificial intelligence in higher education: opportunities, issues, and challenges. In *Human-Centered AI* (pp. 151–162). Chapman and Hall/CRC. DOI: 10.1201/9781003320791-17

Rao, G. T., & Suhasini, N. (2025). Integrating artificial intelligence in higher education to enhance teaching and learning. *Computer Applications in Engineering Education*, *33*(6), e70085. DOI: 10.1002/cae.70085

Rashidi, H. H., Pantanowitz, J., Hanna, M. G., Tafti, A. P., Sanghani, P., Buchinsky, A., Fennell, B., Deebajah, M., Wheeler, S., Pearce, T., Abukhiran, I., Robertson, S., Palmer, O., Gur, M., Tran, N. K., & Pantanowitz, L. (2025). Introduction to artificial intelligence and machine learning in pathology and medicine: Generative and nongenerative artificial intelligence basics. *Modern Pathology*, *38*(4), 100688. DOI: 10.1016/j.modpat.2024.100688 PMID: 39755237

Ray, S., & Saeed, M. (2018). Applications of educational data mining and learning analytics tools in handling big data in higher education. In *Applications of Big Data analytics: Trends, issues, and challenges* (pp. 135–160). Springer International Publishing. DOI: 10.1007/978-3-319-76472-6_7

Revell, T., Yeadon, W., Cahilly-Bretzin, G., Clarke, I., Manning, G., Jones, J., Mulley, C., Pascual, R. J., Bradley, N., Thomas, D., & Leneghan, F. (2024). ChatGPT versus human essayists: An exploration of the impact of artificial intelligence for authorship and academic integrity in the humanities. *International Journal for Educational Integrity*, *20*(1), 18. DOI: 10.1007/s40979-024-00161-8

Rodrigues, M., Silva, R., Borges, A. P., Franco, M., & Oliveira, C. (2025). Artificial intelligence: Threat or asset to academic integrity? A bibliometric analysis. *Kybernetes*, *54*(5), 2939–2970. DOI: 10.1108/K-09-2023-1666

Rodríguez-Ortiz, M. Á., Santana-Mancilla, P. C., & Anido-Rifón, L. E. (2025). Machine Learning and Generative AI in Learning Analytics for Higher Education: A Systematic Review of Models, Trends, and Challenges. *Applied Sciences (Basel, Switzerland)*, *15*(15), 8679. DOI: 10.3390/app15158679

Ross, J., Curwood, J. S., & Bell, A. (2020). A multimodal assessment framework for higher education. *E-Learning and Digital Media*, *17*(4), 290–306. DOI: 10.1177/2042753020927201

Russell, S., & Norvig, P. (2021). *Artificial intelligence: A modern approach* (4th ed.). Pearson.

Sajja, R., Sermet, Y., Cikmaz, M., Cwiertny, D., & Demir, I. (2024). Artificial Intelligence-Enabled Intelligent Assistant for Personalized and Adaptive Learning in Higher Education. *Information (Basel), 15*(10), 596. DOI: 10.3390/info15100596

Shakoor, F. Real-Time AI Responses (December 02, 2024). Available at *SSRN*: DOI: 10.2139/ssrn.5044211

Sharma, D., Shroff, S., Sharma, G., & Sachan, M. R. (2025). *Beyond Grades: Holistic Assessment and Evaluation in Contemporary Education*. Yashita Prakashan Private Limited.

Shwedeh, F. (2024). The integration of artificial intelligence (AI) into decision support systems within higher education institutions. *Nanotechnology Perceptions, 20*(5), 331–357. DOI: 10.26668/businessreview/2024.v9i12.5176

Stenhouse, L. (1975). *An introduction to curriculum research and development*. Heinemann.

Strielkowski, W., Grebennikova, V., Lisovskiy, A., Rakhimova, G., & Vasileva, T. (2025). AI-driven adaptive learning for sustainable educational transformation. *Sustainable Development (Bradford), 33*(2), 1921–1947. DOI: 10.1002/sd.3221

Suskie, L. (2018). *Assessing student learning: A common sense guide*. John Wiley & Sons.

Suskie, L. (2023). Understanding the nature and purpose of assessment. In *Designing better engineering education through assessment* (pp. 3–22). Routledge. DOI: 10.4324/9781003444107-2

Tan, L.Y.; Hu, S.; Yeo, D.J., & Cheong, K.H. A. (2025). A comprehensive review on automated grading systems in STEM using AI techniques. Mathematics, 13(17), 2828., 2828. DOI: 10.3390/math1317282

Tang, K. H. D. (2024). Implications of Artificial Intelligence for Teaching and Learning. *Acta Pedagogia Asiana, 3*(2), 65–79. DOI: 10.53623/apga.v3i2.404

Tholen, G. (2020). Degree power: Educational credentialism within three skilled occupations. *British Journal of Sociology of Education, 41*(3), 283–298. DOI: 10.1080/01425692.2019.1690427

Tlili, A., Shehata, B., Adarkwah, M. A., Bozkurt, A., Hickey, D. T., Huang, R., & Agyemang, B. (2023). What if the devil is my guardian angel: ChatGPT as a case study of using chatbots in education. Smart learning environments,10(1), 15. DOI: 10.1186/s40561-023-00237-x

Tomlinson, C. A. (2017). Differentiated instruction. In *Fundamentals of gifted education* (pp. 279–292). Routledge. DOI: 10.4324/9781315639987-26

Trajkovski, G., & Hayes, H. (2025). Foundations of AI in Educational Assessment. In *AI-Assisted Assessment in Education: Transforming Assessment and Measuring Learning* (pp. 1–58). Springer Nature Switzerland.

Wang, P. (2019). On defining artificial intelligence. Journal of artificial general intelligence, 10(2), 1-37. DOI: DOI: 10.2478/jagi-2019-0002

Weber-Wulff, D., Anohina-Naumeca, A., Bjelobaba, S., Foltýnek, T., Guerrero-Dib, J., Popoola, O., Šigut, P., & Waddington, L. (2023). Testing of detection tools for AI-generated text. *International Journal for Educational Integrity*, *19*(1), 26. DOI: 10.1007/s40979-023-00146-z

Wiggins, G. (1990). The Case for Authentic Assessment. *Practical Assessment, Research & Evaluation*, *2*(1), 2. DOI: 10.7275/ffb1-mm19

Yan, Y. X., Wu, J. P., Nguyen, B. A., & Chen, H. M. (2020, February). The impact of iterative assessment system on programming learning behavior. In *Proceedings of the 2020 9th International Conference on Educational and Information Technology* (pp. 89-94). DOI: 10.1145/3383923.3383939

Yeo, M. A. (2023). Academic integrity in the age of Artificial Intelligence (AI) authoring apps. *TESOL Journal*, *14*(3), e716. DOI: 10.1002/tesj.716

Zawacki-Richter, O., Marín, V. I., Bond, M., & Gouverneur, F. (2019). Systematic review of research on artificial intelligence applications in higher education – where are the educators? *International Journal of Educational Technology in Higher Education*, *16*(1), 39. DOI: 10.1186/s41239-019-0171-0

Zhao, J., Chapman, E., & Sabet, P. G. P. (2024). Generative AI and educational assessments: A systematic review. *Education Research and Perspectives*, *51*, 124–155. https://search.informit.org/doi/10.3316/informit.T2025061800005500592641426. DOI: 10.70953/ERPv51.2412006

KEY TERMS AND DEFINITIONS

Artificial Intelligence (AI): Computer-based systems capable of performing tasks commonly associated with human intelligence, including learning, reasoning, problem-solving, pattern recognition, decision-making, and language processing.

Generative Artificial Intelligence (Generative AI): A form of artificial intelligence capable of generating new content, including text, images, audio, video, and computer code, in response to user prompts.

Assessment Evidence: Information generated through assessment tasks and student performance that academics use to make judgments about what students know, understand, and can do.

Assessment Validity: The extent to which assessment evidence supports appropriate interpretations and uses of assessment results for their intended purposes.

Authentic Assessment: Assessment that requires students to demonstrate knowledge, skills, reasoning, and competence through meaningful, contextualised, and often real-world or professionally relevant tasks.

Trustworthy Assessment Evidence: Assessment evidence that provides a credible basis for making judgments about student learning and competence.

Construct-Irrelevant Variance: Variation in assessment performance caused by factors unrelated to the knowledge, skills, or competence the assessment is intended to measure

Process-Based Assessment: An assessment approach that evaluates evidence generated during the learning and production process rather than relying exclusively on the final product.

Multimodal Assessment: An approach that uses multiple modes through which students can demonstrate learning and competence.

AI Literacy: The knowledge, skills, and capabilities required to understand, use, evaluate, and engage responsibly with artificial intelligence technologies.

AI-Literate Engagement: The critical, purposeful, transparent, and ethical use of generative AI as a learning resource rather than as a substitute for student thinking.

Supervised Assessment: Assessment conducted under controlled conditions in which student performance can be directly observed or verified.

Chapter 9
AI-Generated Feedback as a Pedagogical Tool:
Opportunities and Design Principles

Mustafa Kayyali
http://orcid.org/0000-0003-3300-262X
Maaref University of Applied Sciences, Syria

ABSTRACT

AI-generated feedback is rapidly entering higher education as institutions search for more responsive, scalable, and learner-centered approaches to assessment. Yet its value cannot be reduced to speed, automation, or convenience. This chapter examines AI-generated feedback as a pedagogical tool that can reshape how students interpret their work, revise their thinking, and participate more actively in learning. It explores the opportunities offered by generative AI, including timely formative guidance, personalized explanations, iterative revision support, and expanded access to feedback in large or resource-limited courses. At the same time, it addresses the risks of overdependence, generic responses, hidden bias, weakened teacher judgment, and the possible erosion of meaningful human dialogue. The chapter argues for careful design principles rooted in transparency, contextual sensitivity, student agency, feedback literacy, and human oversight, positioning AI not as a replacement for educators but as a thoughtfully governed partner in assessment design.

INTRODUCTION

Feedback has always occupied a strange, almost paradoxical place in higher education. Everyone agrees that it matters. Teachers spend hours writing it, students

DOI: 10.4018/979-8-3373-9089-5.ch009

wait for it, institutions include it in quality assurance reports, and assessment policies repeatedly describe it as central to learning. Yet, in practice, feedback often arrives late, is written under pressure, and is received by students at a moment when the assignment has already ended emotionally, cognitively, and sometimes even administratively. A student submits an essay, waits two or three weeks, receives a grade, skims the comments, feels either relieved or disappointed, and then moves on. The teacher, meanwhile, has invested considerable effort in producing comments that may never be fully read, understood, or used. This quiet mismatch between the labor of feedback and its actual pedagogical impact has long troubled higher education.

The rise of generative artificial intelligence has entered this unsettled space with unusual force (Caporusso, 2023). AI-generated feedback promises something that traditional feedback systems have often struggled to provide: immediacy, scalability, personalization, and repetition without exhaustion. A student can now receive comments on a draft within seconds. They can ask for clarification, request examples, compare alternative phrasings, or revise their work through several cycles before submitting it. In large classes, where one instructor may be responsible for hundreds of students, AI tools appear to offer a way of narrowing the feedback gap. In writing-intensive courses, design projects, language learning, coding assignments, reflective journals, and even complex problem-solving tasks, generative AI can provide formative responses at a speed and volume that human educators alone cannot realistically sustain.

But the excitement surrounding AI-generated feedback should not blind us to a deeper question: what kind of feedback are we actually designing, and what kind of learner does it help to produce? Feedback is not merely information. It is not a mechanical transfer of corrections from an expert source to a deficient learner. At its best, feedback is a pedagogical encounter. It helps students notice what they could not yet see, name the gap between intention and performance, and imagine a more refined version of their own work. Good feedback does not simply tell students what is wrong; it teaches them how to judge, revise, and think with greater independence (Szmyd & Mitera, 2024). This is why AI-generated feedback cannot be treated as a simple technological upgrade to marking. It must be understood as part of a wider redesign of assessment, learning relationships, academic responsibility, and student agency.

In this sense, the central issue is not whether AI can generate feedback. It clearly can. The more difficult issue is whether the feedback it generates is pedagogically meaningful, contextually appropriate, ethically responsible, and educationally transformative. A polished AI response may look helpful on the surface while remaining too generic to guide genuine improvement (Pooth, 2025). It may produce fluent comments that sound authoritative but misunderstand the task, the discipline, the student's level, or the teacher's expectations. It may encourage students to chase surface-level improvements rather than engage in deeper intellectual revision. Worse still, it may create the illusion of support while quietly weakening the human dialogue that makes feedback emotionally and academically powerful.

This chapter begins from the assumption that AI-generated feedback is neither a miracle solution nor a threat to be rejected outright. It is better understood as a pedagogical instrument whose value depends on the conditions under which it is designed, used, interpreted, and governed. Like any educational tool, it can deepen learning or flatten it. It can support student confidence or increase dependency. It can democratize access to guidance or reproduce hidden inequalities. It can free teachers from repetitive correction or distance them from the very moments where students need human judgment most. The difference lies not in the technology alone, but in the design principles that shape its use.

A major opportunity lies in the formative potential of AI feedback. In many traditional assessment systems, feedback functions as a postscript: it arrives after the performance has been judged (Archan, 2025). AI allows feedback to move closer to the learning process itself. Students can receive guidance while ideas are still forming, while drafts are still unfinished, while misconceptions can still be corrected before they harden into habits. This shift from end-point commentary to ongoing dialogue is especially important in higher education, where students are expected to develop increasingly complex forms of reasoning, disciplinary writing, evidence use, and self-evaluation. When carefully integrated, AI-generated feedback can help students rehearse the internal questions that skilled learners eventually ask themselves: Is my argument clear? Have I supported this claim? Is this evidence strong enough? What assumptions am I making? How could this explanation become more precise?

Yet this opportunity also brings a responsibility. Students need to learn how to read AI feedback critically rather than receive it passively (Thongsan & Anderson, 2025). They must understand that AI responses are not neutral, final, or inherently superior. They are generated through patterns, probabilities, and training data, not through lived teaching experience or moral responsibility. Therefore, feedback literacy becomes essential. Students should be taught how to evaluate the relevance of AI comments, decide which suggestions to accept or reject, and compare AI-generated advice with teacher expectations, peer responses, disciplinary standards, and their own intentions as writers, researchers, or practitioners. Without this critical layer, AI feedback may become another form of invisible authority, wrapped in smooth language and mistaken for truth.

For educators, the challenge is equally significant. AI-generated feedback requires a rethinking of the teacher's role, not its disappearance. Teachers remain responsible for framing tasks, clarifying criteria, interpreting student needs, identifying deeper patterns of misunderstanding, and sustaining the relational dimension of learning. AI may assist with routine comments, early draft responses, language-level suggestions, or reflective prompts, but it cannot replace the professional judgment that connects feedback to curriculum, identity, motivation, ethics, and context. The teacher's role may become less centered on producing every individual comment and more focused on designing feedback ecosystems in which human and AI responses interact productively (Lawrence et al, 2024).

This chapter therefore explores AI-generated feedback as a pedagogical tool situated at the intersection of assessment design, student agency, teacher expertise, and institutional responsibility. It examines the opportunities that generative AI offers for more timely, adaptive, and dialogic feedback, while also confronting the risks of automation, bias, dependency, and superficial personalization. Most importantly, it argues that AI feedback must be guided by human-centered design principles. These principles include transparency, alignment with learning outcomes, contextual sensitivity, student control, iterative use, ethical oversight, and the preservation of meaningful teacher-student dialogue. The future of feedback in higher education should not be imagined as a choice between human care and machine efficiency. The more difficult, and far more interesting, task is to design systems where technology strengthens the human purposes of assessment rather than quietly replacing them.

REFRAMING FEEDBACK IN THE AGE OF GENERATIVE AI: FROM CORRECTION TO PEDAGOGICAL DIALOGUE

Feedback in higher education has too often been treated as a kind of academic aftercare: something offered once the real work has already been done, submitted, judged, and sealed with a grade. It appears at the end of the learning cycle, sometimes with sincerity, sometimes with exhaustion, and often with a quiet hope that students will somehow translate brief marginal notes into future improvement. "Clarify your argument." "More evidence needed." "Good point, but underdeveloped." These comments are familiar, almost ritualistic. They may be true. They may even be useful. Yet they frequently arrive as fragments rather than conversations, as verdicts rather than invitations. The student reads them alone, after the emotional weight of assessment has already fallen. A mark has been assigned. The moment of revision has passed. What remains is a small pile of comments, some encouraging, some cryptic, some painful, and many destined to disappear into the next deadline.

This is the first problem that generative AI forces higher education to confront. Not simply whether machines can produce feedback, but whether traditional feedback practices were ever as pedagogically alive as institutions claimed them to be. The arrival of AI-generated feedback exposes an old weakness with new sharpness (Nassar, 2025). If a system can instantly generate comments that resemble what students often receive from teachers, then perhaps the issue is not only technological imitation; perhaps the deeper issue is that much feedback has already been reduced to formula. It has become thin, compressed, overburdened by workload, and detached from the messy interior of learning. Generative AI did not create this problem. It has merely placed a mirror in front of it.

To reframe feedback in the age of generative AI, then, requires a shift away from seeing feedback as correction alone. Correction has its place, of course. Errors matter. Misused concepts, weak evidence, grammatical confusion, faulty reasoning, poor referencing, and structural disorder cannot simply be celebrated in the name of student freedom. Higher education is not a space where every attempt is equally sound. Standards exist for a reason. Yet correction becomes pedagogically impoverished when it narrows feedback to the detection of deficiency. A student is more than a container of mistakes. A draft is more than a field of errors awaiting harvest. Learning develops through interpretation, uncertainty, struggle, imitation, resistance, and gradual refinement. Feedback, if it is to serve learning rather than merely audit performance, must enter that living process.

Generative AI changes the rhythm of this process because it makes feedback available before the teacher's final judgment. This is one of its most disruptive possibilities (Mourtajji & Chiss, 2025). Students can now submit a paragraph, a plan, a coding attempt, a laboratory reflection, or a research question to an AI system and receive immediate response. Not once, but repeatedly. Not only after completion, but during formation. This seemingly simple temporal shift has deep pedagogical consequences. Feedback no longer has to sit at the end of assessment like a locked door. It can become a companion to drafting, testing, revising, rethinking. It can interrupt the old pattern in which students discover weaknesses only when it is too late to do anything meaningful about them.

Still, immediacy is not the same as wisdom. A fast comment may be shallow. A fluent explanation may be wrong. A confident suggestion may quietly distort the assignment's purpose. This is where the temptation around AI-generated feedback becomes dangerous (Nysom, 2023). Because it speaks smoothly, it can appear more authoritative than it deserves to be. Because it responds patiently, it can seem more caring than it actually is. Because it produces language with ease, it may conceal the absence of genuine understanding. Pedagogical dialogue is not produced by words alone. It depends on orientation, context, judgment, and care. An AI system can simulate many features of dialogue, but the educational value of that simulation depends on whether students are taught how to interrogate it.

The most powerful use of AI-generated feedback may not be in telling students what to fix, but in helping them learn how to ask better questions of their own work. This distinction is subtle, but crucial. A corrective system says: here is what is wrong. A dialogic system asks: what are you trying to say, and where does the work fail to carry that intention? It prompts the student to examine choices. Why this source? Why this structure? Why this claim here, and not later? What would a skeptical reader question? Which part of the argument is doing the heaviest intellectual lifting? These questions do not merely repair a text; they cultivate judgment. They invite students into the habits of mind that characterize mature academic practice.

In that sense, feedback becomes less like a red pen and more like a rehearsal space. Students can try out an idea, receive a response, defend their intention, revise, compare alternatives, and perhaps even reject the advice offered. Rejection matters. A learner who accepts every AI suggestion without thought is not becoming more independent; they are becoming obedient to a polished external voice (Bowen & Watson, 2025). The goal is not to produce students who outsource judgment, but students who can negotiate with feedback, weigh its relevance, and decide what kind of revision genuinely strengthens their work. There is a quiet dignity in that process. It treats students not as passive recipients of improvement, but as emerging participants in disciplinary conversation.

This reframing also changes the teacher's role. In a correction-centered model, the teacher is often positioned as the final inspector of student performance. The teacher identifies flaws, assigns value, and offers recommendations. In a dialogic model supported by generative AI, the teacher becomes something more complex: a designer of feedback environments. This does not diminish professional expertise; it heightens it. Educators must decide when AI feedback is appropriate, what kinds of prompts students should use, how AI responses should be evaluated, which forms of feedback require human attention, and how assessment criteria can be made visible without becoming mechanistic (Chang et al, 2023). The teacher's labor shifts from writing every comment by hand to shaping the conditions under which comments become meaningful.

There is, however, a danger in celebrating this shift too quickly. Institutions may hear "AI feedback" and translate it into workload reduction, cost efficiency, or scalable student support. These goals are not inherently illegitimate, especially in universities where staff are stretched beyond reasonable limits. Yet if efficiency becomes the dominant logic, feedback may become even more alienating than before. Students could find themselves surrounded by automated comments but starved of human recognition. They may receive more words, but less presence. They may be given endless suggestions and still feel unseen. This would be a strange failure: an abundance of feedback with a poverty of relationship.

Pedagogical dialogue requires more than responsiveness. It requires accountability (Lapidot-Lefler, 2025). A teacher can be questioned, challenged, and asked to clarify the reasoning behind a comment. A teacher can remember that a student has struggled with the same issue before, or that a hesitant improvement deserves encouragement. A teacher can sense when a blunt correction would close a student down, and when a sharper challenge might awaken seriousness. Generative AI does not possess this relational memory in any deeply human sense (Rolls, 2024). It may track patterns, but it does not care. It may adapt tone, but it does not bear responsibility. For this reason, AI-generated feedback should be positioned as part of a wider feedback ecology, not as the ecology itself.

A humane model of AI-supported feedback would place students in active relation to multiple voices: their own developing judgment, peer perspectives, teacher expertise, disciplinary standards, and AI-generated prompts. Each voice has a different function. AI can offer immediacy and breadth. Peers can offer readerly response and shared struggle. Teachers can offer expert judgment and ethical presence. Students themselves must gradually learn to orchestrate these voices rather than be overwhelmed by them. Feedback, in this richer sense, becomes not a message delivered to the learner, but a practice enacted by the learner.

This is especially important in higher education, where assessment should not merely certify what students know at a given moment, but help them become capable of future judgment beyond the classroom. A graduate who can improve only when someone else marks errors has not fully learned. A graduate who can seek feedback, interpret it, challenge it, and use it with discernment has acquired something more durable. Generative AI, when designed carefully, can support this movement from dependency to agency. When designed carelessly, it can reverse it.

The age of generative AI invites higher education to recover the unfinished promise of feedback (Otaki, 2023). Not feedback as correction scribbled after the fact. Not feedback as a bureaucratic requirement attached to assessment policy. Not feedback as comforting praise or technical repair alone. Rather, feedback as dialogue: sometimes gentle, sometimes unsettling, often iterative, and always oriented toward the student's growing capacity to see their own work more clearly. The real question is not whether AI can generate comments. It can, and increasingly well. The more demanding question is whether universities can design feedback practices in which those comments become part of a thoughtful pedagogical relationship. That is where the future of AI-generated feedback will be decided—not in the machinery of response, but in the educational imagination that surrounds it.

THE PROMISE OF AI-GENERATED FEEDBACK IN HIGHER EDUCATION ASSESSMENT

The promise of AI-generated feedback in higher education assessment begins, perhaps, with a very ordinary frustration: students need guidance long before teachers are able to provide it. This is not because teachers are careless or indifferent. Quite the opposite. Many educators pour an almost invisible amount of intellectual and emotional labor into feedback, reading drafts late at night, trying to phrase criticism gently, attempting to balance encouragement with rigor, and hoping that a few carefully chosen sentences might nudge a student toward clearer thinking. Yet the conditions of higher education often work against this ideal. Large classes, compressed semesters, administrative burdens, diverse student needs, and the relentless pace of assessment cycles make timely, individualized feedback difficult to sustain. Somewhere between aspiration and workload, feedback loses some of its force.

AI-generated feedback enters this landscape with a powerful, if complicated, promise: it can make feedback more immediate, more frequent, and more available (Venter et al, 2025). A student no longer needs to wait two weeks to discover that their argument lacks coherence, that their evidence does not quite support the claim, or that their introduction announces more than the paper actually delivers. They can receive early comments while the work is still alive, still unfinished, still capable of changing direction. This matters. Learning is highly sensitive to timing. Feedback given after the learner has mentally moved on may have documentary value, but its formative power is weakened. Feedback given during the act of composing, solving, designing, coding, or reflecting can become part of the thinking process itself.

This shift from delayed judgment to ongoing guidance may be one of the most important contributions of generative AI to assessment design. In traditional systems, assessment frequently becomes a closing ceremony. Students submit work, teachers evaluate it, grades are recorded, and feedback appears almost like a postscript (Meinel et al, 2024). AI-generated feedback can unsettle that structure by creating opportunities for pre-submission dialogue. It allows students to test their work before it becomes final. They can ask whether their thesis is sufficiently focused, whether their paragraph development is convincing, whether their methodology is described with enough precision, or whether their conclusion merely repeats earlier points. Such interaction can make assessment feel less like a single performance under pressure and more like an iterative movement toward quality.

The promise is especially visible in formative assessment. Generative AI can support low-stakes cycles of practice in which students revise not because they have failed, but because revision is treated as part of learning (Uanachain & Aouad, 2025). This distinction is small on the surface and enormous underneath. In many academic cultures, students associate feedback with deficiency. Comments reveal what went wrong. Marks expose shortcomings. Red ink, even when digital, carries a certain emotional sting. AI-generated feedback, when carefully designed, can help normalize the idea that good work is made through repeated adjustment. A draft is not an embarrassment. A weak first answer is not a verdict on ability. A confused paragraph is simply material for thought. This can create a more forgiving, exploratory assessment climate, one in which students are less afraid to show unfinished thinking.

Another promise lies in personalization, though the word should be handled carefully. Personalization does not mean that every AI response is automatically meaningful because it is addressed to one student (Sajja et al, 2024). True personalization requires sensitivity to level, purpose, discipline, task, and learner intention. Still, generative AI can offer a form of adaptive explanation that conventional feedback systems often struggle to provide at scale. A student who does not understand a teacher's comment can ask for clarification. A student with weaker academic language can request simpler wording. A more advanced student can ask for a sharper critique. A multilingual learner can explore how phrasing, tone, and disciplinary vocabulary shape meaning. A student working late, anxious before a deadline, may receive guidance at a moment when no tutor, instructor, or writing center appointment is available.

This accessibility is not trivial. Higher education often assumes that students know how to seek help, interpret academic expectations, and translate feedback into revision (Zhan, 2023). Many do not. First-generation students, international students, students returning after long educational gaps, students with disabilities, and students from under-resourced schooling backgrounds may experience feedback as coded language. They hear "be more critical" or "engage more deeply with the literature," but what does that actually mean on the page? AI-generated feedback can, at its best, unpack such phrases into concrete revision moves. It can show examples, ask guiding questions, suggest alternatives, and help students rehearse academic judgment in a lower-pressure setting. In this sense, AI may widen access not simply to comments, but to the hidden grammar of academic quality.

There is also promise in the way AI can support feedback literacy. Students often receive feedback without being taught how to use it. They may correct grammar while ignoring conceptual issues, or they may treat every suggestion as a command. Generative AI can be used to slow down this process. Instead of merely giving advice, it can prompt students to classify feedback, prioritize revisions, compare different versions, and explain why they accepted or rejected certain suggestions (Farrokhnia et al, 2026). A student might ask: Which comments relate to argument? Which relate to structure? Which are about clarity rather than content? What revision would have the greatest impact? These activities move feedback from passive reception to active interpretation. The student is no longer only being corrected; they are learning how correction works.

For teachers, too, AI-generated feedback carries real pedagogical possibilities. It can help identify recurring patterns across student work: weak thesis statements, superficial evidence use, unclear methodological justification, fragmented organization, or limited reflection. Rather than spending all their time repeating the same basic comments, instructors may use AI-supported analysis to redesign teaching interventions. If many students struggle with synthesis, the problem may not be individual weakness but a curricular signal. If students consistently misunderstand a criterion, perhaps the rubric needs clarification. If AI tools can reduce some of the repetitive burden, teachers may have more time for higher-order feedback: the kind that requires disciplinary expertise, ethical sensitivity, and human discernment.

This does not mean that AI should take over the educator's voice. The more interesting possibility is different. AI can handle some first-layer responses, while teachers focus on the deeper pedagogical moments where human judgment matters most (Airaj, 2024). For example, AI may provide preliminary comments on clarity, organization, or alignment with stated criteria, while the teacher responds to originality, conceptual risk, disciplinary nuance, or the student's growth over time. In such a model, AI does not erase teacher feedback; it helps redistribute attention. The teacher becomes less trapped in routine correction and more available for interpretation, mentoring, and intellectual challenge.

The promise of AI-generated feedback also extends to assessment transparency. Students often struggle because expectations remain partly invisible. Rubrics may exist, but they are not always alive in the student's working process. AI can help translate criteria into questions students can apply before submission (Xu et al, 2025). If the criterion asks for critical analysis, the AI can help the learner examine whether they have merely described ideas or actually evaluated relationships, tensions, assumptions, and implications. If the criterion emphasizes evidence, AI can prompt the student to inspect whether each claim is supported, whether sources are integrated rather than dropped into the text, and whether counterarguments have been considered. Assessment criteria then become less like institutional paperwork and more like tools for self-regulation.

Figure 1. Pedagogical Opportunities of AI-Generated Feedback Across Assessment Functions

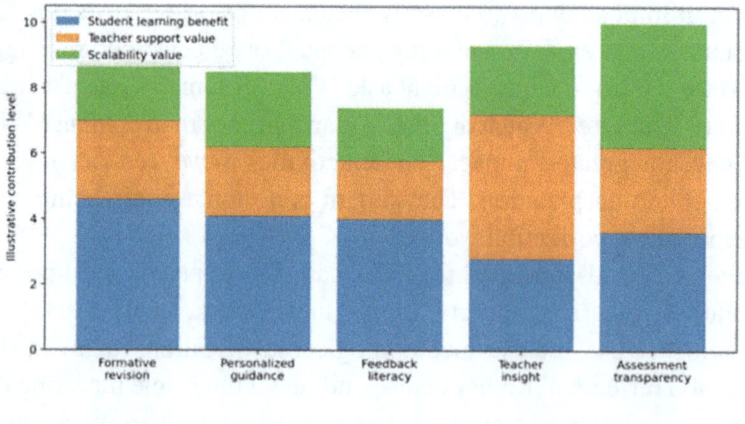

In disciplines beyond writing, the possibilities are equally significant. In programming courses, AI-generated feedback can help students understand why code fails rather than simply pointing to an error. In design education, it can prompt reflection on usability, audience, iteration, and visual logic. In teacher education, it can respond to lesson plans by asking whether objectives, activities, and assessment tasks are aligned. In nursing, engineering, business, or laboratory-based courses, AI can support scenario analysis, reflective decision-making, and explanation of procedural reasoning (Papaneophytou & Nicolaou, 2025). The value lies not in replacing expert assessment, but in multiplying opportunities for students to practice thinking with criteria before they are formally judged.

Yet the promise must be held with sobriety. AI-generated feedback is not valuable because it is new. Higher education has seen many tools arrive wrapped in the language of transformation. Some changed practice; others became expensive ornaments. The value of AI feedback depends on whether it is woven into assessment design with care. It must be aligned with learning outcomes, openly explained to students, reviewed for accuracy, and embedded in activities that require reflection rather than blind acceptance. Otherwise, it risks producing a strange excess: more comments, more suggestions, more textual noise, but not necessarily more learning.

Perhaps the most hopeful vision is one in which AI-generated feedback helps restore feedback to its proper place within learning. Not at the end. Not as punishment. Not as hurried annotation. Not as a private message that students half-read and then forget. Instead, feedback becomes continuous, dialogic, revisable, and shared. It becomes something students do with their work, not something done to them after the work is finished. Generative AI can support this movement because it offers immediacy, adaptability, and scale. But these qualities become educational only when guided by human purpose.

The promise, then, is not that AI will make feedback perfect. It will not. Nor will it remove the need for teachers, peer dialogue, institutional responsibility, or student effort. Its deeper promise is that it may help higher education rethink the architecture of assessment itself. It may allow universities to move from scarce, delayed, one-directional feedback toward richer feedback ecologies where students encounter guidance early, often, and critically. If designed with imagination and restraint, AI-generated feedback can help turn assessment from a terminal act of measurement into a living process of improvement. That is not a small promise. It is, in fact, one of the more compelling reasons to take this technology seriously without surrendering to it.

DESIGNING FEEDBACK THAT SUPPORTS LEARNING, AGENCY, AND REFLECTION

Designing AI-generated feedback for higher education assessment is not simply a matter of making comments faster, longer, or more technically precise (Deepshikha, 2026). That would be an oddly small ambition for such a powerful shift. The real task is more delicate: to design feedback that helps students become more capable of learning from their own work. In other words, feedback should not only repair the assignment in front of the student; it should strengthen the learner behind it. This difference is easy to miss, especially in assessment cultures where feedback is still imagined as a corrective message attached to a completed product. Yet if generative AI is to serve a genuinely pedagogical purpose, its feedback must reach beyond correction and move toward agency, self-questioning, and reflective judgment.

A useful starting point is to ask what students are expected to do with feedback. Too often, the answer is vague. They are expected to "use it," "learn from it," or "improve next time," as if these actions were obvious. They are not. Many students receive feedback as a set of disconnected instructions: add evidence, clarify the argument, improve structure, define key terms, engage more critically. These comments may be accurate, but accuracy alone does not guarantee usefulness. A student may understand that their argument is weak without knowing how to rebuild it (Kapur et al, 2022). They may accept that their analysis is descriptive without recognizing what analytical depth looks like in practice. They may be told to be more critical and still wonder, privately and with some frustration, what "critical" actually means in this discipline, this task, this paragraph, this particular intellectual moment.

This is where feedback design becomes central. AI-generated feedback should be structured not only to identify problems, but to make the next step visible (Nazaretsky et al, 2026). A comment that says, "Your claim needs stronger support," may be true. A more pedagogically useful response would ask the student to locate the claim, identify the evidence currently attached to it, consider whether that evidence proves, illustrates, complicates, or merely accompanies the point, and then decide whether a stronger source, a clearer explanation, or a more modest claim is needed. Such feedback does not simply diagnose weakness; it teaches the student how to think through weakness. It turns feedback into a small act of apprenticeship.

Learning-oriented feedback must also preserve struggle. This may sound strange, since AI tools are often praised for reducing difficulty (Nassar, 2025). But not all difficulty is harmful. Some forms of confusion are productive; they mark the edge of understanding. When AI feedback becomes too directive, too complete, or too eager to solve, it can rob students of the intellectual labor that learning requires. A system that instantly rewrites a poor paragraph may produce a better paragraph, but it may not produce a better writer. A system that explains why the paragraph lacks coherence, offers two possible revision strategies, and asks the student to choose the one that best fits their intention is doing something more educationally honest. It leaves room for effort. It respects the learner's role in the revision.

Agency depends on that room. Students need to feel that feedback is something they can negotiate, not merely obey. In a higher education context, this is particularly important because academic work is not always governed by simple right-or-wrong answers. Arguments can be framed differently. Evidence can be interpreted from competing angles. A methodological decision may be defensible in one research tradition and questionable in another. Even writing style varies across disciplines, genres, and epistemic communities. AI-generated feedback should not flatten this complexity into a single authoritative voice. It should present suggestions as possibilities, invite justification, and encourage students to ask whether a recommendation aligns with their purpose. The phrase "consider revising" is often more pedagogically generous than "revise." A question may open more thinking than a command.

This does not mean feedback should become timid or endlessly relativistic. Students also need clarity. They need to know when something is genuinely underdeveloped, inaccurate, unsupported, or incoherent. The challenge is to combine firmness with invitation. Strong feedback can still be dialogic. It can say, in effect: this part does not yet work, and here are several ways you might examine it. The tone matters, but tone is not merely politeness. It shapes how students relate emotionally to revision. Harsh feedback can produce defensiveness or shame. Overly soft feedback can blur standards. The best feedback carries an unusual balance: it is honest enough to matter and careful enough to keep the learner engaged.

For AI-generated feedback, this balance must be intentionally designed (Nazaretsky et al, 2026). The system should avoid exaggerated praise, generic encouragement, and the kind of smooth, padded language that makes every draft sound "promising" even when it is deeply confused. Students deserve more than comforting vagueness. At the same time, feedback should not imitate the coldness of automated evaluation, where the student feels processed rather than addressed. A humane feedback system should recognize effort without romanticizing it, identify weakness without humiliating the learner, and point toward improvement without pretending that revision is easy. There is something quietly powerful about feedback that says: this is not yet clear, but it can become clearer, and here is how to begin.

Reflection is the bridge between receiving feedback and learning from it. Without reflection, feedback remains external (Abraham, 2022). It may improve the submitted work, but it does not necessarily change the student's habits of thinking. For this reason, AI-generated feedback should be embedded in reflective routines. Students might be asked to write a short response explaining which AI suggestions they accepted, which they rejected, and why. They might compare AI feedback with peer feedback or teacher comments, noting where the voices converge and where they differ. They might identify one recurring issue across several assignments and create a personal revision plan. These activities may seem modest, but they alter the role of feedback. The student becomes an interpreter, not merely a recipient.

Such reflective use is also a safeguard against dependency. One of the quieter risks of AI-generated feedback is that students may begin to treat it as a private authority that must approve their work before they can trust it. This is especially likely when feedback is instant, fluent, and endlessly available. A student can ask again and again: Is this good enough? Is this clearer? Can you improve this? What grade would this receive? At first, this may look like engagement. Beneath the surface, however, it can become a form of cognitive outsourcing. The student's internal evaluative voice weakens because the external voice is always ready. Good design must resist this. AI feedback should gradually move students toward self-assessment, not permanent consultation.

One way to support this movement is through staged feedback. Early in a course, AI responses may be more explanatory and scaffolded, helping students understand criteria, terminology, and revision strategies. As students develop confidence, the feedback can become less directive and more question-based. Instead of telling students what to change, it can ask them to identify the weakest part of their argument, predict what a critical reader might challenge, or explain how their evidence supports their main claim. Over time, the feedback environment should become less like a repair service and more like a mirror that students learn to hold for themselves.

The design of feedback must also account for disciplinary difference. Feedback in engineering design is not the same as feedback in literary analysis. Feedback on a nursing reflection is not the same as feedback on a statistical report. A business case analysis, a laboratory write-up, a lesson plan, and a philosophical essay all carry different expectations about evidence, reasoning, voice, structure, and judgment. Generic AI feedback, however fluent, can miss these differences. It may reward clarity while overlooking disciplinary rigor, or encourage broader explanation when the task requires concise technical precision (Geroimenko, 2025). For AI-generated feedback to support real learning, it must be aligned with the epistemic habits of the field. Rubrics, examples, teacher-designed prompts, and discipline-specific criteria are not decorative additions; they are the conditions that make feedback educationally trustworthy.

There is also a social dimension that should not be ignored. Feedback is not only a cognitive tool; it is part of the relationship between the learner and the academic community. Students learn what counts as quality, seriousness, originality, and care through the responses they receive. If AI feedback becomes the dominant voice in assessment, students may encounter academic standards as automated language rather than as shared human practice. This would be a loss. The better approach is to let AI support the feedback ecology while keeping teachers and peers visibly present. Students should see feedback as a conversation across multiple sources of judgment, each with its own strengths and limits.

Designing feedback that supports learning, agency, and reflection finally requires a certain restraint. Not every task needs AI feedback (Chang et al, 2023). Not every comment needs to be generated instantly. Not every student benefits from the same kind of response. The abundance of AI should not lead to feedback saturation, where learners are buried under suggestions and lose the ability to decide what matters. Sometimes the most useful feedback is brief. Sometimes it is a question. Sometimes it is a teacher's handwritten sentence that cuts directly to the heart of a student's confusion. Sometimes it is silence followed by self-review. Good design knows when to intervene and when to leave space.

The promise of AI-generated feedback will be realized only if it is shaped by a rich understanding of learning itself (Jacobsen & Weber, 2023). Students do not grow simply because comments are available. They grow when feedback helps them notice, decide, revise, and reflect; when it invites them into standards rather than merely measuring them against standards; when it strengthens their capacity to judge their own work with increasing honesty and sophistication. In this sense, the deepest purpose of AI-supported feedback is not to make students dependent on intelligent systems, but to help them become more intelligent participants in their own learning. That is a harder design challenge than automation. It is also a far more worthwhile one.

RISKS, LIMITATIONS, AND ETHICAL CONCERNS IN AI-MEDIATED FEEDBACK PRACTICES

The growing use of AI-mediated feedback in higher education carries an undeniable sense of possibility, but it also brings with it a cluster of risks that cannot be brushed aside as minor technical inconveniences (Hamilton, 2025). Feedback is not a neutral academic accessory. It shapes how students understand their abilities, how they approach revision, how they interpret standards, and sometimes, quite quietly, how they judge their own worth as learners. When feedback becomes mediated through generative AI systems, the question is no longer only whether the comments are useful or efficient (Saini et al, 2024). The deeper question is whether the feedback remains educationally trustworthy, ethically accountable, and genuinely supportive of human learning.

One of the first limitations concerns accuracy. Generative AI systems can produce feedback that sounds polished, confident, and pedagogically reasonable, even when it is partly mistaken (Pratschke, 2024). This is perhaps the most unsettling feature of AI-mediated feedback: its fluency can disguise fragility. A student may receive a comment that appears precise but misreads the assignment, overlooks the teacher's expectations, invents weaknesses that are not there, or praises superficial qualities while missing deeper conceptual errors. In traditional feedback, students may at least know that a teacher's comment comes from someone responsible for the course, familiar with the assessment criteria, and aware of the disciplinary context. AI-generated feedback, unless carefully constrained and monitored, may speak in a voice of authority without possessing the situated judgment that authority requires.

This becomes especially problematic in higher education because academic work is rarely generic. What counts as a strong argument in sociology may not count as strong evidence in biomedical science. A reflective nursing journal, a legal case analysis, an engineering design report, and a philosophical essay all operate with different assumptions about voice, evidence, structure, and validity. AI systems often flatten these distinctions. They may encourage "more detail" when concision is needed, praise "creativity" in a genre that demands procedural accuracy, or suggest a more assertive claim where disciplinary caution is expected. Such feedback can appear helpful while quietly pulling students away from the epistemic culture of their field. The danger is not dramatic. It is subtler than that. It is the slow production of academically tidy but intellectually misplaced work.

Bias is another serious concern. AI systems are trained on large bodies of data that carry the marks of social, linguistic, cultural, and institutional inequality (Zajko, 2022). These marks do not vanish simply because the output is framed as educational support. Feedback may privilege certain forms of academic English, certain rhetorical traditions, certain assumptions about "clarity" or "professionalism," and certain norms of argumentation associated with dominant academic cultures. Students from multilingual, non-Western, Indigenous, working-class, or otherwise marginalized backgrounds may find their voices corrected into conformity rather than developed with respect. There is a difference between helping a student meet disciplinary expectations and erasing the texture of their expression. AI-mediated feedback may not always know that difference.

This risk is particularly acute for international students and multilingual writers (Curry & Lillis, 2024). On the surface, AI can offer valuable language support. It can explain grammar, suggest alternative phrasing, and help students communicate ideas more clearly. Yet if used carelessly, it may also impose a smooth, standardized academic voice that strips away individuality and rhetorical diversity. The student's writing becomes more fluent, perhaps, but also less theirs. In a university sector that increasingly claims to value global perspectives, this matters. Higher education should not invite students from diverse linguistic worlds only to feed their writing into systems that quietly discipline them into sameness.

A further ethical concern lies in dependency. AI feedback is available instantly, patiently, and without visible fatigue (Rudroff, 2024). This can be helpful, but it can also become seductive. Students may begin to consult AI at every stage of thinking: before forming an idea, before trusting a sentence, before deciding whether an argument is strong enough. Over time, the learner's internal evaluative voice may weaken. Instead of asking, "Does this argument work?" the student asks, "Will the system approve this?" Instead of wrestling with ambiguity, they may seek immediate reassurance. This is not learning in its fullest sense. It is a kind of intellectual outsourcing disguised as support.

The paradox is sharp. Feedback is meant to build independence, yet AI-mediated feedback may produce new forms of dependence if students are not taught how to question, filter, and sometimes refuse it. A student who accepts every suggestion from an AI system is not necessarily becoming a stronger learner. They may simply be becoming more compliant. The educational aim should be to cultivate judgment, not obedience. This is why AI feedback must be designed to invite reflection rather than automatic correction. Students should not only receive comments; they should be asked to evaluate those comments, explain their revision choices, and identify where the AI's advice is useful, limited, or irrelevant.

Privacy and data governance also demand careful attention. Feedback often involves unfinished student work, personal reflections, research ideas, clinical scenarios, design prototypes, and sometimes sensitive information about identity, experience, or difficulty. When such material is submitted to AI systems, institutions must ask uncomfortable but necessary questions. Where does the data go? Is it stored? Is it used for model improvement? Who can access it? Can students opt out without penalty? Are they being asked to trade privacy for academic support? These questions should not be buried in long terms-of-service documents that nobody reads. They belong at the center of institutional policy.

There is also a fairness issue. If some students have access to high-quality AI feedback tools while others rely on free, limited, or poorly configured systems, assessment conditions may become uneven. Students with stronger digital literacy may learn how to prompt effectively, refine outputs, and extract better guidance. Others may receive shallow or misleading feedback and not know how to improve it. What appears to be a universal support tool may actually widen gaps between students who know how to use AI strategically and those who do not. In this sense, AI feedback is not automatically inclusive. Inclusion has to be designed, taught, resourced, and monitored.

Teacher workload raises another complicated question. AI is often introduced with the promise of reducing repetitive feedback labor (Kirk, 2025). This may be partly true. It may help teachers avoid writing the same comment dozens of times, identify common problems, or support early-stage drafting. Yet workload reduction can easily become institutional justification for reducing human contact. Universities may be tempted to treat automated feedback as a substitute for teacher engagement, especially in large classes or financially strained systems. This would be a profound misunderstanding. The problem of feedback in higher education is not merely that there are too few comments. It is that students need meaningful encounters with standards, expectations, and human judgment. Replacing exhausted teachers with tireless machines may solve an administrative problem while deepening a pedagogical one.

Accountability becomes blurred when AI feedback causes harm or confusion (McNealis, 2026). If a student follows AI-generated advice and performs poorly, who is responsible? The student? The teacher who allowed the tool? The institution that licensed it? The company that built it? The algorithm that cannot answer for itself? Educational feedback has consequences. It can shape grades, confidence, progression, and academic identity. A system that influences these outcomes must be accountable in more than a symbolic sense. Yet AI-mediated feedback often sits in an ambiguous space: powerful enough to influence learning, but not always governed as carefully as formal assessment.

Another limitation concerns emotional sensitivity. Feedback is affective, not merely cognitive. Students do not receive comments as empty processors of information. They receive them with anxiety, pride, defensiveness, fatigue, hope, and sometimes a long history of feeling academically inadequate. A teacher can notice when a student needs encouragement before critique, or when a confident student needs to be pushed beyond comfortable competence. AI can imitate empathy, but imitation is not the same as moral attentiveness. Its tone may be gentle, but it does not know the student (Vučenović & Maksimović, 2025). It may say "you are doing well," but it does not mean it. For some learners, this may not matter. For others, especially those struggling with confidence, the difference between simulated care and human recognition may be deeply significant.

There is also the risk of feedback saturation. Because AI can generate endless commentary, students may receive too much. Too many suggestions can paralyze revision rather than support it. A draft covered in comments, alternatives, warnings, and possibilities may leave the learner unsure where to begin. Human teachers often make selective judgments: this is the one issue to focus on now; that other weakness can wait. AI systems may lack this pedagogical restraint unless carefully designed (Yue et al, 2022). More feedback is not necessarily better feedback. Sometimes it is noise wearing the costume of help.

The ethical challenge, then, is not to reject AI-mediated feedback outright, but to resist its careless normalization. Institutions should not treat AI feedback as an inevitable upgrade, nor should educators assume that students will naturally use it well. It requires explicit guidance, transparent boundaries, disciplinary alignment, human oversight, and opportunities for critical reflection. Students should know that AI feedback is provisional, not final; suggestive, not sovereign. Teachers should remain visible in the feedback process, especially where judgment, care, originality, and ethical interpretation are required.

Figure 2. Core Human-Centered Design Principles for AI-Generated Feedback

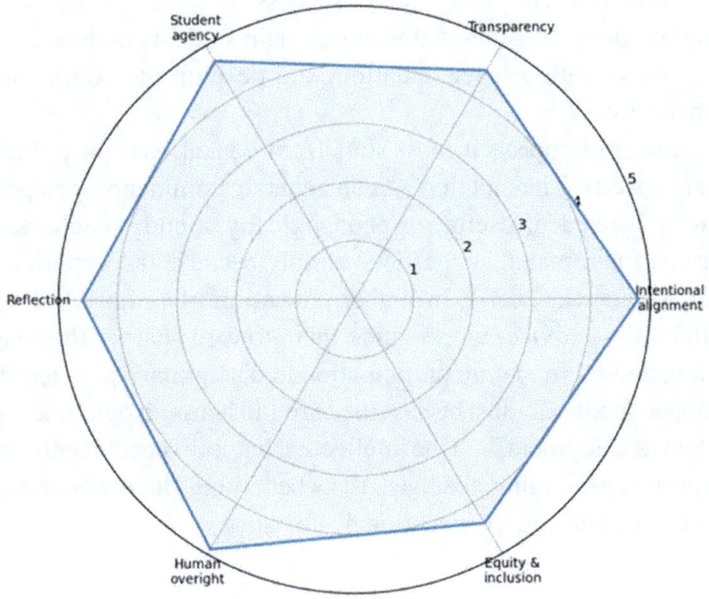

AI-mediated feedback can support higher education, but only if its limitations are kept in view (Zhao, 2024). The danger is not simply that the technology might fail. The greater danger is that it might work well enough to be trusted too quickly, adopted too broadly, and questioned too little. A smooth comment can still be shallow. A rapid response can still be wrong. A personalized suggestion can still be biased. A supportive tone can still conceal the absence of real responsibility. For this reason, the future of AI feedback must be shaped by caution as much as enthusiasm. Good educational design does not ask only what a tool can do. It asks what it may damage, what it may hide, whom it may disadvantage, and what human purposes must remain non-negotiable.

TOWARD HUMAN-CENTERED DESIGN PRINCIPLES FOR AI-GENERATED FEEDBACK

Human-centered design in AI-generated feedback begins with a deceptively simple premise: feedback exists for learners, not for systems (Calidonio, 2025). It is easy, almost dangerously easy, to forget this when generative AI enters the assessment landscape with its speed, fluency, and operational elegance. Institutions may admire the efficiency. Teachers may welcome the relief from repetitive comments. Students may appreciate the immediacy. Yet none of these benefits, valuable as they are, should become the central measure of success. The real question is quieter and more demanding: does AI-generated feedback help students understand their work more deeply, revise with greater intention, and develop the confidence to judge quality for themselves?

A human-centered approach must start from educational purpose rather than technological capacity. The fact that AI can generate comments does not mean that every comment is needed, useful, or pedagogically sound. Feedback should not become a river of automated suggestions simply because the system can produce them (Shi & Aryadoust, 2024). In higher education, the aim is not to surround students with endless advice, but to guide them toward sharper thinking, stronger self-evaluation, and more mature participation in disciplinary practice. This means that AI-generated feedback must be designed around learning outcomes, assessment criteria, student development, and the intellectual habits expected within a particular field. Without such grounding, feedback risks becoming fluent decoration: impressive on the surface, but thin in educational substance.

Figure 3. Cumulative Ethical and Practical Risks in AI-Mediated Feedback

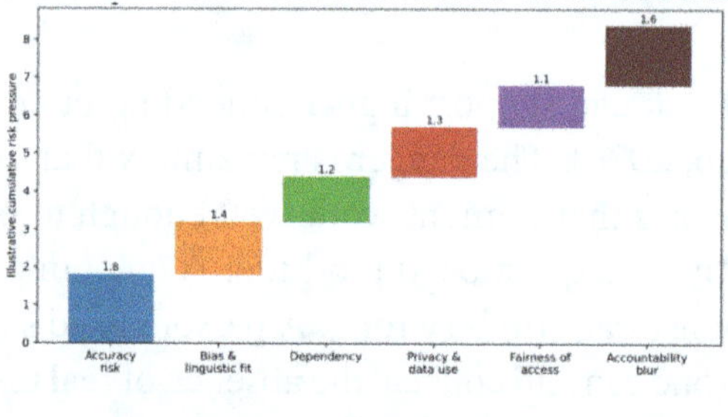

The first principle, then, is intentional alignment. AI-generated feedback should be tied clearly to the purpose of the task. A research essay, a reflective journal, a laboratory report, a clinical case analysis, a business proposal, and a programming assignment do not require the same kind of response (Aithal & Aithal, 2023). Each carries its own logic of quality. In one context, originality may matter most; in another, procedural accuracy; in another, ethical reasoning, evidence selection, methodological clarity, or professional judgment. Generic feedback can mislead students because it gives the impression of relevance while ignoring the hidden architecture of the discipline. A human-centered design does not ask AI to comment vaguely on “clarity” or “improvement.” It asks the system to respond through the actual criteria, language, and epistemic expectations of the course.

Transparency is equally important. Students should know when they are receiving AI-generated feedback, what kind of system is producing it, what its limits are, and how it should be used (Öztürk & Cebi, 2026). There is something ethically fragile about feedback that appears personal but is actually automated, especially when students assume it carries the same authority as a teacher’s judgment. Transparency does not weaken trust; it makes trust possible. Students need to understand that AI feedback is provisional, suggestive, and sometimes flawed. It may be helpful, but it is not sacred. It may notice patterns, but it does not know the learner in the way a teacher can. Once this is made clear, students can approach AI feedback not as a verdict, but as one voice within a wider learning conversation.

A third principle concerns student agency. AI-generated feedback should not turn learners into passive recipients of machine-polished advice. The design should require students to make decisions. Which suggestion is useful? Which one does not fit the purpose of the assignment? Which comment addresses a surface issue, and which points to a deeper weakness in reasoning? Which revision would genuinely improve the work, rather than merely make it sound smoother? These questions matter because agency is not built by receiving more guidance; it is built by learning how to interpret guidance. In this sense, the best AI feedback may be less directive than many people expect. It may ask questions. It may offer options. It may invite comparison. It may deliberately leave space for the student’s judgment to operate.

Reflection should be woven into the feedback process, not added as an afterthought. A student who uses AI-generated feedback should be encouraged, perhaps even required, to explain how they responded to it (Nazaretsky et al, 2026). This could take the form of a short revision note, a reflective commentary, or an annotated draft showing which suggestions were accepted, adapted, or rejected. Such practices prevent AI feedback from becoming an invisible editing service. They also help teachers see how students are thinking about revision, not merely what the revised product looks like. The learning is often in the decision trail: the hesitation, the choice, the justification, the moment when a student says, “I see why this comment matters, but I do not want to follow it exactly because my argument is trying to do something different.” That is not disobedience. That is intellectual growth.

Human oversight remains non-negotiable. AI may assist feedback, but it should not become the final guardian of academic quality. Teachers carry responsibilities that cannot be delegated to a system: interpreting student progress, recognizing originality, noticing emotional difficulty, protecting fairness, and connecting feedback to the broader aims of the course. A teacher can understand when a student’s awkward paragraph contains a genuinely interesting idea. A teacher can see when technically correct work lacks curiosity, or when imperfect work shows real conceptual movement. AI may identify features of a text, but it does not inhabit the moral and relational space of teaching. Human-centered design keeps educators present, not as decorative supervisors, but as active interpreters of learning.

This does not mean teachers must manually control every AI-generated comment. That would defeat much of the practical value. Instead, oversight can be layered. Educators can design prompts, set boundaries, review samples, calibrate feedback against rubrics, monitor patterns, and intervene where stakes are high. AI feedback may be more appropriate for early drafts, practice tasks, formative checkpoints, and low-stakes revision than for final judgments. The higher the consequence, the stronger the need for human review. This layered approach respects both the usefulness of automation and the seriousness of assessment.

Table 1. Design Principles for AI-Generated Feedback in Higher Education

Design Principle	Pedagogical Purpose	Practical Design Implication	Expected Learner Benefit
Intentional alignment	Match feedback to task purpose and assessment goals	Configure prompts and criteria around disciplinary expectations and stage of learning	More relevant and actionable feedback
Transparency	Help students understand what generated the feedback and what its limits are	Disclose AI use, explain criteria, and signal uncertainty where appropriate	Greater trust and critical interpretation
Student agency	Prevent passive compliance and support judgment	Offer options, questions, and revision pathways instead of only fixed commands	Stronger autonomy and decision-making
Reflection	Turn comments into learning rather than mere correction	Embed self-explanation, comparison, and response activities after feedback	Improved feedback literacy and metacognition
Human oversight	Preserve accountability and pedagogical responsibility	Review outputs, sample responses, and intervene when nuance is needed	Higher quality and safer use
Equity and inclusion	Ensure fair access and culturally sensitive feedback	Check language bias, accessibility, and appropriateness for diverse learners	More just and inclusive feedback environments

Equity must also sit at the heart of design. AI-generated feedback should not benefit only the already confident, digitally fluent, or linguistically privileged student (Khasawneh, 2024). Some learners know how to prompt effectively, challenge responses, and extract deeper value from AI tools. Others may accept weak feedback because it sounds authoritative. Some may not have equal access to reliable platforms, stable internet, or institutional guidance. A human-centered model requires training, shared access, clear expectations, and support for students who may be unfamiliar with AI-mediated learning. Otherwise, the technology that claims to democratize feedback may quietly widen the distance between students who can use it strategically and those who cannot.

Language diversity deserves particular care. AI feedback often nudges writing toward standardized academic fluency, which can be helpful but also culturally flattening (Wang, 2026). Students should not be made to feel that intellectual legitimacy requires the erasure of voice. The task is not to preserve every linguistic feature unchanged, nor to impose a bland universal style. It is to help students communicate effectively within academic and professional contexts while still respecting the individuality of expression. Human-centered feedback should distinguish between confusion and difference, between necessary disciplinary convention and unnecessary stylistic conformity. That distinction is delicate. AI alone cannot always be trusted to make it.

Privacy and data responsibility form another essential principle. Student work is not raw material to be casually fed into opaque systems (Wu et al, 2026). Drafts may contain personal reflections, original research ideas, sensitive experiences, clinical observations, or unpublished intellectual labor. Institutions must be clear about what data is submitted, where it is stored, whether it is used for training, and what choices students have. Consent should not be symbolic. Opt-out routes should be meaningful. A student should not have to surrender privacy in order to receive academic support.

Finally, AI-generated feedback should be evaluated continuously. Universities should not assume that because a tool produces impressive comments, it is improving learning. Evidence is needed: Are students revising more thoughtfully? Do they understand criteria better? Are teachers noticing stronger drafts? Are certain groups disadvantaged? Are students becoming more independent, or more dependent? Are comments accurate across disciplines? Are learners overwhelmed by too much feedback? These questions should be asked repeatedly, not once during adoption and then forgotten.

Table 2. Institutional Oversight and Evaluation Framework for AI-Mediated Feedback

Area	Key Question	Suggested Action	Lead Responsibility	Indicator of Success
Accuracy	Is the feedback disciplinarily sound and pedagogically useful?	Audit sample outputs against rubric and expert judgment	Faculty and assessment leads	Low rate of misleading or incorrect guidance
Transparency	Do students know when and how AI feedback is used?	Provide disclosure statements and tool-use guidance	Course leaders and program teams	Students can explain the feedback source and limits
Equity	Are all students benefiting fairly?	Monitor access, language issues, and differential outcomes	Equity offices and teaching teams	Reduced access gaps and inclusive learner experience
Privacy	Is student work handled responsibly?	Adopt secure systems and explicit consent/ data protocols	Institutional governance and IT	Compliance with data policy and student confidence
Teacher workload	Does AI support rather than distort staff work?	Use AI for first-pass assistance while preserving human review	Departments and instructors	Sustainable workload with maintained quality
Continuous evaluation	Is the tool improving learning over time?	Collect student feedback, outcome data, and teacher reflections	Program review teams	Evidence of learning value and responsible refinement

A human-centered model of AI-generated feedback is not anti-technology. It is, in fact, the opposite: it takes the technology seriously enough to design its use with care. It recognizes that feedback is one of the most intimate parts of assessment because it speaks directly to the learner's effort, uncertainty, and possibility. Poorly designed AI feedback may produce efficiency without growth. Carefully designed AI feedback may help students encounter their work with fresh eyes, revise with greater purpose, and gradually internalize the standards of thoughtful academic practice. The difference lies not in the machine's fluency, but in the human wisdom surrounding its use.

CONCLUSION

AI-generated feedback stands at one of the most delicate intersections in contemporary higher education: the meeting point between technological possibility and pedagogical responsibility. Its appeal is easy to understand. Higher education systems are under pressure to serve more students, respond more quickly, personalize learning, reduce delays, and support increasingly diverse academic needs.

In such a context, generative AI appears almost perfectly timed. It can produce comments instantly, adapt explanations to different levels, offer revision prompts, support students outside office hours, and provide a kind of continuous formative presence that many courses have never been able to sustain. For students who often receive feedback too late to use it, this is not a minor improvement. It may change the rhythm of learning itself.

Yet the chapter has argued that speed alone is not pedagogy. Nor is personalization meaningful simply because a system can generate individualized text. The real educational question is whether AI-generated feedback helps students become more capable, reflective, and self-directed learners. Does it deepen their understanding of quality? Does it help them recognize the structure of their own mistakes? Does it encourage revision as a thoughtful act rather than a cosmetic adjustment? Does it protect their agency, or does it quietly train them to wait for machine-generated approval before trusting their own judgment? These questions matter because feedback is never just about improving a single piece of work. It shapes how students understand learning, authority, effort, and themselves.

One of the most important conclusions to draw is that AI-generated feedback should not be treated as a replacement for teacher feedback. This framing is too narrow, too mechanical, and ultimately misleading. The more useful question is how AI can expand the feedback environment around students without eroding the human relationships that give education its depth. In some cases, AI may be best used before submission, helping students test early drafts, identify unclear reasoning, or practice applying criteria. In other cases, it may serve as a supplementary layer after teacher feedback, helping students unpack comments they do not fully understand. It may also support peer review, reflective learning, language development, or self-assessment. But in each of these roles, its value depends on thoughtful design rather than mere availability.

The design of AI-generated feedback must therefore begin with educational intention. Institutions and educators should ask what problem they are trying to solve. Is the aim to improve timeliness? To support revision? To reduce teacher workload? To help students understand assessment criteria? To increase equity in access to guidance? To develop feedback literacy? These aims are not identical, and each requires different forms of implementation. A tool designed to correct grammar is not the same as one designed to stimulate critical reflection. A system that gives rubric-based comments is not the same as one that supports exploratory dialogue. Without clear pedagogical purpose, AI feedback risks becoming a decorative layer added to assessment systems that remain unchanged at their core.

A second conclusion concerns transparency. Students should know when feedback is AI-generated, how it is produced, what its limits are, and how they are expected to use it. Hidden or poorly explained AI use can damage trust, especially if students feel that their work is being processed by systems they do not understand. Transparency is not only a technical matter; it is an ethical and relational one. Students deserve to know whether comments come from a teacher, a machine, or a combination of both. They also need guidance on how to interpret those comments critically. Otherwise, AI-generated feedback may become another opaque authority in academic life, one that speaks confidently but cannot be questioned in the same way a teacher can.

A third conclusion is that feedback literacy must become a central part of AI-driven assessment design. Students need more than feedback; they need the ability to use feedback. This distinction is often overlooked. Many learners, especially those in their early university years, may not know how to translate comments into revision strategies. They may accept weak AI suggestions because they sound fluent, or reject useful ones because they challenge their original intention. They may focus on surface corrections while ignoring deeper conceptual weaknesses. For this reason, AI feedback should be accompanied by activities that require students to compare comments, justify revisions, reflect on choices, and evaluate the usefulness of different forms of guidance. The goal is not simply to give students better answers. The goal is to help them become better judges of quality.

The role of educators remains central in this process. AI may reduce some repetitive burdens, but it cannot assume responsibility for the moral, disciplinary, and relational dimensions of feedback. Teachers understand the history of a course, the emotional texture of a classroom, the hidden struggles behind a student's performance, and the intellectual standards of a discipline in ways that AI systems cannot genuinely possess. A teacher can notice hesitation, growth, frustration, originality, or risk-taking. A teacher can decide when a student needs encouragement more than correction, or when a polished answer hides shallow understanding. These forms of judgment are not peripheral to feedback; they are part of what makes it educational.

At the institutional level, AI-generated feedback demands careful governance. Policies should address data privacy, bias, accessibility, academic integrity, accountability, and quality assurance. It is not enough to introduce tools and assume that responsible use will follow naturally. Institutions must provide training for teachers, orientation for students, and clear boundaries around appropriate use. They should also evaluate whether AI feedback works equally well across disciplines, languages, student backgrounds, and assessment types. A system that benefits confident, digitally fluent students while confusing or disadvantaging others cannot be described as genuinely inclusive. Equity must be designed into AI feedback practices from the beginning, not added later as a corrective gesture.

Ultimately, the promise of AI-generated feedback lies not in making assessment less human, but in giving educators and students new ways to recover what feedback was always meant to be: timely, dialogic, actionable, and connected to growth. Used carelessly, AI may produce a flood of comments with little learning value.

Used wisely, it can help shift assessment away from one-way judgment and toward sustained pedagogical conversation. The difference is subtle but decisive. More feedback is not automatically better feedback. Faster feedback is not automatically deeper feedback. Personalized feedback is not automatically empowering feedback.

The future of AI-generated feedback in higher education will depend on whether universities choose convenience alone or design with care. If AI is used merely to accelerate marking, reduce workload, and standardize responses, its contribution may remain thin, even if technically impressive. But if it is embedded within a richer culture of formative assessment, student reflection, teacher judgment, and ethical oversight, it can become something more valuable: a tool that helps students engage with their own learning while preserving the human purposes at the heart of education. The task ahead is not to surrender feedback to machines, nor to defend older practices simply because they are familiar. The task is to build feedback ecologies in which AI serves learning, teachers remain intellectually and ethically present, and students gradually acquire the confidence to read, question, revise, and grow.

Limitations of the Research

This chapter is conceptual and analytical rather than empirical, and it does not present original experimental, survey, or longitudinal data. The figures and numerical values are illustrative representations derived from the chapter's arguments, not measured findings from a specific intervention. Experiences with AI-generated feedback may vary significantly across disciplines, languages, institutional contexts, technological infrastructures, and student populations. For that reason, the proposed design principles and risks should be interpreted as a guiding framework rather than a universal formula. Future research should test these ideas through classroom-based studies, comparative evaluations, and mixed-method investigations of student learning, teacher workload, and ethical governance.

Recommendations

Higher education institutions should adopt AI-generated feedback as a pedagogical support system rather than as a replacement for teaching judgment. Effective implementation begins with intentional assessment design: educators should decide where AI feedback can enrich formative learning, where teacher feedback is indispensable, and how both can work together across revision cycles. Students should be explicitly taught feedback literacy so that they can question, compare, and use AI-generated comments critically instead of accepting them passively. Institutions should also design for agency by ensuring that feedback offers pathways for reflection, revision, and choice rather than merely prescribing corrections. Human oversight must remain central. Teachers should review patterns in AI feedback, monitor disciplinary accuracy, and intervene where automated responses risk misunderstanding student intent. Privacy, transparency, and equity should be built into governance from the start, with clear policies for data use, disclosure, and accessibility. Universities should evaluate AI feedback continuously through mixed evidence, including student experience, learning outcomes, teacher judgment, and fairness indicators. The most promising future lies not in making feedback less human, but in using AI to create more timely, dialogic, and pedagogically meaningful opportunities for learning.

REFERENCES

Abraham, R. M. (2022). Reflection on improving feedback skills and a framework for moving towards feed forward. *Bangladesh Journal of Medical Science*, *21*(1), 206–212. DOI: 10.3329/bjms.v21i1.56351

Airaj, M. (2024). Ethical artificial intelligence for teaching-learning in higher education. *Education and Information Technologies*, *29*(13), 17145–17167. DOI: 10.1007/s10639-024-12545-x

Aithal, P. S., & Aithal, S. (2023). Application of ChatGPT in higher education and research–A futuristic analysis. [IJAEML]. *International Journal of Applied Engineering and Management Letters*, *7*(3), 168–194. DOI: 10.47992/IJAEML.2581.7000.0193

Archan, D. (2025). (HOW) CAN ARTIFICIAL INTELLIGENCE ENHANCE FORMATIVE FEEDBACK IN HIGHER EDUCATION? In ICERI2025 Proceedings (pp. 3350-3356). IATED.

Bowen, J. A., & Watson, C. E. (2025). *Teaching with AI: A practical guide to a new era of human learning*. JHU Press. DOI: 10.56021/9781421453392

Calidonio, S. L. (2025). Designing Intelligent Feedback: an AI-Augmented Feedback Framework for Prototyping in Design Thinking (Master's thesis, Universidade NOVA de Lisboa (Portugal)).

Caporusso, N. (2023). Generative artificial intelligence and the emergence of creative displacement anxiety. Research in Psychology and Behavior, 3(1).

Chang, D. H., Lin, M. P. C., Hajian, S., & Wang, Q. Q. (2023). Educational design principles of using AI chatbot that supports self-regulated learning in education: Goal setting, feedback, and personalization. *Sustainability (Basel)*, *15*(17), 12921. DOI: 10.3390/su151712921

Curry, M. J., & Lillis, T. (2024). Multilingualism in academic writing for publication: Putting English in its place. *Language Teaching*, *57*(1), 87–100. DOI: 10.1017/S0261444822000040

Deepshikha, D. (2026, December). A systematic review on the future of educational assessment: AI-driven grading and personalised feedback in higher education. In Artificial Intelligence in Education (Vol. 2, No. 2, pp. 75-115). Emerald Publishing Limited.

Farrokhnia, M., Latifi, S., Papadopoulos, P. M., Hogenkamp, L., Gijlers, H., Khosravi, H., & Noroozi, O. (2026). Generative AI offers more, but students revise less: Comparing the effects of teacher and AI feedback on student essay revisions. *International Journal of Educational Technology in Higher Education*, *23*(1), 6. DOI: 10.1186/s41239-026-00579-9

Geroimenko, V. (2025). Foundational Communication Principles: Ensuring Clarity, Precision, and Effectiveness in AI Interaction. In *Beyond and After Prompt Engineering: The Future of AI Communication* (pp. 137–173). Springer Nature Switzerland.

. Hamilton, D. M. (2025). Exploring the Influence of Artificial Intelligence on Teaching Strategies in Higher Education: A Phenomenological Approach.

Jacobsen, L. J., & Weber, K. E. (2023). The promises and pitfalls of ChatGPT as a feedback provider in higher education: An exploratory study of prompt engineering and the quality of AI-driven feedback. *OSF preprints*, 29.

Kapur, M., Hattie, J., Grossman, I., & Sinha, T. (2022, September). Fail, flip, fix, and feed–Rethinking flipped learning: A review of meta-analyses and a subsequent meta-analysis. [). Frontiers Media SA.]. *Frontiers in Education*, *7*, 956416. DOI: 10.3389/feduc.2022.956416

Khasawneh, D. M. A. S. K. (2024). Improving the learning of language proficiency at tertiary education level through AI-driven assessment models and automated feedback systems. *Migration Letters : An International Journal of Migration Studies*, *21*(2), 712–726.

Kirk, A. M. (2025). Teaching Transformed: A Qualitative Exploration of Artificial Intelligence's Impact on Teacher Workload Through Secondary Analysis (Doctoral dissertation, South College).

Lapidot-Lefler, N. (2025). Teacher responsiveness in inclusive education: A participatory study of pedagogical practice, well-being, and sustainability. *Sustainability (Basel)*, *17*(7), 2919. DOI: 10.3390/su17072919

Lawrence, L., Echeverria, V., Yang, K., Aleven, V., & Rummel, N. (2024). How teachers conceptualise shared control with an AI co-orchestration tool: A multiyear teacher-centred design process. *British Journal of Educational Technology*, *55*(3), 823–844. DOI: 10.1111/bjet.13372

McNealis, R. (2026). Shame in the machine: Affective accountability and the ethics of AI. *AI & Society*, *41*(1), 403–413. DOI: 10.1007/s00146-025-02472-x

Meinel, C., Friedrichsen, M., Staubitz, T., Reinhard, S., & Köhler, D. (2024). Assessment methods for online teaching. Scientific Reports of the German University of Digital Science, 3.

Mourtajji, L., & Chiss, N. (2025). GENERATIVE AI: ARE WE READY TO DISRUPT OUR EDUCATIONAL PARADIGMS? In EDULEARN25 Proceedings (pp. 9321-9326). IATED.

Nassar, H. M. (2025). Comparing the quality of AI-generated and instructor feedback in a university writing program (Master's thesis, The American University in Cairo (Egypt)).

Nazaretsky, T., Mejia-Domenzain, P., Swamy, V., Frej, J., & Käser, T. (2026). Who Gives Feedback Matters: Student Biases Towards Human and AI-Generated Formative Feedback. *Journal of Computer Assisted Learning*, *42*(1), e70153. DOI: 10.1111/jcal.70153

Nysom, L. (2023). AI Generated Feedback for Students' Assignment Submissions (Doctoral dissertation, Master's thesis, Aalborg university]. Aalborg university Project Library. https://projekter. aau. dk/projekter/files/547261577/Lars_Nysom_Master_Project. pdf)

. Otaki, B. (2023). Feedback in the era of generative AI.

Öztürk, Y., & Cebi, A. (2026). The potential of AI-generated feedback from the students' perspective: A systematic review. *Assessment & Evaluation in Higher Education*, *51*(1), 41–62. DOI: 10.1080/02602938.2025.2588385

Papaneophytou, C., & Nicolaou, S. A. (2025). Promoting critical thinking in biological sciences in the era of artificial intelligence: The role of higher education. *Trends in Higher Education*, *4*(2), 24. DOI: 10.3390/higheredu4020024

Pooth, R., Sattler, S., Westerberg, F., Pavicic, T., & Kerscher, M. (2025). Transforming Skin Quality Evaluation With AI: From Subjective Grading to Data-Driven Precision. *Journal of Cosmetic Dermatology*, *24*(S4), e70371. DOI: 10.1111/jocd.70371 PMID: 40847895

Pratschke, B. M. (2024). *Generative AI and education: Digital pedagogies, teaching innovation and learning design*. Springer Nature. DOI: 10.1007/978-3-031-67991-9

Rolls, E. T. (2024). The memory systems of the human brain and generative artificial intelligence. *Heliyon*, *10*(11), e31965. DOI: 10.1016/j.heliyon.2024.e31965 PMID: 38841455

Rudroff, T. (2024). Revealing the complexity of fatigue: A review of the persistent challenges and promises of artificial intelligence. *Brain Sciences*, *14*(2), 186. DOI: 10.3390/brainsci14020186 PMID: 38391760

Saini, A. K., Cope, B., Kalantzis, M., & Zapata, G. C. (2024). The future of feedback: Integrating peer and generative AI reviews to support student work. EdArXiv preprint, 1-57. DOI: 10.35542/osf.io/x3dct

Sajja, R., Sermet, Y., Cikmaz, M., Cwiertny, D., & Demir, I. (2024). Artificial intelligence-enabled intelligent assistant for personalized and adaptive learning in higher education. *Information (Basel)*, *15*(10), 596. DOI: 10.3390/info15100596

Shi, H., & Aryadoust, V. (2024). A systematic review of AI-based automated written feedback research. *ReCALL*, *36*(2), 187–209. DOI: 10.1017/S0958344023000265

Szmyd, K., & Mitera, E. (2024). The impact of artificial intelligence on the development of critical thinking skills in students. *European Research Studies*, *27*(2), 1022–1039. DOI: 10.35808/ersj/3876

Thongsan, N. C., & Anderson, N. J. (2025). From Passive Answers to Active Inquiry: How AI Supports Critical Reading in EFL Classrooms. *LEARN Journal: Language Education and Acquisition Research Network*, *18*(2), 795–820. DOI: 10.70730/KMKL8505

Uanachain, D. M. N., & Aouad, L. I. (2025). Generative AI in Education: Rethinking Learning, Assessment & Student Agency for the AI Era. *Thresholds in Education*, *48*(1), 111–132.

Venter, J., Coetzee, S. A., & Schmulian, A. (2025). Exploring the use of artificial intelligence (AI) in the delivery of effective feedback. *Assessment & Evaluation in Higher Education*, *50*(4), 516–536. DOI: 10.1080/02602938.2024.2415649

. Vučenović, T., & Maksimović, M. (2025). The Illusion of Understanding: Digital Empathy and Emotional Mimicry in AI-Driven Education.

Wang, Y. (2026). Enhancing University EFL Learners' Writing Performance: The Role of AI-Enhanced Goal-Setting, Feedback and Social Norm Interventions. *Journal of Computer Assisted Learning*, *42*(1), e70179. DOI: 10.1002/jcal.70179

Wu, M., Liu, W., Wang, Y., Ding, W., & Yao, M. (2026, April). Rethinking User Empowerment in AI Recommender System: Innovating Transparent and Controllable Interfaces. In *Proceedings of the 2026 CHI Conference on Human Factors in Computing Systems* (pp. 1-21). DOI: 10.1145/3772318.3791914

Xu, S., Su, Y., & Liu, K. (2025). Investigating student engagement with AI-driven feedback in translation revision: A mixed-methods study. *Education and Information Technologies*, *30*(12), 16969–16995. DOI: 10.1007/s10639-025-13457-0

Yue, M., Jong, M. S. Y., & Dai, Y. (2022). Pedagogical design of K-12 artificial intelligence education: A systematic review. *Sustainability (Basel)*, *14*(23), 15620. DOI: 10.3390/su142315620

Zajko, M. (2022). Artificial intelligence, algorithms, and social inequality: Sociological contributions to contemporary debates. *Sociology Compass*, *16*(3), e12962. DOI: 10.1111/soc4.12962

Zhan, Y. (2023). What do college students think of feedback literacy? An ecological interpretation of Hong Kong students' perspectives. *Assessment & Evaluation in Higher Education*, *48*(5), 686–700. DOI: 10.1080/02602938.2022.2121380

Zhao, C. (2024). AI-assisted assessment in higher education: A systematic review. *Journal of Educational Technology and Innovation*, *6*(4). Advance online publication. DOI: 10.61414/jeti.v6i4.209

KEY TERMS AND DEFINITIONS

AI-Generated Feedback: feedback produced by generative artificial intelligence systems to guide student revision, reflection, or task improvement.

Ethical AI Feedback: AI-mediated feedback designed and used with attention to accuracy, fairness, transparency, privacy, and accountability.

Feedback Literacy: the learner's capacity to interpret, evaluate, and use feedback productively.

Human Oversight: the continuing responsibility of educators to monitor, interpret, and govern AI-assisted feedback processes.

Human-Centered Design: a design approach that prioritizes learner needs, educational purpose, equity, and meaningful use over technological novelty.

Pedagogical Dialogue: an interactive learning-oriented exchange in which feedback helps students think, question, revise, and grow rather than simply obey corrections.

Student Agency: the ability of learners to make decisions, exercise judgment, and act purposefully in response to feedback.

Chapter 10
Who Is Doing the Thinking?
Adapting a Guiding Rubric for Doctoral Supervision to Keep Pace With Rapid Advances in Generative AI

Michael J. von Maltitz
http://orcid.org/0000-0001-7308-651X
University of the Free State, South Africa

Inger Fabris-Rotelli
http://orcid.org/0000-0002-2192-4873
University of Pretoria, South Africa

Danielle Jade Roberts
http://orcid.org/0000-0001-9473-5822
University of KwaZulu-Natal, South Africa

Ansie Smit
http://orcid.org/0000-0003-0315-0875
University of Pretoria, South Africa

Daniel Maposa
http://orcid.org/0000-0003-2641-0502
University of Limpopo, South Africa

Sonali Das
http://orcid.org/0000-0002-6350-4279
University of Pretoria, South Africa

ABSTRACT

Examining the evolving challenge of doctoral supervision in the age of generative artificial intelligence (GenAI) is framed by the question: who is doing the thinking? As AI tools increasingly mediate research processes, supervisors face growing difficulty in distinguishing genuine student cognition and GenAI-assisted outputs. Building on an existing guiding rubric for doctoral supervision in Statistics, an extension is proposed that integrates the responsible, transparent use of GenAI across the doctoral lifecycle, from topic and literature discovery, through methodology and data

DOI: 10.4018/979-8-3373-9089-5.ch010

analysis, to write-up and defence. The revisions proposed for the rubric shift the role of GenAI from a productivity shortcut to a mechanism for enhancing critical thinking. It introduces expanded criteria emphasising transparency, verification, attribution, and development of AI literacy in students and supervisors. A five-level developmental framework is proposed, progressing from uncritical GenAI use to reflexive GenAI stewardship, cultivating independent, ethically grounded researchers.

INTRODUCTION

In the 1600s René Descartes wrote "I think, therefore I am". In the current era of Generative Artificial Intelligence (GenAI) and Natural Language Processing (NLP) tools, this can be reinterpreted within modern academic learning as a shift from mere existence through thought to validated knowledge through critical and reflective cognition aided by AI tools. Cognition situated within today's academic expectations is thus challenged by the fact that supervisors are unable to distinguish between what is actually learnt, and what is merely presented as a collation of prompt-engineered AI outputs, thus begging the question: "Who is doing the thinking?". The "Who is doing the thinking?" goes hand-in-hand with "What is being thought?". To evaluate the student, supervisors are now challenged between discerning what is being presented for evaluation as a demonstration of learning merely for the degree requirement, versus how that knowledge was con-structed and validated, and then further applied — both with and beyond AI assistance.

The detection of AI usage within academic context can get complicated (Bassett et al., 2026). It can either mean that the material was flatly plagiarised, or to the other extreme that it was generated via systematic engagement with GenAI tools for a specific critically thought-out purpose. While the former can translate to low embodiment of knowledge, the latter can be representative of an exercise in scientific research and learning. Several studies have investigated the implications of the somewhat sudden rise in the usage of AI tools in the context of both postgraduate research and postgraduate research supervision (for example, Cowling et al., 2023; Dai et al., 2023; Huang et al., 2025; Mabirizi, Katushabe, Muhoza, and Rugasira, 2025; Omodan, 2025; Segooa et al., 2025). In most studies, these versatile new tools are argued to benefit both students and supervisors, while simultaneously highlighting the possible ethical accountability issues that they inevitably raise.

In this chapter, we focus specifically on the process of doctoral supervision in the GenAI-era — that is, of the doctoral journey of the student with the supervisor(s) and the use of GenAI in it, while ensuring the graduate attributes are achieved by the end.

A doctoral degree is the process of evolving from "What do I know?" to "How do we know, and how can this be extended to new context?", and is thus a process that inherently requires the *gen-eration of new knowledge*, and which cannot result based only on the collation of existing (digital) resources. Furthermore, the doctoral journey is not solely about producing a thesis, but about de-veloping the attributes expected of a doctoral graduate. In the South African context, the Council on Higher Education (CHE), through its National Review of Doctoral Qualifications[1], identifies five knowledge attributes and four skills attributes that should be developed through doctoral edu-cation. These include, among others, specialised and in-depth knowledge, the ability to make an original contribution to knowledge, ethical awareness, the ability to evaluate and apply appropriate research methodologies, autonomy, effective communication, and critical and analytical thinking. The development of these attributes therefore provides an important lens through which doctoral education should be understood: the thesis is not the ultimate purpose of the doctorate, but one of the principal means through which the development and attainment of doctoral-level capabilities are demonstrated.

Importantly, the CHE further recommends that the assessment of the attainment of doctoral grad-uate attributes should be included in the assessment guidelines accompanying the thesis for exam-ination. This positions the thesis and its examination as an important point at which the attainment of these attributes can be evaluated. However, the increasing integration of GenAI into the research process raises a fundamental challenge to relying predominantly on the completed thesis as evi-dence of their attainment. A thesis may demonstrate a highly polished and technically sophisticated final product without necessarily providing sufficient evidence of how the candidate developed the reasoning, methodological judgement, critical evaluation, problem-solving ability and autonomy represented in that product. Where GenAI has contributed to activities across the research process, including literature synthesis, conceptual development, methodological exploration, coding, sta-tistical analysis, interpretation and academic writing, the final thesis has increasingly become an insufficient proxy for the intellectual development and capabilities of the doctoral candidate.

This shifts the question from whether the thesis meets the expected standard to what evidence demonstrates that the candidate has attained the attributes expected of a doctoral graduate. In an era in which aspects of the research process can be increasingly mediated or performed by GenAI, the challenge for doctoral supervision is therefore not simply to establish whether AI has been used appropriately, but to establish whether the candidate has developed and can independently demonstrate the intellectual capabilities that the doctorate is intended to confer. This suggests a need to move beyond only assessment of the final research product towards a more developmental approach in which evidence of doctoral attribute attainment is gathered and evaluated progressively throughout the PhD journey. This progression is the focus of discussion in this chapter.

Against this backdrop, academics need to be at the forefront of the rapid expansion in GenAI tools. These tools can impact the academic integrity and perceived quality of the PhD degree both positively and negatively. GenAI's benefits include enhanced learning and accessibility to complicated information, improvement in research techniques, research design, and quality of writing, and even the fact that they can provide an initial source of feedback. Potential negative impacts include possible plagiarism of unattributed work, AI hallucinations, and, simply, the overuse of AI-generated constructs. As supervisors, we risk overdependence and blind trust in information provided in these tools without the student validating the information, leading to laziness in critical-thinking. Moreover, these tools are developing at a pace at which assessing the validity and reliability of student submissions becomes problematic.

It is the responsibility of academics to minimise the negative impacts of these tools by fostering an ethical mindset that guides the appropriate use of these powerful tools within the academic community and their respective students. Wright, 2024 mentions that ad-hoc methods of control should be abandoned in favour of a more structured approach to learning how to use and subse-quently monitoring the use of GenAI for both the student and the supervisor. Such an approach, however, needs to extend beyond monitoring GenAI use itself towards monitoring the development and demonstration of the doctoral capabilities that GenAI may increasingly mediate.

The emerging literature on GenAI in doctoral education has increasingly addressed doctoral stu-dents' use of AI, academic integrity, authorship, transparency, ethical use, AI literacy and the changing nature of the supervisory relationship (Betteney et al., 2025; Lu et al., 2025; Mwansa and Ngandu, 2026; Storey, 2026b). As GenAI has become increasingly embedded in everyday academic practice, attention has shifted beyond simply detecting or requiring disclosure of AI use, towards understanding how its use affects learning and the development of doctoral capabilities (Aladsani, 2025). With this shift, evaluating evidence of the PhD candidate's development towards independent research becomes increasingly central to doctoral supervision (Storey, 2026a).

This raises a more fundamental question for doctoral supervision: how can supervisors establish that a candidate is progressively becoming an independent researcher when GenAI may increas-ingly mediate many of the activities through which that development has traditionally been ob-served? Considerably less attention appears to have been given to the developmental implications of GenAI for doctoral graduate attributes; that is, how supervisors can determine whether the capa-bilities expected of a doctoral graduate are progressively being developed and ultimately attained when GenAI may increasingly mediate aspects of the research process. This is distinct from deter- mining whether a student has complied with an institutional policy on AI use. The central question becomes not simply whether GenAI was used appropriately, but what evidence demonstrates that the candidate has developed the knowledge, skills and intellectual autonomy expected at doctoral level.

This gap in practical approaches for assessing the evidence of attainment of doctoral graduate at-tributes is particularly pertinent in the South African context, where the viva voce is not uniformly implemented as a compulsory component of doctoral assessment. Indeed, the CHE has noted that the oral examination of a doctoral thesis is unevenly used across South African higher education institutions and has recommended its inclusion as part of doctoral examination to provide an addi-tional opportunity to assess the graduate attributes specified in the Doctoral Degrees Qualification Standard[2]. In contexts where such an oral examination is not routinely undertaken, there is a par-ticular need for alternative opportunities throughout the doctoral journey to evaluate evidence of the candidate's intellectual ownership, critical reasoning, methodological competence, autonomy and other doctoral-level capabilities.

Several frameworks and guidelines have begun to address responsible GenAI use in postgradu-ate and doctoral research. For example, a systematic review of GenAI in postgraduate research proposed a framework centred on institutional oversight, human-AI collaboration and ethical use (Mabirizi, Katushabe, Muhoza, et al., 2025). The Open University has developed a Position State-ment and Guidance on Generative AI and Doctoral Education, while the University of Auckland has developed Generative Artificial Intelligence in Doctoral Research Guidelines, which provide guidance for doctoral candidates, supervisors, confirmation committees and examiners. Other frameworks have similarly sought to translate responsible AI principles into practical guidance for research, including the ETHICAL framework proposed by Eacersall et al., 2025, which focuses on principles such as transparency, critical engagement with AI outputs, security and research in-tegrity.

We found limited evidence of a framework that systematically maps GenAI use across the stages of the doctoral journey, the capabilities expected of the doctoral candidate at each stage, and the evidence that supervisors can use to assess the progressive development and attainment of those capabilities. It is in this vein that this chapter proposes the extension of the work by von Maltitz et al., 2025, wherein a guiding rubric was developed for a holistic student-supervisor doctoral journey in Statistics. Modifications to the existing guiding rubric in light of GenAI should be designed specifically for doctoral supervision, in recognition of the fact that GenAI tools are here to stay, and that doctoral supervision needs to change the use of GenAI tools from being merely a productivity shortcut, to a rigour-enhancing and insight-amplifying instrument.

While this chapter is focused on GenAI requirements for an expanded guiding rubric for supervi-sion in any postgraduate Statistics field, the concepts emphasised can be generalised to any field inside or outside of the sciences, as the modifications proposed are not discipline-specific, nor do they relate to a portion of the existing guiding rubric that is uniquely contextualised within the field of Statistics.

AI Policies in South Africa

The speed of the availability of new AI tools to students and researchers cannot be matched by human expertise. The importance of timely and adaptive AI policies (or guidelines) should at least be matched, however. Across the South African university landscape, a number of institutions have promptly put AI policies in place for the academic environment, namely the University of Pretoria, University of the Witwatersrand, University of Johannesburg, University of South Africa, North West University, University of KwaZulu-Natal, University of the Free State, Nelson Mandela Uni-versity, University of Cape Town, Stellenbosch University, University of the Western Cape, Cape Peninsula University of Technology, Durban University of Technology, Rhodes University and Sefako Makgatho Health Sciences University. Other institutions in South Africa are very active in engaging in AI with students and stakeholders: University of Limpopo, University of Venda, University of Fort Hare, Tshwane University of Technology, Central University of Technology and the University of Mpumalanga. Universities South Africa has put together guidelines for the university environment, highlighting the overall impact AI has in academia. An important aspect that is under discussion at most institutions in South Africa is the doctoral defence. Many institu-tions have historically only had informal defences, not part of the final assessment process, since the formal completion is ratified through the an external thesis examination. Going forward, the defence may need to be the most important step in ensuring the work presented is the candidate's own, as well as ensuring true doctoral attribute achievement.

The diverse response by institutions in South Africa points to an unstable (but progressing) AI environment in academia. While much AI research is conducted in South Africa (see for example this document and this news), there is little in place on the impact of GenAI in our postgraduate environments, nor for recommendations on how institutions and supervisors can evaluate whether doctoral graduates have attained the skills, competencies and attributes expected of a PhD qualifi-cation when GenAI increasingly mediates the research process.

The remainder of this chapter is structured as follows. First we review the existing guiding rubric for doctoral supervision in Statistics (von Maltitz et al., 2025), with particular attention to its cur-rently limited treatment of GenAI. Next, the possi-ble use of GenAI tools is mapped across five key phases of the Statistics doctoral journey: Discovery, Methodology, Data analysis and version control, Write-up, and Presentation and defence, highlighting how the use of AI tools across each phase can enhance research rigour and quality, without replacing the student's critical think-ing. This is followed by a discussion on the transition from a basic GenAI user to an AI-literate researcher, emphasising desirable difficulties and productive struggle. The next section discusses the proposed expansion of the rubric to include supervisor capability and professional growth, en-suring that supervisors themselves remain AI-literate and are able to guide students effectively. Subsequent sections then consider revised measurement criteria that are proposed to expand the rubric from three achievement levels to five developmental maturity levels, and conclude with strategies for future-proofing the rubric to ensure its continued relevance as AI tools evolve. It is worth noting that the guiding rubric under consideration is not designed as a traditional assessment rubric, but as a tool for progressive growth of the PhD candidate and their supervisory team. The measurement criteria are set as reflective rather than for a traditional assessment purpose.

EXISTING GUIDING RUBRIC

In academic Statistics in South Africa, the increasing attraction of Statistics graduates to industry careers, partly driven by the Fourth Industrial Revolution, has weakened the postgraduate pipeline into academia (Fabris-Rotelli et al., 2022). The consequences of that shift are now being felt across Statistics departments nationally where there are simply not enough experienced, PhD-level academics to meet the supervision needs of the discipline. At the same time, many of the senior academics who have historically provided the bulk of PhD supervision and mentorship are approaching retirement, further reducing the pool of experienced supervisors available to mentor and develop emerging academics. This creates a longer-term capacity challenge for Statistics departments: how do we develop the next generation of supervisors while the traditional sources of supervisory expertise and mentorship are diminishing? The response was:

1. The establishment of StatSNetSA, a national network of Statistics academics that fosters collaboration, supervision capacity, academic development, and postgraduate Statistics re-search and training;
2. The development of a guiding rubric for PhD supervision, emerging from this collaborative network.

The rubric emerged through a multi-year collaborative programme within StatS-NetSA, drawing on the collective experiences of emerging PhD supervisors across

South African Statistics de-partments. It was subsequently refined through scholarly engagement and disciplinary practice (Fabris-Rotelli et al., 2022. The rubric is not intended to function as an assessment instrument for the PhD thesis. Rather, it is a structured, developmental framework that assists supervisors and students with navigating the PhD journey (von Maltitz et al., 2025). It is not solely concerned with whether the final thesis meets the required standard; rather, it asks: Are we developing an indepen-dent researcher? It focuses on research integrity, critical thinking and professional development, while recognising that these capabilities develop progressively throughout the doctoral journey. Importantly, the framework is intended to be used collaboratively by the student and supervisory team, providing a shared basis for discussing progress, identifying areas for further development, and supporting reflective supervisory practice and supervisor development. While the original work is primarily concerned with supervision in doctoral research in the statistical sciences, the rubric could likely be modified and applied within other fields in future research.

Figure 1. The six dimensions of the guiding rubric for PhD supervision in Statistics

Currently, the rubric comprises six interconnected dimensions of doctoral supervision as presented in Figure 1. While the guiding rubric was not built explicitly within a conceptual framework, but rather through a long process of consultation with stakeholders, it does naturally parallel the concepts identified as important in doctoral supervision by Lee, 2008. In this work, five facets are identified as approaches that coexist in doctoral supervision, namely functional, enculturation, critical thinking, emancipation, and developing a quality relationship. A functional approach man-ages the doctoral project by ensuring progression through tasks. Enculturation inducts the student into the discipline/research community. The critical thinking approach challenges the student to analyse, question, and construct arguments. Emancipation facilitates the student's intellectual and personal development so that they might build independence. Relationship development seeks to create a productive and supporting supervisory relationship.

We can map the existing guiding rubric in von Maltitz et al., 2025 onto the approaches identified by Lee, 2008. Section 1: Statistics Identity (Crisis) Opportunities establishes the student's transi- tion from being a student of Statistics to becoming a member of the statistical research community, in parallel with Lee's 2008 enculturation and emancipation. Section 2: Funding, concerned with development of capabilities associated with obtaining and managing research funding, is associated with the functional approach and with emancipation. Section 3: The Thesis Document operationalises critical thinking and increasing intellectual autonomy through the production of the doctoral research document. Thus, it relates to the approaches in critical thinking and eman-cipation. Section 4: Student-Supervisor Relationship mirrors the relationship development ap-proach from Lee, 2008. In Section 5: Standardised Assessment the student needs to demonstrate scholarly judgement, methodological reasoning and research insight in a structured manner, and is thus associated with the critical thinking and functional approaches. However, an emancipatory function also appears, because, by making the expectations of doctoral-level work explicit at the beginning of the process, the rubric reduces the extent to which the student must rely on the super-visor as the sole interpreter of what constitutes a successful PhD. Finally, Section 6: Supervisor/ Student Growth revisits enculturation and emancipation, as it details how a student joins the discipline's community as an independent and capable member.

In the current guiding rubric, a subsection on "The Use of Generative AI" appears under Section 3: The Thesis Document, comprising an introduction, a set of considerations, and three levels of achievement as presented in Figure 2.

Figure 2. Considerations of GenAI in original guiding rubric

The Use of Generative AI		
Responsible parties: student and supervisor. MOU item.		

The exponential expansion of the use of Generative AI in education and research, cannot be ignored, regardless of the stance or policy on AI that the institution has.

- ☐ The institution's policy on the use of AI in research is acknowledged and adhered to.
- ☐ Regardless of whether or not the institution has a formal policy (or an informal policy) for acknowledgement, the student and supervisor need to ensure that the use of generative AI is discussed in the context of research integrity, noting that generative AI can create content that contains false information, made-up references, and biased or prejudiced viewpoints, amongst other things.
- ☐ Generative AI, however, can be extremely beneficial for the research process, and the use of different AI tools should be discussed. This includes tools for correcting language and grammar, tools for finding and summarising topical peer-reviewed literature, and tools for generating, testing and commenting on code, amongst others.
- ☐ It is vital that the student is aware of the fact that every time AI is used in the research process, the content, including code, that it generates needs to be rewritten in the student's own words, understood and defended by the student, verified as true and unbiased by the student, and, if necessary, referenced in the thesis as having been used in the production of the research.

Levels of achievement

☐ Institutional AI policies have not been acknowledged. Generative AI advantages and disadvantages have not been discussed. The supervisor cannot clearly see where and when Generative AI has been used in the dissertation.	☐ Institutional AI policies are acknowledged and adhered to. While the use of AI has been discussed in terms of research integrity, the supervisor cannot see (or is not clear on) where Generative AI has been used.	☐ Institutional AI policies are acknowledged and adhered to and the use of Generative AI has been discussed, with a focus on research integrity. The use of Generative AI is transparent and well referenced in the research product, where necessary.

These three levels of achievement in Figure 2 focus on the use of GenAI, essentially reflecting progression from non-compliance towards transparent and responsible use. However, we now consider this insufficient, as a student may be fully transparent about their use of GenAI while still becoming intellectually dependent on it. We therefore propose the consideration of a five-level developmental continuum, presented later in this chapter, that considers not only transparency and responsible use, but also the extent to which the student retains intellectual ownership of the re- search process. The aim of this chapter is therefore to plan a more comprehensive framework for guiding the use of GenAI in doctoral research (and, by extension, other postgraduate research), using the supervisor-student journey from first registration to graduation as the organising mech-anism, as in the original paper and guiding rubric (von Maltitz et al., 2025). Furthermore, GenAI should be regarded as an evolving component of any similar framework, requiring continued de-velopment in response to the rapidly growing body of research and emerging guidance on the use of these tools in postgraduate research.

The guiding process proposed in this chapter will be informed by a wider field of research on GenAI in supervision than is currently referred to within the original manual, and will ensure the development of the student into a graduate with the skills for effective and ethical use of GenAI in a rapidly evolving environment. We would like to note once more that the research that this chapter is based on is specifically for Statistical research supervision, and the extended guiding rubric is also within these same parameters. However, we also propose to offer more general guidelines for higher education institutions world-wide and to other fields within or outside mathematical sciences.

MAPPING USE ACROSS THE STATISTICS DOCTORAL LIFECYCLE

The number of GenAI tools is numerous, yet identifying useful ones to enhance the quality of doctoral studies throughout a PhD can be like holding water in your hand. These tools are particu-larly susceptible to rapid obsolescence when they are not backed by ongoing, rapid development to remain robust and relevant in a highly competitive environment. GenAI tools developed as 'wrap-pers' for complex LLMs such as ChatGPT and Claude can quickly become obsolete as LLMs improve, with single-purpose tools quickly being replaced by AI agents and agentic AI systems (Hughes et al., 2025).

Assuming the candidate and supervisor are well acquainted with (and are following) the ethical guidelines and regulations regarding the use of GenAI during a doctoral study, it would be ideal to identify AI tools that are proven to be stable, multi-functional, and assist the doctoral candidate's development without writing the thesis for the candidate (von Maltitz et al., 2025).

The lifecycle of a statistics doctoral candidate can be divided into five phases, each with a set of cross-cutting AI tools. We will use these phases to categorise the GenAI tool types that might be used in each of these parts of the doctoral study below.

Phase 1: Discovery

The first phase focuses on exploration and orientation and uses discovery tools. It is in this phase that the topic is scoped within existing and emerging research areas, requiring citation network analysis (e.g. Calero-Medina and Noyons, 2008) to map significant relationships within a given field using scientific references. This allows for the visualisation of the topic's evolution and trajectory, as well as the influence of specific authors and research clusters on this field of study. Citation network analysis requires the positioning of literature topics by integrating evidence-based key findings and summaries of areas of consensus and contention.

While LLMs such as ChatGPT, Claude, Copilot, Gemini, DeepSeek, and Grok can be used to initiate a literature search or review of a particular topic, there are more specific GenAI tools for this purpose. Discovery tools such as ResearchRabbit, Litmaps, and Consensus can help the candidate rapidly assimilate the ever-increasing volume of information available today. Open-source citation tools such as Zotero, which is integrated with ResearchRabbit, make keeping track of references a simpler task, while Scite.ai can be used to test the authenticity and citation track of a particular paper. Using other discovery tools such as Elicit, the candidate should then refine the research gap, generate their own research questions from it, and stress-test the feasibility and novelty of those questions. Other academic GenAI tools include Perplexity AI with an ability to cite sources, web-searches with academic filters, and deep research modes; SciSpace, a platform allowing for interactions with PDF papers, feedback on complex methods, and assistance with formatting documents; NotebookLM, assisting with interrogations of any uploaded documents while GenAI provides answers exclusively from those documents; and Scholarcy, designed to read, summarise, and design flash cards from documents for faster processing of large volumes of literature.

There is an abundance of AI tools that are designed for research assistance, and this allows a researcher to triangulate sources of information and critically assess information provided; a task that is fundamental to learning, and which will be discussed later in this chapter.

Phase 2: Methodology

The second phase of the doctoral study focuses on the conceptualisation and methodological de-sign. This includes the proposal and/or thesis format development, where synthesis tools such as LLMs can be used to draft succinct sections. They can also be useful for guiding the creative process of methodology development by identifying existing statistical methodologies to serve as a foundation and by helping develop new statistical methodologies to address the research ques-tion. GenAI tools ellmer (R) and chatlas (Python) can be used to assist with the required statistical design and simulation, supporting the theoretical justification of methodologies and defining un-derlying data and model assumptions and/or potential violations.

Phase 3: Data analysis and version control

Phase three entails implementing the proposed methodology from Phase 2. This phase relies on intensive code generation, workflow automation, debugging, and error diagnosis, including con-vergence and runtime issues. Generative tools such as GitHub and LLMs are useful for kicking off the coding phase, addressing specific errors, maintaining version control throughout the study, and preserving research. However, GenAI coding capabilities at this point are still unable to provide bug-free code that addresses all the needs of the doctoral candidate, though we should not rule this possibility out in the near future. Even if programming code can be created by GenAI with no risk of error, the intellectual ownership of code presented in a doctoral study remains with the candi-date, and, as a result, the student should be able to understand and defend any and all programming. Depending on the research question posed by the statistical doctoral candidate, the overreliance on GenAI tools for coding assistance must be reviewed and discussed by the candidate and supervisor. R and Python libraries, are useful tools to aid the candidate in model development, implementation and evaluation, including model fit and robustness checks, reproducibility and verification, and fi-nal model validation for prediction or forecasting purposes. Again, ellmer and chatlas could be used in data analysis tasks, and many LLMs can call agents to run code they have created (to do, for ex-ample, independent data analysis tasks). As statisticians, we highly recommend not allowing any GenAI tools to manage the data analysis process without independently understanding, veri-fying, and running any code provided by or run by agents of AIs.

Phase 4: Write-up

The fourth phase requires the synergistic communication of the candidate's research in a thesis document, with a logical sequencing of arguments across a series of chapters that links the results from Phase 3 to the research question, aim, and objectives. Generative tools, including LLMs and Grammarly, can help define a document format, adjust language and tone for academic pur-poses, and clarify ambiguous statements. Tools such as Paperpal help strengthen the logical flow of arguments and identify remaining reasoning gaps, ensuring consistency between the research question, aims, methodology, results, discussion, and conclusions. Using a tool such as Paperpal can significantly improve the candidate's writing skills and reduce costly language editing costs for non-native English-speaking users.

Phase 5: Presentation and defence

The fifth and final phase in the doctoral candidate's degree cycle is the *viva voce* or oral presenta-tion. This is the candidate's opportunity to confidently present, discuss and defend their research to the broader academic community. Although many academic institutions are increasingly relying on the *viva* defence to assess whether the candidate has truly mastered the research and the doctoral research process, GenAI tools can also be used as part of the preparation. LLMs can be used as examination simulation tools to generate mock examiner questions to stress-test decisions made during the thesis. The tools can help to outline the presentation slides and refine the narrative for clarity under time constraints. Using LLMs' voice-activated functionalities, the candidate can also practise improving verbal articulation and statistical reasoning.

Although LLMs are not considered the most academically appropriate tool, it is the modern first go-to for many users when trying to understand a new topic. Similar to consulting with Wikipedia when delving into a new topic, LLMs are strong general-purpose tools to start with, especially when you do not know where to start.

FROM AI USER TO AI-LITERATE RESEARCHER

Desirable difficulties are learning conditions that are at the correct level of difficulty, and they are objectively experienced or perceived as needing increased effort to overcome (de Bruin et al., 2023). According to the originators of these concepts, these desirable difficulties could include varying conditions of learning, interleaving learning on disparate topics, and spacing learning over multiple sessions across longer periods of time (Bjork & Bjork, 2011), all of which are naturally inherent in postgraduate research. For example, the research process for a new graduate researcher can be extremely uncomfortable to begin with; where students are used to being told which learn-ing material to revise or learn, the research process often throws them into 'the deep end' of a research topic to discover relevant material on their own (at least relatively, compared to their un-dergraduate years). The apparent cognitive struggles in learning are considered desired difficulties, since they could increase the time on task, or because they require an attentional response that in turn leads to better remembering (Rosner et al., 2015). The interleaving of having to solve multiple problems of different natures during the research process (finding and summarising literature, collating research, formulating valid questions and methodology to answer the questions, possible data collection, simulation, and analysis, structuring writing and language editing, etc.) also contributes to improved learning (Lin et al., 2011). Moreover, research is — in its very essence — an ill-structured problem, and impasses that cause failures in the learning process have been shown to be productive in eventual long-term learning (Kapur, 2008). It should be noted that even if a student perceives the cognitive effort required to overcome these hurdles is so great that they are struggling to achieve mastery, the process is a positive one: this enhanced perceived difficulty has been shown to be related to delayed positive learning effects (de Bruin et al., 2023).

Now, knowing that we desire some friction in the learning process, we must, in parallel, admit that GenAI tool usage often releases some of the effort required in a learning process to the benefit of academic achievement. This is done through cognitive offloading and tools for shared metacognition (Iqbal et al., 2025). Knowing that GenAI tools can ease the cognitive processes, it is vital that we provide our students with a roadmap to achieving actual long-term learning when these GenAI tools are so readily available to take away uncomfortable cognitive strain. We suggest that the supervisors talk to their students about using GenAI to offload only the time-consuming re-search tasks that might have been subcontracted in a way to lower level researchers or technical experts in non-field-related areas, undergraduates and assistants, in the past. These include tasks like software coding — if this is simply a means to an end, rather than the topic of the research itself — language editing, resource gathering for a literature review, etc. Any task that is central to the building of defensible knowledge in the research process should not be offloaded entirely to GenAI tools, in order to promote the student's long-term learning. In this way, we encourage the transition of a graduate student from an AI user to an AI-literate researcher that understands the need to preserve productive struggle and the harm of outsourcing thinking.

If a student understands that 'seeking discomfort' in learning will enhance the fruits of their labour, they will more likely try to use GenAI to deepen their understanding instead of bypassing learning. Hopefully, they will come to a realisation of when it is that they should not use GenAI. More-over, as Bauer et al. (2025, p. 11) mentions, developing human knowledge and skills should be a priority, especially for tasks that require 'deep understanding, ethical considerations, and creative problem-solving, which cannot be entirely outsourced to AI (e.g., qualitative interpretation requiring contextual understanding and theoretical framing)'.

One of the ways we suggest that students develop these skills is to triangulate sources of information that will be used in their research. This is time-consuming process, and one that is easily overlooked when GenAI tools are used for efficiency gains. Slowing down and carefully considering the information provided by the tool becomes a desired difficulty that may enhance learning. Moreover, the only way that GenAI tools' information can be critiqued effectively is by building and strengthening domain-specific knowledge (Bauer et al., 2025). As educators, we already understand that GenAI tools create the most stimulating outputs when the user knows generally what the answer could be beforehand. It is also important to understand what GenAI can and cannot do, and what GenAI tools inherently do from their training. The former is only assessable by experts in the domain that the tool is venturing into; research refers to it as AI hallucinations (Anh-Hoang et al., 2025; Ji et al., 2023). The latter concerns the far more nefarious manifestations like covert and overt racism based on the language that is used in prompting (Hofmann et al., 2024).

SUPERVISOR CAPABILITY AND PROFESSIONAL DEVELOPMENT

As previously discussed, the original guiding rubric was designed to encapsulate and guide the entire doctoral journey and the supervisor-student relationship, addressing not only the development of the PhD graduate's attributes, but also the growth and development of the supervisor (Fabris-Rotelli et al., 2022). It includes a dedicated section on supervisor and student growth, with defined levels of achievement for the supervisor in areas such as establishing and leveraging networks (e.g. for external assessment and article review) and the composition of diverse external examiner panels, as well as student-focused outcomes for which the supervisor is responsible, including the attainment of learning outcomes, the development of graduate attribute skills, conference partici-pation and participation in funding applications.

In light of rapid advancements in GenAI, this chapter provides the groundwork for expanding the guiding rubric to explicitly incorporate the development of supervisor capability in the responsible and clear use of these tools. This includes fostering GenAI literacy among supervisors, equipping them to guide appropriate use, critically evaluate GenAI-assisted outputs, and identify potential misuse or overreliance in student work. Importantly, the need for such guidance is not limited to novice supervisors. The emergence of GenAI has introduced new supervisory challenges that extend to experienced academics who may themselves be unfamiliar with these technologies. As such, elements of the modified rubric, particularly those relating to GenAI practices, can serve as a valuable framework for both early-career and senior supervisors, supporting them in ensuring that students meaningfully engage with their research and develop the necessary critical and method-ological skills, rather than relying uncritically on AI-generated outputs.

Building on this, the development of supervisor capability in the context of GenAI must be under-stood as both an individual and collective endeavour. The rapid emergence of these tools has, in many cases, exposed generational and technological gaps between supervisors, with early-career academics often more familiar with the practical use of such tools, while more experienced su- pervisors bring disciplinary depth and critical research judgement. Rather than viewing this as a limitation, it presents an opportunity for reciprocal learning and collaboration. Creating structured opportunities for knowledge exchange, including peer learning and informal mentoring, can help bridge these gaps and support a more cohesive supervisory approach to the integration of GenAI. Central to this is the need for supervisors to develop clear, shared norms around the appropriate and ethical use of GenAI in doctoral research. What was once largely implicit now needs to be made explicit: what kinds of GenAI use are acceptable, when and how its use should be disclosed, and how students can show that they genuinely understand and can defend their work. These expecta-tions may differ across levels of supervisory experience. Novice supervisors may focus more on building foundational GenAI literacy and providing structured guidance, while more experienced supervisors may refine judgement and help shape wider disciplinary standards. In co-supervision arrangements, this becomes especially important, as it requires clear agreement between supervi-sors to ensure consistency in guidance and evaluation, and to avoid conflicting expectations for the student.

At an institutional level, the development of supervisor capability should be supported through formal structures, including targeted training in GenAI literacy, clear and practical policy guid-ance, and the provision of tools and frameworks for transparent and ethical GenAI use in research outputs. In parallel, the cultivation of communities of practice offers a valuable mechanism for ongoing learning, allowing supervisors to share experiences and emerging best practices across disciplines. Such communities can also play a critical role in refining and evolving the rubric itself as a responsive and adaptive tool.

Importantly, the integration of GenAI is reshaping the supervisor-student relationship. There is a growing need for open and ongoing discussions about how these tools are used, making the relationship more collaborative and based on transparency and trust. Within this evolving dynamic, supervisors are required to guide students as well as actively engage with how students use GenAI, ensuring the focus stays on developing critical thinking and methodological soundness with a clear sense of ownership over their work. This places greater emphasis on process-oriented forms of assessment, where supervisors seek to establish "who is doing the thinking" through mechanisms such as discussions and defence of AI-assisted work throughout the PhD journey.

Finally, supervisors play an important role as ethical leaders in this space. By using GenAI respon-sibly and transparently in their own academic practice, supervisors help build a culture of integrity and accountability. As these technologies continue to evolve, so too must supervisory practices. The rubric should therefore be viewed as a dynamic framework that supports ongoing professional development and adaptation, ensuring that both supervisors and students are equipped to navigate an increasingly complex and AI-integrated research landscape. To operationalise the ideas above in the guiding rubric itself, we propose a new subsection to be added under Section 7: Supervisor and Student Growth. Titled *"Supervisor and student capability development with Generative AI"* (with responsible parties listed as supervisor, co-supervisor and student, and flagged as an MOU item). The addition makes explicit the need for supervisors at all career stages to build and demonstrate their own working knowledge of AI tools. It will set out practical discussion points around shared norms for ethical use, reciprocal learning between novice and experienced super-visors, consistent guidance in co-supervision arrangements, and ongoing dialogue about who is doing the thinking in any GenAI-assisted work. By placing this alongside the existing GenAI sub-section in Section 3: The Thesis Document, the modified rubric will address both the student's research outputs and the supervisor's professional development in a coherent way. Although the original rubric and this update retain their Statistics focus, the new subsection will be deliberately framed so that it can be adapted to any field of study, offering generalisable guidance for higher education institutions worldwide. This keeps the rubric a living, responsive tool that evolves with the technology.

MEASUREMENT

In this section we finalise the proposed changes to be made in the doctoral supervision guiding rubric in von Maltitz et al., 2025, Section 3: The Thesis Document. Below we outline the pro-posed changes which reflect a more structured approach to GenAI use across the research process and the development of AI-literate doctoral researchers.

Table 1.

Original rubric	Revised rubric
☐ The institution's policy on the use of AI in research is acknowledged and adhered to.	Merged into one item
☐ Regardless of whether or not the institution has a formal policy (or an informal policy) for acknowledgement, the student and supervisor need to ensure that the use of generative AI is discussed in the context of research integrity, noting that generative AI can create content that contains false information, made-up ref-erences, and biased or prejudiced viewpoints, amongst other things.	
☐ Generative AI, however, can be extremely beneficial for the research process, and the use of different AI tools should be discussed. This includes tools for correcting language and grammar, tools for finding and summarising topical peer-reviewed literature, and tools for generating, testing and commenting on code, amongst others.	Edited slightly to incorporate the types of tools identified in this chapter: ☐ Generative AI can be extremely beneficial for the research process, and the use of differ-ent AI tools should be discussed. This includes tools for discovery, methodology, data analysis and version control, write-up, and presentation and defence.
☐ It is vital that the student is aware of the fact that every time AI is used in the research pro-cess, the content, including code, that it gener-ates needs to be rewritten in the student's own words, understood and defended by the stu-dent, verified as true and unbiased by the stu-dent, and, if necessary, referenced in the thesis as having been used in the production of the research.	Splitting of this component into multiple points, encompassing transparency, attribu-tion, and verification: ☐ Students should be aware that any AI tool usage might have to be disclosed when pub-lishing work from their research, or when sub-mitting their PhD. Care should be taken to doc-ument AI tool usage and workflows, and save conversations with LLMs.
	☐ It is important to ask LLMs for references that can be traced to their sources when us-ing these tools, so that the correct attribution of knowledge ownership can be made.
	☐ Information provided by LLMs should be verified as the truth through links provided by those LLMs or through triangulation of infor-mation from multiple sources.
	☐ Wherever possible, LLM content should be rewritten by the student into their own words, in order to encourage deeper understanding of the content, and to maintain the presence of the student's own voice throughout their writing. Naturally, all content presented in a student's research should be defended by that student.

continued on following page

Table 1. Continued

Original rubric	Revised rubric
-	A final point is added to the rubric to encour-age a discussion concerning the evolution from being an AI user to becoming an AI-literate researcher, which means that the following points need to be included: disciplinary under-standing, originality, bias detection, and data confidentiality. ☐ The student and supervisory team should be aware of the fact that LLMs might not be well trained on cutting-edge discipline-specific knowledge, and so any output in a stu-dent's niche research field may be inadequate, regardless of how confident an LLM may seem to be on the topic. Moreover, LLM outputs could be biased if their training data contained any amount of bias. The latter cannot be val-idated, so LLM users should be aware of this possibility.
	☐ Since LLMs are merely complex statistical models, they can only provide information that is technically already owned by other entities, meaning that the originality of output should always be questioned.
	☐ Students and supervisors should understand that without explicit censoring, LLMs will usu-ally include prompt information as future training data. As a result, confidential in-formation should never be discussed in LLM tools unless the student and supervisor are completely satisfied that the LLM option to not train on user data has been activated.

Furthermore, instead of only three achievement levels for this section of the guiding rubric, we propose an expansion toward a wider continuum of developmental maturity levels in Figure 3.

Figure 3. Expanded levels of achievement

Level 1	Level 2	Level 3	Level 4	Level 5
Uncritical use	**Transparent procedural use**	**Critical scholarly use**	**Independent disciplinary judgement**	**Reflexive AI stewardship**
The student and supervisor are not aware of the institutional policies or guidelines for AI use; it is assumed that AI tools have been used in some capacity.	The student and supervisor are aware of the institutional policies or guidelines for AI use, and are recording and referencing AI tool use.	Level 2, plus: AI tools are used extensively to improve critical thinking and depth of learning in the research.	Level 3, plus: the student has become the disciplinary thinker, able to critique the output of LLMs in their discipline in a scholarly manner.	Level 4, plus: the student has developed a deep self-awareness of their own thinking process, and an ethical responsibility for how AI shapes scholarship.

FUTURE-PROOFING

The guidelines and rules set for complying with the requirements for a doctoral degree differ across institutions as well as countries. These are governed by the higher education practices of a country at the time and change as the governance of a country adapts to the fluidity of governments. Rules set are essentially snapshots at a specific time and in terms of doctoral requirements only remain relatively stable for short periods of time, with reactive institutions adapting as necessary to ensure standards are met. Such standards most often aim to comply in some uniform way across the world, with minor internal requirements adjusted as needed for specific internal processes making sense for that specific environment. Across the world, doctoral requirements are relatively static, usually implementing a 'what isn't broken, doesn't need fixing' strategy, due to tedious administrative processes needed for changes. What has worked relatively well in the past can no longer be considered acceptable in the age of GenAI. Static rules assume that the future will behave exactly like the past. GenAI has turned all cognitive thinking upside down, requiring serious and quick responses in research and supervision to ensure the skill sets of a doctoral graduate are still attained. Current doctoral candidates have still possibly progressed through a non-GenAI undergraduate and Masters degree, hopefully ensuring the cognitive level assumed has in fact been obtained. However, in a short time span this assumption of attainment will be at risk and within a single 'generation' of graduates, updated, agile approaches and guidelines are needed.

The guiding rubric proposed next is a first revision of the original, already providing an update due to GenAI growth. Such periodic revision will be needed going forward to ensure the rubric and hence the community of supervisors remain agile and ready for ensuring cognitive growth in the doctoral candidate.

Goodhart's Law (Strathern, 1997) states: "When a measure becomes a target, it ceases to be a good measure." This speaks to the goal of simply complying and not focussing on the growth of a doctoral candidate. Although experienced supervisors may have this goal clearly in their supervision goals, the rise of GenAI presents the risk of the illusion of this being attained. As such, training towards tool-agnostic principles is incredibly important for the PhD journey in a GenAI age.

The guiding rubric has the overarching goal of producing a doctoral graduate with the intended attributes — namely, that of an independent researcher with well-developed cognitive skills, with the ability to continually grow their skill set on their own, and to impart these skills on the next generation of graduates. A static rubric only assessing the final outcome of a doctoral thesis does not achieve this, and neither does the incorrect use of GenAI as a tool during the studies. A guiding rubric leads the candidate and supervisors through a journey of growth, discussion, and critical thinking, ensuring a post-PhD GenAI ecosystem resilient to cognitive laziness and restriction of new knowledge.

The guiding rubric that this research is based on and the changes proposed in this chapter can be adapted to fields other than Statistics. The extension to other Mathematical Sciences, or even other Sciences is relatively straightforward, with research novelty being similarly measured. In other fields a simple adaptation of the guiding rubric's sections on *Statistics Identity (Crisis) Oppor-tunities* and *Standardised Assessment* is required. The sections *Funding, The Thesis Document, Student-Supervisor Relationship* and *Supervisor and Student Growth* are naturally extendable into other fields. The GenAI extensions in the guiding rubric are also essentially applicable to all research.

ACKNOWLEDGEMENTS

The authors acknowledge funding received from National Research Foundation COE-MaSS grants 2025-039-EDU-StatSNetSA, 2022-074-Edu-Network, 2022-023-EDU-DocSASA and 2022-022- EDU-DocRurics, and NITheCS. NITheCS associates Prof Inger Fabris-Rotelli and Prof Sonali Das also acknowledge the support and collaborative opportunities provided by the NITHeCS network.

REFERENCES

Aladsani, H. (2025). Developing postgraduate students' competencies in generative artificial in-telligence for ethical integration into academic practices: A participatory action research. *Interactive Learning Environments, 33*, 5747–5765. . 2025.2487517DOI: 10.1080/10494820

Anh-Hoang, D., Tran, V., & Nguyen, L.-M. (2025). Survey and analysis of hallucinations in large language models: Attribution to prompting strategies or model behavior. *Frontiers in Arti-ficial Intelligence, Volume 8 - 2025*. DOI: 10.3389/frai.2025.1622292

Bassett, M. A., Bradshaw, W., Bornsztejn, H., Hogg, A., Murdoch, K., Pearce, B., & Webber, C. (2026). Heads we win, tails you lose: Ai detectors in education. *Journal of Higher Education Policy and Management, 0*(0), 1–16. . 2622146DOI: 10.1080/1360080X.2026

Bauer, E., Greiff, S., Graesser, A. C., Scheiter, K., & Sailer, M. (2025). Looking beyond the hype: Understanding the effects of ai on learning. *Educational Psychology Review, 37*(1). *Educational Psychology Review*, *45*(2), 45. Advance online publication. DOI: 10.1007/s10648-025-10020-8

Betteney, M., Yin, B., Kpukumu, J., Cox, M. R., Malhi, M., Mulhare, D., Olaifa, M., & Duan, X. (2025). Generative artificial intelligence and the doctoral student: Procedural and ethical considerations. *Compass: Journal of Learning and Teaching in Higher Education*. DOI: 10.21100/compass.v18i1.1618

Bjork, E. L., & Bjork, R. A. (2011). Making things hard on yourself, but in a good way: Creating desirable difficulties to enhance learning. In Gernsbacher, M. A., Pew, R. W., Hough, L. M., & Pomerantz, J. R. (Eds.), *Psychology and the real world: Essays illustrating fundamental contributions to society* (pp. 56–64). Worth Publishers.

Calero-Medina, C., & Noyons, E. C. (2008). Combining mapping and citation network analysis for a better understanding of the scientific development: The case of the absorptive capacity field. *Journal of Informetrics, 2*(4), 272–279. 10.1016/j. joi. 2008.09.005

Cowling, M., Crawford, J., Allen, K., & Wehmeyer, M. (2023). Using leadership to leverage chat-gpt and artificial intelligence for undergraduate and postgraduate research supervision. *Aus-tralasian Journal of Educational Technology, 39*(4), 83–103. . 8598DOI: 10.14742/ajet

Dai, Y., Lai, S., Lim, C. P., & Liu, A. (2023). Chatgpt and its impact on research supervision: In-sights from australian postgraduate research students. *Australasian Journal of Educational Technology*, *39*(4), 74–88. DOI: 10.14742/ajet.8843

de Bruin, A. B. H., Biwer, F., Hui, L., Onan, E., David, L., & Wiradhany, W. (2023). Worth the ef-fort: The start and stick to desirable difficulties (s2d2) framework. *Educational Psychology Review*, *35*(1), 41. Advance online publication. DOI: 10.1007/s10648-023-09766-w

Eacersall, D., Pretorius, L., Smirnov, I., Spray, E., Illingworth, S., Chugh, R., Strydom, S., Stratton-Maher, D., Simmons, J., Jennings, I., Roux, R., Kamrowski, R., Downie, A., Thong, C. L., & Howell, K. A. (2025). Navigating ethical challenges in generative ai-enhanced research: The ethical framework for responsible generative ai use. *Journal of Applied Learning and Teaching*, *8*(2), 102–115. DOI: 10.37074/jalt.2025.8.2.9

Fabris-Rotelli, I., von Maltitz, M. J., Smit, A., Das, S., Roberts, D., Maribe, G., Maposa, D., & Correa, F. M. (2022). Development of an early career academic supervisor in statistics - a discussion towards a guiding rubric. *ORiON, 38*(1), 29–51. https://hdl.handle.net/10520/ ejc-orion_v38_n1_a2

Hofmann, V., Kalluri, P. R., Jurafsky, D., & King, S. (2024). Ai generates covertly racist decisions about people based on their dialect. *Nature*, *633*(8028), 147–154. DOI: 10.1038/s41586-024-07856-5 PMID: 39198640

Huang, Y., Li, S., & Liu, Z. (2025). Can genai complement supervisor support in shaping post-graduates' research experiences? a mixed-methods approach. *Studies in Higher Education*, •••, 1–19. DOI: 10.1080/03075079.2025.2495710

Hughes, L., Dwivedi, Y. K., Malik, T., Shawosh, M., Albashrawi, M. A., Jeon, I., Dutot, V., Ap-panderanda, M., Crick, T., De', R., Fenwick, M., Gunaratnege, S. M., Jurcys, P., Kar, A. K., Kshetri, N., Li, K., Mutasa, S., Samothrakis, S., Wade, M., & Walton, P. (2025). Ai agents and agentic systems: A multi-expert analysis. *Journal of Computer Information Systems*, *65*(4), 489–517. DOI: 10.1080/08874417.2025.2483832

Iqbal, J., Hashmi, Z. F., Asghar, M. Z., & Abid, M. N. (2025). Generative ai tool use enhances aca-demic achievement in sustainable education through shared meta-cognition and cognitive offloading among preservice teachers. *Scientific Reports*, *15*(1), 16610. Advance online publication. DOI: 10.1038/s41598-025-01676-x PMID: 40360573

Ji, Z., Lee, N., Frieske, R., Yu, T., Su, D., Xu, Y., Ishii, E., Bang, Y. J., Madotto, A., & Fung, P. (2023). Survey of hallucination in natural language generation. *ACM Computing Surveys*, *55*(12), 1–38. Advance online publication. DOI: 10.1145/3571730

Kapur, M. (2008). Productive failure. *Cognition and Instruction*, *26*(3), 379–424. DOI: 10.1080/07370000802212669

Lee, A. (2008). How are doctoral students supervised? concepts of doctoral research supervision.

Lin, C.-H., Knowlton, B. J., Chiang, M.-C., Iacoboni, M., Udompholkul, P., & Wu, A. D. (2011). Brain–behavior correlates of optimizing learning through interleaved practice. *NeuroImage*, *56*(3), 1758–1772. DOI: 10.1016/j.neuroimage.2011.02.066

Lu, W., Li, S., & Qian, X. (2025). The impact of artificial intelligence literacy on doctoral students' innovative behaviour from the perspective of technology affordance. *European Journal of Education*. Advance online publication. DOI: 10.1111/ejed.70245

Mabirizi, V., Katushabe, C., Muhoza, G., & Rugasira, J. (2025). A systematic review of the impact of gen-erative ai on postgraduate research: Opportunities, challenges, and ethical implications. *Discover Artificial Intelligence*, *5*(1), 238. DOI: 10.1007/s44163-025-00495-3

Mabirizi, V., Katushabe, C., Muhoza, G., & Rugasira, J. (2025). A systematic review of the impact of generative ai on postgraduate research: Opportunities, challenges, and ethical implica-tions. *Discover Artificial Intelligence*, *5*(1), 238. DOI: 10.1007/s44163-025-00495-3

Mwansa, G., & Ngandu, M. R. (2026). Transforming research supervision: Ethical and literacy imperatives in the era of generative ai. In I. Kariyana & W. Sinkala (Eds.), *Artificial intel-ligence and postgraduate supervision in higher education* (pp. 191–217). ERRCD Forum. DOI: 10.38140/obp4-2026-11

Omodan, B. I. (2025). Redefining the role of supervisors in the era of artificial intelligence: Im-plications for hybrid postgraduate research governance. *Cogent Education*, *12*(1), 2536534. Advance online publication. DOI: 10.1080/2331186X.2025.2536534

Rosner, T. M., Davis, H., & Milliken, B. (2015). Perceptual blurring and recognition memory: A desirable difficulty effect revealed. *Acta Psychologica*, *160*, 11–22. DOI: 10.1016/j.actpsy.2015.06.006 PMID: 26134415

Segooa, M. A., Modiba, F. S., & Motjolopane, I. (2025). Generative artificial intelligence tools to augment teaching scientific research in postgraduate studies. *South African Journal of Higher Education*, *39*(1), 300–320. DOI: 10.20853/39-1-6275

Storey, V. (2026a). Ai dependency vs. doctoral identity: How generative ai is challenging the de-velopment of independent scholarly thinking in doctoral students. *International Journal of AI in Pedagogy, Innovation, and Learning Futures*, *1*(1). Advance online publication. DOI: 10.46787/ijaipil.v2026i1.6971

Storey, V. (2026b). Ai dependency vs. doctoral identity: How generative ai is challenging the development of independent scholarly thinking in doctoral students. *International Journal of AI in Pedagogy, Innovation, and Learning Futures*. . v2026i1.6971DOI: 10.46787/ijaipil

Strathern, M. (1997). 'Improving ratings': Audit in the British University system. *European Review (Chichester, England)*, *5*(3), 305–321.

von Maltitz, M. J., Fabris-Rotelli, I., Smit, A., Roberts, D., Das, S., Maposa, D., & Correa, F. M. (2025). A guiding rubric and usage manual for the doctoral supervisor and doctoral student in the discipline of statistics. *ORiON*, *41*(1), 1–52. DOI: 10.5784/41-1-799

Wright, A. (2024). Postgraduate supervision in a chatgpt world: What's next? *Proceedings of the 10th International Conference on Higher Education Advances (HEAd'24)*, 1–8. DOI: 10.4995/HEAd24.2024.17244

KEY TERMS AND DEFINITIONS

Cognitive Offloading: subcontracting a process in learning to an agent to ease the cogni-tive demand from the learner.

Desired Difficulty: A difficulty in the learning process that increases cognitive demand, and, in turn, learning depth and retention.

Doctoral Supervision: a specialised, intensive mentoring and academic relationship be-tween a senior academic (the supervisor or advisor) and a doctoral candidate.

GenAI: Generative Artificial Intelligence, usually based on Large Language model archi-tecture.

Guiding Rubric: an evaluation tool or scoring guide that explicitly outlines the expecta-tions, criteria, and standards during a research journey

LLM: Large Language model; a statistical neural network model that sequentially predicts the next token in a text based on vast quantities of training data.

NLP: Natural language processing

ENDNOTES

1 https://www.che.ac.za/sites/default/files/inline-files/CHE%20Doctoral%20Degrees%20National%20Reporte_0.pdf

2 https://www.che.ac.za/sites/default/files/inline-files/CHE%20Doctoral%20Degrees%20National%20Reporte_0.pdf

Chapter 11
Artificial Intelligence in Assessment Design for Cantonese Education

Siu-Lun Lee
http://orcid.org/0000-0002-2306-9217
The Chinese University of Hong Kong, Hong Kong

Ziya Zhou
The Hong Kong University of Science and Technology, Hong Kong

Jialu Li
The Hong Kong University of Science and Technology, Hong Kong

ABSTRACT

This chapter explores how artificial intelligence reshapes assessment design in higher education, using Cantonese as a second language as a distinctive lens. Cantonese's tonal and sociolinguistic complexity provides a rigorous case for evaluating AI's role in oral proficiency testing. The discussion highlights the shift toward adaptive, learner-centred formats that move beyond standardised methods. Drawing on Hong Kong's higher education practices, it demonstrates how integrating Automatic Speech Recognition, Large Language Models, and Text-to-Speech enables contextualized tasks, real-time feedback, and alignment with ACTFL and CEFR frameworks. It also addresses challenges of transparency, cultural sensitivity, and human-in-the-loop mediation. Ultimately, AI-driven assessment design fosters flexible, inclusive, and pedagogically robust approaches across multilingual higher education.

DOI: 10.4018/979-8-3373-9089-5.ch011

1. INTRODUCTION

Artificial intelligence (AI) is rapidly reshaping assessment practices in higher education, and Cantonese as a second language offers a distinctive lens through which to examine these changes. While AI is transforming assessment design across diverse academic disciplines, language learning presents unique challenges that require a sophisticated interplay between technical precision and human-centric nuance. Cantonese, with its intricate tonal system and sociolinguistic complexity, provides a rich case for examining AI's potential in assessment, serving as a rigorous test for the accuracy and cultural sensitivity of current generative technologies.

The integration of AI into Cantonese education has transitioned from a theoretical possibility to a pedagogical necessity within the linguistically dense landscape of Hong Kong's higher education. As an international hub, the city's universities face the complex task of providing robust Cantonese instruction to a diverse student body ranging from local speakers, non-local students and heritage learners to international students. However, traditional Cantonese assessment faces persistent hurdles in evaluating tonal precision, pragmatic competence, and sociocultural relevance. These elements are fundamental to the language but difficult to measure through conventional standardised testing.

This chapter situates AI-driven assessment within broader debates on learner-centred pedagogy and multilingual education, exploring the transformative potential of Generative AI (GenAI) as a scalable solution to these long-standing evaluative hurdles. By leveraging modern tools such as prosody-aware automated speech recognition (ASR) and large language models (LLMs), institutions can transition from static, summative assessments toward dynamic, inclusive approaches that provide real-time, personalised feedback. Such a shift not only enhances linguistic accuracy but also addresses the diverse learning trajectories inherent in a multilingual campus.

However, the 'AI revolution' in Cantonese education demonstrates a delicate balance between promise and pitfalls. While AI offers unprecedented efficiency and the potential to increase student motivation and confidence, its implementation raises critical questions regarding algorithmic bias and the preservation of linguistic integrity. Consequently, this study asserts that while AI offers transformative potential for assessment design, its integration must be guided by pedagogical integrity, cultural awareness, and a steadfast commitment to the human-centric nature of language acquisition.

2. LITERATURE REVIEW ON ARTIFICIAL INTELLIGENCE IN LANGUAGE ASSESSMENT

The landscape of applied linguistics is currently undergoing a paradigm shift, transitioning from traditional computational methodologies toward the pervasive integration of Generative Artificial Intelligence (GenAI). This literature review critically synthesises recent scholarship (2024–2026) to map the evolution of the field, the technical capabilities of Large Language Models (LLMs), and the emerging pedagogical and psychometric challenges.

2.1. Evolution and systematic trends

To understand the current artificial intelligence (AI) revolution, one must first contextualise it within the broader history of the discipline. Zakaria and Aryadoust's (2024) scientometric analysis of applied linguistics (1970–2022) provides a vital longitudinal foundation, illustrating how methodological trends have shifted over five decades. This historical grounding is complemented by Esmaeilzadeh et al. (2025), whose systematic review of research from 2020–2024 captures the explosive entry of AI into teaching and assessment. These works suggest that while applied linguistics has always been interdisciplinary, the current 'AI era' represents a distinct break from previous computer-assisted language learning (CALL) frameworks, necessitating a fundamental re-evaluation of research priorities in applied linguistics.

2.2. AI in language assessment

The most contentious and rapidly evolving sub-field within the discipline is language assessment, where the integration of AI is prompting a fundamental re-evaluation of testing paradigms. Jang and Sawaki (2025) argue that the field is currently in the midst of an 'AI revolution' that offers immense promises for personalised learning but simultaneously poses existential challenges to traditional assessment constructs. This revolution is manifested in several key areas. First, regarding automated scoring and feedback, Misgna et al. (2024) provide a technical survey of deep learning-based automated essay scoring (AES), noting a significant advancement from simple error detection to sophisticated, nuanced feedback generation. However, they caution that the 'black box' nature of these complex models remains a primary concern for psychometric validity and transparency.

Second, the efficiency of item generation has been radically altered. Lin and Chen (2024) offer a targeted investigation into ChatGPT's ability to generate multiple-choice reading comprehension items, finding high capability in terms of production speed and linguistic accuracy. Nevertheless, they underscore the necessity of 'human-in-the-loop' validation to ensure item quality and the relevance of distractors. Finally, Zhang et al. (2025) explore the 'dual impact' of AI in post-entry language assessment (PELA), highlighting a critical tension. On one hand, AI provides the 'potential' for scalable, immediate feedback. On the other hand, it also introduces 'pitfalls' regarding academic integrity and the risk of narrowing the construct being measured to only what the machine can reliably detect.

2.3. Pedagogical transformations

Beyond assessment, AI is reshaping classroom experience and learner psychology. Shi et al. (2025) provide a compelling comparative study between ChatGPT and traditional automated writing evaluation (AWE). Their research is particularly significant for its focus on the 'ideal L2 writing self', suggesting that AI interaction does not just improve text quality but also influences a learner's identity and motivation.

However, the success of these tools is contingent upon teacher agency. Hubbard and Schulze (2025) emphasise that the future of language teaching depends on 'sustained integrated professional development'. They argue that without motivating teachers to engage in continuous learning about AI, the technology will remain an external imposition rather than a transformative pedagogical tool.

2.4. Opportunities and future directions

Chuang and Yan (2025) synthesise these themes by categorising the current state of GenAI into opportunities, such as efficiency and personalisation, together with challenges including security, bias, and the devaluation of human creativity. A critical thread running through this recent corpus, particularly in the work of Chuang and Yan (2025), and Jang and Sawaki (2025), is the need to redefine what 'language proficiency' actually means in an age where AI can mediate communication.

These scholarly works collectively suggest that applied linguistics is moving beyond the 'experimental' phase of AI. While older scientometric trends (Zakaria & Aryadoust, 2024) favoured traditional corpus linguistics and sociolinguistic frameworks, the current era is defined by the automation of high-stakes tasks. Despite the rapid expansion of AI in language assessment, a critical gap remains in its application to oral proficiency, particularly within the context of the Chinese language. While automated scoring for written tasks has matured, recent reviews by Esmaeilzadeh et al. (2025) and Jang and Sawaki (2025) indicate that oral interaction remains an underexplored frontier. This scarcity is even more pronounced for Chinese, where typological features, specifically tonal precision and prosody, present unique algorithmic challenges that current Large Language Models (LLMs) often fail to capture with consistent accuracy (Lin & Chen, 2024). However, Wang (2026) points out that much of the existing research continues to prioritise English as a Foreign Language (EFL) context, leaving a significant need for AI-driven diagnostic tools tailored to the phonetic and interactive complexities of Chinese oral proficiency.

3. CANTONESE EDUCATION AND ASSESSMENTS IN HONG KONG

Cantonese is one of the three primary spoken languages in Hong Kong, alongside Putonghua and English (Bolton et al., 2020; Bolton & Lee, 2020). The 2021 Population Census recorded that 88.2% of the population reported Cantonese as their usual spoken language (Hong Kong Government, 2021). This linguistic landscape is formally influenced by the promotion of 'trilingualism and biliteracy', which aims to develop a citizenry proficient in speaking Cantonese, Putonghua, and English, while being literate in written Chinese and English (Bacon-Shone et al., 2025). In this context, Cantonese serves as the essential language for daily life and local identity, Putonghua as the medium for national and regional integration, and English as the bridge to global commerce. Given its status as a dominant medium of communication within this trilingual framework, the language attracts a diverse cohort of learners annually, including international exchange students and working professionals. These learners of Cantonese as a second language represent a global demographic spanning Africa, the Americas, Australia, Europe, and various regions across East and Southeast Asia (Lee, 2004, 2020). Studies on Cantonese as a second language (Lee, 2004, 2020) indicate that students are primarily motivated by professional and cultural factors, seeking to integrate into Hong Kong's workforce while engaging authentically with its vibrant local lifestyle and popular culture.

Within the global discourse on AI and language assessment, Cantonese education in Hong Kong higher education serves as a distinctive case study of the intersection between technology and complex sociolinguistic landscapes. Despite the pervasive dominance of English in academic and professional domains, Cantonese remains the primary vehicle for everyday communication and a foundational pillar of cultural identity (Bauer, 2016). This creates a unique pedagogical environment where the language is simultaneously a 'living' vernacular and a formal subject of academic study. For local students, Cantonese represents a heritage anchor and a vital tool for cultural continuity. For international and non-local learners, it provides the essential 'social capital' needed to penetrate local networks and engage in identity formation (Lee, 2018a, 2019).

However, a primary challenge for Cantonese educators is the absence of a universally standardised, high-stakes assessment framework, comparable to the IELTS for English or the HSK for Putonghua, that accounts for the language's diglossic nature. Cantonese involves a vast spectrum between formal written Chinese and highly idiomatic, spoken vernacular (Lee, 2023a). This complexity requires a sophisticated pedagogical approach capable of assessing not just vocabulary and grammar, but also the nuanced 'tonal precision' and 'pragmatic appropriateness' required for authentic communication within Hong Kong's diverse social spheres.

Over the past decade, Hong Kong's educational sector has addressed these pedagogical gaps by progressively integrating computer-assisted language learning (CALL) into the curriculum. Since 2009, universities have actively promoted e-learning platforms and online resources to supplement formal instruction, aiming to provide learners with more flexible, self-paced environments (King, 2016; Lee, 2018b; Kataoka, 2023). This digital transition reached a critical turning point during the COVID-19 pandemic, which necessitated an immediate shift to remote instruction and resulted in a substantial increase in student and faculty acceptance of blended, technology-mediated learning (Lee, 2022). Building on this momentum, contemporary scholarship suggests that emerging technologies, including internet learning resources and big data for tracking learner errors, can foster the authentic, contextualised experiences necessary for Cantonese acquisition (Chin, 2023; Lee, 2023b).

However, the emergence of generative AI (GenAI) has ignited a profound debate regarding the ethical and pedagogical limits of automation. While AI offers transformative benefits, such as providing real-time prosody feedback to help learners master the six phonemic tones of Cantonese for pedagogical purposes, educators and policymakers remain cautious regarding algorithmic bias and educational equity (Chen, 2023; Liu & Yau, 2023; Lee & Chen, 2024; Lee, 2025). There is a specific concern that AI models trained on 'standard' Cantonese may fail to recognise legitimate regional variations or the unique interlanguage patterns of heritage and ethnic minority learners. As the field moves toward more automated assessment models, the idiomatic richness and tonal nuances of Cantonese remain a rigorous test for AI. To be truly effective, AI-assisted assessment must move beyond simple speech-to-text functionality to become 'prosody-aware', ensuring that the fairness and validity of the assessment construct are maintained in an increasingly digitised educational landscape.

4. THEORETICAL FRAMEWORK FOR LANGUAGE ASSESSMENT

Effective assessment in language education must move beyond discrete knowledge testing to capture communicative competence (Hymes, 1972; Canale & Swain, 1980; Bachman & Palmer, 2010), and GenAI provides new theoretical and practical tools to achieve this. Rather than merely assessing isolated grammatical or phonological accuracy, communicative competence encompasses the strategic, sociolinguistic, and discourse-level skills required to navigate social contexts and negotiate meaning effectively. This necessitates a shift toward evaluating not only what a learner knows about the language's formal structure, but also their ability to deploy those resources flexibly and appropriately in response to a living interlocutor. The theoretical underpinning for modern communicative assessment, particularly in the context of oral proficiency, is rooted in the functional and holistic evaluation of a speaker's ability to use language in real-world situations. Central to this framework are the American Council on the Teaching of Foreign Languages (ACTFL) Proficiency Guidelines and the Oral Proficiency Interview (OPI), which provide a standardised metric for measuring spontaneous, functional speaking ability regardless of when, where, or how the language was acquired.

4.1 The ACTFL proficiency guidelines

The *ACTFL Proficiency Guidelines* serve as a comprehensive descriptive framework that categorises language proficiency into five major levels including Distinguished, Superior, Advanced, Intermediate, and Novice. To provide a more granular view of a learner's progress, each level, with the exception of Superior and Distinguished, is further divided into Low, Mid, and High sub-levels. Unlike traditional achievement-based tests that measure the mastery of a specific curriculum, the ACTFL framework is 'pro-achievement', focusing holistically on what an individual can do with the language across four key criteria. These include 'global tasks and functions', which identify specific communicative goals such as narrating in the past or supporting an opinion; 'context and content', ranging from predictable daily environments to abstract academic settings; 'the degree to which a message is understood by fluent interlocutors' cultural and grammatical norms; and 'text type', which tracks the structural complexity of speech from isolated phrases to cohesive, extended paragraphs (American Council on the Teaching of Foreign Languages, 2026a).

4.2. The Oral Proficiency Interview (OPI)

The operationalisation of this framework occurs through the Oral Proficiency Interview (OPI). The OPI is a criterion-referenced, holistic assessment consisting of a live, 20-to-30-minute telephonic or face-to-face interview between a certified tester and a candidate. The assessment follows a specific structure, which comprises the warm-up, level checks, probes, and wind-down, designed to identify the speaker's ‘floor’ showing what they can do consistently and their ‘ceiling’ indicating the point at which their linguistic system breaks down (Liskin-Gasparro, 2003).

This framework is particularly relevant when discussing the integration of AI in Cantonese or Chinese language assessments. While AI systems struggle with the nuanced ‘accuracy’ and ‘text type’ requirements of tonal, high-context languages, the OPI provides a benchmark for ‘functional’ communication that AI must aim to replicate. The challenge for automated systems is to simulate the ‘probes’ of an OPI rater, which require a high degree of interactive competence and the ability to evaluate a speaker's breakdown when pushed toward abstract or complex tasks. By utilising the ACTFL framework, researchers can ensure that AI-driven assessments remain grounded in established proficiency principles and communicative validity (Liskin-Gasparro, 2003; American Council on the Teaching of Foreign Languages, 2026b).

4.3 The Common European Framework of Reference for Languages (CEFR)

The Common European Framework of Reference for Languages (CEFR) utilises a six-level hierarchy (A1, A2, B1, B2, C1, and C2) categorised into three broad bands, including Basic User, Independent User, and Proficient User. Similar to the ACTFL proficiency guidelines, CEFR is deeply rooted in a ‘can-do’ functional philosophy, emphasising social and communicative action within a European context. In contrast, the ACTFL Proficiency Guidelines, consisting of five main levels, focus on the specific linguistic breakdown of the learner's performance. While the CEFR often evaluates a learner's ability to navigate a specific social situation, ACTFL places a heavier emphasis on the hierarchy of functional language tasks and the structural accuracy required to sustain them. Despite these different starting points, these two frameworks are increasingly used in tandem to provide a comprehensive, multidimensional view of a learner’s proficiency in global higher education (Jones & Saville, 2009; North, 2014).

The proposed assessment system is strategically designed to synchronise global standards with practical assessment methodology by incorporating both the ACTFL Proficiency Guidelines and the CEFR framework. While the CEFR provides a broad, functional ‘can-do’ perspective of the learner’s social and communicative abilities, the ACTFL guidelines offer a detailed linguistic breakdown necessary for tracking progress in a tonal language like Cantonese. By implementing these rigorous frameworks within the Oral Proficiency Interview (OPI) protocol, the system moves beyond simple vocabulary testing to simulate a real-world, conversational environment. This integration ensures that the AI-driven assessment is not only technologically advanced but also pedagogically grounded, delivering results that are internationally recognised, standardised, and reflective of a learner's true communicative competence.

5. LEVERAGING GENAI IN CANTONESE SPEECH RECOGNITION AND PROFICIENCY ASSESSMENT

The integration of Generative AI into Cantonese speech recognition and proficiency assessment represents a significant technical leap, addressing the linguistic complexities that once hindered automated evaluation. Early comparative studies by Peng et al. (2004) established that Cantonese tone recognition is inherently more challenging than Mandarin due to its denser tonal system, which is traditionally categorised into six phonemic tones, and its significantly overlapping pitch contours. These phonetic overlaps often lead to 'tonal ambiguity' in automated systems, where the pitch height and contour of one tone can be easily misidentified as another in rapid, spontaneous speech. Modern GenAI frameworks, however, are beginning to overcome these barriers through sophisticated architectural innovations that move beyond traditional Hidden Markov models toward deep, Transformer-based neural networks.

A cornerstone of this evolution is the application of large-scale, foundation models like OpenAI's *Whisper* (OpenAI, 2022; Radford et al., 2023). An et al. (2026) demonstrate that Whisper's multilingual pre-training and robust encoder-decoder architecture allow it to achieve high-accuracy Cantonese dialect transcription even in diverse and sophisticated acoustic scenarios. This capability provides a robust foundation for transcribing spontaneous learner speech, which is often characterised by disfluencies, non-standard pronunciations, and varying background noise. As pre-trained foundation models, such systems can be further adapted to downstream tasks through post-training or fine-tuning, enabling better alignment with specific assessment objectives. These models enable the second-stage analysis of syntactic and lexical complexity, which are vital components of the ACTFL and CEFR proficiency frameworks.

To transition from mere transcription to nuanced proficiency assessment, current research emphasises the development of 'prosody-aware' and 'phoneme-aware' models. Chen et al. (2025) introduced *CantoASR*, a specialised framework that facilitates collaboration between Automatic Speech Recognition (ASR) and Large Language Models (LLMs). This system specifically incorporates prosodic features to handle the historically low-resource nature of Cantonese, using the LLM's semantic understanding to disambiguate or interpret acoustically ambiguous tonal information. This is further complemented by the work of Zhang et al. (2025), who utilise phoneme-aware hierarchical augmentation and semantic-aware data strategies. Their approach improves recognition accuracy in contexts where training data is scarce, such as specialised academic or professional Cantonese registers. Such advancements are critical for assessment, as they allow AI to distinguish between subtle phonological variations and lexical tone alternations, a phenomenon that Lau and Wong (2024) identify as central to the cognitive and phonological representation of the language in the learner's mind. Recent developments in speech-based large language models suggest a gradual shift from traditional pipeline-based approaches toward more integrated representations, which may offer additional flexibility for capturing prosodic and semantic information. Furthermore, the hardware and computational frameworks supporting these AI models are becoming increasingly efficient, paving the way for ubiquitous, mobile-first assessment tools. Khan et al. (2025) propose the use of Quantum-dot Cellular Automata (QCA) for neural Cantonese speech converters. This suggests a future where high-speed, nanocomputing-based AI tools could provide real-time, low-latency feedback on oral proficiency directly to the learner's device. This move toward edge computing ensures that the complex task of tonal analysis does not require massive server-side latency, making interactive 'AI-tutors' a practical reality for students. In addition to the significant advances in automatic speech recognition (ASR) and large language model (LLM) modules for language learning, text-to-speech (TTS) technology, which synthesises text into spoken language, has been incorporated as a downstream component following ASR and LLM to construct voice-based conversational systems. Compared with text-based dialogues, a voice-based conversational system enables a more interactive learning and assessment environment by providing immediate feedback and speech-based stimulation. Recent studies and technologies, such as *MiniCPM* (https://github.com/OpenBMB/MiniCPM-o), *Seeduplex* (https://seed.bytedance.com/en/seeduplex), and *Gemini Live* (https://gemini.google/tw/overview/gemini-live), have demonstrated the feasibility of low-latency conversational systems.

Collectively, these studies suggest that GenAI is moving beyond simple word recognition toward a holistic, multimodal understanding of Cantonese. By capturing the intricate relationship between tone, prosody, and semantics, these emerging technologies offer a viable pathway for scalable, automated Cantonese oral proficiency testing. Most importantly, these systems allow for the assessment of communicative competence rather than just isolated phonetics, ensuring that automated tools align with the goals of modern, communicative language teaching.

6. THE DESIGN OF AI-DRIVEN CANTONESE LANGUAGE ASSESSMENT

To bridge the gap between emerging GenAI capabilities and the sociolinguistic requirements of the Hong Kong classroom, this project introduces a scalable, curriculum-aligned diagnostic system design that integrates human expertise with AI-driven precision. Moving beyond theoretical models, the system is designed as a practical evaluative tool that prioritises pedagogical alignment and user agency. The development and deployment of this AI-assisted proficiency test are structured into three strategic phases: (1) planning and prototyping, (2) pilot testing, and (3) full-scale implementation. Professional AI consultants support technical development throughout these stages, focusing on the optimisation of key metrics including Word Error Rate (WER), Phoneme Error Rate (PER), and pitch contour similarity. By integrating established frameworks such as the Oral Proficiency Interview (OPI), the ACTFL Oral Proficiency Guidelines, and the Common European Framework of Reference for Languages (CEFR), the project ensures that the automated output is both internationally recognised and educationally valid.

6.1 Phase 1: Planning and Prototyping

In the initial planning and prototyping stage, a multidisciplinary team, comprising a teacher-researcher and two professional AI consultants, collaborates on the overarching design, environment, and data preparation for the AI-assisted Cantonese proficiency test. This phase involves finalising the project scope and conducting a comprehensive review of existing technologies to ensure the architecture remains at the cutting edge of current research. Student helpers are recruited to assist in the collection of diverse Cantonese speech data, which is essential for training the Large Language Models (LLMs). The core technological framework is built upon a tripartite integration of Automatic Speech Recognition (ASR), which converts student speech to text for pronunciation diagnosis. Large Language Models (LLMs) are built to compare performance data against ACTFL/CEFR criteria to dynamically adjust question difficulty; and incorporating Text-to-Speech (TTS) to synthesise LLM-generated questions into natural speech to facilitate a fluid, conversational interface. Following internal structural modelling, the team focuses on model validation, course digitalisation, and user-interface design to ensure the platform is both pedagogically sound and user-friendly. Figure 1 below shows the technological framework and data flow.

Figure 1. Technological framework for AI-driven Cantonese assessment

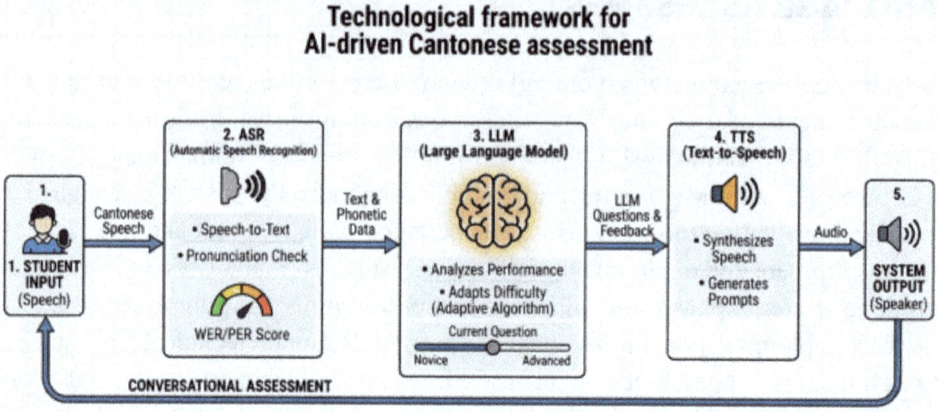

This AI-assisted proficiency test will automatically generate questions of different proficiency levels in speech based on students' speech input. The test operation follows the framework of the Oral Proficiency Interview (OPI). Ratings based on the ACTFL Oral Proficiency Guidelines will be given to each student. Language learning options and suggestions will be given to students when prompted. Once the model was trained and validated, the team focused on system integration and application development, including backend and frontend implementation, and course digitalisation.

6.2 Phase 2: Pilot Testing Stage

The piloting stage involves rigorous testing of the diagnostic tools with small groups of university students in Hong Kong to gather empirical performance data for system refinement. During this phase, the team focuses on technical optimisation, specifically training models to handle language-specific diagnostic tasks and refining the ASR and pitch estimation models to better capture the 'tonal precision' of Cantonese. Key technical components such as automatic speech recognition (evaluated through Word Error Rate), phoneme recognition (Phoneme Error Rate), and pitch estimation (pitch contour similarity) will be optimised. The team collects incremental data to facilitate model post-training, stability testing, and scale-up evaluations. By conducting extensive testing, the team ensures the system can maintain high reliability and low-latency feedback. This iterative process allows for the fine-tuning of the user interface and system architecture based on actual student interactions, ensuring the tool effectively bridges the gap between automated scoring and the lived experience of the learner. Moreover, this stage will incorporate verification by human experts and raters. The performance of the model-based system will be compared against their assessments. Besides, these experts and tutors will be asked to assume the role of learners interacting with the system, to identify any missing elements or limitations within this AI-driven system.

6.3 Phase 3: Full-Scale Implementation Stage

The final phase marks the transition to a full-scale operational environment within a University Cantonese Programme, encompassing over 20 distinct courses. The team continues to validate the test in terms of reliability and validity, as well as to fine-tune the algorithms based on a larger, more diverse pool of student data to ensure long-term stability. This involves verifying the assessment's reliability by ensuring the AI provides consistent ratings across different test sessions and participant cohorts, while confirming its validity by correlating AI-generated scores with human-certified OPI results to ensure the tool accurately measures genuine communicative proficiency. Consistent with the OPI framework, the AI-assisted test interacts with participants through spontaneous speech, automatically providing an ACTFL-based rating for each student. A key innovation in this stage is the dual-target feedback loop, which consists of language learning options and personalised suggestions provided to students upon request, while teachers receive diagnostic reports that identify specific learning needs. This allows educators to provide targeted pedagogical support, ensuring that the 'AI revolution' in Cantonese education remains human-centric and effectively integrated into the institutional fabric.

7. DISCUSSION

The landscape of Cantonese education in Hong Kong's higher education is a critical nexus where the sociolinguistic complexities of a tonal language meet the transformative potential of artificial intelligence. As the preceding review demonstrates, Cantonese presents both the unique psychometric challenges of assessing tonal and pragmatic competence and the significant promise of modern GenAI tools, such as prosody-aware ASR and large language models, in delivering scalable, responsive pedagogical solutions. By synthesising these technological advances with established communicative frameworks, such as the ACTFL guidelines, this initiative aims to catalyse system-level improvements in teaching and learning. Specifically, integrating AI will provide data-driven insights into student performance, enabling more targeted instruction and refining the Cantonese curriculum to meet diverse learner needs. Furthermore, it will enhance accessibility and inclusiveness for local, non-local, and international students by offering personalised, real-time support that was previously labour-intensive. Beyond linguistic gains, the project is designed to promote digital literacy and ethical AI awareness among both students and educators, ultimately establishing a replicable model for AI integration in language education that contributes to the university's strategic goals in innovation and internationalisation.

Following this overview, the discussion proceeds to examine these dimensions through three critical lenses. First, learner-centred evaluation explores how AI-driven diagnostics can move beyond standardised scoring to provide personalised, formative feedback that respects the individual's learning trajectory. Secondly, implications for multilingual higher education situate the Cantonese case within the broader global context, discussing how a localised AI framework can serve as a blueprint for supporting linguistic diversity and inclusive pedagogy in internationalised academic environments. Finally, challenges and ethical considerations address the 'black box' nature of these technologies, specifically confronting issues of algorithmic bias and the preservation of Cantonese linguistic integrity.

7.1. Learner-centred evaluation

The transition toward AI-driven assessment in Cantonese education signals a pivotal move from rigid, summative testing toward a more dynamic, learner-centred evaluation paradigm. By enabling personalised feedback and continuous assessment, AI fosters an evaluative environment that empowers students and accommodates diverse learning trajectories. As Jang and Sawaki (2025) suggest, the 'AI revolution' allows for the creation of assessment frameworks that prioritise formative learning over traditional, high-stakes summative benchmarks. This shift is particularly evident in the capacity of Generative AI to provide individualised feedback that enhances learner agency and engagement, moving significantly beyond generic scoring. Misgna et al. (2024) highlight that deep learning-based systems have advanced to sophisticated feedback generation, serving as a critical pedagogical tool for learners navigating the tonal complexities of Cantonese by providing immediate, granular insights that enable real-time self-correction.

Furthermore, AI-driven evaluation holds the potential to accommodate diverse learner profiles, including heritage learners and ethnic minority students, thereby promoting equity within the Hong Kong educational context. By providing a platform for continuous, low-stakes assessment, AI helps bridge the gap for students with varying levels of prior exposure to Cantonese. This psychological dimension is crucial; Shi et al. (2025) demonstrate that engaging with AI tools can positively influence a student's 'ideal L2 self', and help learners visualise and achieve their linguistic identity in a responsive space. Similarly, Wang (2026) notes that multimodal GenAI increases student engagement in task-based Chinese language learning by facilitating authentic and inclusive practice.

However, the efficacy of this learner-centred approach remains contingent on the quality of the technology and its implementation. While Lin and Chen (2024) affirm that AI can efficiently generate targeted assessment items, the shift toward personalisation must be balanced with transparency. Chuang and Yan (2025) emphasise that the opportunities for tailored evaluation must ensure that students understand the criteria of their assessment to maintain trust. On the teachers' side, as Hubbard and Schulze (2025) argue, the success of a learner-centred model depends on sustained professional development, ensuring educators can use these data-driven insights to provide the targeted, empathetic support necessary for a truly inclusive and equitable multilingual higher education.

7.2. Implications for multilingual higher education

The Cantonese case demonstrates how AI can expand assessment possibilities across multilingual higher education, promoting inclusivity and innovation while highlighting transferable lessons for the global academic community. As Zakaria and Aryadoust (2024) demonstrate, the field of applied linguistics has steadily evolved toward technology-mediated frameworks. The 'AI revolution' described by Jang and Sawaki (2025) now offers a unique opportunity to institutionalise linguistic diversity. By leveraging AI to support a complex heritage and community language like Cantonese, lessons from Cantonese assessment can inform AI-driven design in other language contexts, particularly those involving tonal or low-resource languages that have been historically marginalised in digital pedagogy.

This shift has profound implications for how institutions manage internationalisation and inclusive pedagogy. AI expands inclusivity by supporting diverse learners and reducing barriers to access, providing a scalable solution for students who require personalised linguistic support to navigate their social and academic environments. Zhang et al. (2025) highlight the dual impact of AI in post-entry language assessment (PELA), suggesting that while AI can streamline the screening of diverse student cohorts, it must be implemented carefully to avoid narrowing linguistic constructs. When AI-driven tools facilitate multimodal, task-based learning, these tools foster intercultural competence by allowing international and non-local students to engage authentically with the local linguistic repertoire.

Ultimately, the successful adoption of these technologies in a multilingual context necessitates a collaborative and ethical approach. Cross-institutional collaboration can accelerate innovation while ensuring ethical safeguards, preventing the 'black box' pitfalls often associated with automated systems. As Hubbard and Schulze

(2025) argue, the future of language teaching depends on 'sustained integrated professional development'. In a multilingual university setting, this means training faculty not only in AI literacy but also in the ethical nuances of supporting varied learner profiles. By establishing a replicable model for AI integration, institutions can ensure that technological progress supports, rather than erodes, the rich multilingual landscape of global higher education.

7.3. Challenges and ethical considerations

While the integration of AI into Cantonese education offers transformative potential, it introduces a complex array of challenges and ethical dilemmas that must be rigorously navigated to ensure pedagogical integrity. Despite its potential, AI-driven assessment raises pressing concerns about transparency, cultural sensitivity, and the need to balance automation with human expertise. A primary concern is the 'black box' nature of AI-enabled learning ecologies, which can obscure the logic behind knowledge assessment. Cope et al. (2021) argue that as we move toward these AI-enabled environments, transparency and explainability are critical to maintaining trust in the assessment process. For Cantonese, this is further complicated by the technical difficulty of modelling tonal precision. Kang and Kang (2022) note that while deep learning models can construct sophisticated Chinese teaching systems, their accuracy depends heavily on the quality of data and the underlying algorithms, which may not always align with human linguistic intuition. These risks of bias and over-standardisation highlight the urgent need for careful calibration and oversight to ensure that automated systems do not unfairly penalise natural linguistic variation.

Furthermore, the shift toward AI-driven evaluation raises significant questions regarding academic integrity and the changing nature of the assessment construct. Moqbel and Al-Kadi (2023) provide a theoretical account of foreign language assessment in the age of ChatGPT, highlighting the tension between leveraging AI for efficiency and maintaining validity. These concerns are echoed by Huang et al. (2023), who identify algorithmic bias as a major research trend. To mitigate these risks, cultural sensitivity must guide task design to avoid reinforcing stereotypes or privileging dominant norms, ensuring that the diverse linguistic backgrounds of Hong Kong's student body are respected. For a city like Hong Kong, institutional barriers also play a significant role. Wang and Cheng (2021) identify key barriers, including a lack of teacher readiness and curriculum constraints. These are factors that likely extend to the higher education sector and impact the equitable rollout of such technologies.

Finally, the successful and ethical implementation of AI necessitates a focus on human-AI collaboration. Ji et al. (2023) emphasise that conversational AI should not replace but rather collaborate with human teachers to ensure that the 'human touch' is preserved. Human expertise remains indispensable; AI should augment, not replace, teacher judgment. This is particularly vital when dealing with young or vulnerable learners, as Jeon (2024) suggests that students' emotional experiences with AI are varied and complex. Moreover, Lee (2016) reminds us that 'e-learning readiness' is not uniform, potentially creating new digital divides.

Critically, there is a recurring caution. While AI can generate items (Lin & Chen, 2024) and score essays (Misgna et al., 2024), it cannot yet replicate the nuanced, context-aware judgment of a language professional. The 'pitfalls' identified by Zhang et al. (2025) and the need for professional development highlighted by Hubbard and Schulze (2025) serve as a reminder that the 'AI revolution' in language studies must remain human-centric to maintain ethical and educational integrity. As Pedró et al. (2019) conclude in their UNESCO working paper, while AI presents unprecedented opportunities, the challenges of data privacy, equity of access, and the potential devaluation of human linguistic expertise remain central to the ongoing debate in language policy and practice.

7.3. Future research

Future research should prioritise the empirical validation of AI-integrated assessment systems by conducting rigorous inter-rater reliability studies between certified ACTFL testers and automated models, specifically investigating whether models like *OpneAi Whisper* can accurately identify linguistic 'ceilings' and 'floors' in spontaneous Cantonese speech (An et al., 2026). Alongside these technical benchmarks, longitudinal studies are needed to evaluate the impact of sustained GenAI interaction on the 'Ideal L2 Self' and the reduction of foreign language speaking anxiety among diverse student cohorts over an extended academic period (Shi et al., 2025). Furthermore, a critical area of development lies in bias mitigation; future work must move toward 'Culturally Responsive AI' that recognises dialectal variations, such as those found among heritage learners and ethnic minority students, rather than over-standardising toward a single broadcast norm (Chuang & Yan, 2025). Finally, consistent with the mandate for human-centric innovation, research should focus on operationalising 'Human-in-the-loop' (HITL) assessment frameworks, defining how AI-generated, data-driven insights can best augment, rather than replace, the context-aware judgment of language professionals through sustained integrated professional development (Hubbard & Schulze, 2025).

8. CONCLUSION

The transformation of Cantonese education within the higher education landscape underscores a significant evolution in how tonal languages are taught and evaluated. Cantonese assessment faces persistent challenges in tonal accuracy, pragmatic competence, and sociocultural relevance, necessitating a shift away from traditional, static testing methods. As this chapter has highlighted, AI tools, including advanced speech recognition, automated feedback systems, and interactive conversations, provide scalable solutions to these challenges, offering a level of precision and real-time responsiveness previously unattainable in large-scale language programs.

By integrating these technologies, AI reshapes assessment design by enabling dynamic, learner-centred, and inclusive approaches that move beyond generic scoring toward personalised learning trajectories. The Cantonese education context demonstrates both the promise and the pitfalls of AI-driven evaluation, serving as a microcosm for the broader 'AI revolution' in applied linguistics. While student reception indicates that AI-driven assessment can increase motivation and confidence, the psychological benefits are most pronounced when learners feel supported by a responsive system. However, human mediation remains essential to provide context-aware guidance that algorithms cannot yet replicate.

Finally, AI offers transformative potential for assessment design, but its integration must be guided by pedagogical integrity, cultural awareness, and a commitment to learner-centred education. Moving forward, future directions require balancing technological innovation with pedagogical integrity and cultural sensitivity, ensuring that automated tools enhance rather than diminish the rich linguistic heritage of Cantonese. By maintaining a human-centric focus, multilingual institutions can leverage AI to create an equitable and innovative educational environment that prepares students for a linguistically diverse and technologically advanced future.

REFERENCES

American Council on the Teaching of Foreign Languages. (2026a). *Proficiency Guidelines Overview.* https://www.actfl.org/proficiency-guidelines-overview

American Council on the Teaching of Foreign Languages. (2026b). *Oral Proficiency Interview (OPI).* https://www.actfl.org/assessments/postsecondary-assessments/opi

An, J., Bai, Y., Li, J., Wang, L., Jiang, Y., & Zhang, Y. (2026). Cantonese dialect transcription in diverse sophisticated scenarios via the OpenAI Whisper speech recognition model. In M. Mahmud, M. Doborjeh, K. Wong, A. C. S. Leung, Z. Doborjeh, M. Tanveer (Eds) *Neural Information Processing*. Communications in Computer and Information Science, vol 2294. Springer, Singapore. DOI: 10.1007/978-981-96-7008-6_23

Bachman, L., & Palmer, A. (2010). *Language Assessment in Practice.* Oxford University Press.

Bacon-Shone, J., Bolton, K., & Lee, S. L. (2025). Researching Hong Kong's multilingual landscape. In Durk, G., & Cenoz, J. (Eds.), *The Handbook of Linguistic Landscapes and Multilingualism* (pp. 309–336). John Wiley & Sons.

Bauer, R. (2016). The Hong Kong Cantonese language: Current features and future prospects. *Global Chinese, 2*(2), 115–161. DOI: 10.1515/glochi-2016-0007

Bolton, K., Bacon-Shone, J., & Lee, S. L. (2020). Societal multilingualism in Hong Kong. In Siemund, P., & Leimgruber, J. (Eds.), *Multilingual Global Cities: Dubai, Hong Kong and Singapore* (pp. 160–184). Routledge. DOI: 10.4324/9780429463860-12

Bolton, K., & Lee, S. L. (2020). A socio-historical approach to multilingualism in Hong Kong. In Siemund, P., & Leimgruber, J. (Eds.), *Multilingual Global Cities: Hong Kong, Singapore, and Dubai* (pp. 38–62). Routledge. DOI: 10.4324/9780429463860-4

Canale, M., & Swain, M. (1980). Theoretical bases of communicative approaches to second language teaching and testing. *Applied Linguistics, 1*(1), 1–47. DOI: 10.1093/applin/1.1.1

Chen, D., Lin, Y. C., Huang, Y., Gong, Z., Jiang, D., & Xie, Z. (2025). CantoASR: Prosody-aware ASR-LALM collaboration for low-resource Cantonese. *arXiv preprint arXiv*:2511.04139.

Chen, L. (2023, June 23). Hong Kong rolls out first AI curriculum for junior secondary students, including lessons on ChatGPT, with 'lives definitely affected by artificial intelligence'. *South China Morning Post.*

Chin, A. C. (2023). A corpus-based approach to learning and teaching Cantonese. In Lee, S. L. (Ed.), *The Learning and Teaching of Cantonese as a Second Language* (pp. 184–196). Routledge.

Chuang, P. L., & Yan, X. (2025). Language assessment in the era of generative artificial intelligence: Opportunities, challenges, and future directions. *System, 103846*, 103846. Advance online publication. DOI: 10.1016/j.system.2025.103846

Cope, B., Kalantzis, M., & Searsmith, D. (2021). Artificial intelligence for education: Knowledge and its assessment in AI-enabled learning ecologies. *Educational Philosophy and Theory*, *53*(12), 1229–1245. DOI: 10.1080/00131857.2020.1728732

Esmaeilzadeh, F., Ghahari, S., & Rohani, G. (2025). Artificial intelligence in language teaching and assessment: A systematic review of research (2020-2024). *The Asian Journal of Applied Linguistics*, *9*(1), 1222–1222.

Hong Kong Government. (2021). *Population Census*. Census and Statistics Department.

Huang, X., Zou, D., Cheng, G., Chen, X., & Xie, H. (2023). Trends, research issues and applications of artificial intelligence in language education. *Journal of Educational Technology & Society*, *26*(1), 112–131. https://www.jstor.org/stable/48707971

Hubbard, P., & Schulze, M. (2025). AI and the future of language teaching: Motivating sustained integrated professional development. [IJCALLT]. *International Journal of Computer-Assisted Language Learning and Teaching*, *15*(1), 1–17. DOI: 10.4018/IJCALLT.378304

Hymes, D. H. (1972). On communicative competence. In Pride, J. B., & Holmes, J. (Eds.), *Sociolinguistics* (pp. 269–293). Penguin.

Jang, E. E., & Sawaki, Y. (2025). Advancing language assessment for teaching and learning in the era of the artificial intelligence (AI) revolution: Promises and challenges. *Language Testing*, *42*(4), 361–368. DOI: 10.1177/02655322251348685

Jeon, J. (2024). Exploring AI chatbot affordances in the EFL classroom: Young learners' experiences and perspectives. *Computer Assisted Language Learning*, *37*(1–2), 1–26. DOI: 10.1080/09588221.2021.2021241

Ji, H., Han, I., & Ko, Y. (2023). A systematic review of conversational AI in language education: Focusing on the collaboration with human teachers. *Journal of Research on Technology in Education*, *55*(1), 48–63. DOI: 10.1080/15391523.2022.2142873

Jones, N., & Saville, N. (2009). European language policy: Assessment, learning, and the CEFR. *Annual Review of Applied Linguistics*, *29*, 51–63. DOI: 10.1017/S0267190509090059

Kang, B., & Kang, S. (2022). Construction of Chinese language teaching system model based on deep learning under the background of artificial intelligence. *Scientific Programming*, *2022*(1), 3960023. DOI: 10.1155/2022/3960023

Kataoka, S. (2023). Textbook Cantonese romanization. In Lee, S. L. (Ed.), *The Learning and Teaching of Cantonese as a Second Language* (pp. 196–216). Routledge.

Khan, A., Shaw, R. K., & Bahar, A. N. (2025). A neural Cantonese speech converter using QCA for nanocomputing. *Computers & Electrical Engineering*, *126*, 110536. DOI: 10.1016/j.compeleceng.2025.110536

King, I. (2016, July 16). E-learning is the way forward for quality education. *South China Morning Post*.

Lau, J., & Wong, P. C. (2024). Neural processing of Mandarin and Cantonese lexical tone alternations: Implications for the nature of phonological representations. *Laboratory Phonology*, *15*(1). Advance online publication. DOI: 10.16995/labphon.10293

Lee, S. L. (2004). *History and Current Trends of Teaching Cantonese as a Foreign Language: Investigating Approaches to Teaching and Learning Cantonese* (Doctoral dissertation, University of Leicester).

Lee, S. L. (2016). E-Learning readiness in language learning: Students' readiness survey and normalization process. *Journal of Technology & Chinese Language Teaching*, *7*(2), 23–37.

Lee, S. L. (2018a). Expatriate Cantonese learners in Hong Kong: Adult L2 learning, identity negotiation, and social pressure. In Velliaris, D. (Ed.), *Study Abroad Contexts for Enhanced Foreign Language Learning* (pp. 106–110). IGI Global., DOI: 10.4018/978-1-5225-3814-1.ch007

Lee, S. L. (2018b). Modular approaches in eLearning design. *Journal of Technology and Chinese Language Teaching*, *9*(1), 48–61.

Lee, S. L. (2019). Teaching and learning Cantonese as a second language: Learners' attitudes and learning hurdles. In Wakefield, J. (Ed.), *Cantonese as a Second Language: Issues, Experiences and Suggestions for Teaching and Learning* (pp. 47–66). Routledge.

Lee, S. L. (2020). Learning needs of Cantonese as a second language in Hong Kong tertiary education. *Electronic Journal of Foreign Language Teaching, 17*(2), 460–478. DOI: 10.56040/slle1742

Lee, S. L. (2022). Synchronous online language teaching: A reflection from Hong Kong. In Liu, S. (Ed.), *Teaching the Chinese Language Remotely: Global Cases and Perspectives* (pp. 235–251). Palgrave Macmillan. DOI: 10.1007/978-3-030-87055-3_10

Lee, S. L. (2023a). Teaching literacy skills to Cantonese learners. In Lee, S. L. (Ed.), *The Learning and Teaching of Cantonese as a Second Language* (pp. 67–86). Routledge. DOI: 10.4324/9781003054696

Lee, S. L. (2023b). Learning, teaching and performing Cantonese on the Internet. In Lee, S. L. (Ed.), *The Learning and Teaching of Cantonese as a Second Language* (pp. 216–240). Routledge. DOI: 10.4324/9781003054696

Lee, S. L. (2025). AI-adaptive Chinese Language Learning Environment and Assessments in Hong Kong. In Wachira, P., Liu, X., & Koc, S. (Eds.), *Educational Assessments in the Age of Generative AI* (pp. 119–144). IGI Global. DOI: 10.4018/979-8-3693-6351-5.ch005

Lee, S. L., & Chen, Y. (2024). Discussions of using AI in language education in Hong Kong. In Pan, F. (Ed.), *AI in Language Teaching, Learning, and Assessment* (pp. 133–148). IGI Global. DOI: 10.4018/979-8-3693-0872-1.ch007

Lin, Z., & Chen, H. (2024). Investigating the capability of ChatGPT for generating multiple-choice reading comprehension items. *System, 123*, 103344. Advance online publication. DOI: 10.1016/j.system.2024.103344

Liskin-Gasparro, J. E. (2003). The ACTFL Proficiency Guidelines and the Oral Proficiency Interview: A brief history and analysis of their survival. *Foreign Language Annals, 36*(4), 483–490. DOI: 10.1111/j.1944-9720.2003.tb02137.x

Liu, O., & Yau, C. (2023, March 22). Who needs a teacher? As ChatGPT takes off in Hong Kong, educationists worry about impact on teaching, learning. *South China Morning Post.*

Misgna, H., On, B. W., Lee, I., & Choi, G. S. (2024). A survey on deep learning-based automated essay scoring and feedback generation. *Artificial Intelligence Review*, *58*(2), 36. DOI: 10.1007/s10462-024-11017-5

Moqbel, M. S. S., & Al-Kadi, A. M. T. (2023). Foreign language learning assessment in the age of ChatGPT: A theoretical account. *Journal of English Studies in Arabia Felix*, *2*(1), 71–84. DOI: 10.56540/jesaf.v2i1.62

North, B. (2014). *The CEFR in practice* (Vol. 4). Cambridge University Press.

Open, A. I. (2022). *Introducing Whisper*. OpenAI. https://openai.com/index/whisper/

Pedró, F., Subosa, M., Rivas, A., & Valverde, P. (2019). Artificial intelligence and language learning: Opportunities and challenges. *Working Paper on Language Policy. UNESCO*. https:// unesdoc.unesco.org/ark:/ 48223/pf0000366994

Peng, G., Zheng, H., & Wang, W. Y. (2004, December). Tone recognition for Chinese speech: A comparative study of Mandarin and Cantonese. In *2004 International Symposium on Chinese Spoken Language Processing* (pp. 233-236). IEEE. DOI: 10.1109/CHINSL.2004.1409629

Radford, A., Kim, J. W., Xu, T., Brockman, G., McLeavey, C., & Sutskever, I. (2023, July). Robust speech recognition via large-scale weak supervision. *Proceedings of the 40th International Conference on Machine Learning*, PMLR, 202, 28492-28518.

Shi, H., Chai, C. S., Zhou, S., & Aubrey, S. (2025). Comparing the effects of ChatGPT and automated writing evaluation on students' writing and ideal L2 writing self. *Computer Assisted Language Learning*, •••, 1–28. DOI: 10.1080/09588221.2025.2454541

Wang, T., & Cheng, E. C. K. (2021). An investigation of barriers to Hong Kong K-12 schools incorporating Artificial Intelligence in education. *Computers and Education: Artificial Intelligence*, *2*, 100031. DOI: 10.1016/j.caeai.2021.100031

Wang, Y. (2026). Exploring student engagement with multimodal generative AI in task-based Chinese language learning. *Computer Assisted Language Learning*, •••, 1–26. DOI: 10.1080/09588221.2026.2645428

Zakaria, A., & Aryadoust, V. (2024). A scientometric analysis of applied linguistics research (1970–2022): Methodology and future directions. *Applied Linguistics Review*, *15*(4), 1595–1619. DOI: 10.1515/applirev-2022-0210

Zhang, L., Wu, S., & Wang, Z. (2025). Phoneme-aware hierarchical augmentation and semantic-aware SpecAugment for low-resource Cantonese speech recognition. *Sensors (Basel)*, *25*(14), 4288. DOI: 10.3390/s25144288 PMID: 40732416

Zhang, T., Erlam, R., & de Magalhães, M. B. (2025). Exploring the dual impact of AI in post-entry language assessment: Potentials and pitfalls. *Annual Review of Applied Linguistics*, *45*, 274–293. DOI: 10.1017/S0267190525000030

KEY TERMS AND DEFINITIONS

Artificial Intelligence (AI): Artificial Intelligence (AI) is a broad field of computer science dedicated to creating systems and machines capable of performing tasks that typically require human intelligence, such as visual perception, decision-making, and natural language understanding. Rather than relying solely on explicit, 'hard-coded' programming, modern AI utilises machine learning and neural networks to identify patterns in vast datasets and improve its performance through experience. In the context of higher education and language assessment, AI serves as an overarching framework that powers specific tools, including speech recognition and adaptive algorithms, to automate complex evaluation processes. By simulating cognitive functions, AI enables the shift from static, one-size-fits-all testing toward dynamic systems that can interpret nuance, provide immediate feedback, and scale personalised instruction to a global audience.

Automatic Speech Recognition (ASR): Automatic Speech Recognition (ASR) is a subfield of computer science and computational linguistics that focuses on the translation of spoken language into machine-readable text. By leveraging acoustic and language models, ASR systems analyse the phonological features of an audio signal, such as pitch, duration, and frequency, to identify and transcribe words with increasing precision. In the context of Cantonese, ASR faces unique challenges due to the language's complex tonal system and the frequent use of sentence-final particles. However, modern ASR powered by deep learning and neural networks has become a cornerstone of language assessment, enabling the automated diagnosis of pronunciation accuracy and providing the foundational data necessary for real-time, interactive feedback in digital learning environments.

Cantonese: Cantonese is a major language variety of the Sinitic language family and twidely used in Hong Kong, Macau, and the Guangdong province of Chinese mainland. Within the linguistic landscape of Hong Kong, it serves as the dominant medium for everyday communication, media, and local cultural expression. Characterised by a complex phonological structure involving six distinct lexical tones and a rich array of idiomatic expressions, Cantonese exists in a state of diglossia. While it is the 'living' vernacular of the street and home, it is distinct from the formal written Chinese used in official documents. Beyond its regional roots, Cantonese is used by a vast diaspora in America, Canada, Europe, Malaysia, and Singapore.

Cantonese as a second language: In the Hong Kong context, Cantonese as a Second Language refers to the formal and informal acquisition of Cantonese by individuals for whom it is not their first language. Learners' backgrounds are remarkably diverse, encompassing international exchange students, expatriate working professionals, and non-local students from the Chinese mainland or overseas. Furthermore, Cantonese plays a critical role for the city's ethnic minority communities, for whom Cantonese proficiency is often the primary gateway to integration, enabling them to navigate local education systems, secure employment, and integrate into the broader social life. Given that Cantonese is the primary vehicle for everyday communication and an identity marker, Cantonese education focuses on bridging the gap between classroom grammar and the highly idiomatic, 'living' vernacular required for authentic participation in Hong Kong society.

Communicative competence: Communicative competence is a linguistic and pedagogical concept that refers to a learner's ability to use a language not just with grammatical accuracy, but with social and contextual appropriateness. First coined by sociolinguist Dell Hymes as a critique of purely structural views of language, the term encompasses four key dimensions including grammatical competence (vocabulary and rules), sociolinguistic competence (understanding social context), discourse competence (connecting ideas logically), and strategic competence (the ability to overcome communication gaps). In the context of AI-driven assessment, moving toward communicative competence means evaluating whether a student can successfully navigate a real-world interaction, such as a spontaneous conversation in Cantonese, rather than merely identifying their ability to conjugate verbs or recognise isolated tones in a vacuum.

Computer-assisted language learning (CALL): Computer-Assisted Language Learning (CALL) refers to the search for and study of applications of the computer in language teaching and learning. Rather than being a single method, CALL is a broad pedagogical approach that leverages digital technologies, ranging from interactive software and e-learning platforms to mobile apps and multimedia resources, to enhance linguistic acquisition. In modern higher education, CALL provides learners with a more flexible, self-paced environment, offering immediate feedback and access to authentic materials that traditional classrooms may lack. As the field evolves, CALL has increasingly integrated with artificial intelligence and big data, shifting from simple drill-and-practice exercises toward sophisticated, technology-mediated environments that foster immersion and communicative competence.

E-learning: E-learning, or electronic learning, refers to the delivery of education and training through digital resources, typically facilitated by the internet and electronic devices. Unlike traditional classroom-based instruction, e-learning allows for a more flexible and often asynchronous approach to education, enabling students to access course materials, attend virtual lectures, and participate in collaborative forums from any location. In the context of Hong Kong higher education, e-learning has evolved from serving as a simple repository for digitised handouts to becoming a comprehensive ecosystem of Learning Management Systems (LMS) and interactive platforms. This digital infrastructure proved essential during the shift toward remote instruction, fostering a blended learning culture where technology is used to personalise the educational experience and promote learner autonomy.

Generative Artificial Intelligence (GenAI): Generative Artificial Intelligence (GenAI) refers to a subset of artificial intelligence that focuses on creating new content, such as text, speech, images, or code, rather than simply analysing or classifying existing data. Built upon foundational models and massive datasets, GenAI utilises probabilistic algorithms to predict and synthesise output that mimics human creativity and reasoning. In the sphere of language education, GenAI goes beyond traditional 'static' software by enabling the creation of dynamic, unpredictable conversational scenarios. By integrating GenAI into assessment frameworks, educators can move toward highly personalised learning environments where the AI acts as an intelligent agent, capable of generating authentic dialogues, adapting the difficulty of tasks in real-time, and providing sophisticated, context-aware feedback tailored to each learner's specific proficiency level.

Large Language Models (LLMs): Large Language Models (LLMs) are advanced artificial intelligence systems trained on vast datasets of human language to predict and generate coherent, contextually relevant text. Unlike traditional rule-based software, LLMs utilise deep learning architectures to understand semantic relationships, nuances, and stylistic variations across diverse languages. Within the framework of language assessment, LLMs act as the 'cognitive core', capable of evaluating a learner's output against complex proficiency standards like ACTFL or CEFR. Beyond simple grammar checking, these models can facilitate dynamic interaction by generating adaptive questions and providing nuanced, qualitative feedback, effectively simulating the role of a human interlocutor in a conversational setting.

Oral Proficiency Interview (OPI): The Oral Proficiency Interview (OPI) is a standardised method for assessing spoken language ability through a live, spontaneous conversation between a certified interviewer and a candidate. Rather than testing specific classroom knowledge or memorised vocabulary, the OPI is a performance-based assessment that determines a speaker's functional ability to communicate in real-world contexts. The interview follows a specific structure, comprising an introduction, level checks, probes to test the speaker's ceiling, and a wind-down to elicit a representative sample of speech. This sample is then rated against established frameworks, such as the ACTFL Proficiency Guidelines, to provide a holistic measure of the speaker's global communicative competence, focusing on their ability to handle various social and professional tasks with accuracy and ease.

Proficiency testing: Proficiency testing is an assessment approach designed to measure a person's ability to use a language for real-world communication, regardless of where, when, or how that language was acquired. Unlike achievement tests, which evaluate how well a student has mastered specific material from a classroom curriculum, proficiency testing focuses on spontaneous performance and 'can-do' capabilities. These assessments typically align with standardised frameworks, such as the ACTFL Guidelines or the CEFR, to provide a reliable benchmark of a speaker's functional skill in reading, writing, listening, or speaking. By simulating authentic tasks and scenarios, proficiency testing offers a holistic view of a learner's communicative competence, making it a vital tool for academic placement, professional certification, and the validation of language skills in diverse social and professional contexts.

Putonghua: Putonghua, literally meaning 'common speech', is the official standard language of China. Based on the phonology of the Northern Chinese varieties and the grammar of modern literary Chinese, it serves as the primary medium of national administration, education, and media. In the specific sociolinguistic context of Hong Kong, Putonghua occupies a unique position as one of the three major spoken languages alongside Cantonese and English. While Cantonese remains the dominant vernacular for daily life, Putonghua is increasingly utilised in professional, governmental, and academic spheres, reflecting the city's deep economic and cultural integration with the Chinese mainland.

Reliability and validity: In the context of assessment, reliability and validity are the twin pillars of measurement quality that ensure an evaluation is both consistent and meaningful. Reliability refers to the stability and consistency of a test. A reliable assessment will yield the same results if administered to the same student under similar conditions multiple times. On the other hand, validity concerns the accuracy and relevance of the test, asking whether it actually measures the specific skill or knowledge it claims to assess. For instance, in an AI-driven language assessment, a tool is reliable if it consistently scores a learner's Cantonese proficiency the same way across different sessions, while it is valid if those scores truly reflect the learner's ability to communicate effectively in real-world Hong Kong settings. High reliability is necessary for a good test, but without validity, an assessment may consistently measure the wrong thing.

The ACTFL Proficiency Guidelines: The ACTFL Proficiency Guidelines are a set of descriptions used to evaluate functional language ability across the four skills of speaking, writing, listening, and reading. Developed by the American Council on the Teaching of Foreign Languages, the guidelines categorise proficiency into five main levels including Novice, Intermediate, Advanced, Superior, and Distinguished. Unlike achievement tests that measure what has been learned in a specific curriculum, ACTFL assessments are performance-based, focusing on what a learner can do with the language in spontaneous, real-world situations. Each level describes a specific hierarchy of functional tasks, the range of topics a learner can handle, and the degree of accuracy they can maintain, providing a standardised roadmap for tracking the development of global communicative competence.

The Common European Framework of Reference for Languages (CEFR): The Common European Framework of Reference for Languages (CEFR) is an international standard used to describe language ability across a six-point scale, ranging from A1 for beginners to C2 for those who have mastered a language. Developed by the Council of Europe, the framework provides a common basis for the elaboration of language syllabi, curriculum guidelines, and examinations across the globe. It shifts the focus from purely grammatical knowledge to 'can-do' descriptors, which define what a learner can achieve in real-world communicative contexts. By providing a transparent and coherent set of benchmarks, the CEFR enables educational institutions and employers to compare the language qualifications of candidates from different countries and educational systems with a high degree of consistency.

Text-to-Speech (TTS): Text-to-Speech (TTS) is a type of assistive technology that converts written text into synthesised audible speech. By utilising advanced signal processing and neural network architectures, modern TTS systems can move beyond robotic monologues to produce high-fidelity, natural-sounding audio that replicates human intonation and rhythm. In the context of language assessment, TTS serves as the final link in the conversational chain; it transforms the text generated by AI models into a spoken prompt, allowing the system to act as a responsive interlocutor. For a tonal language like Cantonese, sophisticated TTS is essential for providing learners with accurate phonological models, facilitating a fluid and immersive auditory experience that mimics real-world interaction.

Trilingualism and biliteracy: 'Trilingualism and biliteracy' refers to the overarching linguistic policy and educational goal in Hong Kong, which aims to develop a population capable of speaking three languages, Cantonese, English, and Putonghua, and reading and writing in two languages, Chinese and English. In this unique sociolinguistic framework, Chinese literacy usually involves the use of Traditional Chinese characters, while the spoken component is split between the local vernacular (Cantonese) and the national standard (Putonghua). This policy reflects Hong Kong's identity as a global financial hub and its integration with the Chinese mainland, positioning linguistic versatility as essential social and professional capital. Consequently, language assessment in this context must account for the complex interplay between these codes, ensuring that learners can navigate the city's diverse communicative landscape with both cultural sensitivity and technical accuracy.

Chapter 12
Collaborating With Artificial Intelligence in Higher Education:
Portfolios of Learning Evidence and Interview Assessments

Michael Johan von Maltitz
http://orcid.org/0000-0001-7308-651X
University of the Free State, South Africa

ABSTRACT

This chapter presents a teaching and assessment approach that incorporates generative artificial intelligence (GenAI) into learning while maintaining a focus on students' developing understanding. Drawing on a portfolio-and-interview model implemented in Mathematical Statistics, the approach combines longitudinal portfolios of learning evidence with individual oral interviews. The portfolio records both material collected from external sources, including GenAI where appropriate, and evidence of students' engagement with that material, while the interview provides a complementary opportunity for students to explain and defend their learning. The model is informed by Fink's taxonomy of significant learning, research on desirable difficulties and generative learning, and the AI Assessment Scale. The approach emphasises transparent GenAI use and the cognitive work that remains the responsibility of the student. The chapter describes the creation and assessment of portfolio content, the role of interviews, and practical considerations relating to implementation.

DOI: 10.4018/979-8-3373-9089-5.ch012

INTRODUCTION

Generative artificial intelligence (GenAI) is creating significant challenges for higher education assessment, particularly through the use of large language models (LLMs). Assessment systems and curricula can take considerable time to adapt to technological change, while students may adopt new technologies much more rapidly (Jarni & Gurr, 2024; Kandiko Howson & Kingsbury, 2023; Simelane & Pillay, 2024; Archana et al., 2025; Sousa & Cardoso, 2025; Xiao et al., 2025). The increasing capability of GenAI also creates difficulties for assessment practices that rely primarily on a completed product as evidence of learning. An essay, report, problem solution, theorem proof and application, or other academic artefact may provide limited information about the processes through which the student developed the knowledge presented in that product.

One response to this challenge is to restrict or prohibit the use of GenAI. However, an alternative is to reconsider what assessment is intended to demonstrate and to design learning and assessment activities in which students can engage with GenAI transparently while remaining responsible for their own learning. Such an approach is consistent with the emerging recognition that higher education should prepare students to use AI tools both critically and ethically.

This chapter presents a portfolio-and-interview approach to teaching and assessment in which GenAI can be incorporated into learning activities without making AI detection the primary mechanism for establishing student learning. Portfolios and oral interviews are established forms of authentic assessment, but each has limitations when considered in isolation. On the one hand, a portfolio can provide a rich longitudinal record of student activity and learning, but a completed portfolio may still provide limited evidence of a student's ability to explain or defend what it contains, especially considering the extent that GenAI could be used in the creation of such a product. On the other hand, an oral interview can provide direct evidence of students' understanding, but such a short discussion conducted in isolation provides a relatively brief view of learning and can introduce challenges relating to anxiety and assessor judgement. In the approach described here, the two components are intended to support one another: the portfolio provides a context in which learning develops and becomes visible over time, while the interview places value on students' ability to defend their learning.

The present chapter builds on this empirical evidence and on the author's experience of implementing and refining the approach over several years. The purpose is not to present the portfolio-and-interview model as a universally superior assessment method, but to explain how the two components can be designed to work together and how their principles can be adapted to a higher education environment in which GenAI is readily available. In particular, the chapter considers how the assessment process can shift attention from the production of a final academic product towards the development of learning over time and the development of students' ability to explain what they have learned. In this context, the central question need not be whether a particular product was produced entirely by a student or with assistance from GenAI. Instead, assessment can be designed to generate multiple forms of evidence about what students truly understand and how that understanding was developed. GenAI can therefore be incorporated into the learning process without necessarily reducing the cognitive effort required of students in their learning processes.

The examples in this chapter are primarily drawn from Mathematical Statistics, where the approach has been implemented and studied. This disciplinary context provides particular opportunities for students to develop portfolios containing textbook content, like definitions, theorems and proofs, exercises, problems with solutions, as well as statistical analyses, programming, and reflections. Although the underlying principles may be adaptable to other disciplines, such transferability should be regarded as a proposition for adaptation rather than an established empirical finding of the present research. Different disciplines may require different forms of portfolio evidence, interview questions, assessment criteria and approaches to GenAI use.

The purpose of this chapter is therefore twofold. First, it provides a practical account of how portfolios of learning evidence and interview assessments can be implemented as complementary components of assessment in a higher education environment in which GenAI is readily available. Second, it develops a conceptual basis for understanding how such a teaching and assessment process can maintain a focus on learning over time while allowing students to engage transparently and critically with GenAI.

CONCEPTUAL FRAMEWORK: LEARNING, COGNITIVE ENGAGEMENT AND GENAI

The portfolio-and-interview approach was developed and implemented in Mathematical Statistics courses at the University of the Free State (von Maltitz, 2023, 2026). The portfolio is built throughout the semester and contains evidence of students' developing understanding, including completed work, links to sources, corrections, reflections, and other artefacts through which students document and extend their learning. The distinctive feature of the approach is the way in which the portfolio and interview function together as complementary components of a process-oriented assessment. A portfolio shifts some of the emphasis of assessment away from a single completed product towards the development of learning over time. As students construct, revise, extend and reflect on the content they are choosing to include in their portfolios, this portfolio creation process becomes part of the learning experience. The interview serves a complementary purpose. Students know throughout the portfolio process that they may subsequently be required to explain or defend what they have presented. The interview is therefore not simply a mechanism for checking whether a submitted portfolio represents a student's own work; its anticipated presence can also influence how students engage with the portfolio and with their learning while it is being developed.

The portfolio-and-interview approach is *firstly* informed by Fink's (2003) taxonomy of significant learning, which identifies foundational knowledge, application (and communication), integration, the human dimension, caring and learning how to learn as interrelated dimensions of significant learning. In a mixed-methods study of a second-year Mathematical Statistics course, students completed questionnaires before and after the course addressing dimensions of significant learning based on Fink's (2003) taxonomy. The quantitative analysis found statistically significant increases across all measured dimensions, with the probability represented by Vargha and Delaney's A-statistic that a post-course response would be higher than a pre-course response exceeding 65% for every item (von Maltitz, 2026). The largest increase concerned students' confidence in using statistical terminology, while substantial improvements were also observed in their reported ability to explain, discuss and apply statistical concepts and proofs. The qualitative responses, analysed in more detail in earlier work, provide context for these quantitative findings. Students described improvements in the learning environment, professional communication and their ability to work consistently rather than concentrating their efforts around conventional tests and examinations (von Maltitz, 2023). The evidence therefore suggests that students experienced the portfolio-and-interview approach as supporting significant learning across the dimensions of Fink's taxonomy. While encouraging, the evidence does not, however, establish that the approach produces objectively better learning than all alternative assessment methods, nor does it provide a controlled comparison with other authentic assessment designs. The study used unpaired pre- and post-course responses and had a substantial reduction in questionnaire participation from 51 students at the beginning of the course to 27 at the end. The study also compared students' perceptions of the portfolio-and-interview approach with their perceptions of a more traditional learning and assessment environment. These limitations are important when interpreting the evidence and point towards further research comparing the approach with other authentic assessment designs.

A *second* theoretical consideration addressed by the portfolio -and-interview model concerns the cognitive demands created by the use of GenAI. Tools that can rapidly generate high-quality course content, like example problems and solutions or summaries and evaluations, create opportunities for cognitive offloading. However, GenAI can also be incorporated into activities that require students to question, evaluate, verify, transform and/or integrate the generated content into their learning material. Such activities are consistent with research on desirable difficulties and generative learning, which emphasises active cognitive engagement rather than simply producing a finished product (Bjork & Bjork, 2011; de Bruin et al., 2023; Fiorella & Mayer, 2016). In the approach described here, therefore, the educational value of GenAI depends on how its use affects the cognitive work required of students. When GenAI is incorporated into activities that increase rather than replace the cognitive work required of students, it may contribute to desirable difficulties and, potentially, longer-term learning (Bjork & Bjork, 2011), either because a heightened or changed form of attention is required or simply due to increased time-on-task (Rosner et al., 2015).

A *final* theoretical consideration is how GenAI can be incorporated into this portfolio-and-interview process, with students encouraged to use such tools transparently and critically. The AI Assessment Scale (AIAS) provides a framework for specifying different levels and purposes of AI use within assessment tasks (Perkins et al., 2025). Rather than treating GenAI use itself as the primary assessment problem, this approach shifts attention towards the kinds of learning that assessment should support and the evidence that can be used to demonstrate that learning.

The three perspectives introduced above operate at different but connected levels of the assessment process. Fink's (2003) taxonomy addresses what kinds of learning the assessment is intended to support, including foundational knowledge, application and communication, integration, the human dimension, caring, and learning how to learn. Research on desirable difficulties and generative learning addresses how students engage cognitively with learning activities, particularly the extent to which they actively process, evaluate, organise and integrate information rather than simply receive it (Bjork & Bjork, 2011; de Bruin et al., 2023; Fiorella & Mayer, 2016). The AI Assessment Scale (AIAS) addresses how GenAI may be used in these activities, allowing its role to be specified according to the purpose and cognitive demands of a particular task (Perkins et al., 2025).

Within the portfolio-and-interview model, these perspectives are brought together through the design of the learning activities and the evidence students are required to produce. The portfolio provides a longitudinal context in which students can develop, apply, integrate and reflect on their learning, while collaboration with GenAI content requires students to critically think about AI-generated material rather than simply accept it. The interview then provides an opportunity for students to explain and defend their understanding. The anticipated interview may also influence students' engagement with the portfolio throughout its development, because students know that the material they compile may subsequently need to be explained or defended.

The framework can therefore be represented as a progression from intended learning, through cognitive engagement and appropriately structured GenAI use, to longitudinal evidence of learning and its defence. This relationship is summarised in Table 1. The framework does not assume that GenAI is inherently beneficial or detrimental to learning; rather, its educational value depends on how its use is incorporated into activities and on the cognitive work that remains the responsibility of the student.

Table 1. Conceptual and assessment frameworks for the portfolio-and-interview model

Framework element	Primary question	Application in the model
Fink's taxonomy	What kinds of learning should be supported?	Defines the broader dimensions of learning that students are encouraged to develop and demonstrate.
Desirable difficulties & generative learning	What cognitive engagement should learning activities require?	Encourages students to actively collect, evaluate, organise, apply and integrate information.
AI Assessment Scale	How can GenAI be used in learning activities?	Specifies appropriate forms and levels of GenAI use according to the purpose and cognitive demands of the activity.
Assessment element	Primary question	Application in the model
Portfolio	How can learning development be made visible?	Provides longitudinal evidence of students' developing understanding, application, integration and reflection.
Interview	How can students demonstrate and defend their learning?	Provides direct evidence of students' ability to explain and defend their understanding.
Portfolio + interview	How can different forms of evidence reinforce learning?	Connects learning developed over time with students' ability to articulate and defend that learning.

PORTFOLIO CREATION

The portfolio is developed throughout the semester as a longitudinal record of students' engagement with the course and their developing understanding. It is more than collection (and collation) of completed academic products. Instead, students progressively collect, develop, organise and reflect on researched material as they work towards the learning outcomes of the course. The portfolio therefore provides a record of both the material students encounter and the ways in which they engage with that material during the learning process.

The portfolio contains two broad forms of content. Copied content consists of material obtained or adapted from external sources, including textbooks, lecture material, websites, other digital resources and, where permitted, GenAI. Evidence-of-learning (EoL) content consists of the student's own contributions that make aspects of their engagement with, and developing understanding of, this material visible. The two forms of content are complementary: copied content provides material with which the student can engage, while EoL content records aspects of what the student does with that material during the learning process.

Copied Content

The main content of the portfolio is the material that students collect and collate in the process of meeting the learning outcomes. In Mathematical Statistics or even the broader Mathematical Sciences, for example, this may include lecture material; textbook definitions, theorems and proofs; examples and exercises or problems and solutions; assignments; statistical analyses and computer code; class activities; and other relevant resources. Students are encouraged to build this collection throughout the semester rather than attempting to construct the portfolio retrospectively towards the end of the course. This is because portfolio-building is a time-consuming exercise, promoting learning in a manner that is consistent with evidence supporting time-on-task and distributed practice (Brint & Cantwell, 2010; Cepeda et al., 2006).

Copied content can be incorporated into a portfolio in different ways. Students may transcribe selected material, reproduce or adapt diagrams and examples, include extracts or links to resources, or incorporate material generated using GenAI. The purpose is not to maximise the amount of material collected, but to select and organise content that contributes to the learning outcomes and provides a basis for subsequent engagement. Digital resources make it possible to collect such content much more rapidly through copying and pasting, linking to videos, websites, or interactive apps, or even taking screenshots of those videos or apps. The time saved through these methods can instead be directed towards comparing and collating material from multiple sources.

Because copied content can originate from a range of sources, students should identify the sources from which such material has been obtained. The purpose is to make the origin of portfolio material transparent (and to distinguish it from EoL content). The level of formality required for referencing can be adapted to the purpose of the portfolio and the conventions of the discipline, but students and portfolio assessors should be able to identify where their copied content originated. This principle also applies when GenAI contributes to the development of portfolio material. Where GenAI use is permitted, students should record its use in accordance with the requirements specified for the relevant activity, which may include identifying the tool used and how the resulting material was modified (if at all) and incorporated into the portfolio. Such disclosure provides a record of the role played by GenAI in the development of the portfolio and supports the student's responsibility for the material ultimately presented. The purpose of this referencing is not to suggest that a portfolio is free from academic-integrity concerns. Rather, transparent attribution allows the portfolio to distinguish among material obtained from external sources, material generated or assisted by GenAI, and the student's own EoL content. This distinction is important because the portfolio is intended not only to record what students have encountered, but also to provide evidence of what they have done with that material in the process of learning.

Students should understand that material included in the portfolio may subsequently need to be explained or defended during the interview. The expectation of active defence provides an incentive to engage with copied content sufficiently to understand what has been included, regardless of where that content originated from. The portfolio should therefore represent material that the student is prepared to discuss with an assessor, while the interview provides an opportunity to explore the student's understanding of selected portfolio content.

Evidence-of-Learning Content

Copied content provides the material with which students engage, but its inclusion alone provides limited evidence of what students have learned from it. Evidence-of-learning (EoL) content is student-authored portfolio content that makes aspects of the student's engagement with, and developing understanding of, course material visible; it is any portfolio content that indicates the desired cognitive struggle in the learning process. Proper learning requires effort (Bjork et al., 2013), so another way to identify evidence of learning is to identify where effort was made in the portfolio. While the portfolio content is required to meet the learning outcomes of the course, evidence of learning is required to *show that the learning outcomes were actually met.* Students should be taught that evidence of learning is key to making their content defendable; it is key to turning content into knowledge or understanding. In short, copied content provides material with which students can engage, and EoL content records some of what students do with that material during the learning process.

EoL content is therefore an important complementary component of the portfolio alongside copied content, and it should also develop throughout the semester rather than being added retrospectively to a completed portfolio. This allows the portfolio to record aspects of learning that may otherwise disappear from the final product, including initial misunderstandings, questions, unsuccessful approaches, responses to feedback, and subsequent revisions. In this sense, an imperfect piece of work followed by a well-explained correction may provide particularly useful EoL because it makes a change in understanding visible.

In generating EoL content, students may, for example, triangulate and verify information, annotate copied material, explain a concept in their own words, identify and/or correct an error, connect one concept to another, apply a method to a new problem, evaluate an explanation, reflect on a difficulty they encountered, or describe how their understanding changed. These additions provide evidence of the student's engagement with the material and allow aspects of the learning process to become visible.

Triangulation. With the time-saving inherent in copying content from digital sources, students should be encouraged to compare and collate information – i.e. to triangulate copied content rather than relying uncritically on a single source. In this context, triangulation involves comparing information from multiple sources to evaluate its consistency. These sources may include, amongst others, textbooks, lecture material, peer-reviewed publications, reputable educational resources, discipline-specific forums and appropriately verified open-source resources. Where sources differ (in opinion, process, outcome, *etc.*), students can provide evidence of learning by documenting the investigation surrounding the disagreement and the determination of which interpretation is most appropriate for the context; the comparison itself is one way to generate EoL content. Triangulation is particularly relevant when GenAI is used as a source of copied content. Students engaging with unfamiliar material may not have sufficient prior knowledge to recognise inappropriate GenAI output, be it incorrect, incomplete, or simply outside of the required context. AI-generated explanations, examples, proofs, and problems with solutions should therefore be treated as material requiring evaluation rather than as authoritative content. Comparing such outputs with other credible sources provides one way of requiring students to verify material before incorporating it into their portfolios. In this way, GenAI can become part of the learning activity without replacing the student's responsibility for evaluating the information presented. GenAI is not the source of EoL content, but rather a seed for discussion.

Annotation and explanation. One of the simplest forms of EoL is annotation of copied content. Students can restate a concept in their own words, add omitted steps to a proof or calculation, identify assumptions, add an example, or clarify terminology. Annotation provides an opportunity for students to interact directly with material while retaining the original content as a point of reference (Marshall, 1997). In Mathematical Statistics, for example, a copied proof may be supplemented with explanations of why particular steps are required or how one result follows from another. The copied proof remains copied content; the student's explanatory additions constitute EoL content. With EoL content alongside the proof, an assessor can truly gauge the student's understanding of the tools or tricks used in a proof, or possibly even the history of the proof, giving the assessor a far clearer measure of the student's conceptual understanding.

Review, summary and synthesis. Students can also produce EoL content by reviewing or synthesising material collected from several sources. Where material has been triangulated, for example, a student might summarise areas of agreement, identify differences among sources, or explain why one formulation is more appropriate in a particular context. Summarising and integrating information require students to select and organise material and are consistent with generative approaches to learning (Fiorella & Mayer, 2016). The value of such summaries as EoL content lies less in reproducing the content concisely than in making the student's own interpretation and organisation of that content visible. It should be noted that LLMs are particularly adept at creating summaries, and students should be aware that it is the desired difficulty of personally summarising content that promotes learning. As such, a student's own voice should be encouraged in these endeavours, regardless of language ability.

Application and problem solving. EoL can also be demonstrated through the application of knowledge. In Mathematical Statistics, this may include solving problems, constructing or completing proofs, analysing data, writing or interpreting computer code, generating examples or counterexamples, or applying a statistical method in a new context. A completed solution alone provides some evidence of application, but richer learning evidence can be provided when students explain their reasoning, justify a choice of method, compare alternative approaches, or evaluate the limitations of a solution. Of course, EoL content of this nature will be more likely in later undergraduate courses, and perhaps not at first- and second-year level, where students are not necessarily making methodological choices yet. Similarly, where a problem or solution has been generated using GenAI, the student's evaluation, verification or modification of that material can be considered EoL content even though the original generated material is copied.

Correction and revision. Corrections provide a particularly useful form of EoL content because they can document changes in understanding over time. Students should therefore retain relevant initial work rather than replacing it completely when corrections are made. A correction can show what was originally attempted, what feedback or subsequent reflection identified as problematic, how the student's understanding changed in response, and the final corrected material. This creates a visible sequence from initial understanding, through feedback or reconsideration, to revised understanding. In the implementation described in this chapter, correction of work following formative feedback has become an increasingly important component of the portfolio; von Maltitz (2026) reports that a rubric criterion was subsequently introduced specifically to assess the extent to which students responded to feedback from the formative interview, although this change had not yet been formally evaluated.

Evaluation and integration. EoL content may extend beyond individual items of course content to demonstrate how students understand relationships within and beyond the course. Evaluation can involve comparing approaches, questioning assumptions, assessing the quality of an explanation or solution, or determining where a particular concept fits within the broader structure of the course. These items can also be easily listed as a guide for students if they are struggling to create EoL content. Integration involves connecting course material with other topics, other courses, prior knowledge, personal experience, or even professional applications. This corresponds closely with the integration dimension of Fink's (2003) taxonomy and provides opportunities for students to demonstrate that their understanding extends beyond isolated pieces of information within a singular context. Activities that require students to map relationships across a course can be useful for eliciting this form of EoL content.

Learning logs, journaling and self-reflection. Students may also document aspects of the learning process through work or learning logs, journals or short reflective entries. A learning log can record when particular material was studied, which sources were consulted, difficulties encountered, questions that arose, and how those difficulties were addressed. Journaling can provide a more developed account of students' experiences of learning, although requiring continuous formal journaling may create a substantial feedback burden for assessors, and may also put pressure on the time students have available for building portfolio content that meets the course learning outcomes. In the courses presented by von Maltitz (2023, 2026), there has been a shift towards the use of shorter in-portfolio reflections rather than a separate compulsory journal. Self-reflection is particularly useful when it moves beyond a general statement about whether an activity was easy or difficult. Self-reflection can support metacognitive regulation by encouraging students to monitor and evaluate their understanding, recognise gaps in their learning or misconceptions about content, and then consider how their subsequent learning strategies could be adjusted (Schraw & Moshman, 1995). Such monitoring is educationally important because students do not always accurately judge their own learning or select strategies that support long-term retention (Karpicke et al., 2009). Such reflection can be attached to assignments, corrections, class activities, interview feedback or other portfolio components. Its role is to make the student's interpretation of their own learning process visible rather than to provide evidence of authorship. In von Maltitz (2026), students are provided with a list of questions related to the dimensions of Fink's taxonomy that can be used to stimulate self-reflection responses, making the process much simpler for students not familiar with this practice.

GenAI should generally not be used to generate EoL content on behalf of the student, because its purpose is to make the student's own engagement and reasoning visible. This does not require GenAI to be excluded entirely. Depending on the activity and the specified AIAS level, an LLM might act as a sounding board, generate questions, challenge an explanation, provide formative feedback, suggest alternative approaches, or evaluate a draft against specified criteria. In such cases, the learning evidence lies in what the student subsequently does with that interaction: how they evaluate the response, what they accept or reject, how they revise their work, and what they can explain about the resulting material. As mentioned before, the role of GenAI should always be disclosed, so that the student's own contribution remains distinguishable.

Taken together, these forms of EoL content provide different ways of making aspects of learning visible over time. No individual annotation, summary, application, evaluation, correction, or reflection should be treated as definitive evidence that a learning outcome has been achieved, nor should particular writing characteristics be used to infer whether GenAI was involved. Rather, the accumulation of different forms of EoL content across the portfolio provides a richer basis for assessment, while the interview allows selected evidence and the understanding it represents to be explored through discussion.

INTERVIEW

The interview is the second component of the portfolio-and-interview model and provides an opportunity for students to explain and/or defend the learning represented in their portfolios. In the implementation described in this chapter, individual interviews accompany the formative and final portfolio assessments and are conducted online. Interviews typically last between 15 and 30 minutes and consist of approximately ten questions, although the format can be adapted according to the course, level of study, academic context, and purpose of the assessment. Some of the questions may be *prepared in advance*, having been given to the students during the semester when exploring those components of the course, or having been developed from the individual student's portfolio. Other questions may be *novel to the students*, constructed with the purpose of gauging a student's inherent or latent understanding of course content. The proportions of each type of question could be modified depending on the context.

The interview should not be viewed primarily as a mechanism for determining whether portfolio content was produced by the student or by GenAI. Rather, it provides a second and complementary form of evidence about the student's learning. The portfolio provides longitudinal evidence of engagement and developing understanding, while the interview provides an opportunity for the student to articulate that understanding. Portfolio content can therefore provide a starting point for questioning: students may be asked to explain an annotation, justify a solution, elaborate on a reflection, discuss a correction, compare alternative approaches, or explain material obtained from an external source or GenAI. The emphasis is on what the student understands and can explain about the material they have chosen to include.

The relationship between the portfolio and interview is central to the teaching and assessment model, although neither component is intended merely to compensate for weaknesses in the other. It is worth repeating that the portfolio provides the extended learning environment in which students develop, apply, integrate and reflect on their learning over time, while the interview creates an expectation that this learning may subsequently need to be articulated and defended. As mentioned in the conceptual framework, the interview has a role before it actually takes place: students construct their portfolios knowing that an assessor may ask them about any of the material they include. The anticipated interview provides an incentive for students to engage with portfolio content sufficiently to discuss it, rather than treating portfolio construction solely as the production of an assessable artefact.

The interview can also function as a learning activity rather than only as a summative assessment. Where appropriate, questioning can prompt students to reconsider an answer, identify an error, make a connection, or recognise a gap in their understanding. Moreover, the assessor can give correct answers to any student responses that were initially incorrect. As such, even an end-of-semester interview becomes a formative assessment. Mid-semester, however, such interactions can provide feedback that students subsequently use to revise their portfolios, with the resulting corrections and reflections becoming further EoL content. The relationship between portfolio and interview can therefore be iterative: portfolio evidence informs the interview, while feedback from the interview can contribute to subsequent portfolio development. This formative role has been part of the implementation described in this chapter, although the effectiveness of particular interview practices has not yet been independently evaluated, representing an area of possible future research.

GenAI can be incorporated into preparation for the interview without being used during the assessed conversation itself. Students can, for example, provide an LLM with course objectives, selected portfolio content or example interview questions and ask it to generate questions with which they can practise. They can use the LLM as a conversational partner, ask it to challenge their explanations, request follow-up questions, or compare their responses with suggested answers. Where interview questions are provided to students beforehand, GenAI can similarly be used to explore possible responses and identify areas requiring further study.

The educational value of this use, however, depends on students treating GenAI questions and answers as material for engagement rather than as scripts to memorise. An LLM's suggested response may differ from the level, emphasis, terminology or conversational style expected by the assessor, and its output may require verification. Students should therefore evaluate and adapt the generated material and use the interaction to identify gaps in their own understanding. In terms of the conceptual framework developed earlier, GenAI can serve as a practice or feedback partner while the cognitive responsibility for understanding and defending the material remains with the student.

The interview itself need not prohibit questions about GenAI-assisted portfolio content. Where students have disclosed the use of GenAI, an assessor may ask how it was used, why particular output was accepted or rejected, how information was verified, or what changes the student made to the generated material. Such questions shift the emphasis away from attempting to detect AI use and towards evaluating the student's understanding of, and responsibility for, the material presented. A student who has used GenAI appropriately should therefore be able to discuss that use as part of the learning process.

A discrepancy between the quality of a portfolio and a student's performance in an interview should, however, be interpreted cautiously. Difficulty explaining particular material may provide a reason for further questioning, but should not in itself be treated as evidence of inappropriate GenAI use or academic misconduct. Interview performance can be affected by factors unrelated to authorship or understanding, including anxiety and communication difficulties. Appropriate procedures for interpreting interview evidence, together with considerations of fairness, accessibility, moderation and assessor judgement, are addressed later in the chapter.

IMPLEMENTATION AND QUALITY ASSURANCE

The portfolio-and-interview model requires implementation decisions that extend beyond the design of individual learning activities. In particular, the time required for portfolio assessment and individual interviews affects scalability, while formative feedback and clear assessment criteria influence how students develop their portfolios and respond to assessment. The implementation described in the study this chapter is based on has evolved over several years, and the practices discussed below should therefore be understood as examples from that context rather than as requirements that will necessarily be appropriate in every discipline or institution.

Scalability and Workload

The principal constraint on scaling the portfolio-and-interview model is the time required for individual assessment. Portfolio assessment requires the assessor to review a substantial body of work before the interview, while the interview itself requires dedicated individual contact time with each student. In the implementation described by von Maltitz (2026), a class of approximately 100 students could be assessed by a single lecturer over a concentrated assessment period. Interviews of approximately 30 minutes were combined with portfolio assessments that, with experience, could generally be completed in approximately 20 minutes per student. This represented a substantial workload concentrated around the assessment periods and sometimes required work outside normal teaching hours. These figures should be regarded as implementation experience rather than evidence of a generally applicable capacity limit.

Scaling the approach to larger classes requires additional resources or changes to the assessment process. In a subsequent implementation with approximately 200 students, portfolio assessment was allocated to a teaching assistant while the lecturer conducted the interviews, with the interview period extended to approximately one month. The lecturer reviewed the portfolio and the teaching assistant's assessment before each interview, providing a form of moderation of the portfolio assessment. Other implementations might distribute interviews among several assessors, reduce interview duration, sample portfolio content differently (for example, reviewing only corrections and novel content in the final assessment), or reconsider the number of formative and summative assessment events. Each of these choices has implications for workload and assessment quality and should be determined according to available resources and the purpose of the assessment.

The workload should therefore be made explicit when the model is adopted. For example, 200 individual interviews lasting 15-30 minutes represent approximately 50-100 hours of interview time alone, before portfolio assessment, scheduling, administration and moderation are considered. The model should consequently not be described as inherently scalable. Rather, scalability depends on class size, interview duration, portfolio size, the number of assessment events, available assessors and institutional resources. An implementation that is manageable for a particular lecturer or programme may require substantial modification in another context.

It should be noted that in the implementation by von Maltitz (2023, 2026), the portfolio-and-interview model completely replaces traditional written tests and examinations. Thus, the workload required by the model is offset by the reduction in the time and effort required to create novel tests and examinations, as well as the time required for marking test and examination scripts.

Formative Critique and Feedback

Portfolio construction may be unfamiliar to students who are accustomed to traditional teaching and assessment methods, particularly where they are expected to both collect course material and to generate EoL content while preparing to defend their learning. Formative feedback is therefore an important component of the implementation described here. In addition to the formative portfolio-and-interview assessment, weekly online critiquing sessions have been used to provide students with examples of how portfolios can be developed and improved.

During these sessions, students can volunteer their portfolios for discussion, with a small number reviewed during each session in the same online environment that will be used for interviews. The lecturer works through selected parts of each portfolio, identifies areas that could be improved, highlights effective examples and explains portfolio expectations in the context of students' actual work. Because difficulties encountered by one student may also be experienced by others, discussing selected portfolios allows feedback to be shared across the class rather than repeated individually. Students in the earlier implementation specifically identified these critiquing sessions as useful aspects of the learning environment (von Maltitz, 2023). The sessions should nevertheless be understood as one implementation strategy rather than an essential component of the portfolio-and-interview model.

Formative feedback also connects directly with EoL through correction and revision. Feedback from portfolio critiquing sessions, assignment drafts or the formative interview can identify gaps in content, misunderstandings or opportunities for further development. Students can then retain their initial work, make corrections and document how their understanding changed. In the implementation reported by von Maltitz (2026), the model evolved to include an explicit rubric criterion assessing students' responses to feedback from the formative interview, although the effect of this modification has not yet been formally evaluated. Thus, formative assessment need not operate separately from portfolio creation: the student's response to feedback can itself become part of the longitudinal evidence of learning.

Where students' portfolios are displayed to peers during critiquing sessions, privacy and student expectations should also be considered. In the implementation described here, the sessions are not recorded. Students should know in advance how their work may be shared, and participation in public critique should be managed in accordance with institutional requirements and the educational purpose of the activity.

Assessment, Moderation and Quality Assurance

A clear rubric is important because the portfolio-and-interview model involves judgement across different forms of evidence. In the Mathematical Statistics implementation, the rubric considers aspects such as organisation, required course content, extra material that is considered as EoL content, corrections (responses to feedback), and assignments, together with performance during the interview. The detailed rubric used in the course is provided as supplementary material in von Maltitz (2026). The precise criteria and weightings need not be transferable across disciplines; rather, they should be aligned with the learning outcomes and with the forms of evidence students are expected to produce.

The combination of portfolio and interview evidence is important when interpreting student performance. Remember that a portfolio provides longitudinal evidence accumulated over time, whereas the interview provides a shorter opportunity for students to articulate and defend selected aspects of their understanding. Neither should automatically be treated as definitive when considered in isolation. A discrepancy between the two may indicate that further questioning or feedback is required, but it can have several possible explanations. For example, a student who demonstrates understanding during an interview but has produced limited EoL content may require further guidance in portfolio construction. Conversely, difficulty explaining strong portfolio material may reflect gaps in understanding, but may also be influenced by interview anxiety or communication difficulties. Such discrepancies should therefore not, by themselves, be interpreted as evidence of inappropriate GenAI use or academic misconduct.

Assessment judgement also creates questions of consistency and moderation. Where a single lecturer conducts the assessment, consistency can be supported through a clearly specified rubric, recordings of interviews, and consistent procedures across students. Where multiple assessors are involved in the portfolio assessment, additional calibration is advisable so that assessors develop a shared understanding of the criteria and expected standards. This could include discussing the rubric before assessment, reviewing exemplars, comparing assessments of a sample of portfolios or interviews, and moderating cases in which judgement is uncertain. These procedures are recommendations for implementation; inter-assessor reliability of the portfolio-and-interview model has not yet been formally investigated, and remains open for further research.

Fairness and accessibility should similarly be considered in the design of the interview. If oral communication itself is not the intended learning outcome, differences in fluency, processing speed or confidence should not inadvertently become the primary basis on which disciplinary understanding is judged. Students may also require reasonable accommodations associated with disability, language or interview anxiety. Appropriate arrangements will depend on institutional policies and the intended learning outcomes, but may include reasonable processing time, clarification or repetition of questions, accessible interview technologies, or other approved accommodations. These considerations do not reduce the requirement that students demonstrate understanding; rather, they help ensure that the interview elicits evidence of the learning it is intended to assess.

Privacy and data management require particular consideration where interviews are conducted online or recorded. Students should be informed about whether recordings are made, their purpose, who can access them, and how long they will be retained, with institutional requirements governing consent, storage and data protection followed. Recording may provide useful evidence for moderation or appeals, but it should not be assumed to be necessary in every implementation.

Finally, the rubric and associated procedures should support transparency for students as well as consistency for assessors. In the implementation described by von Maltitz (2026), the completed portfolio rubric is discussed during the interview, allowing students to receive immediate feedback and question possible marking errors. Making assessment criteria available before portfolio construction begins also allows students to understand what forms of content (both copied and EoL) and interview performance will contribute to the assessment. The purpose of quality assurance in this model is therefore not to eliminate professional judgement, but to make that judgement sufficiently transparent, structured and reviewable.

CONCLUSION

The increasing capability and availability of GenAI challenges assessment practices that rely heavily on completed academic products as evidence of student learning. This chapter has presented a portfolio-and-interview approach that responds by placing greater emphasis on the development of learning over time and on students' ability to explain and defend what they have learned. The portfolio provides a longitudinal record in which students collect, develop, organise, apply, integrate, and reflect on copied course material, with various forms of EoL content making aspects of their engagement and developing understanding visible. The interview provides a complementary form of evidence by allowing selected elements of that learning to be explored through oral discussion. Importantly, its anticipated presence can also influence portfolio development, because students know that material they include may subsequently need to be explained or defended.

The contribution of the model lies not in portfolios or oral interviews as individual assessment methods, both of which are well established, but in the way they are combined within a process-oriented approach that can accommodate transparent use of GenAI. GenAI material can form part of the copied content with which students engage, while the creation of learning evidence provides opportunities for students to demonstrate what they have done with that material. The AIAS can be used to specify appropriate levels of GenAI involvement in particular activities, while principles associated with desirable difficulties and generative learning provide a basis for considering the cognitive work that remains the responsibility of the student. The portfolio and interview then provide complementary forms of evidence through which dimensions of significant learning, as described by Fink (2003), can be developed and demonstrated. In this way, the model does not depend on reliably determining whether GenAI contributed to an academic product; instead, it seeks to design learning and assessment activities in which students remain responsible for curating and defending the knowledge represented in their work.

The approach nevertheless has important limitations. It has been developed and studied primarily within Mathematical Statistics at a single higher education institution, and the available empirical evidence should not be interpreted as demonstrating that it produces better learning than alternative authentic assessment approaches. Although the principles underlying the model may be applicable more broadly, transferability to other disciplines should therefore be regarded as a proposition for adaptation rather than an established empirical finding. Different disciplines and institutional contexts may require different forms of portfolio content, different uses of GenAI, different approaches to interviewing, and different assessment criteria. Implementation is also resource dependent: individual interviews and detailed portfolio assessment require substantial assessor time, and larger cohorts may require additional assessors or modifications to the assessment process. Questions of accessibility, fairness, moderation and assessor consistency similarly require attention when the model is adapted to new contexts.

These limitations also identify opportunities for further research. Comparative studies could investigate learning outcomes under the portfolio-and-interview model relative to other authentic assessment approaches, while implementations in other disciplines and institutions could examine which features of the model transfer successfully and which require adaptation. Further research is also needed on the interview component, including its formative role, the relationship between portfolio and interview evidence, and the ways in which anticipation of the interview may influence students' engagement during portfolio development. As the approach is extended to multiple assessors, inter-assessor reliability and moderation also become important areas for investigation. More broadly, future research could examine how different levels and forms of GenAI collaboration affect the cognitive engagement and learning processes that the model is intended to support.

The increasing sophistication of GenAI makes it progressively more difficult to infer student learning from the quality or authorship of a completed academic product alone. The response need not be limited to restricting GenAI or attempting to identify its contribution after the product has been submitted. Assessment can instead be designed to make students' developing understanding visible over time, to require active engagement with the material they encounter or generate, and to provide opportunities for students to express and defend what they have learned. The portfolio-and-interview model presented in this chapter offers one approach to achieving this: shifting the focus from determining who or what produced the product, towards establishing what the student has learned and can defend.

REFERENCES

Archana, S. N., Renjith, V. R., Padmakumar, P. K., C, S., & Aboobaker, N. (2025). Ai assisted learning and research: An exploratory study among university students and scholars. *Discover Education*, *4*(1), 390. DOI: 10.1007/s44217-025-00814-x

Bjork, E. L., & Bjork, R. A. (2011). Making things hard on yourself, but in a good way: Creating desirable difficulties to enhance learning. In Gernsbacher, M. A., Pew, R. W., Hough, L. M., & Pomerantz, J. R. (Eds.), *Psychology and the real world: Essays illustrating fundamental contributions to society* (pp. 56–64). Worth Publishers.

Bjork, R. A., Dunlosky, J., & Kornell, N. (2013). Self-regulated learning: Beliefs, techniques, and illusions. *Annual Review of Psychology*, *64*(1), 417–444. DOI: 10.1146/annurev-psych-113011-143823 PMID: 23020639

Brint, S., & Cantwell, A. M. (2010). Undergraduate time use and academic outcomes: Results from the university of california undergraduate experience survey 2006. *Teachers College Record*, *112*(9), 2441–2470. DOI: 10.1177/016146811011200908

Cepeda, N. J., Pashler, H., Vul, E., Wixted, J. T., & Rohrer, D. (2006). Distributed practice in verbal recall tasks: A review and quantitative synthesis. *Psychological Bulletin*, *132*(3), 354–380. DOI: 10.1037/0033-2909.132.3.354 PMID: 16719566

de Bruin, A. B. H., Biwer, F., Hui, L., Onan, E., David, L., & Wiradhany, W. (2023). Worth the effort: The start and stick to desirable difficulties (s2d2) framework. *Educational Psychology Review*, *35*(1), 41. Advance online publication. DOI: 10.1007/s10648-023-09766-w

Fink, L. D. (2003). *Creating significant learning experiences: An integrated approach to designing college courses*. Jossey-Bass.

Fiorella, L., & Mayer, R. E. (2016). Eight ways to promote generative learning. *Educational Psychology Review*, *28*(4), 717–741. DOI: 10.1007/s10648-015-9348-9

Jarni, N., & Gurr, D. A. (2024). A futures perspective on learning and teaching in higher education: An essay on best and next practices. *Trends in Higher Education*, *3*(3), 793–811. DOI: 10.3390/higheredu3030045

Kandiko Howson, C., & Kingsbury, M. (2023). Curriculum change as transformational learning.

Karpicke, J. D., Butler, A. C., & Roediger, H. L.III. (2009). Metacognitive strategies in student learning: Do students practise retrieval when they study on their own? *Memory (Hove, England)*, *17*(4), 471–479. DOI: 10.1080/09658210802647009 PMID: 19358016

Marshall, C. C. (1997). Annotation: From paper books to the digital library. *Proceedings of the 2nd ACM International Conference on Digital Libraries*, 131–140. DOI: 10.1145/263690.263806

Perkins, M., Roe, J., & Furze, L. (2025). Reimagining the artificial intelligence assessment scale: A refined framework for educational assessment. *Journal of University Teaching & Learning Practice*, *22*(7). Advance online publication. DOI: 10.53761/rrm4y757

Rosner, T. M., Davis, H., & Milliken, B. (2015). Perceptual blurring and recognition memory: A desirable difficulty effect revealed. *Acta Psychologica*, *160*, 11–22. DOI: 10.1016/j.actpsy.2015.06.006 PMID: 26134415

Schraw, G., & Moshman, D. (1995). Metacognitive theories. *Educational Psychology Review*, *7*(4), 351–371. DOI: 10.1007/BF02212307

Simelane, R. M., & Pillay, P. (2024). The evolution of assessment methods in higher education due to the shift to remote learning: A case study. *Research in Educational Policy and Management*, *6*(2), 393–414. DOI: 10.46303/repam.2024.41

Sousa, A. E., & Cardoso, P. (2025). Use of generative ai by higher education students. *Electronics (Basel)*, *14*(7), 1258. DOI: 10.3390/electronics14071258

von Maltitz, M. J. (2023). Encouraging significant learning in mathematical statistics through portfolios of learning evidence and interview assessments. *Proceedings of the 6th International Academic Conference on Education*. DOI: 10.33422/6th.iaceducation.2023.03.105

von Maltitz, M. J. (2026). Portfolios of learning evidence and interview assessments in a mathematical statistics course. *Journal of Statistics and Data Science Education : An Official Journal of the of the American Statistical Association*, *34*(1), 26–35. DOI: 10.1080/26939169.2025.2477151

Xiao, L., Pyng, H. S., Ayub, A. F. M., Zhu, Z., Gao, J., & Qing, Z. (2025). University students' usage of generative artificial intelligence for sustainability: A cross-sectional survey from china. *Sustainability (Basel)*, *17*(8), 3541. DOI: 10.3390/su17083541

KEY TERMS AND DEFINITIONS

Cognitive offloading: subcontracting a process in learning to an agent to ease the cognitive demand from the learner.

Desired difficulty: A difficulty in the learning process that increases cognitive demand, and, in turn, learning depth and retention.

Evidence of learning: student-authored portfolio content that illustrates a student's learning processes and proves that the course learning outcome are met.

GenAI: Generative Artificial Intelligence, usually based on Large Language model architecture.

Interview assessment: a structured online oral interview between of a learner, by an assessor, complementary to the portfolio, to provide additional evidence of the student's understanding.

LLM: Large Language model; a statistical neural network model that sequentially predicts the next token in a text based on vast quantities of training data.

Portfolios of learning evidence: a digital document containing course content and evidence that the student understands that content, and has met the course learning outcomes.

Chapter 13

Ensuring Fairness and Ethical Integrity in AI-Based Assessment Design

Imam Fadli
http://orcid.org/0009-0000-5303-8203
Universitas Islam Negeri Palopo, Indonesia

Nurul Fikriyyah Taqwa
http://orcid.org/0009-0004-3588-1212
Universitas Islam Negeri Palopo, Indonesia

Andi Husni A. Zainuddin
http://orcid.org/0009-0009-1915-6738
Politeknik Dewantara, Indonesia

Amelia Amelia
http://orcid.org/0009-0001-7499-455X
Universitas Islam Negeri Palopo, Indonesia

ABSTRACT

The use of artificial intelligence in assessment design in higher education provides new prospects for economies of scale, personalization and scalable feedback. It is, however, also accompanied by concerning ethical implications around fairness, bias, transparency and accountability of AI-based assessment systems. This paper investigates the problems associated with algorithmic bias in automatic evaluation tools, discussing fairness issues for a varied student population. It focuses on how ethical values such as justice, autonomy and beneficence shape good assessment practice. Safeguards might include the use of bias audits, validation methods and oversight from a human in the loop and culturally responsive design. Strong govern-

DOI: 10.4018/979-8-3373-9089-5.ch013

ment oversight and regulatory convergence are needed for AI-powered assessment to facilitate trust, accessibility and academic integrity. Ethical AI evaluation should eventually become a fusion of technological breakthrough, pedagogical responsibility and social equity.

1. INTRODUCTION: AI IN CONTEMPORARY ASSESSMENT DESIGN

1.1. Growth of AI-Generated Assessments in Higher Education

The integration of artificial intelligence (AI) into higher education has also increased over the last decade, pervading not only teaching and learning strategies but also student assessment protocols (Crompton & Burke, 2023; Liang et al., 2025). In the traditional domain of higher education, assessment development was carried out in a way that relied heavily on human judgment, as they were also responsible for creating tasks, including tests, grading rubrics, feedback processes, and marking criteria (Hooda et al., 2022). However, the need for scalable, effective personalized learning experiences has led institutions to adopt AI-driven technologies to support (and sometimes fully automate) various assessment-related activities. AI-based evaluations here refer to the development of items, adaptive quizzes, assessments of written responses, and automated feedback to learners through algorithms and machine learning systems.

Several factors are contributing to this growth. For one, the proliferation of digital learning environments and learning management systems has given us vast data on students' performance that AI can use to predict what they need to learn next or to customize assessment tasks. Second, the growing adoption of online and hybrid teaching models at large scale has heightened the need for assessments that support high student load and provide timely feedback . Automated assessment tools such as AI-mediated essay scoring, plagiarism detection, and adaptive testing systems have become appealing to institutions seeking to streamline workload while avoiding instructor overload (Iddrisu & Iddrisu, 2025).

Furthermore, developments in natural language processing and the use of generative AI also facilitate the creation of complex assessment systems that can generate human-like questions, simulate real problem-solving, or provide immediate feedback (Fitas, 2025). These developments in ICTs facilitate formative rather than summative assessments, as well as a continuous, circular process that tests learners' abilities without the need for high-stakes testing. Consequently, AI-made assessments are increasingly regarded as an essential feature of contemporary educational design, providing new opportunities for student-centered learning.

While these developments in AI have potential benefits, they also raise fundamental questions of quality, validity, and fairness when TAs are considered (Miller, 2024). As universities experiment with AI in test design, academics' roles change from standalone markers to facilitators and auditors of algorithm-supported systems. It has also highlighted the pressing need to investigate how AI-mediated assessment is reshaping academic standards, learning curricula, and institutional risk. Therefore, understanding the conditions that lead to rapid adoption of AI-based assessments is important for assisting their adoption in line with pedagogical needs and ethics in higher education.

All these studies exemplify the rapid expansion of AI use cases in educational assessment and their potential to improve efficiency and personalize learning experiences. The literature to date has primarily focused on technological capabilities, while paying less attention to integrating ethical principles, fairness, human involvement, and institutional governance into a single framework for assessment design. This divide indicates how we need to think about it — not just as tech innovation, but as grounded in educational responsibility.

1.2. Opportunities and Risks of Automated Evaluation Systems

AI-driven automated assessment systems offer great promise for improving assessment in higher education. The most commonly cited advantage is efficiency (Deepshikha, 2025). Universities often face large class sizes, inadequate teaching resources, and a need for high-quality, rapid feedback. Services such as AI-driven evaluation tools can streamline grading efforts – such as automatically scoring objective tests, evaluating written responses, and returning prompt feedback on performance. It allows educators to spend more time supporting students on an individual level, designing curriculum, and doing other high-level pedagogical work.

Another opportunity lies in personalization. They can also develop adaptive tests that change based on a student's performance level, serving up new questions that match the student's skill set. Adaptive interventions of this kind can be designed to promote deep learning by, for example, diagnosing weaknesses and guiding students into remedial study (Vindigni, 2023). Additionally, automated feedback systems can provide continuous formative assessment, enabling students to monitor their progress and develop skills on the fly. It is how AI-supported evaluation contributes to learner autonomy and self-regulation of learning.

But together with these benefits, the automatic assessors also bring significant threats (Tanberkan et al., 2024). One big issue is algorithmic bias. AI tools for assessments are built using datasets that could mirror historical inequities, assumptions about cultural context, and linguistic norms that may not be equally sensitive to students' groups. For example, automated essay scoring systems could unfairly penalize non-native English speakers or students with diverse socio-cultural backgrounds (Jiang et al., 2024). Such biases can result in unfair assessment, which is contrary to the values of fairness and inclusivity that higher education institutions seek to promote.

There is another danger associated with transparency and accountability. Most AI systems are black boxes; that is, their decision-making is not transparent to educators and students (Katsamakas et al., 2024). Under computer-automated assessment conditions, students experience difficulties in querying or translating their scores, and procedural justice issues arise regarding the ethics of questioning an action. Further, reliance on automation could compromise the teacher's role in context-based assessment and reduce assessment to technical measurements rather than a more facilitative approach to evaluating the learning experience.

There are also issues of academic integrity and trust. As AI is incorporated into assessment practices, students may wonder whether automated systems can truly reflect creativity, critical thinking, or higher-order reasoning. Meanwhile, generative AI resources could give rise to new forms of academic integrity violations, further challenging institutions' efforts to maintain originality in students' work (Francis et al., 2024). Therefore, although automated assessment systems are potentially transformative, their risks need to be rigorously assessed. That is to say, how efficiently one can balance efficiency and fairness with innovation/moral integrity, rather than finding out whether we are closer.

1.3. The Role of Fairness and Ethics in Assessment Practices

Fairness and justice in assessment have always been a cornerstone of fundamental considerations in higher education, given that what we evaluate constitutes an important context for students' learning, academic purposes, and subsequent employment (Uddin & Abu, 2024). Examinations are more than just technical instruments for measuring knowledge; they are also social-pedagogical performances rooted in institutional values, power, relationships, and culture. As AI- and machine-learning-based systems are increasingly employed in assessment design, there is a greater imperative to ensure that ethical considerations and fairness are taken into account.

From the standpoint of assessment objectivity, fairness is a concept that refers to the unbiased treatment of all individuals, such that neither an individual nor a group benefits or is disadvantaged systematically through the methods and criteria of assessment (Alonzo & Teng, 2023). Ethical review practices that incorporate open and inclusive processes, accountability, and respect for learners' diversity (Tierney, 2014). In conventional examination environments, educators have lamented the difficulty of maintaining these principles through meticulous construction, moderation, and subject judgment. But AI-based evaluations come with their own complications, as algorithms sometimes inadvertently reflect biases or obscure the reasoning behind assessment results.

The ethical questions that arise are especially salient when AI systems affect high-stakes decisions, such as course grades, degree completion, or scholarship eligibility (Bulut & Beiting-Parrish, 2024). If AI instruments produce or rate assessments in opaque, inscrutable ways, students may be treated unfairly, with no obvious protocols for recourse. And training and tuning AI systems with student data also raises privacy and consent considerations, requiring institutions to ensure robust governance to protect students' rights.

There is a correlation between fairness and trust in the educational system. Learners are also more likely to engage in learning when they believe assessments are credible, transparent, and fair (Li et al., 2025). On the other hand, unfair AI-mediated evaluation can also induce distrust towards instructors and institutions. It is particularly true in heterogeneous learning communities where students possess different first languages and come from diverse cultural backgrounds and socio-economic statuses. AI-based assessment tools will need to be critically evaluated to ensure they are IF and not used to prop up rather than break down structural inequalities.

Ethical AI-based assessment is not only a technical challenge but also a shared responsibility of educators, researchers, developers, institutions, and policymakers. Involving humans in decision-making and using ethical governance practices, bias-auditing processes, and explainable AI to ensure that Machine Learning (ML) assessment practices align with pedagogical values and uphold trust in education is another essential part of responsible implementation. While AI-assisted assessment has been a rapidly expanding area of research, most studies examine either technological possibilities or discrete ethical issues, such as algorithmic bias, explainability, or privacy. As a result, fair and explainable AI-based student assessments, with human oversight and institutional governance, have limited integration into a consistent ethical-use framework. In this chapter, we bridge these gaps by providing a collective lens for responsible AI adoption in education that supports and advances quality and equitable education while ensuring accountability.

In addition to these disjointed views now peppered across the discipline, this chapter contributes to a developing conversation on ethical artificial intelligence in higher education by presenting an integrated conceptualization of AI-based assessment design. Moving beyond purely technical performance characteristics of AI systems and focusing on ethical principles such as justice, autonomy, beneficence, and accountability, the chapter illustrates how ethics can inform assessment practices to address challenges including algorithmic bias, transparency, institutions, and governance. In addition, it provides a comprehensive schema of the concept that illustrates the need for bias mitigation, human-in-the-loop systems, culturally responsive assessment, and governance frameworks to support trustworthy AI-enabled assessment.

Figure 1.

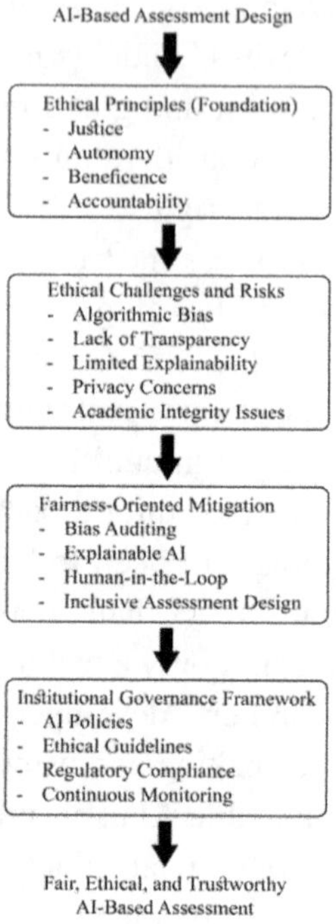

In Figure 1, we present the ethical framework of AI-based assessment in higher education. It shows that the ethical principles of justice, autonomy, beneficence, and accountability form the basis for addressing challenges such as algorithmic bias, transparency, explainability, privacy, and academic integrity. Each of these challenges is mitigated through bias auditing, explainable AI, human-in-the-loop oversight, and inclusive assessment design backed by institutional governance. Combined, these elements support equitable, ethical, and transparent AI-based assessment.

2. ETHICAL FOUNDATIONS IN AI-BASED ASSESSMENT

2.1. Principles of Ethics: Autonomy, Justice, Beneficence and Fidelity

The ethical incorporation of artificial intelligence (AI) into tertiary-level assessment must be grounded in commonly held moral principles that underpin sound decision-making (Williams, 2023). As AI begins to shape the design, administration, and analysis of student assessments, ensuring that these technologies advance educational aims while not trampling on students' rights or undermining institutional integrity is an ethical issue at the heart of assessment. The four principles of autonomy, justice, beneficence, and accountability offer an important organon for appraising AI-assessment systems.

Autonomy is defined as an individual's power to act and choose learning or assessment opportunities (Yusuf et al., 2025). In the case of AI-mediated assessment, autonomy is primarily tied to students' understandings of how assessments are constructed or marked, and to their opportunities to engage meaningfully with evaluations. When AI systems operate invisibly or are imposed on students without their knowledge, students may cede control over their own assessments. If we design for ethical assessment, AI should empower students rather than reduce them to a number.

Fairness and justice, linked to fairness and equity, have been regarded as crucial in the context of assessment (Unal & Hobe, 2025). AI tools have a way of accidentally reflecting social inequalities affirmed in past data or in algorithmic design. For instance, a set of automated scoring tools could disadvantage this type of student if it were trained on limited datasets. Moral justice demands that AI-based evaluation be accessible to succeed in, have the lowest possible levels of discrimination, and be favorable to inclusive examination practices amongst a range of students.

Beneficence includes the duty to maximize benefits and to avoid harm. Efficiency, personalization, and improved feedback are sometimes touted as benefits of AI system assessments (Avci et al., 2025). But beneficence is more than just technological creativity — it entails that AI tools actually enrich student learning, welfare, and growth (Suriano et al., 2025). Institutions should be responsible for verifying that AI does not cause adverse side effects, such as heightening fear and anxiety, misjudging performance, or restricting the quality of the human experience in assessment.

The last is accountability, covering the responsibility for AI-generated decisions. Unlike the conventional test, in which teachers are clearly responsible for test results, AI distribution accounts for shared responsibilities among teachers (and examiners), institutions, programmers, and system designers (Jia & Tu, 2024). Ethical accountability will also require clear governance arrangements that specify who is responsible when AI assessments are biased or inaccurate. Review and appeal mechanisms are crucial to human oversight of automated assessment, ensuring that systems reflect an institution's values and that educational ethics still apply. Combined, these four principles provide a comprehensive ethical framework for assessing the validity and legitimacy of AI-mediated assessment systems.

2.2. Integrity in Assessment and the Ethics of Test Preparation

Academic integrity is a core element of higher education and reflects values such as honesty, trust, fairness, respect, and responsibility (Suriano et al., 2025). With the growing integration of AI into the design and evaluation of assessments, academic integrity presents both new opportunities and profound ethical dilemmas. Responsible AI assessment design will be underpinned by the principle that technology-led innovation should not come at the cost of the authenticity of students' work or confidence in an institutional mode of assessment.

Artificial intelligence-based assessment tools may encourage academic integrity in multiple ways. Automated plagiarism detection tools, such as, support educators in recognizing non-originality in student work and in enforcing good citation habits. Likewise, AI analytics can spot anomalies in student submissions or test-taking activity and reduce cheating across the web (Williams, 2023). Such apps demonstrate how AI can support existing institutional initiatives for ethical academic practice, particularly in the era of large-scale digital learning.

However, AI also poses intricate challenges that can jeopardize academic integrity (Yaakob et al., 2025). Generative AI tools that write essays, solve problems, and even generate responses akin to research results have given rise to new forms of academic misconduct. Students can easily palm off AI-generated work as their own, further muddying the distinction between real assistance and fraudulent representations. These problems ask teachers and schools to disrupt traditional modes of identification and to disaggregate assessment methods that call for independent research, originality, and process-based assessment — ideally, not simply product.

In an AI era, responsible assessment design demands a pedagogical turn toward authenticity (Avci et al., 2025). These include modes of knowledge expression—reflective writing, project-based learning, and oral exams—and practices that expect a higher order of cognitive functioning than rote recall and data manipulation (oral examinations, collaborative problem-solving)—and are therefore less susceptible to AI-enabled malpractice, as they demand contextual engagement and require personal interpretation. Teachers should design tests that reward higher-order cognitive ability, making it harder for automated systems to supplant genuine student understanding.

There is also a significant ethical issue regarding the use of AI in grading and feedback (Kostopoulos et al., 2025). Automated grading is also highly dependent on validation that the tools actually measure what they are intended to measure, rather than merely correlate. If AI gets the student experience wrong, we risk a class of people who will be subjected to unfair grading practices and whose integrity will be weakened. Moreover, an over-reliance on automation may erode educators' professional responsibility and shift assessment away from human judgment.

Institutional responsibility is also central. Universities need to develop guidelines for the acceptable use of AI by students and teachers (Somabut et al., 2025). Ethical guidelines should cover transparency, consent, and the lines between AI-assisted work and academic dishonesty. It's also about teaching our students digital literacy and ensuring they learn to use AI tools and resources ethically and responsibly. And, in the end, academic integrity in assessment that uses AI can't be just about stopping cheaters; it has to foster a culture of ethical learning. Respected assessment practices have to balance innovation with trust, ensuring that AI enriches the quality of education rather than undermines its core values.

2.3. Transparency and Explainability as Ethical Requirements

Transparency and explainability are considered crucial ethical prerequisites for the responsible use of AI in education, especially when used in assessment processes (Du et al., 2024). With AI systems creating more and more test items, grading student work, and offering automated feedback, serious questions arise about how these decisions are made and whether they can be understood, defended, or contested. Without agreed-upon transparency, AI-mediated assessment threatens to erode fairness, trust, and accountability in higher education.

Transparency concerns how open AI processes are and the types of decisions made about everything related to the design of assessment tools, the data used in them, and the outcomes. In standard evaluation mechanisms, grading criteria are open to educators to explain and rationalize evaluation decisions through rubrics and professional judgment (Sperling et al., 2024). But most AI-based assessment systems rely on complex machine learning models that generate outputs that are not directly understandable or interpretable. This "black box" quality has ethical implications when students are assigned grades or feedback without knowing what they were given or how it was assessed.

Explainability builds on transparency, enabling AI to be interpreted in a meaningful way for users (Dikmen et al., 2021). Explanation in AI for assessment needs to provide human-readable rationales for automatically generated scores, present them as relevant contextual information, and facilitate educators in inspecting and confirming system outputs. Interpretability is crucial to procedural justice in the student model, as students are justified in knowing what factors go against them when they receive grades. And if no explanations will suffice, there's little room for appeal or redress of AI-assisted decisions that produce fundamentally unfair outcomes.

Transparency is also related to detecting bias and ensuring fairness. If organizations can't get their hands around that and understand what the AI models are doing, they can't see patterns of discrimination or identify scoring errors. An explainable system enables educators to assess whether particular student groups are unduly disadvantaged and to redress systemic unfairness (R. J. Chen et al., 2023). Therefore, transparency is a question not just of ethical principle but also of a measure for conducting fair assessments.

Research to date consistently points to transparency and explainability as requirements for building trust in AI-based assessment. However, transparency by itself is not a sufficient condition to guarantee ethical evaluation of AI-led applications. Instead, transparency may require complementary mechanisms, such as human oversight and accountability, as well as governance and an institutional framework. The results indicate that explainability should be considered part of a broader ethical ecosystem rather than a standalone element. Hence, transparency and explainability are essential for building students' trust in AI-assisted assessment, as acceptance depends on the legitimacy and clarity of automated decisions (Jia & Tu, 2024). To support responsible implementation, universities should ensure documentation, auditability, and human oversight so that AI complements rather than replaces educators' professional judgment (Savveli et al., 2025).

3. UNDERSTANDING BIAS AND FAIRNESS CHALLENGES

3.1. Algorithmic Bias in Assessment Tools and Datasets

One ethical concern in using AI to design and validate higher education assessments is ensuring that algorithms are free of bias (Kousha & Thelwall, 2022). Bias occurs when an AI consistently makes unfair predictions against specific individuals or groups (Barnes & Hutson, 2024). Where AI-enabled assessment is concerned, that bias may be circularly systemic. Moreover, it can come from the training data on which algorithms are trained, such as design biases already ingrained in an assessment tool and the social-technical environments in which these systems are built and used.

Training data is the primary source of algorithmic bias (Peters & Peters, 2022). AI-based testing instruments, including automated essay scoring systems and adaptive testing apps, depend on large datasets of past student responses and performance scores. If the datasets are not well-balanced and do not represent heterogeneous student profiles, the models can be more effective for some groups of students than others (Kizilcec & Lee, 2022). For example, data that are strongly biased towards native English speakers may negatively affect multilingual learners whose writing styles deviate in linguistic or cultural ways. Likewise, historical assessment data could be marred by current disparities in access to and success within education - if otherwise appropriate AI systems learn from these data, they might perpetuate (or exacerbate) such inequities.

Bias may also occur in measurement and labeling (Baker & Hawn, 2022). In supervised machine learning, an algorithm learns from examples that humans have explicitly labeled. If human judges have inherent racial, gender, class, or proficiency biases, these biases are likely to be reflected in the labels used to train the system (Chen, 2023). As such, AI systems might inherit the subjective refinement that was never meant to become an automated standard.

Another significant source is algorithmic decisions. Developers are required to select which characteristics or factors are more meaningful for evaluation, such as grammar complexity, word count, and response patterns (Lu, 2024). These decisions may reify restricted definitions of academic competence and neglect other ways students can express understanding. An extreme example is an AI-based language testing system that would favor standard forms of expression and place students whose modes of cultural communication differ from the academic mainstream at a disadvantage.

Context bias is also in play. The instruments of assessment are usually developed within an educational system and may not apply equitably across schools, disciplines, or cultures. An algorithm developed for one setting may prioritize unfair outcomes when applied to international/multicultural higher education. It is important to understand these sources of bias when designing ethical AI evaluations. Unless we are vigilant to these issues, ensuring the quality of data, model development, and contextual appropriateness, AI-based assessment tools could mirror existing inequalities rather than fostering equity and inclusion.

Taken together, the literature indicates that algorithmic bias originates from multiple sources, including training data, model design, and implementation contexts. While previous studies propose various technical approaches to reduce bias, fewer examine how pedagogical practices and institutional policies interact with technical interventions to promote equitable assessment. It highlights the importance of adopting multidisciplinary strategies to mitigate bias.

3.2. Equitable Considerations for Diverse Student Groups

The fundamental principle of equity provides students, regardless of their diverse personal backgrounds and learning circumstances, with a fair opportunity to collectively demonstrate achievement (Tai et al., 2022). The use of AI-supported evaluation models raises serious equity concerns, especially for diverse student communities whose ways of being and learning are not sufficiently accounted for in machine-scoring systems. Despite being touted as objective and predictable, AI tools tend to steer people into new forms of exclusion or disadvantage.

One significant equity issue is linguistic diversity. Many assessment AI systems, in particular Automated Writing Evaluation (AWE), are built from the perspective of dominant language use (Stephenson & Harvey, 2022). Students for whom English is a second language may be penalized by what would appear to them as rigid grammatical constructions or rhetorical forms not consistent with their first language. It may lead to lower scores, which are not indicative of content knowledge or critical thinking. Such inequalities erode equitable assessment practices and can deter students who speak multiple languages from participating.

There are also challenges related to cultural diversity (Douglas et al., 2023; Herzog-Punzenberger et al., 2020). The idea that assessment is culture-free does not hold water: students from different cultural backgrounds may bring competing task, argumentation, and expression schemas to bear. AI models that are not exposed to such cultural diversity in their training set can perceive these differences as errors rather than valid linguistic features of academic communication. With the internationalization of higher education, greater equity requires AI-based assessment systems to account for how differing forms of knowledge representation are regarded and presented.

Moreover, AI-induced assessment equity is further confounded by socio-economic inequality (Stephenson & Harvey, 2022). Students from disadvantaged backgrounds will be least likely to have devices, a stable internet connection, or access to AI-based learning. Learning assessment systems that presume equitable access to digital resources are likely also to intensify achievement gaps. Additionally, access issues may arise for students with disabilities in the context of AI assessments if these platforms are not designed to be accessible, such as by enabling compatibility with assistive devices or supporting alternative formats (Chima et al., 2024).

There are also equity concerns with algorithmic profiling (Bešić et al., 2025). Predictive analytics systems can leverage behavioral or performance data to predict student success, and these predictions can be used to characterize certain students as "at risk." While such analytics may be useful for targeted interventions, they also have the potential to stigmatize students and perpetuate deficit-based views. Without AI predictions in check, this might leave diverse learners trapped with lowered expectations or limited opportunities.

Equity demands deliberate inclusive design and continuous monitoring. Don't forget that institutions should also test AI assessment tools with a wide range of people, build in pedagogical and humane scrutiny, and mitigate (Stephenson & Harvey,

2022). Furthermore, equity cannot be automated. It is committed to recognizing diversity as a strength, not an obstacle to be standardized. At the end of the day, ensuring AI-driven assessments are designed fairly is key to preventing innovative technology from, in fact, replicating ingrained prejudices. Higher education must also leverage AI tools to promote equity and honor learner diversity, with fairness as a fundamental principle of academic life.

3.3. Effects of Biased AI Grading on Student Performance and Confidence

Such inequity in AI-based assessment systems can have a serious impact on student outcomes, institutional reputation , and trust (Raza et al., 2025). Evaluation influences academic advancement, graduation from the degree program, and career prospects. When AI-supported assessment yields biased or incorrect results, the implications go beyond technical errors; such mistakes can affect learners' motivation, self-confidence, and lifelong educational paths.

Distorted academic performance: one of the most pressing consequences of unfair AI assessment for students. Biased scoring mechanisms can marginalize certain groups of students, leading to lower grades, missed scholarships, or career advancement obstacles (Yin et al., 2025). These are the kind of inequities that can exacerbate longstanding educational gaps, especially for marginalized students. Feelings of unfair evaluation can lead to disengagement from the course, frustration, and decreased academic self-efficacy among students. It can lead to higher dropout or lower participation in challenging academic streams.

Meanwhile, partial AI judgments also challenge the construct validity of educational measurement. The assessment results are intended to demonstrate students' mastery of new concepts. Yet as AI systems focus on superficial signals, such as writing quality, standardized structure, or response length rather than the depth of understanding, students are wrongly categorized (Lim et al., 2023). It subverts the pedagogical purpose of assessment and, regrettably, can encourage students to game a system in which answers are designed not to serve as evidence of student learning but to admit students into an algorithm.

Trust is another important dimension. Student belief in the fairness and justice of the evaluation process is a fundamental principle of higher education (Bulut & Beiting-Parrish, 2024). But when examinations are perceived as biased, secret, or marked with favoritism, students' trust in the technology and in the educators or institutions that use it can erode. Especially when AI decisions are unexplainable, and students don't have clear avenues for appeal, trust is easily broken. This fracture in trust could lead to resistance toward AI-enhanced learning spaces and slow the acceptance of educational breakthroughs.

And more broadly, unethical AI-assisted assessment practices pose ethical and reputational threats to higher ed institutions. Universities that use unreliable or biased systems may face lawsuits, negative publicity, and a loss of credibility in their claims to pursue diversity and inclusion (Barnes & Hutson, 2024). To avoid these risks, robust governance can be established through bias auditing, transparent assessment processes, and human oversight, whilst students need to know how AI-assisted decisions are made so they can respond to or refute them. These countermeasures bolster the ethical implementation of artificial intelligence (AI) by protecting educational integrity and institutional credibility from compromise.

4. APPROACHES TO ENSURING FAIR AND ETHICAL AI EVALUATION

4.1. Detection, Auditing, and Validation Mechanisms for Biases

To ensure fair AI-supported assessment, systematic methods to detect, measure, and mitigate bias throughout the lifecycle of assessment design and implementation are required (Kolla et al., 2026). Institutions must establish bias-detection, auditing, and measurement strategies to guard against biases embedded in algorithm training data, model formation, and contextual deployment that may impact student outcomes for equity purposes (Fraidan, 2024). These boundaries are important not only as ethical responsibilities to be respected based on 'fairness' and the currency of trust, but also as a matter of academic integrity in automated assessment software.

For them, combating bias begins by defining discrepancies in AI's performance across various student groups (Yin et al., 2025). It includes examining whether the system provides varying scores or feedback for students with different demographic backgrounds (such as gender, ethnicity, language background, socio-economic status, disability). Statistical notions of fairness, for instance, group parity measures or comparisons to the error rates, can then be used to determine (if any) whether particular sub-populations get screwed more than others. For instance, an automatic essay-scoring system might need to be carefully tested so that multilingual learners are not unfairly graded down based solely on linguistic diversity rather than the quality of their content.

Auditing is an essential process of institutional accountability. Algorithmic audits comprise periodic, independent assessments of AI assessment tools to unearth covert biases, unintended regularities, or discriminatory consequences (Cheong, 2024). Examples of the form's audits might include checking training data for inclusive representation, evaluating feature selection methods to remove cultural biases, and testing model outputs across varying environments. Crucially, we should not view the auditing process as an all-or-none exercise; AI models develop over time, and educational contexts shift, which require ongoing surveillance and revision.

Validation methods also ensure that AI-based assessment aligns with pedagogical objectives and educational standards (Rabbi et al., 2024). Validation is the process of establishing evidence that automated testing methods effectively measure the intended learning outcomes and support sound decision-making. AI systems need to be subject to traditional standards of validity in assessment—content validity, construct validity, and consequential validity. For example, an AI is evaluating students' writing, and educators want to know it's testing for critical thinking and argument—not just surface features like vocabulary complexity or sentence length.

In addition, the participatory validation approach has the potential to increase equity (Johnson & McCaffrey, 2023). It has been demonstrated that the participation of teachers, students, and other stakeholders in the evaluation of AI tools helps spot context-related issues that a purely technical audit cannot capture. There is also a need for transparency in audit results and validation outcomes to enable institutions to defend the responsible deployment of AI. In the end, bias detection, auditing, and validation are fundamental steps to protect AI-driven assessment systems from reproducing systemic inequities.

4.2. Human-in-the-Loop Oversight and Educator Responsibility

Although AI technologies provide efficiency and scalability for assessment practices , there is a need for ethical assessment design in higher education to ensure appropriate human oversight (Lindsay et al., 2025). The need for human-in-the-loop underscores the importance of keeping teachers in the loop for AI-assisted formative and summative evaluation, rather than delegating authority to an algorithm. It is human judgment that provides contextual understanding, ethical responsibility, and pedagogical integrity.

AI-driven grading systems are advertised as fair and consistent. However, they fail to capture the complexities of human learning (Balducci, 2024). Machines may be less sensitive to creative, humorous, ironic, and other forms of expression, as well as to varying levels of formality. Teachers, however, may assess work more holistically by considering student performance relative to the learning trajectory and context, or the learner's character. Human supervision is required to ensure the assessment is a pedagogical rather than a purely technical outcome.

Human-in-the-loop monitoring comprises several tasks (Lindsay et al., 2025). Here, "AI-24/7" becomes noisy. The question is how to interpret the AI's evaluation of assessment items and/or its scoring outputs before they influence high-stakes decisions. AI might use imperfect or biased questions, misinterpret students' answers, or offer feedback that does not fit well pedagogically. Teacher review is thus essential to confirm the quality and fairness of automatic assessment units. Furthermore, teachers have a responsibility to promote transparency and communication with students (Gao et al., 2024). Students need to know when AI is used in assessment, how decisions are reached, and how they can challenge them. Human supervision allows students to contest automatic decisions, which helps maintain procedural fairness and trust.

The ethics of governance over AI-supported assessment that exploits new forms of automated decision-making needs to be in the hands of educators for contextualization, so that professional judgment remains dominant (Lim et al., 2023). It takes both AI literacy and institutional guidelines to ensure that AI becomes a decision-support tool—not an evaluator on its own—and that requires faculty development. Good to see how human-in-the-loop oversight mitigates the risks of automation bias, ensuring that assessment practices align with educational values and accountability.

4.3. Inclusive and Culturally Responsive Assessment Design Approaches

Diverse and culturally competent learning design is so critical to achieving equity, yet there's so little of it in machine-learning-based systems (Miller, 2024). The university population is becoming more heterogeneous, with a broader mix of students from diverse language, cultural, social-class, and ability backgrounds. If AI-led analyses are modeled on narrow (or the same) typical or idealized premises about knowledge, communication , and academic excellence, we may be unnecessarily leaving out or disadvantaging students.

The foundation of the practice is one in which diversity is perceived as a core educational asset rather than a challenge to homogenization (Ajjawi et al., 2022). AI systems should be designed and implemented in a manner that supports the expression of learning and the demonstration of knowledge through various means. For instance, AWE tools should be cognizant of multilingual learners' linguistic heterogeneity and avoid equating language proficiency with cognitive capacity. In the same way, culturally responsive assessment recognizes that students may organize arguments, narratives, or problem-solving in different ways depending on their cultural background.

Culturally responsive assessment design also includes ensuring that AI-generated test content is diverse (Nyaaba et al., 2024). Assessment items and cases should avoid favoring particular cultural mores or socio-economic conditions that might not be common among many students. If AIs generate test questions from biased training data, they can reproduce stereotypes or narrow culturally specific examples. Teachers will thus need to evaluate the AI-moderated tests for their relevance, inclusiveness, and cultural sensitivity.

Accessibility is yet another key element (Shailendra et al., 2024). AI assessment platforms that are truly inclusive must accommodate students with disabilities by being compatible with assistive technology and offering flexible assessment formats. An ethical approach to AI development involves universal design for learning, which considers whether assessments measure what students have learned or whether they can navigate technological hurdles.

Participatory approaches to evaluating these assessment tools further improve inclusivity by providing deeper insights into diverse student perspectives. Learners can identify potential fairness and accessibility issues that developers or educators might miss. Combining technical safeguards with educator scrutiny, inclusive assessment design facilitates equitable, valid, and reliable use of AI-enhanced assessment in higher education.

To summarize the preceding discussion, Figure 2 outlines the major ethical risks associated with AI-based assessment, their potential educational impacts, and corresponding mitigation strategies. This synthesis highlights the importance of integrating technical safeguards, pedagogical practices, and institutional governance to promote fair and trustworthy AI-supported assessment.

Figure 2.

Ethical Risk	Potential Educational Impact	Recommended Mitigation Strategy
Algorithmic bias	Unfair grading and unequal learning opportunities	Conduct regular bias auditing and use diverse, representative training datasets
Limited transparency	Reduced trust in AI-assisted assessment decisions	Implement explainable AI techniques and communicate assessment criteria clearly
Inadequate human oversight	Over-reliance on automated decisions and reduced professional judgment	Maintain human-in-the-loop review for high-stakes assessments
Privacy and data security risks	Unauthorized use of student data and loss of confidentiality	Establish robust data governance, privacy policies, and secure data management practices
Academic integrity concerns	Increased misuse of AI tools and compromised assessment validity	Design authentic assessments and implement appropriate AI usage guidelines
Cultural and linguistic bias	Disadvantage for students from diverse linguistic and cultural backgrounds	Apply inclusive and culturally responsive assessment design principles

5. GOVERNANCE, POLICY, AND FUTURE DIRECTIONS

5.1. Institutional Policies for Ethical AI Assessment Adoption

The ethical deployment of AI in higher education assessment is not just a technical issue that can be solved by enough 'safeguards'; it must be driven by robust institutional governance and policy frameworks that guarantee fairness, accountability, and transparency (Ajjawi et al., 2022). Now that AI-powered tech tools are being used more widely across higher ed, including in the design of assessments and even in grading and providing feedback (Jin et al., 2025), institutions should set policies on how to use them responsibly and protect student rights. With no one to regulate it, AI-supported assessment could widen the gap between haves and have-nots, compromise academic honesty, and foster mistrust of school evaluation systems.

Institutional policies provide the basis for how AI should be used in assessment (Plata et al., 2023). These policies need to articulate the intent and reach of AI-based assessment tools so that technology serves pedagogical aims rather than substitutes for human judgment (Choiriyah et al., 2025). For instance, universities could make explicit whether AI systems are deployed solely for formative feedback or also to support high-stakes grading decisions. Policies need to be clear that educators and institutions retain ultimate responsibility for the results of assessments, not machines.

Transparency is a core feature of ethical policy. Universities should demand transparency when AI technologies are used to generate or evaluate questions, to help students understand how their work is being judged (Perkins et al., 2024). Policy should address explanations, so that learners have understandable reasoning behind the machine's scores or other feedback. Additionally, transparent channels of appeal are necessary so that students can question AI-driven decisions and request human reassessment when applicable.

Another key aspect is data governance. AI testing systems depend on student data; privacy, consent, and surveillance are key concerns in their development (Pulijala, 2024). Institutional policies should govern what kinds of information can be collected, how it is stored, and its use, whether for training models or analysis. Students should learn about data practices, and we should establish norms and protections against misuse or unauthorized access.

Faculty development is equally important. Policies should require educators to be trained in AI literacy, ethical considerations, and bias mitigation (Karimi et al., 2023). As a result, teachers can become overdependent on AI output or miss the sight of discriminatory trends. Institutional standards ought to require professional educators to act responsibly and to check human-in-the-loop. In conclusion, the adoption of ethical AI evaluation rests on an organization's proactive commitment to fairness and rigor. Through strong policies, universities can help ensure that

AI-enhanced assessment tools improve the quality of education while respecting equity, accountability, and student trust in higher education assessment practices.

5.2. Regulations, Frameworks and Standards in Educational AI

Beyond institutional policies, ethical AI use in assessment is now increasingly influenced by broader regulatory frameworks and emerging standards (Yan & Liu, 2024). As AI deepens its role in education, governments, industry bodies, and international organizations are developing directives to ensure responsible, fair implementation. Regulatory attention is crucial owing to its influence on high-stakes outcomes (academic progress, certification, and job opportunities), making fairness and accountability core societal issues.

Educational AI regulatory policies usually address transparency, data privacy and discrimination concerns (Cuesta, 2025). Privacy laws, such as the General Data Protection Regulation (GDPR) in Europe, address legal obligations related to data collection and the active consent of individuals for the storage of their personal information. Such rules do matter in an educational context – AI-based testing systems typically handle personal information about students. Institutions must adhere to principles of data minimization and provide students with the right of access and the right to challenge decisions made by algorithms.

Another recent area that regulators seem to be paying attention to is algorithmic accountability (Alrawahna et al., 2025). Policymakers are growing wary of so-called black-box AI systems that make decisions without explainable reasoning. Determine the robustness of predictions based on these observations: Standards for explainable AI require that automated assessment results be interpretable and justifiable, especially those that impact students' grades or progression. A few frameworks suggest a right to human-in-the-loop review, capturing the sense that students should not be subject solely to automated decision-making with no possibility of appeal.

Equity and anti-discrimination criteria are similarly important (Yin et al., 2025). Educational AI tools need to be examined for bias outcomes that cause disadvantage to more vulnerable groups. Fairness audits, impact assessments, and reporting could be mandated for AI systems to prevent the drivers of inequalities from being replicated by them. These standards align with the overall goals and values of inclusive education and social justice.

Ethical AI governance is being advanced by professional organizations and international agencies (Z. Chen, 2023). UNESCO, for example, has published advice on AI ethics that highlights the importance of human rights, inclusion, and sustainability in education technology. Likewise, technical yardsticks for trustworthy AI are under development by standards bodies, including robustness, accountability, and fairness measures.

But regulatory landscapes vary across regions, and the governance of educational AI is still developing. Political development is often slower than technological innovation, leading to oversight gaps (Navneet & Chandra, 2025). Accordingly, it is not enough for universities to simply follow the law, but to be proactive in establishing best ethical practice. Regulatory frameworks and standards ultimately serve as important guardrails to ensure that AI-powered evaluation systems operate responsibly. Harmonizing institutional procedures with these higher-level governance structures is essential to ensure fairness, transparency, and trust in AI-supported higher education assessment.

5.3. Future Research Needs and Sustainable Ethical Assessment Innovation

The future, while still unwritten, must address pending ethical issues and sustainable innovation as the design of AI-mediated assessment proliferates in higher education (Bulut & Beiting-Parrish, 2024). Although current methods are providing promising advances in efficiency and personalization, there is also much to be done regarding fairness, transparency, and long-term educational integrity. Therefore, future research should adopt interdisciplinary methodologies that combine technical aspects with ethical, pedagogical, or socio-cultural dimensions.

One large and important research task is to develop fair-aware AI models. Today's assessment algorithms often fail to generalize well across student subpopulations, leading to unfair predictions (Verwoerd, 2025). In future work, a model designed using more representative datasets should be considered, and fairness constraints to the algorithmic design could be added. Focusing on subtler forms of discrimination (especially for multilingual learners and students with disabilities). Other ways to measure discrimination for diverse cultural groups.

Another hot topic is explainable and interpretable AI. Sustainable ethical evaluation needs a system that provides a good rationale for scores and feedback (Lim et al., 2023). Future work should explore how to achieve explainability without compromising model accuracy, and question the effectiveness of explanations for end users (educators and students). Users' perspectives on AI explanations also play a crucial role in trust building.

Pedagogical aspects of AI assessment will also need to be investigated in subsequent research. Automated assessment must not restrict learning to that which is observable, but must support broader educational aims such as critical thinking, creativity, and reflective learning. Research should investigate how AI can be used to augment assessments in both real-world and formative contexts, rather than reinforcing limited standardized tests (Prompiengchai et al., 2025).

Sustainability is another emerging concern. Progress in ethics cannot be achieved without long-term governance structures, ongoing audit processes , and flexibility in dynamic educational contexts (Anaroua et al., 2025). Studies need to investigate sustainable institutional models of AI governance; this should avoid empty consultative and collaborative exercises and focus on actual, participatory governance with students, educators, and policymakers. Moreover, environmental sustainability concerns related to massive AI systems, such as power-hungry model training, should be put in perspective through a distributed sustainability discourse.

And lastly, future research needs to attend to the global equity of AI testing innovation (Karim et al., 2025). In contexts where resources are low, higher education is likely to have less access to ethical AI tools, which may also widen global educational inequalities. Partnerships in research and open-source models can help drive more equitable access to reliable assessment methods. In summary, sustainable ethical assessment innovation necessitates the continuous development of technology–education values interplay. AI-based assessment in higher education, while benefiting from intelligent systems, can improve by adhering to the principles of fairness, explainability, inclusivity, and governance, maintaining ethical integrity and trust over time.

CONCLUSION

The role of artificial intelligence (AI) is changing how assessment practices are conducted in higher education–making them more efficient, scalable, personalized, and providing timely feedback. These opportunities are only possible when we implement AI within an ethical framework that protects educational values and students' rights. Assessment of Responsible AI goes beyond technical performance information to embed ethical principles, human judgment, transparency, inclusivity, and institutional governance into a coherent assessment ecosystem.

One lacking in multiple synergistic elements of interrelated systems categories, however, is that single individual technical solutions are a poor ethical standard with which to evaluate the trade-offs. This codification of ethical principles, when supplemented with explainable AI, bias mitigation, human-in-the-loop monitoring, and inclusive design and assessment frameworks for adaptive systems, helps keep automated systems aligned with pedagogical goals and their effects on diverse learners. At the institutional level, governance frameworks, alongside clear policies and mechanisms for ongoing evaluation, can reinforce accountability and facilitate the responsible implementation of AI across educational contexts.

Education-based AI technologies will advance, and key to sustainable implementation is collaboration among educators, researchers, developers, institutional

REFERENCES

Ajjawi, R., Tai, J., Boud, D., & Jorre de St Jorre, T. (2022). *Assessment for Inclusion in Higher Education*. Routledge., DOI: 10.4324/9781003293101

Al Fraidan, P. A. (2024). Anticipatory Thinking and AI-Driven Assessments: A Balanced Approach to AI Integration in Education Aligned with Saudi Vision 2030. *African Journal of Biomedical Research, 27*(3), 619–628. DOI: 10.53555/AJBR.v27i3.2560

Alonzo, D., & Teng, S. (2023). Trustworthiness of Teacher Assessment and Decision-Making: Reframing the Consistency and Accuracy Measures. *International Journal of Instruction, 16*(3), 1075–1094. Advance online publication. DOI: 10.29333/iji.2023.16357a

Alrawahna, A. S., Alzghoul, A., & Awad, H. (2025). The Impact of Artificial Intelligence on Public Sector Decision- Making: Benefits, Challenges, and Policy Implications. *International Review of Management and Marketing, 15*(5), 125–138. DOI: 10.32479/irmm.19419

Anaroua, F. I., Li, Q., Tang, Y., & Liu, H. P. (2025). *AI-driven formative assessment and adaptive learning in data-science education: Evaluating an LLM-powered virtual teaching assistant*. https://arxiv.org/abs/2509.20369

Avci, H., Lunn, S. J., & Hazari, Z. (2025). Exploring STEM educators' perspectives on the integration of AI-enabled technologies in teaching and learning. *Computers and Education Open, 9*, 100304. Advance online publication. DOI: 10.1016/j.caeo.2025.100304

Baker, R. S., & Hawn, A. (2022). Algorithmic Bias in Education. *International Journal of Artificial Intelligence in Education, 32*(4), 1052–1092. Advance online publication. DOI: 10.1007/s40593-021-00285-9

Balducci, B. (2024). AI and student assessment in human-centered education. *Frontiers in Education, 9*, 1383148. Advance online publication. DOI: 10.3389/feduc.2024.1383148

Barnes, E., & Hutson, J. (2024). *Navigating the ethical terrain of AI in higher education: Strategies for mitigating bias and promoting fairness*. Forum for Education Studies., DOI: 10.59400/fes.v2i2.1229

Bešić, E., Schulz, L., & Schmid-Meier, C. (2025). *Inclusion and Equity in Artificial Intelligence (AI): Analysis of Educational Policies in Austria, Germany, and Switzerland*. DOI: 10.21203/rs.3.rs-7232992/v1

Bulut, O., & Beiting-Parrish, M. (2024). The Rise of Artificial Intelligence in Educational Measurement: Opportunities and Ethical Challenges. *Chinese/English Journal of Educational Measurement and Evaluation*, *5*(3). Advance online publication. DOI: 10.59863/MIQL7785

Chen, R. J., Wang, J. J., Williamson, D. F. K., Chen, T. Y., Lipkova, J., Lu, M. Y., Sahai, S., & Mahmood, F. (2023). Algorithmic fairness in artificial intelligence for medicine and healthcare. *Nature Biomedical Engineering*, *7*(6), 719–742. Advance online publication. DOI: 10.1038/s41551-023-01056-8 PMID: 37380750

Chen, Z. (2023). Ethics and discrimination in artificial intelligence-enabled recruitment practices. *Humanities and Social Sciences Communications 2023 10:1, 10*(1), 567-. DOI: 10.1057/s41599-023-02079-x

Cheong, B. C. (2024). Transparency and accountability in AI systems: Safeguarding wellbeing in the age of algorithmic decision-making. *Frontiers in Human Dynamics*, *6*, 1421273. DOI: 10.3389/fhumd.2024.1421273

Chima, A. E., Abimbola Eden, C., Chisom, O. N., Adeniyi, I. S., & Scientia, M. (2024). Integrating AI in education: Opportunities, challenges, and ethical considerations. Https://Magnascientiapub.Com/Journals/Msarr/Sites/Default/Files/MSARR-2024-0039.Pdf, *10*(2), 006–013. DOI: 10.30574/msarr.2024.10.2.0039

Choiriyah, S., Ramadhan, S., Nugroho, A., Pembangunan, H. R. P., & Muharom, F. (2025). Artificial intelligence-driven learning assessment in faculties of education: An exploratory study. *Munaddhomah: Jurnal Manajemen Pendidikan Islam*, *6*(3), 482–495. DOI: 10.31538/munaddhomah.v6i3.1937

Crompton, H., & Burke, D. (2023). Artificial intelligence in higher education: The state of the field. *International Journal of Educational Technology in Higher Education*, *20*(1), 22. Advance online publication. DOI: 10.1186/s41239-023-00392-8

Cuesta, J. (2025). Gender bias in Artificial Intelligence. *Journal of Economic Policy Reform*. Advance online publication. DOI: 10.1080/17487870.2025.2579039

Deepshikha, D. (2025). A comprehensive review of AI-powered grading and tailored feedback in universities. In *Discover Artificial Intelligence*. DOI: 10.1007/s44163-025-00517-0

Dikmen, M., Burns, C., de Bruijn, H., Warnier, M., Janssen, M., Afchar, D., Melchiorre, A. B., Schedl, M., Hennequin, R., Epure, E. V., Moussallam, M., Leventi-Peetz, A.-M., Östreich, T., Giroux, M., Kim, J., Lee, J. C., Park, J., Hsu, T.-C., & Abelson, H. Mildaintrainings. (2021). Explainable Artificial Intelligence (XAI): Concepts, taxonomies, opportunities and challenges toward responsible AI. *Information Fusion*.

Douglas, K. A., Neumann, K., & Elena Oliveri, M. (2023). Contemporary Approaches to Assessment of Engineering Competencies for Diverse Learners. *International Handbook of Engineering Education Research*, 690–709. DOI: 10.4324/9781003287483-37

Du, H., Sun, Y., Jiang, H., Islam, A. Y. M. A., & Gu, X. (2024). Exploring the effects of AI literacy in teacher learning: An empirical study. *Humanities & Social Sciences Communications*, *11*(1), 559. Advance online publication. DOI: 10.1057/s41599-024-03101-6

Fitas, R. (2025). Inclusive education with AI: Supporting special needs and tackling language barriers. *AI and Ethics*, *5*(6), 5729–5757. Advance online publication. DOI: 10.1007/s43681-025-00824-3

Francis, N. J., Jones, S., & Smith, D. P. (2024). Generative AI in Higher Education: Balancing Innovation and Integrity. In *British Journal of Biomedical Science*. DOI: 10.3389/bjbs.2024.14048

Gao, R., Merzdorf, H. E., Anwar, S., Hipwell, M. C., & Srinivasa, A. (2024). *Automatic assessment of text-based responses in post-secondary education: A systematic review*. https://arxiv.org/abs/2308.16151

Herzog-Punzenberger, B., Altrichter, H., Brown, M., Burns, D., Nortvedt, G. A., Skedsmo, G., Wiese, E., Nayir, F., Fellner, M., McNamara, G., & O'Hara, J. (2020). Teachers responding to cultural diversity: case studies on assessment practices, challenges and experiences in secondary schools in Austria, Ireland, Norway and Turkey. *Educational Assessment, Evaluation and Accountability 2020 32:3, 32*(3), 395–424. DOI: 10.1007/s11092-020-09330-y

Hooda, M., Rana, C., Dahiya, O., Rizwan, A., & Hossain, M. S. (2022). Artificial Intelligence for Assessment and Feedback to Enhance Student Success in Higher Education. *Mathematical Problems in Engineering*, *2022*, 1–19. Advance online publication. DOI: 10.1155/2022/5215722

Iddrisu, H. M., & Iddrisu, S. A. (2025). Teacher Readiness to Use AI Tools in the Classroom. *International Journal of Research in Education and Science*, *11*(3), 494–510. Advance online publication. DOI: 10.46328/ijres.1314

Jia, X. H., & Tu, J. C. (2024). Towards a New Conceptual Model of AI-Enhanced Learning for College Students: The Roles of Artificial Intelligence Capabilities, General Self-Efficacy, Learning Motivation, and Critical Thinking Awareness. *Systems*, *12*(3), 74. Advance online publication. DOI: 10.3390/systems12030074

Jiang, Y., Hao, J., Fauss, M., & Li, C. (2024). Detecting ChatGPT-generated essays in a large-scale writing assessment: Is there a bias against non-native English speakers? *Computers & Education, 217*, 105070. Advance online publication. DOI: 10.1016/j.compedu.2024.105070

Jin, Y., Yan, L., Echeverria, V., Gašević, D., & Martinez-Maldonado, R. (2025). Generative AI in higher education: A global perspective of institutional adoption policies and guidelines. *Computers and Education: Artificial Intelligence*, *8*(4), 100348. DOI: 10.1016/j.caeai.2024.100348

Johnson, M. S., & McCaffrey, D. F. (2023). Evaluating Fairness of Automated Scoring in Educational Measurement. In *Advancing Natural Language Processing in Educational Assessment* (pp. 142–164). Taylor and Francis., DOI: 10.4324/9781003278658-12

Karim, N. A., Mat, C. M., Suhailah, I., & Noor, M. (2025). A Methodological Framework for AI-Integrated Alternative Assessments in Engineering Education. *Jurnal Kejuruteraan*, *37*(2), 807–819. DOI: 10.17576/jkukm-2025-37(2)-20

Karimi, H., Khawaja, S., Karimi, H., & Khawaja, S. (2023). The Impact of Artificial Intelligence on Higher Education in England. *Creative Education*, *14*(12), 2405–2415. DOI: 10.4236/ce.2023.1412154

Katsamakas, E., Pavlov, O. V., & Saklad, R. (2024). *Artificial Intelligence and the Transformation of Higher Education Institutions: A Systems Approach*. Sustainability., DOI: 10.3390/su16146118

Kizilcec, R. F., & Lee, H. (2022). Algorithmic fairness in education. *The Ethics of Artificial Intelligence in Education: Practices, Challenges, and Debates*, 174–202. DOI: 10.4324/9780429329067-10

Kolla, A. C., Takale, D. G., Mahalle, P. N., Sule, B., & Deshmukh, G. (2026). Mitigating Algorithmic Bias in Facial Recognition Technology: A Deep Learning Approach to Fairness in AI. In *Lecture Notes in Networks and Systems: Vol. 1457 LNNS* (pp. 423–438). Springer, Singapore. DOI: 10.1007/978-981-96-7496-1_34

Kostopoulos, G., Gkamas, V., Rigou, M., & Kotsiantis, S. (2025). *Agentic AI in Education: State of the Art and Future Directions*. IEEE., DOI: 10.1109/ACCESS.2025.3620473

Kousha, K., & Thelwall, M. (2022). *Artificial intelligence technologies to support research assessment: A review*. https://arxiv.org/abs/2212.06574

Li, J., Qu, L., Cai, T., Zhao, Z., Al Hasan Haldar, N., Krishna, A., Kong, X., Romero Macau, F., Chakraborty, T., Deroy, A., Lin, B., Blackmore, K., Noman, N., Cheng, J., Cui, N., & Xu, J. (2025). AI-generated content in cross-domain applications: Research trends, challenges and propositions. *Knowledge-Based Systems, 330*, 114634. Advance online publication. DOI: 10.1016/j.knosys.2025.114634

Liang, J., Stephens, J. M., & Brown, G. T. L. (2025). A systematic review of the early impact of artificial intelligence on higher education curriculum, instruction, and assessment. In *Frontiers in Education*. DOI: 10.3389/feduc.2025.1522841

Lim, T., Gottipati, S., & Cheong, M. (2023). *Artificial Intelligence in Today's Education Landscape: Understanding and Managing Ethical Issues for Educational Assessment*. DOI: 10.21203/rs.3.rs-2696273/v1

Lindsay, E. D., Zhang, M., Johri, A., & Bjerva, J. (2025). The Responsible Development of Automated Student Feedback with Generative AI. *IEEE Global Engineering Education Conference, EDUCON*. DOI: 10.1109/EDUCON62633.2025.11016572

Lu, W. (2024). Inevitable challenges of autonomy: ethical concerns in personalized algorithmic decision-making. *Humanities and Social Sciences Communications 2024 11:1, 11*(1), 1321-. DOI: 10.1057/s41599-024-03864-y

Miller, Wi. (2024). Adapting to AI: Reimagining the Role of Assessment Professionals. *Intersection: A Journal at the Intersection of Assessment and Learning*. DOI: 10.61669/001c.121439

Navneet, S. K., & Chandra, J. (2025). *Rethinking Autonomy: Preventing Failures in AI-Driven Software Engineering*. https://arxiv.org/abs/2508.11824

Nyaaba, M., Zhai, X., & Faison, M. Z. (2024). Generative AI for Culturally Responsive Science Assessment: A Conceptual Framework. *Education Sciences 2024, Vol. 14, Page 1325, 14*(12), 1325. DOI: 10.3390/educsci14121325

Perkins, M., Furze, L., Roe, J., & Macvaugh, J. (2024). The Artificial Intelligence Assessment Scale (AIAS): A Framework for Ethical Integration of Generative AI in Educational Assessment. *Journal of University Teaching & Learning Practice, 21*(06), 21. DOI: 10.53761/q3azde36

Peters, U., & Peters, U. (2022). Algorithmic Political Bias in Artificial Intelligence Systems. *Philosophy & Technology 2022 35:2, 35*(2), 25-. DOI: 10.1007/s13347-022-00512-8

Plata, S., De Guzman, M. A., & Quesada, A. (2023). Emerging Research and Policy Themes on Academic Integrity in the Age of Chat GPT and Generative AI. [AJUE]. *Asian Journal of University Education, 19*(4), 743–758. Advance online publication. DOI: 10.24191/ajue.v19i4.24697

Prompiengchai, S., Narreddy, C., & Joordens, S. (2025). *A Practical Guide for Supporting Formative Assessment and Feedback Using Generative AI.* https://arxiv.org/abs/2505.23405

Pulijala, S. (2024). Artificial Intelligence in Governance: Opportunities, Challenges, and Ethical Implications for Public Administration. *IJFMR - International. Journal of Multidisciplinary Research, 6*(6), 29990. Advance online publication. DOI: 10.36948/ijfmr.2024.v06i06.29990

Rabbi, H., Ehsan, U., Khan, R. A., Yasmeen, R., & Sehatkahani, M. A. (2024). *Development and validation of an AI-based model to predict the assessment outcomes of pre-clinical MBBS/BDS students.* DOI: 10.21203/rs.3.rs-5277982/v1

Raza, F. A., Singh, A. D., Kovilpillai, J. J. S., Hamdan, A., & Rajaratnam, V. (2025). Safeguarding integrity in AI-enhanced education: Stakeholder perspectives on accuracy, validity, and ethics in ASEAN. *European Journal of STEM Education, 10*(1), 22. DOI: 10.20897/ejsteme/17307

Savveli, I., Rigou, M., & Balaskas, S. (2025). From E-Government to AI E-Government: A Systematic Review of Citizen Attitudes. In *Informatics*. DOI: 10.3390/informatics12030098

Shailendra, S., Kadel, R., & Sharma, A. (2024). *Framework for Adoption of Generative Artificial Intelligence (GenAI) in Education.* https://arxiv.org/abs/2408.01443

Somabut, A., Tuamsuk, K., Lowatcharin, G., Traiyarach, S., & Kwangmuang, P. (2025). Preparing for the AI era: Science teachers' readiness and professional development needs for generative AI integration in secondary education. *Social Sciences & Humanities Open, 12*, 102259. Advance online publication. DOI: 10.1016/j.ssaho.2025.102259

Sperling, K., Stenberg, C.-J., McGrath, C., Åkerfeldt, A., Heintz, F., & Stenliden, L. (2024). In search of artificial intelligence (AI) literacy in teacher education: A scoping review. *Computers and Education Open, 6*, 100169. DOI: 10.1016/j.caeo.2024.100169

Stephenson, B., & Harvey, A. (2022). Student Equity in the Age of AI-Enabled Assessment: Towards a politics of inclusion. In *Assessment for Inclusion in Higher Education: Promoting Equity and Social Justice in Assessment* (pp. 120–130). Taylor and Francis. DOI: 10.4324/9781003293101-14

Suriano, R., Plebe, A., Acciai, A., & Fabio, R. A. (2025). Student interaction with ChatGPT can promote complex critical thinking skills. *Learning and Instruction*, *95*, 102011. Advance online publication. DOI: 10.1016/j.learninstruc.2024.102011

Tai, J., Ajjawi, R., Boud, D., & de St Jorre, T. J. (2022). Promoting Equity and Social Justice through Assessment for Inclusion. In *Assessment for Inclusion in Higher Education: Promoting Equity and Social Justice in Assessment* (pp. 9–18). Taylor and Francis. DOI: 10.4324/9781003293101-3

Tanberkan, H., Özer, M., & Gelbal, S. (2024). Impact of artificial intelligence on assessment and evaluation approaches in education. *International Journal (Toronto, Ont.)*.

Tierney, R. D. (2014). Fairness as a multifaceted quality in classroom assessment. *Studies in Educational Evaluation*, *43*, 55–69. Advance online publication. DOI: 10.1016/j.stueduc.2013.12.003

Unal, A., & Hobe, J. (2025). Preservice Teachers' Readiness for Integrating AI in Elementary Classrooms. *Journal of Education and Training Studies*, *13*(4), 34. Advance online publication. DOI: 10.11114/jets.v13i4.7785

Verwoerd, J. C. (2025). *Balancing Innovation and Ethics: A Framework for Responsible AI Integration in Educational Assessment*. DOI: 10.20944/preprints202508.1696.v1

Vindigni, G. (2023). Adaptive and Re-adaptive Pedagogies in Higher Education: A Comparative, Longitudinal Study of Their Impact on Professional Competence Development across Diverse Curricula. *European Journal of Theoretical and Applied Sciences*. DOI: 10.59324/ejtas.2023.1(4).66

Williams, R. T. (2023). The ethical implications of using generative chatbots in higher education. *Frontiers in Education*. Advance online publication. DOI: 10.3389/feduc.2023.1331607

Yaakob, M. A., Abdullah, M. R., Masruh, M. L. M., Yaacob, K. M. S. bin K., Azman, F. M. N., Suarni, A., & Hasanudin. (2025). Empowering Framework Sunnah Values: An Ethical Framework for Research in the Age of Artificial Intelligence (AI). *International Journal of Research and Innovation in Social Science*. DOI: 10.47772/IJRISS.2025.92900008

Yan, Y., & Liu, H. (2024). Ethical framework for AI education based on large language models. *Education and Information Technologies 2024 30:8, 30*(8), 10891–10909. DOI: 10.1007/s10639-024-13241-6

Yin, Z., Chinta, S. V., Wang, Z., Gonzalez, M., & Zhang, W. (2025). *FairAIED: Navigating Fairness, Bias, and Ethics in Educational AI Applications.* https://arxiv.org/abs/2407.18745

Yusuf, H., Money, A., & Daylamani-Zad, D. (2025). Pedagogical AI conversational agents in higher education: A conceptual framework and survey of the state of the art. *Educational Technology Research and Development*, *73*(2), 815–874. Advance online publication. DOI: 10.1007/s11423-025-10447-4

Chapter 14
Ethical Guardrail Framework for Generative AI In Academic Assessment:
Ensuring Fairness, Transparency, and Authenticity

Kevin Manu George
http://orcid.org/0009-0000-4995-3660
Christ (Deemed to be) University, Bangalore, India

Shivani Thapliyal
http://orcid.org/0000-0002-7285-2830
Christ (Deemed to be) University, Bangalore, India

ABSTRACT

This chapter reviews how the development of generative artificial intelligence (Gen-AI) has quickly become embedded in the assessment of higher education and the consequences of this development on validity, reliability, and academic integrity. Although Gen-AI allows evaluating with a high level of scalability, adapting feedbacks, and guided by data, it also poses severe threats, such as algorithmic bias, lack of transparency, hallucinated results, and undermined authentic learning. In this chapter, according to the authors, the conceptual and normative approach is used in order to synthesize literature, policy frameworks and pedagogical theory in order to overcome these difficulties. It suggests an Ethical Guardrails Framework which inserts the transparency, bias reduction, human-in-the-loop validation and

DOI: 10.4018/979-8-3373-9089-5.ch014

accountability controls into the AI-driven assessment systems. The framework makes Gen-AI an aiding force and not a substitute to human judgment making it fit within the institutional governance and international ethics.

1. INTRODUCTION

The landscape of teaching, learning, and assessment, in higher education, has been transformed quickly by generative artificial intelligence (GenAI). The ability of large language models to create sophisticated essays, explanations, computer code, summaries, feedback and more academic writing has made them a valuable set of tools. This increased availability of this tool has then led to many important questions about academic integrity and authorship in studies, fairness and transparency, and the use of artificial intelligence in the learning process. Yet, at the root of the issue for higher education is the question of how assessment will continue to offer valid and meaningful evidence of student learning, where generative AI has a role in producing assessed work.

Assessment is largely about making informed judgements about what one considers students' knowledge, understanding and capability to do. An assessment's value goes beyond just the task it takes and the grade it yields, it is about the quality of evidence it yields and the defensibility of the interpretations made from that evidence. Validity is thus a major concern in assessment. For Messick (1995), validity is the justification of interpretations made from assessment performance and for Kane (2013) it is a construction and evaluation of an argument that supports the interpretations and uses of the assessment results. In this view, evidence for assessment needs to be aligned with the desired learning construct in such a way that judgments about student achievement can be made.

This relationship between assessment performance and evidence of learning is complicated by the emergence of GenAI. The student's own written answer, for instance, could be very sophisticated in language, structure and arguments, and still include significant components of a generative AI system. The extent to which such a reaction reflects the student's own analytical skills depends on the assessment's construct and the extent to which the student is allowed to use AI. Many would say that it is not just the "use of artificial intelligence", but the way it is used which could impact the interpretation that can be reasonably drawn from the assessment evidence.

This distinction will be important especially given the varying impact of GenAI based on the assessment purpose. Unrestricted AI-generated text can also be distracting by introducing construct-irrelevant influences and cause a disconnection between observed performance and the intended construct. However, an assessment that is meant to assess a student's capacity to utilise, critique or manage the use of AI in a work environment would be entirely appropriate for AI involvement. Therefore, simply considering the use of AI as unethical or universally wrong is not sufficient to assess or design an assessment policy.

The challenge goes beyond validity to the authenticity of assessment. In authentic assessment, relationships between learning activities and the practices, contexts, and performances that students might experience outside of school are created, and the assessment process is oriented towards these relationships (Gulikers, Bastiaens, & Kirschner, 2004; Wiggins, 1998). As AI becomes more prevalent in the workplace, there is a tension for assessment designers. Narrowing what technologies students might be using in their work settings can limit the contextual authenticity of the task, but using AI to complete the cognitive activity under assessment could also undermine a task's meaningful assessment of individual competence. In AI-rich environments, therefore, it is important to consider what is being assessed, what role AI is playing in the task, and what evidence is needed to be shown to demonstrate competence.

Besides, Generative AI presents a disruption to traditional thinking around the production of assessment evidence. Evidence-centred approaches to assessment focus on the connection between claims about the learner, evidence needed to substantiate claims, and the tasks used to elicit evidence (Mislevy, Almond, & Lukas, 2003). In some cases, the use of AI has contributed significantly to the creation of a final assessment product, and the final product itself might no longer be sufficient evidence for some learning claims. This raises questions about how assessment tasks can reflect the process of reason, decision making, reflection, evaluation and independent judgement.

This is very important because assessment is also a tool for students to evaluate the quality of their work. When students are able to access systems that generate seemingly sophisticated academic products, assessment literacy and evaluative judgement play a larger role. Students are expected to critically assess the accuracy, relevance, credibility, limitations, and appropriateness of information generated by AI, not take it for granted. Carless and Boud (2018) and Tai et al. (2018) have studied the importance of students' ability to comprehend standards and make judgement about the quality of work. Recent research on generative AI also indicates that evaluative judgement is becoming a pivotal skill in AI-supported learning environments (Bearman, Tai, & Dawson, 2024).

These changes suggest that there is a need to go beyond AI governance principles to tackle the ethical challenges posed by GenAI. Current approaches focus on issues of transparency, fairness, accountability, explainability, and human oversight (Floridi et al., 2018; UNESCO, 2021; OECD, 2019). These principles may give some guidance on how ethical considerations are translated into design of assessment but by themselves cannot explain the impact of GenAI on the validity, authenticity, and interpretation of assessment evidence. However, over the past few years, there has been a growing interest in the field of assessment reform that extends beyond the focus on AI detection to more questions concerning validity, authentic assessment, assessment redesign, and evidence of learning (Bearman & Ajjawi, 2023; Ellis et al., 2024; Hao et al., 2024; Kaldaras, Akaeze, & Reckase, 2024; Lye & Lim, 2024).

This chapter addresses this by moving the conversation about ethical AI from AI governance to assessment theory. The chapter starts with established concepts of assessment and how they are affected by the challenges of GenAI, rather than starting with general concepts of ethics and applying them to higher education. It addresses four interrelated questions: What does it mean to be a valid assessment in an AI-rich environment? When AI becomes a part of professional practice, what does it mean to be an authentic performer? What proof is required to substantiate student learning claims? And how will assessment remain fair, transparent and have human evaluative judgement while recognising legitimate use of AI?

2. BACKGROUND AND CONTEXT

2.1 The Changing Landscape of Higher Education Assessment

Assessment is a key feature of higher education since it serves as evidence by which teachers evaluate the knowledge, skills, understanding and capabilities of students. There has been a paradigm shift in how assessment is delivered and managed with digital technologies, but there is a further paradigm shift with generative artificial intelligence (GenAI) that can provide a direct contribution to the creation of assessed work. This alters the linkage between learning outcomes and learning evidence for making decisions about learning.

2.2 Assessment Validity in an AI-Rich Environment

With the advent of GenAI, one of the critical questions is, does assessment evidence continue to support the intended interpretation of the student learning (Messick, 1995; Kane, 2013)? The use of AI does not negate the validity of an assessment, but rather the effectiveness of using AI depends on the type of learning construct being evaluated and the role given to AI. So the key question is whether the assessment is a reliable indicator of the skills it aims to measure.

2.3 Evidence of Learning

The evidence-centred approaches focus on how learning claims, the evidence needed to support those claims and the tasks that elicit that evidence are linked

(Mislevy, Almond, & Lukas, 2003). However, when the output is subject to the influence of GenAI, this relationship can become more complex, as the student's knowledge and reasoning may not be the main influence on the final product. The design of assessments may thus require the inclusion of other evidence (e.g., reflection, explanation, process documentation, or demonstration) as these are needed to support the intended learning claim.

2.4 Authenticity and Generative AI

Authentic assessment is linked to real life practices and contexts outside of the school environment (Gulikers, Bastiaens, & Kirschner, 2004; Wiggins, 1998). GenAI adds a conflict between authenticity and independent performance as AI is becoming ubiquitous in the workplace, and unchecked AI use can mask what is being evaluated. Thus, the design of the assessment should take into account the purpose of learning and real context, and decide which position the AI will hold.

2.5 Assessment Literacy and Evaluative Judgement

Assessment literacy and evaluative judgement are also more important in the context of GenAI. Students should assess AI-generated content for accuracy, relevance, credibility, and suitability for the subject. It is already acknowledged that the development of feedback literacy and evaluative judgement is a vital part of student learning (Carless & Boud, 2018; Tai et al., 2018). AI-based assessment can thus offer students opportunities to assess and apply AI outputs.

2.6 Ethical and Equity considerations

GenAI raises further issues around fairness, access, transparency, bias and accountability. Students may not have equal access to AI tools and AI literacy may vary, which may affect their performance on assessments; the output of the AI might contain errors or bias. Such anxieties are especially important when we consider that assessment has implications for students. Thus, rather than being assessed on their own, the broader principles of AI ethics have to be understood within the context of existing assessment requirements.

2.7 Towards Assessment-Centred Ethical Guardrails

AI governance frameworks already highlight key principles like fairness, transparency, accountability, and human oversight (Floridi et al., 2018; UNESCO, 2021; OECD, 2019). These principles do not, however, cover the validity and meaningfulness of assessment as a result of AI. This chapter, therefore, takes an assessment-centred approach where ethical guardrails become anchored in the following: Validity, Authenticity, Evidence of learning, Fairness, Evaluative judgement, Consequences, and Accountability. GenAI is thus not only considered an ethical threat but also a phenomenon that calls for a reevaluation of assessment theory and design.

3. REVIEW OF LITERATURE

3.1 Assessment Validity

To grasp the implications of generative artificial intelligence (GenAI) in higher education, it is essential to first understand its validity under a theoretical framework. Validity is fundamentally related to the extent to which evidence and theoretical argumentation are supporting the interpretations and uses that are drawn from assessment performance (Messick, 1995; Kane, 2013). So even if a task seems relevant or yields a numerical score, it is not valid as an assessment. Instead, validity is the extent to which the evidence produced by the assessment is reasonably associate to claims of knowledge, skills, or capabilities it is designed to assess.

Messick's (1995) unified conception of validity emphasises that validity incorporates considerations of construct representation and construct-irrelevant variance. Construct-irrelevant variance refers to performance being affected by factors that are not related to the construct being assessed, whereas construct representations refer to whether the assessment adequately represents the intended construct. This is very important in AI-assisted evaluation. When an assessment is designed to evaluate a student's independent analytical writing, but a lot of the performance is dependent on generative AI, then the output of the assessment may include parts that are not reflective of the student's independent analytical writing. However, if the intended construct involves the use of effective AI, limiting the use of AI might itself create construct irrelevant influences.

Kane's (2013) argument-based approach also conceptualizes validity as a series of inferences that link observed performance to the decisions or interpretations that are made based on that performance. It is useful for this perspective in an AI-rich environment, as the adoption of GenAI could impact various steps in this inferential chain. For instance, if the learner's written submission is very complex, the teacher might assume the student has a high level of analytical skills. However, inferences made from the evidence of performance to the level of capability may be strengthened if the submission appears to have been produced in significant part by AI.

The central assessment question is not whether AI has been used but whether the use of AI impacts on the defensibility of the intended interpretation of the assessment. The same AI application can be suitable for one assessment, or unsuitable for another, depending on the type of assessment and the circumstances in which students are expected to use the AI

Consequential implications of validity also exist. The assessment results may impact students' progression, certification, employment, and future opportunities. Thus, the implications of assessment practices cannot be detached from choices made about the use of AI. An assessment-centered approach to GenAI should, therefore, consider the impact of the technology on the meaning of the evidence, the premises of assessment judgements, and the implications of the judgements. This offers a theoretical grounding for the treatment of validity as a prime ethical constraint in assessment with AI.

3.2 Evidence-Centred Assessment

The second important theoretical underpinning for the understanding of assessment in AI-rich environments is evidence-centred assessment. Mislevy, Almond, and Lukas (2003) think of assessment as a domain that is shaped by the claims about the students that are made, the evidence needed to support those claims, and the tasks that are created that elicit that evidence. This strategy offers a helpful framework for rethinking assessment when generative AI can be directly incorporated into student work.

An assessment starts with a statement of what the learner knows, understands and is able to do. The educator then determines the evidence that needs to be collected to support that claim and then creates a task by which that evidence can be observed. First Claim then Evidence then Task is a form of this relationship. A teacher might want to set up that the pupil can critically analyze the various business strategies on his or her own. Relevant evidence can include the student's capacity to analyze information, to find solutions, to rationalize decisions, and to provide justification for a recommendation. This evidence can be elicited in a written report.

The model is complicated by the fact that GenAI can help create the assessment response without demonstrating the learner's reasoning or knowledge. Therefore, a polished final report may give evidence of the quality of the product, but not be enough to give evidence of the student's individual analytical process. The issue is not about the use of AI itself, but rather whether the evidence provided by the task is still adequate to substantiate the desired claim.

This view takes the conversation about assessment of AI away from detection. Rather than the question of whether an authentic text is an AI-generated product, the question educators should ask is what evidence is required to support the learning claim. If a final product is not adequate, assessment can include additional evidence types like drafts, oral explanations, reflective accounts, demonstrations, process documentation, or evaluating AI-generated products.

The evidence-centred view also advocated for differentiated solutions to applying AI. When using AI tools in an intentional way to investigate and communicate a problem, the AI output can be considered part of the assessment evidence, provided it is aligned with the problem's purpose. The assessment conditions may need to limit the use of AI if the claim involves independent thinking without technological support. Hence, the correct use of GenAI depends on the relationship of the claim, evidence, and task and not on a blanket rule of "allowed" or "not allowed".

This framework offers a valuable conceptual foundation for the redesign of assessments. It implies, that the assessment tasks should continue to produce adequate and relevant evidence of learning if AI is to be used in an ethical manner. This means evidence of learning becomes a key "guardrail" to prevent the unintentional erosion of the link between assessment performance and the learning claims resulting from it while technology is a part of the solution.

3.3 Authentic Assessment and Learning Theory.

But one more theoretical lens for exploring the influence of GenAI in higher education is provided by authentic assessment. Authentic assessment attempts to build meaningful links among learning activities, what kind of activities might a student encounter, standards, and performances that take place outside of school. Gulikers, Bastiaens and Kirschner (2004) name a number of dimensions of authenticity: the authenticity of the task, physical context, the social context, the form of assessment, and the assessment criteria. In the same way Wiggins (1998) calls for assessment that asks students to show something useful instead of the reproducing of information.

With the advent of GenAI, this sense of authenticity becomes problematic. AI technological tools are being widely integrated in professional and knowledge-based activities. Employers might require workers to engage with generative systems in a variety of settings, such as research, writing, coding, analysis, communication, decision making, etc. in many work areas/domains. If and when the use of AI is completely banned during assessment, this situation can then then significantly alter the contours of the assessment environment that remains today. But, unrestricted use of AI can pose the counter problem when the assessment aims to evaluate student skills that they can delegate to the AI system to execute on their behalf.

This tension highlights the danger that might be found in thinking that banning or allowing AI is synonymous with being authentic. The question to ask is whether the task conditions are suitable for the evidence for the measured competence. An assessment that asks students to develop their own argument, for instance, might not allow extensive use of AI support. An assessment that tests students' critical assessment and evaluation of AI-generated information, however, could have an AI as a component of the authentic task.

Designing assessments must start first with the learning outcomes and then, based on these outcomes, design what portion technology will have in the product. In his review, Biggs and Tang (2011) focus on constructive alignment between the intended learning, teaching and learning activities and assessment. In such an environment with AI, it is crucial for educators to reflect on the consistency of the use of GenAI tools with the ability being assessed. Also, focus on assessment criteria is important for achieving authenticity. When a student is asked to incorporate AI into a professional task, evaluations can be based on outputs from AI in addition to the quality of decisions made concerning the use of AI. These might include creating effective prompts, checking the information, determining a limitation, analysing outputs and making decisions.

Therefore, the GenAI can be utilized to go beyond the simple question of whether or not students used AI during an assessment. The bigger question is, whether the assessment reflects the proper human performance in an increasingly AI-driven landscape. Authenticity then goes to the role of being a strong ethical obstructor to ensure that the conditions for assessment are educationally defensible and are correlated with the conditions or practices for which a student is being prepared.

3.4 Assessment Literacy & Evaluative Judgement

Theoretically, assessment in the AI-rich environment can be understood by using assessment literacy and evaluative judgement. Assessment literacy is a student and teacher understanding of the purpose, standards, criteria, processes and evidence of assessment. Evaluative judgement specifically means the ability to make judgement decisions regarding quality of work products. The capacities are important as assessment not just a way for teachers to evaluate pupils, but also a way for pupils to evaluate and develop the skills to improve themselves.

Carless and Boud (2018) stress the value of student feedback literacy and students' ability to interpret, apply and respond to feedback. Evaluative judgement is also believed to be an important capability in education which helps students to identify and judge for quality, as suggested by the authors of the report, Tai et al., (2018). As students work with generative AI, these ideas become more and more pertinent.

An AI can generate answers that seem elegant, authoritative, coherent and well-formed but draw untrue facts and/or incorrect reasoning, refer to nonexistent sources or show a restriction of context. Students need to have more than just the technical expertise to use AI systems. They need to be able to critique and judge whether the AI-generated response is accurate, relevant, well supported, and fits the disciplinary context.

It alters possibilities for the role of assessment. But instead of considering AI as a threat to student learning, classroom assessments can be created to ask students to make evaluative judgements regarding AI-generated products. For instance, the students may have to find vulnerabilities in an argument produced by the AI, check the credibility of the sources it used, evaluate it against credible information, correct their own arguments, and justify their corrections.

This is supported by recent research on generative AI and evaluative judgement, which suggests a new set of skills should be equipped to making valid judgements of the quality of work in contexts where AI has become a significant factor in the creation of that work (Bearman, Tai & Dawson, 2024). Assessment can then move from measuring just the creation of an answer, to measuring how students interpret, challenge, "improve" and defend answers they have created using technological assistance.

It is also important in terms of the perspective that it will have on teachers. It is essential for teachers to have assessment literacy to know when the use of AI will enhance learning and when it will undermine the assessed construct that they're trying to assess. They need to be able to identify situations where using AI is an acceptable part of the assessment and situations where there is a need for independent work to be demonstrated.

Therefore, understanding the importance of assessment literacy and evaluative judgement must be included within an ethical practice of GenAI. While banning tech alone won't suffice, so will a lack of judgment for students and faculty to both use and question and evaluate AI. This introduces evaluative judgement as a additional element of the proposed assessment centred system of guards.

4. GENERATIVE AI AND THE TRANSFORMATION OF ASSESSMENT

Generative Artificial Intelligence (GenAI) is reshaping the landscape of higher education assessment by impacting the way students complete assessment tasks, as well as how educators interpret the evidence that comes out of those tasks. Earlier technologies in education were mainly for the delivery, administration, or evaluation of assessments, while GenAI can actually be used to create written, visual, analytical, and computational outputs. This presents a reason to reflect on existing beliefs and theories linking student achievement to proof of learning. The debate over the validity of assessments, reconstruction of assessments, authenticity of assessments, and evaluative judgement has been growing in recent years, as we have started to think more about valid assessment, redesign assessment, authenticity, and evaluative judgement (Bearman & Ajjawi, 2023; Ellis et al., 2024; Hao et al., 2024). The impact of GenAI is thus far not equal on all types of assessment. They rely on the purposes for which students are being prepared, the format of the assessment, the purpose of using AI, and the evidence needed to support claims of student achievement.

Figure 1. **From Assessment Theory to Ethical Requirements**

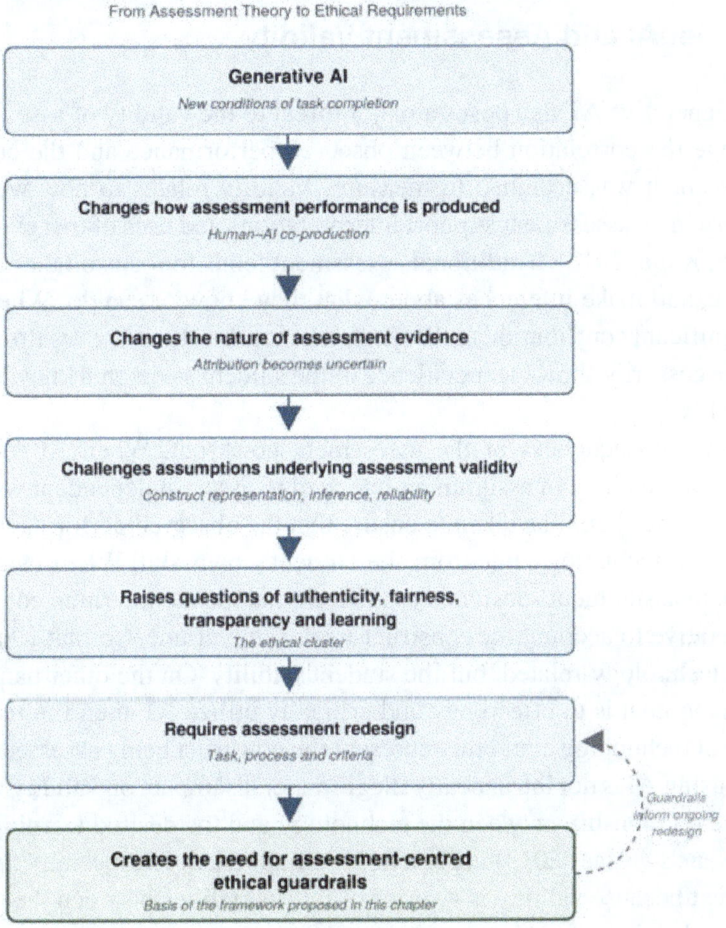

The same assessment may impact the measures of independent writing versus an assessment tailored to measure the ability to critically evaluate AI generated information. This is not an issue of whether or not to allow the use of AI, but how the use of AI can be made to be aligned with the purpose and validity of assessment. This needs to change from a technology-focused question to analysis focused on assessment. The remainder of the document looks at how GenAI engages with six key aspects of assessment: validity, evidence of learning, authenticity, academic integrity, fairness and equity, and evaluation judgement. These dimensions highlight the need for more than just institutional measures or limitations to respond to GenAI ethically. They need assessments that can produce meaningful, equitable and defensible evidence of learning and are designed for a world where students are increasingly interacting with intelligent digital systems.

4.1 GenAI and Assessment Validity

Generative AI also poses a major threat to the validity of assessments as it may change the correlation between observed performance and the construct that the assessment was designed to measure. Validity relates to how well evidence and theory in an assessment support interpretations and uses of that evidence (Messick, 1995; Kane, 2013). Traditional assessment tends to focus on the what students are doing, and make inferences about what they know or can do. When GenAI makes a significant contribution to that performance, however, the resulting product might not necessarily show clear evidence of the student's personal knowledge, reasoning, or skills.

The consequences of the assessment construct. When AI-generated work is incorporated into an assignment intended to assess independent written communication, care should be taken to ensure that the observed performance does not stem from the technology but from the student's own skill.When using AI-generated work in assignments designed to measure independent written communication, it's imperative to account for construct-irrelevant variance so that what gets observed isn't technology-related, but the student's ability. On the other hand, if the desired learning goal is to effectively and critically utilize AI, then limiting access to this type of technology could misrepresent the construct being assessed. This is to show that using AI is not intrinsically illegitimate. It's impact on validity varies according to the relationship between the technology and the desired learning outcome.

Kane's (Kane, 2013) argument-based approach is especially applicable in this context because validity is a series of interpretations between the observed behaviors and claims of student competence. These interpretations could be impacted by GenAI if a polished product is considered proof of something the student has not been able to produce on their own. For instance, a student could submit a thorough analytical report that was created with significant support from AI. The report could be well written and the assessment claim accurate, but the evidence might not be adequate to support the assessment claim when it is about the student's independent analytical reasoning.

The challenge is not just detecting AI written content, but also identifying the quality of the writing. The question, therefore, is not if, but how, to determine the quality of the writing. AI detection systems can alert to the presence of AI, but their detection does not mean that the assessment interpretation is invalid. A more basic question is: is there enough evidence from which the teacher can draw a conclusion that supports the desired statement of learning?

This can be tackled by the design of assessment to be more explicit about learning outcomes and evidence. When applicable, teachers can add oral explanations, process evidence, drafts, reflections, demonstrations, and/or critical evaluation of AI output. These methods may not be used for all constructs, but rather may be used depending on the construct.

So, for GenAI, educators need to rethink about validity as an ongoing relationship among construct, task, technology, evidence, and interpretation. This creates a sense of assessment validity as an ethical concern and forms the theoretical underpinning for the proposed Ethical Guardrails Framework.

4.2 GenAI and Evidence of Learning

As GenAI becomes more prevalent, it is important to ask the question of "what constitutes good evidence of student learning? Evidence-centred assessment is a view of assessment as a relationship between claims about learners, the evidence required to support those claims, and the tasks that would elicit the evidence (Mislevy, Almond & Lukas, 2003). Such a relationship is becoming even more relevant when the AI systems are directly involved in the creation of assessment outputs.

A traditional written assignment can yield a final product that represents what a student knows, reasons, can research, and can communicate. Where one or more of the elements of the product are a product of a generative AI system, however, the connection between the product and the student's underlying capabilities may become less clear. A good essay may show that a good product is possible, but it can't show that the student has the knowledge or reasoning on his own to create a good product.

But it is not to say that the end products have disappeared. Instead, the evidentiary standards for specific evaluations might require re-evaluation. If the intended learning claim involves a process (e.g. reasoning, decision making, critical analysis, independent problem solving), teachers might need further evidence which makes the process more visible. This could be in the form of drafts, reflective explanations, oral questioning, demonstration, working notes, decision rationale, or assessment of AI-generated content.

With this method, the role of AI detection is also altered. Detection aims to identify whether there is AI involvement in an output or whether an output is influenced by AI. Assessment for ECA, on the other hand, questions whether the evidence that is available is adequate to support the learning claim. The difference matters, because a situation might exist in which the use of AI is wholly suitable for an assessment. An example of this is an assessment that explicitly asks students to "produce a first response using GenAI and then assess its accuracy, make edits, and provide reasons for their edits. In a task like this, evidence of learning might be in the student's evaluation and reasoning, rather than in the AI-generated response.

Hence, the first step in the design of assessment is to ask, what does the student have to do to support the educator's educational claim? The type and amount of evidence should be based on the answer. This view helps to inform more flexible and purposeful assessment redesign. Wherever AI is available, a teacher can determine if there is adequate evidence provided from the final product or if further evidence is needed to demonstrate learning and understanding. In higher education, in which assessment may have multiple functions among them, it is especially so.

The product itself is no longer the focus and the underlying evidence of assessment judgement becomes a central focus. Making sure that assessment provides adequate evidence of learning not only becomes an ethical duty but also a critical boundary condition for the use of AI in assessment.

4.3 GenAI and Authenticity

In the context of widespread access to generative AI, there's a growing significance of rethinking assessment in terms of authenticity. Authentic assessment aims at creating genuine links between learning activities and world or workplace contexts, practices, standards, and performances that students will encounter outside of school (Gulikers, Bastiaens, & Kirschner, 2004; Wiggins, 1998). However, with the advent of GenAI, this principle is becoming increasingly complex as AI is increasingly becoming a part of professional and knowledge-based activities.

A ban on AI in assessment could thus impose constraints on conditions that are different from those in today's professional practice. If you're a business graduate, a marketing professional, a programmer, a researcher, a finance professional, a designer, or a communicator, you're likely to be using AI in your workflows on a frequent basis. When considering the importance of authentic assessment, the use of technology in the assessment process may not be suitable to remove technology from an activity if it is a component of the professional job.

Meanwhile, the use of AI in an unrestricted manner can compromise authenticity when the central ability an assessment is designed to assess is the same ability that it is using. For instance, if an assignment is intended to assess the student's independent capacity to construct and present an argument, using GenAI to generate a large portion of the argument could hinder the student's ability to demonstrate his/

her independent skill. The resulting work may look like a professional product and may offer some evidence of the individual's ability, but not much.

It is therefore important to carefully consider the role of AI in the task. So what is the question? Is there AI? Is there using AI? The question is: Is there using AI, in the context for which students are being prepared, and is that usage authentic? Students can use AI as a productivity or research tool in some assessments, as this is a legitimate use. In the latter, AI might be limited due to the fact that the ultimate goal is to perform independently.

This separation also provides room for new possibilities of authentic assessment. Students might be asked to assess AI business recommendations, recognize gaps and flaws in AI business analyses, audit sources of information, rewrite AI-generated code, or explain their rationale behind making decisions when incorporating AI. These tasks can be a more accurate reflection of current workplace practice and still measure discipline knowledge and judgment.

The design of the assessment then must ensure consistency between intended learning objectives, real contexts, assessment tasks and assessment criteria (Biggs & Tang, 2011). If AI is used in a meaningful and responsible way within the context of real-world professional practice, then, assessment criteria can be designed to measure the effectiveness and responsible use of the technology, rather than just whether or not the students used it.

This demands authenticity to be reconsidered rather than thrown away in the case of GenAI. The goal should be to develop assessment contexts that are representative of meaningful professional and disciplinary practice and in which students have responsibility for the competencies being evaluated. When it comes to meaningful assessment, then, authenticity emerges as a moral boundary to avoid when considering the use of AI.

4.4 GenAI and Academic Integrity

Academic Integrity has traditionally been linked to values like Honesty, Correct Attribution, Originality, and Responsible Scholarship. However, the advent of GenAI has complicated these tenets as students are now able to produce significant chunks of academic writing on tools that are easily accessible and increasingly powerful. Therefore the issue of unauthorised assistance, authorship, plagiarism and misrepresentation has surfaced as a prominent concern in higher education.

But tackling GenAI as a problem of academic dishonesty is only part of the picture in terms of its implications for assessment. The method of relying on AI-generated text has come into question recently, as have measures that concentrate on individual breaches. The central assessment concern is whether conditions under which a task is completed are consistent with the intended learning outcomes and whether the expectations communicated to students are consistent with the central assessment concern and the task conditions (Bearman & Ajjawi, 2023; Ellis et al., 2024).

4.5 How AI can contribute to an equal opportunity workplace

Adapting Generative AI (GenAI) in higher education involves equipping institutions with the balance of equity, access, and robust assessment design. Fair assessment means that a student's learning outcomes are evaluated based on what learning outcomes they intended to achieve and not based on the difference in AI literacy, access to high quality tools, language and subject differences in algorithms. Where the competency with AI is not a formal learning objective, then the design of the assessment should not allow technological disparity to influence performance. Institutions should offer clear boundaries and consistent guiding principles and criteria in assigning grades on a case-by-case basis, rather than blanket bans that will worsen inequities.

At the same time, with the emergence of LLM models that are fluent but also prone to making mistakes, the role of evaluative judgement—the capacity to make critical assessment of quality and validity of work (Carless & Boud, 2018; Tai et al., 2018) becomes increasingly relevant. Evaluations need to move beyond the simple generation task to include questioning, verification, critique and defence of outputs created by GenAI (Bearman, Tai, & Dawson, 2024).

Teachers also need to be assessment literate, to determine if students have applied critical thinking or to simply take what the machine suggests. The integrity of assessments relies on a different principle: that of not preventing students from using AI, but from using AI in ways that are unethical, unjustified, or fail to assess the content critically.

5. RESEARCH GAP

Research on the use of AI in higher education has focused on automated grading, adaptive testing, predictive analytics, and increasing efficiency. Far less has been considered, however, is whether AI-supported assessment serves as a valid source of evidence for higher-order thinking, disciplinary knowledge, and genuine learning. This leads to a need for moving beyond the technical performance to assessment validity and authenticity.

The second gap is between AI Ethics and Assessment Practice. The principles of fairness, transparency, accountability and human oversight are strongly anchored in both UNESCO (2021) and OECD (2019) frameworks. But these principles are generally articulated in the governance domain and not effectively articulated into assessment design decisions. The literature thus offers little guidance on how to put the ethical principles into practice in everyday assessment practice.

Additional gaps in linking assessment theory, AI capabilities, ethical governance and institutional practice need to be addressed. Assessment scholarship is not a new concept and it is rich with foundations of construct validity, authentic assessment and learning oriented assessment (Biggs & Tang, 2011; Wiggins, 1998) and the literature of AI governance covers the technological and ethical risks. But these views are rarely considered together as part of a holistic assessment-centred view.

Lastly, there is still not enough concrete advice for redesigning assessments for GenAI. Most of the discussion is about detecting, academics dishonesty or productivity instead of designing valid assessments that allow for appropriate usage of AI without losing the evidence of learning.

This chapter thus provides an argument for an assessment-centred Ethical Guardrails Framework that links assessment theory to AI Ethics and to actual assessment design, thus offering a structured set of principles to ensure the validity, authenticity, fairness, transparency, evaluative judgement and accountability of AI-enabled higher education.

6. CHAPTER PROPOSITIONS

The above literature review shows that there is a considerable degree of disunity among the studies that cover AI-enhanced assessment, artificial intelligence ethics, and natural pedagogic development. In order to give analytical clarity and theoretical guidance, this chapter develops three propositions that are interrelated and which form the basis of the framework development that follows.

Proposition 1: Generative AI essentially questions the authenticity of classical academic assessment models.

Generative AI machines can create coherent essays, solve quantitative problems, generate code, and simulate the process of analytical reasoning. These systems are at the cognitive output level and not at the mechanical support level as compared to the older automation tools. This implies that the conventional forms of assessment especially take-home essays, standardized examinations, and problem-based submissions are no longer reliable as a proxy of individual student cognition. In previous assessments, authenticity has alluded to the fact that work presented is an internalized knowledge and worked reasoning of a student (Wiggins, 1998). This suggestion does not presuppose that AI eradicates authenticity, however, it rather destabilizes assessment models based on output verification and not the process verification. The issue is not only technical then, but epistemological: the institutions have to re-evaluate what constitutes demonstrable learning in the context of AI-mediated situations.

Proposition 2: Ethical risks in AI-enhanced evaluation go beyond academic malpractice to organizational issues of prejudice, lack of transparency, and failure to govern.

Current discourse tends to use the notion of cheating or plagiarism as the most common way of discussing generative AI. Although the issue of academic integrity is valid (Cotton et al., 2023), the ethical risk environment is more extensive. Algorithms can replicate historical discrimination in the training data (O'Neil, 2016). Adaptive learning analytics can prioritize the process of measurable behaviour over greater cognitive involvement (Siemens and Baker, 2012). The use of AI-driven proctoring technologies can potentially introduce the surveillance as an aspect of teaching with detrimental effects on student autonomy and a disproportionate impact on marginalized groups (Selwyn, 2019).

In addition, such governance models as those suggested by UNESCO (2021) also focus on transparency, accountability, and human control as the core values. However, institutional implementation is not always planned in terms of auditability and explainability. The solution to these risks needs operational design measures and not normative proclamations only.

Proposition 3: It is not necessary to limit pedagogical innovation by including ethical guardrails into AI-based systems of assessment.

One of the most widespread responses of the institutions to generative AI has been ban or enhanced surveillance. Nonetheless, constructivist and authentic assessment theories indicate that assessment redress, instead of restraint, can be a more sustainable solution (Biggs, 1996; Wiggins, 1998). Among the epistemic integrity preservation, the incorporation of ethical guardrails, including human-in-the-loop assessment, transparency conditions, iterative submissions, and reflective elements, would be needed to allow innovation in AI-supported learning practices.

7. METHODOLOGICAL APPROACH

The chapter uses a conceptual research methodology and a qualitative approach to analyze the implications of generative artificial intelligence (GenAI) on assessment in higher education and to create an assessment-centred Ethical Guardrails Framework. No primary empirical data collection and experimental testing is involved in the study. Rather, it makes sense of and draws upon existing assessment scholarship, new assessment research on GenAI, and pertinent literature on AI ethics and governance, to uncover tensions in conceptual frameworks and establish a theoretically informed framework.

The methodological approach is based on four complementary strategies which are conceptual research design, synthetic review of literature, policy and framework analysis (PFA) and normative analytical reasoning. These approaches work together to ground the chapter in assessment theory and the new challenges that GenAI has introduced. The methodology starts at the beginning of the assessment question, namely, validity, authenticity, evidence of learning, fairness, evaluative judgement, and accountability, and explores how GenAI impacts these concepts.

The intent here is not to assess the positive or negative impact of GenAI in education. Rather, the analysis questions how assessment can remain a reliable source of evidence of student learning as more and more AI systems are involved in the creation, review, and interpretation of student work. This framework brings together theory and ethics with practical guidelines for designing assessments and institutional practice.

7.1 Conceptual Research Design

The main methodological approach is conceptual research that involves the development, elaboration and integration of theoretical constructs instead of gathering new empirical observations. This approach is suitable as GenAI has raised new questions on assessment validity, authenticity, authorship, evidence of learning, and the role of human judgement which cannot be answered solely by technological performance measures.

The conceptual design brings together three main areas, namely assessment theory, GenAI capabilities, and ethical governance. Assessment scholarship is the theoretical underpinning for the understanding of validity, authenticity, evidence of learning, assessment design, and evaluative judgement. Studies on GenAI suggest ways in which AI systems can create, edit, analyse and facilitate academic work, which will shift the focus of assessment tasks to the evidence that these tasks create. The principles found in AI ethics and governance literature include those on transparency, fairness, accountability, human oversight, and responsible use.

The combination of the above domains transcends the individual analysis of the capability of AI and its institutional policy. In the case of a student having a written response generated by GenAI, for instance, the capability of generating a high quality written response is not just treated as a technological advancement; it is studied and analyzed in terms of whether the written response still constitutes valid evidence of the student's intended learning. Likewise, transparency is viewed as a principle of AI governance, not only from a general perspective, but also concerning the students' understanding of assessment processes and defensibility of assessment decisions.

The conceptual framework that is created in this study, therefore, is meant to be a theoretical framework and not a valid instrument for empirical research. Its propositions and guardrails offer a foundation for future empirical studies on their applicability in various disciplines, assessment types, and institutional contexts.

7.2 Synthetic Literature Review

We adopt a synthetic literature review method to unite relevant academic literature from the assessment, GenAI and AI ethics fields instead of considering them as distinct disciplines. The literature is organized around the assessment questions and constructs, enabling the literature to directly inform the development of the framework.

The first strand consists of assessment theory, specifically, research into validity, authenticity, assessment design, evidence of learning, feedback and evaluative judgement. The theoretical framework for exploring the relationship between assessment evidence and intended claims to student learning comes from the work of Messick (1995), Kane (2013), Mislevy, Almond, and Lukas (2003), Wiggins (1998), and Gulikers, Bastiaens, and Kirschner (2004).

The second strand is dedicated to the latest research on GenAI and assessment in higher education. This literature review explores the potential impact of LLM on the validity of assessment, assessment redesign, academic work and evaluative judgement. The studies by Bearman & Ajjawi, 2023, (Bearman et al (2024), Ellis et al. (2024), Hao et al. (2024), Kaldaras, Akaeze, and Reckase (2024), and Lye and Lim (2024) stand out for their focus on the broader aspects of assessment validity and redesign, rather than just the detection of AI and academic dishonesty.

The third strand focuses on academic integrity, AI ethics and algorithmic governance. This literature adds thoughts regarding fairness, transparency and accountability, bias, human oversight, and the responsible use of AI. The governance landscape is set against the backdrop of UNESCO (2021), OECD (2019) and relevant AI ethics scholarship.

In the final, scholarship on feedback literacy and evaluative judgement will be considered to investigate how students can critically appraise the products of AI, instead of merely accepting them. The synthesis of these strands highlights areas of convergence and tension and helps to inform the conceptual framework of the proposed guardrails.

7.3 Policy and Framework Analysis

The chapter carries out a targeted policy and framework assessment of international principles of AI governance. The contextual and normative sources, primarily UNESCO (2021) and OECD (2019), are not used as assessment scholarship.

It explores the interpretation of key principles of fair and just assessments including transparency, fairness, accountability, human oversight, and privacy in the context of higher education assessment. One way to achieve transparency could be to inform students about when they are using AI in their writing and how assessment is being aided by AI. It can mean that institutions and teachers remain accountable for the consequences of assessment decisions which can be made automatically, and that human oversight can ensure that outputs from automated systems undergo proper academic judgement.

The policy analysis is thus not an exhaustive list of international principles. Rather, it poses the question of how these principles are connected to existing essay requirements. This is critical since if a governance principle cannot be linked to the design, administration, interpretation, and/or impact of assessment, then the principle has limited value in practice.

The analysis thus facilitates the implementation of general principles of governance of AI into mechanisms for assessment. These mechanisms involve disclosure, human review, opportunities for appeal, mechanism for monitoring bias, appropriate data governance and assessment designs that produce adequate evidence of learning. The policy literature, therefore, serves to support and enrich a theoretical argument, not to shape it.

7.4 Normative-Analytical Approach

The last methodological aspect is a normative-analytical approach which is employed in order to look at what the assessment practices and institutional arrangements ought to be if GenAI is used. Normative analysis focuses on the question of whether practice is valid, fair, authentic, transparent, accountable, and autonomous for the students.

The tensions of the times when the various assessment aims/ethical considerations clash are particularly examined. For instance, automated assessment can be more efficient, but may raise issues of transparency or interpretability of decisions. AI proctoring can enhance assessment security and privacy concerns, as well as heighten concerns about surveillance. Likewise, in some situations, unrestricted use of AI could be a true example of professional behavior, while in others, it might be evidence of poor performance and not reflect independent use of AI tools.

The conflict shows how ethically judging the use of AI is not a binary decision of either prohibit AI or welcome AI. These conflicts reveal the reasons why ethical judgment of AI is not only a matter of accepting AI or rejecting it. Rather, the context of the learning construct, role of AI, evidence needed to substantiate the assessment claim, and the implications of the assessment decision will determine the appropriate response.

One major conclusion that the analysis suggests is that humans are responsible for consequential assessment decisions. AI can provide support in providing feedback, analysis, content creation, or administrative duties, but it's important that the analysis and interpretation of evidence, and making high-stakes judgements, remain appropriately subject to human academic oversight.

7.5 Ethical Guardrails Framework Proposal

The four methodological strategies are the foundation for the Ethical Guardrails Framework. Conceptual research lays the foundation for theoretical framework, synthetic literature review links assessment scholarship and recent research in the field of GenAI, policy analysis identifies principles of assessment governance and normative analysis transforms these principles into assessment specific conditions. It therefore aims to go 'beyond the catch-all requests for responsible AI to establish concrete, assessment-driven guardrails for safeguarding the validity, authenticity, fairness, evidence of learning, and accountability of AI while allowing for appropriate pedagogical innovation.

Figure 2. Ethical Guardrail Framework for Generative AI in Academic Assessment

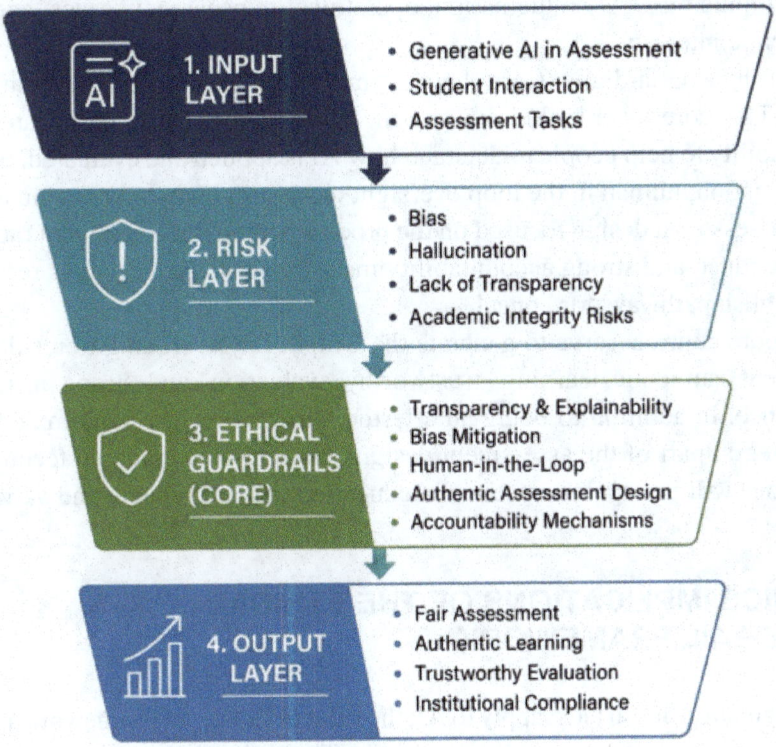

The main normative and structural input of the current chapter is the proposed Ethical Guardrails Framework of AI-mediated academic assessment. It is developed as a reaction to the epistemic, ethical, and governance-related issues presented by generative AI to the assessment system of higher education. The framework supports a design-based approach to governance as opposed to prohibitionist or surveillance-based approaches, directly incorporating ethical limitations into the structure of assessment. It is based on globally accepted standards of AI ethics as stipulated by the OECD (2019) and the UNESCO (2021), as well as assessment validity theory and responsible innovation scholarship. The framework presupposes that generative AI is not a momentary upheaval but a structural change of knowledge production, and as such, ethical governance needs to be at the level of assessment design, as opposed to the level of policy statements or enforcement mechanisms.

The suggested approach to assessing generative AI goes through four phases that maintain academic validity and integrity. The framework at the bottom, called the Input Layer, considers how Generative AI tools are being used for deployment, how students are engaging with AI, and how particular assessment tasks are designed.

If unchecked, these inputs become part of the Risk Layer, revealing key risks such as algorithmic bias, AI hallucination, operational transparency issues, and threats to academic integrity.

The Ethical Guardrails (Core) layer is implemented as a countermeasure to the threats. This core level includes 5 key measures of protection: transparency and explainability to help people understand how AI is applied and evaluated, proactive bias mitigation, human in the loop oversight to support high-stakes evaluation, authentic assessment design focused on the process behind the assessment rather than a final product, and strong accountability measures that clarify who is responsible and establish pathways for appeal.

The core controls serve to generate the Output Layer, leading to results of fair assessment, authentic learning, trustworthy evaluation, and strong institutional compliance. In addition to being an afterthought, this architecture embeds ethics as an integral part of the assessment design, ensuring that potential technological disruptions will be regular practices in education that are reliable and valid.

8. ETHICS IMPLICATIONS OF THE ETHICAL GUARDRAIL FRAMEWORK

AI regulation doesn't just apply to AI: the Ethical Guardrail Framework applies to academic assessment design and governance. The main takeaway is that generative AI will force institutions to rethink what constitutes legitimate evidence of student learning. The framework does not focus exclusively on the problem of misconduct; it emphasizes the validity, authenticity, transparency, fairness and human judgment of assessment.

8.1 Implications for Assessment Design and Pedagogy

The framework also emphasises a focus beyond the end product and the learning process. With generative AI, learning can create fluent outputs, making it more difficult to establish whether students have learned the desired knowledge and skills. Assessment may, therefore, involve drafts and reflections, oral explanations, staged submissions, problem-solving activities and context-appropriate applications. When it is acceptable to use AI, the student should acknowledge the use of AI, assess AI outputs and show an understanding of his/her disciplinary reasoning. This helps foster true learning experiences and further build AI literacy, such as how to detect bias, fact-check information, and understand the potential drawbacks of AI-generated content.

8.2 Implications for Faculty Practice.

Instructional tasks and assessments should be built around giving students meaningful and relevant evidence of learning, rather than on the detection of AI. Professional development is needed on the issues of AI literacy, assessment redesign, awareness of bias, data protection, and the evaluation of AI-assisted tools. While the use of AI can help with feedback or formative tasks, there should be meaningful human oversight of decisions regarding grades or progression. Every educator is still held accountable for making interpretations and using professional judgment.

8.3 Institutional Implications

The integration of AI guidance into assessment, curriculum, academic integrity, and student-support policies should be incorporated into the institution's practices. Policies should clearly differentiate between forbidden, allowed, and usage in context uses of AI and describe the disclosure requirements. Institutions should also test AI-powered assessment technologies to ensure accuracy, lack of bias, privacy, explainability, and human oversight. The level of governance should match the level of assessment stakes, data sensitivity, level of AI involvement, and potential liability for errors.

8.4 Implications for fairness and equity

Students have access to and knowledge of AI to varying degrees, which can result in inequalities. Institutions must ensure that all the tools required to use AI are available and that the specific conditions of access are not a prerequisite for the assessment. Although AI-detection tools can be helpful, they should not be used as a definitive measure – they can be inaccurate and categorize legitimate actions as inappropriate. Authorship should be evaluated by more than one type of evidence and human evaluation.

8.5 Policy, Quality Assurance, and Future Research

Assessment practices involving AI should be integrated into a comprehensive strategy for educational quality assurance. Regular validations of assessment, student experiences, emerging threats, and AI policy effectiveness in institutions are necessary. Further studies could investigate the impact of process-based and reflective assessment on achieving greater validity and authenticity, students and educators understanding of AI policies, and the effects of AI on learning, feedback, and fairness in various disciplines and institutional settings.

Overall Implication is that it's not just a way to regulate AI. It offers an assessment-centred framework for determining the conditions, and the timing, for the use of AI without undermining the credibility of evidence of learning. It poses the central question as "How can assessment ensure that meaningful learning is visible, valid, authentic and fairly evaluated in an AI enabled environment?

9. LIMITATION AND FUTURE RESEARCH

The findings of this study have some limitations that should be taken into account when interpreting the Ethical Guardrail Framework. First, the framework is conceptual in nature and is built on the synthesis and critical interpretation of existing literature researching generative artificial intelligence, academic assessment, ethics and educational governance. It is not based on primary empirical information from students, faculty members or institutional administrators. For this reason, the proposed guardrails are theoretically based concepts and not empirically based relationships. The efficacy of their application, thus, should be explored in various educational settings.

Second, generative AI has a temporal constraint due to its rapidly evolving nature. The use of AI continues to be a rapidly changing landscape, as do assessment practices, institutional policies, and regulatory expectations. The framework is a result of a current technological context, and might need to be adapted when AI systems are more capable, multimodal, autonomous, and integrated into educational platforms. The framework should be seen, then, as a changeable set of rules, not a permanent set.

Third, there is a diversity of higher education institutions, which results in diversities of assessment practices both within the different fields of education and across diverse educational levels, different types of higher education institutions and different cultural contexts. An appropriate guardrail for an essay-based humanities assessment is not necessarily directly applicable to laboratory work, programming, or professional practice, or to performance-based assessment. The framework, therefore, sets out general principles, rather than specific prescriptions in a given discipline. Additional context to implement.

Another drawback is that determining authenticity and authorship in AI-driven assessments is challenging. While process-based assessment, oral defence, reflective activities, and disclosure requirements can help provide more evidence of engagement, there is no definitive way to ensure that there is no uncertainty about the level of AI use. Likewise, AI-detection technologies should not be taken as a definite proof of inappropriate use. The framework does not aim to eliminate assessment risks, but minimizes them.

The study also acknowledges that there are conflicting goals in ethical evaluation. The more opportunities provided for transparency, monitoring and verification might enhance the integrity of the assessment but might also increase the workload of students, teachers, students' surveillance or increase the workload of teachers or administrative costs. Likewise, limiting the use of AI can help safeguard specific assessment items and reduce opportunities for students to acquire skills in the use of AI. Proportionality and contextual judgement, rather than universal restrictions are therefore crucial for effective implementation.

The framework needs to be tested for its validity in practice in different assessment designs and institutional contexts, which should be analyzed in future research. Research could be conducted on the effectiveness of reflective commentaries, staged submissions, oral defence, and problem-solving in a context on evidence of learning when compared to traditional product-based assessments. Longitudinal studies could also explore the long-term impact of AI-based assessment on student learning, evaluative judgement, academic integrity, and teachers' practices. Future studies should explore the equity considerations, such as differences in AI access and AI literacy, as well as how students and educators understand disclosure and acceptable-use policies. This would enable the Ethical Guardrail Framework to be further refined, validated and adapted as assessment practices and AI technology continues to develop.

10. CONCLUSION

A key struggle in higher education assessment is the proliferation of capabilities demonstrated by generative artificial intelligence. The question isn't just if students are using AI, it is if current assessment methods are still able to generate valid assessment data for learning when technologies can generate high-quality academic products. The focus of this study has been to consider generative AI not just as a problem of academic integrity or institutional technology management, but as a challenge for evaluation.

To address this challenge, this study has developed an Ethical Guardrail Framework that centres the principles of assessment validity, authenticity, transparency, fairness, and human judgement in the use of AI to support assessment. It suggests that rather than trying to ban or identify AI usage, the focus should be on determining if assessment activities are still measuring intended learning outcomes. There are other forms of evidence that can be assessed to demonstrate genuine learning and disciplinary reasoning, including process oriented assessment, reflective activities, staged submissions, oral explanation, contextualised problem-solving, and transparent disclosure.

It is also shown that assessment redesign is not enough to achieve ethical assessment. Faculty need to have the right AI and assessment literacy, institutions need the right governance and data-protection mechanisms, and students need to have equal access to knowledge and resources about AI. Especially in situations where AI systems have impact on high-stakes evaluation decisions, human judgment plays a crucial role. Ethical guardrails should not be a straitjacket but principles to inform responsible decisions regarding when and how AI can be involved in assessment.

In a key way, the framework doesn't presume generative AI is incompatible with academic evaluation. The impact will vary based on the learning construct being assessed and the purpose for using AI in the assessment. Wherever the aim of assessment is to measure independent reasoning or unaided performance, AI could threaten validity, and wherever the aim of assessment is to measure critical use of AI, then using AI as a legitimate part of the assessment could be valid.

Finally, there's an opportunity to rethink higher education's demonstration of knowledge, capability, and learning in the era of generative AI. The aim of the future of assessment should therefore not be a duel between the educator and the technology that can detect AI-generated content. Rather, it should be designed in a manner that makes learning visible, allows for meaningful human judgment, and creates clear and fair playing field for technological involvement. The Ethical Guardrail Framework supports this shift by linking together principles underpinning ethics and assessment factors into a platform for institutions to engage in technological innovation while maintaining the integrity and learning intent of assessment.

REFERENCES

Bearman, M., & Ajjawi, R. (2023). Automated feedback and assessment in higher education: A review of current trends. *Assessment & Evaluation in Higher Education*.

Bearman, M., Tai, J., Dawson, P., Boud, D., & Ajjawi, R. (2024). Developing evaluative judgement for a time of generative artificial intelligence. *Assessment & Evaluation in Higher Education*, *49*(6), 908–922. DOI: 10.1080/02602938.2024.2335321

Biggs, J., & Tang, C. (2011). *Teaching for quality learning at university* (4th ed.). Open University Press.

Carless, D., & Boud, D. (2018). The development of student feedback literacy: Enabling uptake of feedback. *Assessment & Evaluation in Higher Education*, *43*(8), 1315–1325. DOI: 10.1080/02602938.2018.1463354

Ellis, C., Dawson, P., Bearman, M., Boud, D., Ajjawi, R., & Tai, J. (2024). Assessment reform in the age of artificial intelligence. *Assessment & Evaluation in Higher Education*. Advance online publication. DOI: 10.1080/02602938.2024.2385343

Floridi, L., Cowls, J., Beltrametti, M., Chatila, R., Chazerand, P., Dignum, V., Luetge, C., Madelin, R., Pagallo, U., Rossi, F., Schafer, B., Valcke, P., & Vayena, E. (2018). AI4People—An ethical framework for a good AI society. *Minds and Machines*, *28*(4), 689–707. DOI: 10.1007/s11023-018-9482-5 PMID: 30930541

Gulikers, J. T. M., Bastiaens, T. J., & Kirschner, P. A. (2004). A five-dimensional framework for authentic assessment. *Educational Technology Research and Development*, *52*(3), 67–86. DOI: 10.1007/BF02504676

Hao, J., von Davier, A. A., Yaneva, V., Lottridge, S., von Davier, M., & Harris, D. J. (2024). Transforming assessment: The impacts and implications of large language models and generative AI. *Educational Measurement: Issues and Practice*, *43*(3), 5–16. DOI: 10.1111/emip.12602

International Center for Academic Integrity. (2021). *The fundamental values of academic integrity*.

Kaldaras, L., Akaeze, H. O., & Reckase, M. D. (2024). Developing valid assessments in the era of generative artificial intelligence. *Frontiers in Education*, *9*, 1399377. DOI: 10.3389/feduc.2024.1399377

Kane, M. T. (2013). Validating the interpretations and uses of test scores. *Journal of Educational Measurement*, *50*(1), 1–73. DOI: 10.1111/jedm.12000

Lye, C. Y., & Lim, L. (2024). Generative artificial intelligence in tertiary education: Assessment redesign principles and considerations. *Education Sciences*, *14*(6), 569. DOI: 10.3390/educsci14060569

Messick, S. (1995). Validity of psychological assessment: Validation of inferences from persons' responses and performances as scientific inquiry into score meaning. *The American Psychologist*, *50*(9), 741–749. DOI: 10.1037/0003-066X.50.9.741

Mislevy, R. J., Almond, R. G., & Lukas, J. F. (2003). *A brief introduction to evidence-centered design*. ETS Research Report Series. Educational Testing Service., DOI: 10.1002/j.2333-8504.2003.tb01908.x

OECD. (2019). *OECD principles on artificial intelligence*. OECD Publishing.

Selwyn, N. (2019). *Should robots replace teachers? AI and the future of education*. Polity Press.

Tai, J., Ajjawi, R., Boud, D., Dawson, P., & Panadero, E. (2018). Developing evaluative judgement: Enabling students to make decisions about the quality of work. *Higher Education*, *76*(3), 467–481. DOI: 10.1007/s10734-017-0220-3

UNESCO. (2023). *Recommendation on the ethics of artificial intelligence*. UNESCO Publishing.

Wiggins, G. (1998). *Educative assessment: Designing assessments to inform and improve student performance*. Jossey-Bass.

World Bank. (2021). *Artificial intelligence in education: Challenges and opportunities for sustainable development*.

World Economic Forum. (2020). *Global AI governance: A guide for policymakers*.

Compilation of References

Abbas, M., Khan, T. I., & Jam, F. A. (2025). Avoid excessive usage: Examining the motivations and outcomes of generative artificial intelligence usage among students. *Journal of Academic Ethics*, *23*(4), 2423–2442. DOI: 10.1007/s10805-025-09659-3

Abraham, R. M. (2022). Reflection on improving feedback skills and a framework for moving towards feed forward. *Bangladesh Journal of Medical Science*, *21*(1), 206–212. DOI: 10.3329/bjms.v21i1.56351

Abuzied, A. I. H., & Nabag, W. O. M. (2023). Structured viva validity, reliability, and acceptability as an assessment tool in health professions education: A systematic review and meta-analysis. *BMC Medical Education*, *23*(1), 531. DOI: 10.1186/s12909-023-04524-6 PMID: 37491301

Adabor, E. S., Addy, E., Assyne, N., & Antwi-Boasiako, E. (2025). Enhancing sustainable academic course delivery using AI in technical universities: An empirical analysis using adaptive learning theory. *Sustainable Futures : An Applied Journal of Technology, Environment and Society*, *10*, 100828. Advance online publication. DOI: 10.1016/j.sftr.2025.100828

Adams Becker, S., Cummins, M., Davis, A., Freeman, A., Hall Giesinger, C., & Ananthanarayanan, V. (2017). *NMC horizon report: 2017 higher education edition*. The New Media Consortium., DOI: 10.1111/cura.12022

Adeoye, M. A., Prastikawati, E. F., & Riwayatiningsih, R. (2025). Beyond traditional testing: Exploring the efficacy of adaptive assessments in shaping future learners. *Journal of Nonformal Education*, *11*(1), 153–169. DOI: 10.15294/jone.v11i1.19934

Afolabi, I. Y., Ugah, J. O., Igwe, J. S., & Nwali, M. E.Afolabi I.YUgah J.OIgwe J.SNwali M.E. (2025). Development of an ai-driven adaptive learning management system using data analytics. *International Journal of Scientific Research in Modern Science and Technology*, *4*(7), 52–63. DOI: 10.59828/ijsrmst.v4i7.349

Agomuoph, F. (2023, May 18). *Professor flunks entire class based on ChatGPT's false claims. Digital Trends.* https://www.digitaltrends.com/computing/chatgpt-dupes-professor-trying-to-catch-ai-plagiarism/

Agostini, D., & Picasso, F. (2024). Large language models for sustainable assessment and feedback in higher education: Towards a pedagogical and technological framework. *Intelligenza Artificiale*, *18*(1), 121–138. DOI: 10.3233/IA-240033

Ahmad, S. F., Alam, M. M., Rahmat, M. K., Mubarik, M. S., & Hyder, S. I. (2022). Academic and Administrative Role of Artificial Intelligence in Education. *Sustainability (Basel)*, *14*(3), 1101. DOI: 10.3390/su14031101

Ahmed, A. M., & Mejri, M. (2025). Generative AI for cybersecurity awareness training. Proceedings, 1–10. DOI: 10.1109/IECON58223.2025.11221870

Ahmed, Z., Shanto, S. S., Khanom Rime, M. H., Morol, M. K., Fahad, N., Hossen, J., & Abdullah-Al-Jubair, M. (2024). The generative AI landscape in education: Mapping the terrain of opportunities, challenges and student perception. *IEEE Access : Practical Innovations, Open Solutions*, *1*, 147023–147050. Advance online publication. DOI: 10.1109/ACCESS.2024.3461874

Ahmer, S. (2025). Designing adaptive lessons with GenAI to meet diverse learning preferences.

Airaj, M. (2024). Ethical artificial intelligence for teaching-learning in higher education. *Education and Information Technologies*, *29*(13), 17145–17167. DOI: 10.1007/s10639-024-12545-x

Aithal, P. S., & Aithal, S. (2023). Application of ChatGPT in higher education and research–A futuristic analysis. [IJAEML]. *International Journal of Applied Engineering and Management Letters*, *7*(3), 168–194. DOI: 10.47992/IJAEML.2581.7000.0193

Ajjawi, R., Tai, J., Boud, D., & Jorre de St Jorre, T. (2022). *Assessment for Inclusion in Higher Education*. Routledge., DOI: 10.4324/9781003293101

Akbar, M. S. (2025). Beyond detection: designing AI-resilient assessments with automated feedback tool to foster critical thinking. *arXiv preprint arXiv:2503.23622*.

Al Fraidan, P. A. (2024). Anticipatory Thinking and AI-Driven Assessments: A Balanced Approach to AI Integration in Education Aligned with Saudi Vision 2030. *African Journal of Biomedical Research*, *27*(3), 619–628. DOI: 10.53555/AJBR.v27i3.2560

Aladsani, H. (2025). Developing postgraduate students' competencies in generative artificial in-telligence for ethical integration into academic practices: A participatory action research. *Interactive Learning Environments, 33*, 5747–5765. . 2025.2487517DOI: 10.1080/10494820

Alali, R. M., & Wardat, Y. (2024). *Opportunities and challenges of integrating generative artificial intelligence in education.* International Journal of Religion., DOI: 10.61707/8y29gv34

Alderson, J. C., & Wall, D. (1993). Does washback exist? *Applied Linguistics, 14*(2), 115–129. DOI: 10.1093/applin/14.2.115

Aleven, V., McLaughlin, E. A., Glenn, R. A., & Koedinger, K. R. (2016). Instruction based on adaptive learning technologies. In Mayer, R. E., & Alexander, P. A. (Eds.), *Handbook of research on learning and instruction* (pp. 522–560). Routledge., DOI: 10.4324/9781315736419

Alfaleh, M. (2026). Sustainable AI-Driven Assessment in Higher Education: A Systematic Review of Fairness, Transparency, Pedagogical Innovation, and Governance. *Sustainability (Basel), 18*(2), 785. DOI: 10.3390/su18020785

Al-Maskari, A., Al Riyami, T., & Ghnimi, S. (2024). Factors affecting students' preparedness for the fourth industrial revolution in higher education institutions. *Journal of Applied Research in Higher Education, 16*(1), 246–264. DOI: 10.1108/JARHE-05-2022-0169

AlMohsen, F. (2025). Ethical integration of generative AI in higher education assessments. Advances in Computational Intelligence and Robotics Book Series, 275–288. DOI: 10.4018/979-8-3693-7332-3.ch017

Aloisi, C. (2023). The future of standardised assessment: Validity and trust in algorithms for assessment and scoring. *European Journal of Education, 58*(1), 98–110. DOI: 10.1111/ejed.12542

Alon-Barkat, S., & Busuioc, M. (2021). Human-AI interactions in public sector decision making: Automation bias and selective adherence to algorithmic advice. *Journal of Public Administration: Research and Theory, 33*(1), 153–159. DOI: 10.1093/jopart/muac007

Alonzo, D., & Teng, S. (2023). Trustworthiness of Teacher Assessment and Decision-Making: Reframing the Consistency and Accuracy Measures. *International Journal of Instruction, 16*(3), 1075–1094. Advance online publication. DOI: 10.29333/iji.2023.16357a

Alotaibi, N. S. (2024). The impact of AI and LMS integration on the future of higher education: Opportunities, challenges, and strategies for transformation. *Sustainability (Basel), 16*(23), 10357. DOI: 10.3390/su162310357

Alrawahna, A. S., Alzghoul, A., & Awad, H. (2025). The Impact of Artificial Intelligence on Public Sector Decision- Making: Benefits, Challenges, and Policy Implications. *International Review of Management and Marketing, 15*(5), 125–138. DOI: 10.32479/irmm.19419

Alshanetsky, E. (2025). When AI Dissolves Trust: Education Can Pioneer New Infrastructure. *Society, 62*(6), 982–987. DOI: 10.1007/s12115-025-01149-x

Alsharefeen, R., & Al Sayari, N. (2025, June). Examining academic integrity policy and practice in the era of AI: A case study of faculty perspectives. *Frontiers in Education, 10*, 1621743. Advance online publication. DOI: 10.3389/feduc.2025.1621743

Alter, A. L., Oppenheimer, D. M., Epley, N., & Eyre, R. N. (2007). Overcoming intuition: Metacognitive difficulty activates analytic reasoning. *Journal of Experimental Psychology. General, 136*(4), 569–576. DOI: 10.1037/0096-3445.136.4.569 PMID: 17999571

Al-Zahrani, A. M., & Alasmari, T. M. (2024). Exploring the impact of artificial intelligence on higher education: The dynamics of ethical, social, and educational implications. *Humanities & Social Sciences Communications, 11*(1), 1–12. DOI: 10.1057/s41599-024-03432-4

American Council on the Teaching of Foreign Languages. (2026a). *Proficiency Guidelines Overview*. https://www.actfl.org/proficiency-guidelines-overview

American Council on the Teaching of Foreign Languages. (2026b). *Oral Proficiency Interview (OPI)*. https://www.actfl.org/assessments/postsecondary-assessments /opi

American Educational Research Association (AERA), American Psychological Association (APA), & National Council on Measurement in Education (NCME). (2014). *Standards for educational and psychological testing*. American Educational Research Association. DOI: 10.2307/j.ctvr43hg2

American Psychological Association. (2025). *APA journals policy on generative AI*. https://www.apa.org/pubs/journals/resources/publishing-tips/policy-generative-ai

Amirjalili, F., Neysani, M., & Nikbakht, A. (2024, March). Exploring the boundaries of authorship: A comparative analysis of AI-generated text and human academic writing in English literature. [). Frontiers Media SA.]. *Frontiers in Education, 9*, 1347421. DOI: 10.3389/feduc.2024.1347421

An, J., Bai, Y., Li, J., Wang, L., Jiang, Y., & Zhang, Y. (2026). Cantonese dialect transcription in diverse sophisticated scenarios via the OpenAI Whisper speech recognition model. In M. Mahmud, M. Doborjeh, K. Wong, A. C. S. Leung, Z. Doborjeh, M. Tanveer (Eds) *Neural Information Processing*. Communications in Computer and Information Science, vol 2294. Springer, Singapore. DOI: 10.1007/978-981-96-7008-6_23

Ananny, M., & Crawford, K. (2018). Seeing without knowing: Limitations of the transparency ideal and its application to algorithmic accountability. *New Media & Society*, *20*(3), 973–989. DOI: 10.1177/1461444816676645

Anaroua, F. I., Li, Q., Tang, Y., & Liu, H. P. (2025). *AI-driven formative assessment and adaptive learning in data-science education: Evaluating an LLM-powered virtual teaching assistant*. https://arxiv.org/abs/2509.20369

Andrew, M., & Mueller, B. (2025). Is that all there is?" Work-integrated learning educators meet GenAI: upskilling journeys to "the deep end. In *Handbook of Artificial Intelligence in Higher Education* (pp. 300–314). Edward Elgar Publishing. DOI: 10.4337/9781035338764.00028

Anh-Hoang, D., Tran, V., & Nguyen, L.-M. (2025). Survey and analysis of hallucinations in large language models: Attribution to prompting strategies or model behavior. *Frontiers in Arti-ficial Intelligence, Volume 8 - 2025*. DOI: 10.3389/frai.2025.1622292

Antara, P., Mohd Beta, R. M. D., Ibrahim, N. A. & Talip, I. (2025, October 23). Beyond the algorithm: Towards a human-centered AI pedagogy. *International Journal of Research and Innovation in the Social Sciences.* DOI: 10.47772/IJRISS.2025.903SEDU0570

Apostolopoulos, I. D., Tzani, M., & Aznaouridis, S. I. (2023). ChatGPT: ascertaining the self-evident. The use of AI in generating human knowledge. arXiv preprint arXiv:2308.06373.

Archan, D. (2025). (HOW) CAN ARTIFICIAL INTELLIGENCE ENHANCE FORMATIVE FEEDBACK IN HIGHER EDUCATION? In ICERI2025 Proceedings (pp. 3350-3356). IATED.

Archana, S. N., Renjith, V. R., Padmakumar, P. K., C, S., & Aboobaker, N. (2025). Ai assisted learning and research: An exploratory study among university students and scholars. *Discover Education*, *4*(1), 390. DOI: 10.1007/s44217-025-00814-x

Archer, A., & Breuer, E. (Eds.). (2015). *Multimodality in writing: The state of the art in theory, methodology and pedagogy*. Brill., DOI: 10.1163/9789004297197

Archer, E. (2017). The Assessment Purpose Triangle: Balancing the Purposes of Educational Assessment. *Frontiers in Education*, *2*, 41. DOI: 10.3389/feduc.2017.00041

Ardito, C. G. (2025). Generative AI detection in higher education assessments. *New Directions for Teaching and Learning*, *2025*(182), 11–28. DOI: 10.1002/tl.20624

Arslan, B., Lehman, B., Tenison, C., Sparks, J. R., López, A. A., Gu, L., & Zapata-Rivera, D. (2024). Opportunities and challenges of using generative AI to personalize educational assessment. *Frontiers in Artificial Intelligence*, *7*, 1460651. Advance online publication. DOI: 10.3389/frai.2024.1460651 PMID: 39434872

Aruna Jasmine, J., Nisha Jenipher, V., Richard Jimreeves, J. S., Ravindran, K., & Dhinakaran, D. "A traceability set up using digitalization of data and accessibility," International Conference on Intelligent Sustainable Systems (ICISS), IEEE Xplore, Tirunelveli, India, pp. 907-910, 2021. DOI: DOI: 10.1109/ICISS49785.2020.9315938

Athar, M. E. (2025, May). The constructive, over reliant and irresponsible use of artificial intelligence tools in academia: Personality correlates and implications for academic integrity. *Computers in Human Behavior Reports*, *18*, 100679. Advance online publication. DOI: 10.1016/j.chbr.2025.100679

Audrin, C., & Audrin, B. (2022). Key factors in digital literacy in learning and education: A systematic literature review using text mining. *Education and Information Technologies*, *27*(6), 7395–7419. DOI: 10.1007/s10639-021-10832-5

Australian Government Tertiary Education Quality and Standards Association. (2026, February 28). *What is academic integrity?* https://www.teqsa.gov.au/students/understanding-academic-integrity/what-academic-integrity

Avci, H., Lunn, S. J., & Hazari, Z. (2025). Exploring STEM educators' perspectives on the integration of AI-enabled technologies in teaching and learning. *Computers and Education Open*, *9*, 100304. Advance online publication. DOI: 10.1016/j.caeo.2025.100304

Avilés Mariño, E., & Sarasa Cabezuelo, A. (2025). AI-Enhanced PBL and Experiential Learning for Communication and Career Readiness: An Engineering Pilot Course. *Algorithms*, *18*(10), 634. DOI: 10.3390/a18100634

Awashreh, R., Al-Naqbi, S., & Gharib, M. (2024). Ethical decision making by Arab universities' advisory and shadow committees: Forms of corruption, implications, and solutions. *Kurdish Studies*, *12*(1), 4197–4209.

Babu, M. S. (2025). AI-Driven Educational Assessments: Navigating the Intersection of Innovation, Equity, and Ethical Concerns for Future Learning. Journal of Cultural Analysis and Social Change, 1368-1382.

Bachman, L. F., & Palmer, A. S. (1996). *Language testing in practice: Designing and developing useful language tests*. Oxford University Press.

Bachman, L. F., & Palmer, A. S. (2010). *Language assessment in practice: Developing language assessments and justifying their use in the real world*. Oxford University Press.

Bachman, L., & Palmer, A. (2010). *Language Assessment in Practice*. Oxford University Press.

Bacon-Shone, J., Bolton, K., & Lee, S. L. (2025). Researching Hong Kong's multilingual landscape. In Durk, G., & Cenoz, J. (Eds.), *The Handbook of Linguistic Landscapes and Multilingualism* (pp. 309–336). John Wiley & Sons.

Bahari, A. (2025). Balancing syntactic complexity and clarity: The role of AI in enhancing academic writing proficiency. *Saudi Journal of Language Studies*, *5*(4), 271–290. DOI: 10.1108/SJLS-10-2024-0062

Baker, R. S., & Hawn, A. (2021). Algorithmic bias in education. *International Journal of Artificial Intelligence in Education*, *32*(4), 1052–1092. DOI: 10.1007/s40593-021-00285-9

Baker, R. S., & Inventado, P. S. (2014). Educational data mining and learning analytics. In Larusson, J. A., & White, B. (Eds.), *Learning analytics: From research to practice* (pp. 61–75). Springer., DOI: 10.1007/978-1-4614-3305-7_4

Balducci, B. (2024). AI and student assessment in human-centered education. *Frontiers in Education*, *9*, 1383148. Advance online publication. DOI: 10.3389/feduc.2024.1383148

Balfour, S. P. (2013). Assessing Writing in MOOCs: Automated Essay Scoring and Calibrated Peer Review. 8. https://files.eric.ed.gov/fulltext/EJ1062843.pdf

Bandi, A., Adapa, P. V. S. R., & Kuchi, Y. E. V. P. K. (2023). The power of generative ai: A review of requirements, models, input–output formats, evaluation metrics, and challenges. *Future Internet*, *15*(8), 260. DOI: 10.3390/fi15080260

Banerjee, J., Franceshina, F., & Smith, A. M. (2007). Documenting features of written language production typical at different IELTS band score levels In IELTS Academic Writing Task 2. In Taylor, L., & Flavey, P. (Eds.), *IELTS Research Reports* (Vol. 7, pp. 191–237). Cambridge ESOL.

Banks, M. (2019). Fighting the tyranny of the pixel: The visual culture reader as a resource for the methodological development of visual research. *Visual Studies*, *34*(2), 181–190. DOI: 10.1080/1472586X.2019.1653223

Bannister, P., Alcalde, Peñalver, E. & Santamaria Urbieta, A. (2024). International students and generative artificial intelligence: A cross-cultural exploration of HE academic integrity policy. *Journal of International Students, 14*(3), 149-170. ISSN: ISSN-2162-3104

Baraniuk, R. G., Burrus, C. S., Johnson, D. H., & Jones, D. L. (2016). Adaptive assessment and training using the Web. *Proceedings of the IEEE International Conference on Acoustics, Speech, and Signal Processing*, *6*, 3868–3871. DOI: 10.1109/ICASSP.1997.604701

Barnes, E., & Hutson, J. (2024). *Navigating the ethical terrain of AI in higher education: Strategies for mitigating bias and promoting fairness.* Forum for Education Studies., DOI: 10.59400/fes.v2i2.1229

Barocas, S., Hardt, M., & Narayanan, A. (2019). *Fairness and machine learning: Limitations and opportunities.* MIT Press., DOI: 10.7551/mitpress/12200.001.0001

Basit, I., Safdar, U., & Malik, F. (2025).Artificial intelligence and academic integrity: A study of faculty perceptions in higher education. *Policy Journal of Social Science Review* 3(4), 212-221. ISSN 3006-4627.

Bassett, M. A., Bradshaw, W., Bornsztejn, H., Hogg, A., Murdoch, K., Pearce, B., & Webber, C. (2026). Heads we win, tails you lose: Ai detectors in education. *Journal of Higher Education Policy and Management, 0*(0), 1–16. . 2622146DOI: 10.1080/1360080X.2026

Bassett, M. A., Bradshaw, W., Bornsztejn, H., Hogg, A., Murdoch, K., Pearce, B., & Webber, C. (2026). Heads we win, tails you lose: AI detectors in education. *Journal of Higher Education Policy and Management*, •••, 1–16. DOI: 10.1080/1360080X.2026.2622146

Bauer, E., Greiff, S., Graesser, A. C., Scheiter, K., & Sailer, M. (2025). Looking beyond the hype: Understanding the effects of AI on learning. *Educational Psychology Review*, *37*(2), 45. DOI: 10.1007/s10648-025-10020-8

Bauer, R. (2016). The Hong Kong Cantonese language: Current features and future prospects. *Global Chinese*, 2(2), 115–161. DOI: 10.1515/glochi-2016-0007

Bayne, S. (2015). Teacherbot: Interventions in automated teaching. *Teaching in Higher Education*, *20*(4), 455–467. DOI: 10.1080/13562517.2015.1020783

Bearman, M., & Ajjawi, R. (2023). Automated feedback and assessment in higher education: A review of current trends. *Assessment & Evaluation in Higher Education.*

Bearman, M., Ajjawi, R., Boud, D., Tai, J., & Dawson, P. (2022). *Re-imagining university assessment in a digital world.* Springer Nature.

Bearman, M., Dawson, P., Bennett, S., Hall, M., Molloy, E., Boud, D., & Joughin, G. (2022). How university teachers design assessments: A cross-disciplinary study. *Higher Education, 74*(1), 49–64. DOI: 10.1007/s10734-016-0027-7

Bearman, M., Tai, J., Dawson, P., Boud, D., & Ajjawi, R. (2024). Developing evaluative judgement for a time of generative artificial intelligence. *Assessment & Evaluation in Higher Education, 49*(6), 908–922. DOI: 10.1080/02602938.2024.2335321

Bender, E. M., Gebru, T., McMillan-Major, A., & Shmitchell, S. (2021). On the dangers of stochastic parrots: Can language models be too big? *Proceedings of the 2021 ACM Conference on Fairness, Accountability, and Transparency*, 610-623. DOI: 10.1145/3442188.3445922

Bertram Gallant, T. (2008). *Academic integrity in the twenty-first century: A teaching and learning imperative.* Jossey-Bass., DOI: 10.1002/9781118638521

Bešić, E., Schulz, L., & Schmid-Meier, C. (2025). *Inclusion and Equity in Artificial Intelligence (AI): Analysis of Educational Policies in Austria, Germany, and Switzerland.* DOI: 10.21203/rs.3.rs-7232992/v1

Betteney, M., Yin, B., Kpukumu, J., Cox, M. R., Malhi, M., Mulhare, D., Olaifa, M., & Duan, X. (2025). Generative artificial intelligence and the doctoral student: Procedural and ethical considerations. *Compass: Journal of Learning and Teaching in Higher Education.* DOI: 10.21100/compass.v18i1.1618

Bhardwaj, S., & Sharma, I. (2025). Exploring the effects of AI-powered personalized classroom management strategies. In *Transforming education with AI-powered personalized learning* (pp. 25–48). IGI Global., DOI: 10.4018/979-8-3693-5443-8.ch002

Biggs, J., & Tang, C. (2011). *Teaching for quality learning at university* (4th ed.). Open University Press.

Biggs, J., & Watkins, D. (2001). Insights into teaching the Chinese learner. In Watkins, D., & Biggs, J. (Eds.), *Teaching the Chinese learner: Psychological and pedagogical perspectives* (pp. 277–300). Comparative Education Research Centre., DOI: 10.1007/978-94-011-3620-1_16

Bin-Nashwan, S. A., Sadallah, M., & Bouteraa, M. (2023). Use of Chat-GPT in academia: Academic integrity hangs in the balance. *Technology in Society, 75*, 102370. Advance online publication. https://www.sciencedirect.com/science/article/pii/S0160791X23001756. DOI: 10.1016/j.techsoc.2023.102370

Bjork, E. L., & Bjork, R. A. (2011). Making things hard on yourself, but in a good way: Creating desirable difficulties to enhance learning. In Gernsbacher, M. A., Pew, R. W., Hough, L. M., & Pomerantz, J. R. (Eds.), *Psychology and the real world: Essays illustrating fundamental contributions to society* (pp. 56–64). Worth Publishers.

Bjork, R. A., Dunlosky, J., & Kornell, N. (2013). Self-regulated learning: Beliefs, techniques, and illusions. *Annual Review of Psychology, 64*(1), 417–444. DOI: 10.1146/annurev-psych-113011-143823 PMID: 23020639

Black, K., & Warhurst, R. (2025). Democratising the curriculum: inclusive learning through students' ownership of assessment. In Handbook of Inclusive Learning and Teaching in Business and Management. Cheltenham, UK: Edward Elgar Publishing. Retrieved May 27, 2026, from DOI: 10.4337/9781035325733.00008

Blackboard. (2026). *SafeAssign*. https://safeassign.blackboard.com/

Black, P., & Wiliam, D. (1998). Assessment and classroom learning. *Assessment in Education: Principles, Policy & Practice, 5*(1), 7–74. DOI: 10.1080/0969595980050102

Black, P., & Wiliam, D. (2009). Developing the theory of formative assessment. *Educational Assessment, Evaluation and Accountability, 21*(1), 5–31. DOI: 10.1007/s11092-008-9068-5

Blodgett, S. L., Barocas, S., Daumé, H.III, & Wallach, H. (2020). Language (technology) is power: A critical survey of "bias" in NLP. *Proceedings of the 58th Annual Meeting of the Association for Computational Linguistics*, 5454-5476. DOI: 10.18653/v1/2020.acl-main.485

Blommerde, T., Bright, W., Musgrave, E., Mitchell, R., & Heselton, R. (2024). AI detectors in universities: Time to turn them off and embrace AI for enhanced learning. *Educational Developments, 25*(4), 8–11.

Bolton, K., Bacon-Shone, J., & Lee, S. L. (2020). Societal multilingualism in Hong Kong. In Siemund, P., & Leimgruber, J. (Eds.), *Multilingual Global Cities: Dubai, Hong Kong and Singapore* (pp. 160–184). Routledge. DOI: 10.4324/9780429463860-12

Bolton, K., & Lee, S. L. (2020). A socio-historical approach to multilingualism in Hong Kong. In Siemund, P., & Leimgruber, J. (Eds.), *Multilingual Global Cities: Hong Kong, Singapore, and Dubai* (pp. 38–62). Routledge. DOI: 10.4324/9780429463860-4

Bond, M., Zawacki-Richter, O., & Nichols, M. (2020). Revisiting five decades of educational technology research: A content and authorship analysis. *British Journal of Educational Technology, 51*(3), 1854–1877. DOI: 10.1111/bjet.12899

Boral, K., & Mondal, K. K. (2025). Comparing AI-Generated Responses: A Study on ChatGPT, Gemini, and Copilot in Education. *Journal of Educational Technology Systems, 54*(2), 291–309. DOI: 10.1177/00472395251368385

Boud, D., Ajjawi, R., Dawson, P., & Tai, J. (Eds.). (2018). *Developing evaluative judgement in higher education: Assessment for knowing and producing quality work*. Routledge., DOI: 10.4324/9781315109251

Boud, D., & Falchikov, N. (2007). *Rethinking assessment in higher education: Learning for the longer term*. Routledge. DOI: 10.4324/9780203964309

Boud, D., & Soler, R. (2016). Sustainable assessment revisited. *Assessment & Evaluation in Higher Education, 41*(3), 400–413. DOI: 10.1080/02602938.2015.1018133

Bouguettaya, S., Pupo, F., Chen, M., & Fortino, G. (2025). A meta-survey of generative AI in education: Trends, challenges, and research directions. *Big Data and Cognitive Computing, 9*(9), 237. DOI: 10.3390/bdcc9090237

Bovill, C. (2020). Co-creation in learning and teaching: The case for a whole-class approach in higher education. *Higher Education, 79*(6), 1023–1037. DOI: 10.1007/s10734-019-00453-w

Bowen, J. A., & Watson, C. E. (2025). *Teaching with AI: A practical guide to a new era of human learning*. JHU Press. DOI: 10.56021/9781421453392

Bozkurt, A., Karadeniz, A., Baneres, D., Guerrero-Roldán, A. E., & Rodríguez, M. E. (2021). Artificial intelligence and reflections from educational landscape: A review of AI studies in half a decade. *Sustainability (Basel), 13*(2), 800. DOI: 10.3390/su13020800

Brem, A., & Hörauf, D. (2025). Artificial creativity? AI's short-and long-term impact on creativity. *Research Technology Management, 68*(2), 54–58. DOI: 10.1080/08956308.2025.2450756

Brint, S., & Cantwell, A. M. (2010). Undergraduate time use and academic outcomes: Results from the university of california undergraduate experience survey 2006. *Teachers College Record, 112*(9), 2441–2470. DOI: 10.1177/016146811011200908

Bruner, J. (1990). *Acts of meaning*. Harvard University Press.

Buchanan, J., Hill, S., & Shapoval, O. (2024). ChatGPT hallucinates non-existent citations: Evidence from economics. *The American Economist, 69*(1), 80–87. Advance online publication. DOI: 10.1177/05694345231218454

Buele, J., & Llerena-Aguirre, L. (2025, July). Transformations in academic work and faculty perceptions of artificial intelligence in higher education. *Frontiers in Education, 10*, 1603763. Advance online publication. DOI: 10.3389/feduc.2025.1603763

Bulut, O., & Beiting-Parrish, M. (2024). The Rise of Artificial Intelligence in Educational Measurement: Opportunities and Ethical Challenges. *Chinese/English Journal of Educational Measurement and Evaluation, 5*(3). Advance online publication. DOI: 10.59863/MIQL7785

Caena, F., & Redecker, C. (2019). Aligning teacher competence frameworks to 21st century challenges: The case for the European Digital Competence Framework for Educators. *European Journal of Education, 54*(3), 356–369. DOI: 10.1111/ejed.12345

Calero-Medina, C., & Noyons, E. C. (2008). Combining mapping and citation network analysis for a better understanding of the scientific development: The case of the absorptive capacity field. *Journal of Informetrics, 2*(4), 272–279. 10.1016/j.joi. 2008.09.005

Calidonio, S. L. (2025). Designing Intelligent Feedback: an AI-Augmented Feedback Framework for Prototyping in Design Thinking (Master's thesis, Universidade NOVA de Lisboa (Portugal)).

Canale, M., & Swain, M. (1980). Theoretical bases of communicative approaches to second language teaching and testing. *Applied Linguistics, 1*(1), 1–47. DOI: 10.1093/applin/1.1.1

Caner, H. N. (2025). AI detection tools: A systematic review of empirical evidence and their implications for education. *Khazar Journal of Humanities and Social Sciences, 28*(4), 4. DOI: 10.5782/2223-2621.1580

Caporusso, N. (2023). Generative artificial intelligence and the emergence of creative displacement anxiety. Research in Psychology and Behavior, 3(1).

Carless, D. (2015). *Excellence in university assessment: Learning from award-winning practice*. Routledge., DOI: 10.4324/9781315740621

Carless, D., & Boud, D. (2018). The development of student feedback literacy: Enabling uptake of feedback. *Assessment & Evaluation in Higher Education, 43*(8), 1315–1325. DOI: 10.1080/02602938.2018.1463354

Carroll, S. R., Garba, I., Figueroa-Rodríguez, O. L., Holbrook, J., Lovett, R., Materechera, S., Parsons, M., Raseroka, K., Rodriguez-Lonebear, D., Rowe, R., Sara, R., Walker, J. D., Anderson, J., & Hudson, M. (2023). The CARE principles for indigenous data governance. Open Scholarship Press Curated Volumes: Policy. *Data Science Journal, 19*(1), 43. DOI: 10.5334/dsj-2020-043 PMID: 37810187

Carter, S., Bennett, S., Hawkins, J., & Southam, D. (2025). Programmatic assessment: A literature review of challenges, opportunities and useful tools to support student transition to the workplace. *Assessment & Evaluation in Higher Education*, •••, 1–18. DOI: 10.1080/02602938.2025.2567538

Castro, R. (2019). Blended learning in higher education: Trends and capabilities. *Education and Information Technologies*, *24*(4), 2523–2546. DOI: 10.1007/s10639-019-09886-3

Cath, C., Wachter, S., Mittelstadt, B., Taddeo, M., & Floridi, L. (2018). Artificial intelligence and the 'good society': The US, EU, and UK approach. *Science and Engineering Ethics*, *24*(2), 505–528. DOI: 10.1007/s11948-017-9901-7

Cepeda, N. J., Pashler, H., Vul, E., Wixted, J. T., & Rohrer, D. (2006). Distributed practice in verbal recall tasks: A review and quantitative synthesis. *Psychological Bulletin*, *132*(3), 354–380. DOI: 10.1037/0033-2909.132.3.354 PMID: 16719566

Chan, C. K. Y. (2023). A comprehensive AI policy education framework for university teaching and learning. *International Journal of Educational Technology in Higher Education*, *20*(1), 38. Advance online publication. DOI: 10.1186/s41239-023-00408-3

Chang, D. H., Lin, M. P. C., Hajian, S., & Wang, Q. Q. (2023). Educational design principles of using AI chatbot that supports self-regulated learning in education: Goal setting, feedback, and personalization. *Sustainability (Basel)*, *15*(17), 12921. DOI: 10.3390/su151712921

Charles, K. A., Yousuf, A., Chua, H. C., Matthews, S., Harnett, J., & Hinton, T. (2025). AI in action: Changes to student perceptions when using generative artificial intelligence for the creation of a multimedia project-based assessment. *European Journal of Pharmacology*, *998*, 177508. DOI: 10.1016/j.ejphar.2025.177508 PMID: 40086582

Charmaz, K. (2014). *Constructing grounded theory* (2nd ed.). Sage.

Chechitelli, A. (2023, June 6). *Understanding the false positive rate for sentences of our AI writing detection capability*. Turnitin Blog. https://www.turnitin.com/blog/understanding-

Chen, D., Lin, Y. C., Huang, Y., Gong, Z., Jiang, D., & Xie, Z. (2025). CantoASR: Prosody-aware ASR-LALM collaboration for low-resource Cantonese. *arXiv preprint arXiv*:2511.04139.

Chen, L. (2023, June 23). Hong Kong rolls out first AI curriculum for junior secondary students, including lessons on ChatGPT, with 'lives definitely affected by artificial intelligence'. *South China Morning Post.*

Chen, Z. (2023). Ethics and discrimination in artificial intelligence-enabled recruitment practices. *Humanities and Social Sciences Communications 2023 10:1, 10*(1), 567-. DOI: 10.1057/s41599-023-02079-x

Chen, A. M., Kleppinger, E. L., Churchwell, M. D., & Rhoney, D. H. (2024). Examining competency-based education through the lens of implementation science: A scoping review. *American Journal of Pharmaceutical Education, 88*(2), 100633. DOI: 10.1016/j.ajpe.2023.100633 PMID: 38092089

Chen, J., Huang, K., Lai, C., & Jin, T. (2025). The Impact of GenAI-Based Collaborative Inquiry on Critical Thinking in Argumentation: A Case Study of Blended Argumentative Writing Pedagogy. *TESOL Quarterly, 59*(S1), S150–S182. DOI: 10.1002/tesq.3407

Chen, R. J., Wang, J. J., Williamson, D. F. K., Chen, T. Y., Lipkova, J., Lu, M. Y., Sahai, S., & Mahmood, F. (2023). Algorithmic fairness in artificial intelligence for medicine and healthcare. *Nature Biomedical Engineering, 7*(6), 719–742. Advance online publication. DOI: 10.1038/s41551-023-01056-8 PMID: 37380750

Cheong, B. C. (2024). Transparency and accountability in AI systems: Safeguarding wellbeing in the age of algorithmic decision-making. *Frontiers in Human Dynamics, 6*, 1421273. DOI: 10.3389/fhumd.2024.1421273

Chicago Manual of Style. (2026). *Citation, documentation of sources.* https://www.chicagomanualofstyle.org/qanda/data/faq/topics/Documentation/faq0422.html

Chima, A. E., Abimbola Eden, C., Chisom, O. N., Adeniyi, I. S., & Scientia, M. (2024). Integrating AI in education: Opportunities, challenges, and ethical considerations. Https://Magnascientiapub.Com/Journals/Msarr/Sites/Default/Files/MSARR-2024-0039.Pdf, *10*(2), 006–013. DOI: 10.30574/msarr.2024.10.2.0039

Chin, A. C. (2023). A corpus-based approach to learning and teaching Cantonese. In Lee, S. L. (Ed.), *The Learning and Teaching of Cantonese as a Second Language* (pp. 184–196). Routledge.

Chiu, T. K. (2024). Future research recommendations for transforming higher education with generative AI. *Computers and Education: Artificial Intelligence, 6*, 100197. DOI: 10.1016/j.caeai.2023.100197

Chiu, T. K. F. (2026). Human-Centric Artificial Intelligence Pedagogy (HCAP) framework developed from TPACK through integration of artificial intelligence literacy and competency. *Interactive Learning Environments*, 1–16. DOI: 10.1080/10494820.2026.2615818

Chiu, T. K., Ahmad, Z., Ismailov, M., & Sanusi, I. T. (2024). What are artificial intelligence literacy and competency? A comprehensive framework to support them. *Computers and Education Open*, *6*, 100171. DOI: 10.1016/j.caeo.2024.100171

Choiriyah, S., Ramadhan, S., Nugroho, A., Pembangunan, H. R. P., & Muharom, F. (2025). Artificial intelligence-driven learning assessment in faculties of education: An exploratory study. *Munaddhomah: Jurnal Manajemen Pendidikan Islam*, *6*(3), 482–495. DOI: 10.31538/munaddhomah.v6i3.1937

Chookaew, S., Kitcharoen, P., Howimanporn, S., & Panjaburee, P. (2024). Fostering student competencies and perceptions through artificial intelligence of things educational platform. *Computers and Education: Artificial Intelligence*, *7*, 100308. DOI: 10.1016/j.caeai.2024.100308

Chuang, P. L., & Yan, X. (2025). Language assessment in the era of generative artificial intelligence: Opportunities, challenges, and future directions. *System*, *103846*, 103846. Advance online publication. DOI: 10.1016/j.system.2025.103846

Cohen, D. K. (1987). Educational technology, policy, and practice. *Educational Evaluation and Policy Analysis*, *9*(2), 153–170. DOI: 10.3102/01623737009002153

Conole, G. (2013). *Designing for learning in an open world*. Springer., DOI: 10.1007/978-1-4419-8517-0

Contrino, M. F., Reyes-Millán, M., Vázquez-Villegas, P., & Membrillo-Hernández, J. (2024). Using an adaptive learning tool to improve student performance and satisfaction in online and face-to-face education for a more personalized approach. *Smart Learning Environments*, *11*(6), 6. Advance online publication. DOI: 10.1186/s40561-024-00292-y

Cook-Sather, A., Bovill, C., & Felten, P. (2014). *Engaging students as partners in learning and teaching: A guide for faculty*. Jossey-Bass., DOI: 10.1002/tl.20106

Cope, B., & Kalantzis, M. (2015). *A pedagogy of multiliteracies: Learning by design*. Palgrave Macmillan., DOI: 10.1057/9781137539724

Cope, B., Kalantzis, M., & Searsmith, D. (2021). Artificial intelligence for education: Knowledge and its assessment in AI-enabled learning ecologies. *Educational Philosophy and Theory*, *53*(12), 1229–1245. DOI: 10.1080/00131857.2020.1728732

Corbin, T., Dawson, P., Nicola-Richmond, K., & Partridge, H. (2025). Where's the line? It's an absurd line: Towards a framework for acceptable uses of AI in assessment. *Assessment & Evaluation in Higher Education, 50*(5), 705–717. DOI: 10.1080/02602938.2025.2456207

Cowling, M., Crawford, J., Allen, K., & Wehmeyer, M. (2023). Using leadership to leverage chat-gpt and artificial intelligence for undergraduate and postgraduate research supervision. *Aus-tralasian Journal of Educational Technology, 39*(4), 83–103. . 8598DOI: 10.14742/ajet

Crawford, J., Cowling, M. and Allen, K.-A. (2023) Leadership is needed for ethical ChatGPT: character, assessment, and learning using artificial intelligence AI. *Journal of University Teaching & Learning Practice 20*(3), 02.

Crawford, J., Cowling, M., & Allen, K. A. (2023). Leadership is needed for ethical ChatGPT: Character, assessment, and learning using artificial intelligence (AI). *Journal of University Teaching & Learning Practice*, 20(3), 02. DOI: 10.53761/1.20.3.02

Crawford, K., & Paglen, T. (2019). Excavating AI: The politics of images in machine learning training sets. *AI & Society, 36*(4), 1105–1116. DOI: 10.1007/s00146-019-00934-z

Crockett, R., & Howe, R. (2024). The inherent uncertainties of AI-text detection and the implications for education institutions: An overview. In Mahmud, S. (Ed.), *Academic integrity in the age of artificial intelligence* (pp. 175–198). IGI Global. DOI: 10.4018/979-8-3693-0240-8.ch010

Crompton, H., & Burke, D. (2023). Artificial intelligence in higher education: The state of the field. *International Journal of Educational Technology in Higher Education, 20*(1), 1–22. DOI: 10.1186/s41239-023-00392-8

Cronbach, L. (1970). *Essentials of psychological testing* (3rd ed.). Harper.

Cuban, L. (2001). *Oversold and underused: Computers in the classroom*. Harvard University Press., DOI: 10.4159/9780674030107

Cuesta, J. (2025). Gender bias in Artificial Intelligence. *Journal of Economic Policy Reform*. Advance online publication. DOI: 10.1080/17487870.2025.2579039

Curry, M. J., & Lillis, T. (2024). Multilingualism in academic writing for publication: Putting English in its place. *Language Teaching, 57*(1), 87–100. DOI: 10.1017/S0261444822000040

Dai, Y., Lai, S., Lim, C. P., & Liu, A. (2023). Chatgpt and its impact on research supervision: In-sights from australian postgraduate research students. *Australasian Journal of Educational Technology*, *39*(4), 74–88. DOI: 10.14742/ajet.8843

Dalalah, D., & Dalalah, O. M. (2023). The false positives and false negatives of generative AI detection tools in education and academic research: The case of ChatGPT. *International Journal of Management Education*, *21*(2), 100822. DOI: 10.1016/j.ijme.2023.100822

Darbyshire, P., & Beitsayadeh, C. (2025). Enhancing Student Success through GAI and Predictive Analytics. *International Journal for Educational Media and Technology*, *19*(2). https://www.ijemt.org/index.php/journal/article/view/392

Davalos, J., & Yin, L. (2024, October 18). *AI detectors falsely accuse students of cheating with big consequences.* Businessweek. https://news.bloomberglaw.com/private-equity/ai-detection-tools-are-falsely-accusing-students-of-cheating

Dawson, P. (2020). *Defending assessment security in a digital world.* Routledge. DOI: 10.4324/9780429324178

Dawson, P., Henderson, M., Mahoney, P., Phillips, M., Ryan, T., Boud, D., & Molloy, E. (2019). What makes for effective feedback: Staff and student perspectives. *Assessment & Evaluation in Higher Education*, *44*(1), 25–36. DOI: 10.1080/02602938.2018.1467877

de Bruin, A. B. H., Biwer, F., Hui, L., Onan, E., David, L., & Wiradhany, W. (2023). Worth the ef-fort: The start and stick to desirable difficulties (s2d2) framework. *Educational Psychology Review*, *35*(1), 41. Advance online publication. DOI: 10.1007/s10648-023-09766-w

De Wit, H., & Altbach, P. G. (2021). Internationalization in higher education: Global trends and recommendations for its future. *Policy Reviews in Higher Education*, *5*(1), 28–46. DOI: 10.1080/23322969.2020.1820898

Deck, L., Schoeffer, J., De-Arteaga, M., & Kühl, N. (2024). A critical survey on fairness benefits of explainable AI. In *Proceedings of the 2024 ACM conference on fairness, accountability, and transparency 1579*-1595. DOI: 10.1145/3630106.3658990

Dede, C. (2006). Scaling up: Evolving innovations beyond ideal settings to challenging contexts of practice. In Sawyer, R. K. (Ed.), *The Cambridge handbook of the learning sciences* (pp. 551–566). Cambridge University Press., DOI: 10.1017/CBO9780511816833.034

Deepa, S. (2022c). Options in multiple choice questions: Oh Really! Yours sincerely Adult learners! *Language and Language Teaching: A peer reviewed journal.* Vol 11.2.22. (pp 81-86.)

Deepa, S. (2022a). Thought seeds in anthrogogic learning contexts. *Journal of Indian Education, 48*(2), 58–70.

Deepa, S. (2022b). Verbal disposition: The need for language potentiality in anthrogogic spaces. *Journal of English Language Teaching, 64*(6), 17–24. DOI: 10.66121/x2e8ay04

Deepa, S. (2026). Principles of anthrogogic language education. In Deepa, S., & Durairajan, G. (Eds.), *Anthrogogy in Use: A Handbook for Language Educators* (pp. 3–26). Orient BlackSwan.

Deepa, S., & Ambati, A. (2026). Anthrogogic Contexts and Student Sense of Plausibility in Language Materials. In Sarkeshikian, A. (Ed.), *Exploring the Psychology of Language Materials Development* (pp. 245–278). IGI Global Scientific Publishing., DOI: 10.4018/979-8-3373-2995-6.ch008

Deepa, S., & Durairajan, G. (2023). Learning through assessment in anthrogogic contexts: Wash-forward. In Gokturk-Saglam, A. L., & Sevgi-Sole, E. (Eds.), *Emerging practices for online language assessment, exams, evaluation, and feedback* (pp. 99–118). IGI Global., DOI: 10.4018/978-1-6684-6227-0.ch006

Deepa, S., & Durairajan, G. (2025a). Students and Teachers as Equal Learning Collaborators: Reflections on an Anthrogogic Course in India. In Aftab, A. (Ed.), *Materials for Language Assessment* (pp. 91–111). Cambridge Scholars Publishing., https://www.cambridgescholars.com/product/978-1-0364-5693-1

Deepa, S., & Durairajan, G. (2026). Language learner versus user in anthrogogic contexts: The case of idioms in multiple choice items. In Tomlinson, B., & Masuhara, H. (Eds.), *Materials Development for L2 Communicative Ability: Theory and Practice* (pp. 393–406). Bloomsbury Academic.

Deepshikha, D. (2026, December). A systematic review on the future of educational assessment: AI-driven grading and personalised feedback in higher education. In Artificial Intelligence in Education (Vol. 2, No. 2, pp. 75-115). Emerald Publishing Limited.

Deepshikha, D. (2025). A comprehensive review of AI-powered grading and tailored feedback in universities. *Discover Artificial Intelligence, 2025*(5), 251. DOI: 10.1007/s44163-025-00517-0

Deepshikha, D. (2026). *A systematic review on the future of educational assessment: AI-driven grading and personalised feedback in higher education.* Artificial Intelligence in Education., DOI: 10.1108/AIIE-03-2025-0036

Dewey, J. (1910). *How we think*. Prometheus Books. DOI: 10.1037/10903-000

Dhinakaran, D., Edwin, S., Gopalakrishnan, S., Selvaraj, D., & Lalitha, S. D. (2025). UNCA: A Neutrosophic-Based Framework for Robust Clustering and Enhanced Data Interpretation. *International Journal of Neutrosophic Science*, *25*(4), 176–192. DOI: 10.54216/IJNS.250415

Dhinakaran, D., Gopalakrishnan, S., Selvaraj, D., Girija, M. S., & Prabaharan, G. (2025). Mining privacy-preserving association rules using transaction hewer allocator and facile hash algorithm in multi-cloud environments. *MethodsX*, *14*, 103317. DOI: 10.1016/j.mex.2025.103317 PMID: 40331027

Dhinakaran, D., Kumar, D. A., Dinesh, S., Selvaraj, D., & Srikanth, K. Recommendation System for Research Studies Based on GCR, *2022 International Mobile and Embedded Technology Conference (MECON)*, Noida, India, (2022) 61-65, DOI: 10.1109/MECON53876.2022.9751920

Dhinakaran, D., Ramani, R., Edwin Raja, S., & Selvaraj, D. (2026). Enhancing clinical data security with the contextual polynomial-based data protection model (CPDPM). *Biomedical Signal Processing and Control*, *111*, 108329. DOI: 10.1016/j.bspc.2025.108329

Dikmen, M., Burns, C., de Bruijn, H., Warnier, M., Janssen, M., Afchar, D., Melchiorre, A. B., Schedl, M., Hennequin, R., Epure, E. V., Moussallam, M., Leventi-Peetz, A.-M., Östreich, T., Giroux, M., Kim, J., Lee, J. C., Park, J., Hsu, T.-C., & Abelson, H. Mildaintrainings. (2021). Explainable Artificial Intelligence (XAI): Concepts, taxonomies, opportunities and challenges toward responsible AI. *Information Fusion*.

DiPaulo, D. (2022). Do preservice teachers cheat in college, too? A quantitative study of academic integrity among preservice teachers. *International Journal for Educational Integrity*, *18*(1), 3. DOI: 10.1007/s40979-021-00097-3

Doğan, M., Celik, A., & Arslan, H. (2025). AI in higher education: Risks and opportunities from the academician perspective. *European Journal of Education*, *60*(1), e12863. DOI: 10.1111/ejed.12863

Dollinger, M., Lodge, J. M., & Coates, H. (2019). Co-creation in higher education: Towards a conceptual model. *Journal of Industry-University Collaboration*, *1*(1), 45–59. DOI: 10.1108/JIUC-01-2018-0003

Dolský, M. (2025). Reassembling Learning Collectives: An Ethnography of Student Entanglements with Generative AI in Czech Higher Education.

Douglas, K. A., Neumann, K., & Elena Oliveri, M. (2023). Contemporary Approaches to Assessment of Engineering Competencies for Diverse Learners. *International Handbook of Engineering Education Research*, 690–709. DOI: 10.4324/9781003287483-37

Drachsler, H., & Greller, W. (2016). Privacy and analytics: It's a DELICATE issue. *Proceedings of the 6th International Conference on Learning Analytics & Knowledge*, 89-98. DOI: 10.1145/2883851.2883893

Du, H., Sun, Y., Jiang, H., Islam, A. Y. M. A., & Gu, X. (2024). Exploring the effects of AI literacy in teacher learning: An empirical study. *Humanities & Social Sciences Communications*, *11*(1), 559. Advance online publication. DOI: 10.1057/s41599-024-03101-6

Durairajan, G. (2026). Principles of anthrogogic testing and assessment: The need for joyful humane practices. In Deepa, S., & Durairajan, G. (Eds.), *Anthrogogy in use: A handbook for language educators* (pp. 27–55). Orient BlackSwan.

Durning, S. J., Dong, T., Ratcliffe, T., Schuwirth, L., Artino, A. R.Jr, Boulet, J. R., & Eva, K. (2016). Comparing open-book and closed-book examinations: A systematic review. *Academic Medicine*, *91*(4), 583–599. DOI: 10.1097/ACM.0000000000000977 PMID: 26535862

Dwivedi, Y. K., Hughes, L., Ismagilova, E., Aarts, G., Coombs, C., Crick, T., Duan, Y., Dwivedi, R., Edwards, J., Eirug, A., Galanos, V., Ilavarasan, P. V., Janssen, M., Jones, P., Kar, A. K., Kizgin, H., Kronemann, B., Lal, B., Lucini, B., & Williams, M. D. (2023). So what if ChatGPT wrote it? Multidisciplinary perspectives on opportunities, challenges and implications of generative conversational AI for research, practice and policy. *International Journal of Information Management*, *71*, 102642. DOI: 10.1016/j.ijinfomgt.2023.102642

Eacersall, D., Pretorius, L., Smirnov, I., Spray, E., Illingworth, S., Chugh, R., Strydom, S., Stratton-Maher, D., Simmons, J., Jennings, I., Roux, R., Kamrowski, R., Downie, A., Thong, C. L., & Howell, K. A. (2025). Navigating ethical challenges in generative ai-enhanced research: The ethical framework for responsible generative ai use. *Journal of Applied Learning and Teaching*, *8*(2), 102–115. DOI: 10.37074/jalt.2025.8.2.9

Eaton, S. E. (2023). ChatGPT and other AI text generators: Strategies for promoting academic integrity. *Innovations in Education and Teaching International.* Advance online publication. DOI: 10.1080/14703297.2023.2190148

Eaton, S. E. (2025). Neurodiversity and academic integrity: Toward epistemic plurality in a post plagiarism era. *Teaching in Higher Education*, 1–20. DOI: 10.1080/13562517.2025.2583456

Editors Academy of Management Learning and Education. (2024). From the editors: Critical thinning in the age of generative AI. *Academy of Management Learning and Education Journal*, 23(3). 373-378. DOI: 10.5465/amle.2024.0338

EL Fougour, W., & Erradi, M. (2025). Enhancing formative assessment with AI. Advances in Computational Intelligence and Robotics Book Series, 307–332. DOI: 10.4018/979-8-3373-7579-3.ch010

Elkhatat, A. M., Elsaid, K., & Almeer, S. (2023). Evaluating the efficacy of AI content detection tools in differentiating between human and AI-generated text. *International Journal for Educational Integrity, 19*(1), 17. DOI: 10.1007/s40979-023-00140-5

Elliot, N. (2016). A theory of ethics for writing assessment. *Journal of Writing Assessment, 9*(1). Advance online publication. DOI: 10.5281/zenodo.55756

Ellis, C., Dawson, P., Bearman, M., Boud, D., Ajjawi, R., & Tai, J. (2024). Assessment reform in the age of artificial intelligence. *Assessment & Evaluation in Higher Education*. Advance online publication. DOI: 10.1080/02602938.2024.2385343

Ellis, R. A., Goodyear, P., O'Hara, A., & Prosser, M. (2020). Students' experiences of e-assessment in higher education: The ecology of assessment for learning. *Assessment & Evaluation in Higher Education, 45*(2), 316–330. DOI: 10.1080/02602938.2019.1638117

Elsayed, H. (2024). The impact of hallucinated information in large language models on student learning outcomes: A critical examination of misinformation risks in AI-assisted education. *Northern Reviews on Algorithmic Research, Theoretical Computation, and Complexity, 9*(8), 11–23.

Elshall, A. S., & Badir, A. (2025). Balancing AI-assisted learning and traditional assessment: The FACT assessment in environmental data science education. *Frontiers in Education, 10*, 1596462. Advance online publication. DOI: 10.3389/feduc.2025.1596462

Ertmer, P. A., & Ottenbreit-Leftwich, A. T. (2010). Teacher technology change: How knowledge, confidence, beliefs, and culture intersect. *Journal of Research on Technology in Education, 42*(3), 255–284. DOI: 10.1080/15391523.2010.10782551

Esmaeilzadeh, F., Ghahari, S., & Rohani, G. (2025). Artificial intelligence in language teaching and assessment: A systematic review of research (2020-2024). *The Asian Journal of Applied Linguistics, 9*(1), 1222–1222.

European Network for Academic Integrity. (2018, October 26). *Glossary for academic integrity.* https://www.academicintegrity.eu/wp/glossary/

Eynon, R. (2021). What should be the role of AI in education? *AI & Society*, *36*(4), 1199–1203. DOI: 10.1007/s00146-020-01040-4

Eysenbach, G. (2023). The Role of ChatGPT, Generative Language Models, and Artificial Intelligence in Medical Education: A Conversation With ChatGPT and a Call for Papers. *JMIR Medical Education*, *9*, e46885. https://mededu.jmir.org/2023/1/e46885. DOI: 10.2196/46885 PMID: 36863937

Fabris-Rotelli, I., von Maltitz, M. J., Smit, A., Das, S., Roberts, D., Maribe, G., Maposa, D., & Correa, F. M. (2022). Development of an early career academic supervisor in statistics - a discussion towards a guiding rubric. *ORiON, 38*(1), 29–51. https://hdl.handle.net/10520/ ejc-orion_v38_n1_a2

Facione, P. (1990). *Delphi report.* Committee on Pre-College Philosophy, American Psychological Association. https://assessment.trinity.duke.edu/documents/Delphi_Report.pdf

Fagbohun, O., Iduwe, N. P., Abdullahi, M., Ifaturoti, A., & Nwanna, O. M. (2024). Beyond traditional assessment: Exploring the impact of large language models on grading practices. Journal of Artificial Intelligence. *Machine Learning and Data Science*, *2*(1), 1–8. DOI: 10.51219/JAIMLD/oluwole-fagbohun/19

Farrokhnia, M., Latifi, S., Papadopoulos, P. M., Hogenkamp, L., Gijlers, H., Khosravi, H., & Noroozi, O. (2026). Generative AI offers more, but students revise less: Comparing the effects of teacher and AI feedback on student essay revisions. *International Journal of Educational Technology in Higher Education*, *23*(1), 6. DOI: 10.1186/s41239-026-00579-9

Feng, S. (2025). Group interaction patterns in generative AI-supported collaborative problem solving: Network analysis of the interactions among students and a GAI chatbot. *British Journal of Educational Technology*, *56*(5), 2125–2145. DOI: 10.1111/bjet.13611

Ferguson, R. (2012). Learning analytics: Drivers, developments and challenges. *International Journal of Technology Enhanced Learning*, *4*(5-6), 304–317. DOI: 10.1504/IJTEL.2012.051816

Ferrara, E. (2024). The butterfly effect in artificial intelligence systems: Implications for AI bias and fairness. *Machine Learning with Applications*, *15*, 100525. Advance online publication. DOI: 10.1016/j.mlwa.2024.100525

Ferreira, W. J., & Richetto, K. C. D. S. (2025). Education towards equity: Adapting assessment practices in the multicultural context of mathematics education. *Educar em Revista, 41*, e93725. DOI: 10.1590/1984-0411.93725

Fink, L. D. (2003). *Creating significant learning experiences: An integrated approach to designing college courses*. Jossey-Bass.

Fiorella, L., & Mayer, R. E. (2016). Eight ways to promote generative learning. *Educational Psychology Review, 28*(4), 717–741. DOI: 10.1007/s10648-015-9348-9

Fitas, R. (2025). Inclusive education with AI: Supporting special needs and tackling language barriers. *AI and Ethics, 5*(6), 5729–5757. Advance online publication. DOI: 10.1007/s43681-025-00824-3

Fixsen, D. L., Naoom, S. F., Blase, K. A., Friedman, R. M., & Wallace, F. (2005). *Implementation research: A synthesis of the literature*. University of South Florida., DOI: 10.1037/e525602012-001

Flahive, E. (2026). Assessment in Higher Education: Purpose, Practice, and Feedback. In Linguistics and Language Teaching Conference 2024 (p. 196). Zayed University Press.

Flanagan, J. C. (1954). The critical incident technique. *Psychological Bulletin, 51*(4), 327–358. DOI: 10.1037/h0061470 PMID: 13177800

Floridi, L., Cowls, J., Beltrametti, M., Chatila, R., Chazerand, P., Dignum, V., Luetge, C., Madelin, R., Pagallo, U., Rossi, F., Schafer, B., Valcke, P., & Vayena, E. (2018). AI4People, An ethical framework for a good AI society: Opportunities, risks, principles, and recommendations. *Minds and Machines, 28*(4), 689–707. DOI: 10.1007/s11023-018-9482-5

Fortuna, A., Prasetya, F., Dwingo Samala, A., Rawas, S., Criollo, S., Kaya, D., & Nabawi, N. (2025). Artificial intelligence in personalized learning: A global systematic review of current advancements and shaping future opportunities. *Social Sciences & Humanities Open, 12*, 102114. Advance online publication. DOI: 10.1016/j.ssaho.2025.102114

Fošner, A., & Aver, B. (2025). AI chatbots in higher education: Students' beliefs and concerns. *Sustainable Futures: An Applied Journal of Technology, Environment and Society, 9*, 100734. Advance online publication. DOI: 10.1016/j.sftr.2025.100734

Foucault, M. (1991). *Discipline and Punish: The Birth of the Prison*. Vintage Books. (Original work published 1978)

Francis, N. J., Jones, S., & Smith, D. P. (2024). Generative AI in Higher Education: Balancing Innovation and Integrity. In *British Journal of Biomedical Science*. DOI: 10.3389/bjbs.2024.14048

Frank, R., Black, P. E., & Jeff, C. (2025). Testing by Talking: Rethinking Oral Examinations. *American Journal of Pharmaceutical Education, 89*(12), 101892. Advance online publication. DOI: 10.1016/j.ajpe.2025.101892 PMID: 41177357

Freeman, R. E., Phillips, R., & Sisodia, R. (2020). Tensions in stakeholder theory. *Business & Society, 59*(2), 213–231. DOI: 10.1177/0007650318773750

Fyfe, P. (2023). How to cheat on your final paper: Assigning AI for student writing. *AI & Society, 38*(4), 1395–1405. DOI: 10.1007/s00146-022-01397-z

Gao, R., Merzdorf, H. E., Anwar, S., Hipwell, M. C., & Srinivasa, A. (2024). *Automatic assessment of text-based responses in post-secondary education: A systematic review*. https://arxiv.org/abs/2308.16151

Gardner, J., & Brooks, C. (2018). Student success prediction in MOOCs. *User Modeling and User-Adapted Interaction, 28*(2), 127–203. DOI: 10.1007/s11257-018-9203-z

Gay, G. (2018). *Culturally responsive teaching: Theory, research, and practice* (3rd ed.). Teachers College Press.

Gegg-Harrison, W. (2023). Against the use of GPTZero and other LLM-detection tools on student writing. *Write Rethink*. https://writerethink.medium.com/against-the-use-of-gptzero-and-other-llm-detection-tools-on-student-writing-b876b9d1b587

Gerlich, M. (2025). AI tools in society: Impacts on cognitive offloading and the future of critical thinking. *Societies (Basel, Switzerland), 15*(1), 6. Advance online publication. DOI: 10.3390/soc15010006

Geroimenko, V. (2025). Foundational Communication Principles: Ensuring Clarity, Precision, and Effectiveness in AI Interaction. In *Beyond and After Prompt Engineering: The Future of AI Communication* (pp. 137–173). Springer Nature Switzerland.

Ghosh, S., Brooks, B., Ranmuthugala, D., & Bowles, M. (2020). Authentic Versus Traditional Assessment: An Empirical Study Investigating the Difference in Seafarer Students' Academic Achievement. *Journal of Navigation, 73*(4), 797–812. DOI: 10.1017/S0373463319000894

Gikandi, J. W., Morrow, D., & Davis, N. E. (2011). Online formative assessment in higher education: A review of the literature. *Computers & Education, 57*(4), 2333–2351. DOI: 10.1016/j.compedu.2011.06.004

Giray, L., Jacob, J., Encanto, V., & Mansilungan, C. J. (2026). Cheating writing with generative AI: Exploring student motivations using the Theory of Planned Behavior. *Journal of Academic Ethics, 24*(1), 1–23. DOI: 10.1007/s10805-025-09695-z

Glaser, E. M. (1941). *An experiment in the development of critical thinking*. Teacher's College, Columbia University.

Gligorea, I., Cioca, M., Oancea, R., Gorski, A.-T., Gorski, H., & Tudorache, P. (2023). Adaptive Learning Using Artificial Intelligence in e-Learning: A Literature Review. *Education Sciences, 13*(12), 1216. Advance online publication. DOI: 10.3390/educsci13121216

Goldhamer, M. E. J., Martinez-Lage, M., Black-Schaffer, W. S., Huang, J. T., Co, J. P. T., Weinstein, D. F., & Pusic, M. V. (2022). Reimagining the clinical competency committee to enhance education and prepare for competency-based time-variable advancement. *Journal of General Internal Medicine, 37*(9), 2280–2290. DOI: 10.1007/s11606-022-07515-3 PMID: 35445932

Gomes, E. (2026). *The AI that isn't: AI bias against neurodivergent and non-native writers*. Elise. https://www.elisegomes.com/en/post/the-ai-that-isn-t-false-ai-positives-and-the-harm-to-neurodivergent-writers

Gonsalves, C. (2025). Addressing student non-compliance in AI use declarations: Implications for academic integrity and assessment in higher education. *Assessment & Evaluation in Higher Education, 50*(4), 592–606. DOI: 10.1080/02602938.2024.2415654

Gonsalves, C. (2025). Contextual Assessment Design in the Age of Generative AI. *Journal of Learning Development in Higher Education*, (34). Advance online publication. DOI: 10.47408/jldhe.vi34.1307

Govender, R., & Rajkoomar, M. (2021). A multimodal model for learning, teaching and assessment in higher education. COVID-19: Interdisciplinary explorations of impacts on higher education,57. DOI: 10.52779/9781991201195/04

Grinschgl, S., Papenmeir, F., & Meyeroff, H. (2021). Consequences of cognitive offloading: Boosting performance, but diminishing memory. *Quarterly Journal of Experimental Psychology, 74*(9), 1477–1496. DOI: 10.1177/17470218211008060 PMID: 33752519

Gruenhagen, J. H., Sinclair, P. M., Carroll, J., Baker, P. R., Wilson, A., & Demant, D. (2024). The rapid rise of generative AI and its implications for academic integrity: Students' perceptions and use of chatbots for assistance with assessments. *Computers and Education: Artificial Intelligence, 7*, 100273. DOI: 10.1016/j.caeai.2024.100273

Grunwald, A. (2018). Societal engagement in the age of artificial intelligence. *AI & Society, 33*(3), 477–478. DOI: 10.1007/s00146-018-0846-4

Gulikers, J. T. M., Bastiaens, T. J., & Kirschner, P. A. (2004). A five-dimensional framework for authentic assessment. *Educational Technology Research and Development, 52*(3), 67–86. DOI: 10.1007/BF02504676

Gustilo, L., Ong, E., & Lapind, M. R. (2024). Algorithmically-driven writing and academic integrity: Exploring educators' practices, perceptions and policies in the AI era. *International Journal for Educational Integrity, 20*(3), 3. Advance online publication. DOI: 10.1007/s40979-024-00153-8

Habib, S., Vogel, T., Anli, X., & Thorne, E. (2024). How does generative artificial intelligence impact student creativity? *Journal of Creativity, 34*(1), 100072. Advance online publication. DOI: 10.1016/j.yjoc.2023.100072

Hadra, M., Cambridge, K., & Mesbah, M. (2026). Evaluating the accuracy and reliability of AI content detectors in academic contexts. *International Journal for Educational Integrity, 22*(1), 4. DOI: 10.1007/s40979-026-00213-1

Haggard, P. (2019). The neurocognitive bases of human volition. *Annual Review of Psychology, 70*(1), 9–28. DOI: 10.1146/annurev-psych-010418-103348 PMID: 30125134

Hamidi, H., Hejran, A. B., Sarwari, A., & Edigeevna, S. G. (2024). The effect of outcome based education on behavior of students. *European Journal of Theoretical and Applied Sciences, 2*(2), 764–773. DOI: 10.59324/ejtas.2024.2(2).68

Han, B., Coghlan, S., Buchanan, G., & McKay, D. (2025). Who is helping whom? Student concerns about AI-teacher collaboration in higher education classrooms. *Proceedings of the ACM on Human-Computer Interaction*, USA, *9*(2), 1-32. DOI: 10.1145/371110

Hanna, M. G., Pantanowitz, L., Jackson, B., Palmer, O., Visweswaran, S., Pantanowitz, J., Deebajah, M., & Rashidi, H. H. (2025). Ethical and bias considerations in artificial intelligence/machine learning. *Modern Pathology, 38*(3), 100686. Advance online publication. DOI: 10.1016/j.modpat.2024.100686 PMID: 39694331

Hannigan, T., McCarthy, I. P., & Spicer, A. (2024). Beware of botshit: How to manage the epistemic risks of generative chatbots. *Business Horizons, 4678265*(5), 471–486. Advance online publication. DOI: 10.1016/j.bushor.2024.03.001

Han, Y., Ren, W., & Li, X. (2026). Can artificial intelligence assistance enhance creativity in university students? An experimental study. *New Ideas in Psychology, 82*, 101246. DOI: 10.1016/j.newideapsych.2026.101246

Hao, J., von Davier, A. A., Yaneva, V., Lottridge, S., von Davier, M., & Harris, D. J. (2024). Transforming assessment: The impacts and implications of large language models and generative AI. *Educational Measurement: Issues and Practice*, *43*(3), 5–16. DOI: 10.1111/emip.12602

Harrington, L. (2024). Comparison of generative artificial intelligence and predictive artificial intelligence. *AACN Advanced Critical Care*, *35*(2), 93–96. Advance online publication. DOI: 10.4037/aacnacc2024225 PMID: 38848562

Harvard University. (2025). *Student handbook academic integrity*. https://oaisc.fas.harvard.edu/find-resources/

Hassen, M. (2025). The impact of AI on students' reading, critical thinking, and problem-solving skills. *American Journal of Education and Information Technology*, *9*(2), 82–90. DOI: 10.11648/j.ajeit.20250902.12

Hattie, J., & Timperley, H. (2007). The power of feedback. *Review of Educational Research*, *77*(1), 81–112. DOI: 10.3102/003465430298487

Hazra, R., Chatterjee, P., & Ghosh, S. (2026). Assessment and Feedback Through Generative AI Intelligent Tutoring Systems. In Collaborative Paradigms of Generative AI and Human Intelligence for Equitable Learning Futures (pp. 121-148). IGI Global Scientific Publishing. DOI: 10.4018/979-8-3373-6063-8.ch005

Heidari Tabrizi, H., & House, J. (2025). Moving Beyond Conventional Tests: Performance Assessment as an Alternative for Evaluating Students' Academic Translations. Contrastive Pragmatics, 1-32. DOI: 10.1163/26660393-bja10139

Heijne-Penninga, M., Kuks, J. B. M., Hofman, W. H. A., & Cohen-Schotanus, J. (2008). Influence of open-book tests on study behaviour: A discrete choice experiment. *Advances in Health Sciences Education : Theory and Practice*, *13*(2), 263–273. DOI: 10.1007/s10459-006-9038-y PMID: 17063381

Henderson, M., Selwyn, N., & Aston, R. (2017). What works and why? Student perceptions of 'useful' digital technology in university teaching and learning. *Studies in Higher Education*, *42*(8), 1567–1579. DOI: 10.1080/03075079.2015.1007946

Herodotou, C., Rienties, B., Hlosta, M., Boroowa, A., Mangafa, C., & Zdrahal, Z. (2020). The scalable implementation of predictive learning analytics at a distance learning university: Insights from a longitudinal case study. *The Internet and Higher Education*, *45*, 100725. DOI: 10.1016/j.iheduc.2020.100725

Herzog-Punzenberger, B., Altrichter, H., Brown, M., Burns, D., Nortvedt, G. A., Skedsmo, G., Wiese, E., Nayir, F., Fellner, M., McNamara, G., & O'Hara, J. (2020). Teachers responding to cultural diversity: case studies on assessment practices, challenges and experiences in secondary schools in Austria, Ireland, Norway and Turkey. *Educational Assessment, Evaluation and Accountability 2020 32:3, 32*(3), 395–424. DOI: 10.1007/s11092-020-09330-y

Hochstetter-Diez, J., Negrier-Seguel, M., Diéguez-Rebolledo, M., Candia-Garrido, E., & Vidal, E. (2025). From Mapping to Action: SmartRubrics, an AI Tool for Competency-Based Assessment in Engineering Education. *Sustainability (Basel), 17*(13), 6098. DOI: 10.3390/su17136098

Hofmann, V., Kalluri, P. R., Jurafsky, D., & King, S. (2024). Ai generates covertly racist decisions about people based on their dialect. *Nature, 633*(8028), 147–154. DOI: 10.1038/s41586-024-07856-5 PMID: 39198640

Holmes, W., Anastopoulou, S., Schaumburg, H., & Mavrikis, M. (2022). *Technology-enhanced personalised learning: Untangling the evidence*. Robert Bosch Stiftung. DOI: 10.25656/01:25412

Holmes, W., Bialik, M., & Fadel, C. (2019). *Artificial Intelligence in Education Promises and Implications for Teaching and Learning* (1st ed.). Center for Curriculum Redesign.

Holmes, W., Bialik, M., & Fadel, C. (2019). *Artificial intelligence in education: Promises and implications for teaching and learning*. Center for Curriculum Redesign., DOI: 10.1007/s40593-021-00237-x

Holmes, W., & Porayska-Pomsta, K. (2022). *The ethics of artificial intelligence in education: Practices, challenges, and debates*. Routledge., DOI: 10.4324/9780429329067

Holstein, K., & Doroudi, S. (2021). Equity and artificial intelligence in education: Will "AIEd" amplify or alleviate inequities in education? *arXiv preprint*. /arXiv.2104.12920DOI: 10.48550

Holstein, K., Hong, G., Tegene, M., McLaren, B. M., & Aleven, V. (2018). The classroom as a dashboard: Co-designing wearable cognitive augmentation for K-12 teachers. *Proceedings of the 8th International Conference on Learning Analytics and Knowledge*, 79-88. DOI: 10.1145/3170358.3170377

Holstein, K., McLaren, B. M., & Aleven, V. (2019). Co-designing a real-time classroom orchestration tool to support teacher-AI complementarity. *Journal of Learning Analytics, 6*(2), 27–52. DOI: 10.18608/jla.2019.62.3

Holzinger, A. (2016). Interactive machine learning for health informatics: When do we need the human-in-the-loop? *Brain Informatics*, *3*(2), 119–131. DOI: 10.1007/s40708-016-0042-6

Hong Kong Government. (2021). *Population Census*. Census and Statistics Department.

Hooda, M., Rana, C., Dahiya, O., Rizwan, A., & Hossain, M. S. (2022). Artificial intelligence for assessment and feedback to enhance student success in higher education. *Mathematical Problems in Engineering*, *2022*(1), 5215722. DOI: 10.1155/2022/5215722

Hsu, T. C., & Lao, N. (2025). From Policy to Pedagogy–Building Human-Centered AI Literacy Across Educational Contexts. *Informatics in Education*, *24*(4), 645–651. DOI: 10.15388/infedu.2025.00

Huang, J., Xin, Y. P., & Chang, H. H. (2025). The application of machine learning to educational process data analysis: A systematic review. *Education Sciences*, *15*(7), 888. Advance online publication. DOI: 10.3390/educsci15070888

Huang, X., Zou, D., Cheng, G., Chen, X., & Xie, H. (2023). Trends, research issues and applications of artificial intelligence in language education. *Journal of Educational Technology & Society*, *26*(1), 112–131. https://www.jstor.org/stable/48707971

Huang, Y., Li, S., & Liu, Z. (2025). Can genai complement supervisor support in shaping post-graduates' research experiences? a mixed-methods approach. *Studies in Higher Education*, •••, 1–19. DOI: 10.1080/03075079.2025.2495710

Hubbard, P., & Schulze, M. (2025). AI and the future of language teaching: Motivating sustained integrated professional development. [IJCALLT]. *International Journal of Computer-Assisted Language Learning and Teaching*, *15*(1), 1–17. DOI: 10.4018/IJCALLT.378304

Hughes, L., Dwivedi, Y. K., Malik, T., Shawosh, M., Albashrawi, M. A., Jeon, I., Dutot, V., Ap-panderanda, M., Crick, T., De', R., Fenwick, M., Gunaratnege, S. M., Jurcys, P., Kar, A. K., Kshetri, N., Li, K., Mutasa, S., Samothrakis, S., Wade, M., & Walton, P. (2025). Ai agents and agentic systems: A multi-expert analysis. *Journal of Computer Information Systems*, *65*(4), 489–517. DOI: 10.1080/08874417.2025.2483832

Hung, C. T., Wu, S. E., Chen, Y. H., Soong, C. Y., Chiang, C. P., & Wang, W. M. (2024). The evaluation of synchronous and asynchronous online learning: Student experience, learning outcomes, and cognitive load. *BMC Medical Education*, *24*(1), 326. DOI: 10.1186/s12909-024-05311-7 PMID: 38519950

Hutson, J., Taft, J. G., Barocas, S., & Levy, K. (2018). Debiasing desire: Addressing bias & discrimination on intimate platforms. *Proceedings of the ACM on Human-Computer Interaction*, 2(CSCW), 1-18. DOI: 10.1145/3274342

Hymes, D. H. (1972). On communicative competence. In Pride, J. B., & Holmes, J. (Eds.), *Sociolinguistics* (pp. 269–293). Penguin.

Ibrahim, K. (2023). Using AI-based detectors for control AI-assisted plagiarism in ESL writing: "The Terminator vs. the machines. *Language Testing in Asia, 13*(46), 46. Advance online publication. DOI: 10.1186/s40468-023-00260-2

Iddrisu, H. M., & Iddrisu, S. A. (2025). Teacher Readiness to Use AI Tools in the Classroom. *International Journal of Research in Education and Science, 11*(3), 494–510. Advance online publication. DOI: 10.46328/ijres.1314

Ifenthaler, D., & Yau, J. Y. K. (2020). Utilising learning analytics to support study success in higher education: A systematic review. *Educational Technology Research and Development, 68*(4), 1961–1990. DOI: 10.1007/s11423-020-09788-z

Ilgun Dibek, M., Sahin Kursad, M., & Erdogan, T. (2025). Influence of artificial intelligence tools on higher order thinking skills: A meta-analysis. *Interactive Learning Environments, 33*(3), 2216–2223. DOI: 10.1080/10494820.2024.2402028

Ilieva, G., Yankova, T., Ruseva, M., & Kabaivanov, S. (2025). A framework for generative AI-driven assessment in higher education. *Information (Basel), 16*(6), 472. DOI: 10.3390/info16060472

Ince, A. H., & Özbay, S. (2025). AI-Enhanced Adaptive Testing: Integrating Response Time with IRT Models. *KSII Transactions on Internet and Information Systems, 19*(8). Advance online publication. DOI: 10.3837/tiis.2025.08.005

Indiana University of Pennsylvania. (2026). *Types of violations.* https://www.iup.edu/academicaffairs/for-faculty/academic-integrity/types-of-violations.html

International Center for Academic Integrity. (2014). Fundamental values of academic integrity. {Pamphlet}. https://www.academicintegrity.org/aws/ICAI/pt/sp/values

International Center for Academic Integrity. (2021). *The fundamental values of academic integrity.*

Iqbal, J., Hashmi, Z. F., Asghar, M. Z., & Abid, M. N. (2025). Generative ai tool use enhances aca-demic achievement in sustainable education through shared meta-cognition and cognitive offloading among preservice teachers. *Scientific Reports, 15*(1), 16610. Advance online publication. DOI: 10.1038/s41598-025-01676-x PMID: 40360573

Irons, A., & Elkington, S. (2021). *Enhancing learning through formative assessment and feedback*. Routledge. DOI: 10.4324/9781138610514

Islam, M., Hasan, M. M., & Mahmud, R. (2024). EFL teachers' perceptions of AI's impact on academic integrity and pedagogy in Bangladeshi universities. *Language Literacy: Journal of Linguistics, Literature, and Language Teaching*, *8*(2), 564–579. DOI: 10.30743/ll.v8i2.10082

Ismail, A., Tanweer, M., & Farooq, S. (2024). Transforming assessments with generative AI. Advances in Educational Technologies and Instructional Design Book Series, 379–404. DOI: 10.4018/979-8-3693-2418-9.ch014

Iswari, N. M. S. (2025). Personalized learning system based on artificial intelligence to enhance learning effectiveness: A bibliometric analysis. *G-Tech*, *9*(3), 1436–1446. DOI: 10.70609/g-tech.v9i3.7355

Jacobsen, L. J., & Weber, K. E. (2023). The promises and pitfalls of ChatGPT as a feedback provider in higher education: An exploratory study of prompt engineering and the quality of AI-driven feedback. *OSF preprints*, 29.

Jamieson, S., & Moore Howard, R. (2019). Rethinking the relationship between plagiarism and academic integrity. *International Journal of Technologies in Higher Education*, *16*(2), 69. Advance online publication. DOI: 10.18162/ritpu-2019-v16n2-07

Janardhana, D. R., Arif, H., Bhat, U. H., Rukmini, T., Hanumanthappa, H., & Gaikwad, V. (2025). Personalized learning systems using AI enhancing adaptive education. *International Journal of Environmental Sciences*, •••, 668–676. DOI: 10.64252/ps80c806

Jang, E. E., & Sawaki, Y. (2025). Advancing language assessment for teaching and learning in the era of the artificial intelligence (AI) revolution: Promises and challenges. *Language Testing*, *42*(4), 361–368. DOI: 10.1177/02655322251348685

Jarni, N., & Gurr, D. A. (2024). A futures perspective on learning and teaching in higher education: An essay on best and next practices. *Trends in Higher Education*, *3*(3), 793–811. DOI: 10.3390/higheredu3030045

Jeon, J. (2024). Exploring AI chatbot affordances in the EFL classroom: Young learners' experiences and perspectives. *Computer Assisted Language Learning*, *37*(1–2), 1–26. DOI: 10.1080/09588221.2021.2021241

Jervis, C. G., & Brown, L. R. (2020). The prospects of sitting 'end of year' open book exams in the light of COVID-19: A medical student's perspective. *British Journal of Educational Technology*, *51*(5), 1865–1870. DOI: 10.1111/bjet.12980 PMID: 32432953

Jewitt, C. (2008). Multimodality and literacy in school classrooms. *Review of Research in Education*, *32*(1), 241–267. DOI: 10.3102/0091732X07310586

Jha, M., & Atif, A. (2025). Reimagining pedagogy for the GenAI era: Frameworks, challenges and institutional strategies. *Australasian Journal of Educational Technology*, *41*(5), 56–73. DOI: 10.14742/ajet.10645

Jiang, Y., Hao, J., Fauss, M., & Li, C. (2024). Detecting Chat-GPT-generated essays in a large-scale writing assessment: Is there a bias against non-native speakers? *Computers & Education*, *217*, 105070. Advance online publication. DOI: 10.1016/j.compedu.2024.105070

Jiang, Y., Xie, L., & Cao, X. (2025). Exploring the effectiveness of institutional policies and regulations for generative AI usage in higher education. *Higher Education Quarterly*, *79*(4), e70054. DOI: 10.1111/hequ.70054

Jia, X. H., & Tu, J. C. (2024). Towards a New Conceptual Model of AI-Enhanced Learning for College Students: The Roles of Artificial Intelligence Capabilities, General Self-Efficacy, Learning Motivation, and Critical Thinking Awareness. *Systems*, *12*(3), 74. Advance online publication. DOI: 10.3390/systems12030074

Jia, X., Li, P., & Li, W. (2025, February 24). The role of creative mindsets in the relationship between metacognitive experience and divergent thinking: A metacognitive perspective. *Journal of Intelligence*, *13*(3), 27. Advance online publication. DOI: 10.3390/jintelligence13030027 PMID: 40137059

Ji, H., Han, I., & Ko, Y. (2023). A systematic review of conversational AI in language education: Focusing on the collaboration with human teachers. *Journal of Research on Technology in Education*, *55*(1), 48–63. DOI: 10.1080/15391523.2022.2142873

Jin, Y., Yan, L., Echeverria, V., Gašević, D., & Martinez-Maldonado, R. (2025). Generative AI in higher education: A global perspective of institutional adoption policies and guidelines. *Computers and Education: Artificial Intelligence*, *8*(4), 100348. DOI: 10.1016/j.caeai.2024.100348

Ji, Z., Lee, N., Frieske, R., Yu, T., Su, D., Xu, Y., Ishii, E., Bang, Y. J., Madotto, A., & Fung, P. (2023). Survey of hallucination in natural language generation. *ACM Computing Surveys*, *55*(12), 1–38. Advance online publication. DOI: 10.1145/3571730

Johansen, M. W., Goddiksen, M. P., Clavien, C., Hogan, L., Olsson, I. A. S., Santos, J. B., dos Santos, R. A., Wall, P. J., Sandøe, P., & Lund, T. B. (2026, March). Academic integrity across educational levels: Exploring students' engagement with grey-zone and non-compliant practices in four European countries. *PLoS One*, *21*(3), e0342227. Advance online publication. DOI: 10.1371/journal.pone.0342227 PMID: 41779692

Johns Hopkins University. (2026). *Neurodivergence at a glance*. https://imagine.jhu.edu/blog/2022/10/05/neurodivergence-at-a-glance/

Johnson, T. K. A. (2024). Humanization in Higher Education: A Grounded Theory Study on the Impact That Customer Service Practices Have on the Student Academic Journey (Doctoral dissertation, Morgan State University).

Johnson, M. S., & McCaffrey, D. F. (2023). Evaluating Fairness of Automated Scoring in Educational Measurement. In *Advancing Natural Language Processing in Educational Assessment* (pp. 142–164). Taylor and Francis., DOI: 10.4324/9781003278658-12

Johnstone, S. M., & Soares, L. (2014). Principles for developing competency-based education programs. *Change*, *46*(2), 12–19. DOI: 10.1080/00091383.2014.896705

Jones, N., & Saville, N. (2009). European language policy: Assessment, learning, and the CEFR. *Annual Review of Applied Linguistics*, *29*, 51–63. DOI: 10.1017/S0267190509090059

Jönsson, A. (2024). Prompting for progression: How well can GenAI create a sense of progression in a set of multiple-choice questions?.

Kaddouri, M., Mhamdi, K., Jabri, A., Boukare, M., & Jmad, S. (2025). Generative artificial intelligence and assessment of learning. Advances in Educational Technologies and Instructional Design Book Series, 277–326. DOI: 10.4018/979-8-3693-6527-4.ch010

Kaldaras, L., Akaeze, H. O., & Reckase, M. D. (2024). Developing valid assessments in the era of generative artificial intelligence. *Frontiers in Education*, *9*, 1399377. Advance online publication. DOI: 10.3389/feduc.2024.1399377

Kandiko Howson, C., & Kingsbury, M. (2023). Curriculum change as transformational learning.

Kane, M. T. (2013). Validating the interpretations and uses of test scores. *Journal of Educational Measurement*, *50*(1), 1–73. DOI: 10.1111/jedm.12000

Kang, B., & Kang, S. (2022). Construction of Chinese language teaching system model based on deep learning under the background of artificial intelligence. *Scientific Programming*, *2022*(1), 3960023. DOI: 10.1155/2022/3960023

Kapur, M. (2008). Productive failure. *Cognition and Instruction*, *26*(3), 379–424. DOI: 10.1080/07370000802212669

Kapur, M., Hattie, J., Grossman, I., & Sinha, T. (2022, September). Fail, flip, fix, and feed–Rethinking flipped learning: A review of meta-analyses and a subsequent meta-analysis. [). Frontiers Media SA.]. *Frontiers in Education*, *7*, 956416. DOI: 10.3389/feduc.2022.956416

Karadağ, N. (2023). The impact of artificial intelligence on online assessment: A preliminary review. *Journal of Educational Technology & Online Learning*, *6*(4), 822–837. DOI: 10.31681/jetol.1351548

Karakose, T., & Tulubas, T. (2025). The role of educational leaders in the age of artificial intelligence (AI). *Educational Process: International Journal*, *16*(1), e2025267. DOI: 10.22521/edupij.2025.16.267

Karimi, H., Khawaja, S., Karimi, H., & Khawaja, S. (2023). The Impact of Artificial Intelligence on Higher Education in England. *Creative Education*, *14*(12), 2405–2415. DOI: 10.4236/ce.2023.1412154

Karim, N. A., Mat, C. M., Suhailah, I., & Noor, M. (2025). A Methodological Framework for AI-Integrated Alternative Assessments in Engineering Education. *Jurnal Kejuruteraan*, *37*(2), 807–819. DOI: 10.17576/jkukm-2025-37(2)-20

Karnabi, S. (2025). Exploring International Master's Students' Perceptions on the Use of Generative AI tools for.

Karpicke, J. D., Butler, A. C., & Roediger, H. L.III. (2009). Metacognitive strategies in student learning: Do students practise retrieval when they study on their own? *Memory (Hove, England)*, *17*(4), 471–479. DOI: 10.1080/09658210802647009 PMID: 19358016

Kasneci, E., Sessler, K., Küchemann, S., Bannert, M., Dementieva, D., Fischer, F., Gasser, U., Groh, G., Günnemann, S., Hüllermeier, E., Krusche, S., Kutyniok, G., Michaeli, T., Nerdel, C., Pfeffer, J., Poquet, O., Sailer, M., Schmidt, A., Seidel, T., & Kasneci, G. (2023). ChatGPT for good? On opportunities and challenges of large language models for education. *Learning and Individual Differences*, *103*, 102274. DOI: 10.1016/j.lindif.2023.102274

Katsamakas, E., Pavlov, O. V., & Saklad, R. (2024). Artificial intelligence and the transformation of higher education institutions: A systems approach. *Sustainability (Basel), 16*(14), 6118. DOI: 10.3390/su16146118

Keith-Spiegel, P. (1994). Teaching psychologist and the new APA ethics code: Do we fit in? *Professional Psychology, Research and Practice, 25*(4), 362–268. DOI: 10.1037/0735-7028.25.4.362 PMID: 12186089

Khaliq, A., Muhammad, N., & Qamar, N. (2025). Enhancing Student Engagement and Academic Performance through AI-Based Tutoring Systems: A Comparative Study of Traditional vs. AI-Driven Education Models. *The Critical Review of Social Sciences Studies, 3*(4), 824–834. DOI: 10.59075/m9g5pc96

Khan, A., Shaw, R. K., & Bahar, A. N. (2025). A neural Cantonese speech converter using QCA for nanocomputing. *Computers & Electrical Engineering, 126*, 110536. DOI: 10.1016/j.compeleceng.2025.110536

Khare, Y. (2023). Generative AI vs Predictive AI: What is the Difference. Analytics Vidhya. https://www. analyticsvidhya. com/blog/2023/09/generative-ai-vs-predictive-ai/

Khasawneh, D. M. A. S. K. (2024). Improving the learning of language proficiency at tertiary education level through AI-driven assessment models and automated feedback systems. *Migration Letters : An International Journal of Migration Studies, 21*(2), 712–726.

Khatter, A., Thalaachawr, K., & Blyth, M. (2024). Student engagement and fostering ownership of learning. *Journal of Applied Learning & Teaching, 7*(1), 291–302. https://search.informit.org/doi/10.3316/informit.T2025091900007891326081625

Khine, M. S. (2024). Using AI for Adaptive Learning and Adaptive Assessment. In Khine, M. S. (Ed.), *Artificial Intelligence in Education*. Springer., DOI: 10.1007/978-981-97-9350-1_3

Khlaif, Z. N., Odeh, A., & Bsharat, T. R. K. (2024). Generative AI-powered adaptive assessment. Advances in Educational Technologies and Instructional Design Book Series, 157–176. DOI: 10.4018/979-8-3693-6397-3.ch007

Khlaif, Z. N., Alkouk, W. A., Salama, N., & Abu Eideh, B. (2025). Redesigning assessments for AI-enhanced learning: A framework for educators in the generative AI era. *Education Sciences, 15*(2), 174. Advance online publication. DOI: 10.3390/educsci15020174

Khlaif, Z. N., Ayyoub, A., Hamamra, B., Bensalem, E., Mitwally, M. A., Ayyoub, A., Hattab, M. K., & Shadid, F. (2024). University teachers' views on the adoption and integration of generative AI tools for student assessment in higher education. *Education Sciences*, *14*(10), 1090. DOI: 10.3390/educsci14101090

King, I. (2016, July 16). E-learning is the way forward for quality education. *South China Morning Post*.

Kirk, A. M. (2025). Teaching Transformed: A Qualitative Exploration of Artificial Intelligence's Impact on Teacher Workload Through Secondary Analysis (Doctoral dissertation, South College).

Kizilcec, R. F., & Lee, H. (2022). Algorithmic fairness in education. *The Ethics of Artificial Intelligence in Education: Practices, Challenges, and Debates*, 174–202. DOI: 10.4324/9780429329067-10

Kizilcec, R. F., & Lee, H. (2022). Algorithmic fairness in education. In Khosrow-Pour, M. (Ed.), *Encyclopedia of information science and technology* (5th ed., pp. 1–15). IGI Global., DOI: 10.4018/978-1-7998-9220-5.ch132

Knight, S., Shum, S. B., Ryan, P., Sándor, Á., & Wang, X. (2020). Designing academic writing analytics for civil law student self-assessment. *International Journal of Artificial Intelligence in Education*, *28*(1), 1–28. DOI: 10.1007/s40593-016-0121-0

Knox, J. (2020). Artificial intelligence and education in China. *Learning, Media and Technology*, *45*(3), 298–311. DOI: 10.1080/17439884.2020.1754236

Kochmar, E., Vu, D. D., Belfer, R., Gupta, V., Serban, I. V., & Pineau, J. (2022). Automated Data-Driven Generation of Personalized Pedagogical Interventions in Intelligent Tutoring Systems. *International Journal of Artificial Intelligence in Education*, *32*(2), 323–349. DOI: 10.1007/s40593-021-00267-x

Koenecke, A., Nam, A., Lake, E., Nudell, J., Quartey, M., Mengesha, Z., Toups, C., Rickford, J. R., Jurafsky, D., & Goel, S. (2020). Racial disparities in automated speech recognition. *Proceedings of the National Academy of Sciences of the United States of America*, *117*(14), 7684–7689. DOI: 10.1073/pnas.1915768117

Kofinas, A. K., Tsay, C.-H., & Pike, D. (2025). The impact of generative AI on academic integrity of authentic assessments within a higher education context. *British Journal of Educational Technology*, *56*(6), 2522–2549. DOI: 10.1111/bjet.13585

Koh, K. H. (2017). Authentic Assessment. In Kathy Hytten (ed.), Oxford Research Encyclopedia of Education (New York, NY, online edn, Oxford Academic, 9 June 2016 -), DOI: 10.1093/acrefore/9780190264093.013.22

Kolla, A. C., Takale, D. G., Mahalle, P. N., Sule, B., & Deshmukh, G. (2026). Mitigating Algorithmic Bias in Facial Recognition Technology: A Deep Learning Approach to Fairness in AI. In *Lecture Notes in Networks and Systems: Vol. 1457 LNNS* (pp. 423–438). Springer, Singapore. DOI: 10.1007/978-981-96-7496-1_34

Kostopoulos, G., Gkamas, V., Rigou, M., & Kotsiantis, S. (2025). *Agentic AI in Education: State of the Art and Future Directions*. IEEE., DOI: 10.1109/ACCESS.2025.3620473

Kotsis, K. T. (2025). Integrating artificial intelligence into higher education curricula: Challenges and opportunities for science-based programs. International Journal of Artificial Intelligence Engineering and Transformation, 6(1), 04-12. DOI: 10.54660/IJAIET.2025.6.1.04-12

Kousha, K., & Thelwall, M. (2022). *Artificial intelligence technologies to support research assessment: A review*. https://arxiv.org/abs/2212.06574

Kramm, N., & McKenna, S. (2023). AI amplifies the tough question: What is higher education really for? *Teaching in Higher Education*, *28*(8), 2173–2178. DOI: 10.1080/13562517.2023.2263839

Kress, G. (2010). *Multimodality: A social semiotic approach to contemporary communication*. Routledge., DOI: 10.4324/9780203970034

Krishna, K., Song, Y., Karpinska, M., Wieting, J., & Iyyer, M. (2023). Paraphrasing evades detectors of ai-generated text, but retrieval is an effective defense. *Advances in Neural Information Processing Systems*, *36*, 27469–27500. DOI: 10.52202/075280-1195

Kuhail, M. A., Alturki, N., Alramlawi, S., & Alhejori, K. (2023). Interacting with educational chatbots: A systematic review. *Education and Information Technologies*, *28*(1), 973–1018. DOI: 10.1007/s10639-022-11177-3

Kulik, J. A., & Fletcher, J. D. (2016). Effectiveness of intelligent tutoring systems: A meta-analytic review. *Review of Educational Research*, *86*(1), 42–78. DOI: 10.3102/0034654315581420

Kumar, K. P., Ponnuchamy, K., Bala, N. M., Santhoshini, M. V., Himasri, K., & Jagadeesh, K. (2025). An AI-Powered Smart Learning Platform Integrating Adaptive Assessments, Personalized Learning Paths, and Performance Analytics, 2025 4th International Conference on Applied Artificial Intelligence and Computing (ICAAIC), Salem, India, 2025, pp. 1283-1288, DOI: 10.1109/ICAAIC64647.2025.11330782

Lancaster, T. (2023). Academic integrity challenges in the era of ChatGPT. *Journal of Academic Ethics*. Advance online publication. DOI: 10.1007/s10805-023-09478-1

Lapidot-Lefler, N. (2025). Teacher responsiveness in inclusive education: A participatory study of pedagogical practice, well-being, and sustainability. *Sustainability (Basel), 17*(7), 2919. DOI: 10.3390/su17072919

Lau, J. Y. F. (2024). Revisiting the origin of critical thinking. *Educational Philosophy and Theory, 57*(7), 724–733. DOI: 10.1080/00131857.2024.2320199

Lau, J., & Wong, P. C. (2024). Neural processing of Mandarin and Cantonese lexical tone alternations: Implications for the nature of phonological representations. *Laboratory Phonology, 15*(1). Advance online publication. DOI: 10.16995/labphon.10293

Lave, J., & Wenger, E. (1991). *Situated learning: Legitimate peripheral participation*. Cambridge University Press. DOI: 10.1017/CBO9780511815355

Lawrence, L., Echeverria, V., Yang, K., Aleven, V., & Rummel, N. (2024). How teachers conceptualise shared control with an AI co-orchestration tool: A multiyear teacher-centred design process. *British Journal of Educational Technology, 55*(3), 823–844. DOI: 10.1111/bjet.13372

Leaton Gray, S., Edsall, D., & Parapadakis, D. (2025). AI-Based Digital Cheating At University, and the Case for New Ethical Pedagogies. *Journal of Academic Ethics, 23*(4), 2069–2086. DOI: 10.1007/s10805-025-09642-y

Lee, A. (2008). How are doctoral students supervised? concepts of doctoral research supervision.

Lee, S. L. (2004). *History and Current Trends of Teaching Cantonese as a Foreign Language: Investigating Approaches to Teaching and Learning Cantonese* (Doctoral dissertation, University of Leicester).

Lee, A. V. Y. (2023). Supporting students' generation of feedback in large-scale online course with artificial intelligence-enabled evaluation. *Studies in Educational Evaluation, 77*, 101250. Advance online publication. DOI: 10.1016/j.stueduc.2023.101250

Lee, A. V. Y. (2025). The double-edged sword of generative AI for assessment: efficiency versus homogenization. In *Navigating Generative AI in Higher Education* (pp. 128–143). Edward Elgar Publishing. DOI: 10.4337/9781035337873.00012

Lee, S. L. (2016). E-Learning readiness in language learning: Students' readiness survey and normalization process. *Journal of Technology & Chinese Language Teaching, 7*(2), 23–37.

Lee, S. L. (2018a). Expatriate Cantonese learners in Hong Kong: Adult L2 learning, identity negotiation, and social pressure. In Velliaris, D. (Ed.), *Study Abroad Contexts for Enhanced Foreign Language Learning* (pp. 106–110). IGI Global., DOI: 10.4018/978-1-5225-3814-1.ch007

Lee, S. L. (2018b). Modular approaches in eLearning design. *Journal of Technology and Chinese Language Teaching*, *9*(1), 48–61.

Lee, S. L. (2019). Teaching and learning Cantonese as a second language: Learners' attitudes and learning hurdles. In Wakefield, J. (Ed.), *Cantonese as a Second Language: Issues, Experiences and Suggestions for Teaching and Learning* (pp. 47–66). Routledge.

Lee, S. L. (2020). Learning needs of Cantonese as a second language in Hong Kong tertiary education. *Electronic Journal of Foreign Language Teaching*, *17*(2), 460–478. DOI: 10.56040/slle1742

Lee, S. L. (2022). Synchronous online language teaching: A reflection from Hong Kong. In Liu, S. (Ed.), *Teaching the Chinese Language Remotely: Global Cases and Perspectives* (pp. 235–251). Palgrave Macmillan. DOI: 10.1007/978-3-030-87055-3_10

Lee, S. L. (2025). AI-adaptive Chinese Language Learning Environment and Assessments in Hong Kong. In Wachira, P., Liu, X., & Koc, S. (Eds.), *Educational Assessments in the Age of Generative AI* (pp. 119–144). IGI Global. DOI: 10.4018/979-8-3693-6351-5.ch005

Lee, S. L., & Chen, Y. (2024). Discussions of using AI in language education in Hong Kong. In Pan, F. (Ed.), *AI in Language Teaching, Learning, and Assessment* (pp. 133–148). IGI Global. DOI: 10.4018/979-8-3693-0872-1.ch007

Lee, S., Choe, H., Zou, D., & Jeon, J. (2026). Generative AI (GenAI) in the language classroom: A systematic review. *Interactive Learning Environments*, *34*(1), 335–359. DOI: 10.1080/10494820.2025.2498537

Leon, M. (2024). Generative AI as a new paradigm for personalized tutoring in modern education. *International Journal of Integrating Technology in Education*, *15*(3), 49–63. DOI: 10.5121/ijite.2024.13304

Le, X. (2024). Assessment reform in higher education: An ethical approach to harness the power of generative artificial intelligence. *Education Research and Perspectives*, *51*, 156–185. DOI: 10.70953/ERPv51.2412007

Liang, J., Stephens, J. M., & Brown, G. T. L. (2025). A systematic review of the early impact of artificial intelligence on higher education curriculum, instruction, and assessment. In *Frontiers in Education*. DOI: 10.3389/feduc.2025.1522841

Liang, W., Yuksekgonul, M., Mao, Y., Wu, E., & Zou, J. (2023). GPT detectors are biased against non-native English writers. *Patterns (New York, N.Y.)*, *4*(7), 1–4. DOI: 10.1016/j.patter.2023.100779 PMID: 37521038

Li, J., Qu, L., Cai, T., Zhao, Z., Al Hasan Haldar, N., Krishna, A., Kong, X., Romero Macau, F., Chakraborty, T., Deroy, A., Lin, B., Blackmore, K., Noman, N., Cheng, J., Cui, N., & Xu, J. (2025). AI-generated content in cross-domain applications: Research trends, challenges and propositions. *Knowledge-Based Systems*, *330*, 114634. Advance online publication. DOI: 10.1016/j.knosys.2025.114634

Lim, K. (2024). Assessing beyond grades: Unravelling the implications on student learning and engagement in higher education. *Assessment & Evaluation in Higher Education*, *49*(5), 665–679. Advance online publication. DOI: 10.1080/02602938.2024.2314703

Lim, T., Gottipati, S., & Cheong, M. (2023). *Artificial Intelligence in Today's Education Landscape: Understanding and Managing Ethical Issues for Educational Assessment*. DOI: 10.21203/rs.3.rs-2696273/v1

Lin, C. C., Huang, A. Y. Q., & Lu, O. H. T. (2023). Artificial intelligence in intelligent tutoring systems toward sustainable education: A systematic review. *Smart Learning Environment*, *10*(41), 41. Advance online publication. DOI: 10.1186/s40561-023-00260-y

Lin, C.-H., Knowlton, B. J., Chiang, M.-C., Iacoboni, M., Udompholkul, P., & Wu, A. D. (2011). Brain–behavior correlates of optimizing learning through interleaved practice. *NeuroImage*, *56*(3), 1758–1772. DOI: 10.1016/j.neuroimage.2011.02.066

Lindsay, E. D., Zhang, M., Johri, A., & Bjerva, J. (2025). The Responsible Development of Automated Student Feedback with Generative AI. *IEEE Global Engineering Education Conference, EDUCON*. DOI: 10.1109/EDUCON62633.2025.11016572

Lin, H., & Chen, Q. (2024). Artificial intelligence (AI)-integrated educational applications and college students' creativity and academic emotions: Students and teachers' perceptions and attitudes. *BMC Psychology*, *12*(1), 487. DOI: 10.1186/s40359-024-01979-0 PMID: 39285268

Lin, Z., & Chen, H. (2024). Investigating the capability of ChatGPT for generating multiple-choice reading comprehension items. *System*, *123*, 103344. Advance online publication. DOI: 10.1016/j.system.2024.103344

Lipnevich, A. A., & Smith, J. K. (2022). *The Cambridge handbook of instructional feedback.* Cambridge University Press., DOI: 10.1017/9781009180344

Liskin-Gasparro, J. E. (2003). The ACTFL Proficiency Guidelines and the Oral Proficiency Interview: A brief history and analysis of their survival. *Foreign Language Annals, 36*(4), 483–490. DOI: 10.1111/j.1944-9720.2003.tb02137.x

Liu, O., & Yau, C. (2023, March 22). Who needs a teacher? As ChatGPT takes off in Hong Kong, educationists worry about impact on teaching, learning. *South China Morning Post.*

Liu, L. (2025). Beyond one-size-fits-all: An AI-driven approach for personalized quizzes using clustering and ChatGPT. *International Journal of Information and Education Technology (IJIET), 15*(9), 1768–1776. DOI: 10.18178/ijiet.2025.15.9.2378

Lodge, J. M., Kennedy, G., & Lockyer, L. (2018). Digital learning environments, the science of learning, and the relationship between the teacher and the learner. In Lodge, J. M., Horvath, J. C., & Corrin, L. (Eds.), *Understanding and shaping student learning* (pp. 1–14). Springer., DOI: 10.1007/978-3-319-72669-5_1

Lodge, J. M., & Thompson, K. (2024). Generative artificial intelligence and learning analytics. *Journal of Learning Analytics, 11*(1), 1–8. DOI: 10.18608/jla.2024.8255

Lu, W. (2024). Inevitable challenges of autonomy: ethical concerns in personalized algorithmic decision-making. *Humanities and Social Sciences Communications 2024 11:1, 11*(1), 1321-. DOI: 10.1057/s41599-024-03864-y

Luckin, R. (2025). Nurturing human intelligence in the age of AI: Rethinking education for the future. *Development and Learning in Organizations, 39*(1), 1–4. DOI: 10.1108/DLO-04-2024-0108

Luckin, R., & Cukurova, M. (2019). Designing educational technologies in the age of AI: A learning sciences-driven approach. *British Journal of Educational Technology, 50*(6), 2824–2838. DOI: 10.1111/bjet.12861

Luckin, R., Holmes, W., Griffiths, M., & Forcier, L. B. (2016). *Intelligence unleashed: An argument for AI in education.* Pearson.

Luckin, R., Holmes, W., Griffiths, M., & Forcier, L. B. (2016). *Intelligence unleashed: An argument for AI in education.* Pearson. DOI: 10.13140/RG.2.2.30194.84164

Lund, B., & Wang, T. (2023, January). *Chatting about ChatPGT*: How *may AI and GPT impact academia and libraries*. Library Hi Tech News. https://www.researchgate.net /profile/Brady-Lund/publication/367161545_Chatting_about_ChatGPT_How_ may_AI_and _GPT_impact_academia_and_libraries/links/6412235c315df-b4cce80f0e4/ Chatting-about-ChatGPT-How-may-AI-and-GPT-impact-academia-and-libraries.pd

Lund, B. D., Lee, T. H., Mannuru, N. R., & Arutla, N. (2025a). AI and academic integrity: Exploring student perceptions and implications for higher education. *Journal of Academic Ethics*, *23*(3), 1545–1565. DOI: 10.1007/s10805-025-09613-3

Lund, B., Mannuru, N. R., Teel, Z. A., Lee, T. H., Ortega, N. J., Simmons, S., & Ward, E. (2025b, September). Student perceptions of AI-assisted writing and academic integrity: Ethical concerns, academic misconduct, and use of generative AI in higher education. *AI in Education*, *1*(1), 2. DOI: 10.3390/aieduc1010002

Luo, J. (2025). How does GenAI affect trust in teacher-student relationships? Insights from students' assessment experiences. *Teaching in Higher Education*, *30*(4), 991–1006. DOI: 10.1080/13562517.2024.2341005

Luo, J., Zheng, C., Yin, J., & Teo, H. H. (2025). Design and assessment of AI-based learning tools in higher education: A systematic review. *International Journal of Educational Technology in Higher Education*, *22*(1), 42. DOI: 10.1186/s41239-025-00540-2

Lu, W., Li, S., & Qian, X. (2025). The impact of artificial intelligence literacy on doctoral students' innovative behaviour from the perspective of technology affordance. *European Journal of Education*. Advance online publication. DOI: 10.1111/ejed.70245

Lye, C. Y., & Lim, L. (2024). Generative artificial intelligence in tertiary education: Assessment redesign principles and considerations. *Education Sciences*, *14*(6), 569. DOI: 10.3390/educsci14060569

Mabirizi, V., Katushabe, C., Muhoza, G., & Rugasira, J. (2025). A systematic review of the impact of gen-erative ai on postgraduate research: Opportunities, challenges, and ethical implications. *Discover Artificial Intelligence*, *5*(1), 238. DOI: 10.1007/s44163-025-00495-3

Macfadyen, L. P., Dawson, S., Pardo, A., & Gaševic, D. (2020). Embracing big data in complex educational systems: The learning analytics imperative and the policy challenge. *Research & Practice in Assessment*, *9*, 17–28.

Maciel, R. S. P., Valle, P. H. D., Santos, K. S., & Nakagawa, E. Y. (2024). Systems interoperability types: A tertiary study. *ACM Computing Surveys*, *56*(10), 1–37. DOI: 10.1145/3659098

Magis, D., Yan, D., & Von Davier, A. A. (2017). *Computerized adaptive and multistage testing with R: Using packages catR and mstR*. Springer., DOI: 10.1007/978-3-319-69218-0

Magne, V., Vince, S., Mace, R., & Hooper, S. (2025). AI as a dialogic partner: Rethinking feedback in higher education. *Assessment & Evaluation in Higher Education*, •••, 1–15.

Mahamad, S., Chin, Y. H., Zulmuksah, N. I. N., Haque, M. M., Shaheen, M., & Nisar, K. (2025). Technical review: Architecting an AI-driven decision support system for enhanced online learning and assessment. *Future Internet*, *17*(9), 383. DOI: 10.3390/fi17090383

Mahmoud, E. (2025). Artificial intelligence solutions and college students' assessment: Exploring potential influences on their creative thinking skills. *Journal of Information Systems Engineering and Management*, 2468-4376. ISSN: 2468-4376

Mahmud, S. K., & Kurt, M. (2026). Enhancing Inclusive Sustainability-Oriented Learning in Higher Education Using Adaptive Learning Platforms and Performance-Based Assessment. *Sustainability (Basel)*, *18*(3), 1489. DOI: 10.3390/su18031489

Maity, S., & Deroy, A. (2024). Generative AI and its impact on personalized intelligent tutoring systems. https://doi.org/DOI: 10.35542/osf.io/kawr5

Mallik, S., & Gangopadhyay, A. (2023). Proactive and reactive engagement of artificial intelligence methods for education: A review. *Frontiers in Artificial Intelligence*, *6*, 1151391. Advance online publication. DOI: 10.3389/frai.2023.1151391 PMID: 37215064

Mammadova, I., Ismayilli, F., Aliyeva, E., & Mammadova, N. (2025). The Role of Artificial Intelligence in Shaping Assessment Practices in Higher Education. *Educational Process: International Journal*, *18*(1), e2025439. DOI: 10.22521/edupij.2025.18.439

Mancuso, V., Sarcinella, E. D., Bruni, F., Arlati, S., Di Santo, S. G., Cavallo, M., Cipresso, P., & Pedroli, E. (2024). Systematic review of memory assessment in virtual reality: Evaluating convergent and divergent validity with traditional neuropsychological measures. *Frontiers in Human Neuroscience*, *18*, 1380575. DOI: 10.3389/fnhum.2024.1380575

Mani, Z. A. (2025). Transitioning to competency-based education in nursing: A scoping review of curriculum review and revision strategies. *BMC Nursing*, *24*(1), 1111. Advance online publication. DOI: 10.1186/s12912-025-03319-y PMID: 40855546

Manokore, K., Manokore, A. S., & Chigora, T. B. (2024). Educational assessments in the age of generative AI. Advances in Educational Marketing, Administration, and Leadership Book Series, 59–92. DOI: 10.4018/979-8-3693-6351-5.ch003

Manu, A. (2024). Generative AI as a disruptor. In *Transcending imagination* (pp. 147–162). Chapman and Hall/CRC. DOI: 10.1201/9781003450139-15

Marey, A., Arjmand, P., Alerab, A. D. S., Eslami, M. J., Saad, A. M., Sanchez, N., & Umair, M. (2024). Explainability, transparency and black box challenges of AI in radiology: Impact on patient care in cardiovascular radiology. *The Egyptian Journal of Radiology and Nuclear Medicine*, *55*(1), 183. DOI: 10.1186/s43055-024-01356-2

Mariam, G., Adil, L., & Zakaria, B. (2024). The integration of artificial intelligence (ai) into education systems and its impact on the governance of higher education institutions. *International Journal of Professional Business Review*, *9*(12), 13. DOI: 10.26668/businessreview/2024.v9i12.5176

Marshall, C. C. (1997). Annotation: From paper books to the digital library. *Proceedings of the 2nd ACM International Conference on Digital Libraries*, 131–140. DOI: 10.1145/263690.263806

Martin, F., Sun, T., & Westine, C. D. (2020). A systematic review of research on online teaching and learning from 2009 to 2018. *Computers & Education*, *159*, 104009. DOI: 10.1016/j.compedu.2020.104009

Matheis, P., & Jubin, J. (2025). Assessment renaissance: authentic design in the era of generative AI. In *Generative AI in Higher Education*. Edward Elgar Publishing., DOI: 10.4337/9781035326020.00020

May, T. A., Provinzano, K., Koskey, K. L. K., Sondergeld, C. J., Stone, G. E., Archer, J., & Rimkunas, N. (2025). Expanding the team: Integrating generative artificial intelligence into the assessment development process. *Applied Sciences (Basel, Switzerland)*, *15*(18), 9976. DOI: 10.3390/app15189976

McAdoo, T., Denneny, S., & Lee, C. (2025, September 9). *Citing generative AI in APA style: Part I reference formats*. APA Style Blog. https://apastyle.apa.org/blog/cite-generative-ai-references

McIntosh, T. R., Susnjak, T., Liu, T., Watters, P., Xu, D., Liu, D., & Halgamuge, M. N. (2025). From Google Gemini to OpenAI Q*(Q-Star): A survey on reshaping the generative artificial intelligence (AI) research landscape. *Technologies*, *13*(2), 51. DOI: 10.3390/technologies13020051

McNealis, R. (2026). Shame in the machine: Affective accountability and the ethics of AI. *AI & Society*, *41*(1), 403–413. DOI: 10.1007/s00146-025-02472-x

McNely, B. J., & Teston, C. B. (2015). Tactical and strategic: Qualitative approaches to the digital humanities. In Ridolfo, J., & Hart-Davidson, W. (Eds.), *Rhetoric and the digital humanities* (pp. 111–126). University of Chicago Press., DOI: 10.7208/chicago/9780226177274.003.0008

McTighe, J., Doubet, K. J., & Carbaugh, E. M. (2020). *Designing authentic performance tasks and projects: Tools for meaningful learning and assessment*. ASCD.

Meinel, C., Friedrichsen, M., Staubitz, T., Reinhard, S., & Köhler, D. (2024). Assessment methods for online teaching. Scientific Reports of the German University of Digital Science, 3.

Mekheimer, M. (2025). Generative AI-assisted feedback and EFL writing: A study on proficiency, revision frequency and writing quality. *Discover Education*, *4*(1), 170. Advance online publication. DOI: 10.1007/s44217-025-00602-7

Melisa, R., Ashadi, A., Triastuti, A., Hidayati, S., Salido, A., Ero, P. E. L., & Fuad, Z. A. (2025). Critical thinking in the age of AI: A systematic review of AI's effects on higher education. *Educational Process: International Journal*, *14*(1), e2025031. DOI: 10.22521/edupij.2025.14.31

Memarian, B. & Doleck, T. (2024). A review of assessment for learning with artificial intelligence. Computers in Human Behavior: Artificial Humans. DOI: 10.1016/j.chbah.2023.100040

Merriam Webster Dictionary. (2026). *Construct*. https://www.merriam-webster.com/dictionary/construct

Messick, S. (1989). Validity. In Linn, R. L. (Ed.), *Educational measurement* (3rd ed., pp. 13–103). American Council on Education/Macmillan.

Messick, S. (1995). Validity of psychological assessment: Validation of inferences from persons' responses and performances as scientific inquiry into score meaning. *The American Psychologist*, *50*(9), 741–749. DOI: 10.1037/0003-066X.50.9.741

Miller, Wi. (2024). Adapting to AI: Reimagining the Role of Assessment Professionals. *Intersection: A Journal at the Intersection of Assessment and Learning*. DOI: 10.61669/001c.121439

Miller, E., & Konstantinou, I. (2022). Using reflective, authentic assessments to embed employability skills in higher education. *Journal of Work-Applied Management, 14*(1), 4–17. DOI: 10.1108/JWAM-02-2021-0014

Mimoudi, A. (2025). Generative AI to bridge the educational divide: Personalized learning and challenges. *Social Sciences & Humanities Open, 12*, 102140. DOI: 10.1016/j.ssaho.2025.102140

Mingay, D. (2026, January 9). *After being falsely branded an AI plagiarist how can I accuse students?* The Times Higher Education. https://www.timeshighereducation.com/opinion/after-being-falsely-branded-ai-plagiarist-how-can-i-accuse-students

Misgna, H., On, B. W., Lee, I., & Choi, G. S. (2024). A survey on deep learning-based automated essay scoring and feedback generation. *Artificial Intelligence Review, 58*(2), 36. DOI: 10.1007/s10462-024-11017-5

Mishra, D. R., & Varshney, D. (2024, April). Academic integrity in higher education: Faculty perceptions, strategies, and digital challenges in the digital age. *International Journal of All Research Education and Scientific Methods, 12(*4). ISSN 2455-6211.

Mislevy, R. J., Almond, R. G., & Lukas, J. F. (2003). *A brief introduction to evidence-centered design*. ETS Research Report Series. Educational Testing Service., DOI: 10.1002/j.2333-8504.2003.tb01908.x

Mittelstadt, B. D., Allo, P., Taddeo, M., Wachter, S., & Floridi, L. (2016). The ethics of algorithms: Mapping the debate. *Big Data & Society, 3*(2), 2053951716679679. DOI: 10.1177/2053951716679679

MLA Style Center. (2026). *How do I cite generative AI in MLA style?* https://style.mla.org/citing-generative-ai-updated-revised/

Mokhtar, T., & Manganelli, J. (2026). *Coexistence and Coevolution of Humans and Intelligent, Adaptive Environments*. CRC Press. DOI: 10.1201/9781003441953

Montebello, M. (2025). Rethinking Pedagogy and Assessment in the Age of Generative AI.

Montebello, M. (2025). Rethinking Pedagogy and Assessment in the Age of Generative AI. In *Artificial Intelligence*. IntechOpen., DOI: 10.5772/intechopen.1012982

Montenegro, E., & Jankowski, N. A. (2020). A new decade for assessment: Embedding equity into assessment praxis. *Occasional Paper No. 42*. National Institute for Learning Outcomes Assessment. DOI: 10.7282/t3-kbtn-ex80

Moqbel, M. S. S., & Al-Kadi, A. M. T. (2023). Foreign language learning assessment in the age of ChatGPT: A theoretical account. *Journal of English Studies in Arabia Felix*, *2*(1), 71–84. DOI: 10.56540/jesaf.v2i1.62

Morrell, L. J. (2021). Iterated assessment and feedback improves student outcomes. *Studies in Higher Education*, *46*(3), 485–496. DOI: 10.1080/03075079.2019.1643301

Morris, R., Perry, T., & Wardle, L. (2021). Formative assessment and feedback for learning in higher education: A systematic review. *Review of Education*, *9*(3), e3292. DOI: 10.1002/rev3.3292

Moruzzi, C. (2025). Artificial intelligence and creativity. *Philosophy Compass*, *20*(3), e70030.1 of 8 DOI: 10.1111/phc3.70030

Mor, Y., Craft, B., & Hernández-Leo, D. (2015). The art and science of learning design [Editorial]. *Research in Learning Technology*, *21*. Advance online publication. DOI: 10.3402/rlt.v21i0.22513

Mor, Y., & Winters, N. (2007). Design approaches in technology-enhanced learning. *Interactive Learning Environments*, *15*(1), 61–75. DOI: 10.1080/10494820601044236

Mourtajji, L., & Chiss, N. (2025). GENERATIVE AI: ARE WE READY TO DISRUPT OUR EDUCATIONAL PARADIGMS? In EDULEARN25 Proceedings (pp. 9321-9326). IATED.

Mudenda, S. (2025). Impact of Artificial Intelligence on College and University Students: A Global Transformation of the Education System. *Creative Education*, *16*(11), 1801–1828. DOI: 10.4236/ce.2025.1611112

Mulaudzi, L. V., & Hamilton, J. (2025). Lecturer's perspective on the role of AI in personalized learning: Benefits, challenges, and ethical considerations in higher education. *Journal of Academic Ethics*, *23*(4), 1571–1591. DOI: 10.1007/s10805-025-09615-1

Mulder, R., Baik, C., & Ryan, T. (n.d.) *Rethinking assessment in response to AI.* https://melbourne-cshe.unimelb.edu.au/ai-aai/home/ai-assessment/designing-assessment-tasks-that-are-less-vulnerable-to-ai

Mumtaz, S., Carmichael, J., Weiss, M., & Nimon-Peters, A. (2025). Ethical use of artificial intelligence-based tools in higher education: Are future business leaders ready? *Education and Information Technologies*, *30*(6), 7293–7319. DOI: 10.1007/s10639-024-13099-8

Murff, M. J. (2025). AI-Enabled Innovations in Automated Essay Scoring and Feedback Systems. Theses and Dissertations. 10933. https://scholarsarchive.byu.edu/etd/10933

Mwansa, G., & Ngandu, M. R. (2026). Transforming research supervision: Ethical and literacy imperatives in the era of generative ai. In I. Kariyana & W. Sinkala (Eds.), *Artificial intel-ligence and postgraduate supervision in higher education* (pp. 191–217). ERRCD Forum. DOI: 10.38140/obp4-2026-11

Nallamothu, T. K. (2024). The age of smart living how AI is shaping our daily lives in real time. *International Journal of Research and Applied Innovations*, *7*(5), 11456–11468. DOI: 10.34218/IJAIRD_02_02_017

Nassar, H. M. (2025). Comparing the quality of AI-generated and instructor feedback in a university writing program (Master's thesis, The American University in Cairo (Egypt)).

Navneet, S. K., & Chandra, J. (2025). *Rethinking Autonomy: Preventing Failures in AI-Driven Software Engineering*. https://arxiv.org/abs/2508.11824

Nazaretsky, T., Mejia-Domenzain, P., Swamy, V., Frej, J., & Käser, T. (2026). Who Gives Feedback Matters: Student Biases Towards Human and AI-Generated Formative Feedback. *Journal of Computer Assisted Learning*, *42*(1), e70153. DOI: 10.1111/jcal.70153

Ncube, P. D. N., Dzvapatsva, G. P., Matobobo, C., & Ranga, M. M. (2026). Redefining student assessment in AI-infused learning environments: A systematic review of challenges and strategies for academic integrity. *AI and Ethics*, *6*(68), 68. Advance online publication. DOI: 10.1007/s43681-025-00871-w

Newton, P. E., & Shaw, S. D. (2014). *Validity in educational and psychological assessment*. SAGE Publications., DOI: 10.4135/9781446288856

Ng, D. T. K., Leung, J. K. L., Chu, K. W. S., & Qiao, M. S. (2021). AI Literacy: Definition, Teaching, Evaluation and Ethical Issues. *Proceedings of the Association for Information Science and Technology*, *58*(1), 504–509. DOI: 10.1002/pra2.487

Ngila, F. (2023, July 5). *The UK's top universities reached an agreement on how to deal with generative AI*. Tech and Innovation. https://qz.com/russel-uk-universities-generative-ai-students-1850603771

Nguyen Thanh, B., Vo, D. T. H., Nguyen Nhat, M., Pham, T. T. T., Thai Trung, H., & Ha Xuan, S. (2023). Race with the machines: Assessing the capability of generative AI in solving authentic assessments. *Australasian Journal of Educational Technology, 39*(5), 59–81. DOI: 10.14742/ajet.8902

Nguyen, Q. H. (2023). AI and plagiarism: Opinion from teachers, administrators and policymakers. *Proceedings of the AsiaCALL International Conference*, Vietnam, *4*, 75–85. DOI: 10.54855/paic.2346

Nilson, L. B., & Stanny, C. J. (2023). *Specifications Grading: Restoring Rigor, Motivating Students, and Saving Faculty Time* (2nd ed.). Routledge., DOI: 10.4324/9781003447061

Nkealah, N. (2023). Unravelling an assessment puzzle: Reflections on reconciling effective assessment and workload management in South African higher education. *Assessment & Evaluation in Higher Education, 48*(8), 1092–1102. DOI: 10.1080/02602938.2023.2173139

Noble, S. U. (2018). *Algorithms of oppression: How search engines reinforce racism.* NYU Press., DOI: 10.18574/nyu/9781479833641.001.0001

Noroozi, O., Haddadian, G., Gao, X., Schunn, C., Alqassab, M., & Banihashem, S. K. (2025). The value of GenAI for peer feedback provision: Student perceptions and impacts. *International Journal of Educational Technology in Higher Education, 22*(1), 61. DOI: 10.1186/s41239-025-00558-6

North, B. (2014). *The CEFR in practice* (Vol. 4). Cambridge University Press.

Northern Michigan University Center for Teaching and Learning. (2026). *Creating AI-resistant assignments, activities and assessments (designing out).* https://nmu.edu/ctl/creating-ai-resistant-assignments-activities-and-assessments-designing-out

Nyaaba, M., Zhai, X., & Faison, M. Z. (2024). Generative AI for Culturally Responsive Science Assessment: A Conceptual Framework. *Education Sciences 2024, Vol. 14, Page 1325, 14*(12), 1325. DOI: 10.3390/educsci14121325

Nyagope, T. S. (2024). Massification at higher education institutions; challenges associated with teaching large classes and how it impacts the quality of teaching and learning in South Africa. *International Journal of Environmental, Sustainability, and Social Science, 5*(1), 209–220. DOI: 10.38142/ijesss.v5i1.852

Nysom, L. (2023). AI Generated Feedback for Students' Assignment Submissions (Doctoral dissertation, Master's thesis, Aalborg university]. Aalborg university Project Library. https://projekter. aau. dk/projekter/files/547261577/Lars_Nysom_Master_Project. pdf)

O'Neil, C. (2016). *Weapons of math destruction: How big data increases inequality and threatens democracy*. Crown., DOI: 10.1080/2330443X.2018.1436530

Obizue, M. N., Otuonye, C. E., & Daw, A. (2025). Massification and internationalization of higher education: problems and prospects. International journal of economics, finance, accounting and management, 1(2), 14-30. https://journals.iempsglobal.org/index.php/IJEFAM/article/view/34

Ochs, E. (1979). Planned and unplanned discourse. IN T. Givon (Ed.). Syntax and semantics. Vol. 12. Discourse and syntax. (pp. 51-80. Academic Press. Spolsky, B. (1989). Conditions for second language learning: Introduction to a general theory. Oxford University Press

OECD. (2019). *OECD principles on artificial intelligence*. OECD Publishing.

Ofori-Boateng, R., Aceves-Martins, M., Wiratunga, N., & Moreno-Garcia, C. F. (2024). Towards the automation of systematic reviews using natural language processing, machine learning, and deep learning: A comprehensive review. *Artificial Intelligence Review*, *57*(200), 200. Advance online publication. DOI: 10.1007/s10462-024-10844-w

Olaniyan, J., Verkijika, S. F., & Obagbuwa, I. C. (2025). NLP-Based restoration of damaged student essay archives for educational preservation and fair reassessment. *Electronics (Basel)*, *14*(16), 3189. Advance online publication. DOI: 10.3390/electronics14163189

Omodan, B. I. (2025). Redefining the role of supervisors in the era of artificial intelligence: Im-plications for hybrid postgraduate research governance. *Cogent Education*, *12*(1), 2536534. Advance online publication. DOI: 10.1080/2331186X.2025.2536534

Open, A. I. (2022). *Introducing Whisper*. OpenAI. https://openai.com/index/whisper/

Open, A. I. (2026a, March 22). *Create a masters' level case analysis with five questions that is AI-resistant. ChatGPT.* https://chatgpt.com/?utm_source=google&utm_medium=paid_search&utm_campaign =GOOG_C_SEM_GBR_Core_CHT_TST_ACQ_PER_MIX_ALL_NAMER_US_EN_031126&c_id=23637266097&c_agid=196969197591&c_crid=799723648506&c_kwid=kwd-1927051708782&c_ims= &c_pms=1026339&c_nw=g&c_dvc=c&gad_source=1&gad_campaignid=23637266097&gbraid=0AAAAA-I0E5epYRlgKduzSFX-sQOYZrHef1&gclid =Cj0KCQjwpv7NBhCzARIsADkIfWxDJjoqHUIN0piKd-KEuMidNeKrijJxK7yIxxo2OYST42UoXiXurfI8aAtfyEALw_wcB

Open, A. I. (2026b, March 22). *How do I make university student assessments AI-resistant?* ChatGPT. https://chatgpt.com/?utm_source=google&utm_medium=paid_search&utm_campaign=GOOG_C_SEM_GBR_Core_CHT_TST_ACQ_PER_MIX_ALL_NAMER_US_EN_031126&c_id=23637266097&c_agid=196969198031&c_crid=799723648692&c_kwid=kwd-693063707937&c_ims=&cpms=1026339&c_nw=g&c_dvc=c&gad_source=1&gad_campaign id=23637266097&gbraid=0AAAAA-I0E5epYRlgKduzSFXsQOYZrHef1&gc lid=Cj0KC-Qjwpv7NBhC zARIsADkIfWypQK5HNuacRkifSNdZESQ7RdWBUiW_X8B6X-saJMCOCrkIeYxBKvN waAqvc EALwwcB

Oroh, E. Z., Ali, M. I., Pelenkahu, N., Usman, H., & Rorintulus, O. A. (2025). Authentic assessment in higher education to increase critical thinking and develop metacognitive awareness. *Studies in English Language and Education, 12*(2), 827–844. DOI: 10.24815/siele.v12i2.45077

Ouyang, F., Zheng, L., & Jiao, P. (2022). Artificial intelligence in online higher education: A systematic review of empirical research from 2011 to 2020. *Education and Information Technologies, 27*(6), 7893–7925. DOI: 10.1007/s10639-022-10925-9

Owan, V. J., Abang, K. B., Idika, D. O., Etta, E. O., & Bassey, B. A. (2023). Exploring the potential of artificial intelligence tools in educational measurement and assessment. *Eurasia Journal of Mathematics, Science and Technology Education, 19*(8), em2307. Advance online publication. DOI: 10.29333/ejmste/13428

Owoseni, A., Kolade, O., & Egbetokun, A. (2024). Applications of generative AI in summative assessment. In *Generative AI in higher Education: Innovation strategies for teaching and learning* (pp. 97–122). Springer Nature Switzerland. DOI: 10.1007/978-3-031-60179-8_4

Öztürk, Y., & Cebi, A. (2026). The potential of AI-generated feedback from the students' perspective: A systematic review. *Assessment & Evaluation in Higher Education, 51*(1), 41–62. DOI: 10.1080/02602938.2025.2588385

Palalas, A., Pegrum, M., Gunawardena, C. N., Robertson, R. S., & Ventura, J. (2025). The 'Tragic Dilemma'of GenAI in Education: An Exploratory Human-AI Conversation. *Postdigital Science and Education, 7*(4), 1451–1477. DOI: 10.1007/s42438-025-00600-w

Pang, W., & Wei, Z. (2025). Shaping the Future of Higher Education: A Technology Usage Study on Generative AI Innovations. *Information (Basel), 16*(2), 95. DOI: 10.3390/info16020095

Papamitsiou, Z., & Economides, A. A. (2014). Learning analytics and educational data mining in practice: A systematic literature review of empirical evidence. *Journal of Educational Technology & Society*, *17*(4), 49–64.

Papaneophytou, C., & Nicolaou, S. A. (2025). Promoting critical thinking in biological sciences in the era of artificial intelligence: The role of higher education. *Trends in Higher Education*, *4*(2), 24. DOI: 10.3390/higheredu4020024

Pardo, A., Jovanovic, J., Dawson, S., Gašević, D., & Mirriahi, N. (2019). Using learning analytics to scale the provision of personalised feedback. *British Journal of Educational Technology*, *50*(1), 128–138. DOI: 10.1111/bjet.12592

Park, Y., & Derakhshan, A. (2026). From Gutenberg to the classroom: Large-scale generation and validation of vocabulary-controlled EFL reading materials. *Language Testing in Asia*, *16*(1), 13. Advance online publication. DOI: 10.1186/s40468-026-00429-5

Pasquale, F. (2015). *The black box society: The secret algorithms that control money and information.* Harvard University Press., DOI: 10.4159/harvard.9780674736061

Paulsen, L., & Lindsay, E. (2024). Learning analytics dashboards are increasingly becoming about learning and not just analytics-A systematic review. *Education and Information Technologies*, *29*(11), 14279–14308. DOI: 10.1007/s10639-023-12401-4

Pedró, F., Subosa, M., Rivas, A., & Valverde, P. (2019). Artificial intelligence and language learning: Opportunities and challenges. *Working Paper on Language Policy. UNESCO.* https:// unesdoc.unesco.org/ark:/ 48223/pf0000366994

Peng, G., Zheng, H., & Wang, W. Y. (2004, December). Tone recognition for Chinese speech: A comparative study of Mandarin and Cantonese. In *2004 International Symposium on Chinese Spoken Language Processing* (pp. 233-236). IEEE. DOI: 10.1109/CHINSL.2004.1409629

Penn State University. (2026). *University College academic integrity procedures.* https://www.campuses.psu.edu/university-college-academic-integrity-procedures

Perelman, L. (2020). E-rater® doesn't rate: The validity of automated essay-scoring programs. *Journal of Writing Assessment*, *13*(1). Advance online publication. DOI: 10.5281/zenodo.3747603

Perkins, M. (2023). Academic integrity considerations of AI large language models in the post-pandemic era: ChatGPT and beyond. *Journal of University Teaching & Learning Practice*, *20*(2), 1–10. DOI: 10.53761/1.20.02.07

Perkins, M., Furze, L., Roe, J., & Macvaugh, J. (2024). The Artificial Intelligence Assessment Scale (AIAS): A Framework for Ethical Integration of Generative AI in Educational Assessment. *Journal of University Teaching & Learning Practice, 21*(06), 21. DOI: 10.53761/q3azde36

Perkins, M., & Roe, J. (2023). Decoding academic integrity policies: A corpus linguistics investigation of AI and other technological threats. *Higher Education Policy, 37*(3), 633–650. DOI: 10.1057/s41307-023-00323-2

Perkins, M., Roe, J., & Furze, L. (2025). Reimagining the artificial intelligence assessment scale: A refined framework for educational assessment. *Journal of University Teaching & Learning Practice, 22*(7). Advance online publication. DOI: 10.53761/rrm4y757

Perkins, M., Roe, J., Postma, D., McGaughran, J., & Hickerson, D. (2023). Detection of GPT-4 generated text in higher education: Combining academic judgement and software to identify generative AI tool misuse. *Journal of Academic Ethics*. Advance online publication. DOI: 10.1007/s10805-023-09490-5

Peters, U., & Peters, U. (2022). Algorithmic Political Bias in Artificial Intelligence Systems. *Philosophy & Technology 2022 35:2, 35*(2), 25-. DOI: 10.1007/s13347-022-00512-8

Plata, S., De Guzman, M. A., & Quesada, A. (2023). Emerging Research and Policy Themes on Academic Integrity in the Age of Chat GPT and Generative AI. [AJUE]. *Asian Journal of University Education, 19*(4), 743–758. Advance online publication. DOI: 10.24191/ajue.v19i4.24697

Poellhuber, B., Roy, N., & Lepage, A. (2024). Artificial intelligence in higher education: opportunities, issues, and challenges. In *Human-Centered AI* (pp. 151–162). Chapman and Hall/CRC. DOI: 10.1201/9781003320791-17

Ponomarioviené, J., Jakavonytė-Staškuvienė, D., & Torterat, F. (2025). Implementing competency-based education through the personalized monitoring of primary students' progress and assessment. *Education Sciences, 15*(2), 252. DOI: 10.3390/educsci15020252

Pooth, R., Sattler, S., Westerberg, F., Pavicic, T., & Kerscher, M. (2025). Transforming Skin Quality Evaluation With AI: From Subjective Grading to Data-Driven Precision. *Journal of Cosmetic Dermatology, 24*(S4), e70371. DOI: 10.1111/jocd.70371 PMID: 40847895

Popenici, S. A., & Kerr, S. (2017). Exploring the impact of artificial intelligence on teaching and learning in higher education. *Research and Practice in Technology Enhanced Learning*, *12*(1), 1–13. DOI: 10.1186/s41039-017-0062-8

Pratama, A. R. (2025). The accuracy-bias trade-offs in AI text detection tools and their impact on fairness in scholarly publication. *PeerJ. Computer Science*, *11*, e2953. DOI: 10.7717/peerj-cs.2953 PMID: 40989485

Pratschke, B. M. (2024). *Generative AI and education: Digital pedagogies, teaching innovation and learning design*. Springer Nature. DOI: 10.1007/978-3-031-67991-9

Prinsloo, P., & Slade, S. (2016). Student vulnerability, agency, and learning analytics: An exploration. *Journal of Learning Analytics*, *3*(1), 159–182. DOI: 10.18608/jla.2016.31.10

Prinsloo, P., & Slade, S. (2017). An elephant in the learning analytics room: The obligation to act. *Proceedings of the 7th International Conference on Learning Analytics & Knowledge*, 46-55. DOI: 10.1145/3027385.3027406

Prompiengchai, S., Narreddy, C., & Joordens, S. (2025). *A Practical Guide for Supporting Formative Assessment and Feedback Using Generative AI*. https://arxiv.org/abs/2505.23405

Pulijala, S. (2024). Artificial Intelligence in Governance: Opportunities, Challenges, and Ethical Implications for Public Administration. *IJFMR - International. Journal of Multidisciplinary Research*, *6*(6), 29990. Advance online publication. DOI: 10.36948/ijfmr.2024.v06i06.29990

Quach, K. (2023, September 23). *Colleges snub Turnitin's AI-writing detector over fears it will wrongly accuse students*. The Register. https://www.theregister.com/2023/09/23/turnitin_ai_detection/#:~:text=Various%20American%20universities%2C%20however%2C%20including,cheating%2C%20as%20noted%20by%20Bloomberg

Quinlan, K. M., Sellei, G., & Fiorucci, W. (2025). Educationally authentic assessment: Reframing authentic assessment in relation to students' meaningful engagement. *Teaching in Higher Education*, *30*(3), 717–734. DOI: 10.1080/13562517.2024.2394042

Rabbi, H., Ehsan, U., Khan, R. A., Yasmeen, R., & Sehatkahani, M. A. (2024). *Development and validation of an AI-based model to predict the assessment outcomes of pre-clinical MBBS/BDS students*. DOI: 10.21203/rs.3.rs-5277982/v1

Radford, A., Kim, J. W., Xu, T., Brockman, G., McLeavey, C., & Sutskever, I. (2023, July). Robust speech recognition via large-scale weak supervision. *Proceedings of the 40th International Conference on Machine Learning*, PMLR, 202, 28492-28518.

Rahiman, H. U. & Kodikal, R. (2024). Revolutionizing education: Artificial intelligence empowered learning in higher education. Cogent Education. 11:1, 2293431, DOI: DOI: 10.1080/2331186X.2023.2293431

Rani, D., & Rani, M. D. (2025). Adaptive Assessment: Personalizing Evaluation in the Digital Age. *International Journal of Engineering Science & Humanities, 15*(4), 506–513.

Ranieri, M., Raffaghelli, J. E., & Bruni, I. (2023). Data literacy in teacher education: A scoping review and conceptual framework. *Teaching and Teacher Education, 125*, 104049. DOI: 10.1016/j.tate.2023.104049

Rao, G. T., & Suhasini, N. (2025). Integrating artificial intelligence in higher education to enhance teaching and learning. *Computer Applications in Engineering Education, 33*(6), e70085. DOI: 10.1002/cae.70085

Rashidi, H. H., Pantanowitz, J., Hanna, M. G., Tafti, A. P., Sanghani, P., Buchinsky, A., Fennell, B., Deebajah, M., Wheeler, S., Pearce, T., Abukhiran, I., Robertson, S., Palmer, O., Gur, M., Tran, N. K., & Pantanowitz, L. (2025). Introduction to artificial intelligence and machine learning in pathology and medicine: Generative and nongenerative artificial intelligence basics. *Modern Pathology, 38*(4), 100688. DOI: 10.1016/j.modpat.2024.100688 PMID: 39755237

Ray, S., & Saeed, M. (2018). Applications of educational data mining and learning analytics tools in handling big data in higher education. In *Applications of Big Data analytics: Trends, issues, and challenges* (pp. 135–160). Springer International Publishing. DOI: 10.1007/978-3-319-76472-6_7

Raza, F. A., Singh, A. D., Kovilpillai, J. J. S., Hamdan, A., & Rajaratnam, V. (2025). Safeguarding integrity in AI-enhanced education: Stakeholder perspectives on accuracy, validity, and ethics in ASEAN. *European Journal of STEM Education, 10*(1), 22. DOI: 10.20897/ejsteme/17307

Regan, P. M., & Jesse, J. (2019). Ethical challenges of edtech, big data and personalized learning: Twenty-first century student sorting and tracking. *Ethics and Information Technology, 21*(3), 167–179. DOI: 10.1007/s10676-018-9492-2

Reidenberg, J. R., & Schaub, F. (2018). Achieving big data privacy in education. *Theory and Research in Education, 16*(3), 263–279. DOI: 10.1177/1477878518805308

Revell, T., Yeadon, W., Cahilly-Bretzin, G., Clarke, I., Manning, G., Jones, J., Mulley, C., Pascual, R. J., Bradley, N., Thomas, D., & Leneghan, F. (2024). ChatGPT versus human essayists: An exploration of the impact of artificial intelligence for authorship and academic integrity in the humanities. *International Journal for Educational Integrity*, *20*(1), 18. DOI: 10.1007/s40979-024-00161-8

Rholetter, W. (2024). *Academic integrity*. EBSCO Knowledge Advantage Research Starters. https://www.ebsco.com/research-starters/education/academic-integrity

Rhoney, D. H., Chen, A. M., Churchwell, M. D., Daugherty, K. K., Jarrett, J. B., Kleppinger, E. L., Nawarskas, J. J., Sibicky, S. L., Stowe, C. D., & Meyer, S. M. (2024). The need for competency-based education. *American Journal of Pharmaceutical Education*, *88*(6), 100706. DOI: 10.1016/j.ajpe.2024.100706 PMID: 38705241

Richmond, L. L., & Taylor, R. G. (2025). The benefits and potential costs of cognitive offloading for retrospective information. *Nature Reviews Psychology*, *4*(5), 312–321. DOI: 10.1038/s44159-025-00432-2

Risko, E. F., & Gilbert, S. J. (2016). Cognitive offloading. *Trends in Cognitive Sciences*, *20*(9), 676–688. DOI: 10.1016/j.tics.2016.07.002 PMID: 27542527

Rodrigues, M., Silva, R., Borges, A. P., Franco, M., & Oliveira, C. (2025, March). Artificial intelligence: Threat or asset to academic integrity? A bibliometric analysis. *Kybernetes, International Journal of Cybernetics. Kybernetes*, *54*(5), 2939–2970. DOI: 10.1108/K-09-2023-1666

Rodríguez-Ortiz, M. Á., Santana-Mancilla, P. C., & Anido-Rifón, L. E. (2025). Machine Learning and Generative AI in Learning Analytics for Higher Education: A Systematic Review of Models, Trends, and Challenges. *Applied Sciences (Basel, Switzerland)*, *15*(15), 8679. DOI: 10.3390/app15158679

Roll, I., & Wylie, R. (2016). Evolution and revolution in artificial intelligence in education. *International Journal of Artificial Intelligence in Education*, *26*(2), 582–599. DOI: 10.1007/s40593-016-0110-3

Rolls, E. T. (2024). The memory systems of the human brain and generative artificial intelligence. *Heliyon*, *10*(11), e31965. DOI: 10.1016/j.heliyon.2024.e31965 PMID: 38841455

Rosner, T. M., Davis, H., & Milliken, B. (2015). Perceptual blurring and recognition memory: A desirable difficulty effect revealed. *Acta Psychologica*, *160*, 11–22. DOI: 10.1016/j.actpsy.2015.06.006 PMID: 26134415

Ross, J., Curwood, J. S., & Bell, A. (2020). A multimodal assessment framework for higher education. *E-Learning and Digital Media, 17*(4), 290–306. DOI: 10.1177/2042753020927201

Rubel, A., & Jones, K. M. (2016). Student privacy in learning analytics: An information ethics perspective. *The Information Society, 32*(2), 143–159. DOI: 10.1080/01972243.2016.1130502

Rudolph, J., Tan, S., & Tan, S. (2023). ChatGPT: Bullshit spewer or the end of traditional assessments in higher education? *Journal of Applied Learning and Teaching, 6*(1), 342–363. DOI: 10.37074/jalt.2023.6.1.9

Rudroff, T. (2024). Revealing the complexity of fatigue: A review of the persistent challenges and promises of artificial intelligence. *Brain Sciences, 14*(2), 186. DOI: 10.3390/brainsci14020186 PMID: 38391760

Russell Group. (2023). *Russell Group principles on the use of generative AI tools in education.* https://www.russellgroup.ac.uk/policy/policy-briefings/principles-use-generative-ai-tools-education

Russell, S., & Norvig, P. (2021). *Artificial intelligence: A modern approach* (4th ed.). Pearson.

Sai Aswin, B. G., Vishnubala, S., Dhinakaran, D., Kumar, N. J., Udhaya Sankar, S. M., & Mohamed Al Faisal, A. M. (2023). "A Research on Metaverse and its Application," 2023 World Conference on Communication & Computing (WCONF), RAIPUR, India, pp. 1-6, DOI: 10.1109/WCONF58270.2023.10235216

Saini, A. K., Cope, B., Kalantzis, M., & Zapata, G. C. (2024). The future of feedback: Integrating peer and generative AI reviews to support student work. EdArXiv preprint, 1-57. DOI: 10.35542/osf.io/x3dct

Sajja, R., Sermet, Y., Cwiertny, D., & Demir, I. (2025). Integrating AI and learning analytics for data-driven pedagogical decisions and personalized interventions in education. Technology, knowledge and learning, 1-31. DOI: 10.1007/s10758-025-09897-9

Sajja, R., Sermet, Y., Cikmaz, M., Cwiertny, D., & Demir, I. (2024). Artificial Intelligence-Enabled Intelligent Assistant for Personalized and Adaptive Learning in Higher Education. *Information (Basel), 15*(10), 596. DOI: 10.3390/info15100596

Salinas-Navarro, D. E., Vilalta-Perdomo, E., Michel-Villarreal, R., & Montesinos, L. (2024). Designing experiential learning activities with generative artificial intelligence tools for authentic assessment. *Interactive Technology and Smart Education, 21*(4), 708–734. DOI: 10.1108/ITSE-12-2023-0236

Samoili, S., Cobo, M. L., Gomez, E., De Prato, G., Martinez-Plumed, F., & Delipetrev, B. (2021). *AI watch. Defining artificial intelligence 2.0.* Publications Office of the European Union., DOI: 10.2760/019901

Savveli, I., Rigou, M., & Balaskas, S. (2025). From E-Government to AI E-Government: A Systematic Review of Citizen Attitudes. In *Informatics*. DOI: 10.3390/informatics12030098

Sayeed, S. (2026, January 19). *Can AI detectors mistake neurodivergent writing for AI-generated text?* AI Writing. https://deceptioner.site/blog/can-ai-detectors-flag-neurodivergent-writing-styles

Schicktanz, S., Welsch, J., Schweda, M., Hein, A., Rieger, J. W., & Kirste, T. (2023). AI-assisted ethics? Considerations of AI simulation for the ethical assessment and design of assistive technologies. *Frontiers in Genetics, 14*, 1039839. Advance online publication. DOI: 10.3389/fgene.2023.1039839 PMID: 37434952

Schraw, G., & Moshman, D. (1995). Metacognitive theories. *Educational Psychology Review, 7*(4), 351–371. DOI: 10.1007/BF02212307

Schwartz, S. H. (2012). An overview of the Schwartz Theory of Basic Values. *Online Readings in Psychology and Culture,* 2(1). htp://DOI: 10.9707/2307-0919.1116

Schwartz, R., Dodge, J., Smith, N. A., & Etzioni, O. (2020). Green AI. *Communications of the ACM, 63*(12), 54–63. DOI: 10.1145/3381831

Seale, J. (2020). *Simplifying accessibility in educational technologies and practices.* Routledge., DOI: 10.4324/9780429398650

Segooa, M. A., Modiba, F. S., & Motjolopane, I. (2025). Generative artificial intelligence tools to augment teaching scientific research in postgraduate studies. *South African Journal of Higher Education, 39*(1), 300–320. DOI: 10.20853/39-1-6275

Selwyn, N. (2019). *Should robots replace teachers? AI and the future of education.* Polity Press.

Selwyn, N. (2022). The future of AI and education: Some cautionary notes. *European Journal of Education, 57*(4), 620–631. DOI: 10.1111/ejed.12532

Selwyn, N., Hillman, T., Bergviken Rensfeldt, A., & Perrotta, C. (2020). Digital technologies and the automation of education: Key questions and concerns. *Postdigital Science and Education, 2*(3), 541–547. DOI: 10.1007/s42438-020-00150-7

Shailendra, S., Kadel, R., & Sharma, A. (2024). *Framework for Adoption of Generative Artificial Intelligence (GenAI) in Education.* https://arxiv.org/abs/2408.01443

Shakoor, F. Real-Time AI Responses (December 02, 2024). Available at *SSRN*: DOI: 10.2139/ssrn.5044211

Sharma, D., Shroff, S., Sharma, G., & Sachan, M. R. (2025). *Beyond Grades: Holistic Assessment and Evaluation in Contemporary Education.* Yashita Prakashan Private Limited.

Sharma, S., & Gupta, B. (2023). Investigating the role of technostress, cognitive appraisal and coping strategies on students' learning performance in higher education: A multidimensional transactional theory of stress approach. *Information Technology & People*, *36*(2), 626–660. DOI: 10.1108/ITP-06-2021-0505

Sheffield Hallam University. (2026). *Definitions of academic misconduct.* https://www.shu.ac.uk/myhallam/university-life/university-rules-and-regulations/student-conduct/academic-conduct-regulation/definitions-of-academic-misconduct

Shermis, M. D., & Burstein, J. (Eds.). (2013). *Handbook of automated essay evaluation: Current applications and new directions*. Routledge., DOI: 10.4324/9780203122761

Shi, H., & Aryadoust, V. (2024). A systematic review of AI-based automated written feedback research. *ReCALL*, *36*(2), 187–209. DOI: 10.1017/S0958344023000265

Shi, H., Chai, C. S., Zhou, S., & Aubrey, S. (2025). Comparing the effects of ChatGPT and automated writing evaluation on students' writing and ideal L2 writing self. *Computer Assisted Language Learning*, •••, 1–28. DOI: 10.1080/09588221.2025.2454541

Shute, V. J. (2008). Focus on formative feedback. *Review of Educational Research*, *78*(1), 153–189. DOI: 10.3102/0034654307313795

Siemens, G., & Long, P. (2011). Penetrating the fog: Analytics in learning and education. *EDUCAUSE Review*, *46*(5), 30–32.

Simelane-Mnisi, S. (2023). Effectiveness of LMS digital tools used by the academics to foster students' engagement. *Education Sciences*, *13*(10), 980. DOI: 10.3390/educsci13100980

Simelane, R. M., & Pillay, P. (2024). The evolution of assessment methods in higher education due to the shift to remote learning: A case study. *Research in Educational Policy and Management*, *6*(2), 393–414. DOI: 10.46303/repam.2024.41

Singh, H. K. D., & Mohamad, S. K. (2025). *Designing an AI-Resilient Assessment Framework in Open and Distance Learning*. Innovative Teaching and Learning Journal., DOI: 10.11113/itlj.v9.202

Skripchuk, J. (2025). *Effective Help-Seeking in Programming Outside the Classroom: Challenges, Motivations, and Pedagogy*. North Carolina State University.

Slade, S., & Prinsloo, P. (2013). Learning analytics: Ethical issues and dilemmas. *The American Behavioral Scientist, 57*(10), 1510–1529. DOI: 10.1177/0002764213479366

Smerdon, D. (2024). AI in essay-based assessment: Student adoption, usage, and performance. *Computers and Education: Artificial Intelligence, 7*, 100288. Advance online publication. DOI: 10.1016/j.caeai.2024.100288

Smith, C. D., Worsfold, K., Davies, L., Fisher, R., & McPhail, R. (2013). Assessment literacy and student learning: The case for explicitly developing students 'assessment literacy'. *Assessment & Evaluation in Higher Education, 38*(1), 44–60. DOI: 10.1080/02602938.2011.598636

Smolansky, A., Cram, A., Raduescu, C., Zeivots, S., Huber, E., & Kizilcec, R. F. (2023). Educator and Student Perspectives on the Impact of Generative AI on Assessments in Higher Education. In Proceedings of the Tenth ACM Conference on Learning @ Scale (L@S '23). Association for Computing Machinery, New York, NY, USA, 378–382. DOI: 10.1145/3573051.3596191

Sol, K., Sok, S., & Heng, K. (2025). *Rethinking assessment in higher education in the age of generative AI. Encyclopedia of educational innovation.* Springer., DOI: 10.1007/978-981-13-2262-4_327-1

Somabut, A., Tuamsuk, K., Lowatcharin, G., Traiyarach, S., & Kwangmuang, P. (2025). Preparing for the AI era: Science teachers' readiness and professional development needs for generative AI integration in secondary education. *Social Sciences & Humanities Open, 12*, 102259. Advance online publication. DOI: 10.1016/j.ssaho.2025.102259

Song, J., & Liu, S. (2025, July 1). Dark personality traits are associated with academic misconduct, frustration, negative thinking, and generative AI use habits: The case of Sichuan art universities. [P]. *BMC Psychology, 13*(1), 633. DOI: 10.1186/s40359-025-02949-w PMID: 40598633

Sousa, A. E., & Cardoso, P. (2025). Use of generative ai by higher education students. *Electronics (Basel), 14*(7), 1258. DOI: 10.3390/electronics14071258

Southavilay, V., Yacef, K., Reimann, P., & Calvo, R. A. (2013). Analysis of collaborative writing processes using revision maps and probabilistic topic models. *Proceedings of the 3rd International Conference on Learning Analytics and Knowledge*, 38-47. DOI: 10.1145/2460296.2460307

Sperling, K., Stenberg, C.-J., McGrath, C., Åkerfeldt, A., Heintz, F., & Stenliden, L. (2024). In search of artificial intelligence (AI) literacy in teacher education: A scoping review. *Computers and Education Open, 6*, 100169. DOI: 10.1016/j.caeo.2024.100169

Stalnaker, J. M., & Stalnaker, R. C. (1934). The effect of open-book examinations. *School and Society*, *39*, 533–535.

Stenhouse, L. (1975). *An introduction to curriculum research and development.* Heinemann.

Stephenson, B., & Harvey, A. (2022). Student Equity in the Age of AI-Enabled Assessment: Towards a politics of inclusion. In *Assessment for Inclusion in Higher Education: Promoting Equity and Social Justice in Assessment* (pp. 120–130). Taylor and Francis. DOI: 10.4324/9781003293101-14

Stillman, T. (2025). Maintaining academic integrity through AI-trap questions. *Journal of Educators Online,* 22(4). EISSN-1547-500. https://www.thejeo.com/archive/archive/2025_223~2/25rea0023_jeo_sept_30_stillmanpdf

Stoney Brook University. (2026). *Categories of academic dishonesty.* https://www.stonybrook.edu/commcms/academic_integrity/faculty-and-staff/categories-of-academic-dishonesty.php

Storey, V. (2026b). Ai dependency vs. doctoral identity: How generative ai is challenging the development of independent scholarly thinking in doctoral students. *International Journal of AI in Pedagogy, Innovation, and Learning Futures.* . v2026i1.6971DOI: 10.46787/ijaipil

Storey, V. (2026a). Ai dependency vs. doctoral identity: How generative ai is challenging the de-velopment of independent scholarly thinking in doctoral students. *International Journal of AI in Pedagogy, Innovation, and Learning Futures*, *1*(1). Advance online publication. DOI: 10.46787/ijaipil.v2026i1.6971

Strathern, M. (1997). 'Improving ratings': Audit in the British University system. *European Review (Chichester, England)*, *5*(3), 305–321.

Strielkowski, W., Grebennikova, V., Lisovskiy, A., Rakhimova, G., & Vasileva, T. (2025). AI-driven adaptive learning for sustainable educational transformation. *Sustainable Development (Bradford)*, *33*(2), 1921–1947. DOI: 10.1002/sd.3221

Strubell, E., Ganesh, A., & McCallum, A. (2019). Energy and policy considerations for deep learning in NLP. *Proceedings of the 57th Annual Meeting of the Association for Computational Linguistics*, 3645-3650. DOI: 10.18653/v1/P19-1355

Su, F., O'Dea, M., Wood, M., & Seidl, E. (2026). Embracing a new world: authentic assessment designs in an age of generative artificial intelligence (GenAI). Perspectives: Policy and Practice in Higher Education, 1-12.

Sullivan, M., Kelly, A., & McLaughlan, P. (2023). ChatGPT in higher education: Considerations for academic integrity and student learning. *Journal of Applied Learning and Teaching*, *6*(1), 31–40. DOI: 10.37074/jalt.2023.6.1.17

Suna, H. E., & Özer, M. (2025). Assessment in higher education in the era of generative AI. Advances in Computational Intelligence and Robotics Book Series, 241–274. DOI: 10.4018/979-8-3373-7579-3.ch008

Suriano, R., Plebe, A., Acciai, A., & Fabio, R. A. (2025). Student interaction with ChatGPT can promote complex critical thinking skills. *Learning and Instruction*, *95*, 102011. Advance online publication. DOI: 10.1016/j.learninstruc.2024.102011

Suskie, L. (2018). *Assessing student learning: A common sense guide*. John Wiley & Sons.

Suskie, L. (2023). Understanding the nature and purpose of assessment. In *Designing better engineering education through assessment* (pp. 3–22). Routledge. DOI: 10.4324/9781003444107-2

Szmyd, K., & Mitera, E. (2024). The impact of artificial intelligence on the development of critical thinking skills in students. *European Research Studies*, *27*(2), 1022–1039. DOI: 10.35808/ersj/3876

Tai, J., Ajjawi, R., Boud, D., & de St Jorre, T. J. (2022). Promoting Equity and Social Justice through Assessment for Inclusion. In *Assessment for Inclusion in Higher Education: Promoting Equity and Social Justice in Assessment* (pp. 9–18). Taylor and Francis. DOI: 10.4324/9781003293101-3

Tai, J., Ajjawi, R., Bearman, M., Boud, D., Dawson, P., & Jorre de St Jorre, T. (2023). Assessment for inclusion: Rethinking contemporary strategies in assessment design. *Higher Education Research & Development*, *42*(2), 483–497. DOI: 10.1080/07294360.2022.2057451

Tai, J., Ajjawi, R., Boud, D., Dawson, P., & Panadero, E. (2018). Developing evaluative judgement: Enabling students to make decisions about the quality of work. *Higher Education*, *76*(3), 467–481. DOI: 10.1007/s10734-017-0220-3

Tan, L.Y.; Hu, S.; Yeo, D.J., & Cheong, K.H. A. (2025). A comprehensive review on automated grading systems in STEM using AI techniques. Mathematics, 13(17), 2828., 2828. DOI: 10.3390/math1317282

Tanberkan, H., Özer, M., & Gelbal, S. (2024). Impact of artificial intelligence on assessment and evaluation approaches in education. *International Journal (Toronto, Ont.)*.

Tang, K. H. D. (2024). Implications of Artificial Intelligence for Teaching and Learning. *Acta Pedagogia Asiana, 3*(2), 65–79. DOI: 10.53623/apga.v3i2.404

Tariq, M. U. (2024). Advancing inquiry-based learning through generative AI-enabled assessments. Advances in Educational Marketing, Administration, and Leadership Book Series, 179–206. DOI: 10.4018/979-8-3693-6351-5.ch007

Tarisayi, K. S. (2024, March). Strategic leadership for responsible artificial intelligence adoption in higher education. *CTE Workshop Proceedings, 11,* 4-14. DOI: 10.55056/cte.616

Tarun, B., Du, H., Kannan, D., & Gehringer, E. F. (2025). Human-in-the-loop systems for adaptive learning using generative AI. arXiv. /arxiv.2508.11062DOI: 10.1109/FIE63693.2025.11328658

Teixeira, B., Carvalhais, L., Pinto, T., & Vale, Z. (2025). Explainable AI framework for reliable and transparent automated energy management in buildings. *Energy and Building*, *374*, 116246. Advance online publication. DOI: 10.1016/j.enbuild.2025.116246

The-false-positive-rate-for-sentences-of-our-ai-writing-detection-capability

Tholen, G. (2020). Degree power: Educational credentialism within three skilled occupations. *British Journal of Sociology of Education*, *41*(3), 283–298. DOI: 10.1080/01425692.2019.1690427

Thongsan, N. C., & Anderson, N. J. (2025). From Passive Answers to Active Inquiry: How AI Supports Critical Reading in EFL Classrooms. *LEARN Journal: Language Education and Acquisition Research Network*, *18*(2), 795–820. DOI: 10.70730/KMKL8505

Tierney, R. D. (2014). Fairness as a multifaceted quality in classroom assessment. *Studies in Educational Evaluation*, *43*, 55–69. Advance online publication. DOI: 10.1016/j.stueduc.2013.12.003

Tlili, A., Shehata, B., Adarkwah, M. A., Bozkurt, A., Hickey, D. T., Huang, R., & Agyemang, B. (2023). What if the devil is my guardian angel: ChatGPT as a case study of using chatbots in education. Smart learning environments,10(1), 15. DOI: 10.1186/s40561-023-00237-x

Tomlinson, C. A. (2017). Differentiated instruction. In *Fundamentals of gifted education* (pp. 279–292). Routledge. DOI: 10.4324/9781315639987-26

Tondeur, J., Van Braak, J., Sang, G., Voogt, J., Fisser, P., & Ottenbreit-Leftwich, A. (2012). Preparing pre-service teachers to integrate technology in education: A synthesis of qualitative evidence. *Computers & Education*, *59*(1), 134–144. DOI: 10.1016/j.compedu.2011.10.009

Topping, K. J., Gehringer, E., Khosravi, H., Gudipati, S., Jadhav, K., & Susarla, S. (2025). Enhancing peer assessment with artificial intelligence. *International Journal of Educational Technology in Higher Education*, *22*(1), 3. DOI: 10.1186/s41239-024-00501-1

Trajkovski, G., & Hayes, H. (2025). Foundations of AI in Educational Assessment. In *AI-Assisted Assessment in Education: Transforming Assessment and Measuring Learning* (pp. 1–58). Springer Nature Switzerland.

Treviranus, J. (2018). Learning differences and digital equity. In *The Cambridge handbook of computing education research* (pp. 420–443). Cambridge University Press., DOI: 10.1017/9781108654555.016

Tripp, D. (1993). *Critical incidents in teaching: Developing professional judgement*. Routledge.

Trott, D. C. (1991, October). *Anthrogogy.* (Paper presentation). Meeting of the American Association for Adult and Continuing Education, Montreal, Quebec.

Trust, T., Maloy, R. W., & Edwards, S. (2023). Learning about AI through five big ideas: A guide for secondary teachers. *TechTrends*, *67*(2), 325–334. DOI: 10.1007/s11528-022-00809-4

Tsai, Y. S., Rates, D., Moreno-Marcos, P. M., Muñoz-Merino, P. J., Jivet, I., Scheffel, M., Drachsler, H., Kloos, C. D., & Gašević, D. (2020). Learning analytics in European higher education, Trends and barriers. *Computers & Education*, *155*, 103933. DOI: 10.1016/j.compedu.2020.103933

Turner, C. E., & Purpura, J. E. (2016). Learning-oriented assessment in second and foreign language classrooms. In Tsagari, D., & Banerjee, J. (Eds.), *Handbook of second language assessment* (pp. 255–274). De Gruyter Mouton., DOI: 10.1515/9781614513827-018

Tutor, B. O. D., Lopez-Tutor, M. J., & Bernardo, L. M. A. (2025, June). Motivations of tertiary-level students to use generative artificial intelligence (GenAI) to cheat. *International Conference on Frontiers of Educational Technologies Proceedings*, Singapore, 509-519. Springer. DOI: 10.1007/978-981-95-2521-8_36

Uanachain, D. M. N., & Aouad, L. I. (2025). Generative AI in Education: Rethinking Learning, Assessment & Student Agency for the AI Era. *Thresholds in Education, 48*(1), 111–132.

Ültanır, E. (2012). An epistemological glance at the constructivist approach: Constructivist learning in Dewey, Piaget, and Montessori. *International Journal of Instruction, 5*(2). ISSN: 1694-609X

Unal, A., & Hobe, J. (2025). Preservice Teachers' Readiness for Integrating AI in Elementary Classrooms. *Journal of Education and Training Studies, 13*(4), 34. Advance online publication. DOI: 10.11114/jets.v13i4.7785

UNESCO. (2021). *AI and education: Guidance for policymakers.* UNESCO. https://unesdoc.unesco.org/ark:/48223/pf0000376709

UNESCO. (2023). *Recommendation on the ethics of artificial intelligence.* UNESCO Publishing.

University of Chicago. (2026). *Generative AI at UChicago.* https://genai.uchicago.edu/resources/faculty-and-instructors/strategies-for-designing-ai-resistant-assignments

University of Edinburgh. (2026). *Academic misconduct.* https://registryservices.ed.ac.uk/academic-services/staff/discipline/academic-misconduct

University of Massachusetts Boston. (2026). T*ypes of academic integrity errors.* https://www.umb.edu/academics/provost/academic-integrity/integrity-errors/

University of Northern Michigan. (2026). *Creating AI-resistant assignments, activities and assessments (designing out).* Center for Teaching and Learning. https://nmu.edu/ctl/creating-ai-resistant-assignments-activities-and-assessments-designing-out

University of Washington at Saint Lewis. (2026). *AI resilient assignments.* https://ctl.wustl.edu/resources/ai-resistant-assignments/

van der Linden, W. J., & Glas, C. A. (Eds.). (2010). *Elements of adaptive testing.* Springer., DOI: 10.1007/978-0-387-85461-8

Venter, J., Coetzee, S. A., & Schmulian, A. (2025). Exploring the use of artificial intelligence (AI) in the delivery of effective feedback. *Assessment & Evaluation in Higher Education, 50*(4), 516–536. DOI: 10.1080/02602938.2024.2415649

Verwoerd, J. C. (2025). *Balancing Innovation and Ethics: A Framework for Responsible AI Integration in Educational Assessment.* DOI: 10.20944/preprints202508.1696.v1

Villasenor, J. (2023). How ChatGPT can improve education, not threaten it. *Scientific American*. Advance online publication. DOI: 10.1038/scientificamerican0323-12

Vindigni, G. (2023). Adaptive and Re-adaptive Pedagogies in Higher Education: A Comparative, Longitudinal Study of Their Impact on Professional Competence Development across Diverse Curricula. *European Journal of Theoretical and Applied Sciences*. DOI: 10.59324/ejtas.2023.1(4).66

Voigt, P., & Von dem Bussche, A. (2017). *The EU General Data Protection Regulation (GDPR): A practical guide*. Springer., DOI: 10.1007/978-3-319-57959-7

von Maltitz, M. J. (2023). Encouraging significant learning in mathematical statistics through portfolios of learning evidence and interview assessments. *Proceedings of the 6th International Academic Conference on Education*. DOI: 10.33422/6th.iaceducation.2023.03.105

von Maltitz, M. J. (2026). Portfolios of learning evidence and interview assessments in a mathematical statistics course. *Journal of Statistics and Data Science Education : An Official Journal of the of the American Statistical Association*, *34*(1), 26–35. DOI: 10.1080/26939169.2025.2477151

von Maltitz, M. J., Fabris-Rotelli, I., Smit, A., Roberts, D., Das, S., Maposa, D., & Correa, F. M. (2025). A guiding rubric and usage manual for the doctoral supervisor and doctoral student in the discipline of statistics. *ORiON*, *41*(1), 1–52. DOI: 10.5784/41-1-799

Voogt, J., Fisser, P., Pareja Roblin, N., Tondeur, J., & van Braak, J. (2015). Technological pedagogical content knowledge – A review of the literature. *Journal of Computer Assisted Learning*, *29*(2), 109–121. DOI: 10.1111/j.1365-2729.2012.00487.x

Wahle, J. P., Ruas, T., Kirstein, F., & Gipp, B. (2022, December). How large language models are transforming machine-paraphrased plagiarism. *Proceedings of the 2022 Conference on Empirical Methods in Language Processing, Society for Computational Linguistics*, Abu Dhabi, UAE. https://aclanthology.org/2022.emnlp-main.62/

Wainer, H., Dorans, N. J., Flaugher, R., Green, B. F., & Mislevy, R. J. (2000). *Computerized adaptive testing: A primer* (2nd ed.). Lawrence Erlbaum Associates., DOI: 10.4324/9781410605931

Waked, S. N., Abdelsalem, A., Wagar Ashraf, M., & El Alaoui, K. (2024). T*he impact of falsely detecting AI-generated text on academic assessment. Proceedings of the* International Society *for Technology, Education and Science*, Antalya Turkey. https://eric.ed.gov/default.aspx?q=descriptor%3A%22Plagiarism%22&ff1=pubSpeeches%2FMeeting+Papers&id=ED673127

Waladi, C., & Lamarti, M. S. (2024). Adaptive AI-driven assessment for competency-based learning scenarios. In *Innovative instructional design methods and tools for improved teaching* (pp. 215–226). IGI Global Scientific Publishing., DOI: 10.4018/979-8-3693-3128-6.ch010

Wang, P. (2019). On defining artificial intelligence. Journal of artificial general intelligence, 10(2), 1-37. DOI: DOI: 10.2478/jagi-2019-0002

Wang, S., & Huang, Y. (2025). Facilitation or Inhibition: The impact of generative artificial intelligence on college students' creativity. *Frontiers of Education in China*, *20*(1), 38–53. DOI: 10.3868/s110-020-025-0003-0

Wang, T., & Cheng, E. C. K. (2021). An investigation of barriers to Hong Kong K-12 schools incorporating Artificial Intelligence in education. *Computers and Education: Artificial Intelligence*, *2*, 100031. DOI: 10.1016/j.caeai.2021.100031

Wang, Y. (2026). Enhancing University EFL Learners' Writing Performance: The Role of AI-Enhanced Goal-Setting, Feedback and Social Norm Interventions. *Journal of Computer Assisted Learning*, *42*(1), e70179. DOI: 10.1002/jcal.70179

Wang, Y. (2026). Exploring student engagement with multimodal generative AI in task-based Chinese language learning. *Computer Assisted Language Learning*, •••, 1–26. DOI: 10.1080/09588221.2026.2645428

Wang, Y., Liu, O. L., & Zhao, C. M. (2020). Evaluating automated essay scoring in mass assessment of English writing in China: Accuracy, validity, and fairness. *Educational Measurement: Issues and Practice*, *39*(3), 26–35. DOI: 10.1111/emip.12346

Warren, S. J., Boston Vogt, E., Tincher, B., & Yang, J. (2026). Enhancing quality assurance through strategic artificial intelligence integration: A framework for higher education digital transformation. *Quality Assurance in Education*, *34*(2), 205–222. DOI: 10.1108/QAE-09-2024-0183

Watson, A. P. (2024). Hallucinated citation analysis: Delving into student-submitted AI-generated sources at the University of Mississippi. *The Serials Librarian*, *85*(5-6), 172–280. DOI: 10.1080/0361526X.2024.2433640

Webb, M., & Galamba, A. (2026). Transforming pedagogy with GenAI-supported formative assessment: Challenges for teacher education. *British Journal of Educational Technology*, *57*(3), 690–706. DOI: 10.1111/bjet.70051

Weber-Wulff, D., Anohina-Naumeca, A., Bjelobaba, S., Foltýnek, T., Guerrero-Dib, J., Popoola, O., Šigut, P., & Waddington, L. (2023). Testing of detection tools for AI-generated text. *International Journal for Educational Integrity*, *19*(1), 26. DOI: 10.1007/s40979-023-00146-z

Wei, X. (2024, July 3). *How AI detects student engagement to transform classrooms.* Digital Promise. https://digitalpromise.org/2024/07/03/how-ai-detects-student-engagement-to-transform-classrooms/

Wenger, E. (1998). *Communities of practice: Learning, meaning, and identity.* Cambridge University Press., DOI: 10.1017/CBO9780511803932

Whittaker, M., Crawford, K., Dobbe, R., Fried, G., Kaziunas, E., Mathur, V., West, S. M., Richardson, R., Schultz, J., & Schwartz, O. (2019). *AI now report 2018.* AI Now Institute at New York University.

Wiegle, S. (2002). *Assessing writing*. Cambridge University Press. DOI: 10.1017/CBO9780511732997

Wiggins, G. (1990). The Case for Authentic Assessment. *Practical Assessment, Research & Evaluation*, *2*(1), 2. DOI: 10.7275/ffb1-mm19

Wiggins, G. (1993). *Assessing student performance: Exploring the purpose and limits of testing*. Jossey-Bass.

Wiggins, G. (1998). *Educative assessment: Designing assessments to inform and improve student performance*. Jossey-Bass.

Williams, J. E., & III, J. D. (2016). Student privacy in learning analytics. In C. Haythornthwaite, R. Andrews, J. Fransman, & E. M. Meyers (Eds.), *The SAGE handbook of e-learning research* (pp. 438-457). SAGE Publications. DOI: 10.4135/9781473955011.n21

Williams, J. B. (2006). The place of open-book, online exams in supporting deep learning. *Australasian Journal of Educational Technology*, *22*(1), 1–14. DOI: 10.14742/ajet.1299

Williams, J. B., & Wong, A. (2009). The efficacy of final examinations: A comparative study of closed-book, open-book and cheat sheet examinations. *Assessment & Evaluation in Higher Education*, *34*(3), 335–345. DOI: 10.1080/02602930801956029

Williamson, B. (2018). The hidden architecture of higher education: Building a big data infrastructure for the 'smarter university'. *International Journal of Educational Technology in Higher Education*, *15*(1), 1–26. DOI: 10.1186/s41239-018-0094-1

Williamson, B., Bayne, S., & Shay, S. (2020). The datafication of teaching in higher education: Critical issues and perspectives. *Teaching in Higher Education*, *25*(4), 351–365. DOI: 10.1080/13562517.2020.1748811

Williamson, B., & Eynon, R. (2020). Historical threads, missing links, and future directions in AI in education. *Learning, Media and Technology*, *45*(3), 223–235. DOI: 10.1080/17439884.2020.1798995

Williams, R. T. (2023). The ethical implications of using generative chatbots in higher education. *Frontiers in Education*. Advance online publication. DOI: 10.3389/feduc.2023.1331607

Wilson, J., & Roscoe, R. D. (2020). Automated writing evaluation and feedback: Multiple metrics of efficacy. *Journal of Educational Computing Research*, *58*(1), 87–125. DOI: 10.1177/0735633119830764

Winne, P. H., & Baker, R. S. (2013). The potentials of educational data mining for researching metacognition, motivation and self-regulated learning. *JEDM-Journal of Educational Data Mining*, *5*(1), 1–8. DOI: 10.5281/zenodo.3554619

World Bank. (2021). *Artificial intelligence in education: Challenges and opportunities for sustainable development.*

World Economic Forum. (2020). *Global AI governance: A guide for policymakers.*

Wright, A. (2024). Postgraduate supervision in a chatgpt world: What's next? *Proceedings of the 10th International Conference on Higher Education Advances (HEAd'24)*, 1–8. DOI: 10.4995/HEAd24.2024.17244

Wu, Y. (2024). Critical thinking pedagogics design in an era of ChatGPT and other AI Tools-Shifting from teaching" what" to teaching" why" and" how." *Journal of Education and Development*, 8(1). ISSN 2529-7996

Wu, M., Liu, W., Wang, Y., Ding, W., & Yao, M. (2026, April). Rethinking User Empowerment in AI Recommender System: Innovating Transparent and Controllable Interfaces. In *Proceedings of the 2026 CHI Conference on Human Factors in Computing Systems* (pp. 1-21). DOI: 10.1145/3772318.3791914

Wu, Y. (2026, February). Future-proofing medical assessment: Evaluating collaborative intelligence in the age of artificial intelligence. *Academic Medicine*, *101*(2), 152–159. DOI: 10.1093/acamed/wvaf039 PMID: 41620848

Xiao, L., Pyng, H. S., Ayub, A. F. M., Zhu, Z., Gao, J., & Qing, Z. (2025). University students' usage of generative artificial intelligence for sustainability: A cross-sectional survey from china. *Sustainability (Basel)*, *17*(8), 3541. DOI: 10.3390/su17083541

Xia, Q., Weng, X., Ouyang, F., Lin, T. J., & Chiu, T. K. F. (2024). A scoping review on how generative artificial intelligence transforms assessment in higher education. *International Journal of Educational Technology in Higher Education*, *21*(1), 40. DOI: 10.1186/s41239-024-00468-z

Xu, Y., Ding, Z., Zhang, Z., Zhou, L., Zhou, Y., & Ge, Z.-G. (2025). Personalized learning resources created by generative artificial intelligence: A systematic review. Proceedings, 84–89. DOI: 10.1109/ICETT66247.2025.11137092

Xu, Y., Zhu, J., Wang, M., Qian, F., Yang, Y., & Zhang, J. (2024). The impact of a digital game-based AI chatbot on students' academic performance, higher-order thinking, and behavioral patterns in an information Technology Curriculum. 14(15), 6418; .DOI: 10.3390/app14156418

Xu, B., Li, J., & Zhang, S. (2022). Artificial intelligence in academic writing: Opportunities, limitations, and ethical concerns. *Journal of Educational Technology & Society*, *25*(4), 76–89.

Xu, S., Su, Y., & Liu, K. (2025). Investigating student engagement with AI-driven feedback in translation revision: A mixed-methods study. *Education and Information Technologies*, *30*(12), 16969–16995. DOI: 10.1007/s10639-025-13457-0

Xu, Z. (2024). *AI in education: Enhancing learning experiences and student outcomes.* Applied and Computational Engineering., DOI: 10.54254/2755-2721/51/20241187

Yaakob, M. A., Abdullah, M. R., Masruh, M. L. M., Yaacob, K. M. S. bin K., Azman, F. M. N., Suarni, A., & Hasanudin. (2025). Empowering Framework Sunnah Values: An Ethical Framework for Research in the Age of Artificial Intelligence (AI). *International Journal of Research and Innovation in Social Science*. DOI: 10.47772/IJRISS.2025.92900008

Yadav, R., Huzooree, G., Yadav, M., & Gangodawilage, D. (2025). Generative AI for personalized learning content creation. Advances in Computational Intelligence and Robotics Book Series, 107–130. DOI: 10.4018/979-8-3693-8744-3.ch005

Yan, Y., & Liu, H. (2024). Ethical framework for AI education based on large language models. *Education and Information Technologies 2024 30:8*, *30*(8), 10891–10909. DOI: 10.1007/s10639-024-13241-6

Yan, D., Von Davier, A. A., & Lewis, C. (Eds.). (2014). *Computerized multistage testing: Theory and applications*. CRC Press., DOI: 10.1201/b16858

Yan, L., Greiff, S., Teuber, Z., & Gašević, D. (2024). Promises and challenges of generative artificial intelligence for human learning. *Nature Human Behaviour*, *8*(10), 1839–1850. DOI: 10.1038/s41562-024-02004-5

Yan, L., Pammer-Schindler, V., Mills, C., Nguyen, A., & Gašević, D. (2025). Beyond efficiency: Empirical insights on generative AI's impact on cognition, metacognition and epistemic agency in learning. *British Journal of Educational Technology*, *56*(5), 1675–1685. DOI: 10.1111/bjet.70000

Yan, Y. X., Wu, J. P., Nguyen, B. A., & Chen, H. M. (2020, February). The impact of iterative assessment system on programming learning behavior. In *Proceedings of the 2020 9th International Conference on Educational and Information Technology* (pp. 89-94). DOI: 10.1145/3383923.3383939

Yeganeh, L. N., Fenty, N. S., Chen, Y., Simpson, A., & Hatami, M. (2025). The future of education: A multi-layered metaverse classroom model for immersive and inclusive learning. *Future Internet*, *17*(2), 63. DOI: 10.3390/fi17020063

Yeo, M. A. (2023). Academic integrity in the age of Artificial Intelligence (AI) authoring apps. *TESOL Journal*, *14*(3), e716. DOI: 10.1002/tesj.716

Yilmaz, M., Temur, H. B., Emmungil, L., Çelik, E., Gauthier, A., & Cukurova, M. (2026). Supporting self-regulated learning through generative AI feedback in online higher education: The importance of student perceptions of the source of feedback. *International Journal of Educational Technology in Higher Education*, *23*(1), 16. DOI: 10.1186/s41239-026-00592-y

Yin, Z., Chinta, S. V., Wang, Z., Gonzalez, M., & Zhang, W. (2025). *FairAIED: Navigating Fairness, Bias, and Ethics in Educational AI Applications*. https://arxiv.org/abs/2407.18745

Young, V. A. (2014). Other people's English and a other rhetorical dispositions. In Schroeder, C., Fox, H., & Bizzell, P. (Eds.), *ALT DIS: Alternative discourses and the academy* (pp. 49–60). Boynton/Cook., DOI: 10.2307/j.ctt5hjqkx.7

Yue, M., Jong, M. S. Y., & Dai, Y. (2022). Pedagogical design of K-12 artificial intelligence education: A systematic review. *Sustainability (Basel)*, *14*(23), 15620. DOI: 10.3390/su142315620

Yusuf, H., Money, A., & Daylamani-Zad, D. (2025). Pedagogical AI conversational agents in higher education: A conceptual framework and survey of the state of the art. *Educational Technology Research and Development*, *73*(2), 815–874. Advance online publication. DOI: 10.1007/s11423-025-10447-4

Zajko, M. (2022). Artificial intelligence, algorithms, and social inequality: Sociological contributions to contemporary debates. *Sociology Compass*, *16*(3), e12962. DOI: 10.1111/soc4.12962

Zakaria, A., & Aryadoust, V. (2024). A scientometric analysis of applied linguistics research (1970–2022): Methodology and future directions. *Applied Linguistics Review, 15*(4), 1595–1619. DOI: 10.1515/applirev-2022-0210

Zaky, H. (2026). Reimagining Higher Education: The Promise and Challenges of Competency-Based Learning in the Digital Age. Available at *SSRN* 6131446. http://dx.doi.org/DOI: 10.3390/knowledge6030015

Zaphir, L., Lodge, J. M., Lisec, J., McGrath, D., & Khosravi, H. (2024). How critically can an AI think? A framework for evaluating the quality of thinking of generative artificial intelligence. *arXiv preprint arXiv:2406.14769.*

Zawacki-Richter, O., Marín, V. I., Bond, M., & Gouverneur, F. (2019). Systematic review of research on artificial intelligence applications in higher education – where are the educators? *International Journal of Educational Technology in Higher Education, 16*(1), 1–27. DOI: 10.1186/s41239-019-0171-0

Zenisky, A. L., & Hambleton, R. K. (2012). Developing test score reports that work: The process and best practices for effective communication. *Educational Measurement: Issues and Practice, 31*(2), 21–26. DOI: 10.1111/j.1745-3992.2012.00231.x

Zhang, L., Wu, S., & Wang, Z. (2025). Phoneme-aware hierarchical augmentation and semantic-aware SpecAugment for low-resource Cantonese speech recognition. *Sensors (Basel), 25*(14), 4288. DOI: 10.3390/s25144288 PMID: 40732416

Zhang, L., Yang, S., & Carter, R. A. (2020). Personalized learning and ESSA: What we know and where we go. *Journal of Research on Technology in Education, 52*(3), 253–274. DOI: 10.1080/15391523.2020.1728448

Zhang, Q. (2024). Harnessing artificial intelligence for personalized learning pathways: A framework for adaptive education management systems. *Applied and Computational Engineering, 82*(1), 167–172. DOI: 10.54254/2755-2721/82/20241102

Zhang, T., Erlam, R., & de Magalhães, M. B. (2025). Exploring the dual impact of AI in post-entry language assessment: Potentials and pitfalls. *Annual Review of Applied Linguistics, 45*, 274–293. DOI: 10.1017/S0267190525000030

Zhan, Y. (2023). What do college students think of feedback literacy? An ecological interpretation of Hong Kong students' perspectives. *Assessment & Evaluation in Higher Education, 48*(5), 686–700. DOI: 10.1080/02602938.2022.2121380

Zhao, C. (2024). AI-assisted assessment in higher education: A systematic review. *Journal of Educational Technology and Innovation, 6*(4). Advance online publication. DOI: 10.61414/jeti.v6i4.209

Zhao, J., Chapman, E., & Sabet, P. G. P. (2024). Generative AI and educational assessments: A systematic review. *Education Research and Perspectives*, *51*, 124–155. https://search.informit.org/doi/10.3316/informit.T2025061800005500592641426. DOI: 10.70953/ERPv51.2412006

Zhao, L., Zhao, B., & Li, C. (2023). Alignment analysis of teaching–learning-assessment within the classroom: How teachers implement project-based learning under the curriculum standards. *Disciplinary and Interdisciplinary Science Education Research*, *5*(1), 13. DOI: 10.1186/s43031-023-00078-1

About the Contributors

Andi Husni A. Zainuddin is an academic and researcher who recently joined Politeknik Dewantara. While she has recently transitioned to this institution and has yet to publish research under her new affiliation, she brings a wealth of expertise from her extensive tenure at IAIN Palopo. Her research primarily focuses on Education, Social Science, and English Language Teaching (ELT), with a notable scholarly impact of 148 citations and an h-index of 6. Her work explores contemporary issues such as online assessment and the Merdeka Curriculum. She remains dedicated to advancing modern pedagogical methods that bridge academic excellence with regional cultural values.

Amelia is a researcher in the field of English Language Teaching (ELT) with a strong interest in digital technology integration, instructional design, and vocational education. She actively conducts research on innovative teaching models, particularly the implementation of digital tools to enhance language learning outcomes. Her recent works focus on technology-enhanced learning, blended learning, and pedagogical strategies for vocational and higher education contexts. She is currently involved in academic writing, curriculum development, and teacher training programs.

D. Dhinakaran, is an Associate Professor in the Department of Computer Science and Engineering at Vel Tech Rangarajan Dr. Sagunthala R&D Institute of Science and Technology, Chennai. He holds a B.E., M.E., and Ph.D. in Computer Science from Anna University. His research expertise includes Privacy-Preserving Data Mining, Artificial Intelligence, Internet of Things (IoT), MANETs, Cloud Computing, and Image Processing. A prolific researcher, he has presented over 30 papers at international conferences, published more than 60 articles in reputed international journals, and filed three patents. He has been honoured as one of the Top 2% Scientists globally by Elsevier and Stanford University. He is actively supervising Ph.D. scholars and serves as a reviewer for reputed international journals and conferences, reflecting his strong commitment to academic excellence and research advancement. His innovative contributions and dedication to academia have made a significant impact on the evolving fields of Computer Science and Engineering.

Shree Deepa makes primary arguments and contributions to Indian ELT, Assessment, Inclusive education, IKS and Anthrogogy. She is widely popular for her cutting edge research contributions and is a sought after resource person.

Geetha Durairajan is a retired professor from EFL University, Hyderabad, India. She is an internationally renowned scholar in ELT and Language Assessment. She has been more productive academically post retirement.

Imam Fadli is an accomplished English educator and lecturer with strong academic achievements, holding both Bachelor's and Master's degrees in English Education from IAIN Palopo, graduating with outstanding GPAs. He has extensive experience as an English mentor, tutor, and university lecturer. Imam is also skilled in digital content creation, graphic design, videography, and website management. His academic excellence is reflected through multiple awards, international conference presentations, and research publications, demonstrating his dedication to education and professional development.

Colleen Halupa is a retired Air Force Officer. She has a doctorate in curriculum and instruction and has been a dean and academic program director for numerous academic programs in business and healthcare. She is a writer and researcher in online learning, pedagogy, assessment and academic honesty.

Kristofina Junias is a Lecturer in the Department of Technical and Vocational Education and Training (TVET) at the Namibia University of Science and Technology (NUST), Namibia. She holds a PhD in Curriculum Studies from Stellenbosch University, South Africa, a Master of Education in Curriculum Studies, a Bachelor of Education in Educational Foundations, and a Diploma in Science Education from the University of Zimbabwe. Prior to joining academia, she served for more than seven years as a Senior TVET Curriculum Development Coordinator at the Namibia Training Authority (NTA), where she played a key role in the development and review of competency-based curricula and qualifications. Her areas of research interest include curriculum studies, assessment and evaluation, technical and vocational education and training (TVET), higher education, quality assurance, educational technology, and skills development.

Siu-lun Lee is Principal Lecturer at the Chinese University of Hong Kong. He is an experienced teacher and administrator of Chinese language programmes, with extensive involvement in curriculum development and linguistic research. His academic interests include applied linguistics, Cantonese studies, Chinese linguistics, educational technology, language teaching pedagogy, multilingualism, sociolinguistics. He is editor of the learning and teaching of Cantonese as a second language and author of the Modern Cantonese series published by Routledge.

Daniel Maposa is a Professor of Statistics in the Department of Statistics and Operations Research, University of Limpopo. He holds a PhD degree in Statistics, MSc in Statistics and Operations Research and Honours in Applied Mathematics. He also holds a postgraduate certificate in SARIMA Research Ethics and Integrity from Wits and a certificate in Doctoral Supervision from Stellenbosch University. He is President of the South African Statistical Association (SASA), Chairperson of Ethics Committee at the University of Limpopo. He has been a member of the International Statistical Institute (ISI) and SASA for over 15 years. His research interests are in Extreme Value Theory (EVT), Time Series Forecasting, and Machine Learning. Daniel Maposa has published over 60 accredited journal articles in reputable journals including Springer Nature and 12 DHET-accredited conference proceedings. He has two book chapters in his name. In his research activities, Daniel Maposa has attended and presented his research work globally including in New Zealand, Australia, China, Switzerland, Brazil, Morocco, Malaysia, and The Netherlands, among others.

Danielle Jade Roberts holds a PhD in Applied Statistics. She has vast experience in teaching, curriculum development, research and student supervision in applied statistics and data science. She takes a data-driven approach to solve real world problems using statistics, machine learning and technology, with a focus on public health and other societal challenges in resource-limited settings in Africa. Danielle's extensive knowledge spans various statistical and data science techniques, including but not limited to joint models, spatial models, and both supervised and unsupervised learning models. Her research aims to assist stakeholders and policymakers in optimizing the distribution of scarce resources through more focused strategies. She is one of the founding members of the newly formed network on Statistics Supervision in South Africa (StatSNetSA). She is a regular reviewer for international ISI journals and currently serves on the Executive Committee of the South African Statistical Association (SASA).

S. Edwin Raja, Associate Professor, Department of Computer Science and Engineering in Vel Tech Rangarajan Dr.Sagunthala R&D Institute of Science and Technology, Chennai. He has completed his Ph.D. in Information and Communication Engineering from Anna University-chennai in the year 2021. He obtained his M.Tech. (Network Engineering) in the year 2010 from Kalasalingam University, Krishnan kovil and B.E. (Computer Science and Engineering) in the year 2006 from C.S.I Institute of Technology, Thovalai. He has more than thirteen plus years of teaching experience and his area of interests are Cyber Security, Big Data Analytics, Machine Learning & Computer Networks. He has published more than 4 research articles in various journals and conferences. Also, he has published 3 patents, acted as reviewer in reputed journals.

Ansie Smit is a senior lecturer at the University of Pretoria with a background in Mathematical Statistics. She lecturers in both the Department of Geology and the Department of Statistics. Her focus areas are hazard and risk assessment, geostatistics and statistical education.

Nurul Taqwa An English and Linguistics Lecturer with one year of experience in higher education, specializing in language studies, academic writing, and communication skills. Demonstrated strong abilities in public speaking, problem-solving, and teamwork. Actively participated in various academic and institutional events as an adjudicator, supervisor, and speaker, which have strengthened the leadership and interpersonal skills. Contributed to several research articles, reflecting the commitment to academic excellence and continuous professional growth.

Michael J. von Maltitz is an Associate Professor in the Department of Mathematical Statistics and Actuarial Science at the University of the Free State (UFS), South Africa. He obtained his PhD in Mathematical Statistics at the UFS in 2015 and has since split his research focus to include experimentation in teaching and learning in the field of Mathematical Statistics. He is a founding member of StatSNetSA, a research group dedicated to development and retention of academic statisticians in South Africa, and is an active member of the IASE and ISI.

Index

A

H

I

L

www.ingramcontent.com/pod-product-compliance
Lightning Source LLC
LaVergne TN
LVHW062028101126
852251LV00005B/50